NOTES ON THE GREEK TEXT OF LEVITICUS

SOCIETY OF BIBLICAL LITERATURE
SEPTUAGINT AND COGNATE STUDIES SERIES

Series Editor
Bernard A. Taylor

Editorial Advisory Committee

N. Fernández Marcos, Madrid
I. Soisalon - Soininen, Helsinki
E. Tov, Jerusalem

Number 44

NOTES ON THE GREEK TEXT OF LEVITICUS

by
John William Wevers

NOTES ON THE GREEK TEXT OF LEVITICUS

by

John William Wevers

Scholars Press
Atlanta, Georgia

NOTES ON THE GREEK TEXT OF LEVITICUS

by
John William Wevers

© 1997
Society of Biblical Literature

Library of Congress Cataloging-in-Publication Data
Wevers, John William.
    Notes on the Greek text of Leviticus / by John William Wevers.
       p.   cm. — (Septuagint and cognate studies series ; no. 44)
    Includes bibliographical references and indexes.
    ISBN 0-7885-0324-3 (cloth ; alk. paper)
    1. Bible. O.T. Leviticus. Greek—Versions—Septuagint.
    2. Bible. O.T. Leviticus—Translating. I. Title. II. Series.
BS1254.G7S448   1997
222'.130486—dc21   96-47348
                                            CIP

    ISBN 1-58983-157-8 (pbk. : alk. paper)

Printed in the United States of America
on acid-free paper

Table of Contents

Introductory Statement ix
Sigla xxx
Notes 1
Appendix A: Proposed Changes in Lev 483
Appendix B: Terms for Sacrifices 484
Index of Greek Words and Phrases 488
Index of Hebrew Words and Phrases 500
Index of Grammatical and Textual Items 509
General Index 515

This book is dedicated to former students of mine who have long since become my Departmental colleagues.

INTRODUCTORY STATEMENT

I. Character of the Lev translation

1.0. Almost a century and a half ago Zacharias Frankel observed "Der Vertent des Buches Leviticus ist an vielen Stellen Exeget, and wo er treu übersetzt, wird von dem Stoffe so überwältigt, dass er den Genius der Sprache, in welche er übersetzt, unbeachtet lässt."[1] A bit later on he states even more bluntly: "Er scheint von dem Stoffe so sehr überwältigt worden zu sein, dass er von den Regeln und der Redeweise der griechischen Sprache unbewusst haüfig abglitt."[2] That the translator did on occasion depart from the accepted rules and normal practices of Greek grammar is undoubtedly true, though I am sceptical about the reason for this departure given by Frankel; I suspect the reason to be far less exalted; he simply was not a careful grammarian.

As a translation, Lev is more of an isolate type of translation than a contextual one.[3] A purely "isolate" translation would simply be a word for word set of equivalences for Hebrew lexemes in the Greek with little regard for the context in which such were used. Terms such as "isolate" and "contextual" are not used in an absolute sense; rather one can say that, compared to Gen and Exod, Lev is much more isolate than contextual in character.

Though this assessment should not be overstated, it is true that Hebraisms abound. A monolingual Greek reader would not readily understand such oddities as ἀνδρὶ ἀνδρὶ ᾧ ἂν γένηται (15:2) as referring "to any man to whom there should happen," or what was meant by κοίτη σπέρματος at 15:16,17; even the common θανάτῳ θανατούσθω at 20:2 (already found at Exod 21:12,15) would sound strange to Greek ears.

This last example illustrates an attempt to reproduce a common Hebrew syntagm in which a cognate free infinitive (מות) precedes a finite verb (ימות) by

---

1. Ueber den Einfluss der palästinischen Exegese auf die alexandrinische Hermeneutik (Leipzig, 1851), 122.
2. Idem, p.126.
3. I use the terminology introduced by Albert Pietersma, Manual for NETS Translators (Ada, Mich, 1996), 12. He speaks of a continuum of a scale from one extreme to the other as applicable to various translation units, so that "each unit may be expected to show its own distinctive profile."

which the verbal notion is stressed; what is meant is that "he shall surely die." This Hebrew syntagm has no corresponding pattern in Greek, and LXX translators usually render such free infinitives either by a cognate dative noun or a cognate participle. It might be noted that occasionally the translator does not use a cognate participle but an idiomatic synonym. I note e.g., 14:48 ἐὰν δὲ παραγενόμενος εἰσέλθῃ ὁ ἱερεύς "But should the priest on arrival enter."

In spite of the many Hebraisms, it needs to be stressed that the translator did not procede mechanically, and though the syntax is more often translation Greek than compositional, the translator did try to make sense. The text must have communicated to its Alexandrian audience, and it becomes the modern reader to try to understand what its composer intended.

1.1. Lexically the most extreme type of Hebraism is the calque, i.e. a word chosen from the target language to represent the lexemic content of the equivalent source word. Probably the most often-cited example of the calque is that of διαθήκη used to represent the Hebrew ברית. The word διαθήκη is never used throughout the Alexandrian Scriptures in the Greek sense of the word, but only in the sense of ברית. In other words, to understand the Greek word one must consult the Hebrew, not the Greek, dictionary. Other examples of calques in Lev are ἀνάθεμα for חרם "anything devoted to destruction, under the ban," θάνατος for דבר "pestilence," κοίτη for שכבה "emission of semen," πώγων for זקן "chin, beard," σάρξ for בשר "flesh," but also as "penis," and ὕσσωπος for אזוב "hyssop."

1.2. Characteristic of Lev, though possibly distressing to the strict grammarian, is the use of αὐτό and αὐτά as default pronouns. Whenever the translator was at a loss for an antecedent he used the neuter pronoun. Thus at 5:16 αὐτό is twice used, first to refer to ὃ ἥμαρτεν ἀπὸ τῶν ἁγίων, and the second one to τὸ ἐπίπεμπτον. Or at 6:10 αὐτό is used, but must refer to κατακάρπωσιν which is feminine. At 6:34 the pronoun in καὶ περιελεῖ αὐτά apparently refers to the contents of the verse as a whole (probably except for the first item); similarly αὐτά in v.36 twice refers in general to the parts of sacrifices eligible for food.[4]

1.3. The translator also created a number of neologisms, and I noted the following examples: 7:2 αἴνεσις for תודה; 15:4 (ὁ) γονορρυής for הזב; 16:8 ἀποπομπαῖος for עזאזל; 18:23 (κοίτην σου εἰς) σπερματισμόν for שכבה; 19:10

---

[4]. Huber 33—38 gives numerous examples of incongruence either of gender or of number. But even his lists are incomplete.

ἐπανατρυγάω for עוֹלֵל; 19:19 κατοχεύω for הרביע; 19:23 περικαθαρίζω for ערל; 19:27 (ποιέω) σισόην for הקיף; 21:4 βεβηλόω for Ni of חלל.

A number of hapax legomena also obtain in Lev. The following list has been identified: 1:15 στραγγίζω; 5:9 καταστραγγίζω; 6:23 ὁλόκαυτος; 8:20 κρεανομέω; 11:10 ἐρεύγομαι; 11:22 ἀττάκη; ὀφιομάχη; 11:30 μυγαλῆ; καλαβώτης; σαύρα; ἀσπάλαξ; 11:35 κυθρόπους; 15:8 προσσιελίζω; 18:23 σπερματισμός; 19:26 ὀρνιθοσκοπέω; 20:15 κοιτασία; 21:20 κυρτός; 22:22 μυρμηκιῶντα; ψωραγριῶντα; 22:23 κολοβόκερκον; 22:24 ἐκτομίας; 22:26 φθάρμα; 24:22 δικαίωσις; 25:46 κατόχιμος; 26:1 λίθος σκοπός; 26:26 σιτοδεία; 27:27 τίμημα.

1.4. At times the translator betrays a lack of certainty on cultic matters. He apparently did not understand what precisely the term אשה meant as sacrifice. It is at times confused with the מנחה (e.g. at 2:2,3), where it becomes θυσία, and at times with עלה (e.g. 4:35 5:12) where ὁλοκαυτώματα is used. Nor does he understand what is meant by the תנופה or the collocation הניף תנופה. Sometimes he uses ἐπιτίθημι ἐπίθεμα (twice), but elsewhere there occur ἀποφέρω ἀφαίρεμα (8:27), ἀφαιρέω ἐπίθεμα (8:29), ἀφαιρέω ἀφαίρεμα (9:21), ἀφόρισμα ἀφορίζω (at 10:15), and ἀφορίζω ἀφόρισμα (14:12).

Sometimes Lev lacks the clarity of MT. At 3:4 it is clear that what the priest is to turn aside (יסירנה) is "the lobe on the liver along with the kidneys." But the Greek does not render the suffix, simply having περιελεῖ. What is to be removed is not stated; it might be the entire κάρπωμα of vv.3b—4 or only v.4b as in MT. Or to give but one more example, at 4:15 the elders are to place their hands on the head of the bullock; then שחט the bullock, i.e. "one shall slay" the bullock. The actual slaying is naturally the work of an individual, but LXX renders the verb by the plural, σφάξουσιν. Thus the elders of the assembly are to do the butchering as well, which must have created a great deal of confusion at the altar indeed!

1.5. Particularly characteristic of the translator's work is his love of variation. At 2:13 מנחה occurs twice, the first one is rendered by the standard θυσία, but the second one by θυσιασμάτων for which see Appendix B. Normally Lev uses κρίμα to translate משפט, but at 24:22 the translator used a hapax legomenon, δικαίωσις. For הקריב "bring a sacrifice" he uses either προσφέρω (52 times) or προσάγω (37 times), purely for variety's sake. There is no distinction intended between the two whatsoever. Or to mention but one more, though many dozens could be listed, the verb הקטיר is used in the sense of "to offer up a sacrifice" throughout the book. From 1:9 up to 2:16 he translates it as ἐπιτίθημι; he then changes to ἀναφέρω at 2:16 which he uses consistently (eight times) through 4:31. Then three cases of ἐπιτίθημι obtain through 6:12. There follow again eight cases of ἀναφέρω through 9:10, then ἐπιτίθημι occurs three times (9:13—17), and finally ἀναφέρω returns through 17:6. I can discover no exegetical reason for these changes; they merely represent the translator's love for variety.

1.6. But this is not always the case. At 9:20 החזות is rendered by τὰ στηθύνια, but in the next verse by the singular τὸ στηθύνιον. In v.20 the breast is cut up in pieces, but in v.21 the breast as a whole is being dedicated. In ch.11 the word מים is sometimes rendered by the singular and sometimes by the plural. The translator is, however, making an important distinction. Whenever the word refers to water as the home of aquatic life he uses the plural ὕδατα; otherwise the singular ὕδωρ occurs throughout.

In fact, the translator at times intentionally departs from the usual rendering. At 15:33 reference is made to a man who cohabits with טמאה, which is usually rendered by ἀκάθαρτος (74 out of 81 times). The rendering ἀποκαθημένης is unique; the unclean one is "a woman who sits apart," a reference to the isolation required of a woman in her menses.

At 26:19 גאון עזכם "the arrogance of your strength" refers to your arrogant reliance on strength. LXX has τὴν ὕβριν τῆς ὑπερηφανίας ὑμῶν "the insolence of your arrogance," a creative and fine rendering. In the following verse ותם לריק כחכם "your strength is expended in vain" is translated by ἔσται εἰς κενὸν ἡ ἰσχὺς ὑμῶν. A rendering of תם taken in the sense of "be finished, come to an end" would be tautological with εἰς κενον, and so the translator used the neutral ἔσται.

2.1. *Clarification of the text*. Changes are often made in order to clarify the Hebrew text. Many of these are merely a matter of simplification. Thus at 19:22 MT has the verb נסלח modified by a מן phrase, מחטאתו, i.e. "atonement shall be made for him for his sin." LXX omits the מן entirely and makes ἡ ἁμαρτία the subject: "the sin shall be forgiven him." Earlier at v.3 the Hebrew reads ... איש תיראו "each one of you shall fear." LXX simplifies by using a third person singular verb ἕκαστος ... φοβείσθω.

At 20:9 the protasis contains both כי and אשר, "should anyone who." LXX has simplified with its ἄνθρωπος ἄνθρωπος ὃς ἄν, i.e. has disregarded the כי

entirely. And at 24:22 MT has two clauses: "there shall be one judgment for you; כגר כאזרח יהיה." LXX makes a single clause out of these: "there shall be one judgment for proselytes and native born."

2.2. Far more significant are attempts at clarification which render the intent of a passage more precise. At 1:15 and 5:9 it is required for the sacrifice of birds that the blood be drained out of the carcass (Ni of מצה). Birds, however, are small, and contain very little blood, so LXX translated the verb by (κατα)στραγγιεῖ "shall squeeze out (the blood)." At 4:3 הכהן becomes ὁ ἀρχιερεύς, which is a fuller and more accurate designation, and at 6:32(7:2) the priest must sprinkle the blood על המזבח, whereas LXX more precisely has προσχεεῖ ἐπὶ τὴν βάσιν τοῦ θυσιαστηρίου "he must pour out the blood about the base of the altar." The gloss in v.31, the immediately preceding verse, τοῦ κριοῦ, makes the νόμος "regulation" of the אשם pertain more specifically to "the ram of the אשם."

At 8:15 MT states that Moses took את הדם and then placed it on the horns of the altar. The Alexandrian more exactly designated the blood as partitive: ἀπὸ τῆς αἵματος "some of the blood." At 9:19 among the parts of the sacrificial animal placed on the altar is the enigmatic המכסה "that which covers." This seems incomplete, and LXX adds both a subject and an ἐπί modifier; it reads τὸ στέαρ τὸ κατακαλύπτον ἐπὶ τῆς κοιλίας "the fat which covers the abdomen," which makes excellent sense.

At 13:5 after a seven-day period of quarantine for a diseased person, it is said ראהו הכהן "and the priest shall examine him," but LXX substitutes τὴν ἀφήν for the suffix. After all, it is the affected skin that must be examined, not the person as such. At 21:9 a charge is made against the daughter of a priest that she was defiling את אביה, but the translator changed this to "τὸ ὄνομα of her father"; it is her father's reputation that has been damaged. The sacrifice אשה occurs twice in 23:36. In v.a it is rendered by the plural ὁλοκαυτώματα, but in v.b by the singular. In v.a the reference is to the sacrifice(s) for seven days, but in v.b the אשה is only for the eighth day.

It is said concerning the lamps in the tabernacle at 24:4 "יערך before Yahweh תמיד." The verb is made personal in the Greek by καύσετε, but more significantly the imprecision of תמיד is changed to ἕως τὸ πρωΐ; the lamps did not burn continually; they would hardly burn in broad daylight; see Exod 27:21: ἀφ' ἑσπέρας ἕως πρωΐ. At 24:16 MT says "whether proselyte or native-born בנקבו

שם he shall be put to death." LXX specifies with greater precision "when he pronounces τὸ ὄνομα κυρίου let him die." And at 27:27 the protasis refers to בבהמה הטמא "unclean cattle." But v.26 had specified such firstborn as אם שור אם שה, i.e. ἐάν τε μόσχον ἐάν τε πρόβατον, for which the description κτηνῶν would be incorrect, but the rendering τῶν τετραπόδων τῶν ἀκαθάρτων in Lev could not be faulted.

2.3. Often what is clearly implicit in MT is rendered explicit in LXX. At 5:8 MT says "and he must bring them to the priest, והקריב one for a sin offering." Though the subject of the first clause is the worshiper, it is the priest who performs the sacrifice; LXX makes this clear by specifying the subject: (προσάξει) ὁ ἱερεύς. At 13:36 MT makes two statements: "the priests must make an examination for yellow hair" and "טמא הוא." LXX makes the latter a ὅτι clause: ὅτι ἀκάθαρτός ἐστιν, i.e. because "it (or he) is unclean." Similarly at 21:21 LXX added a ὅτι to indicate the implicit relationship of the judgment מום בו to v.a which preceded it.

At 16:15 the priest "must slaughter the kid for the sin offering of the people," to which LXX added ἔναντι κυρίου. That the slaughter should take place in the sanctuary is implied, but LXX makes this certain by its "before the Lord." And at 25:31b it is said concerning houses in unwalled villages גאלה תהיה לו. Though this is obviously a general rule, LXX makes certain that "they shall διὰ παντός be redeemable," i.e. it will always be redeemable.

3.1. *Rationalizations.* That the Alexandrian did not woodenly translate his text word-for-word without regard for the context is fully clear; he approached his text in rational fashion quite aware of the context in which a passage stood.

At 9:4 MT has the unique notion of מנחה בלולה בשמן. מנחה is regularly rendered by θυσία, but here the parallel at 7:2, σεμίδαλιν πεφυραμένην ἐν ἐλαίῳ, seemed more fitting, and the translator adopted this "emendation" of "fine flour" for "grain sacrifice." That the translator did not simply render word-for-word in unthinking fashion, but studied the context is also seen at 13:49 in comparison with vv.51—53, 57—59. In MT the passage concerns a נגע צרעת appearing in a garment. In v.49 the relevant collocation reads בבגד או בעור (או בשתי או בערב או בכל כלי עור) "in the garment or the leather or the warp or the woof or any article of leather." In vv.51—53, 57—59 the phrase או בעור does not occur. LXX has changed the order of the items in v.49 to read ἐν τῷ δέρματι ἢ ἐν τῷ ἱματίῳ ἢ ἐν τῷ στήμονι ἢ ἐν τῇ κρόκῃ. In other words, LXX throughout has the collocation "either in the warp or in the woof" immediately following "in the garment," a more logical order indeed.

In 25:39—40 regulations concerning the treatment of an indentured fellow-Israelite are given. MT says: "לא תעבד בו the work of an עבד," but "as a hireling or a native-born ... יעבד עמך." LXX translates the verb עבד differently in the two verses. In v.39 it has οὐ δουλεύσει σοι (δουλείαν οἰκέτου) "not shall he do for you the work of a δοῦλος." But in v.40 the verb reads ἐργᾶται (παρὰ σοί), i.e. work as a hireling alongside you, but not as of inferior rank.

At 25:52 the Masoretes made the first cut in the verse after לו, which is accented with an *ethnach*, i.e. וחשב לו belongs to v.a, rather than to v.b. Admittedly this seems strange, and modern translations generally follow LXX which makes καὶ συλλογιεῖται αὐτῷ begin the apodosis, i.e. "then it shall be reckoned to him according to his years"; the reference is to the amount of ransom to be paid for the release of an indentured Israelite.

At 26:30 the divine threat includes inter alia "I will put את גלוליכם פגרי על פגריכם," i.e. "your corpses upon the corpses of your dung idols." Since idols are unreal, the notion of "their corpses" is bizarre, and the translator changed the figure to read: τὰ κῶλα ὑμῶν ἐπὶ τὰ κῶλα τῶν εἰδώλων ὑμῶν "your limbs on the limbs of your idols." Incidentally, κῶλα was adopted by later translators as well, and the word became the usual rendering for פגרים.

3.2. Passages which might be considered inconsistent may often be rendered in a more consistent way by Lev. Thus at 4:13 the protasis concerns "the community ישגו, and the matter is hidden from the eyes of the assembly." V.14 then continues that this נודעה "becomes known." The condition is thus one of the community sinning by inadvertence. LXX, however, in the light of the γνωσθῇ of v.14 defines ישגו by ἀγνοήσῃ, i.e. the inadvertent sin is a matter of ignorance.

At times change in number creates an odd text. E.g. at 19:33 MT says: "And if a resident alien should reside with you (אתך) in your land (בארצכם), not may you oppress (תונו) him." The translator renders the entire verse in second personal plural. Similarly at 24:5—7 the text is recorded in second person singular in MT, i.e. as applying only to Aaron. This is inconsistent with v.3, where the Aaronids are given orders, and their duties outlined in the plural. LXX has changed the singular verbs of vv.5—7 into the plural so as to be consistent with the order to the Aaronids in v.3. In 25:31 MT is inconsistent in number.

The subject of v.a is בתי "houses," but the verb is יחשב in the Ni. Furthermore, in v.b the verb is יצא. LXX renders them all in the plural: αἱ οἰκίαι ... λογισθήτωσαν ... ἐξελεύσονται.

Consistency may, however, be a matter of one's point of view. The word מושבתיכם occurs seven times in the book (3:17 7:26[16] 23:3,14,17,21,31), and only at 23:31 is it rendered by a plural noun: ἐν πάσαις κατοικίαις ὑμῶν. In all other cases the noun is singular, though modified by ὑμῶν. After all, none of "you" has more than "one" dwelling.

3.3. The translator is intent on avoiding any possible misunderstanding on the part of the reader, in fact, at times actually "correcting" the text. Thus at 23:20 it is theoretically possible to understand the two ל phrases as apposite in the collocation "they shall be holy ליהוה לכהן." Of course, Yahweh is not the priest, but the gloss added at the end, τῷ προσφέροντι αὐτά, αὐτῷ ἔσται, makes even such a theoretical reading impossible.

At 26:41 an exiled people is presupposed. God says: "And I will go with them in hostile fashion, and הבאתי them into the land of their enemies." Since the people are already exiled, the verb "I will bring" is contradictory, and the translator changed it to ἀπολῶ "I will destroy."

At 9:22 MT lists the following sacrifices as having been performed by Aaron: החטאת והעלה והשלמים. LXX has changed the second one to the plural, τὰ ὁλοκαυτώματα, retaining only the first one τὸ περὶ τῆς ἁμαρτίας as singular. The translator, being aware of the plurality of burnt offerings according to ch.1, "corrected" the text to the plural noun.

According to 15:1 "the Lord spoke to Moses and Aaron as follows." In MT v.2 continues with דברו, but LXX has λάλησον. After all, only one of the brothers, presumably Moses, would actually speak to the Israelites, and so LXX also continued with καὶ ἐρεῖς for ואמרתם.

In MT at 16:20 reference is made to Aaron's bringing forward the live goat after having completed making atonement for the adytum, the tabernacle and the altar. Afterwards, he is to transfer ritually all the evils and sins of the Israelites on to the head of the goat. But no reference at all is made to the Aaronids who are particularly mentioned in v.33. The translator rectified this omission by adding καὶ περὶ τῶν ἱερέων καθαριεῖ before the sending away of the live goat into the desert.

3.4. That the translator had reverence for the sacred text nevertheless, or possibly because of this reverence, he did on occasion intentionaly change the text; in other words, he put into Greek what he thought God actually meant to say. Thus at 5:7 MT speaks of an אשמו which חטא. But for sin, not a trespass offering but a sin offering was needed; accordingly, LXX interprets the passage by περὶ τῆς ἁμαρτίας αὐτοῦ ἧς ἥμαρτεν.

At 8:2 Moses is ordered to take Aaron and his sons with him ואת הבגדים. But the ritual described begins with the robing of the high priest, and only afterwards at v.13, are the sons clothed. So the translator renders הבגדים by τὰς στολὰς αὐτοῦ, i.e. the clothes of Aaron. And at 16:10 the live kid יעמד, which the Masoretes vocalized as Ho, thus "shall be made to stand (alive before Yahweh)." The translator changed this to στήσει αὐτόν, i.e. the priest must set him, as though the verb were a Hi with suffix. According to LXX the priest plays an active role in the matter.

3.5. It is hardly surprising that in the translation of such a difficult book as the Hebrew Leviticus, the translator at times misunderstood the Hebrew text. Sometimes this resulted in a confused text, and MT is much clearer than LXX. A few examples must suffice.

At 14:10 MT states (תמימים) וכבשה אחת (בת שנתה תמימה) יקח שני כבשים, i.e. "two male lambs ... and one female lamb." LXX somehow misunderstood this; it reads δυὸ ἀμνοὺς ἐνιαυσίους ἀμώμους καὶ πρόβατον ἒν ἐνιαύσιον ἄμωμον. Why he should render כבשים by ἀμνούς (quite correctly), but כבשה uniquely by πρόβατον is baffling. The latter is otherwise always correctly rendered by ἀμνάς. It might be noted that the translator added ἐνιαυσίους as a necessary characteristic of ἀμνούς; this is readily intelligible as a case of leveling.

At 19:16 the Hebrew is difficult. It says "not תעמד against the blood of your neighbour." What the verb "to stand" intends here is not immediately clear, and the translator simply tried to make sense with his "οὐκ ἐπισυστήσῃ against the blood of your neighbour." That in the context the word תעמד should mean "conspire" makes good sense. At v.30 LXX vocalized the Hebrew differently from the Masoretes. MT read "מקדשי you must fear"; i.e. you must have reverence for my sanctuary. LXX understood מקדשי as a prepositional phrase as its ἀπὸ τῶν ἁγίων μου shows; what LXX says is "be fearful of (i.e. show reverence for) my holy things." A similar misunderstanding occurs at 20:3 where MT has שם קדשי "my holy name." The Greek has a surprising τὸ ὄνομα τῶν ἡγιασμένων μοι "the name of those sanctified for me." Did the translator read שם מקדשי by dittography of mu, i.e. a plural Pu participle with suffix?

At 21:5 MT says about priests that "they may not create baldness (i.e. shave) their heads." The context refers to prohibited mourning rites for the dead. LXX did not fully understand this, but tried to make good sense of it by using a double accusative, φαλάκρωμα and τὴν κεφαλήν, modifying "you may not shave," and adding an interpretive gloss, ἐπὶ νεκρῷ, at the end.

And to give but one more example: at 22:9, MT has a difficult text in which pronominal references seem odd. It reads: "they must guard את משמרתי, that not they might take on guilt עליו and die בו because יחללהו." One would have expected third feminine singular pronouns referring to משמרתי, but they are all masculine. There is no sensible masculine singular antecedent, and the references must be postcedent to קדש in v.10. The translator solved this by using his default pronoun αὐτά in each case, for which see 1.2. above. Since he had rendered משמרתי by the plural μου τὰ φυλάγματα a smooth text resulted, but it does not equal MT.

4.0. *Leveling*. All the Pentateuch translators engage in the practice of leveling the text, and Lev is no exception. I need give only a few examples of this phenomenon.

At 2:8 MT begins with a second person verb, הבאת, and for v.b changes to third person, הקריבה. Since the last word in v.a is ליהוה, a third person "he must bring it" might grammatically refer to יהוה, which common sense would naturally reject. LXX levels the entire verse to third person, which thereby voids any notion that the Lord should be bringing a sacrifice. At 13:27 after translating the final clause, נגע צרעת הוא, LXX adds ἐν τῷ ἕλκει ἐξήνθησεν, which is a case of leveling with v.20. At 21:13 MT states that a priest must marry a woman בבתוליה. LXX not only has παρθένον but adds ἐκ τοῦ γένους αὐτοῦ, which levels with v.14.

Often leveling is ex par, i.e. from a parallel passage. At 19:3 MT has אמו ואביו. LXX reverses the two nouns, both here and at 21:2. This is not a case of male chauvenism, but rather one of ex par influence, e.g. of the Decalogue. At 20:26 for קדוש אני יהוה LXX adds ὁ θεὸς ὑμῶν after κύριος. In fact, the self-identification formula אני יהוה often appears in the long form "I am the Lord your God" throughout the Holiness Code (chh.18—26), for which see 7.7 below. And at 24:15 for תדבר לאמר the Greek has καὶ ερεῖς πρὸς αὐτούς for לאמר, a formulaic pattern which occurs 13 times in Lev.

5.0. *Updating*. I have found little indication in Lev which might reflect the life and times of the Alexandrian translator. At 19:35 measures of length, weight and quantity are given resp as מדה, משקל and משורה. The translator did render these by good Alexandrian terms as μέτροις, σταθμίοις and ζυγοῖς. A μέτρον was a general word for measure and was used to register length or size or content, whereas a στάθμιον was a standard measure of weight, and ζυγόν "yoke" was used in the plural for a balance used for weighing metals. ζυγὰ δίκαια (v.36) demands accurate weights for the balance or scale. Reference is also made in v.36 to צדק הין. At 23:13 the word הין also occurs, and is there transliterated by ἵν, but at 19:36 the weight is translated by χοῦς, a well-known measure of capacity, especially of liquids; compare the cognate verb χέω "to pour."

5.1. The notion of Torah may well be reflected at 24:12. MT orders the placing in custody of the blasphemer לפרש להם על פי יהוה "to clarify for them according to a word of Yahweh." The Greek interprets this by διακρῖναι αὐτὸν διὰ προστάγματος κυρίου. The פי of Yahweh presumably refers to an oracle, a spoken word, but to the translator judgment was to be given through a statute of the Lord. In other words, a body of law, a Torah, is implied, and its προστάγματα are to be applied.

A similar state of affairs may be understood at 26:46. This constitutes the subscription to the chapter: "These are the statutes and the judgments והתורת which Yahweh set between him and the Israelites in Mt. Sinai by means of Moses." The translator, however, does not translate התורת by οἱ νομοι, but by ὁ νόμος. What was revealed on Mt. Sinai was Torah, a body of law, not simply instructions.

6.1. *Exegetical matters*. Of greater interest are cases betraying an exegetical mindset on the part of the translator. Some of these involve reinterpreting or correcting MT over against what it actually says. Ch.1 deals with burnt offerings. Vv.3—4 refer to a worshiper who presents his offering from (his) cattle, brings it to the sanctuary, and places his hand on the head of the animal. Then v.5 continues with ושחט the animal, after which it is the Aaronids who must deal with the blood; then v.6 reverts to the worshiper with הפשיט the burnt offering and נתח it in pieces, with vv.7—8 again switching to the Aaronids who are to perform at the altar. In LXX these verbs are all in the plural: σφάξουσιν, ἐκδείραντες, μελιοῦσιν. Since these are done ἔναντι κυρίου, i.e. within the sanctuary and at the altar, these operations must be done by priests, not by the lay worshiper. The next section, vv.10—13, refers to the worshiper presenting a sheep. Once again, שחט and נתח occur in the singular, but the translator changes them to the plural.

6.2. At 9:15 the word ויחטאהו occurs in a context where it must be taken to mean "and he offered it (i.e. the kid) as a sin offering," which is then modified by כראשון "as in the first case," i.e. a reference to the first sacrifice recorded in v.8, the sin offering on his own behalf. LXX has interpreted the verb differently. The Pi of חטא often means "to purify," and so the rendering καὶ ἐκαθάρισεν αὐτόν is used, which must mean "and he performed the rite of purification with it"; apparently this refers to the rite with the blood in v.9, i.e. "dipping the finger into the blood, and daubing the horn of the altar, and then pouring out the remainder of the blood at the base of the altar. It is possible to understand MT in this way, though it hardly represents its intent.

On the other hand, at 20:9 MT may represent an inexactitude which LXX has understood correctly. The protasis details a person who might curse את אביו ואת אמו. The Greek changes this to "his father ἤ his mother." MT has "both and," but LXX makes the bad-mouthing (κακῶς εἴπῃ) refer to either parent. This is probably what the Hebrew precept intended.

6.3. Some renderings are due to the difference between the structure of the source and of the target language. At 12:3 the Hebrew states that on the eighth day "the flesh of his (the male baby's) foreskin shall be circumcized (ימול Ni)." The translator made the verb active περιτεμεῖ τὴν σάρκα τῆς ἀκροβυστίας αὐτοῦ. The subject is not stated, but the context can only refer to γυνή of v.1. The Hebrew ימול is masculine, but the recasting of the syntagm makes use of the fact that in Greek the verb is not inflected for gender. One could of course also understand an indefinite subject, but this is quite unnecessary; the mother was fully able to perform the rite.

At 20:20 the translator was faced with a lexical item for which Greek had no single equivalent. The incest law concerns the דדה whose shame belongs to the דד, i.e. an agnate aunt and uncle. But the distinction between a relative of the matriarchal line and that of the patriarchal, particularly for the male is difficult to make in Greek without an explanatory gloss. The דדה the translator interpreted by using the feminine of the adjective συγγενής, thus τῆς συγγενούς. The word דדו he then rendered by τῆς συγγενείας, which in the context could only be his uncle, the husband of the συγγενούς αὐτοῦ. A valiant attempt indeed!

6.4. At 7:20(10) MT uses a common formulaic penalty for certain cultic offences, in this case the eating of meat from the זבח השלמים; the penalty reads: הנפש ההוא נכרתה מעמיה, "that person shall be cut off from his people." That such banishment could mean death is taken for granted by LXX, which translates the verb by ἀπολεῖται, thus "shall die, be killed." The same rendering recurs in LXX vv.11,15,17 and 23:30.

6.5. At 9:24 LXX found MT's statement that the people ירנו "shouted for joy," an inappropriate response to the divine theophany,[5] and substituted ἐξέστη "be astonished, amazed," as a more reverent reaction. The LXX reading shows a translator who is not simply rendering Hebrew into Greek, but is trying to reflect what the canonical text must have intended.

Such care is also reflected at 16:13. On the day of atonement Aaron must inter alia "put incense on the fire before Yahweh and the ענן הקטרת shall cover the propitiatory and he will not die." The word ענן occurs 90 times in the Hebrew Bible, and the usual word used to render it is νεφέλη (78 times). Here, however, it is rendered by ἀτμίς "mist, vapor," which, except for Ezek 8:11, is a unique rendering. An ἀτμίς would hardly hide the ἱλαστήριον from sight; it would merely hover over it. The translator thinks of the incense cloud as distinct from normal clouds, as e.g. the cloud in which the Lord reveals himself in v.2.

6.6. Another unique rendering in Lev obtains at 26:31. The collocation ריח ניחח occurs 45 times, and the Greek ὀσμὴ εὐωδίας is a true calque, which occurs solely as its rendering. It is descriptive of sacrifices to the Lord, a sweet or lovely savor for deity to enjoy. But at 26:31 in a context of divine displeasure God says: "I will not smell בריח ניחחכם." Only here is the negative particle used in connection with "smelling your sweet savor," and the translator, fully understanding that the phrase described sacrifices, used τῶν θυσίων as a substitute for ניחח; this according to the Alexandrian was what God meant to say: "I will not smell the savor of your sacrifices."

6.7. Two exegetical niceties occur in the account of the death of Nadab and Abioud, who offered strange fire on the altar. At 10:3 a divine oracle is communcated to Aaron which demands proper worship: "Among those who approach me (i.e. for worship) I must be considered holy; and in the presence of all העם I will be glorified." The usual LXX rendering for עם is λαός (1621 times) or ἐθνός (159 times),[6] but here העם is parallel to קרבי "those approaching me," and the unusual rendering συναγωγῇ is used (occurs elsewhere for עם only at Num

---

5. Frankel, op. cit. 130 says "die eigentliche Bedeutung 'jauchzen' schien die dieser göttliche Manifestation night decent."
6. According to the count in Dos Santos.

32:15). It is the people approaching for worship who are meant; it is the people as the cultic assembly that is here appropriate.

In v.6 the Lord allowed all but the surviving priests to bewail את השרפה אשר שרף יהוה "the burning which Yahweh burned," i.e. whom he destroyed by fire. LXX makes fully clear that the fire was not the fire consuming the sacrifice on the altar by its rendering τὸν ἐμπυρισμὸν ὃν ἐνεπυρίσθησαν ὑπὸ κυρίου; the fire was that by which they (i.e. Nadab and Abioud) were consumed by the Lord.

6.8. The pericope 24:10—23 deals with a specific case of a half-breed born of an Israelite mother but fathered by an Egyptian, who (v.11) יקב את השם ויקלל "he blasphemed the Name and cursed." LXX correctly rendered this by ἐπονομάσας ... τὸ ὄνομα κατηράσατο "by pronouncing the name he cursed." The basis for condemning such is given at v.15: "anyone who curses אלהיו shall bear חטאו," i.e. this is a capital offence, such a one must die. LXX renders אלהיו by θεόν. The translator apparently felt that a half-breed might well not consider Yahweh to be his God. Nonetheless, having cursed the Lord God, θανάτῳ θανατούσθω (v.16).

7.0. *Theological realia*. Though Lev is much more of an isolate type of rendering than Gen or Exod, the point of view of the translator does appear here and there. His theological presuppositions can often be detected in his choice of lexeme for a particular concept, or in his prejudicial choice of certain renderings, even in slight changes of text which a close comparison of text and translation might reveal.

7.1. At 3:13 the worshiper must, when he brings a goat as offering to Yahweh, place his hand on its head, and שחט אתו before the tabernacle. In other words, he (the worshiper) is to slaughter it. In the next clause "the Aaronids must sprinkle its blood." The Greek has the worshiper put (his) hands on its head, καὶ σφάξουσιν αὐτό; it is the priests who are to do the slaughtering, not the worshiper. Similarly at 4:24 for the ruler, and at 4:29 for the layman who sins inadvertently, ושחט occurs, but is in both cases changed to the plural καὶ σφάξουσιν. The Alexandrian insists on the priestly slaughter of the sin offering; it is thus part of the cultic duties of the priests.

7.2. The notion of God's לחם occurs a number of times in the book, but Lev assiduously avoids the notion of "the bread of God,"as though God might be in need of food. The translator deals with it in various ways. When all else fails he simply omits it. At 3:16 the priest must sacrifice לחם אשה לריח ניחח. For this collocation Lev has κάρπωμα ὀσμὴν εὐωδίας τῷ κυρίῳ (the dative is a pious gloss); there is no equivalent for לחם. At 7:3(13) the prepositional phrase על חלת לחם חמץ occurs as modifying יקריב; the reference is to the תודת שלמיו offering. LXX translates the phrase by ἐπ' ἄρτοις ζυμίταις "with leavened loaves." The word ἄρτοις renders חלת, not לחם which is again omitted. And at 8:26 in the ordination ritual, a sacrifice was demanded which included inter alia one חלת מצה and one חלת לחם שמן. The Greek reads ἄρτον ἕνα ἄζυμον καὶ ἄρτον ἐξ ἐλαίου ἕνα; again לחם is not rendered.

The most common rendering of לחם as part of God's sacrifice is δῶρα, the usual rendering for קרבן. This is the case at 21:8,17,21,22 and 22:25. The only other case in which לחם appears is at 3:11, where MT states that the priest shall offer it לחם אשה ליהוה, but the Greek has ὀσμὴν εὐωδίας κάρπωμα κυρίῳ. This could be textual in origin; in fact, at 8:21,28 κάρπωμα also follows ὀσμὴ(ν) εὐωδίας, and at 2:9 3:5,16 6:15 κάρπωμα precedes the phrase. In any event, the general picture is consistent; the translator avoids any notion of God's bread. In an Egyptian environment during the Ptolemaic period such a notion might well be considered pagan.

7.3. At 8:31 Moses is speaking; he says "אשר צויתי לאמר: Aaron and his sons may eat it." But such orders did not come from Moses himself, and so Lev says ὃν τρόπον συντέτακταί μοι. After all, the words came from the Lord. Similarly at 10:13 MT reads כן צויתי. The Masoretes were careful to vocalize this as Pu, but the Greek makes this clear by means of a passive verb in its οὕτως γὰρ ἐντέταλταί μοι.

7.4. AT 13:11 the translator flatly contradicts MT. In the case of chronic "leprosy" in the skin of one's flesh, the priest must declare such a one unclean. V.b then continues with לא יסגרנו כי טמא הוא, which seems odd indeed. This seems to state clearly "he must not isolate him because he is unclean," which goes contrary to the general instructions of the chapter; see e.g. vv.4—5. In any event, LXX simply omits the negative: "he must isolate him because he is unclean."

7.5. To the Alexandrian the language of 16:16 was overly vigorous. Reference is there made to "the tent of meeting השכן," i.e. which dwelt (with them). How could the tabernacle be thought of in such personal terms? By rendering the word by the passive participle of κτίζω the personification of the tent of witness is avoided. Lev reads concerning the tent τῇ ἐκτισμένῃ (ἐν αὐτοῖς), i.e. "which was set, built among them."

7.6. The Hebrew text of 18:21 forbids giving any of one's seed להעביר למלך. The word מלך is here intended as the name of the god Moloch to whom child sacrifice was reputedly offered, thus "to cause to pass through (fire) to Molech." Apparently the translator misread the *resh* of להעביר as a *daleth*, translating the structure by λατρεύειν ἄρχοντι. The name מלך was not recognized as such, but was taken as the usual word for "king." What LXX means is "not may you give any of your seed to do cultic service to a ruler." This did make sense in the Alexandria of the Ptolemaic period, during which the pretention of divinity by the Ptolemies was accepted by the Egyptians; it would have been impolitic to forbid cultic reverence to the king, i.e. to Ptolemy, but the indefinite ἄρχων was safer.

7.7. Typical of chh.18—26, commonly called the Holiness Code, is the frequent occurrence of the divine self-identification formula, either in the short form, אני יהוה, with 24 cases, or the long formula אני יהוה אלהיכם (19 instances). The translator, however, much preferred the long formula. All cases of the long formula in MT are also long in LXX, but of the 24 short forms, only eleven are short in the Greek, with 12 substituting the long form, and one being omitted. The reason for the popularity of the long form may be due to the use of a third pattern אני יהוה מקדשכם "I Yahweh am the one who sanctifies you," a formula which occurs a number of times as well. That Yahweh is your God, i.e. the one who sanctifies you, does contextualize the bare identification אני יהוה/ἐγὼ κύριος as "your God."

7.8. Other cases occur in which somehow a disrespectful view of deity might be stimulated by MT. At 26:33 God threatens his disobedient people with והריקתי אחריכם חרב "And I will unsheathe after you a sword." The graphic picture of deity actually drawing a sword from the sheathe (to chase) after his people was offensive to the translator. He paraphrases by καὶ ἐξαναλώσει ὑμᾶς ἐπιπορευομένη ἡ μάχαιρα "and the sword being drawn (literally on the march) shall destroy you." The notion that God should draw the sword has been completely removed by LXX.

21:8a reads וקדשתו כי את לחם אלהיך הוא מקריב. The address is to the people as a unit, and the suffix refers to the priest. A problem occurs with the first word. The normal understanding would be "and you (the people) shall sanctify him," which could hardly have been intended. To avoid such a bizarre possibility the translator has reinterpreted the clause by καὶ ἁγιάσει αὐτόν. By making the verb third person the subject becomes God: "And he shall sanctify him." Of course, the Hebrew verb must have intended "and you must regard him as holy." For לחם see comment above at 7.2.

At 26:23—24 the word קרי occurs. In v.23 the context is the people's hostile attitude towards God: והלכתם עמי קרי "and you walk with me in hostility." This LXX renders more or less adquately by ἀλλὰ πορεύησθε πρός με πλάγιοι. In v.24, however, it is God who will himself walk with you בקרי. This becomes θυμῷ πλαγίῳ "in hostile anger." The gloss θυμῷ is added to avoid the notion of treachery, crookedness on God's part. In v.28 this recurs and is softened by a parallel statement "and I will chasten you sevenfold according to your sins." That the distinction in the word as applied to man vs God is intentional is clear from vv.40—41, where the clauses of vv.23—24 recur making the same distinction, πλάγιοι vs ἐν θυμῷ πλαγίῳ.

7.9. At 26:44 God speaks of בריתי אתם "my covenant with them." The Lev translator shared with other translators of the Pentateuch a careful avoidance of the notion that God should speak of his covenant as a pact between two equals. The divine covenant with man was unidirectional; it was a covenant τὴν πρὸς αὐτούς. The Alexandrians never rendered ברית by συνθήκη, but always by διαθήκη. Such a διαθήκη was a gracious gift directed towards mankind. Other examples of a divine διαθήκη πρός someone may be found in other Pentateuchal books, e.g. at Gen 6:18 9:11 Exod 6:4 Dt 5:2 7:2.

7.10. At 21:23 the priest who has some מום (blemish, defect) is forbidden inter alia to approach the altar lest he should profane מקדשי "my sanctuaries." The Masoretes have vocalized the word as a plural. The Greek not only makes the word singular, but also makes it clear that the sanctuary is a single sanctuary by its τὸ ἅγιον τοῦ θεοῦ αὐτοῦ. The translator was of course fully aware of the Deuteronomic insistence on a single sanctuary, and his interpretation of מקדשי is an intentional identification as "the sanctuary (i.e. the holy place) of his God."

8.0. The passages discussed in this introductory statement will, I trust, convince the reader of the usefulness of studying Lev as an exegetical tool. It constitutes our earliest extant exegetical source for understanding the difficult text of Leviticus; it reflects the understanding of the Biblical text by diaspora Jewry in Alexandria in the third century BCE. This understanding may not always be clear; it certainly was not always what the original writers of the Hebrew parent text intended, but it was theirs, and it is both a valid and a fascinating area of study for its own sake.

II. Character of this volume

This is now the fourth volume of Notes on a LXX book of the Pentateuch. What had been said of the earlier volumes concerning presuppositions underlying the Notes is equally appropriate for the Notes on the Greek Leviticus; furthermore, I have taken the introductory remarks of my earlier volumes (more particularly of the Notes on Deuteronomy) and simply adapted them to this one.

9.0. The text commented on is not that of Rahlfs (Ra), but that of the Göttingen LXX.[7] The Ra text was not a critical text; it was a student edition, a *Handausgabe*, based mainly on the text of Codex B (Vaticanus) with its obvious errors corrected. A few readings from Codex A as well as occasional O (hexaplaric) readings and some L (Lucianic or pseudo-Lucianic) readings for certain books constitute a small apparatus. Rahlfs never intended this text to be anything more than an interim text, one that would eventually be replaced by the critical texts of the Göttingen Septuaginta.

It is the volumes of the Göttingen LXX that represent the state of the art; these are based on new collations of all the relevant texts available, including all the extant papyri remains as well as the texts of the sub-versions. What the Göttingen texts provide is as close an approximation to the original LXX as possible, limited only by the inadequacies of the editor.

It is this text which is analyzed. No attempt is made to review scholarly opinions, since it was thought to be much more appropriate to read the LXX text itself than to read about it. The text is far more important than what scholars say about it, and this is equally true of what the author of these Notes has to say.

The professional Greek scholar will probably find my Notes overly elementary and repetitive, but they are not intended for the professional. I have written these Notes to help serious students of the Pentateuch who want to use the LXX text with some confidence, but who are themselves neither specialists in LXX studies nor in Hellenistic Greek. Such students might well need help in understanding the LXX text over against the Hebrew, and it is hoped that such students might find these Notes a useful guide.

9.1. The point of departure for these Notes is that of Lev, i.e. of the Greek text of Leviticus in the Göttingen Septuagint; see the preceding footnote. The

---

7. Leviticus, SEPTUAGINTA Vetus Testamentum Graecum Auctoritate Academiae Scientiarum Gottingensis edidit John William Wevers. II, 2. Göttingen, 1986.

problem faced by the translator was how to render the intent of the Hebrew parent text into a Greek form which his synagogal audience and readers would understand. To do this well presupposes an artist who fully understood both the limitations and the possibilities of the two linguistic codes involved, viz. Hebrew and Hellenistic Greek.[8] Stress is intentionally placed on how well the translator carried out his work, thus on how he constructed his Greek text, on how and whether he avoided transfering the characteristics of the source language to the target language. Accordingly the Notes concentrate throughout on the morphological, syntactic and semantic levels of language.

9.2. Since Lev is by nature a translation text, a careful comparison at all levels between the presumed parent Hebrew and the resultant Greek texts is basic to the Notes. I have taken the parent text as the consonantal text of MT except where the evidence makes such a parent text unlikely. This consonantal text is an actual text, and throughout an attempt has been made to avoid speculative reconstructions as much as possible, even though at times these might be most attractive.

Other ancient texts which were compared throughout as well were the Samaritan Hebrew (Sam), the Onkelos Targum as representing the Babylonian tradition, and the Pseudo-Jonathan and Neophyti Targums as representing the Jerusalem form of the Targums. Also compared were published Qumran fragments as well as the Peshitta (Syriac) and the Vulgate (Latin) translations. These as a group constitute the ancient witnesses.

9.3. The Notes deal principally with the work of the translator, i.e. they are concerned with how the translator, the original LXX, interpreted the text; they have disregarded how later users of the LXX interpreted the text. To have reviewed how Josephus, Philo and the Church Fathers of the early centuries understood the LXX would simply have duplicated the fine work on Leviticus of P.Harlé and D.Pralon.[9] Needless to say I have consulted their work at every juncture, and have profited immeasurably from this careful piece of work, but my point of departure is quite different from their volume, and the two works are to

---

8. For a comparison of these two codes see my Notes on the Greek Text of Exodus, pp.vii—xiv, as well as my "The Use of Versions for Text Criticism: the Septuagint" in La Septuaginta en la Investigacion Contemporanea (V Congreso de la IOSCS), editado por Natalio Fernández Marcos (Madrid, 1894), pp.15—24.
9. La Bible d'Alexandrie. 3. Le Lévitique, Traduction du texte grec de la Septante, Introduction et Notes par Paul Harlé et Didier Pralon. Paris, 1988.

a great extent in complementary distribution. Harlé-Pralon have also given a full translation of Deut, whereas I have not done so. I have limited translations to difficult passages, wherever such might facilitate one's understanding of how the translator understood the Hebrew text.[10]

9.4. I have used the term "tradition" throughout to represent the development of the original LXX text, the autographon, from its original form as reconstructed for the critical text up to its form (or forms) in the fifteenth century, when the invention of movable type made possible the production of multiple identical copies of a text, thereby revolutionizing textual development. The tradition in its multiple forms is summarized in the first apparatus of the Göttingen edition(s).

9.4.1. But those for whom the LXX was sacred scripture did not have the original text as it left the hands of the translator, nor did they have the Göttingen text as its approximation. The countless users of the LXX throughout the centuries only had copies, in fact, copies of copies. Such readers had manuscripts which represented later forms of the LXX text. These manuscripts are all eclectic in nature, i.e. they are based on a complicated and often untraceable textual genealogy.

9.4.2. I have not recorded all the evidence for such variant readings in painstaking detail, but rather made generalizations concerning patterns of support, which are explained under 9.4.4—7 below.[11] The interested reader will find details of support in the first apparatus of the Göttingen edition. I have also simplified the evidence and largely disregarded scattered support by concentrating on support by textual families. I have used "textual families" in a quantitative sense, i.e. support by at least half of the members of a textual family as given in 9.4.3. below.

The first apparatus of the Göttingen editions constitutes a digest of this textual history of the LXX. That text underwent a most complicated history of revisions, which is reflected in the texts of the text families. The first apparatus is actually a summary of a living text. What the synagogue, and later the church,

---

10. The IOSCS is actively engaged in planning and preparing a translation of the Greek O.T. into English.
11. I have explained some of these larger generalizations in my "The Göttingen Pentateuch: Some Post-partem Reflections," in VII Congress of the International Organization for Septuagint and Cognate Studies, edited by Claude Cox (Atlanta, 1991), pp.51—60.

used was that living and developing tradition. When the ancient writers quoted and commented on the scriptures, these scriptures were part of that living tradition.

9.4.3. The following table details these families with their members; the numbers follow those of the Rahlfs catalogue.[12]

O = G-58-376-426(from 16:1) Arab Syh
oI = 15-64-381-618-708
oII = 29-72-82-707 Arm
O' = $O + oI$; $O^{\mathrm{)}}$ = $O + oII$; $O'^{\mathrm{)}}$ = $O + oI + oII$; $o I^{\mathrm{)}}$ = $oI + oII$

C = 16-46-77-131-500-529-739
cI = 57-73-320-413-528-550-552-761
cII = 52-313-414-417-422-551-615
C' = $C + cI$; $C^{\mathrm{)}}$ = $C + cII$; $C'^{\mathrm{)}}$ = $C + cI + cII$; $c I^{\mathrm{)}}$ = $cI + cII$

b = 19-108-118-314-537

d = 44-106-107-125-610

f = 53-56-129-246-664

n = 54-75-127-458-767

s = 30-85-130-321-343-344-346-730

t = 74-76-84-134-370

x = 71-509-527-619

---

12. A. Rahlfs, Verzeichnis der griechishen Handschriften des Alten Testaments, für das Septuaginta-Unternehmen aufgestellt. MSU 2. Berlin, 1915. The Unternehmen has been keeping the Verzeichnis up-to-date, and Detlef Fraenkel has been assigned the task of preparing a revised edition by the Committee directing the affairs of the Unternehmen.

y = 121-318-392

z = 68-120-122-126-128-407-628-630

Uncials: A B F M V

Papyri: 801 802 809 858 931 936 947 954

Unclassified Codices = 18 55 59 319 416 424 426(to 16:1) 642 646 646¹ 799

Versions = Arab(ic), Arm(enian), Eth(iopic), Co(ptic) which includes Bo(hairic) and Sa(hidic), La (= Vetus Latina), Pal(estinian-syriac), and Syh (= Syrohexaplar)

9.4.4. A variant may be identified as a one, two or three family variant. Thus a *b x z* reading means that the reading is supported by all or a majority of the manuscripts of the *b x* and *z* families; it may also have scattered support from other manuscripts or from the versions, but that is disregarded. When such readings are identified as e.g. a *b* reading, what is meant is that the reading has been judged to be a *b* family reading. But should more than three families support a reading it is simply called a *popular* reading, whereas if the support includes over half of all witnesses, i.e. of manuscripts and versions, it is designated a *majority* reading.

9.4.5. Since the uncial texts, A B F M V, and the papyri, constitute on the whole the oldest Greek manuscript witnesses I have often listed them as well, e.g. A F *b f s*. Except for the later F^a and F^b readings, uncial support is only listed if it is unclouded; thus "corrector" readings of uncial manuscripts are usually disregarded.

Occasionally the + sign is used to signal manuscript support; it is to be understood as meaning "along with scattered support." Thus the designation F+ means that a reading is found in codex F as well as in scattered manuscript(s) not identifiable as constituting a textual family or families.

9.4.6. From the table in 9.4.3. it appears that a large number of manuscripts constitute the Catena text. The edition has subdivided these witnesses into a main group, *C*, and two subordinate groups, *cI* and *cII*. Since most readers will probably not be interested in Catena criticism these have usually all been subsumed under the siglum *C* throughout the Notes.

9.4.7. Frequent reference is also made to a Byzantine text. The term applies to the family readings which characterize the text of the Byzantine lectionaries in the Pentateuch.[13] A Byzantine textual reading means a reading supported by all or at least two of *d n t*.

10.0. Certain information has been almost routinely relegated to footnotes, not because it is unimportant, but rather because it is not central to the Notes.

10.1. The Notes do not detail reasons for choosing the readings of Lev in favor of variant readings, except where I now consider the Lev reading as secondary. Such arguments concerning the originality of the text are fully discussed in my THGL Chapter 4 (The Critical Text [Lev]),[14] and such matters are all referred to in footnotes where the relevant page of THGL is given. The user who is not interested in such matters can simply disregard these references.

10.2. Materials gleaned from the second apparatus of the Göttingen edition are also routinely placed in footnotes. Readings from The Three, Aq, Sym and Theod, are given, mainly without comment. In the edition these materials are presented precisely as the manuscripts have the reading, even when they are clearly faultily transmitted. I have seen fit to make judgments on these readings, and to make corrections in the footnotes in order to help the reader to understand them.

The relegation of readings to the footnotes does not constitute a judgment on the value of their evidence; it is solely due to the fact that the Notes deal with the LXX text, whereas the readings of the second apparatus are in essence extra-Septuagintal materials, usually gleaned from the margins of LXX texts, the Church Fathers, or of Syh. Such readings have in the long course of LXX tradition history often influenced that tradition, sometimes actively invading it, especially through Origen's hexapla. But their origins are rooted in the Hebrew rather than the LXX tradition, and their interests were revisional. They are thus of importance in understanding the text history rather than the text of LXX, and so should be carefully distinguished from LXX itself.

---

13. See Chapter 11, "The Lectionary Texts" in the author's Text History of the Greek Genesis, MSU XI (Göttingen, 1974), 176—185.
14. Text History of the Greek Leviticus, MSU XIX (Göttingen, 1986), 72—132.

11.0. It should be emphasized that the Notes are not simply another commentary in the usual sense of the term. Rather they examine in detail how the Greek translator interpreted his parent Hebrew text. In other words, Lev is essentially an exegetical document, and this exegesis can only be grasped by a close attention to the linguistic mode which Lev exploits. In fact, the LXX text is the first document we have in the long history of the exegesis of the Hebrew Bible. What one must look for in particular are fine points of clarification made where the Hebrew is not fully clear, or matters where the Greek text appears to deviate from the apparent meaning of the source text. Whenever Lev strays from the obvious intent of the Hebrew, it has been noted, and I have often suggested a possible reason for such deviation.

One should not automatically presuppose a different parent text when differences between the Greek and the Hebrew obtain; rather one should first seek for and pursue other explanations. It is only through such details that a picture of the attitudes, the theological prejudices, as well as of the cultural environment of these Jewish translators can emerge. It is in the confidence that readers will learn to discover something about what these Alexandrian translators thought their Hebrew Torah meant, or ought to mean, that these Notes are presented.

12.0. As in the case of the earlier volumes no bibliography (except for the Sigla which follows this introductory statement) is included in this volume. It was never the author's intention to present a picture of the state of the art, but rather to provide the serious student some help in his/her comparison of MT and LXX. For readers who must have a detailed bibliography the work of Cécile Dogniez and the earlier Brock, Fritsch, Jellicoe Bibliography may be consulted.[15]

The sigla table which follows contains references to works which I found especially useful in preparing the Notes. Occasional studies not given in the Sigla, but referred to in the Notes are given with full bibliographical details in the footnotes.

13.0. The reader will note that, as in the case of my Genesis and Deuteronomy Notes, an Appendix A has been added listing suggested changes in the critical text of the Göttingen volume. I trust that the list will not be taken as

---

15. Bibliography of the Septuagint: Bibliographie de la Septante (1970–1993) par Cécile Dogniez, Avec une préface de Pierre-Maurice Bogaert. Leiden, 1995; A Classified Bibliography of the Septuagint, compiled by S.P.Brock, C.T.Fritsch and S.Jellicoe. Leiden, 1973.

evidence that the editor could not make up his mind, but rather as illustrating that the establishment of a critical text is not a case of *ipse dixi*, but a never-ending application of one's critical faculties to the task. Reworking the text from a new point of view has given new insights, and the Appendix simply demonstrates the undeniable fallibility of the editor.

A second Appendix deals with Lev's terms for the various sacrifices which constitute a major part of the book. By gathering these materials together, the reader may more easily comprehend, not only how the translator viewed the sacrificial system as a whole, but also whether, or in how far, the terminology represented the same system as that of MT.

14.0. It would be remiss of me were I not to acknowledge gratefully the debt I owe to my colleagues in the Department of which I have long been a member, who have sustained me with their friendship and support for more than forty years, and in whose midst I have continued to work in spite of official retirement from the University. In particular I wish to acknowledge those former students of mine who have joined the faculty of the Department of Near Eastern Studies at the University of Toronto. It is to these that I have dedicated this volume as a small token of my affection and gratitude. These particular colleagues are together with their areas of special study the following: Paul Dion (History and Culture of Syria-Palestine), Grant Frame (Assyriology), Libby Garshowitz (Exegetical Literature of Spanish Jewry), Kirk Grayson (Assyriology), Ted Lutz (Hebrew Biblical Literature), Al Pietersma (Septuagint), Don Redford (Egyptology), and John Revell (Masoretic Hebrew Grammar).

I must also add that I am most grateful to Bernard Taylor, the editor of IOSCS, who again generously offered to proofread my finished manuscript, and thereby saved me from many embarrassing errors. He is, however, in no way responsible for what I have written; for that I assume full and sole responsibility.

15.0. As in the case of the parallel volumes on Genesis, Exodus and Deuteronomy, which appeared in this series, the author prepared camera ready copy. The software used was Nota Bene 4.2 plus Lingua, and was printed on an HP LaserJet IV. I also owe thanks to the technical expertise of John Oldham at the New York office of Nota Bene who provided me with the necessary correction for a glitch in the NB software, but I owe Paul J. Bodin of Berkeley, CA, formerly of Union Theol. Seminary, NYC, a particular debt of gratitude for his help in overcoming difficulties with the software used; his expertise was freely shared, and I appreciate his friendship and advice at those times when I felt rather desperately in need of it.

Sigla

- AASF = Annales Academiae Scientiarum Fennicae
- Aejmelaeus = Aejmelaeus, A., Parataxis in the Septuagint: A Study of the Renderings of the Hebrew Coordinate Clauses in the Greek Pentateuch. AASF: Dissertationes Humanarum Litterarum 31. Helsinki, 1982.
- Aq = Aquila
- Aristeas = Aristeas to Philcrates (Letter of Aristeas), edited and translated by M. Hadas. New York, 1973
- Bauer = Arndt, W.P. and Gingrich, F.W., A Greek-English Lexicon of the New Testament and Other Early Christian Literature, transl. and adapt. from W. Bauer, Griechisch-Deutsches Wörterbuch zu den Schriften des Neuen Testaments und der übrigen urchristlichen Literatur, 4te Aufl., 1952. Chicago, 1957; 2nd ed. revised and augmented by F.W.Gingrich and F.W.Danker from the 5te Aufl.
- BDB = Brown, F., Driver, S.R. and Briggs, C.A., A Hebrew and English Lexicon of the Old Testament, with an Appendix containing the Biblical Aramaic. Boston and New York, 1907
- BHS = Biblia Hebraica Stuttgartensia, ed. K.Elliger et W.Rudolph. Stuttgart, 1977; Fasciculus 2: Exodus et Leviticus praeparavit G.Quell. 1973
- Bl-Debr = Blass, F., Debrunner, A. u. Rehkopf, Fr., Grammatik des neutestamentlichen Griechisch, 14te völlig neubearb. Aufl. Göttingen, 1975
- Boisacq = Boisacq, E., Dictionaire étymologique de la langue Grecque. Paris, 1938
- Cox, Hex = Cox, Claude E., Hexaplaric Materials Preserved in the Armenian Version, SCS 21, Atlanta, 1986
- idem, VI Congress = Cox, Claude, ed., VI Congress of the International Organization for Septuagint and Cognate Studies: Jerusalem 1986, SCS 23, Altanta, 1986
- idem, VII Congress = Cox, Claude, ed.,VII Congress of the International Organization for Septuagint and Cognate Studies: Leuven 1989, SCS 31, Atlanta, 1991
- Crönert = Crönert, W., Memoria Graeca Herculanensis, Lipsiae, 1903
- Daniel = Daniel, S., Recherches sur le vocabulaire de culte dans le Septante. Études et Commentaires 61. Paris, 1966

- De Septuuginta = Pietersma A. and Cox, C., edd., De Septuaginta: Studies in honour of John William Wevers on his sixty-fifth birthday. Mississauga, Ont, 1984
- DJD XII = Discoveries in the Judean Desert XII; Qumran Cave 4 VII: Genesis to Numbers by E.Ulrich and F.M.Cross, + J.R.Davila, N.Jastram, J.E.Sanderson, E.Tov and J.Strugnell. Oxford, 1994
- Dogniez-Harl = Dogniez, C. et Harl, M., Le Deutéronome: Traduction du texte grec de la Septante, Introduction et Notes. La Bible d'Alexandrie 5. Paris, 1992
- Dorival = Dorival, G., Les Nombres: Traduction du texte grec de la Septante, Introduction et Notes. La Bible d'Alexandrie 4. Paris, 1994
- Dos Santos = Elmar Camilo Dos Santos, An Expanded Hebrew Index for the Hatch-Redpath Concordance to the Septuagint, Jerusalem, n.d.
- Field = Field, Fr., Origenis Hexaplorum quae supersunt. Oxonii, 1867-1875
- Freedman = Freedman, D.N., Variant Readings in the Leviticus Scroll from Qumran Cave 11, CBQ 36(1974), 525—534
- Gispen = Gispen, W.H., Het Boek Leviticus. Kommentaar of het Oude Testament. Kampen, 1950

Greenspoon-Munnich = Greenspoon, L. and Munnich, O., edd., VIII Congress of the International Organization for Septuagint and Cognate Studies: Paris 1992, SCS 41, Atlanta, 1995

- GK = Gesenius' Hebrew Grammar as edited and enlarged by the late E.Kautzsch. Second English edition revised by A.E.Cowley. Oxford, 1910
- Harlé-Pralon = Harlé, P. et Pralon, D., Le Lévitique: Traduction du texte grec de la Septante, Introduction et Notes. La Bible d'Alexandrie 3. Paris, 1988
- Hesych = Hesychii Alexandrini Lexicon recensuit et emendavit Kurt Latte. Hauniae, 1953, 1966
- Hesychius = Hesychius, Presbyter in Jerusalem, Commentarius in Leviticum
- Helbing = Helbing, R., Die Kasussyntax der Verba bei den Septuaginta. Göttingen, 1928
- Helbing, Gramm. = Helbing, R., Grammatik der LXX: Laut- und Wortlehre. Göttingen, 1907
- Holladay = Fragments from Hellenistic Jewish Authors. Vol.I: Historians by C.R.Holladay. Texts and Translations no.20. Pseudepigrapha no.10. Chico, CA, 1983

- HR = Hatch, E. & Redpath, H.A., A Concordance to the Septuagint and the other Greek Versions of the O.T. I-II, Suppl. Oxford, 1897-1906
- Huber = Huber, K., Untersuchungen über den Sprachcharacter des griechischen Leviticus. Giessen, 1916.
- IOSCS = International Organization for Septuagint and Cognate Studies
- Johannessohn, Gebrauch = Johannessohn, M., Der Gebrauch der Präpositionen in der Septuaginta. MSU 3,3. Berlin, 1926
- KB = Koehler, L. and Baumgartner, W., Lexicon in Veteris Testamenti Libros. Leiden, 1953.
- Lampe = Lampe, G.W.H., A Patristic Greek Lexicon, Oxford, 1961
- Later Revisers = οἱ λοιποί or οἱ λ´
- Lee = Lee, J.A.L., A Lexical Study of the Septuagint Version of the Pentateuch. Chico, 1983
- Lev = The text in Leviticus, SEPTUAGINTA Vetus Testamentum Graecum Auctoritate Academiae Scientiarum Gottingensis edidit John William Wevers. II, 2. Göttingen, 1986.
- LS = Liddell, H.G., Scott, R., & Jones, H.S., A Greek-English Lexicon, 9th ed., Oxford, 1940
- Mayser = Mayser, E., Grammatik der griechischen Papyri aus der Ptolemäerzeit. I., Leipzig, 1906. II 1, Berlin, 1926. II 2, 1933/34. II 3, 1934. 2 Aufl. I 1, 1970. I 2, 1938. I 3, 1936
- Milgrom = Leviticus 1—16. A New Translation with Introduction and Commentary, by Jacob Milgrom. Anchor Bible 3. New York, 1991
- MSU = Mitteilungen des Septuaginta-Unternehmens
- MT = Masoretic Text as found in BHS
- NIV = New International Version
- NJPS = TANAKH The Holy Scriptures; The New JPS Translation According to the Traditional Hebrew Text
- NRSV = New Revised Standard Version
- Note at Dt = Wevers, J.W., Notes on the Greek Text of Deuteronomy. Atlanta, 1995
- Note at Exod = idem, Notes on the Greek Text of Exodus. Atlanta, 1990
- Note at Gen = idem, Notes on the Greek Text of Genesis. Atlanta, 1993
- Pesh = Peshiṭta. The O.T. in Syriac according to the Peshiṭta Version. Part I, fasc 2. Leviticus by D.J.Lane. Leiden, 1991

- Porter = Porter, S.E. Verbal Aspect in the Greek of the New Testament with Reference to Tense and Mood. Studies in Biblial Greek, Vol.I. New York, 1989
- Prijs = Prijs, L., Jüdische Tradition in der Septuaginta. Leiden, 1948
- Ra = Rahlfs, A., Septuaginta, Stuttgart,1935
- Reider-Turner = An Index to Aquila by the late J.Reider, completed and revised by N.Turner. Supplements to VT, Vol.XII, Leiden, 1966
- Sam = Samaritan Pentateuch. Der hebräische Pentateuch der Samaritaner, herausg. von A. von Gall. Giessen, 1918
- SBL = Society of Biblical Literature
- Schl = Schleuser, J.F., Novus Thesaurus philologico-criticus, sive Lexicon in LXX et reliquos interpretes Graecos ac Scriptores Apocryphos V.T. Lipsiae, 1820-1821
- Schwyzer = Schwyzer, E., Griechische Grammatik auf der Grundlage von Karl Brugmanns griechischer Grammatik. Handbuch der Altertumswissenschaft. II.1.Band I:3.Auflage, und Band II:2.Auflage. München, 1959
- SCS = SBL: Septuagint and Cognate Studies Series (Scholars Press)
- Sollamo = Sollamo, R., Renderings of Hebrew Semiprepositions in the Septuagint, AASF: Dissertationes Humanarum Litterarum 19. Helsinki, 1979
- Sollamo, Rep = Sollamo, R., Repetition of the Possessive pronouns in the Septuagint, SCS 40. Atlanta, 1995
- SS = Soisalon-Soininen, I., Studien zur Septuaginta-Syntax, AASF 237. Helsinki, 1987
- SS Inf = idem, Die Infinitive in der Septuaginta. AASF 132, 1. Helsinki, 1965
- Suidas = (Suda). Suidae Lexicon, Graece & Latine ... Aemilii Porti. Cantabrigiae, 1705
- Suppl.V.T. = Supplements to Vetus Testamentum
- Syh = The Syrohexaplar
- Sym = Symmachus
- Targ = The Targums Pseudo-Jonathan, Neophiti, and Onkelos
- Tar^J = Targum Pseudo-Jonathan of the Pentateuch: Text and Concordance. E.G.Clarke. Hoboken, NJ, 1984
- Tar^O = Targum Onkelos. Sperber, A., The Bible in Aramaic based on Old Manuscripts and Printed Texts. Vol.I. The Pentateuch according to Targum Onkelos. Leiden, 1959
- Tar^P = The Palestinian Targum. A. Díez Macho, Levítico, NEOPHYTI 1: Targum Palestinense ms de la Biblioteca Vaticana. Tomo III. Madrid, 1971

- Thack = Thackeray, H.St.J., A Grammar of the Old Testament in Greek according to the Septuagint: I. Introduction, Orthography and Accidence. Cambridge, 1909
- The Others = οἱ λοιποί or οἱ λ´
- The Three = οἱ γ´
- Theod = Theodotion
- THGD = Wevers, J.W. Text History of the Greek Deuteronomy, MSU 13, Göttingen, 1978
- THGE = idem, Text History of the Greek Exodus, MSU 21, Göttingen, 1992
- THGG = idem, Text History of the Greek Genesis, MSU 11. Göttingen, 1974
- THGL = idem, Text History of the Greek Leviticus, MSU 19. Göttingen, 1986
- THGN = idem, Text History of the Greek Numbers, MSU 16. Göttingen, 1982
- Tov = Tov, E., The Text-Critical Use of the Septuagint in Biblical Research, Jerusalem Biblical Studies 3. Jerusalem, 1981
- Ulrich = Ulrich, E.C., The Septuagint Manuscripts from Qumran: a Reappraisal of Their Value, SCS 33. (Atlanta, 1992), 49—80
- VT = Vetus Testamentum
- Vulg = The Vulgate. Biblia Sacra: Vulgatae Editionis Sixti V Pont. Max. iussu recognita et Clementis VIII auctoritate edita. Romae, 1965
- Walters = Walters, P., The Text of the Septuagint, edited by D.W.Gooding. Cambridge, 1973
- ZürB = Die Zürcher Bibel

NOTES

1:1 The book begins with a divine summons to Moses. The verb ἀνεκάλεσεν is rarely used in OT, and occurs only here in the book; in fact, it translates the verb קרא only three times in the Pentateuch (also at Exod 31:2 35:30 where it was used of God summoning Beseleel as architect for the tabernacle), and once elsewhere in OT (at Jos 4:4 where Yesous calls up 12 tribal appointees to carry memorial stones before the ark). The compound is used in its literal sense "to call up, summon"; Moses is left with no option but to obey. The verb is modified in MT by אל משה, which Lev correctly rendered by Μωυσῆν. Hex with misguided fidelity to MT added a προς before the noun to represent the preposition, but the verb is better served by an accusative designating the person summoned.

For the translation of אהל מועד by τῆς σκηνῆς τοῦ μαρτυρίου see Note at Exod 27:21. The direct speech marker introduces v.2.

1:2 Moses is ordered to speak to the Israelites and say to them. This pattern of "speak to ... and say to them" occurs ten times in the book. On occasion (five times) λέγων is substituted for the second clause, but the two are, however, never combined. What he is to say is contained in what follows up through the end of ch.3. A new section begins with "And the Lord spoke to Moses saying" at the beginning of ch.4. The remainder of ch.1 deals with three kinds of δῶρα "gifts," which Lev uses to translate קרבן, a word which appears in the Pentateuch here for the first time. The word occurs, except for two citations in Ezek, only in Lev (40 times) and Num (24 times). Except for 7:5 (where the verb δωρεῖται is used) it is throughout OT always translated by δῶρον/-ρα.[1] The translator understood the word as referring to any kind of gift, hence uses the plural. When these become specific, as in vv.3,10,14, the singular is used.

The subject of the conditional structure is ἄνθρωπος ἐξ ὑμῶν, which constitutes a simplification of MT in which מכם occurs after כי יקריב rather than immediately after אדם.[2] Hex corrects the word order to fit MT by

---
1. Aq and Sym here translate by προσφοράν.
2. Milgrom suggests that מכם limits אדם to the Israelites, i.e. excludes proselytes. But as he also points out, at times אדם occurs without such modification. I suspect that since Israelites are addressed throughout, whether מכם occurs or not makes no real difference in sense.

transposing the prepositional phrase after προσαγάγῃ, but this perpetuates the lack of clarity of MT's text. The preposition is a partitive ἐξ, as are the three cases of ἀπό that occur within the apodosis later in the verse.[3]

The verb for "bring (a sacrifice)," the Hi of קרב, occurs twice in the verse, but is translated by different verbs, by προσαγάγῃ and by προσοίσετε. The two are exact synonyms as can be seen from their usage in the book. To bring an offering is usually shown by the Hi of קרב, though occasionally the causative of בוא is used. προσάγω is used 36 times for the former, and five times for the latter in Lev, whereas προσφέρω occurs 50, and 12 times resp.[4] Obviously, which of the two verbs is to be used is a matter of indifference to the translator.

The apodosis begins by defining these gifts as being ἀπὸ τῶν κτηνῶν, "from cattle," with which the two following phrases are in apposition; thus the cattle are defined as being either βοῶν or προβάτων. It is also possible to understand ἀπὸ τῶν κτηνῶν as modifying προσαγάγῃ of the protasis, in which case one must disregard the comma preceding the phrase. The Masoretes did not understand it in this way, and the punctuation of the critical text follows the understanding of the Masoretes.

In the tradition, the A F b x y+ text read προσφερη for προσαγάγῃ; this may well be a case of leveling with προσοίσει in the apodosis. Since the two are exact synonyms one generally prefers to follow the text which is better supported in the tradition. The Byz text had added η before the second ἀπό phrase, as well as changed the καί before the third phrase to η; The B f z+ text added και before the second phrase. These variants arise from the copyists wrongly wanting to join the three phrases together as coordinate in some way.

1:3 The particle ἐάν here represents אם; as an introductory particle to represent "if" it occurs far more frequently in the book than does כי (as v.2); in fact, it occurs 91 times; either, however, may introduce a condition and be rendered by ἐάν. The condition is given as a nominal clause of which the predicate is ὁλοκαύτωμα "holocaust, burnt offering," which was to be completely burned. This is the usual rendering for עלה in the book, occurring 45

---

3. See SS 165—167.
4. According to HR.

times.[5] Other renderings are ὁλοκαύτωσις (six times), ὁλοκάρπωσις (once), κάρπωσις (twice), and κάρπωμα (six times, all in ch.1).

If it is to be an acceptable (δεκτόν) sacrifice, it must be a male animal without blemish. The popular addition of αυτο after προσάξει is probably hex in origin, since MT reads יקריבנו. The Hebrew verb appears twice, but as in v.2, is translated differently, i.e. by προσάξει and by προσοίσει; see comment at v.2. The sacrifice must be brought to the door of the tent of testimony. The "door" area must refer not simply to the entrance of the tent, but also to the courtyard area in front of it, where people could gather to present their sacrifices. This sacrifice is intended לרצנו "for his acceptance," i.e. acceptance on his (i.e. of the one presenting the sacrifice) behalf. Lev translates this freely by an adjective δεκτόν.[6] It is not clear what the adjective modifies, either ὁλοκαύτωμα or δῶρον, though I suspect that the translator thought of "his gift" as being acceptable. Hex has added αυτω to render the suffix of לרצנו, which would then mean "acceptable to God." Byz has added αυτο εξιλασασθαι, which is an import from v.4.

1:4 The worshiper is to lay the hand on the head of the καρπώματος; it is of course his own hand which he uses, but since MT has ידו hex has added an αυτου under the asterisk to represent the suffix.[7] Precisely what is meant by the laying on of the hand is uncertain, but it probably entails some symbolic transfer from the worshiper to the sacrifice by which action the worshiper identifies himself with the animal to be sacrificed.[8] Possibly it means that the worshiper offers himself thereby, dedicating himself to God's service by this cultic symbol.

Since this action has something to do with making the καρπώματος δεκτὸν αὐτῷ ἐξιλάσασθαι περὶ αὐτοῦ the transfer may refer to the transfer of guilt. In MT v.b is introduced by *waw*, but the translator disregarded the conjunction. It should also be noted that the antecedent for both pronouns is the

---

5. According to my count in HR. The statistics in HR unfortunately need some revision, for which see Appendix B. On the rendering of עלה in Lev see Daniel 242—244.
6. See SS 98. Sym translates by τῇ εὐδοκίᾳ αὐτοῦ.
7. For Lev commonly omitting the suffix with χείρ see the discussion in SS 95—96.‘
8. Milgrom maintains that since only one hand is used, transference is excluded; he regards its use here as merely indicating ownership; see pp.181—182.

worshiper himself. If it is to be acceptable for him so as to make atonement on his behalf, the guilt has to have been transferred; the worshiper must indeed be atoned for. The verb ἐξιλάσκομαι was first used in Gen 32:20, where Jacob says "ἐξιλάσομαι his face by means of gifts sent on ahead." Obviously the verb there means "to propitiate"; Jacob intends to placate Esau's possible grudge against him by means of a large gift. The verb is then used absolutely at Exod 30:10: "make propitiation on the horns (of the incense altar)," but at vv.15—16 the verb is modified by περὶ τῶν ψυχῶν ὑμῶν, and at 32:30 by περὶ τῶν ἁμαρτίων ὑμῶν. Throughout OT ἐξιλάσκομαι renders כפר almost exclusively; it is clear that Alexandrian Jewry understood כפר in the sense of "to make atonement, propitiate."

Why the עלה should be rendered by κάρπωμα here as well as in vv.9,13,14 and 17, but never elsewhere in the book is puzzling.[9] The noun is cognate to the root καρπο— "to enjoy the fruits of."[10] Does this then mean that the burnt offering is viewed from God's point of view, rather than that of the worshiper, i.e. as a sacrifice which God enjoys? It certainly is called an ὀσμὴ εὐωδίας τῷ κυρίῳ in vv.9,13 and 17.

1:5 MT distinguishes between the number of the opening verb which is singular and that of the remaining verbs. In MT the worshiper slaughters the μόσχον himself, but the offering of the blood and the dashing of it on the altar round about is the function of the Aaronid priests. LXX levels the number throughout to the plural, so that the Aaronid priests also do the slaughtering.

According to MT the priests are to splash or dash the blood on the altar round about. The verb in LXX is προσχεοῦσιν, which is not exactly the same in meaning; it means "to pour out near or towards," but it is the usual rendering throughout the OT; in fact, only once is προσχέω used in OT to render another verb, and it may be taken as a calque for זרק, in which case the verb

---

9. See THGL 74.
10. The cognate noun κάρπωσις occurs in Holladay 63 in Demetrius the Historian, fragm.1 along with the infinitive καρπῶσαι as well as the the compound ὁλοκαρπῶσαι. The context is the story of Abraam's sacrifice of Isaak, in which the latter infinitive is used to describe Abraam's sacrifice οφ Isaac. There follows the statement of his being forbidden ὑπὸ ἀγγέλου, κριὸν αὐτῷ πρὸς τὴν κάρπωσιν παραστησαντος ... τὸν δὲ κριον καρπῶσαι. On p.130 an Eupolemas fragment describes Solomon's going down to Shiloh after completing the building of the temple καὶ θυσίαν τῷ θεῷ εἰς ὁλοκάρπωσιν προσαγαγεῖν βοῦς χιλίους.

must be rendered by "splash" or "dash," i.e. as equivalent to זרק. Similarly, θυσιαστήριον may be taken as a calque for מזבח, though only for legitimate Israelite altars. βωμός, the Classical word for altar, is used only for non-Israelite, illegitimate, heathen altars, and does not occur in Lev. The altar referred to is located at the doors of the tent of witness. Though "doors" are attested for the tent, the plural is here peculiar. MT more logically has a singular פתח, but all Greek witnesses in the tradition attest to the plural genitive, τῶν θυρῶν; the number of the word used to render פתח seems to be a matter of complete indifference to the translator.[11] For θυρῶν see discussion at v.3.

1:6 In MT the verbs are singular; it is the worshiper who acts. LXX, however, follows Sam in using the plural; it is the priests who are responsible for the cultic activity involved. The participle ἐκδείραντες shows attendant circumstance, thus "having flayed the burnt offering, they cut it up." A popular A variant has the simplex form, but this involves no semantic difference. Both forms occur in the OT only as translation of the Hi of פשט. The Hebrew insists that they (the priests) are to cut it up into its pieces. LXX simply has κατὰ μέλη, but hex has added αυτου under the asterisk to equal the Hebrew suffix. By κατὰ μέλη is meant "according to the natural parts (of the sacrificial animal)," i.e. in accordance with its framework or skeleton.

1:7 The translator understood נתנו correctly as meaning "place, put," and used ἐπιθήσουσιν to render it. The syntax of οἱ ἱερεῖς (appositive of οἱ υἱοὶ Ἀαρών) differs from MT, which has הכהן. The singular can only be in apposition to אהרן. LXX follows the text of Sam; Pesh and Tar^N also read the plural noun.

Whether ἐπιστοιβάσουσιν "they shall pile up" or the simplex is original is uncertain; the simplex is an A F M majority reading, but the B reading of the compound is also well-supported. In such doubtful cases when no other deciding factors are present I have chosen the oldest attested reading as original, viz. that of B*. The verb occurs only three times, and that only in this chapter (also vv.8,12), and each time it renders the verb ערך, which is elsewhere usually rendered by παρατάσσω (24 times). MT, as well as Tar,

---

11. See THGL 73.

speak of arranging the firewood (עצים/ξύλα) on the fire, whereas the translator speaks of piling up the firewood; what he probably had in mind was stoking the fire; by piling on the firewood the fire would be sustained, for which comp 6:12—13, but see also 6:8 and 12.

1:8 After having prepared the altar for the sacrifice, the Aaronid priests are to "pile up τὰ διχοτομήματα καί the head and the suet." Why the translator should change from μέλη to the synonym διχοτομήματα, which occurs only here in the book, is unclear. The words mean the same, and apparently the translator simply prefered variation so as to avoid monotony. MT lacks the conjunction before את ראש. Since "the head and the suet" make little sense as appositives to διχοτομήματα,[12] ἐ ῢὸ את and ואת must be understood as being the preposition "with." LXX must have read ואת, the text of Sam, which is supported by Tar^N and Pesh as well.[13]

The final relative clause in MT, "which is on the altar," has האש for its antecedent, but LXX makes it refer to עצים, i.e. τὰ ὄντα refers to τὰ ξύλα, not to τοῦ πυρός. This is not an impossible reading of the Hebrew, but an אשר clause intervenes, and a reader would not normally understand it in this fashion. Actually ms 376 has changed τὰ ὄντα to του, which then does equal MT, a change which could be either hex or simply an exegetical change. It might be noted that ἐπί here governs the genitive, whereas in vv.5,7,9 it governs the accusative. The distinction observed is that ἐπί with the genitive modifies ὄντα, but in vv.5,7,9 the phrase modifies a verb of movement, προσχεοῦσιν (v.5), and ἐπιθήσουσιν (vv.7,9).

1:9 Since v.9 contrasts with v.8, it is introduced by a δέ structure. The intestines and the feet are first to be washed with water before they are placed on the altar. MT has a singular construction: ירחץ במים והקטיר הכהן, which is a structure similar to the opening of v.1, i.e. two coordinate verbs, but with the subject appearing only after the second verb. The Masoretes were troubled by this structure, and so placed במים under the *ethnach*. But this is an odd reading of the text indeed, since there is no antecedent for ירחץ, and it presupposes that the worshiper does the washing. Both NJPS and NRSV have

---

12. The Three all read ύΓόPt.
13. Kenn 1,69,80,198 also read ואת.

understood the subject as indefinite (for which one would normally expect a plural verb), and render it by "its entrails and (its) legs shall be washed with water." LXX has levelled the entire structure with the plurals of vv.5—8. Furthermore, it has omitted the suffixes of קרבו וכרעיו as unnecessary to the sense. Hex has in both cases added αυτου under the asterisk to equal the suffixes in MT. But of greater consequence is LXX's rendering of הקטיר "burn up into smoke" by ἐπιθήσουσιν, i.e. "the priests shall place all these (τὰ πάντα) on the altar," an equation occurring 12 times in Lev, for which see Note at Exod 29:13. Clearly the translator understood הקטיר to mean "to present an offering (on an altar)."[14]

The sacrifice is then triply described as a κάρπωμα, a θυσία and an ὀσμὴ εὐωδίας to the Lord.[15] For κάρπωμα as a translation of עלה see comment at v.4. θυσία occurs nine times in the book for אשה (or אש) commonly rendered by "fire offering."[16] More commonly (19 times) it is rendered by κάρπωμα, and even by ὁλοκαύτωμα (seven times). Clearly the translator understood the term as a general one for a sacrifice, presumably one that was burned up. The third phrase, ὀσμὴ εὐωδίας, occurs frequently both in Lev and Num, and is a calque for ריח ניחוח, for which see Notes at Gen 8:21 and Exod 29:18.[17]

1:10 Vv.10—13 deal specifically with the sacrifice of προβάτων (cf v.2) in contrast to the βοῶν of vv.3—9. By צאן the animals which are herded by the shepherd are intended in distinction from בקר "cattle." In MT the צאן are divided into two classes, הכשבים "sheep" or העזים "goats." LXX has shown this division by its ἀπό τε τῶν ἀρνῶν καὶ (instead of או) τῶν ἐρίφων. LXX has also omitted rendering the repeated preposition before the second noun.

Though in general the prescriptions for the προβάτων are much like those for the βοῶν, some differences can be noted. LXX speaks of τὸ δῶρον αὐτοῦ τῷ κυρίῳ, but MT has no equivalent for τῷ κυρίῳ, and hex has ac-

---

14. See THGL 73.
15. For ὀσμὴ εὐωδίας see Daniel 188—197.
16. Milgrom rightly objects to the rendering "fire offering," and suggests "food gift," which I find equally unacceptable. The term δῶρον is never used to render it, nor is the אשה necessarily food. Possibly one might simply use "an offering," since LXX used a wide variety of words to render it.
17. See Daniel 176,188. Instead of εὐωδίας Aq has ἀναπαύσεως, and Theod renders by εὐαρεστήσεως. According to Procopius The Others read εὐδοκίας, which in my opinion seems unlikely to be correct. See also the discussion in Milgrom 162—163.

cordingly placed it under the obelus; the translator's parent text followed that of Sam, but see also v.2. In contrast to v.3 where יקריבנו was rendered by προσάξει, leaving it to hex to add a rendering for the suffix, here Lev has προσάξει αὐτό. In v.4 the text has "and he shall place the hand upon the head τοῦ καρπώματος," whereas here αὐτοῦ is used. It should be noted, however, that the entire clause is missing in MT. LXX has harmonized the text with that of the first section.

1:11 As in v.5 the opening verse is in the singular, which creates a difficulty as to the reference. In v.5 it referred to the worshiper bringing the offering, whereas the action which dealt with the disposal of the blood was effected by the Aaronid priests. And in v.5 the slaughtering was presumably done at the door(s) of the tent of meeting, but here it is done at the north side of the altar where laymen were not allowed. All of this is voided by LXX which levels to the plural, i.e. the priests perform all the actions; cf comment at v.5. Presumably one can understand שחט as having an indefinite subject as might conceivably be done for v.5 and for ירחץ in v.9, but cf comments ad loc. The problem of singular verbs is continued for MT in v.12 as well.

Why the slaughter of the offering should take place "at the side of the altar towards the north" is not clear.[18] The Greek has translated על ירך by ἐκ πλαγίων; see also Num 3:29,35. πλάγιος more commonly renders צד, and for the notion of "side" only the neuter plural is used throughout OT.

For the second clause see the discussion at v.5 of which it is an abbreviated version both in MT and LXX, the latter being a word-for-word rendering of MT.

1:12 For the consistent plural over against MT see comments on the parallel vv.6—8. At v.6 נתח ... לנתחיה was rendered by cognates: μελιοῦσιν ... κατὰ μέλη, but here LXX has changed the verb to διελοῦσιν, probably for the sake of variation.[19] At v.6 the suffix of לנתחיה (referring to העלה) was not translated and αυτου, referring to τὸ ὁλοκαύτωμα, was supplied under the asterisk by hex. Here the suffix is masculine, referring to קרבנו of v.10, but κατὰ μέλη occurs without an αυτου, which is once again supplied under the asterisk

---

18. For על ירך Aq has ἐπὶ μηρόν, and Sym interprets by τὸ ὀπίσω τὸ κατὰ μέρος.
19. Sym, however, reads μελιοῦσιν.

by hex.[20] As in the case of αὐτό, its antecedent is τὸ δῶρον of v.10. As in v.8 this is followed by "καί the head and the suet," but this time the preposition את is preceded by a conjunction, and could hardly be interpreted as the preposition meaning "with." Since the two verses are obviously related, the originality of את at v.8 is highly questionable. That the LXX text of v.8 influenced the rendering here is clear from the fact that MT has changed את הראש ואת הפדר to ואת ראשו ואת פדרו. Hex has added an αυτου to both nouns; for the former the asterisk is also attested. The remainder of the verse is the same as in v.8 in MT, but in LXX the last אשר had been rendered by τὰ ὄντα in v.8, and here simply by τά, again presumably for the sake of variety.[21]

1:13 For the first clause which is the same as in v.9 except for the δέ becoming a καί structure here, see comments ad loc. MT differs in the two clauses, however, in that the two coordinate nouns are here articulated nouns without pronominal suffixes.

In v.b the verbs necessarily change to the singular, since the subject is stated as ὁ ἱερεύς; this contrasts with v.9, which read ἐπιθήσουσιν οἱ ἱερεῖς, although MT had והקטיר הכהן. Here the verbal notion is divided into two coordinate verbs: "προσοίσει (for הקריב) all these and ἐπιθήσει (for הקטיר) on the altar." For הקטיר see comment at v.9. For the triple description of the sacrifice also see comments at v.9. It might be noted that MT differs at this point in adding הוא after עלה; LXX has an ἐστιν in both cases simply for good sense; see also v.17.

1:14 The remainder of the chapter deals with the burnt offering of birds. The protasis begins with ἐὰν δέ (as in v.10), which is the usual rendering for ואם (69 times out of 73 cases) in Lev. Over against the nominal clause of the protasis in MT the Greek has rendered קרבנו by προσφέρῃ δῶρον "should one offer a gift"; by adding the verb the pronominal suffix becomes completely otiose, and even hex did not supply an αυτου.[22] The verb then has a double accusative, which I would render "one should present an offering as a gift (to

---

20. See SS 97.
21. See THGL 72.
22. See SS 93.

the Lord)." An A B 936 x+ variant has the verb in second person, προσφερης, but this cannot be intended; the entire chapter is in third person.²³ The apodosis is introduced by καί in imitation of the Hebrew. The sacrifice is limited to two types of birds, τρυγόνων "turtledoves," which is a calque for תרים, or περιστερῶν "doves," which uniquely renders בן היונה here; it normally renders יונה. Whether בן היונה actually means "young dove" as is often alleged is uncertain; I suspect that the phrase also simply means "doves."²⁴ In both cases the sacrifice is designated by an ἀπό phrase; the ἀπό, like its counterpart מן, is partitive. What is meant is "a turtledove or a dove."

1:15 The priest is to "bring (it) to the altar." LXX does not translate the pronominal suffix to the verb, and hex has added αυτο under the asterisk to equal MT.²⁵ An A F O f x+ variant changes πρός to επι under the influence of the recurring ἐπὶ τὸ θυσιαστήριον in the chapter (vv.5,7,9,11,13), but here MT has אל, not על. After all, the bird must be processed before being placed on the altar. Only after he (the priest) had pinched off the head, does he place (it) ἐπὶ τὸ θυσιαστήριον. MT reads ראשו, and most witnesses add αυτου after κεφαλήν, which is probably recensional, though it might simply have been added ad sensum. For ἐπιθήσει rendering הקטיר see comment at v.9.

The last clause in MT reads ונמצה דמו על קיר המזבח "and its blood shall be drained out on the wall of the altar." LXX has reinterpreted the Ni נמצה positively by an active verb, by which דמו becomes a modifier. Its στραγγιεῖ τὸ αἷμα makes the priest the subject: "he shall squeeze out the blood." Hex has added an αυτου to represent the suffix in MT. The verb στραγγίζω is a hapax legomenon as is the compound καταστραγγίζω at 5:9; both render the Ni of מצה in Lev, but it would be methodologically wrong to posit semantic differences between the Greek and the Hebrew words, beyond the change in voice. The modifying prepositional phrase also differs in LXX; it reads πρὸς τὴν βάσιν (of the altar) "at the base of the altar."²⁶ The base of the altar is far more common than its wall; in fact, it occurs 10 times in Lev, though only once more with πρός (4:18; but with παρά and ἐπί four times each). In fact,

---

23. See THGL 124.
24. Theod Aq translate מן בן היונה by ἀπὸ τῶν υἱῶν τῆς περιστερᾶς, and Sym has ἀπὸ νεοσσῶν περιστερᾶς.
25. See THGL 105,124.
26. The Three all attest to παρὰ τὸν τοῖχον.

at 5:9 an ἐπί phrase modifies the compound καταστραγγιεῖ. The change of "wall" to "base" in LXX is obviously intentional. Dion has made the interesting suggestion that a Rabbinic tradition (m.Zebaḥ 2:1) has it that blood placed on the wall might allow some of it to touch the top of the altar, which would render the offering invalid. This might well have been the stimulus for the translator to use the more common designation "base."²⁷

1:16 Its crop is to be removed along with נצתה. LXX has omitted the suffix of מראתו, which has been supplied by hex as αυτου.²⁸ Precisely what נצתה means is not clear. Tar have it refer to the contents of the crop, i.e. partially digested food, but this is obviously a contextual translation. LXX translates it by (σὺν) τοῖς πτεροῖς, i.e. as the plural of נוצה "feathers."²⁹ Since LXX did not render the suffix, hex has supplied an αυτου under the asterisk. The problem with the LXX translation is its disregard of the suffix of נצתה; this must refer to מראתו, but a crop does not have feathers.³⁰ Presumably LXX is based on the Sam tradition which has a masculine suffix, i.e. referring to עוף of v.14.

In the second clause αὐτό is difficult to understand, and the majority variant, αυτα, voids the problem by referring to the coordinate pair, πρόλοβον and πτεροῖς. But αὐτό has no obvious antecedent, unless it be taken as an ad sensum reference to the mass of crop and feathers, i.e. waste. The singular must, however, be original; it is the more difficult reading, and the old uncials A B (and G) support it. Furthermore, the translator does use the neuter singular pronoun much more widely than is commonly presupposed, particularly when the antecedent is not overly clear.³¹

1:17 Rather than dividing the sacrifice as in the case of cattle (v.6) or of sheep (v.12), a bird is to be torn open by the wings. After all, a bird is too small to be cut into parts. LXX reads ἐκ τῶν πτερύγων, i.e. (it is to be torn) out of the

---

27. P.E.Dion, JBL CVI (1987), 478—492.
28. Aq rendered the noun by ⌐ñ ≤á⌐ σ⌴ᵃ ÷ ≤ÿñ, whereas Theod Sym translate the word by τὴν φῦσαν.
29. Sym (and Theod?) supports this understanding with σὺν τοῖς πτίλοις.
30. Milgrom 170—171 proposes the novel notion that מראה refers to the "crissum" rather than to the crop, and that "its feathers" refers to the adjoining tail feathers. There is no ancient evidence, however, for understanding the word in this way, and LXX also supports the traditional rendering of "crop."
31. See the discussion in Huber 33ff.

wings. Only thereafter must the priest place it (for הקטיר אתו; see note at v.9) on the altar. Here the αὐτό has a clear referent; it must be a πετεινόν (i.e. ἀπὸ τῶν πετεινῶν). BHS does not support the καί of καὶ οὐ διελεῖ, but a number of mss, as well as Sam, do read ולא, and this is also supported by Tar^J, Pesh and Vulg.

For the triple description of the sacrifice see comment at vv.9,13.

Chapter 2

2:1 MT introduces the verse with ונפש כי, i.e. "As for a person if." LXX simplifies this by its ἐὰν δὲ ψυχή. The use of ψυχή as subject of προσφέρῃ demonstrates conclusively that it simply means "a person," and like its Hebrew equivalent can be either male or female. MT refers to the sacrifice as קרבן מנחה; LXX translates this bound phrase by a double accusative, thus "should a person bring a gift as a sacrifice to the Lord." A d+ variant does change θυσίαν to the genitive θυσιας, which would equal MT more precisely. θυσία is regularly used to render מנחה, a word used to designate a grain or meal offering in contrast to the animal sacrifices of ch.1.[1] In fact, except for 2:13 where מנחה occurs twice but Lev uses θυσιασμάτων for the second one, and at 9:4 where σεμίδαλιν occurs instead of מנחה, for which see comment ad loc, מנחה is always translated by θυσία in the book. Ch.2 is devoted entirely to the regulations dealing with the מנחה/θυσία. This sacrifice is similar in function to the עלה of ch.1 in Lev, but has traditionally been thought to be the sacrifice for the poor. Not everyone could afford a sacrificial animal, and for such a grain sacrifice would be acceptable.

It is then said of such a ψυχή that σεμίδαλις ἔσται τὸ δῶρον αὐτοῦ, i.e. since such a ψυχή is usually a male, αὐτοῦ is used as pronoun, though grammatically one would expect the feminine. The feminine was avoided in the Hebrew as well, probably to make certain that its antecedent not be understood to be מנחה/θυσία. Note that the verbs יצק and נתן are both masculine, though their subject is נפש. The sense is fully clear; αὐτοῦ can only refer to the worshiper. The base of the sacrifice is to be σεμίδαλις "fine, wheat flour," which is a calque for סלת; in fact, סלת is only rendered by σεμίδαλις in the OT.

The subject continues for the second part of the verse. To be a sacrifice the flour must have olive oil poured on it and frankincense placed on it. The second αὐτό probably has δῶρον as antecedent as well, rather than ἔλαιον. The *b* text has αυτην for both cases of αὐτό, thereby making θυσία the antecedent. LXX ends with θυσία ἐστιν which has no counterpart in MT, but is based on the מנחה הוא of Sam.[2]

---

1. Aq Sym render מנחה by δῶρον, whereas the anonymous ἡ προσφορά was probably intended to represent קרבן; cf 1:3.
2. The word מנחה is also extant in 4QExod-Lev^f; see DJD XII 143—144.

2:2 The subject of οἴσει must still be the worshiper; see comment at v.1. MT has a pronominal suffix, which LXX does not render, and hex has added αυτο under the asterisk to make up for it. The second and third clauses have as subject ὁ ἱερεύς, which does not appear until after the verb ἐπιθήσει of the third clause, for which see comment at 1:1. This imitates MT, but it is confusing, since one could easily understand the worshiper to be the one who removes a handful, and only common sense forces one to a proper attribution of the action to the officiating priest.

The priest then first grabs a handful of the fine flour "from it," together with the oil and all its incense. The antecedent of the pronoun αὐτῆς throughout the verse is θυσία. The phrase ἀπ' αὐτῆς represents a locative phrase in MT, משם "from there," but the translation is sensible. πλήρη τὴν δράκα "a handful" represents מלא קמצו, and hex has added αυτου under the asterisk to equal the untranslated suffix.³ Two partitive מן phrases, מסלתה ומשמנה,⁴ are rendered not only without genitive pronouns,⁵ but also by different prepositions: ἀπό ... σύν. Hex has added αυτης under the asterisk to both nouns.

For ἐπιθήσει see comment at 1:9. The handful is called "its memorial," and only it is offered up on the altar as a θυσία, ὀσμὴ εὐωδίας to the Lord. Why this sacrifice should be called a μνημόσυνον is not clear. This is the regular translation of אזכרה in Lev, except for 24:7, where it is translated by ἀνάμνησιν.⁶ The meaning of the Hebrew is no clearer than is that of the Greek. Is it something to stir God's memory, or is it in recognition of some divine gift in the past? Both NJPS and NRSV translate it as "a token offering", and RSV and NIV, as "memorial portion," but it remains unclear.⁷ What is clear is that the translator thought it meant a remembrance, a memorial.

That LXX is often quite inconsistent is obvious from its use of θυσία both for מנחה as well as here for אשה, for which see comment at 1:9.

---

3. Aq translates literally by πλήρωμα δρακὸς αὐτοῦ; Sym has πλήρης τῆς δρακός, and Theod revised LXX to πλήρης τὴν δράκα.
4. See SS 165–166.
5. See SS 97.
6. See Harlé-Pralon 40.
7. Milgrom 181–182 suggests that the term is related to זכר "remembrance" i.e. "referring to the fact that the entire cereal offering should really go up in smoke, and that the portion that does is *pars pro toto*." But this is no more than a suggestion; he translates the word by "token portion."

2:3 The partitive מן is rendered by ἀπό (τῆς θυσίας),⁸ but what is intended would be better rendered by omitting the preposition which must be branded a Hebraism. A popular variant text added το before the preposition to make better Greek out of it, but the Hebraic text is clearly original.

That the remainder of the מנחה/θυσία is the portion set aside for the Aaronids makes it very holy, ἅγιον τῶν ἁγίων ἀπὸ τῶν θυσίων (for אשׁי) κυρίου. The point of the superlative expression is that it is completely removed from profane use; it is devoted entirely to priestly use.⁹ In fact, the superlative term is reserved for those sacrifices which are intended solely for use by priests or for God alone; other sacrifices are simply ἅγια.¹⁰ The term occurs 13 times in the book.

2:4 I would suggest that the comma is in the wrong place in the critical text; a comparison with vv.5 and 7 makes clear that it belongs afer κλιβάνῳ; this is also the interpretation of the Masoretes who placed תנור under the *ethnach*. The protasis then reads: "and if one should bring as gift a sacrifice baked in an oven." For the translation of קרבן מנחה by a double accusative see comment at v.1. Instead of ἐν κλιβάνῳ an A B+ variant reads εκ λιβανου, which is obviously inspired palaeographically.¹¹ In MT the verb is in second person, תקרב. An A F *ol y z*+ variant corrects προσφέρῃ to προσφερης. This need not be a recensional variant based on the Hebrew, but may be due to the influence of second person references in vv.5—7.¹²

That it was at first blush uncertain where the apodosis should begin promoted a popular A B expansion, δωρον κυριω, before ἐκ σεμιδάλεως; this then would solve the problem by reading "the gift to the Lord (should be) of fine flour." It has, however, no support in MT, and the more difficult shorter text is original.¹³ The apodosis is in the accusative, presumably with the προσφέρῃ of

---

8. See SS 165—166.
9. The prepositional phrase is rendered by Aq as ἀπὸ πυρῶν κυρίου, by Sym as ἀπὸ τῶν καρπωμάτων κυρίου, and in Theod as ἀπὸ τῶν τοῦ πυρὸς κυρίου.
10. See Harlé-Pralon 30.
11. See THGL 68.
12. See THGL 124.
13. See THGL 106.

the protasis carried over to it, thus "(one must offer it) from fine flour, unleavened loaves ...."

These offerings baked in an oven may be of two kinds: unleavened cakes mixed with olive oil[14] and unleavened wafers besmeared with oil. Note that LXX does not distinguish between חלות and לחם; both are translated by ἄρτους. In fact, חלה is translated by ἄρτος 12 out of 14 times.[15]

2:5 Vv.5 and 6 concern a fried sacrifice, i.e. a θυσία ἀπὸ τηγάνου. The word τήγανον never appears as τάγηνον in OT, but which is the earlier spelling is uncertain.[16] In MT this is a sacrifice על a griddle rather than from it, whereas LXX reads "sacrifice from a frying-pan." In any event, the cakes of v.5 are to be made of fine flour mixed with olive oil, as well as unleavened. The matter is prescriptive as the future ἔσται implies. The B+ variant, εστιν, is decidedly secondary; it is merely a thoughtless error.

2:6 The verse begins with פתות vocalized as a free infinitive. The translator correctly understood the infinitive as contextual. Since the coordinate clause begins with ויצקת "and you must pour," the future verbs διαθρύψεις and ἐπιχεεῖς correctly render MT. The root פתת is a hapax legomenon, but the infinitival noun פת is well-known as meaning "fragment, piece, bit," and the rendering διαθρύψεις "you must crumble" is correct. The infinitive is modified by אתה, and the pronoun refers to מנחה. The translator, however, used the plural, whereas a literal rendering would have read αυτην; presumably he used αὐτά by attraction to κλάσματα for פתים as a second modifier of the verbal notion.[17]

MT ends the verse abruptly with מנחה הוא, but LXX has θυσία ἐστὶν κυρίῳ. The addition is not surprising, since nominal clauses ending sections usually end with with τῷ κυρίῳ; cf 1:9,13,17 2:2 3:16, or simply with κυρίῳ as at 2:12,16 3:5,11. The obelus in cod G is on the wrong word; it should have been on κυρίῳ, not ἐστίν.

---

14. The Others read κολλύρας instead of ἄρτους.
15. According to the count of Dos Santos.
16. Both are recognized in LS.
17. The Three all read ψωμούς instead of κλάσματα.

2:7 The bound phrase מנחת מרחשת is translated in unusual fashion by a noun plus an ἀπό phrase, a correct intuition; it is a sacrifice from a stew-pan.[18] The Greek θυσία ἀπὸ ἐσχάρας apparently means "a sacrifice from a grate or grating." This distinguishes it from the τηγάνου of v.5; in modern terms the distinction would be a barbecued sacrifice vs one that was fried in a pan.

2:8 MT begins with a second person verb, והבאת, but in v.b changes to third person והקריבה ... הגישה. LXX levels to third person, using προσοίσει "present," an equation which occurs 12 times in the book;[19] it is used more commonly for הקריב. Actually והבאת may well be a palaeographically inspired error due to its being followed by את. A 4Q text reading והביא is probably original.[20] F Byz correct to second person, προσοίσεις. The verb προσοίσει occurs twice; in the first clause it is modified by τὴν θυσίαν ... τῷ κυρίῳ, and in the coordinate clause it is modified simply by πρὸς τὸν ἱερέα, which is confusing.[21] MT had distinguished the two not only in person but also in choice of verb: "you shall bring them ... (to Yahweh)," and "he shall present it to the priest." But the subject of הקריבה can hardly be Yahweh. To avoid such a bizarre understanding LXX not only levelled the verbs to third person, but also the actual verbs, thereby preserving an ambiguity, but not the dangerous one inherent in MT. The translator simply transferred the ambiguity to the modifiers, τῷ κυρίῳ vs πρὸς τὸν ἱερέα, relying on the reader's common sense to keep the chronology straight: the offering is of course to the Lord, but the mechanics of such an offering is to present it to the priest, who in turn will bear it to the altar. The second προσφέρει translated only the verb in הקריבה, and hex added αυτο under the asterisk to represent the suffix.

The sacrifice being brought is described by ἣν ἂν ποιήσῃ ἐκ τούτων, a possible rendering of the consonantal text of MT, though the Masoretes had vocalized תעשה as a Ni 3rd feminine singular with מנחה as subject. What LXX conveys is "which (i.e. the sacrifices) he might make from these (i.e. the components of the sacrifice, viz. fine flour and oil)." The pronoun τούτων refers to the σεμίδαλις and ἐλαίῳ of v.7. The Byz text has changed the verb to a second person verb consistent with its change of both cases of προσοίσει to second per-

---

18. See SS 69.
19. According to HR.
20. 4QLev^b; see DJD XII 179—180.
21. For the unusual πρός construction with προσφέρω see THGL 77.

son and the change of θυσίαν to θυσιαν σου. This text has personalized the worshiper by using direct address throughout the verse wherever possible. The verb is changed to a present tense, ποιη, in A B b+, but the present subjunctive occurs only rarely in Lev, and when it does it stresses linear action. The aorist is to be preferred here.[22]

The last clause of MT is reduced to a participial construction denoting attendant circumstance, and is subordinated to the opening clause of v.9. The translator has also used the participle intransitively, i.e. "And having approached the altar," but MT has a Hi verb plus suffix, הגישה "he shall bring it near (to the altar)." A b reading has corrected the participle to προσεγγιει αυτην, which shows Hebrew influence, probably mediated through one of The Three. An n+ gloss has added ο ιερευς, but this is otiose, since the main clause in v.9 also designates the subject as ὁ ἱερεύς.

2:9 The verse begins asyndetically in view of the subordination of the preceding structure; cf comment on v.8. A b reading has added και, for which see the comment on v.8 on the correction of the last clause in the b text. The officiating priest "shall remove (MT has הרים "raise, lift off") from the sacrifice its τὸ μνημόσυνον." The use of ἀφαιρέω to render the causative of רום occurs seven times in the book; the translator fully understood that "lifting from" meant "removing." For the memorial offering see the discussion at v.2. For ἐπιθήσει as rendering of הקטיר see comment at 1:9.

The description of the sacrifice in v.b is identical to that in v.2 for MT, but here אשה is rendered not by θυσία but by κάρπωμα, for which see Note at Deut 18:1. For אשה see comment at 1:9. κάρπωμα must reflect the root καρπο- "to enjoy the fruits of," and so like the next term, ὀσμὴ εὐωδίας, the sacrifice is probably intended for the Lord's enjoyment.[23]

In the tradition, a popular M text read οσμην instead of ὀσμή. This would simplify v.b by making it modify ἐπιθήσει, but the nominative is original; see v.2, and comp 1:9,13,17.

---

22. See THGL 125 for the defence of the aorist.
23. Theod and Aq have πυρόν for אשה. Ms 130 also attributes the reading to Sym, but I suspect this to be an error for Theod, i.e. based on a confusion of *sigma* and *theta*. Compare f.n. at v.3.

2:10 V.10 is identical to v.3 in MT, but the translator preferred variation.[24] For the intent of this verse see comments at v.3. There והנותרת was translated by καὶ τὸ λοιπόν, but here by τὸ δὲ καταλειφθέν. For קדש v.3 reads ἅγιον, but at v.10 LXX has the plural ἅγια, which, however, a b+ variant "corrects" to the singular. And the final phrase, מאשי יהוה, was there rendered by ἀπὸ τῶν θυσιῶν κυρίου, but here by ἀπὸ τῶν καρπωμάτων κυρίου.[25] A b n text has θυσιων for καρπωμάτων, obviously under the influence of v.3.

2:11 No sacrifice may be offered which is leavened. In MT כל המנחה is the subject of לא תעשה, i.e. "no sacrifice may be made (with leaven)," but LXX turns this around by changing the verb to a 2nd plural, ποιήσετε, and inflecting "every sacrifice" in the accusative: "You shall not make any sacrifice (with leaven)." The πᾶσαν θυσίαν is then defined by a relative clause ἣν ἂν προσφέρητε τῷ κυρίῳ. The plural second person verb must be addressed to the priests; this applies to the entire paragraph, vv.11–13. The γάρ clause gives the reason for not permitting the preparation of a leavened sacrifice, viz., neither leaven nor honey may be offered as a sacrifice to the Lord, presumably because both, in contrast to salt, are subject to spoilage. Note that LXX uses two different words for "leaven," ζυμωτόν in the prohibition to represent חמץ, but ζύμην in the γάρ clause for שאר. The former refers to that which is leavened, whereas ζύμη is the leaven itself. MT's prohibition uses תקטירו as verb, here translated by προσοίσετε,[26] which is then modified by καρπῶσαι. The complementary infinitive as an interpretation of the noun אשה is unique; one would have expected the noun κάρπωμα, for which see comment at 1:9.

In the tradition, Byz simplified (ἀπ') αὐτοῦ as αυτων, thereby referring to both ζύμην and μέλι; this was probably promoted by the plural αὐτά of v.12 which see. The Byz text also tried to make better sense out of the infinitive καρπῶσαι by adding θυσιαν after it. Both variants are rationalizing attempts to simplify the more difficult LXX text.

2:12 A general rule about leaven and honey. "As a δῶρον ἀπαρχῆς you may offer them to the Lord, but (δέ) such may not be made to go up on the altar for a

---

24. For a discussion of this tendency on the part of Lev see the discussion in THGL 72–74.
25. Theod attests to τοῦ πυρός, whereas Aq has πυρῶν (κυρίῳ).
26. See THGL 73.

sweet smelling savor to the Lord." The singular passive verb is adequate for rendering the יעלו of MT which must be taken as having an indefinite plural subject. At vv.1,4 קרבן מנחה was rendered by a double accusative, but here the bound phrase is more literally translated by δῶρον plus a genitive modifier. The κυρίῳ at the end of the verse has no equivalent in MT, and is, accordingly, put under the obelus in hex. Since the sacrifices are throughout devoted to the Lord, the addition is easily explained as being ex par. First fruits may be sweet or leavened, and may be offered to the Lord, but they may not be sacrificed.

2:13 For the rendering of קרבן מנחתך comp the comment at v.12. Over against the prohibitions of vv.11,12, the people are positively enjoined to have their sacrifices salted with salt. In MT the order is an active one: "with salt תמלח,"[27] as over against the passive of LXX. LXX has the entire verse in second person plural, rather than the singular of MT by which the duty to salt the sacrifices falls upon the worshiper; in LXX it is the task of the priests. This is a good case of leveling, since the preceding verses were also plural (in both MT and LXX). The use of salt in sacrifices contrasts with that of leaven and honey, since salt is indeed a preservative.

Of such importance is salt that it is called "the salt of the Lord's covenant," with which compare the "covenant of salt" at Num 18:19.[28] The idiom used is rather odd Greek in its use of διαπαύσετε. What LXX says is that "you may not bring to an end, cause to rest, the covenant of salt from your sacrifice." The verb is used in an attempt to translate the Hebrew תשבית "make to rest," which with מן means "to withhold." The verb διαπαύω occurs elsewhere in OT only once (Hos 5:13), but not for השבית. The Byz text used a different compound, καταπαυσετε, which is the more usual rendering for השבית. Greek presents the prohibition asyndetically as in Sam, over against MT, so it is probably a textual matter. LXX has also changed MT's אלהיך to κυρίου. Throughout the chapter reference is made only to "the Lord," and the change is probably simply a case of leveling the text.

Whether the dative κυρίῳ τῷ θεῷ ὑμῶν is original in the last clause or not is by no means certain. The majority text does not have it, nor does Philo, nor is it

---

27. For ἀλί as an instrumental dative see SS 122.
28. See Dorival ad loc.

supported by MT. On the other hand, codd A and B both support the plus, and when in doubt one prefers to follow the lead of the oldest uncials.

The concept "salt" occurs three times in the verse, the first two, ἁλί and ἅλα, are derived from ἅλς, and the last one is the neuter ἅλας. There is no difference lexically between the two. Confusion among copyists obtained with ἅλα, which popularly became αλας, and ἅλας became αλα in *O b n+*. In all cases the oldest witnesses were adopted as critical text.

2:14 With v.14 LXX returns to the singular of MT. The offering of first fruits is to be "fresh ears roasted, crushed (or ground)."[29] Codd A and B have an odd doublet for νέα, adding απαλον before it.[30] For "roasted" MT has קלוי באש, but LXX only translates the participle, πεφρυγμένα.[31]

LXX has added καί before προσοίσεις. This means that the description of the offering of first fruits given above has no verb, but stands by itself as a nominal structure constituting the apodosis, and for sense one must understand something like "it is to be," or "it must consist of." In MT there is no problem, since תקריב has no conjunction before it, and the verb is modified by the description of the offering demanded, i.e. "If you offer a sacrifice ... you must bring fresh ears ...." In the Greek the καί clause is coordinated with the first two clauses of v.15. LXX also differs from MT in having τῷ κυρίῳ after ἐρεικτά; this is obviously ex par. Its omission by a *b* text is probably recensional.

2:15 The text is essentially the same as v.1b, but put into second person, and with pronouns adjusted to the context, and so instead of ונתת as the opening word, LXX has καὶ ἐπιχεεῖς "and you shall pour," which admittedly is contextually more fitting for olive oil than "and you shall put," and instead of αὐτό (twice referring to δῶρον), the text reads αὐτήν referring to the θυσίαν of v.14.

2:16 Up to this point ἐπιτίθημι was used by the translator to translate הקטיר; for this see comment at 1:9. Here Lev changes to ἀναφέρω; i.e. והקטיר is rendered by καὶ ἀνοίσει. This verb is used consistently (eight times) up through 4:31, after

---

29. For χίδρα The Three apparently read ἔριγμα (retroverted from Syh), and instead of ἐρεικτά Aq Sym have ἀπαλόν.
30. See THGL 108—109.
31. Aq and Sym adopt the LXX and add (ἐν) πυρί; Theod has ὄπτον instead of πεφρυγμένα.

which LXX returns to ἐπιτίθημι (three cases: 4:35 5:12 6:12), then back to ἀναφέρω (eight cases through 9:10), then ἐπιτίθημι (at 9:13,14,17), and thereafter ἀναφέρω again (9:20 16:25 17:6).[32] Admittedly ἀναφέρω "to offer up" is much closer to הקטיר than ἐπιτίθημι.

For τὸ μνημόσυνον see comment at v.2. For a discussion of the pattern ἀπὸ τῶν χίδρων σὺν τῷ ἐλαίῳ see comments and references at v.2. Unlike v.2 hex did not add genitive pronouns to the nouns in spite of the Hebrew pronominal suffixes of גרשה and שמנה. For κάρπωμα as a translation of אשה see comment at v.9.[33]

---

32. See THGL 73.
33. Theod Aq render אשה by πυρόν, an etymological rendering based on אש "fire."

Chapter 3

3:1 Ch.3 describes the regulations concerning the θυσία σωτηρίου, which is LXX's translation of זבח שלמים, a term which has been variously rendered as thankoffering, peace offering, salvation sacrifice, thanksgiving sacrifice, fellowship sacrifice, and more recently as sacrifice of well-being (by NRSV and NJPS). I would suggest that what the Greek means is still another, viz. a sacrifice for deliverance. What the Greek intends is a sacrifice offered as a token of gratitude for deliverance of some kind; this is what the term σωτήριον implies.¹ The entire chapter, except for the subscription (v.17) is in third person; i.e. a new section is presented, and the subject must be the worshiper; similarly, the antecedent of αὐτοῦ, though not stated, must be the worshiper as well. It should also be noted that θυσία does not render מנחה in this chapter, but זבח, the root of which means "to slaughter"; in other words, a זבח is an animal sacrifice.

The protasis is explicated by a more specific ἐὰν μέν clause, "if in fact he would bring it ἐκ τῶν βοῶν."² What is meant is an animal sacrifice.³ MT has a nominal clause, הוא מקריב, but LXX has rendered the participle not by the usual present indicative, but by an aorist subjunctive;⁴ cf also v.7. Undoubtedly MT intended הוא as the subject, but Lev rendered it by αὐτό modifying προσαγάγῃ, and referring to δῶρον,⁵ but an A B O b+ variant has αυτου, an obvious mistake which would modify βοῶν i.e. "his cattle," and could hardly have been intended. An n+ reading has αυτος, which does equal MT, and may well have been mediated through a reviser's text.⁶

LXX has also expanded the protasis, by adding τῷ κυρίῳ after "his gift," which hex placed under the obelus. The parent text may well have had the ליהוה attested by a Qumran ms.⁷

---

1. The Others translate שלמים literally by εἰρηνικῶν; cf שלום "peace." See also Harlé-Pralon 37.
2. The preposition is clearly partitive, reflecting the מן of MT; see SS 161.
3. Theod Aq have ἀπὸ τοῦ βουκολίου, and Sym has ἀπὸ τῶν βοῶν.
4. See THGL 95.
5. See THGL 98.
6. Theod does read αὐτός, whereas Aq has αὐτοῦ. Sym does not have an equivalent. The verb that follows also differs from LXX's προσαγάγῃ: Theod Aq have an indicative, προσφέρει, and Sym has ἢ προσφέρων.
7. By 4QLev^b; see DJD XII 180.

As in the case of the burnt offerings (cf 1:3), sacrifices for deliverance must also be ἄμωμον; when applied to sacrifices this means that they have no physical blemishes or defects. The Hebrew תמים suggests wholeness, completeness, and may also refer to moral or spiritual perfection; in Lev, however, it applies to sacrifice, for which the term refers only to physical wholeness.

3:2 Lev simply renders סמך "shall lean" by the less colorful ἐπιθήσει, and neglects the suffixes for ידו and קרבנו. In the tradition, αυτου has been supplied for both nouns, the former by a majority text, and for the latter under the asterisk by hex.[8] Furthermore, LXX also insists that the worshiper place both hands (τὰς χεῖρας) on the head of the gift, whereas MT has a singular noun.[9]

The פתח of the tent of testimony occurs 27 times in the book; it is always in the singular, but LXX uses the plural for a third of these; once, 8:31, αὐλῇ is substituted, and all the others are in the singular. There seems to be no rationale for the use of the plural. In fact, the tent of testimony is never modified by the plural "doors," but only by the singular פתח throughout the Pentateuch, nor is there a common context for the plural cases.[10] Sometimes the altar is located at the door, but in other cases it refers to the location where a worshiper is to bring a sacrifice and give it to the priest; see comment at 1:3. The translator makes no distinction between "door" and "doors" of the tent of testimony. A *b* reading does correct τὰς θύρας to την θυραν to equal MT. It is the worshiper rather than the priests who is to slaughter (σφάξει) αὐτό, referring to the δῶρον.

The number of the verb changes for the third clause; it is not the worshiper, but rather the Aaronid priests who must manipulate the blood of the sacrifice; they must προσχεοῦσιν "pour (it) out on the altar τῶν ὁλοκαυτωμάτων round about." In fact, only priests were allowed to approach the altar. The *C'* *f*+ variant προχεουσιν is simply a palaeographically inspired mistake. MT has no equivalent for the genitive noun, and hex has recognized this by placing the

---

8. See SS 95.
9. Milgrom 150—153 maintains that there is an essential difference between leaning with both hands in the case of the scapegoat (16:21) and leaning with one hand as in other sacrifices. Whether this distinction is valid or not may be uncertain, but it was irrelevant to Alexandrian Jewry as represented by LXX, which makes no such a distinction.
10. See THGL 73.

phrase under the obelus. As in the case of 5:12 where τῶν ὁλοκαυτωμάτων was also added, the source for it must have been 4:7,25,30, since it only occurs in these verses. The phrase מזבח העלה also occurs elsewhere at 4:10,34, where העלה is rendered by τῆς καρπώσεως and τῆς ὁλοκαυτώσεως resp.

3:3—4 MT orders the worshiper to bring an offering for Yahweh from the sacrifice for deliverance, for which see comment at v.1. For אשה rendered by κάρπωμα see comment at 2:9. LXX changes the subject with its plural προσάξουσιν to the Aaronid priests. It is they who are to take from the sacrifice a κάρπωμα for the Lord. Not only does this contradict 7:20, where it is the worshiper's hands which bring the καρπώματα to the Lord, and it is he who must bring the fat which is on the breast and the lobe of the liver as a gift before the Lord, but this also creates a considerable difficulty of interpretation for what follows. V.4 ends with περιελεῖ, which apparently refers to the worshiper. Precisely what is it that the worshiper is to remove together with the kidneys? Two possibilities present themselves: a) that περιελεῖ governs all of vv.3b—4, i.e. the fat covering the abdomen up through the lobe which is on the liver. The difficulty with this understanding is that καὶ τοὺς δύο νεφρούς is then repeated in σὺν τοῖς νεφροῖς; and b) that the verb only governs τὸν λοβὸν τὸν ἐπὶ τοῦ ἥπατος σὺν τοῖς νεφροῖς; the καί introducing this structure would then coordinate with the καί introducing v.3a. This interpretation is also difficult because the priests are to bring as an offering to the Lord the fat which covers ... τῶν μηρίων, which includes the two kidneys, which is inconsistent with the fact that it is the worshiper who removes the kidneys. I suspect that the former interpretation is easier than the latter. Thus the entire κάρπωμα is to be set aside, after which the instructions in v.5 are to be carried out.

The parts constituting the sacrifice are on the whole clear, though the Greek is not fully obvious. The first item is the fat which covers the קרב. The Hebrew קרב refers to the entrails, but the Greek κοιλίαν simply means a cavity, and is applied to the abdomen or the belly. The fat that covers is then the fatty net which is spread over the abdomen, which does indeed cover the intestines. As to the fat on the kidneys, this is also identified as τὸ ἐπὶ τῶν μηρίων; probably what is intended is "that which is alongside the loins," though admittedly this interprets the preposition in two different senses: "that which is *upon* them, that which is *alongside* the loins."[11] It should also be noted that MT is much clearer than LXX. The verb in MT has a feminine suffix, יסירנה "he shall turn it aside." The suffix must refer to יתרת "the lobe (of the liver)," but by failing to render the suffix LXX created syntactic confusion. In fact, in MT it is quite clear that the fact that the suffix refers to יתרת also resolves the repetitiveness of על הכליות. In the second case of the phrase it modifies "the lobe of the liver," thus "he shall remove it (i.e. the lobe of the liver) besides the kidneys."

3:5 LXX has added the designation οἱ ἱερεῖς to the subject in MT, "the Aaronids," and the addition is ex par; cf v.2. MT has as modifier for the verb an אתו, grammatically referring to אשה, which the translator interpreted by the plural αὐτά, correctly understanding what was to be offered up as the sum total of the components of the κάρπωμα. For ἀνοίσουσιν see comment at 2:16. The verb is modified by three ἐπί phrases, resp governing τὸ θυσιαστήριον, τὰ ὁλοκαυτώματα and τὰ ξύλα, with the last one in turn modified by τὰ ἐπὶ τοῦ πυρός. As in v.4 the preposition cannot be understood in the same sense throughout. That the sacrifices should be offered up *on* the altar is sensible; the Hebrew's המזבחה can here only be understood in a locative sense.[12] But the sacrifice can hardly be offered up on the burnt offerings, and this ἐπί must be understood as "alongside," and the "burnt offerings" must refer to the daily holocausts discussed in 6:14—18. The next two phrases can be rendered by "upon the firewood which is on the fire." In the tradition, an A B *x* gloss, επι του θυσιαστηριου, obtains after πυρός, but in spite of support by the two oldest uncials it must be secondary; it is an otiose statement stating that the fire was on the altar, which is obvious.[13]

For v.b see comments at 1:9. Here the dative κυρίῳ is, however, unarticulated, though a majority text does add the article. But the old uncials lack it, and the variant text was probably created ex par.

3:6 Vv.6—11 parallel vv.1—5. Instead of the gift being from τῶν βοῶν, it is now from τῶν προβάτων. The protasis has τὸ δῶρον as subject of a nominal clause with ἀπὸ τῶν προβάτων as predicate. The syntax of the following structure is

---

11. See Gispen ad loc.
12. See GK 90d.
13. See THGL 106—107.

peculiar; though it describes τὸ δῶρον it is in the accusative. I would suggest that the προσοίσει is proleptically understood, thus "(when presenting) a sacrifice for deliverance to the Lord, male or female, he shall present it without blemish." This is much clearer in MT which reads (ליהוה) לזבח שלמים "for a sacrifice ...."[14]

This apodosis is similar to, but not identical with, that of v.1. The phrase ἔναντι κυρίου occurred in v.1, but it is lacking here, since MT too lacks the phrase. Similarly, "male or female" differs from v.1, but renders MT which reads זכר או נקבה.

3:7 This verse has no parallel in vv.1—5. It specifies the gifts ἀπὸ τῶν προβάτων of v.6 as being ἄρνα, the accusative of ἄρην "lamb."[15] The protasis is a nominal clause in MT, הוא מקריב, which LXX rendered by an aorist subjunctive, προσαγάγῃ, without translating the pronominal subject,[16] and hex has supplied it under the asterisk as αυτος.[17] In the apodosis αὐτό must refer to δῶρον; Byz changed the reference by its αυτον to ἄρνα. The reference intended by אתו could be either כבש or קרבנו, though the latter is nearer, and the interpretation of LXX is likely correct.

3:8 The Greek text is the same as v.2, except for the addition of αὐτοῦ after δῶρον here, and the omission of τῶν ὁλοκαυτωμάτων modifying "altar." For the interpretation see comments at v.2. It is clear that except for the changes mentioned, the translator followed the Greek of v.2 rather than MT of v.8; note the identification of the Aaronids as οἱ ἱερεῖς as well as the addition of τὰς θύρας before "the tent of witness"; cf also v.13.

In the tradition, hex added αυτου after τὰς χεῖρας to equal the suffix of ידו, and the majority tradition, including O, changed the phrase to the singular την χειρα, which corresponds to the singular noun in MT. Differences between LXX and MT were noted by hex, which added αυτου after αἷμα under the asterisk to equal דמו of MT, as well as placing οἱ ἱερεῖς under the obelus to signalize its lack of correspondence in MT.

---

14. The Others follow MT more closely with εἰς θυσίαν εἰρηνικῶν.
15. Aq has ἀμνόν, and Sym, πρόβατον.
16. See THGL 98.
17. Retroverted from Syh.

3:9 V.9a is much like the first clause in v.3,[18] but does not change ליהוה/κυρίῳ to τῷ θεῷ. The majority text corrects to κυριω, but this is probably ex par, rather than hex. It is by now clear that the translator preferred variation to set patterns. The change to τῷ θεῷ is neither textual nor theological; it simply shows LXX's impatience with set patterns.[19] V.3b is included at the end of v.9 with two differences: it begins with καί, and it omits πᾶν. In the tradition, καὶ τὸ στέαρ τὸ κατακαλύπτον τὴν κοιλίαν is omitted by an A B b+ text, but this is due to homoiarchon, since the next phrase also begins with καὶ τὸ στέαρ.[20] A further variant is the addition of παν before the last τὸ στέαρ. Since MT reads כל החלב one might think this majority text to be hex, but it apparently is already to be found in ms 802 from the first century BCE, and must constitute a very early, prehexaplaric correction of the text.[21]

But between the opening clause and the materials at the end of the verse MT has חלבו האליה תמימה לעמת העצה יסירנה, for which LXX has τὸ στέαρ καὶ τὴν ὀσφὺν ἄμωμον σὺν ταῖς ψόαις περιελεῖ αὐτό. The suffix of the first Hebrew word was not translated, but it probably promoted the καί, which has no Hebrew counterpart, i.e. as though reading חלב והאליה. אליה is actually the broad tail of the Oriental sheep, and it also occurs at 7:3(6:33) 8:25 9:19, and is throughout translated by ὀσφύς, which means "loins."[22] The tail/loins must also be "spotless," i.e. ἄμωμον.[23] In MT תמימה is almost certainly intended adverbially, i.e. as "wholly, entirely," which the translator, however, did not understand. He took the word in the usual sense of ἄμωμον, though the notion that the ὀσφύν should be ἄμωμον is rather inappropriate.

The Hebrew העצה is a hapax legomenon and is usually interpreted as "the spine"; compare the Arabic ʿuṣʿuṣ which means "tail bone, coccyx." LXX translated it by ταῖς ψόαις "loin muscles." The translator may well not have understood the word and simply made a contextual translation. The suffix of יסירנה must refer to אליה, but the translator has the neuter, which is probably

---

18. Instead of τοῦ σωτηρίου κάρπωμα Aq reads τῶν εἰρηνικῶν πυρόν.
19. For a discussion of this characteristic of Lev see THGL 72—75.
20. See THGL 111—112.
21. See THGL 19.
22. The Others render the word more exactly by τὸ κέρκιον.
23. Aq has τελείαν, whereas Sym has ὁλόκληρον. Both mean "whole, complete."

intended as an indefinite neuter, referring to the foregoing, i.e. the fat and the loins.[24] A *b* variant reads αυτην, which equals MT by referring to ὀσφύν.

3:10 This verse is identical to v.4 in MT, and LXX only changed τοὺς δύο to ἀμφοτέρους τούς, illustrating the translator's love of variation.[25]

3:11 LXX begins the verse asyndetically over against MT. This is corrected by 802(vid) Byz by preposing a καί. As at v.9 support by 802 proves that this is not a usual recensional correction, but is prehex in origin.[26] The verbal suffix of והקטירו, for which the parent text was probably the והקטר of 4QLev[b][27] rather than MT, is not translated, leaving ἀνοίσει without an object; the translator "fixed this up" by putting ὀσμήν in the accusative,[28] thus "the priest shall offer up ... a sweet smelling savor."[29] The suffix of הקטירו is singular, and probably refers to the אשה of v.9, which word, however, consists of a list of components, and is best rendered for sense by "them." For המזבחה taken in a locative sense, and accordingly rendered by an ἐπί plus accusative noun, see comment at v.5. Unique in the context is the word לחם "bread," probably in the sense of "food." MT says "The priest shall burn them (הקטירו) on the altar as food." LXX apparently has substituted ὀσμὴν εὐωδίας for לחם. Why the translator avoided rendering לחם is not clear; possibly the notion that sacrifice should provide food for the deity smacked too much of pagan (Egyptian) practices, and the substitution of ὀσμὴν εὐωδίας was a "safe" interpretation. Furthermore, this also levelled with v.5, though transposing the phrase with κάρπωμα, and changing it to the accusative;[30] comp also v.16.[31]

3:12 Vv.12—16 are parallel to vv.6—11, but concern τῶν αἰγῶν rather than τῶν προβάτων. In MT, however, the protasis differs slightly in that "his gift" is not "from the goats" as one might expect (as in vv.1,6), but simply עז "a goat."

---

24. See Huber 35.
25. See THGL 72.
26. See THGL 19.
27. See DJD XII 180—181.
28. See THGL 120.
29. For ἀναφέρω translating הקטיר see comment at 2:10.
30. See THGL 119—120.
31. See the discussion in Daniel 139—141 on LXX's dealing with לחם as an אשה to Yahweh.

LXX, however, levels with v.6 with its ἀπὸ τῶν αἰγῶν. In the tradition, a majority F M variant text adds τω κυριω after "his gift," probably under the influence of v.1.

That vv.12—16 are parallel to vv.6—11 was clear from a *b* text which summarized the apodosis plus vv.13—16 simply by κατα την αυτην συνταξιν "in the same fashion." The apodosis is introduced by καί in imitation of MT, but the translator does not render the suffix of the verb הקריבו. Hex added αυτο under the asterisk to make up for it, using the neuter to refer to δῶρον.

3:13 In MT this verse is identical with v.8, which see, except that v.8 had identified ראשו as ראש קרבנו, and LXX follows the change to ראשו with τὴν κεφαλὴν αὐτοῦ as well; cf comments at v.8.

The second clause in LXX differs from that of MT mainly in that the subject has changed. The singular שחט presupposed the worshiper slaughtering his sacrifice, but LXX with its plural σφάξουσιν presupposes the named subject of the next clause, οἱ υἱοὶ ᾿Ααρὼν οἱ ἱερεῖς, as effecting it. This contrasts with vv.2 and 8, where σφάξει obtains. LXX is unique among the ancient witnesses in singling out the goat for priestly slaughter. LXX also differs from MT in reading ἔναντι κυρίου παρὰ τὰς θύρας τῆς σκηνῆς instead of לפני אהל as the locale for the slaughter. This may then explain why the translator has the Aaronid priests performing the slaughter; "before the Lord" means at the altar, to which the layman was not given access. The worshiper in v.8 might do the slaughter near the doors of the tent, but not at the altar, i.e. not before the Lord. For the variant readings adding αυτου to "the hands," and changing the phrase to the singular, see comment at v.8.

The last clause in the verse is exactly the same as in v.8, both in MT as well as the slightly different text for the Greek. As in v.8 hex added αυτου under the asterisk after αἷμα to represent the suffix of דמו; cf comments at v.8.

3:14 LXX begins with καὶ ἀνοίσει ἀπ᾿ αὐτοῦ κάρπωμα. The αὐτοῦ refers to the δῶρον, which, as the parallel sections dealing with "cattle" and "sheep" show, involved the sacrifice for deliverance. The translator apparently was not as attentive as he should have been, since MT does not read והקטיר but והקריב. Furthermore, he also omitted קרבנו, which hex supplied under the asterisk as δωρον αυτου.[32]

---

32. For the unique failure to render קרבן see Daniel 122.

The Hi of קרב occurs 89 times in the book and in 87 of these it is rendered either by προσφέρω or by προσάγω.³³ But between 2:16 and 4:31 ἀναφέρω occurs for הקטיר eight times; cf comment at 2:16. That the translator wrongly had והקטיר in mind is more than likely. And in this context, as the parallels in vv.3 and 9 show, an ἀπ' phrase alone is appropriate, whereas the A B F *b* *n*+ variant επ is due to the idiom "offer up on the altar," as at v.5,11,16.³⁴ I would translate the clause "And he shall take up from it a sacrifice for the Lord."

For v.b, which is exactly the same as v.9 except for adding πᾶν before the last τὸ στέαρ, see comments ad loc.

3:15 This verse is exactly the same as vv.4 and 10 in MT, but LXX differs from the LXX of v.10 on three points: it has πᾶν before τὸ στέαρ; it omits τὸν ἐπί (τοῦ ἥπατος), and it follows the περιελεῖ of v.4 rather than περιελών; see comments at vv.4 and 10.³⁵ Grammatically uncertain is the modification of περιελεῖ, but it seems likely that τὸν λοβὸν ... νεφροῖς was intended. This was also the interpretation of the Masoretes who placed הכסלים under the *ethnach*. Neither MT nor LXX make clear the fate of the kidneys; are they removed as in v.b or are they part of the offering placed on the altar as in v.a?

In the tradition, most witnesses read τους δυο rather than ἀμφοτέρους τούς, but the support of the three oldest uncials, A B G, is decisive for establishing the critical text. An A *n*+ text omits πᾶν, in which it equals MT. With τὸ στέαρ appearing frequently throughout the chapter, the omission is probably simply ex par in origin. It should also be noted that the majority text did read τον επι before τοῦ ἥπατος under the influence of the parallel passages. The shorter text is here also supported by the three oldest uncials; see above.

3:16 This verse is paralleled in vv.5 and 11, but there are substantial differences. LXX, as at v.11, ignores the suffix of the verb; here the suffix is plural, הקטירם, and hex has added αυτα to represent it in the tradition. The omission resulted, as at v.11, in ὀσμήν being inflected in the accusative, i.e. as object of ἀνοίσει, though here as a second accusative, along with κάρπωμα.³⁶ For המזבחה rendered

---

33. See THGL 73.
34. See THGL 77.
35. The Three all read τοὺς δύο instead of ἀμφοτέρους τούς.
36. See THGL 120.

by an ἐπί phrase, see comment at v.5. As in v.11, לחם follows immediately, but it is completely disregarded by LXX, and hex has added αρτον under the asterisk to equal it.[37] At v.11 ὀσμὴν εὐωδίας took its place, but this has an equivalent here in the prepositional phrase לריח ניחח, which, however, follows לחם אשה. Here LXX reads κάρπωμα ὀσμὴν εὐωδίας, i.e. transposes κάρπωμα before ὀσμὴν εὐωδίας; cf comments at v.11. In the tradition, an A B F O b n+ variant text reads οσμη ex par; see v.5 and 1:9,13,17 2:2,9. LXX has τῷ κυρίῳ after εὐωδίας, in which it follows Sam; MT only has ליהוה at the end of the verse, which LXX also supports.

The critical text takes πᾶν ... fin as a separate clause, i.e. "all the fat belongs to the Lord." A substantial majority of witnesses omits the article τό, which supports MT: כל חלב, and the LXX is uncertain. The articulated phrase is, however, supported by the oldest witnesses, A B F M, though it could be argued that the article is ex par. It was, however, felt to be prudent in doubtful cases to follow the oldest witnesses. It also makes excellent sense in that the articulated phrase perforce refers to all the fat mentioned earlier, whereas the unarticulated phrase theoretically might include the fat of non-sacrificial animals as well.

3:17 V.17 is a subscribed summary of the chapter. It consists of two statements: a) that the regulation is valid for all time and place, and b) that no fat nor blood may be eaten.

The verse opens with νόμιμον εἰς τὸν αἰῶνα which renders the bound phrase חקת עולם.[38] חקה "statute" occurs 26 times in the book. When the word modifies a verb (11 times) it is translated seven times by προστάγματα, once each by νόμος, δικαιώματα and νόμιμα, and once it is omitted (see comment at 26:15). Whenever it stands in a nominal clause (15 times) it is always rendered by νόμιμον. This is followed by εἰς τὰς γενεὰς ὑμῶν. The γενεάς may be viewed as the component parts from a temporal point of view of τὸν αἰῶνα. The final phrase of the first statement is ἐν πάσῃ κατοικίᾳ ὑμῶν "in your every household." MT has the noun in the plural, but LXX intentionally individuates, i.e. each of you is a member of a single household, and the πάσῃ means that all your individual households are to be involved in observing the νόμιμον. In the

---

37. See Daniel 139—141.
38. See SS 69.

tradition, the first phrase has become νομιμον αιωνιον in Byz, but the rarer phrase of LXX must be original.

The second statement is "you may not eat any fat nor any blood." The future ἔδεσθε is prohibitive.[39] This prohibition underlines a basic principle underlying this chapter, viz. that fat and blood belong to the Lord. The fat must then be burned on the altar, and the blood must be poured out near it. The principle is not a summation of the first three chapters, since chapter two concerns only vegetable/grain sacrifices, and so it can apply only to this chapter.

---

39. See Porter 419—420.

Chapter 4

4:2 This verse can be construed as a general condition for the entire chapter, that of someone who commits a sin inadvertently. The regulations that follow are typical cases, that of a high priest, the community, a ruler, an ordinary citizen. Here such are all grouped under ψυχή/נפש "person, someone." The Greek term is a calque for נפש, a term commonly misunderstood as "soul," but better understood as a sentient being, a person. That ψυχή is a calque is clear from the translation of נפש in the OT: of the 735 cases of נפש translated into Greek,[1] 695 are rendered by ψυχή, five by a reflexive pronoun (σεαυτοῦ), and the remaining 35 are scattered among a motley 26 different equivalents, including four transliterations; see comment at 2:1. The preposing of ἐάν by the subject ψυχή without an intervening pronoun such as ἥ or ἥτις is unusual, though it does occur also at 5:15,21.

The verb used for sin is the common rendering for the root חטא, ἁμάρτῃ, and it is modified by the adverb ἀκουσίως "inadvertently." This renders the phrase בשגגה, and is its usual rendering.[2] LXX, however, uniquely inserts ἔναντι κυρίου between the verb and the adverb, i.e. without counterpart in MT, or in any other ancient witnesses. But it is a proper intuition, since it involves the מצות of the Lord.[3] LXX sets ἁμάρτῃ in its proper perspective. Since the verse is a general condition it is proper to define the nature of ἁμάρτῃ as being "before the Lord." Hex has quite correctly placed the phrase under the obelus. The verb is modified by an ἀπό phrase.[4] The modification by ἀπό is highly unusual, and probably indicates the occasion from which sin is committed,[5] thus sin over against any of the statutes of the Lord. Most wit-

---

1. The count is that of Dos Santos.
2. Aq and Sym have ἐν ἀγνοίᾳ, thereby preserving the syntactic structure of the Hebrew.
3. Milgrom 230—231 distinguishes מצות from משפטים as religious laws which only God can punish over against civil wrongs which can be dealt with in the courts. It is, however, a distinction which LXX did not carry out, since it does not render these terms in a consistent fashion.
4. The preposition is partitive; see SS 161. So is the preposition in the phrase ἀπ' αὐτῶν later in the verse; cf *ibid* 166.
5. See LS sub ἀπό III.6.

nesses modify τῶν προσταγμάτων by παντων, which does equal MT, but the translator may well have considered this otiose in view of the last clause in the verse. מצות is not commonly rendered by προστάγματα (only twice in Lev, and only 11 times in OT). One would expect εντολων here (158 times in OT);[6] in fact, it only renders מצוה in Lev (eight times).

The relative clause refers to προσταγμάτων. The Ni verb תעשינה is in unusual fashion rendered by δεῖ plus an active infinitive; it does, however, adequately translate the intent of MT which may be rendered by "which may not be done." The final clause in MT contains two מן phrases: מאחת מהנה. LXX interprets the first of these neatly by ἕν τι "any one." The second phrase is partitive, and is literally rendered by ἀπ' αὐτῶν; I would have thought a simply genitive pronoun would have been adequate.

4:3 Vv.3—12 deal with the sin offering for the high priest. The translator introduces the condition by ἐὰν μέν, the latter particle being used to express certainty. Since it is the high priest who sins, the μέν is used to note that it is really so, thus "if in fact." The Greek designates him as ὁ ἀρχιερεὺς ὁ κεχρισμένος "the anointed high priest." The Byz text changed ἀρχιερεύς to ιερευς; this is probably recensional in origin. MT simply speaks of "the anointed priest," but the translator rightly understood it as applicable only to the high priest, in view of the case of his sinning τοῦ τὸν λαὸν ἁμαρτεῖν, which probably means "so that the people are sinful,"[7] i.e. are in a state of being sinful and in need of expiation; in any event, the only priest whose actions would involve the people as a whole must be the high priest. The structure is an interpretation of לאשמת העם probably meaning "for effecting the guilt of the people,"[8] or possibly in a more general sense "to the hurt of the people." Since in MT's bound phrase העם comes second, hex has reordered τὸν λαόν after the infinitive as well.

The apodosis is introduced by καί in imitation of MT; the high priest "must bring on behalf of his sin which he sinned a bullock from the cattle." The animal must be without blemish. In MT it must be brought to Yahweh לחטאת "for a sin offering,"[9] but the translator levelled with his earlier περὶ τῆς ἁμαρτίας αὐτοῦ,

---

6. According to HR.
7. See Harlé-Pralon ad loc, and also Daniel 315, note 57.
8. Aq has a more literal rendering: εἰς πλημμέλησιν τοῦ λαοῦ "for the fault, error of the people."
9. For its consistent translation in LXX see THGL 117.

which, however, represented על חטאתו.[10] It should also be noted that the majority text omits αὐτοῦ, which equals MT; the text of Lev is not fully certain.[11] The αὐτοῦ was adopted, since A and B both supported it.

4:4 The high priest must bring the bullock to the door of the tent of testimony ἔναντι κυρίου. The double designation παρὰ τὴν θύραν τῆς σκηνῆς τοῦ μαρτυρίου, for which see comment at 1:3, and ἔναντι κυρίου, which designates the altar area, could only apply to a priest. The altar is παρά the door, i.e. near, next to it; see comment at 3:13. The altar is designated as "the altar of burnt offerings" in v.7. The importance of priestly action being done "before the Lord" is stressed by LXX even more than by MT. In MT it occurs with הביא, and then in the last clause with שחט as well. LXX also added ἔναντι κυρίου for the middle clause, i.e. he must place his hand on the head of the animal *before the Lord* as well, i.e. at the altar. Hex put the phrase under the obelus, since it has no equivalent in MT. A number of text families has omitted the phrase, possibly through mediate Hebrew influence. Note that here ידו is rendered by the singular τὴν χεῖρα αὐτοῦ as over against 3:3,8, illustrating how the translator saw no significance in "hand" vs "hands." For ἐπιθήσει rendering סמך, see comment at 3:2.

4:5 The subject is now called "the anointed priest," a variation from the term used in v.3. That the translator doted on variation is clear from his rendering of הכהן המשיח, first as ὁ ἀρχιερεὺς ὁ κεχρισμένος in v.3, but here as ὁ ἱερεὺς ὁ χριστός. He is also called ὁ τετελειωμένος τὰς χεῖρας, undoubtedly based on Sam which reads אשר מלא את ידו, with LXX not rendering the suffix as commonly.[12] The structure represents an idiom taken from the mystery religions as "the one who has the hands consecrated or validated,"[13] and means "the one who was ordained to office." The idiom derives ultimately from Exod 29:9: καὶ τελειώσεις τὰς χεῖρας Ἀαρών....; see Note ad loc. The structure, which is in apposition to the subject, was placed under the obelus in hex to indicate its absence from MT.

---

10. But περί can render ל as well; see Johannessohn 220.
11. See THGL 93—94.
12. See SS 95—96.
13. See Bauer sub τελειόω 3.

The priest is to take some of the blood—note the partitive ἀπό—and bring it into the tent of witness. The stress is placed on the priest's bringing the blood into the tent by subordinating לקח to an attendant participle. In the tradition, εἰς has become επι in A B b f+, but this is a careless mistake. Lev normally used εἰς with εἰς-compounds.[14]

4:6 The priest is to dip his finger into the blood. LXX does not render the suffix of אצבעו, and hex added αυτου after δάκτυλον to equal it. In the second clause LXX also has τῷ δακτύλῳ in which it follows the Sam text באצבעו, again failing to render the suffix. Incidentally, Lev never renders the suffix of אצבעו, since it is always obvious whose finger is involved. This has no equivalent in MT, and A B b omit it entirely, thereby equalling MT. Whether or not this was omitted under Hebrew influence is unknown, but that the omission is secondary is certain. Only an original reading could have followed the Sam text. That some of the versions do add a genitive pronoun has nothing to do with the fact that Sam had a suffix; the pronoun is merely ad sensum.

In the second clause an ἀπό phrase modifies the verb προσρανεῖ; this is a clear case of a partitive preposition, and it should be translated "some of (the blood)."[15] Note once again the importance of this being done ἔναντι κυρίου. This sevenfold sprinkling is to be done κατὰ τὸ καταπέτασμα τὸ ἅγιον "before the holy curtain," which is rather an odd way of representing the Hebrew את פני פרכת הקדש;[16] one would have expected the bound phrase to have required a genitive του αγιου, i.e. "(curtain) of the sanctuary."[17]

4:7 For ἀπο see comment at v.6. Over against MT, LXX designates the blood as τοῦ μόσχου, a quite unnecessary addition, since there is only one source of blood given in the context. Hex has placed the plus under the obelus to show that it is an addition. The priest is to put some of the blood on the horns of the altar,[18] thereby rendering the entire altar ceremonially cleansed. Unfortunately, why

---

14. See THGL 77—78.
15. See SS 161.
16. See SS 65.
17. The anonymous marginal s reading σὺν τῷ προσώπῳ τοῦ καταπετάσματος is typically Aq.
18. For "horns of the altar" see R.D.Haak, "altars" A.1. in The Anchor Bible Dictionary I 163.

altars had these projections at their corners remains unknown. The altar involved is called τοῦ θυμιάματος τῆς συνθέσεως "of the burning of the compound." By συνθέσεως the compound of spices of which incense was made is meant, for which see Exod 30:34—38 and the Notes ad loc. So what is meant is "the altar for the burning of the incense." The word often occurs in modification of θυμίαμα in the Pentateuch as a translation of "burning of סמים" (Exod 31:11 35:19 Lev 16:12 Num 4:16), and comp v.18 and 2Par 13:11.

In MT לפני יהוה modifies the verb נתן, i.e. the priest is to put some of the blood ... "before Yahweh." But LXX renders the phrase as a modifier of θυσιαστηρίου (though θυμιάματος is grammatically possible as well) by its τοῦ ἔναντι κυρίου. It is, of course, true that the incense altar was ἔναντι κυρίου as was the altar of burnt offerings; both were within the tent of witness; see the relative clause which follows.

In the second clause the preposed modifier is πᾶν τὸ αἷμα τοῦ μόσχου. Of course, what is meant is all the blood that remained after the sprinkling and daubing on the part of the priest. This is to be poured out at the base of the altar τῶν ὁλοκαυτωμάτων "of burnt offerings." In the tradition, different readings are supported: της ολοκαρπωσεως, της καρπωσεως, and της ολοκαυτωσεως, but LXX is supported by the old uncials A and B, and is probably original. The phrase מזבח העלה occurs six times in this chapter; העלה is rendered by the plural τῶν ὁλοκαυτωμάτων at vv.7,25 and 30, by the plural τῶν καρπώσεων at v.18, but by singulars at v.10 (τῆς καρπώσεως) and v.34 (τῆς ὁλοκαυτώσεως). Why the translator should vary the translation to this extent is only explicable by his love of variety; all that concerned him was that the altar was a place for offering animal sacrifice(s).

4:8 The word חטאת can mean either sin or sin offering.[19] Greek speakers found it difficult to distinguish between the two. The Lev translator, however, did well with the latter here for the פר החטאת "the bullock of the sin offering" by his τοῦ μόσχου τοῦ τῆς ἁμαρτίας.[20] The verb περιελεῖ is used here and in v.19 to render

---

19. Milgrom 253—254 is certainly correct is maintaining that the translation of חטאת by "sin-offering" is incorrect; he suggests instead that it should be called a "purification offering." This would be more accurate for the Hebrew term, but since LXX uses the term ἁμαρτίας I shall continue to use "sin offering" throughout even for the Hebrew term so as to avoid confusion, with, however, the reservation expressed.
20. For a fuller discussion of "sin offering" in Lev see THGL 117.

ירים, a unique equation in OT. Elsewhere in Lev it is used to render the causative stems of the root סור. Possibly the translator is merely leveling with 3:4,9,10,15 4:9,31,35.

V.b is identical in MT with the parallels in 3:3,9,14, where קרב is rendered by κοιλία. The translator here used τὰ ἐνδόσθια and τῶν ἐνδοσθίων, merely for variation. For the interpretation of v.b see comments at 3:3.

4:9 Except for ὅ ἐστιν instead of τό (ἐπὶ τῶν μηρίων) and the final αὐτό, this verse is identical with 3:4; cf comments ad loc.

4:10 Since comparison is at issue (ὃν τρόπον), the verb is inflected in the present middle of ἀφαιρέω, thus "as it is being taken." The Hebrew has יורם, which an anonymous source (probably Aq) translated literally by ὑψοῦται. The verb is singular, but must refer to vv.8—9, taken as a collective whole; what is referred to is the general practice with respect to the bullock which pertains τοῦ τῆς θυσίας τοῦ σωτηρίου. The translator effected this by the initial τοῦ. MT had (משור) זבח השלמים, i.e. it had no equivalent for the τοῦ, which together with the present tense verb ensured the notion of common practice. To make the relationship of the ὃν τρόπον clause clearer it would be better to change the comma after σωτηρίου in the critical text to a colon.

The second clause then orders the sacrifice on the מזבח העלה. This had been translated in v.7 by τοῦ θυσιαστηρίου τῶν ὁλοκαυτωμάτων, but now it becomes "the altar τῆς καρπώσεως," which is found elsewhere in OT only at v.18; cf comment at v.7. This kind of variation is typical of Lev, and no special value should be attached to it; it is simply "the altar of sacrifice."[21] Over against MT's הקטירם LXX simply has ἀνοίσει; the translator felt no need to specify, since the context made it clear what was to be sacrificed. Hex, however, added αυτο, a singular pronoun to agree with the singular at the end of v.9; cf the comment above about the singular verb in v.a. A *b* variant added the plural αυτα, thereby equally MT more exactly.

4:11—12 Only if the two verses are read together can sense be made. V.11 strings together a group of modifiers to an eventual verb in v.12: "they shall

---

21. See THGL 74.

bring out." But the verb is followed by ὅλον τὸν μόσχον (for את כל הפר), which in the context must be understood as the overall term for the modifiers listed in v.11. What "the whole bullock" must mean is all the remains of the animal, i.e. minus those parts that had been sacrificed as described in vv.3—10.

These remains comprise the list in v.11, i.e. "the skin ... and all its flesh along with the head, the legs (literally "the extremities"), the belly and the dung." The Greek has disregarded the suffixes for ראשו, כרעיו, קרבו and פרשו as being otiose. Hex has added an αυτου under the asterisk for the first one, κεφαλῇ, but not for the last three. All of v.11 is then a preposed modifier: "As for the skin ... dung."

V.12 continues with καὶ ἐξοίσουσιν ... ἐκχεοῦσιν ... κατακαύσουσιν, with no subject given, i.e. these are indefinite plurals, as in "They say," "Man sagt," "on dit." MT has all the corresponding verbs in the singular, which means that the priest (i.e. the high-priest) himself is to take care of the disposal of the waste materials. The Greek avoids committing itself, quite intentionally, one suspects, allowing for the possibility that other sanctuary people might well carry out these duties. Such indefinite plurals are best rendered in English by the passive, thus "and the whole bullock shall be brought out ... and it shall be burned ...."

The "clean place" to which these remains are to be brought is defined in MT as אל שפך הדשן "to the ash heap," which LXX renders freely by οὗ ἐκχεοῦσιν τὴν σποδιάν "where ashes are poured out." There it (the αὐτόν refers to ὅλον τὸν μόσχον) is to be burned on the kindling by fire.[22]

That the translator knew what שפך הדשן meant is clear from the final clause: ἐπὶ τῆς ἐκχύσεως τῆς σποδιᾶς καυθήσεται "on the ash heap shall it be burned." The passive verb reflects the Masoretic Ni, which in turn gives a good basis for understanding the plural verbs as indefinite plurals.

4:13 Vv.13—21 describe the second case of inadvertent sin, that of the entire community. The subject is given as πᾶσα συναγωγὴ Ἰσραήλ. The Byz text has articulated συναγωγή, but this violates Lev usage. The phrase "community of Israel" is articulated only when it is not preceded by "all."[23] The Byz text has also added υιων before Ἰσραήλ. This is the more usual expression in the Pentateuch. Usage is as follows: in Exod 11 instances with υιων vs one without;

---
22. For the instrumental ἐν (πυρί) see SS 117.
23. See THGL 87.

in Lev the proportions are four to two, and in Num, 11 vs one; only in Dt is the ratio reversed: one vs three. The Byz reading is clearly an ex par intrusion. The verb ישגו means "to do something wrong inadvertently;" LXX stresses the fact of ignorance by its choice of ἀγνοήσῃ "act in ignorance." The Byz text changed this to αμαρτη ακουσιως, probably under the influence of v.2, though it may have been an intentional attempt at greater precision.[24] Incidentally, the A B *b* x+ text represents a conflation of the two, creating the tautological αγνοηση ακουσιως, which could hardly have been intended.

Furthermore, the matter is hidden from the community's notice, i.e. no one has noticed, caught on to the matter. The word for "community" has changed in MT from עדת to קהל. Though the terms are not fully synonymous Lev makes no distinction between the two, again using συναγωγή; in fact, Lev always renders קהל (11 times) and עדה (five times) by the same word.

This inadvertent action is further defined as doing "one of all the Lord's commandments which may not be done," i.e. did something that was forbidden.[25] This action is πλημμελήσωσιν "they shall be in error, at fault." In MT the relative clause modifies מצות "commandments" as the number of the verb תעשינה shows. But LXX has ἣ οὐ ποιηθήσεται; this modifies "one" μίαν. A *b* reading "corrects" this to αι ου ποιηθησονται to equal MT. An A B *b* x+ text changes πλημμελήσωσιν to the indicative; this would make the clause the beginning of the apodosis. This might be possible if the verb γνωσθῇ of v.14a were also changed to the indicative, which a *b* text actually does.

4:14 V.14a is still part of the protasis, i.e. of v.13: "and the sin by which they were sinning should become known to them." The verb in the relative clause, ἥμαρτον, is modified by ἐν αὐτῇ, which refers to ἁμαρτία, thus "by which they sinned." MT has עליה which must have either אחת or חטאת as referent. The preposition is unexpected, and LXX has simplified the phrase by an instrumental ἐν.

The apodosis is introduced by καί in imitation of MT. The subject is still συναγωγή, here for קהל.[26] The verb is in the plural, הקריבו, since the subject is "the congregation," but LXX renders in strict concord by the singular προσάξει.

---

24. See THGL 129.
25. For the partitive use of ἀπό with numbers see SS 166.
26. The anonymous reading ἡ ἐκκλησία is the regular rendering of קהל by Aq.

The sacrifice is the same as in the case of the high priest in v.3, though with small differences. Over against v.3 τῷ κυρίῳ is absent as well as the αὐτοῦ modifying ἁμαρτίας. For περὶ τῆς ἁμαρτίας rendering לחטאת see comment at v.3.[27] The ἄμωμον has no equivalent in MT, and is probably based on v.3, though it should be noted that Sam also reads תמים.

The last clause also has a plural verb rendered by a Greek singular as in the preceding clause. The Hebrew simply has "before the tent of meeting," but LXX inserts τὰς θύρας. For the plural "doors (of the tent of witness)" see comment at 3:2. Its parallel in 3:4a has the singular, realized αὐτόν as τὸν μόσχον, and added ἔναντι κυρίου at the end. MT has no counterpart to the τὰς θύρας at all, simply reading לפני אהל מועד.

4:15 The זקני העדה "the elders of the assembly" is rendered by οἱ πρεσβύτεροι τῆς συναγωγῆς. The term זקן "elder" only occurs three times in the book; at 19:32 it is also rendered by πρεσβυτέρου. At 9:1 it is rendered by γερουσία "senate," which also occurs at 9:3, but without Hebrew equivalent. The elders, as representatives of the people, are to place their hands on the head of the bullock before the Lord, i.e. at the sanctuary; here the phrase can hardly mean "at the altar," but is intended as a variant to παρὰ τὰς θύρας τῆς σκηνῆς τοῦ μαρτυρίου of v.14, i.e. at the sanctuary; see comment at 3:13. The placing of the hands on the head of the sacrificial animal presumably symbolizes the transfer of the guilt of the people to the animal. Only thereafter שחט the bullock before Yahweh, i.e. "one shall slay the bullock." That the singular is used is logical; the actual butchery would be the work of an individual, an understanding which the translator missed, since he levelled to the plural verb; the elders did the slaying, which is logistically somewhat difficult to contemplate.

4:16 The "anointed priest" follows the translation of v.5 rather than that of v.3. That he should bring some of the blood[28] into the sanctuary is sensible. Why the Byz text should have changed εἰς to ἐπί is unclear, particularly since MT has אל.

---

27. See also THGL 117.
28. For the partitive use of ἀπό see SS 161.

4:17 This verse is paralleled in v.6 in MT, but with three differences. Instead of מן הדם v.17 has בדם; v.6 has added מן הדם after והזה, and for its פרכת הקדש v.17 has הפרכת.

For the first clause LXX, as in v.4, has τὸν δάκτυλον, and hex corrects to equal MT by adding αυτου. On the other hand, it added τοῦ μόσχου after "blood," which hex placed under the obelus, since it has no counterpart in the Hebrew. The modification of βάψει by an ἀπό phrase is obviously due to the Hebrew טבל modified by מן. I would understand the ἀπό/מן as partitive, i.e. "dip into some of the blood." See also 14:16 for the same structure.

The second clause follows the Sam tradition by its κατενώπιον τοῦ καταπετάσματος τοῦ ἁγίου. Hex placed τοῦ ἁγίου under the obelus, since MT does not have the הקדש of Sam. What is unclear in the Greek is the status of ἁγίου; it can be either an adjective, which would equal its status in v.6, or it could be a noun, which would equal Sam. It is quite impossible to determine what the translator had in mind, though the parallel in v.6 would suggest its adjectival intent. The use of κατενώπιον is unexpected for את, and it is unique in the Pentateuch.[29]

4:18 For ἀπὸ τοῦ αἵματος see comment at v.17; it is obviously partitive. For the first clause see comments at v.7, whose text is somewhat different. Here the Greek follows MT in omitting τοῦ μόσχου, but follows Sam in having τῶν θυμιαμάτων τῆς συνθέσεως modifying θυσιαστηρίου. Apparently the translator interpreted Sam in reading קטרת as a plural noun, in contrast to his rendering of the word as a singular at v.7. It does prove that the source of the longer text was not the Greek text of v.7, but a Hebrew one. And over against τοῦ ἔναντι κυρίου of v.7, LXX translated MT's relative clause "which (is) before Yahweh" literally by ὅ ἐστιν ἐνώπιον κυρίου, which here must mean "in the sanctuary itself." For the understanding of v.a see the comments at v.7.

The second clause in MT is identical with that of v.7, except that it lacks הפר modifying "blood," i.e. it has only הדם. The Greek, however, illustrates our translator's fondness for variation as a comparison between the two renderings would show. This is clear from the translation of העלה by (τοῦ θυσιαστηρίου) τῶν καρπώσεων;[30] see the discussion at v.10. The "altar" is then located τοῦ ὄντος

---

29. See Harlé-Pralon ad loc.
30. For which see THGL 74.

(πρὸς τῇ θύρᾳ τῆς σκηνῆς τοῦ μαρτυρίου). The O text wrongly changes the genitive to the nominative το ον; this makes it parallel to the ὅ structures which precede and modify the earlier θυσιαστηρίου, "which is the one which is near ...." An odd variant is that of the A B x+ text which reads των instead of τοῦ ὄντος; this can only be taken as a careless mistake for the O reading, i.e. το ον read as τον but spelled as των. The clause also illustrates the difference between πρός plus the accusative over against the dative: "All the blood he shall pour πρὸς τὴν βάσιν," but the altar is the one which is πρὸς τῇ θύρᾳ; with the accusative, movement may be implied, but with the dative, it is position, i.e. "near the door."

4:19 LXX does not render the suffix of חלבו, and a popular hex(?) text adds αυτου to στέαρ. For ἀνοίσει see comment at 2:16, and for ἐπὶ τὸ θυσιαστήριον see comment at 3:5. The subject of the verb must be ὁ ἱερεύς of v.18.

4:20 LXX translates the structure עשה ל by ποιέω plus an accusative,[31] which is good Classical usage.[32] Actually, the Byz text has rendered the pattern throughout by ποιεῖν plus the dative, which is a recensional (Theod?) correction towards the Hebrew. For τοῦ τῆς ἁμαρτίας see comment at v.8.[33] The כן clause continues with a יעשה ל construction, which LXX idiomatically renders by a passive ποιηθήσεται. Hex has added αυτω under the asterisk to equal the לו of MT.

The importance of these regulations is expressed by the second part of the verse. The ritual sacrifice by the priest means that he makes atonement on their behalf (i.e. of the sinning people). For the meaning of ἐξιλάσεται see the discussion at 1:4. Precisely how the atonement is effected, whether by transfer of the sin to the head of the animal or by the pouring out of the blood before the Lord, is not said. The end towards which all of this moves is given in the final clause: "and the sin shall be pardoned for them."[34] MT simply has ונסלח להם, and hex has placed ἡ ἁμαρτία under the obelus; the addition in LXX is an ad sensum clarification. The notion of ἀφεθήσεται "be pardoned" in effect removes con-

---

31. I can find little justification for translating ποιεῖν by "sacrifice," as Harlé-Pralon ad loc; it simply means "to treat, deal with."
32. For the first לפר Sym retains LXX's τὸν μόσχον, but Theod changes this to the dative, τῷ μόσχῳ, and Aq translated by τῇ δαμάλῃ.
33. And see the discussion at THGL 117.
34. See Bauer sub ἀφίημι 2.

has placed ἡ ἁμαρτία under the obelus; the addition in LXX is an ad sensum clarification. The notion of ἀφεθήσεται "be pardoned" in effect removes consequences of the inadvertent sin which the people had committed, and restores the relationship between God and the people which had been damaged, to one of full communion once again.

4:21 The verbs in MT are all in the singular and refer to the priest, but are in the plural in LXX, for which see comment at v.12. את הפר is translated by τὸν μόσχον ὅλον; the ὅλον has no counterpart in MT, and hex has put it under the asterisk; its source is probably v.12, where, however, it precedes τόν. But here it must be taken as neuter, i.e. adverbially, thus "entirely, wholly."[35] In the second clause אתו is realized as τὸν μόσχον; the reference is correct, though a pronoun would have been sufficient. The translator simply levelled with the first clause. The rendering "the bullock τὸν πρότερον" interprets הראשון "the first" correctly by the comparative, since there was only one earlier animal sacrificed in the chapter; see vv.3—11.

The use of ἁμαρτία is highly unusual here. The Hebrew חטאת can hardly mean "sin," but must mean "sin offering." One would have expected the translator to have used something like η (περι) της αμαρτιας so as to make it refer to the sacrifice. Rendering the clause as "it is the sin of the community" does not make much sense here, and the double-entendre of the Hebrew has been taken over by the translator; cf also v.24. On the other hand, it is likely that the genitive ἁμαρτίας is original, as is argued at v.24; here too it is the majority reading, and the A B+ minority text supporting the nominitive should be considered a grammatical simplification. Accordingly, the critical text should be corrected to ἁμαρτίας.

4:22 Vv.22—26 deal with a ruler who sins inadvertently. Though MT introduces the protasis by אשר, presumably as a temporal conditional particle, LXX levels with the other sections of the chapter by its ἐὰν δέ. LXX articulates ἄρχων, thereby signifying the class, whereas MT simply has נשיא "a leader." The term probably refers to the leader of a clan. For καὶ ποιήσῃ ... ποιηθήσεται see comments at v.13, where exactly the same structure obtains.[36] Quite unexpected is the

---
35. See LS sub ὅλος I.4.
36. For the ἤ clause Sym has ἤ ἐστιν ἄδικος ποιεῖν (retroverted from Syh).

rendering of אלהיו by τοῦ θεοῦ αὐτῶν, and a popular variant has changed the pronoun to αυτου. The αὐτῶν can only make sense in the larger context as reference to the "community of Israel" of vv.13—21. It must be original, since it is the more difficult reading. No copyist would change an original αυτου which would obviously refer to ἄρχων, to the plural.

Also questionable is the doublet καὶ ἁμάρτῃ occurring before καὶ πλεμμελήσῃ. It has no correspondent in MT, and it is omitted by a majority of witnesses. On the other hand, why would a copyist or reviser add it? It is repetitive, serves no obvious purpose, and it is supported by the oldest witnesses, A and B. What is does do is recall the first verb of the protasis. It then serves as an intermediate step; the sin is inadvertent and it is recognized as such, after which a feeling of guilt or error is experienced.

The ἀκουσίως is oddly placed after ποιθήσεται, but this is where MT has its equivalent.[37] It can modify either ἁμάρτῃ 1° or ποιήσῃ; it probably was intended to modify ποιήσῃ, as its position in the verse would seem to indicate.

4:23 MT begins with a correlative או which LXX interprets as καί. The או is probably to be taken in the sense of אם.[38] On the other hand, the correlative conjunction may indicate that as an alternative to v.22's ואשם he is made aware of his inadvertent sin by someone else. The translator took it in the sense of אם, i.e. as a further condition; thus he sinned, was in error, and the sin became known to him.

The apodosis is introduced by καί following MT practice. His gift is to be "a χίμαρον from the goats, a male without blemish." The word χίμαρος usually means a he-goat, but when it is ἐξ αἰγῶν, probably "a kid." It is the usual rendering in OT for שעיר. In the tradition, a popular gloss is added at the end: περι αμαρτιας; it is ex par, e.g. v.32.

4:24 The subject of the verb must be the ἄρχων, and as usual the suffix of ידו is not rendered,[39] since the reference can only be to the ruler. The majority text does add an αυτου, but this is clearly recensional in origin. For the significance of placing the hand on the head of the animal see comment at v.15.

---

37. Aq and Sym render בשגגה by ἐν ἀγνοίᾳ.
38. This is how Rashi understands it. He says כמו אם i.e. "the same as if."
39. See SS 95—96.

In MT the verbs in the second clause and in the relative clause are singular. It is the ruler who slays the kid as a sacrifice, but this all has to be done "before Yahweh," by which is probably intended "within the sanctuary," where only priests (or Levites) were allowed to function. LXX follows Sam, which has the indefinite plural; this may well have been changed to avoid the notion of a layman slaughtering before the Lord; comp comment at 1:11. One can conveniently render such by a passive transform: "and it shall be slaughtered ἐν τόπῳ where τὸ ὁλοκαυτώματα are slaughtered before the Lord." The plural noun represents העלה correctly as a collective. In the tradition, the Byz text articulates τόπῳ; this is a simplification of the text based on the limiting οὗ clause, but it is quite unnecessary.

V.b consists of חטאת הוא in MT, and must mean "it is a sin offering." This is distinguished in Lev from חטאת meaning "sin" by using the genitive case or by περί plus the genitive noun.[40] The reading taken as original in Lev must then be secondary, an early simplification of the text. One does not expect a genitive noun as the subject of ἐστιν, and the urge to drop the final *sigma* gave way to the A B F+ reading. I would now consider ἁμαρτίας original not only here, but also at v.21 and at 5:9,12.

4:25 This verse is paralleled in v.18, which see. LXX coalesces the first two clauses, ונתן ... ולקח, into one clause with the single verb ἐπιθήσει. The Byz text tried to correct this by adding και ληψεται before και ἐπιθήσει, but this equals MT only partially. For κέρατα see comment at v.7. For τοῦ τῆς ἁμαρτίας see comment at v.8. LXX never translates the suffix of אצבעו, since it is obviously always one's own finger, though hex has added αυτου under the asterisk.[41] It should be noted that Origen also added και δωσει here. But LXX had actually omitted ולקח, not ונתן, by its single καὶ ἐπιθήσει. It once again demonstrates how mechanically Origen operated in creating the hexapla. It is only a *b* variant text, which substituted ληψεται for ἐπιθήσει, and added και επιθησει here, which is equal to MT. For τῶν ὁλοκαυτωμάτων (twice) see comment at v.24. For the last clause see comments at v.7. It differs from v.7 in reading τὸ πᾶν (αἷμα) rather than πᾶν τό. It should be noted that BHS does not support the πᾶν, though many mss, Sam and Tar^ON do have כל. As to the position of παν between the article

---
40. See THGL 117.
41. See SS 96.

and the noun, it is transposed with the article by *d+*, which is stylistic, not textual in origin; see vv.7,18,19,26 over against vv.7,8,30 and 31.

4:26 For parallels to v.a see v.19 and v.10. For init ... θυσιαστήριον see v.19. Over against v.19, however, it has αὐτοῦ after στέαρ, but lacks περιελεῖ ἀπ᾽ αὐτοῦ for which MT also follows the shorter text. Both MT and LXX add "the fat of the sacrifice for deliverance" at the end of v.9. For θυσίας σωτηρίου see discussion at 3:1. For v.b see comments at v.20b. The two do differ substantially, however. Since in v.26 the offering is for an ἄρχων, περὶ αὐτοῦ is automatic rather than the plural of v.20. So too αὐτῷ obtains rather than αὐτοῖς. Lacking in v.20 is the modifier ἀπό τῆς ἁμαρτίας αὐτοῦ, but it does add ἡ ἁμαρτία as subject for ἀφεθήσεται. All but the last-named one are due to the parent text. The phrase ἀπὸ τῆς ἁμαρτίας αὐτοῦ is odd as modifying ἐξιλάσεται. The collocation probably means "he shall make atonement because of his sin."[42]

4:27 Vv.27—35 describe the regulations pertaining to an individual ἐκ τοῦ λαοῦ τῆς γῆς who might sin inadvertently; the term "the people of the land" refers to the common people, ordinary folk. The section consists of two parts: vv.27—31 concern an offering of a χίμαιραν ἐκ αἰγῶν; vv.32—35 concern an offering of a προβάτων. The term ψυχὴ μία simply means "a person, an individual;" see comments at v.2 and at 2:1. For the modification of ποιῆσαι cf comments at v.13 on the modification of ποιήσωσιν; the two are identical except for the adjustment in number for the final verb. Here, however, LXX follows Sam (and v.13) in reading πασῶν before "his commandments."[43]

4:28 V.28a is identical in the Greek with v.14 except for the necessary adjustment in number; cf comments ad loc.

The apodosis for vv.27—28a begins with v.b, and is in imitation of MT introduced by καί. Over against the cases thus far, for which a spotless male was to be offered, a spotless female animal is required for the ordinary citizen, a χίμαιραν from the goats. In MT a change to the feminine is also made with v.28. The antecedent, נפש, is disregarded throughout; "his" sin becomes known to

---

42. See LS sub ἀπό III.6.
43. Kenn 101,136,232ᶜ also read מכל מצות instead of ממצות.

"him," which "he" sinned, etc. LXX follows MT, as is clear from the use of αὐτῷ. MT has קרבנו as the first modifier for הביא, which LXX omitted, but hex has added its translation, το δωρον αυτου, under the asterisk.[44] חטאתו occurs twice in the verse, and the translator has sensibly disregarded the suffixes as being otiose.[45] Hex in both cases added an αυτου to represent them. It should also be noted that θήλειαν ἄμωμον does not conform to the word order of MT which has תמימה נקבה. The transposition of the phrase to equal MT obtains in O Byz+, and this is obviously a hex correction.[46] The term θήλειαν is actually otiose, since χίμαιραν is feminine, but it equals MT's נקבה. It does contrast with the masculine χίμαρον of v.23, which is apparently reserved as the sacrifice for an ἄρχων.

4:29 As in the other cases the worshiper is to place the hand (for ידו) on the head of the sacrificial animal, which is uniquely called τοῦ ἁμαρτήματος αὐτοῦ (for החטאת);[47] (for the laying on of the hand see comment at 1:4). Of course, it means "his sin offering," but nowhere else is it called this in OT; the word is identical in meaning with ἁμαρτία. It simply illustrates once again Lev's love for variation. Oddly enough, Origen neither omitted αὐτοῦ nor is there an obelus extant to indicate its absence in MT. In fact, in the next clause את החטאת is rendered by τὴν χίμαιραν τὴν τῆς ἁμαρτίας. Obviously Origen did not recognize the distinction between τὴν τῆς ἁμαρτίας and τῆς ἁμαρτίας which Lev makes; see comment at v.8. As expected, hex has put χίμαιραν τήν under the obelus as a structure for which MT has no counterpart. As usual, hex has also added αυτου after "the hand" to represent the suffix.

Since the second clause orders the slaying of the kid of the sin offering the verb is again put into the plural, for the rationale of which see the comments at 3:3—4. Lev again illustrates the urge towards clarifying expansions by its rendering of במקום העלה by ἐν τόπῳ οὗ σφάζουσιν τὰ ὁλοκαυτώματα.

4:30 The first clause has the priest taking ἀπό (some of) its blood with the finger. The ἀπό is again obviously used partitively.[48] Lev again omits the suffix with

---
44. For a reasoned explanation for this omission see Daniel 123—124, note 18.
45. See SS 97.
46. See THGL 103.
47. See the discussion of this point in Daniel 304.
48. See SS 161.

bodily parts, as here in the case of האצבעו, for which it always omits the suffix.[49] The majority text does add αυτου, which is either a hex correction or an ad sensum gloss. For the verse in general see comments at v.25. Lev did abbreviate the reference to the "base of the altar of burnt offerings," by omitting the last prepositional phrase. A popular text has added των ολοκαυτωματων, but this has no basis in MT; it is, in fact, based on Sam which reads מזבח העלה. The source of the asterisk in two s mss is not clear, and may well be misplaced in the mss, e.g. from αυτου referred to above as a majority reading. Neither O nor Syh, the major representatives of hex readings, witness to the plus; it is not hex.

4:31 The preposed modifier, את כל חלבה, is rendered without regard to the suffix by πᾶν τὸ στέαρ, but this time hex did not "correct" the phrase by adding a genitive pronoun. At first blush the present tense of the verb in the ὃν τρόπον clause is unexpected in view of the הוסר of the parent text, but it is idiomatically correct; it signifies what is the usual case, i.e. "as the fat is (normally) removed from the sacrifice for deliverance." For ἐπὶ τὸ θυσιαστήριον rendering המזבחה see comment at 3:5. For v.b see comments at v.20.

4:32 לחטאת is rendered by περὶ ἁμαρτίας, which phrase is used to designate the sin offering,[50] and should be translated "for a sin offering." The A B O x+ variant text, εις αμαρτιαν, is probably a hex correction; in any event, it is a reading based on a revision towards the Hebrew. Whether ἁμαρτίας was originally articulated is uncertain; the majority text does read της αμαρτιας, and constitutes the more usual reading.[51]

The apodosis is not introduced by a conjunction, since MT lacks its usual introductory waw. For the required offering as θῆλυ see comment at v.28.

4:33 This verse is paralleled in v.29, but instead of the unique τοῦ ἁμαρτήματος αὐτοῦ the translator reverts to τοῦ (referring to δῶρον) τῆς ἁμαρτίας to render החטאת, for which see comment at v.8. As usual, hex corrects τὴν χεῖρα by adding αυτου to render ידו. For the change in number of the verbs in v.b see comment at 3:3—4. At v.29 σφάξουσιν was modified by τὴν χίμαιραν τὴν τῆς

---

49. See SS 119—120.
50. See THGL 117.
51. See the discussion in THGL 78.

ἁμαρτίας, but here LXX only has αὐτό (to represent אתה), and fails to render the following modifier לחטאת. Hex has, however, added περι αμαρτιας to equal it. For the remainder of the verse see comment at v.29.

4:34 Comp comments on v.30 for this verse. The two verses differ primarily in that the two coordinate clauses of v.30 are coalesced into one by subordinating the first one into a participial structure. Our verse also spells out "some of the blood" as being τοῦ τῆς ἁμαρτίας instead of the pronoun αὐτῆς, and the altar is described as τῆς ὁλοκαυτώσεως rather than as τῶν ὁλοκαυτωμάτων,[52] which is also added after τοῦ θυσιαστηρίου 2° over against MT. Since the suffix of ידו refers to προβάτων, LXX perforce has αὐτοῦ, not αὐτῆς as well.

4:35 For the first clause see comments at v.31. One difference between the two is the recognition of the suffix in חלבה here by αὐτοῦ; also the ὃν τρόπον clause is expanded by the modifier προβάτου after στέαρ, and by reading ἐκ τῆς θυσίας τοῦ instead of ἀπὸ θυσίας.

With the second clause a section begins in which ἐπιτίθημι is used to render הקטיר, for which see comment at 2:16. A hex correction changes the word order of αυτὸ ὁ ἱερεύς to conform to that of MT: הכהן אותם. Note that LXX changed the plural pronoun to the singular, since only πᾶν αὐτοῦ τὸ στέαρ is referred to. MT's plural apparently presupposes various pieces of fat as at vv.8–9, which are, however, not mentioned here. Surprising is the rendering of אשי by the singular τὸ ὁλοκαύτωμα; cf comment at 1:9. It has been corrected by C' Byz+ to the plural to equal MT. The translator may well have used the singular under the influence of αὐτό; see comment above.

For v.b see discussion at v.20, from which it differs in some details. It has added περὶ τῆς ἁμαρτίας after ἱερεύς for על חטאתו; hex has added αυτου to represent the suffix in MT.[53] Furthermore, necessary changes in number were made to fit the context.

---

52. See THGL 74.
53. See SS 97 and THGL 112.

Chapter 5

5:1 Vv.1—4 contain a series of conditions, for which vv.5—6 are the apodosis. For ψυχή see comments at 2:1 and 4:2; it follows ἐὰν δέ rather than preceding it as in MT ונפש כי. כי is rightly taken as equivalent to the conditional particle ἐάν.[1] The coordinate ἁμάρτῃ καὶ ἀκούσῃ imitates MT, but the second verb identifies what the ἁμάρτῃ consists of, i.e. the sin involves hearing a spoken adjuration under certain specific conditions. In fact, the ἁμάρτῃ consists of vv.1—4. The fact that it is φωνὴν ὁρκισμοῦ means that the adjuration was publicly made; the unusual collocation reproduces the קול אלה of MT literally.

That Lev often disregards grammatical concord is clear from the masculine οὗτος which refers to ψυχή which is feminine.[2] The statement καὶ οὗτος ... σύνοιδεν constitutes a further definition; he has heard an adjuration, and is a potential witness, i.e. being a witness means that either he has seen or has become acquainted (with the matter). What constitutes all this as sin is ἐὰν μὴ ἀπαγγείλῃ, i.e. if he does not report the matter.

The apodosis is straightforward: λήμψεται τὴν ἁμαρτίαν,[3] which represents נשא עונו "he shall incur (his) guilt." That ἁμαρτία also equals "guilt" is shown by its rendering of עון 26 times in the Pentateuch, of which 11 are found in Lev.[4] LXX does not render the suffix, which is quite unnecessary in Greek. Hex, however, adds αυτου under the asterisk to equal it.

5:2 V.2 constitutes a second sin, but the Greek equals MT only for the opening words "or a person who might touch any unclean matter," after which it differs considerably from MT.[5] For the first defilement in MT: "Either a corpse of an unclean wild animal," LXX has two possible sources: ἢ θνησιμαίου ἢ θηριαλώτου

---

1. See THGL 74.
2. For numerous examples of incongruence in gender in Lev see Huber 33—36.
3. Harlé-Pralon ad loc call it a calque, but this is an exaggeration. That ἁμαρτία can encompass the notion of "guilt" as well as "error" is attested already in Plato and Aristotle; see LS sub ἁμαρτία 2.
4. Milgrom 295 makes the interesting point that "incurring guilt" always implies that punishment will come from God, not man.
5. According to Procopius Theod read the relative clause as *quicunque inquinaverit se verbo impuro*, and Aq, as *qui conspurcaverit se verbo aliquo inquinato*.

ἀκαθάρτου, i.e. the reference to חיה is interpreted as an alternative: "or torn by a wild animal." Pollution is, according to LXX, possible by touching an ordinary corpse or one caused by a wild animal. In either case it is ἀκαθάρτου, though this is not overly clear, since ἀκαθάρτου follows θηριαλώτου, and could be taken as modifying only it.

The remainder of the verse covers the second and third defilements of MT, but in reverse order and in the plural. MT reads: "either a corpse of an unclean בהמה or a corpse of unclean שרץ." The translator clearly took both nouns as collectives, though changing שרץ to βδελυγμάτων "abominations."[6] The Greek has also rendered בנבלת in both cases by the plural τῶν θνησιμαίων. What LXX reads is "either unclean corpses of abominations or the unclean corpses of cattle." An A B x+ text has added to the confusion by adding η των before βδελυγμάτων, i.e. reading "or of corpses or of unclean abominations." Origen attempted to correct the LXX by transposing the two structures, but only a *b* variant equals MT adequately with η θνησιμαιου κτηνους ακαθαρτου η θνησιμαιου ερπετου ακαθαρτου, a text obviously recensional in origin, probably deriving from one of The Three. In the tradition, both βδελυγμάτων and κτηνῶν are articulated, the former by an A B *oI x+* text, the latter by an *O s+* reading. Neither is original text as the odd, unbalanced support shows.[7] This is also out of line with MT, where "unclean" does not modify "corpse," but rather בהמה and שרץ resp. To say that corpses are unclean is tautological; what is at issue is the uncleanness of cattle and of creeping things. The translator was obviously rather confused. The Byz text has also added another αψηται after the second ἀκαθάρτων, presumably to remind the reader of the verb governing all these alternatives.

V.b in MT reads ונעלם ממנו והוא טמא ואשם "and it is hid from him, and he is unclean and guilty," which is unrecognized by LXX. Since vv.3 and 4 have similar conditions added, the omission can only be judged an error on the translator's part. It must be admitted that the translator either did not seem to understand this verse at all well or was careless to a fault in his rendering. Hex has added a translation of the Hebrew under the asterisk as και λαθη απ αυτου και αυτος μεμιανται και πλημμεληση.

---

6. Aq and Sym correct this to ἑρπετῶν (retroverted from Latin).
7. See the discussion in THGL 86.

5:3 Unusual is the modification of ἄψηται by an ἀπό phrase (elsewhere only at 15:10); a genitive modifier is usual (26 our of 28 times in the book).⁸ In fact, the first ἀπό phrase is explicated by a second one ἀπὸ πάσης ἀκαθαρσίας αὐτοῦ, which is in turn modified by a relative clause. MT distinguishes the two modifiers, the first by a ב phrase which is the usual modification required by the verb נגע, and the second one by a ל phrase. This is probably to be taken as an explication of the ב phrase, as LXX clearly understood it by rendering both by ἀπό phrases. Thus this might be rendered "even by any uncleanness by which he by touching is defiled." In the tradition, the second ἀπό phrase is popularly given as an alternate by adding η before it: "or any of his pollutions." The relative clause in MT simply means "by which he becomes unclean," but LXX clarifies this by its addition of a participle ἧς ἂν ἁψάμενος μιανθῇ.

The second part of the verse qualifies the condition by "and he is unaware of it, but afterwards he becomes aware and becomes guilty." The μετὰ τοῦτο is a free interpretation of the parent text which has the pronoun הוא. In fact, in the next verse the והוא is closely rendered by καὶ οὗτος. The problem arises from the grammatical structure of the Hebrew, in which three clauses are presented at the same level: ונעלם ממנו "and it is hidden from him," והוא ידע "and he knew," and ואשם "and he is guilty." What the translator did was to make clear that the awareness of the offence was subsequent to his unawareness. He was simply trying to clarify the chronological relation between the two states of consciousness.

5:4 The translator paralleled this condition with v.2 by using a relative pronoun in place of כי. Unusual is the translation of לבטא "to speak rashly" by an attributive participle διαστέλλουσα modifying ψυχή, thus "a person (who swears), saying out loud (literally "uttering by lips")⁹ that he will do evil or good." Lev varies the parallel infinitive by using the compound κακοποιῆσαι in the first case but an adverb plus simplex, καλῶς ποιῆσαι, for the second, though an F M s x z+ text does level it to the compound καλοποιησαι by attraction to the first case. The standard employed for the doing evil or good is given as κατὰ πάντα ὅσα ἂν διαστείλῃ ὁ ἄνθρωπος μεθ' ὅρκου "according to everything which the man uttered under oath." The comitative expression modifying the verb is an idiomatic

---

8. See THGL 115.
9. Using an instrumental dative, τοῖς χείλεσιν; cf SS 119.

rendering of an instrumental בשבעה.[10] Lev expands the parent text rather oddly by rendering ונעלם ממנו "and he is unaware of it" by λάθῃ αὐτὸν πρὸ ὀφθαλμῶν. The prepositional phrase has no actual basis in MT,[11] though I would argue that it constitutes a good free rendering of the Hebrew; I would render the clause by "and it should escape his notice." Hex has omitted the phrase so as to equal MT more exactly. Over against v.3, Lev here translates והוא literally by καὶ οὗτος.

For the final clause the translator has ἁμάρτῃ instead of אשם. Outside the contextual ἁμαρτεῖν in 4:3, where the translator uses the root five times within the verse, the Pentateuch never uses ἁμαρτάνω to translate אשם. Could it be that the translator is simply carrying on his desire for variation, i.e. not wanting to repeat γνῷ καὶ πλημμελήσῃ of v.3? The use of ἕν τι τούτων is also unusual; the τούτων refers to the four conditions outlined in vv.1—4. ἁμαρτάνω can take the accusative, but it is highly unusual; one expects a genitive. The genitive of the structure is a partitive.[12]

5:5 V.4 ended with מאלה and v.5 begins with והיה כי יאשם לאחת מאלה. The translator has disregarded the opening five words because of honoioteleuton, although admitedlly it is repetitive, and its omission does leave a sensible text, with LXX proceding immediately to v.b, which is the apodosis. Hex has filled in the lacuna under an asterisk by και εσται οτι πλημμελησει εις εν απο τουτων.

What the sinner by inadvertence is to do first of all is to declare the sin περὶ ὧν ἡμάρτηκεν κατ' αὐτῆς. MT has as modifier of והתודה "then he shall confess אשר חטא עליה." The על phrase depends on the verb, i.e. he must make confession about it, i.e. he confesses about what he has sinned. The use of ἐξαγορεύσει "make known, declare" to render התודה reflects a true understanding of the nature of confession, which must be spoken, declared; in other words, it can not be silent. The translator used περὶ ὧν to refer to any of the cases in vv.1—4, presumably reflecting the מאלה with which v.4 ends, but since עליה/κατ' αὐτῆς had no antecedent in the shorter text, an antecedent was provided in τὴν ἁμαρτίαν, which has no equivalent in MT. In good English a rendering of κατ' αὐτῆς must be avoided: "he must declare whatever sins he has

---

10. See SS 128.
11. The Others omit it.
12. See SS 166.

sinned." Presumably the declaration must be made to God, since the conditions portrayed in vv.1—4 are all sins against deity; how this declaration was to take place or where is not said, though apparently it was to be prior to the bringing of a sacrifice; cf v.6.[13]

5:6 The verb οἴσει is modified by two περί clauses which are in apposition: "on behalf of whatever he is guilty of over against the Lord, on behalf of the sin which he sinned." In the first of these, the translator faced the problem of translating את אשמו. The word אשם, on the analogy of חטאת signifying either "sin" or "sin offering," also can be taken to mean either "guilt" or "the guilt sacrifice."[14] Note how the translator, again on the analogy of his rendering of חטאת as a sin offering, translates אשם in the latter sense, either with a περί phrase or with a simple genitive; comp v.15. In the second περί structure τῆς ἁμαρτίας fails to render the suffix of חטאתו, but hex added an αυτου under the asterisk to make up for it.

The punctuation in the Göttingen text is faulty in that the comma before ἀμνάδα belongs after it. The offering that must be brought is either a female lamb from the flock or a female kid (χίμαιραν refers to a female) from the herd of goats. For the rendering of לחטאת by περὶ ἁμαρτίας see comment at 4:3.

The Hebrew of v.b consists of only one clause, as over against 4:35 which added ונסלח לו as a second clause. LXX, however, follows 4:35b exactly in its MT form, except for adding ἡ ἁμαρτία at the end as subject for ἀφεθήσεται. Sam also has the longer text, though without an expressed subject at the end; in other words, the source of v.b must be 4:35b.

5:7 Vv.7—13 deal with cases in which the one who sins inadvertently is too poor to bring the sacrificial animal required by v.6. The condition of poverty at the first level is given in the protasis in v.7. MT has "and if his hand does not extend sufficiently for a sheep;" what is meant is if his means are insufficient for a sheep. The Greek has a slightly different idiom to convey this notion: "but if his hand is insufficiently strong for a sheep;" this does convey what MT intends.

---

13. R.Sollamo in Greenspoon-Munnich 48 considers the κατ' αὐτῆς one of "a number of clumsy and/or unintelligible renderings," making ψυχή the possible antecedent of the pronoun, which would be unintelligible indeed.
14. Milgrom 303 argues that the term can also mean punishment or penalty.

Uncertain is the original tense of the verb. In the critical text ἰσχύσῃ was adopted for two reasons. Throughout ch.4 all protases had used only aorist subjunctives. Furthermore, cod B supported the aorist here as well, though only as B*, i.e. a corrector had changed it to the present. In the tradition, the majority A F M text witness to the present tense ισχυη instead of the aorist. Furthermore, in the next protasis (v.11) the present is used, with only one late ms reading a variant aorist. I would now argue that the present tense is also original here, and that the text should read ἰσχύῃ rather than ἰσχύσῃ. That cod B is not to be trusted is clear from its support of the articulation of πρόβατον in the same clause. The evidence is weak, with only B F^b 15 x witnessing to το προβατον; furthermore, MT has שה, an unarticulated noun.[15] In MT the שה is the free element of the bound phrase די שה, which LXX realized idiomatically by εἰς πρόβατον.[16] The apodosis begins with οἴσει, i.e. without an apodotic καί which MT's והביא would support. The verb is modified by περὶ τῆς ἁμαρτίας αὐτοῦ ἧς ἥμαρτεν; this does not represent MT's את אשמו אשר חטא, which collocation is unique in the book, whereas "(his) sin which he sinned" occurs at 4:3,23,28 as well as twice at 19:22. For exactly the same collocation see 4:3. I suspect that the translator was troubled by the notion of sinning an אשם, whereas sinning sin made fine sense.

What the indigent worshiper may substitute for an animal sacrifice are two turtledoves or two young doves.[17] The two are intended to be κυρίῳ "for the Lord." A popular text which is probably hex in origin articulates κυρίῳ, since the preposition of ליהוה is sometimes shown by the dative article, and Origen often corrected κυρίῳ when it represented ליהוה by articulating it.

That two birds are required is explained by one serving as περὶ ἁμαρτίας, i.e. serving as a sin offering, and one intended for a burnt offering. It should be noted that the sin offering also was divided. Certain parts were burned on the altar, and the rest was designated for the ash heap; see ch.4, and especially vv.11—12.

5:8 LXX has added ὁ ἱερεύς as subject of the second clause over against MT, thereby making certain that the reader would not continue the subject of the first

---

15. See THGL 86.
16. See SS 69.
17. For preferring the contracted form νοσσούς rather than the Attic νεοσσους throughout the Pentateuch see Walters 79—80.

clause for the second, which would be the normal way of reading the passage. Only the priest is allowed to make the actual sacrifice. Hex has placed ὁ ἱερεύς under the obelus, since it has no equivalent in MT. The modifier of the verb is τὸ περὶ τῆς ἁμαρτίας πρότερον, in which πρότερον (see also v.10 τὸ δεύτερον) is nominalized as a neuter noun used adverbially, and constitutes a reference to the first of the pair of birds "the one for a sin-offering in v.7"; cf comment at 4:8.

Again for the third clause LXX specifies the subject as ὁ ἱερεύς, which hex also placed under the obelus to show that it does not occur in MT. For "pinch off (its) head" see comment at 1:15. Here the description is fuller than in ch.1, where the priestly action was limited to ἀποκνίσει τὴν κεφαλήν, to which this verse has added αὐτοῦ ἀπὸ τοῦ σφονδύλου καὶ οὐ διελεῖ. The noun normally means "vertebra," rendering the Hebrew ערפו "its neck," and contextually LXX must mean "the neck" as well. The variant σπονδυλου is a later spelling of the word. Hex has added αυτου to represent the suffix of the Hebrew word, which the translator disregarded as being unnecessary. An added detail demands that the wringing of the bird's neck should stop short of separating the head.

5:9 That ἀπό is used partitively here is obvious,[18] since the next clause refers to τὸ δὲ κατάλοιπον τῆν αἵματος. The priest must sprinkle some of the blood of the sin offering on the wall of the altar. For τοῦ περὶ τῆς ἁμαρτίας see comment at 4:18.[19]

The second clause is introduced by a contrastive δέ construction; the remainder of the blood he (i.e. the priest) shall squeeze out upon the base of the altar. The compound καταστραγγιεῖ is a hapax legomenon in OT,[20] but does not differ from the simplex στραγγίζω in meaning, a good example of the tendency towards compounding in Hellenistic Greek. The translator's choice of verb illustrates his tendency to greater exactness. MT has ימצה vocalized by the Masoretes as a Ni, "shall be drained out." But birds do not have a great deal of blood, particularly after some of it has already been used to sprinkle on the altar's walls, so the translator makes the verb active, thereby having the priest squeeze out the remaining drops of blood still in the carcass.

---

18. See SS 161.
19. See the discussion in THGL 117.
20. According to Harlé-Pralon it is a creation of Lev.

For considering ἁμαρτία secondary to the majority ἁμαρτίας see comment at 4:21. Actually not only do A B M support the original genitive, but so does the Qumran text, 802, which dates from the first century BCE.[21] In MT the nominal clause is a simple statement of fact: it is a sin offering. The Greek makes this the reason for the instructions; it is a γάρ clause, thus "because it is a sin offering."

5:10 The verb ποιήσει is modified by a double accusative in imitation of MT: "and the second (of the pair of birds) he shall treat as a burnt offering ὡς καθήκει." I would translate the ὡς clause as "in the usual manner." It represents כמשפט "according to prescription."[22] The verb means "is customary."

In the second part of the verse ἐξιλάσεται is modified by two περί phrases, which I would translate as "and the priest shall make atonement for him for his sin which he sinned." An AB+ text omitted the first phrase, περὶ αὐτοῦ, but both are needed for good sense, and both have counterparts in MT: עליו and מחטאתו. The O text has changed the second περί to απο, presumably a recensional change intended to represent the מן more exactly.[23] For ἐξιλάσεται and ἀφεθήσεται see comments at 4:20.

5:11 For MT's תשיג "should extend (to)," LXX has εὑρίσκῃ,[24] which was paralleled in v.7 by ἰσχύσῃ (... τὸ ἱκανόν, but see comment ad loc), where MT's verb was תגיע. It should be noted that the verb εὑρίσκῃ is a present subjunctive; "not finding (i.e. not affording) a brace[25] of birds" is a regular state of affairs, and the present tense emphasizes this.[26] In the structure בני היונה the בני simply designates membership in the class or species; the phrase simply means "pigeons." LXX has taken this to mean "offspring of the dove," i.e. νοσσοὺς περιστερῶν, "pigeon chicks" or "young pigeons."

The apodosis as usual is marked by the future indicative οἴσει, here introduced by an apodotic καί to equal the Hebrew. The verb is doubly modified by

---

21. Contrary to THGL 120–121.
22. The anonymous reading κατὰ τὴν κρίσιν is almost certainly the reading of Aq.
23. For περὶ αὐτοῦ as original text see THGL 112.
24. For which see THGL 131.
25. See THGL 72.
26. Lev has αὐτοῦ before ἡ χείρ for ידו; the majority text has transposed it to equal the Hebrew order. This need not be a hex correction, since the usual order in the book has the pronoun following the noun; it may well be simply ex par.

accusatives: τὸ δῶρον αὐτοῦ and τὸ δέκατον τοῦ οἰφὶ σεμίδαλιν, thus "as his gift the tenth of an ephah of fine flour." The Hebrew measure האפה is translated by τοῦ οἰφί, an Egyptian measure similar, though not identical, in sound to the Hebrew.[27]

The priest must not ἐπιχεεῖ oil on it. The C'+ tradition has changed this verb as well as ἐπιθήσει in the next clause to second person verbs, but a second person reference is contextually out of order. Note that v.12 begins with καὶ οἴσει, which the C' text does not change to second person. This follows Sam's יצק rather than MT's ישים; admittedly to "pour" oil on the flour is a more appropriate action than to "place" oil on it.[28] Since it is a sin offering, i.e. περὶ ἁμαρτίας, the flour is to be unadorned by oil or frankincense. The b n+ text has changed both cases of αὐτό to αυτην; this constitutes an attempt to "correct" the text in order to refer to ἁμαρτίας, but the neuter refers to δῶρον, and as the more difficult text is to be preferred. The variant text is closer to MT in which the suffix refers to חטאת.

5:12 This verse also uses αὐτό, though the majority text has αυτην.[29] But the parallel to v.11 οἴσει τὸ δῶρον αὐτοῦ makes it likely that the reference in Lev is intended. It might also be noted that the oldest texts, A B F G, all support the neuter.

For καὶ δραξάμενος ... δράκα see comments at 2:2. For τὸ μνημόσυνον ... θυσιαστήριον also see comments at 2:2. It should be noted that αὐτῆς modifying μνημόσυνον must refer to σεμίδαλιν, and is best understood as an objective genitive, as Daniel rightly pointed out.[30] Uncertain is the originality of τῶν ὁλοκαυτωμάτων. MT has על אשי and the majority text has an επι before it, which may well be the better text. It would be easily omitted by copyists, since the phrase "altar of burnt offerings" is an oft-recurring phrase. On the other hand, the addition of επι to equal MT, e.g. by hex, is equally possible. The shorter text is well-suppported, inter alia, by A B, the oldest uncials, and the more difficult shorter text could be original. On the other hand, the Hebrew makes the text of Lev unlikely to be original. If MT had read על עלה or על עולת,

---

27. According to LS it is equal to four χοίνικες. The *choenix* was a dry measure used for grains; see sub χοῖνιξ.
28. Pesh also reads *nswk* "pour."
29. The Three all have αὐτήν.
30. Pp.232—233.

this might be possible, but for a translator to come up with "altar of burnt offerings" as a rendering for מזבחה על אשי is highly improbable. I would now read ἐπί before τῶν ὁλοκαυτωμάτων; comp also 4:35 where exactly the same Hebrew text obtains; see comment ad loc.

For ἁμαρτίας as original rather than ἁμαρτία see comment at v.9 and especially at 4:21.

5:13 For init ... ἥμαρτεν see comments at v.10. Unusual is the rendering of מאחת מאלה.[31] LXX renders this by ἐφ' ἑνὸς τούτων in which the preposition has the sense of "in respect of, concerning,[32] thus "in respect of anyone of these." The majority variant has changed ἐφ' to αφ, which is probably a recensional correction.

V.b. in MT reads והיתה לכהן כמנחה "And it will be the priest's like the meal offering." The Greek defines the subject as τὸ καταλειφθέν; after all, part of it had already been sacrificed as τὸ μνημόσυνον (v.12), and in the interests of strict accuracy, only what was left could belong to the officiating priest; see especially 2:3,10. Usually מנחה was rendered by θυσία (34 times out of 36 in Lev; it also occurs 31 times for זבח), but this was not sufficiently exact for the translator who defined ἡ θυσία as consisting of τῆς σεμιδάλεως, probably a reflection of ch.2 in which regulations for the meal offerings were discussed; the θυσίας usually consisted inter alia of σεμίδαλις; see vv.2,4,5,7.

5:15 For ψυχή see comments at 2:1 and 4:2. The protasis has coordinate verbal structures λάθῃ αὐτὸν λήθῃ καὶ ἁμάρτῃ ἀκουσίως "(if) it should actually escape his notice, and he should sin inadvertently." The αὐτόν has no equivalent in MT, and is an ad sensum addition in LXX; it refers to ψυχή, but since a male person is intended the masculine pronoun is used.[33] This first clause differs considerably from MT which reads נפש כי תמעל מעל "should a person actually commit an act of treachery."[34] Since λανθάνω often occurs as a rendering for עלם some have

---
31. See GK 119w, Note 2 in which the partitive מן before אחת is explained as equivalent to the Latin *ullus*.
32. See LS sub ἐπί A.III.4.
33. See the discussion in Huber 32.
34. Milgrom 345—361 maintains that מעל means "sacrilege" either against "holy things" or against "oaths." Whether or not he is right is not clear to me, but what is clear is that LXX did not understand it in this way.

suggested that the translator misread the relevant text as תעלם עלם,[35] but this is by no means certain in view of the coordinate expression. Since this is a case of sinning inadvertently, it is not a case of perfidy or treachery as the verb מעל implies, but a mistake. The matter escaped his notice; he overlooked it; he forgot. I would suggest that the translation is an exegetical matter rather than a textual one.[36] Actually the verb מעל has no pattern of equivalents in LXX at all. The verb occurs 35 times in OT, but has sixteen different renderings, of which ἀθετέω is the most frequent with six occurrences.[37] For ἀκουσίως see comment at 4:2.[38] The ἀπό phrase modifies ἁμάρτῃ.[39] Just what the "holy things of the Lord" intended is not clear, but in any event what is involved is related to the Lord; the inadvertent sinning concerns not fellow-man, but deity. In the tradition, C' s change ἁμάρτῃ to the first aorist form αμαρτηση.

The apodosis is introduced by καί, and is clearly apodotic as its change to the future indicative shows. τῆς πλημμελείας is the regular rendering in the book for אשם when it refers to the sacrifice; it refers to the trespass offering, but see below. Except for v.18 where εἰς πλημμέλειαν occurs, it is always in the genitive, whether with or without an article and sometimes preceded by περί or by an article used as a pronoun. The offering was to consist of a ram without blemish ἐκ the flock,[40] τιμῆς ἀργυρίου σίκλων τῷ σίκλῳ τῶν ἁγίων "valued in shekels of silver according to the shekel of holy things." The term τιμῆς is regularly used to render בערכך "according to your estimate" in the book. The dative, τῷ κυρίῳ, is a rendering of a ב of instrument.[41] The term τῶν ἁγίων is by no means certain as LXX. MT has the singular הקדש, and the term "shekel of the sanctuary" is well-known. The genitive plural is supported by A B 121, a combination often occurring idiosyncratically in Lev, but here it is clearly the more difficult reading. The singular genitive του αγιου is supported by only one Greek ms and can hardly be taken as original; it may well be a recensional correction. All other Greek witnesses read τω αγιω, thus "according to the holy shekel,"

---

35. E.g. Harlé-Pralon ad loc. See also the discussion in Walters 262,264.
36. Aq renders the construction by παραβῇ παρέβασεν.
37. Accordng to Dos Santos.
38. Aq renders this by ἐν ἀγνοίᾳ.
39. According to SS 161 the ἀπό is partitive, thus "in respect to one of."
40. The ἐκ is partitive; see SS 165.
41. See SS 129.

which I suspect to be a corruption of τῶν ἁγίων. The περί structure is a paraphrastic rendering of the Hebrew לאשם.

5:16 V.16a further defines the apodosis. Not only is the guilty one to offer a trespass offering, but for whatever he failed to do (ἥμαρτεν) of the holy things, he must make restitution. It might be noted that as in v.15 the plural τῶν ἁγίων is used to render הקדש, and here with no variation in the tradition.[42] That the variant text of A B b+, αποτισαι, is secondary is obvious from the syntactical context. This verb, along with the coordinate προσθήσει, must be future; it is still part of that which the guilty one must carry out.[43] The structure τὸ ἐπίπεμπτον represents את חמישתו, but LXX does not translate the suffix.[44] The neuter pronoun αὐτό occurs twice in the verse with no specific antecedent. This is used sporadically by the translator without stating exactly what "it" means,[45] and here it refers to what he is to give, i.e. he will add the fifth to it (i.e. the total), and give it (i.e. the entire restitution) to the priest.

The second part of the verse is similar to vv.6 and 10, but see especially comments at 4:20. It differs from those references in its ἐν τῷ κριῷ τῆς πλημμελείας, which clearly represents an instrumental use of ἐν,[46] thus "by means of the ram of the trespass offering."

5:17 MT begins rather oddly with ואם נפש כי, and modern translators disregard either the אם or the כי: NRSV has "if any of you"; NIV, "if a person," and NJPS, "and when a person." LXX has καὶ ψυχή, ἢ ἄν, a construction also obtaining at 7:11(21) and 20:6. For the former, MT has ונפש כי, and for the latter, והנפש אשר. Whether the parent text here was MT cannot be determined, since the structure ואם נפש כי occurs only here. In the tradition, B F G z+ articulate ψυχή, but when it stands as headword for a protasis it is never articulated.[47]

---

42. The ἀπό is obviously partitive; see SS 167.
43. See THGL 127.
44. See SS 64.
45. See the discussion in Huber 34—35.
46. See SS 120.
47. See the discussion in THGL 86.

The verse as a whole constitutes the protasis of a conditional clause, and its apodosis follows in v.18.⁴⁸ The ἀπό phrase modifies μίαν, and is thus partitive.⁴⁹ The relative clause interprets the Ni תעשינה in an active sense as (ὧν οὐ δεῖ ποιεῖν, which is idiomatic and correct. For τὴν ἁμαρτίαν as rendering for עונו see comment at 5:1. Here, however, the majority text which adds αυτου is not necessarily hex in origin, though of course it may be.

5:18 The apodosis is in imitation of the Hebrew introduced by καί and the first clause is a shortened version of v.15b, which see. Note particularly τιμῆς ἀργυρίου "valued in silver," but MT has no equivalent for ἀργυρίου; it simply has בערכך, the meaning of which is unclear. The translator borrowed ἀργυρίου from the parallel in v.15 in order to hint at the meaning, and it may well refer to a monetary substitute for the ram, thus "or its value in money." Over against v.15 it has not only omitted τῆς πλημμελείας αὐτοῦ τῷ κυρίῳ as well as σίκλων τῷ σίκλῳ τῶν ἁγίων, but also substituted for the rest of the verse εἰς πλημμέλειαν πρὸς τὸν ἱερέα.

For καὶ ἐξιλάσεται ... ἱερεύς and καὶ ἀφετήσεται αὐτῷ see comments at 4:20. The atonement is intended περὶ τῆς ἀγνοίας αὐτοῦ ἧς ἠγνόησεν "concerning his mistake which he had not perceived," an attempt to render על שגגתו אשר שגג "concerning his inadvertent action which he had committed." To this is added καὶ αὐτὸς οὐκ ᾔδει. Obviously the stress in both MT and LXX is on the lack of intention on the part of the transgressor.

5:19 MT begins with אשם הוא which reflects the לאשם of v.18; thus: "it is a trespass offering." This is followed by אשם אשם, and the translator by inadvertence overlooked the initial clause because of homoioteleuton. The Masoretes vocalized the repeated vocables resp as a free infinitive plus verb, thus "he has actually committed a trespass (over against Yahweh)." The translator rendered this by the verb ἐπλημμέλησεν plus a cognate accusative, and then contextualized the statement by means of the γάρ particle. In other words, in LXX v.19 is the basis for the demands of v.18. The statement is repetitive in view of the protasis in v.17, thus "because he has committed an error, he must bring a ram ...."

---

48. Milgrom 334 considers the last clause of the verse as beginning the apodosis. This he bases on his belief (295—297) that cases of אשם involve the perpetrator in ונשא עונו. The Masoretes disagree with this as their accentuation here shows. The translator also made this part of the protasis, as the subjunctive inflection of the verb shows.
49. See SS 166.

Chapter 6

6:2(5:21) Vv.1—6 still deal with πλημμέλεια, and accordingly are part of ch.5 in MT. For ψυχὴ ἐάν see comment at 4:2. For מעל מעלה see comment at 5:15; here it is translated by παριδὼν παρίδῃ "should actually disregard." That the collocation is rendered literally here does give point to those who believe a different parent text to have obtained at 5:15; cf comments ad loc. In MT the verb is modified by ביהוה, i.e. "trespass against Yahweh," but this would be inappropriate for παρίδῃ, and the translator used τὰς ἐντολὰς κυρίου as something which someone might disregard or neglect. What this neglect of the Lord's commandments might consist of is illustrated by what follows in the remainder of this verse and the next one. One might falsify[1] matters which concern the neighbour (τὰ πρὸς τὸν πλησίον): a.) ἐν παραθήκῃ, or b.) περὶ κοινωνίας, or c.) περὶ ἁρπαγῆς, or d.) ἠδίκησέν τι τὸν πλησίον. "The matters which concern the neighbour" translates בעמיתו, a term referring to a clansman. Lev does not distinguish between עמית and רע, translating both by πλησίον. The term occurs twice in the verse; in both cases MT has a third masculine singular suffix which LXX never translates. Of the 16 cases of πλησίον in Lev only σου occurs in modification of the noun, but αυτου never does. In both cases here hex has added αυτου under the asterisk to represent the suffix.

παραθήκη refers to a deposit entrusted to someone; it is a פקדון, which occurs elsewhere only at Gen 41:36, where it is said of food becoming לפקדון for the land. There it is translated by the participle πεφυλαγμένα "preserved"; see Note ad loc. The second possibility concerns κοινωνίας "joint-ownership," which is intended to render תשומת יד. The term is a hapax legomenon, and its exact meaning is uncertain. LXX took it as something held in common; it is usually thought to refer to a pledge, but this notion is derived from the context alone, i.e. as something related to פקדים. The third term, ἁρπαγῆς "plunder, booty" stands for גזל "robbery," whereas the last term, ἠδίκησέν τι τὸν πλησίον,[2] renders עשק את עמיתו. The verb ἀδικέω can take a double accusative "to wrong someone in something," so here "he did his neighbour some wrong."

---
1. Instead of ψεύσηται Aq read ἀρνήσεται.
2. The Three read ἐσυκοφάντησεν as a more exact rendering of עשק.

6:3(5:22) This continues the list of possible deceptions. Possibly one might have found something that was lost, and then ψεύσηται περὶ αὐτῆς "would make a false report about it."

The Masoretes have made the first cut within the last statement. By placing שקר under the ethnach, ונשבע על שקר "and he would swear in a false manner" is taken with v.a, i.e. "he would lie about it and swear swear falsely" are tied together with respect to the finding of something that was lost. Modern translators disregard this cut, and understand what follows "about one of all matters which man might do so as to sin by these" as modifying נשבע, in my opinion rightly. Certainly LXX makes the swearing an oath concern ἑνὸς ἀπὸ πάντων ὧν ἂν ποιήσῃ ὁ ἄνθρωπος κ.τ.λ. τούτων refers to πάντων; the statement is then a general one covering not only the various possibilities for neglecting the commandments of the Lord listed, but anyone of all the things mentioned and unmentioned by which mankind might sin.

In the tradition, the article of ὁ ἄνθρωπος is omitted by most witnesses, but the oldest ones, A B and F, have the article, and it correctly renders האדם of MT. Instead of the aorist infinitive the Byz *oI z* text witnesses to the present αμαρτανειν, but there is no compelling reason for designating "to sin" as a process, and the aorist is to be preferred. The prepositional phrase בהנה is translated literally by ἐν τούτοις. The *b* text has εν αυτοις which represents a stylistic change to a more idiomatic Greek, and is secondary.

6:4(5:23) V.4 together with the first part of v.5 constitute the protasis of a condition, with the apodosis beginning with καὶ ἀποτείσει in v.5. The grammatical pattern is καὶ ἔσται ἡνίκα ἂν plus subjunctive verbs ἁμάρτῃ καὶ πλημμελήσῃ καὶ ἀποδῷ plus modifiers ..., καί plus future indicative verb. The condition described is that of one guilty of the trespasses described in vv.2—3 who wants to undo the wrong done, i.e. ἀποδῷ τὸ ἅρπαγμα ... τὸ ἠδίκημα ... τὴν παραθήκην ... τὴν ἀπώλειαν. Omitted from the list is κοινωνίας of v.2. For τὸ ἅρπαγμα see comment on ἁρπαγῆς of v.2. For τὸ ἀδίκημα see comment on ἠδίκησέν τι τὸν πλησίον at v.2.[3] For παραθήκην see comment at v.2, and for τὴν ἀπώλειαν see comment at v.3. In the tradition, the *b* text has reinterpreted the verse by chang-

---

3. Aq and The Others read τὴν συκοφαντίαν; cf footnote at v.2.

ing ἀποδῷ to the future indicative αποδωσει; this would make this the onset of the apodosis. But LXX correctly interpreted MT, and is original.

6:5(5:24) LXX's failure to render the opening או is probably simply a mistake on the part of the translator; since the preceding word, מצא, ends with an *aleph* confusion would be possible. Or was the translator influenced by v.3 where the finding of something lost is followed both by ψεύσηται and καὶ ὀμόσῃ ....? Hex, represented solely by ms 426, added η at the beginning of the verse to represent the Hebrew conjunction. Actually, the omission of או may well have been intentional. Without it, what follows becomes a summary statement. What LXX has as the last part of the protasis of v.4 is then: "(even) from every matter concerning which he swore unjustly." MT has no equivalent for "matter," and LXX follows the דבר of Sam, which is also supported by Pesh and the מכל מדעם of Tar^J. Hex has placed πράγματος under the obelus to show its absence in MT. For ἀδίκως the equivalent in MT is not על שקר as in v.3, but לשקר; LXX rightly does not differentiate between the two phrases; they are fully synonymous.

The apodosis is introduced by καί, imitating MT. For the neuter singular pronoun αὐτό as object of ἀποτείσει see comment at 5:16. The change by *b* of αὐτό to αυτα betrays an attempt at greater accuracy; after all, a number of trespasses were listed in the protasis. In MT the pronoun אתו is explicated by the prepositional phrase בראשו, but LXX disregarded the preposition, reading τὸ κεφάλαιον as an appositive to αὐτό. Hex has added αυτου under the asterisk to represent the suffix. The noun refers to the capital or principal, which must naturally be repaid. For καὶ τὸ πέμπτον προσθήσει ἐπ' αὐτό see comment at 5:16. Most witnesses read the compound επιπεμπτον; both the simplex and the compound are used to designate a 20% interest rate, or penalty, but the oldest witnesses, A and B, read the simplex, and this is probably the older reading. The majority text has also added, possibly, though not necessarily, hex, an αυτου to represent the suffix of חמשתיו;[4] presumably MT's plural noun is the result of a transposition of שת and י; comp חמישתו of 5:16.[5] LXX perforce follows the singular noun of Sam; the plural would be an odd text indeed. The restitution is to be made τίνος ἐστίν, representing לאשר הוא, i.e. to the one to whom it belonged, to its owner. This is followed by αὐτῷ referring to τίνος. The guilty

---

4. See SS 97.
5. Many Hebrew mss read the singular noun.

one must repay him at the time when he is convicted. MT has a suffix to the verb, יתננו, which hex represented by adding an αυτο.⁶ The repayment is to be made ביום אשמתו, at the time that he becomes aware of his guilt. LXX uses a legal term, the passive of ἐλέγχω, thus "on which day he was convicted." The translation is unique in OT.

6:6(5:25) For the meaning of the genitive τῆς πλημμελείας see comment at 5:15. τιμῆς occurs here without ἀργυρίου for בערכך, for which see comment at 5:18. Here it is modified by εἰς ὅ ἐπλημμέλησεν indicating that for which assessment is made. LXX reordered MT's איל תמים מן הצאן by placing the adjective after the prepositional phrase. Hex reordered ἀπὸ τῶν προβάτων ἄμωμον to agree with the more usual order of MT.

Since οἴσει was already modified by τῷ κυρίῳ, the phrase אל הכהן seemed to contradict the ליהוה modifier. LXX simplified the matter by disregarding the second prepositional phrase, as did Sam; hex, however, added προς τον ιερεα under the asterisk at the end of the verse to equal MT. Modern translators avoid the problem by understanding ליהוה as modifying אשמו, but MT has יביא between the two words; furthermore, the Masoretes divided the verse at this point, placing ליהוה under the *ethnach*. From 4:16 it becomes clear that restitution is actually made to the priest, i.e. the τιμῆς, whereas the τῆς πλημμελείας, as a sacrifice is made to the Lord. The shorter text overlooks an important distinction.

6:7(5:26) For init ... ἱερεύς see comments at 4:20. The atonement here is to be made ἔναντι κυρίου; by this phrase the place of the sacrifice is designated as being in the sanctuary.

LXX has simplified the syntax of the second part of the verse. The relative clause in MT reads אשר יעשה לאשמה בה. LXX has rendered this by coordinate verbs (ὧν) ἐποίησεν καὶ ἐπλημμέλησεν (αὐτῷ). The Greek text is much clearer than MT, making the point that when one did (anyone of all these) he trespassed by it. The relative pronoun is genitive plural by attraction to its antecedent πάντων. The majority text has εν before αὐτῷ, which is probably a recensional correction towards MT.

---

6. See SS 98.

6:9(2) The initial ἔντειλαι Ἀαρὼν καὶ τοῖς υἱοῖς αὐτοῦ apparently covers the section ending with 8:36: "and Aaron and his sons did all the things which the Lord commanded Moses." A majority text has added the dative article τω before Ἀαρών. Since MT reads את אהרן the variant could be recensional in origin, but LXX is fully adequate; Ἀαρών can only be dative. The reason for giving orders to Aaron and his sons, at least for chh.6 and 7, is clear. The regulations dealing with the various sacrifices throughout concern the function of the priests in the performance of the sacrifices.

The ritual of the burnt offering is covered in vv.9—13. Each of the various sacrifices is introduced by the formulaic οὗτος ὁ νόμος of .... The term νόμος (for תורת) I have translated by "ritual."[7]

LXX has rendered the next structure: הוא through בקר in a word for word fashion, and the syntax is difficult. I would take the first ἐπί phrase as defining the ὁλοκαύτωσις: "This is the burnt offering in its burning on the altar the entire night up to the morning." The Hebrew מוקדה is understood by the translator to consist of a noun and suffix, though the Masoretes understood the final *he* as denoting a feminine noun. The noun is a hapax legomenon, and its *ma-* prefix is usually taken to represent place, thus "hearth,' i.e. the hearth of the altar. The translator, however, took it as an infinitival noun with suffix; καῦσις simply means "burning."

The final clause in MT has no equivalent for οὐ σβεσθήσεται. LXX has levelled with vv.12,13, where the clause does occur with an equivalent לא תכבה in MT. The added clause insures that the intent of "the fire of the altar shall burn on it" be understood as a perpetual fire. The addition is rightly put under the obelus in hex to indicate its absence in MT.

6:10(3) The parent text of χιτῶνα λινοῦν is uncertain. Admittedly LXX has no αυτου inserted, which might suggest Sam's מדי rather than the מדו of MT, but a leveling with the coordinate περισκελὲς λινοῦν may well explain the lack of a genitive pronoun in any case. The priest is to don both a linen tunic and linen drawers. The latter are to be donned περὶ τὸ σῶμα αὐτοῦ. The term σῶμα only translates בשר in the book. Here בשר refers to the male pudenda, and σῶμα may

---

7. As is done by NRSV and NJPS. NIV used "regulations." Older translations used "law," "Gesetz," "loi," but a more contextual rendering is preferable.

be understood in the same way. In Lev the word occurs 20 times, of which 11 are from ch.15 where בשר is the source of the semen flow. Elsewhere it usually obtains in a context of that which must be washed. Here the intent of the περισκελές is to avoid uncovering a priest's shame as he goes up the altar steps; cf Exod 20:26 and 28:38(42).

The priest is to remove the κατακάρπωσιν, which is defined by a relative clause, ἣν ἂν καταναλώσῃ τὸ πῦρ τὴν ὁλοκαύτωσιν. The term κατακάρπωσιν obtains only here and in the next verse, and from the context must mean the ashes from the burnt offering. The term may well be a coinage of Lev, deriving it from κατακαρπόω "to sacrifice a burnt offering." The κατακάρπωσις is then what remains on the altar after the sacrifice has been made. This is also clear from the relative clause, which I would translate by "the burnt offering which the fire would have consumed." This is an unusual construction in which the appositive τὴν ὁλοκαύτωσιν occurs within the clause. LXX understood the phrase על המזבח differently. In MT it modifies העלה, i.e. what is consumed is the burnt offering on the altar. LXX makes the phrase modify ἀφελεῖ, rendering it by ἀπὸ τοῦ θυσιαστηρίου.[8] The point is to remove the ashes from the altar, and place αὐτό besides the altar. Here again the neuter pronoun is used, even though the reference is to κατακάρπωσιν, a feminine noun.[9]

In the tradition, the b f+ text changes κατακάρπωσιν to the more common ολοκαρπωσιν, which is obviously wrong; furthermore, in the next verse the κατα compound is retained. The b text also alleviates the odd relative clause by omitting τὴν ὁλοκαύτωσιν. The Byz text attempted to clarify the passage by changing the noun to ολοκαρπωσιν, presumably signalling by this change its relation to the antecedent κατακάρπωσιν. The F M majority text "corrected" αὐτό to the grammatically proper αυτην, but αὐτό is original LXX.

6:11(4) MT then orders the priest to remove את בגדיו and don other בגדים; the reference must be to the מדו בד and the מכנסי בד of the preceding verse. LXX, however, introduces a different term, τὴν στολήν, by which only the outer cloak is usually intended; cf the noun "stole," whereas the χιτῶνα of v.10 is actually an undergarment, worn next to the skin. Here the term must be used generically as "raiment," or more particularly, "vestments," since he is ordered to remove τὴν

---

8. See the discussion in Daniel 169—170.
9. See Huber 34—35.

στόλην, which must refer to the garments of the previous verse. The linen garments are only to be worn inside the sanctuary, but here the priest must leave the tent and remove the κατακάρπωσιν outside the camp to a ritually clean place.

6:12(5) The verb καυθήσεται renders the Ho תוקד, which it renders literally; it too may be translated by "shall be made to burn." It contrasts with the active καύσει later in the verse, which represents the active בער. The verb is modified by ἐπ' αὐτοῦ. B F ol s y z+ read απ αυτου which is barely sensible. What is odd about the variant text is the amount of support it engendered.[10] The fire is to be a perpetual one: καὶ οὐ σβεσθήσεται. The καί has no counterpart in MT, but the previous word is בו, and dittography would have produced ולא, i.e. καὶ οὐ.

The verb καύσει is transitive, as the ξύλα "firewood" shows. What is meant is that the priest is to stoke the fire with firewood τὸ πρωὶ πρωί. The repetition of πρωί is in imitation of the Hebrew in which the repetition denotes distributive force, i.e. "each morning" or "morning by morning."[11] This is done ἐπ' αὐτό. The prepositional phrase follows ὁ ἱερεύς, whereas in MT the order is הכהן עליה. The majority text has reversed the order, which is probably recensional in origin. The majority text also changed the pronoun to the genitive, probably under the influence of ἐπ' αὐτοῦ in the first clause. The verse has ἐπ' plus pronoun four times, successively with αὐτοῦ, αὐτό, αὐτοῦ, αὐτό; these represent resp בו followed by three cases of עליה. In the Greek the antecedent in each case is "the altar," i.e. a neuter noun, but this is not the case for the instances of עליה. For the first two it must be האש, and for the last one, it is העלה. The last phrase modifies ἐπιθήσει for which the majority text also reads επ αυτου. In this case the accusative is certainly original. Whenever ἐπιθήσει is modified by an ἐπί phrase in Lev (61 out of 64 times), it always governs the accusative.[12]

For ἐπιθήσει rendering הקטיר see the discussion at 2:16.[13] Not only is the priest to arrange the burnt offering, he must also sacrifice on it the fat τοῦ σωτηρίου; for the sacrifice for deliverance see comment at 3:1.

---

10. See THGL 78.
11. See GK 123d.
12. See the discussion in THGL 98.
13. See THGL 73.

6:13(6) Here the notion of οὐ σβεσθήσεται is fully stated; a πῦρ διὰ παντός shall be made to burn. The verse is introduced by καί over against MT, which hex has placed under the obelus.

6:14(7) Vv.14—18 deal with the ritual of the meal offering, i.e. the θυσίας, for which ch.2 had given detailed instructions. MT begins with וזאת, but LXX has no conjunction, and hex has added the equivalent καί.

The word מנחה is followed by a free infinitive; this simply sets out the verbal notion without any inflection to show its syntactic function. In such cases the context must determine its use.[14] Here a subject is given: בני אהרן as well as a pronominal modifier: אתה with המנחה as its antecedent. LXX renders this acceptibly by means of a relative clause, though including an unnecessary αὐτήν to represent אתה within it. It may be rendered as "which the Aaronids must bring before the Lord in front of the altar."

6:15(8) The parallel to this instruction is at 2:2, which see. קמצו means "his fist," and at 2:2 it is preceded by מלא, hence "fistful," with the following ἀπό as a partitive,[15] i.e. "some of the fine flour of the meal offering." Hex has added an αυτου under the asterisk after δρακί to represent the Hebrew suffix. Unusual is the ἀπ' αὐτοῦ. One would expect απ αυτης, since the antecedent must be θυσίας, but LXX simply imitated ממנו of MT (where ממנה of Sam would also be simpler). In MT, however, the masculine can be understood as referring to the contents of the sacrifices.[16] Why the translator should imitate such a grammatical feature is not clear, since a masculine pronoun is not really sensible in LXX. The verb is in the singular, since only one Aaronid would be involved in the ritual. The Greek continues with two σύν phrases, whereas MT differentiates; for the first σύν phrase it has a partitive מן structure, i.e. "some of its oil," and for the second phrase MT reads ואת כל הלבנה, but LXX has καὶ σὺν τῷ λιβάνῳ αὐτῆς, i.e. does not render the כל but adds αὐτῆς. What the translator has done is to level the two phrases completely. MT then defines "all its incense" by a relative clause אשר על המנחה. Since the translator had levelled the two phrases, he wanted to make the relative clause apply to both phrases; this he did in a novel

---

14. See GK §113.4.
15. See SS 161.
16. According to Milgrom 392, who reminds one that שמן is masculine.

way. He rendered the pronoun by τὰ ὄντα, with the accusative modifying the verb ἀφελεῖ. Syntactically τὰ ὄντα is in apposition to the two σύν phrases.

The second part of the verse uses ἀνοίσει for הקטיר, for which see comments at 2:16. LXX follows Sam's המזבח אשה with its ἐπὶ τὸ θυσιαστήριον κάρπωμα rather than MT's המזבה.[17] It should be noted that the Sam text occurs in MT at 2:2. For κάρπωμα rendering אשה see comment at 2:9; at 2:2 אשה is translated by θυσία. This κάρπωμα is defined by an appositive ὀσμὴν εὐωδίας. In the tradition, the A B+ variant has the nominative οσμη, probably under the influence of 2:2, where θυσία ὀσμὴ εὐωδίας occurred; this cannot be correct here, since the structure modifies ἀνοίσει. The verb has a further modifier in τὸ μνημόσυνον αὐτῆς, for which see comment at 2:2. The antecedent of αὐτῆς must be θυσίας.

6:16(9) The δέ is contrastive; the preceding verse referred to what was to be offered up on the altar, but now what remains will be food for the priests. The subject of יאכלו is "Aaron and his sons," but LXX has a singular verb ἔδεται, which follows the יאכל of Sam. The singular is also possible by attraction to the nearer element of a compound subject. The singular verb βρωθήσεται could be considered as congruent either with τὸ καταλειφθέν or with the neuter plural ἄζυμα, but MT has מצות תאכל, i.e. it intended "it (i.e. what is left) may be eaten as unleavened cakes," and this is what the translator must have intended as well. The "holy place" is specified as being in the αὐλῇ of the tent τοῦ μαρτυρίου, for which see Note at Exod 27:21, and for the αὐλῇ see Notes at 27:9—15. In the tent they (i.e. Aaron and his sons) are to eat αὐτήν. The reference is not fully clear; grammatically it should be θυσίας, but sensibly it should be τὸ καταλειφθέν or possibly ἄζυμα. An F[b] x+ variant text solves this by changing the pronoun to αυτα, i.e. the ἄζυμα. The αὐτήν was probably chosen by the translator in agreement with the suffix in MT's יאכלוה, in which the pronoun refers to נותרת, but that is Hebrew, not Greek.

6:17(10) "It is not to be baked as leavened." For leaven as forbidden in the meal offering see the discussion at 2:11. MT reads "As their portion I have given it מאשי." The Greek has tried to clarify this; it reads "μερίδα αὐτήν I have given

---

17. GK 118g speaks of this "being an accusative *loci*, which explains nothing, since MT does not inflect for case.

αὐτοῖς ἀπὸ τῶν καρπωμάτων κυρίου." The αὐτήν refers to the θυσίας of v.16; cf the discussion ad loc on αὐτῆς. The μερίδα αὐτήν replaces חלקם. Since αὐτήν already obtains before the verb the אתה becomes redundant, and LXX has substituted αὐτοῖς ad sensum. LXX also changed "my sacrifices" to τῶν καρπωμάτων κυρίου; this constitutes a leveling with v.18 where מאשי יהוה does occur; the same leveling obtains in Sam and Vulg. For καρπωμάτων see comment at 1:9.

Such a portion is very holy.[18] The old combination A B 121 has omitted ἐστιν, but this is not Lev.[19] Comparable in holiness are τὸ τῆς ἁμαρτίας "the sin offering" for which see comment at 4:8,[20] and τὸ τῆς πλημμελείας "the trespass offering," for which see comment at 5:15.

6:18(11) πᾶν ἀρσενικόν is a calque for the Hebrew כל זכר.[21] MT identifies "every male" as בבני אהרן. To the translator this was insufficiently exact, since according to v.16 Aaron and his sons, not just the sons of Aaron, were to eat what was left of the meal offering, and so LXX makes the participants τῶν ἱερέων.[22] The verb ἔδονται disagrees in number with its subject πᾶν ἀρσενικόν. This is an ad sensum congruence with the collective notion of πᾶν.[23]

The following collocation is purely nominal, and is difficult to analyze syntactically. It reads "an eternal prescription for your generations ἀπὸ τῶν καρπωμάτων κυρίου/מאשי יהוה." The context demands that the preposition be taken in the sense of the Latin *de* "concerning." The structure is hardly an SP clause; it simply sets out a nominal structure with no predicate. Presumably it is to be taken as a description of the preceding clause, and I would suggest it should be understood as an interruptive "—an eternal prescription (or usage) for your generations concerning the sacrifices of the Lord."

The final clause affirms the contagious nature of the holy. Anyone who might touch αὐτῶν ἁγιαθησεται. The pronoun's referent is the καρπωμάτων

---

18. For the distinction between ἅγια τῶν ἁγίων and ἅγιον see Harlé-Pralon 30.
19. For compelling evidence of this as a secondary omission see THGL 112.
20. See especially the discussion in THGL 117.
21. According to Harlé-Pralon ad loc.
22. Gispen has the notion that this statement was intended to exclude women, and that the original text was בכהנים, but this is dubious. Rather it was probably intended to refer to all members of the priestly class, i.e. all male descendants of Aaron, not only those serving in the sanctuary.
23. See Huber 38.

κυρίου, declared ἅγια τῶν ἁγίων in v.17. Such a one is thereby sanctified, consecrated.[24]

6:19(12) Vv.19—23 concern the meal offerings specifically to be brought by and for the priests.

6:20(13) The section starts out without the standard "This is the ritual," but procedes directly to the instructions concerning the δῶρον of the priests which they are to offer at the time of their consecration. The text reads Ἀαρὼν καὶ τῶν υἱῶν αὐτοῦ, but "his sons" refers to his successors in the office of high priest; this is clear from v.22, which see. MT speaks of the occasion ביום המשח אתו, a difficult construction in which אתו must be taken as the subject of the Ni infinitive, i.e. "in the day that he is anointed," or possibly better "from the day that he is anointed."[25] LXX found the structure difficult as well, and interpreted the infinitive by χρίσης, thus "in the day in which you anointed him." The reference of αὐτόν seems to be to the high priest, i.e. to Aaron and his successors. In the tradition, an occasional ms has a plural pronoun instead of αὐτόν. The use of a second singular verb is not to be pressed, since it is simply a substitute either for an indefinite, or better still, for a passive, verb.

The meal offering to be presented is the tenth of an οἰφί of fine flour. The phrase εἰς θυσίαν follows Sam's למנחה. MT lacks the preposition, and hex has omitted εἰς to equal it. For οἰφί see comment at 5:11. The priestly offering is to be διὰ παντός, i.e. a perpetual offering. This is explicated by what follows: half of the offering τὸ πρωί and half, τὸ δειλινόν, i.e. the morning and evening sacrifices.

6:21(14) The first clause is well-rendered: "on a griddle shall it be prepared with oil." This is followed in MT by מרבכת תביאנה תפיני, which is difficult, but the first two words probably mean "well-soaked shall you bring it," which LXX rendered with a third person verb by πεφυραμένην οἴσει αὐτήν "kneaded he must bring it," the participle and pronoun referring to the θυσίαν of v.20.[26] For תפיני,

---

24. See Bauer sub ἁγιάζω 2.
25. See the extensive discussion in Gispen ad loc; that the preposition ב can mean "from" is clear from Ugaritic; see also the discussion and references in Milgrom 397.
26. Sym translated the participle by πεπλατυσμένην "flattened out."

a hapax legomenon the meaning of which is unknown, LXX has ἐλεκτά "turned, rolled"; the translator simply guessed at the meaning on the basis of the root פנה "to turn"; the interpretation is unlikely to be correct; at least a rolled meal-sacrifice is not, as far as I know, attested elsewhere. The sacrifice in any event is as one of פתים "of pieces," i.e. θυσίαν ἐκ κλασμάτων.²⁷ The verse ends with θυσίαν εἰς ὀσμὴν εὐωδίας κυρίῳ, whereas MT has תקריב ריח ניהה ליהוה; LXX is at best a free rendering; possibly the translator having already written οἴσει αὐτήν felt that תקריב was tautologous,²⁸ and so created a parallel to the preceding "a sacrifice from pieces," i.e. substituting θυσίαν for the verb. On the other hand, it may well be that a different parent text lay behind LXX.²⁹

In the tradition, the *n* text has ζεστην as a doublet reading for πεφυραμένην. Instead of ἐλικτά *C'* *n* *s*+ read ερικτα "powdered, crushed"; though this was probably palaeographically inspired, it did make rather better sense for a meal offering than ἐλικτά. The *b* text changed θυσίαν 2° to προσοισει; this was obviously influenced mediately by the Hebrew תקריב.

6:22(15) MT begins with a conjunction, but LXX has an asyndetic clause. Hex has made up for this by adding a και at the beginning. The subject of the opening clause is "the priest, the one anointed in his place out of his sons." The ἐκ is partitive; one of the high priest's sons is to succeed him.³⁰ The pronoun αὐτήν refers to θυσίαν; see v.21. This is a regulation for all time, a νόμος αἰώνιος,³¹ viz., that "it must be wholly consumed." MT reads חק עולם ליהוה which would mean "a perpetual due to Yahweh." By omitting ליהוה LXX takes on a different meaning. A majority text added τω κυριω; this is clearly recensional, probably hex in origin. The verb ἐπιτελεσθήσεται occurs only here as a rendering for Ho הקטר, but then the Ho for this verb is most unusual. Elsewhere it only occurs once, as a participle at Mal 1:11. The translation is probably exactly right; it shall be made to go up in smoke, i.e. be wholly consumed.³² In the tradition, the majority text has an article before ἀντ' αὐτοῦ, i.e. "the priest, the one anointed,

---

27. Aq has δῶρον ψωμῶν, and Theod rendered by δῶρον κλασμάτων.
28. See the discussion at THGL 120.
29. See THGL 73.
30. See SS 165–166.
31. Theod has νόμμον αἰώνιον.
32. For this adverbial understanding see also Daniel 265.

the one in his place," but this is the result of dittography in an uncial text; note the letters ΟΣ ending the preceding word χριστός; it is not original.

6:23(16) MT has a neat turn of phrase. In the preceding verse כליל is used adverbially, ἄπαν "wholly." Here it is nominalized as ὁλόκαυτος "a holocaust," i.e. a burnt offering.[33] The priestly offering must be a burnt offering, even though it is a meal offering.[34] What this involves is that οὐ βρωθήσεται. In MT this is syndetic, but LXX introduced it with καί. In the tradition, ὁλόκαυτος is not stable. The n+ text has ολοκαυστος, whereas d has ολοκαυτωματα, and t has ολοκαυτωματος, but the hapax legomenon ὁλόκαυτος is undoubtedly original.

6:25(18) Vv.25—30 deal with the priestly regulations for the sin offering. For חטאת in the sense of sin offering, which occurs twice, τῆς ἁμαρτίας is used when it modifies νόμος,[35] but when it modifies the verb σφάξουσιν, the translator uses τὸ περὶ τῆς ἁμαρτίας, since a simple genitive would be bad Greek. The translator also twice avoids a passive construction in favor of an indefinite active plural, i.e. οὗ σφάζουσιν τὸ ὁλοκαύτωμα and σφάξουσιν τὸ περὶ τῆς ἁμαρτίας; this is semantically valid as a rendering of a passive. In MT the verbs used are תשחט in the Ni, but LXX distinguished the two; the first verb is in the present tense, since it reflects the general custom: "Where they (usually) slay the burnt offering," while the second one gives the regulation and is inflected in the future: "they shall slaughter." The place of slaughter is ἔναντι κυρίου, i.e. in or at the sanctuary.

In the tradition, a popular text articulates 'Ααρών with τῳ, but this is unnecessary in view of καὶ υἱοῖς αὐτοῦ which follows. The z text reads προς before "Aaron"; this could be recensional in view of MT's אל אהרן. The popular variant σφαξουσιν for σφάζουσιν is an error palaeographically inspired by a cursive parent; it is not overly sensible. The change of ἅγια to the singular by b+ may be due to Hebrew influence, but it is not original. ἅγια ἁγίων occurs 11 times in the book, whereas ἅγιον τῶν ἁγίων occurs only at 2:3 and refers to λοιπόν, and ἅγιον ἁγίων at 27:28 modifies ἀνάθεμα and must be singular.

---

33. According to Hes, Aq has *integrum erit*, probably for τέλεια ἔσται.
34. See Daniel 265.
35. Theod and Sym also use (τῆς) ἁμαρτίας (retroverted from Latin). For a discussion of the passage as a whole and of the variants in the text tradition see THGL 117.

6:26(19) The officiating priest shall eat it. LXX translates the Pi participle המחטא by ὁ ἀναφερών, which MT specifically applies to the sin offering.³⁶

For v.b see comments on the parallel passage at v.16b. LXX translates MT word for word.

6:27(20) The contagious character of sacrifice is insisted on in this verse: "everyone who touches its flesh shall be rendered holy." The translator intentionally used a passive to translate the Qal of קדש, since the act of touching confers holiness. The genitive pronoun αὐτῆς refers to the "sin offering" of v.25.

The construction of v.b is peculiar. I would take the first clause as a pendant nominative, and would translate it: "and as for the one who might have had some of its blood sprinkled on the garment." The ἀπό must be understood as partitive,³⁷ since it is "some of its blood" which is the subject of the verb "sprinkled." As in the case of v.a the αὐτῆς must refer to the sin offering of v.25. The ᾧ must ultimately refer to ὁ ἱερεύς of v.26, and the garment is of course his, though neither MT nor LXX note it, it being obvious.

The LXX text represents a possible understanding of the Hebrew, though it is likely that the relative pronouns in MT are meant to have impersonal reference. MT probably intended "whatever touches" and "whatever might have had ..." for the two cases of אשר.

The main structure has as subject ὃ ἂν ῥαντισθῇ ἐπ' αὐτό, referring to ἱμάτιον: "that on which was sprinkled." The besprinkled garment must not be removed; the blood must remain "in a holy place," and there the garment must be washed. The word תכבס was vocalized by the Masoretes as Pi, thus "you must wash." The translator understood it vocalized as Pu, i.e. as passive, which is just as likely to have been intended by the writer. In the A B+ text the subject has been changed from ὅ to ὅς; it is not the garment, but the one who wore it who must be washed. This is clearly secondary. The tradition did have great trouble with πλυθήσεται. Itacism produced πληθησεται and πληθυσεται. The *lambda* was misread as *alpha* to produce πανθησεται, and a z+ text had the garment burned (καυθησεται).

---

36. Theod rendered the participle by ἱλάζων; the anonymous περιαμαρτίζων is almost certainly Aq; cf 9:15, and comp the reading of The Others at 8:15 and 14:49.
37. See SS 158.

6:28(21) The subject of the relative clause must be τὸ περὶ τῆς ἁμαρτίας of v.25. It is the sin offering which is boiled to make it edible for the priests.³⁸ If the container which was used was of clay, it had to be smashed. But if it was a bronze container, this was hardly possible, and other means had to be taken to rid it of any vestige of the sacrificial meat.

In MT the apodosis consists of two verbs vocalized as Pu, and introduced by a *waw*. LXX has no apodotic καί, and understood both verbs as active. ἐκτρίψει "rub thoroughly, rub out" is a good rendering for מרק "to scour."³⁹ The apodosis may be rendered: "he must scour it and wash (it) out with water." In realizing the verbs as active the translator had to add an αὐτό after the first verb in order to make sense.

6:29(22) The structure πᾶς ἄρσην ἐν τοῖς ἱερεῦσιν does not imply that there were also female priests. The synonym αρσεν is a variant of ἄρσην, but it is neuter, and C' d+ read παν αρσεν. That copyists did not differentiate between the two is attested by the occurrence both of πας αρσεν in s t+ and of παν αρσην in f+. They all mean "every male." In MT "every male shall eat אתה," i.e. the חטאת. LXX has the plural αὐτά, which agrees with κρεῶν of v.27. For ἅγια τῶν ἁγίων see comment at 2:3. It might be noted that when anything is called "very holy" it is only of priestly concern; here it is the priests who alone may eat the flesh.

6:30(23) The subject is plural, (πάντα) τὰ περὶ τῆς ἁμαρτίας, though MT has a singular חטאת. It is a general statement, and the plural makes good sense.⁴⁰ What is meant is "no sin offering may be eaten." The noun is modified by a relative clause: "from whose blood may have been brought into the tent of testimony ...." The ὧν ... αυτῶν structure is a Hebraism, and the ἀπό is partitive;⁴¹ it is some of their blood which might have been taken into the tent. The verb is further modified by a purposive infinitive ἐξιλάσασθαι, for which see comment at 4:20. Once a sin offering is brought in for making atonement, it may not be eaten; it must be burned up by fire. Note the use of the compound κατακανθήσεται to

---

38. Theod read ἐψεθῇ, and The Others had ἐψεθήσεται.
39. Sym rendered מרק by σμήξει.
40. See THGL 117.
41. See SS 161.

show complete destruction; the compound verb is, however, regularly used in the book for the burning of sacrifices.

6:31(7:1) The ritual of the trespass offering is formally presented in vv.31—40, though materially vv.38—40 are general observations on priestly benefits. MT begins the section in the usual fashion with וזאת תורת האשם. LXX, however, takes pains to make clear that האשם is the actual animal which is sacrificed by rendering the word by τοῦ κριοῦ τοῦ περὶ τῆς πλημμελείας "of the ram of the trespass offering," which is based on the instructions for the offering in 5:15, which see.[42] Hex has placed τοῦ κριοῦ τοῦ περί under the obelus, since this does not correspond to MT.

For the plural ἅγια (τῶν ἁγίων) see comment at v.25. As at v.25 the b text has the singular αγιον, thereby equalling MT.

6:32(7:2) For v.32a see comments on the parallel passage at v.25. The only difference between the two is that here τὸν κριὸν τῆς πλημμελείας describes the sacrificial animal, whereas at v.25 the reference is to τὸ περὶ τῆς ἁμαρτίας. That the translator levelled with v.25 is especially clear from ἔναντι κυρίου which has no equivalent here, but equals לפני יהוה of v.25. Here it was placed under the obelus by hex. Hex also placed τὸν κριόν under the obelus, for which see comment in v.31.

The change in number to the singular προσχεεῖ shows an actual change of subject. The singular indicates the officiating priest, since only the priest could deal with the blood of a sacrificial animal; see 1:5,11,15 3:2,8,13 4:5—7,16—18,25,30,34 5:9 6:27,30. Instead of MT's "upon the altar (round about)," LXX has ἐπὶ τὴν βάσιν τοῦ θυσιαστηρίου. This is not surprising, since, whenever reference has been made to blood being poured by a priest, it is never "upon the altar," but always "upon the base of the altar"; see 4:18,25,30,34. In MT the verb modified is יזרק "he shall toss, dash," but LXX uses προσχεεῖ "he shall pour towards (or on)." In the OT זרק occurs 31 times, and is translated in 12 different ways, but in 19 cases it is προσχέω which is used; in fact, all but one of the rest are unique renderings, only πάσσω occurring twice.[43] προσχέω is used

---
42. See also Daniel 304.
43. According to the count in Dos Santos.

almost solely (with the exception of Deut 12:27) for translating זרק.[44] Clearly the verb is used with the semantic coloration of the Hebrew. In MT the verb is modified by את דמו, but LXX has only τὸ αἷμα, and hex supplying αυτου to represent the suffix. That the blood is that of the slaughtered ram is, of course, obvious in any case.

6:33(7:3) The priest is also to offer up all its fat; the pronoun αὐτοῦ refers to the κριόν of v.2. In MT this is explicated by a consecution of items continuing through v.4a. The list contains "the אליה, and the fat which covers the intestines," as well as from v.4a "the two kidneys and the fat which is on them which is at the loins." The Greek introduces all this by a καί, and it is not fully clear what is meant, but it probably was not intended to coordinate with στέαρ, but rather to explicate it. The first item is usually understood to refer to the fatty, broad tail of the sheep. It occurs four times in the book (also at 3:9 8:25 9:19), and is always translated by ὀσφύς "loins." Possibly the Alexandrian was uncertain of the meaning of the word.[45]

For the second item LXX has a doublet based on Sam; the longer text is also found in 4:8, and comp 3:9. It not only has "and all the fat which covers the intestines," but adds καὶ πᾶν τὸ στέαρ τὸ ἐπὶ τῶν ἐνδοσθίων "and all the fat which is about the intestines," which exactly equals the text of 4:8, except that there the first πᾶν fails, as does MT and Sam. Hex has placed the doublet under the obelus. It is likely that the shorter text of MT is a case of parablepsis based on homoioteleuton of הקרב.

6:34(7:4) The list continues as in MT, except that הכסלים "the loins" has become τῶν μηρίων "thighs" or "thigh bones," ὀσφύν having been used for אליה.

In MT v.b begins with "and the lobe on the liver" as the *ethnach* on the preceding word and the verbal suffix of יסירנה show; the suffix being feminine singular must refer to היותרת. But the Greek is not clear at all, since it has περιελεῖ αὐτά. I would understand the plural pronoun either as referring to the entire verse except for the first item, i.e. to "the fat which is on them, which is next to the thighs, and the lobe which is on the liver, together with the kidneys

---

44. According to HR.
45. The Others did know the word, and used τὸ κέρκιον.

(he shall remove them)," or as intending only v.b, thus "as for the lobe ... together with the kidneys, he shall remove them."

6:35(7:5) For ἀνοίσει as a translation of הקטיר see comment at 2:16. The reference in αὐτά must refer to all the things listed in vv.33—34. The term המזבחה occurs 24 times in the book, and it is always translated by ἐπὶ τὸ θυσιαστήριον. In other words, the translator understood the postpositive he as indicating location, place where.[46] For κάρπωμα rendering אשה, see comment at 2:9. For the rendering of אשם by περὶ πλημμελείας see comment at 5:15. The majority text has added οσμη ευωδιας after κάρπωμα, which is obviously secondary, and ex par; cf 1:9,13,17 2:2,9 3:5,16 23:13,18.

6:36(7:6) The translator recognized the preposition in בכהנים as meaning "from, out of," and rendered the word by ἐκ τῶν ἱερέων. The use of αὐτά (twice) does not conform to the Hebrew, which has third masculine singular reference throughout, i.e. to אשה. The neuter plural pronouns must be general references to the parts of the sacrificial ram eligible for food.[47] For the eating in a holy place more exactly specified, see vv.16,26. In MT this instruction is a passive one, יאכל in the Ni: "it shall be eaten." LXX transforms it into an active one with an indefinite plural verb: "they shall eat them," which is equally suitable.

For the popular variant παν αρσεν see comment at v.29. The structure ἔδονται αὐτά has been changed in a popular variant to βρωθήσεται, which, since it is supported by all the usual hex text representatives, O'' Arm Syh, may well be recensional; it does equal MT.

6:37(7:7) This verse well illustrates how the translator differentiated between the double meanings of חטאת and אשם. When these terms intend a sacrifice rather than "sin" and "trespass" resp, he inflected the terms in the genitive, and then nominalized the terms either by τὸ περί or simply by τό. I would translate v.a by "as the sin offering, so the trespass offering, they have one rule." Not surprisingly the tradition tended towards leveling the two nominals, either by omitting περί, or by adding it where it was absent. But the translator once again showed his fondness for variation.

---

46. Cf GK 90d.
47. As Harlé-Pralon suggest.

That rule which was common to the two rituals was "the priest who would make atonement with it shall have it." The use of ἐν αὐτῷ is quite correct, since both nominals in the first part of the verse are neuter singular, i.e. either the sin offering or the trespass offering.⁴⁸ Syntactically, ὁ ἱερεύς plus the relative clause is a pendant nominative, and the αὐτῷ of ἔσται αυτῷ refers to the pendant. The subject of ἔσται must be the sin or trespass offering of v.a. The relative clause does not say "who performs the sacrifice," but chooses that which is significant for the worshiper in the ritual, viz. "who makes atonement with it."

6:38(7:8) The verse opens with a pendant nominative, which is marked off by the *ethnach* in MT: "And (as for) the priest who offers a person's burnt offering." What is then said about such a priest is that "he will have the skin of the burnt offering which he (referring to ἀνθρώπου) brings to the priest." The structure is only awkward if a) one fails to recognize the pendant structure of v.a, and b) if one does not recognize that αὐτός refers to ἀνθρώπου. The translator has specifically added αὐτός over against MT to make that point clear. A popular variant, probably Byz in origin, has transposed it with the verb, thereby placing it immediately before αὐτῷ, thus emphasizing the two who are involved, the ἀνθρώπου and the priest. This had been clear in MT from לכהן following the verb, which, however, the translator omitted, preferring an αὐτός before the verb. The *b* text actually added τω ιερει after the verb; this is obviously recensional in origin.

6:39(7:9) LXX levels the verbal action of "in the oven" and "on a hearth⁴⁹ or a griddle" by ποιηθήσεται, though MT uses the Ni of תאפה "shall be baked" for the oven and נעשה "prepared" for the second, and only the second one is correctly rendered by ποιηθήσεται. Why the translator should have avoided rendering the first verb correctly by "shall be baked" in favor of using ποιηθήσεται twice is puzzling. It is, of course, true that "being baked" is also being "prepared," but elsewhere אפה is more exactly rendered by the verb πέσσω; see 2:4 6:17 23:17 26:26. The *O* text has "corrected" the first ποιηθήσεται to πεφθήσεται to equal MT. Clearly this was the choice of Origen in his hex. LXX follows MT exactly with πᾶσα θυσία for the first, and simply πᾶσα for the alter-

---

48. The ἐν is instrumental; see SS 119—120.
49. Instead of ἐσχάρας Theod reads καυστῇ.

native; of course, this too meant "every (sacrifice)." For κλιβάνῳ see 2:4; for ἐσχάρας see 2:7, and for τηγάνου, 2:5.

The second part of the verse shows the translator once again varying his translation. It consists of two ל phrases followed by יהיה. LXX renders the first one, לכהן המקריב אתה, by a genitive, but the second one, לו, by a dative, though the intent, "belonging to," is the same for both. A popular variant has clarified the text considerably by changing αὐτῷ to αυτου, whereas the *b* text has changed the first one to τω ιερει τω προσφεροντι, which is a more literal rendering of MT, and is undoubtedly recensional.[50]

6:40(7:10) MT has as subject כל מנחה בלולה בשמן וחרבה "every meal offering mixed with oil and a dry one" i.e. "or a dry meal offering." LXX has a rather neat way of putting it. Instead of בלולה it has ἀναπεποιημένη "made up," and for the "dry (sacrifice)" it has μὴ ἀναπεποιημένη "not made up." It is thus a case of prepared with or without oil. These all belong "to all the Aaronids, to each one equally." The accusative τὸ ἴσον is adverbial, and is a good idiomatic rendering for איש כאחיו.

---

50. Harlé-Pralon tried to distinguish the two phrases by calling the genitive τοῦ causal. It does make for a smooth translation: "parce que c'est le prêtre qui l'apporte, elle sera à lui," but this is not what MT intended, nor in my opinion did the translator intend it.

Chapter 7

7:1(11) Vv.1—11 deal with the ritual of the sacrifice for deliverance; see comment at 3:1 for the term θυσίας σωτηρίου. The *b* group has των ειρηνικων for השלמים, for which see footnote at 3:1. The verse begins asyndetically over against the וזאת of MT. LXX follows the indefinite plural of Sam with its προσοίσουσιν rather than the singular יקריב of MT. In either event, the subject is not specified, though a possible plural antecedent does exist in the preceding verse, viz. τοῖς υἱοῖς 'Ααρών. In MT no antecedent for יקריב obtains, and one must render it indefinitely, i.e. by "which one might offer." It is, however, also quite clear that the plural of LXX was not intended to denote priestly offerings, but rather lay ones; see comment at v.5.

7:2(12)1 Vv.2—5 deal with a deliverance sacrifice which one offers περὶ αἰνέσεως "for praise," a neologism chosen by Lev to render תודה.[1] The word is not an exact translation, since תודה means "thanks" rather than "praise."[2] LXX introduces the protasis with ἐὰν μέν. The μέν particle expresses certainty, and here I would render it by "(if) specifically"; what the translator does is to specify in particular the kind of sacrifice for deliverance being described.

The apodosis is introduced by the apodotic καί, and signalized by a future indicative verb προσοίσει, modified by ἐπὶ τῆς θυσίας τῆς αἰνέσεως as well as by accusative nouns. The ἐπί here must be intended in the sense of על "along with;" since the שלמים offering is a burnt offering, the praise sacrifice must indicate an extra, viz., "loaves of fine-flour,[3] made up with oil, and unleavened cakes well-smeared with oil, and fine-flour kneaded with oil."

In MT the loaves are also unleavened, and the majority text added αζυμους after ἄρτους; the text does not seem to be hex in origin, but it is fully supported

---

1. Aq preferred ἐπὶ εὐχαριστίας as a more exact rendering.
2. Harlé-Pralon ad loc suggest that the word was chosen rather than the Classical αἶνος to represent the "sens complexes de *todāh* avec ses deux significations conjointes et «gratitude» and «proclamation,»" and accordingly translate αἰνέσεως by «la reconnaissance.» This seems to me a reading of the Hebrew into the Greek. Nor does the subsequent use of the word αἴνεσις bear this out. It means "praise," which might then include gratitutde for deliverance.
3. See SS 63 and its reference to Mayser in footnote 5.

by Byz; in any event, the longer text equals MT and the αζυμους is probably recensional in origin. The Byz text also reinterpreted the loaves which were made up with oil, by its αναπεποιημενης, i.e. agreeing with σεμιδάλεως, thus loaves, consisting of "fine flour made up with oil." Whether one can speak of "fine-flour αναπεποιημενης" is questionable; it might seem rather to be a case of attraction to the σεμιδάλεως which immediately precedes it. The last item in MT is סלת מרבכת חלות בלולת בשמן, but LXX omitted a rendering of חלות בלולת. According to Syh hex inserted κολλύρας ἀναμεμιγμένας[4] to equal MT. For the meaning of מרבכת see comment at 6:21.

7:3(13) LXX begins with ἐπ' ἀρτοῖς ζυμίταις for the longer plus in MT: על חלת לחם חמץ. Hex has changed ἐπ' (ἀρτοῖς) to επι κολλυρων (αρτων αζυμιτων) with the noun under the asterisk, thus "along with loaves of unleavened bread." Why Origen should have changed ζυμίταις to αζυμιτων is incomprehensible, since the loaves are clearly meant to consist of leavened, not unleavened, bread; it must simply be an error on his part. For the plural τὰ δῶρα αὐτοῦ see comment at 1:2. Such loaves are to be offered along with the sacrifice αἰνέσεως σωτηρίου, which I would understand to mean "of praise for deliverance." MT has שלמיו for the last word, but LXX has omitted the suffix.[5] The majority text has added αυτου at the end; this is probably hex in origin.[6]

7:4(14) The initial verb in MT is modified by ממנו, which the Greek omitted as otiose. Hex added απ αυτου after προσάξει to represent it, but the shorter text is not only sufficient, it is stylistically better Greek. The preposition after ἕν is partitive as good sense also dictates.[7] So one from all his gifts is to be brought as an ἀφαίρεμα, a word which occurs eight times in the book, of which five are for תרומה. Though this rendering is etymologically determined, what is meant is something removed (i.e. raised) from common usage to a sacred one; one might

---
4. Retroverted from Syh.
5. The Others translate שלמיו by εἰρηνικῶν αὐτοῦ.
6. According to SS 98 "ist der Anlass zur Weglassung des Pronomens wahrscheinlich der, dass das Suffix zu einer Konstructverbindung gehört und das Ganze bestimmt, so dass eine mechanische Wiedergabe zu einer falscher Verbindung führen würde." This is possible, but the commonality of the omission of such suffixes by LXX makes such a clever notion unlikely. Furthermore, I doubt that the suffix actually refers to more than simply σωτηρίου.
7. See particularly SS 167.

render it by "dedicatory gift." The Hebrew word also occurs at 22:12, where it is rendered by τῶν ἀπαρχῶν; see comment ad loc. For the term and its relation to the root רום, see Note at Exod 29:27. The αὐτοῦ modifying δώρων is an ad sensum addition, probably added by LXX in exchange for the omitted ממנו; see above. Its omission by ms 376 could be hex, though I suspect it to be simply an error by its copyist.

The ἀφαίρεμα will belong to the priest officiating at the sacrifice for deliverance. This is clear from the fact that the priest is the one who pours out the blood; for προσχέοντι as rendering for זרק, see comment at 6:32.

7:5(15) That the praise sacrifice is a sacrifice for deliverance is clear from the fact that it has τὰ κρέα; see ch.3. The αὐτῷ ἔσται has no basis in MT, and though it seems identical to the αὐτῷ ἔσται of v.4b its reference cannot be to the priest. It has actually been added intentionally to contrast with the preceding clause; it must refer to the worshiper, as the plural verb in the last clause demands. LXX does not render the suffix of שלמיו, but has replaced it by αὐτῷ ἔσται; in other words, that it is his (i.e. the worshiper's) is made particularly clear by paralleling the αὐτῷ ἔσται of v.4b. The ביום קרבנו is sensibly rendered by καὶ ἐν ᾗ ἡμέρᾳ δωρεῖται. Only here is the noun rendered by a relative clause, but a literalistic "in the day of his gift(s)" would hardly make sense. The καί was introduced because of the αὐτῷ ἔσται immediately before it; this necessitated a new clause.

The verb in the last clause is in the plural: "not shall they (i.e. the worshiper and his friends) leave from it (any thing) until morning." MT has the singular יגיח "shall he (i.e. the officiating priest) leave." The plural verb of LXX means that the worshiper(s) must see to the disposal of anything remaining of the sacrifice by morning.

In the tradition, the Byz text has changed ἀπ' αὐτοῦ to απ αυτων, probably to agree with the plural τὰ κρέα as antecedent, whereas Lev agrees with σωτηρίου.

7:6(16) This verse speaks of two kinds of σωτηρίου sacrifices: εὐχήν "a votive offering" and the ἑκούσιον "voluntary (or free-will) offering." The regulation is the same for both. The protasis begins with καὶ ἐάν, which is much less common

(12 times) in the book than ἐὰν δέ (85 times).⁸ In the tradition, B O x+ read καν, but crasis never occurs in the book except for κἀγώ at 26:24, and only καὶ ἐάν can be considered Lev here.⁹ The translator has taken זבח as a verb, rather than as noun as the Masoretes did; what MT says is "And if the sacrifice of his gift is a votive offering or a voluntary offering." The change of εὐχήν to the nominative ευχη by A B b+ must be taken as a careless mistake. Overlooking a final *nu* in cursive script is a particularly frequent error, since it is often written as a short superlinear line over the final vowel.¹⁰ The protasis may be rendered: "And if he should sacrifice his gift as a votive or voluntary offering"; this does render the intention of MT accurately. It might be noted that קרבנו is rendered unusually by a singular noun; cf comment at 1:2. The subject is the worshiper.

The apodosis begins with a relative clause which constitutes the timer for the main verb βρωθήσεται, thus "in which day he would bring his sacrifice, it must be eaten."¹¹ The timer has coordinated with it καὶ τῇ αὔριον "and on the next day"; in other words, the eating of the sacrifice may be spread over two days. In MT this fragment is part of a clause coordinate with the first part of the apodosis: והנותר ממנו יאכל; thus "and on the next day, that which is left of it shall be eaten." In other words, MT says "in the day that he brings his sacrifice, it shall be eaten, and on the next day, that which is left of it shall be eaten." The next verse begins with והנותר as well, and the translator inadvertently skipped from the first והנותר to the second. Hex has added a translation of the missing structure under the asterisk in the next verse after καὶ τὸ καταλειφθέν as απ αυτου βρωθησεται και το καταλειφθεν.

7:7(17) The καταλειφθέν now applies to what is left beyond αὔριον to the third day. This differs from MT in that ἕως ἡμέρας τρίτης obtains for ביום השלישי. The Masoretes have divided the verse, so that "in the third day" modifies the verb rather than the participle נותר. MT intends as subject "that which (still) remains of the meat of the sacrifice"; of that is predicated that "it must be burned by fire on the third day."¹² In any event, such remnants must be burned by fire.

---

8. See THGL 102.
9. See THGL 100.
10. See also THGL 121.
11. Without rendering the preposition ב by εν; see SS 110.
12. See SS 110.

7:8(18) MT has the verbal figure האכל יאכל vocalized as Ni by the Masoretes, thus "if there should actually be eaten." LXX probably read the free infinitive with Sam as אכל, since it reads an active construction, thus "(but if) he should actually eat." The verb is modified by a partitive ἀπό phrase ἀπὸ τῶν κρεῶν "some of the meat."[13] In MT a fuller prepositional phrase obtains: מבשר זבח שלמיו "some of the meat of the sacrifice for his deliverance," which constitutes the subject of the Ni structure. The shorter text of LXX may be due to a shorter parent text,[14] or it is an intentional abbreviation by the translator, since the context makes it fully obvious that one is discussing the ritual of the sacrifice for deliverance; cf the introductory clause in v.1. Hex added της θυσιας του σωτηριου αυτου to equal the full text of MT.[15]

The apodosis has two clauses: "it will not be accepted αὐτῷ who offers it" and "it will not be reckoned to him." This interprets MT quite differently from that of the Masoretes. MT has no equivalent for the αὐτῷ, and the majority text actually omits it, thereby simplifying the text by leaving τῷ προσφέροντι αὐτό directly modifying δεχθήσεται, but the more difficult text is clearly original. The Masoretes have accented the text with a *segholta* on ירצה, and a *rebiaʿ* on אתו, both disjunctive accents. What the Masoretes intended was "it will not be received, and as for the one offering it, it will not be reckoned to him." In the tradition, the *f* text has an exegetical gloss preceding δεχθήσεται which is commentary: αθυτον εστιν "it is unfit for sacrifice."

But MT has its own comment: פגול יהיה "it will be a foul thing," i.e. unclean and therefore unfit for sacrifice. The term is difficult, and its meaning is uncertain.[16] LXX renders the phrase by μίασμά ἐστιν "it is a defilement."[17]

V.b is a general conclusion: "but the person whoever might eat of it shall bear τὴν ἁμαρτίαν." The term ἁμαρτία not only means "sin," but may also designate the guilt which results from sin.[18] Here it renders עונה "its guilt," and must refer to the guilt resulting from failing to observe the regulation concerning

---

13. See SS 161.
14. As THGL 73 suggests.
15. For the rendering of שלמים in Lev as a whole see THGL 117—118.
16. See Milgrom 422 for a discussion of the term.
17. Aq makes it an ἀπόβλητον, whereas Theod transliterates it by φεγγουλ. The Others (which probably then refers to Sym) read ἀργόν.
18. See LS sub ἁμαρτία 2.

sacrificial meat left over to the third day. LXX does not render the suffix; it is quite unnecessary in Greek.[19]

7:9(19) Uncleanness is also contagious. "Whatever meat might touch anything unclean may not be eaten"; in fact, "it must be burned up by fire."
   V.b begins with והבשר, which at best can be understood as a pendant subject, i.e. "And as for the meat." What must be intended is meat other than that which has touched something unclean. LXX simply disregarded it as redundant, as did Pesh and Vulg; hex has added και τα κρεα under the asterisk to equal MT. LXX accordingly reads only πᾶς καθαρὸς φάγεται τὰ κρέα. Everyone who is καθαρός is ceremonially clean, and so may eat "the meat." The use of the article with κρέα is significant. Initially κρέα is unarticulated, thus "And (whatever) meat," but here τὰ κρέα refers specifically to the sacrificial meat which has touched something impure.

7:10(20) Dire consequences will befall any one who does not follow these regulations according to this and the following verse. V.10 refers to a person eating of the meat of the sacrifice for deliverance while he is in an unclean state, i.e. καὶ ἡ ἀκαθαρσία αὐτοῦ ἐπ' αὐτοῦ. Such a sacrifice is described as ὅ ἐστιν κυρίου, which translates אשר ליהוה only here and in v.11. Normally ליהוה is translated by the dative (τῷ) κυρίῳ. In fact, of the 101 cases of ליהוה in the book, 93 are rendered by the dative.[20] In the tradition, the F M majority text actually reads the dative as well. The translator must have had some special reason for the genitive here, and I suggest that the stress lies on the fact that these sacrifices belong to the Lord. Other cases of ליהוה need not stress possession, but rather "for" or "to Yahweh."
   The apodosis presents a severe penalty for any infraction: "that person ἀπολεῖται ἐκ τοῦ λαοῦ αὐτῆς." The idiom ἀπολεῖται ἐκ is unusual, and the preposition reflects the Hebrew preposition in מעמיה. But MT's verb is נכרתה "shall be cut off"; what is intended by the Hebrew is excommunication from the clan, which LXX interprets as "perishing, dying"; undoubtedly such excommunication from the clan meant virtual death. The LXX, however, makes it "shall be destroyed out of his people." But another possibility is that ἐκ be taken

---

19. See SS 97.
20. See THGL 80.

as "author or occasion of a thing," or even as agent of a passive verb.²¹ The penalty would then mean "that person shall perish by the hand of the people." It might be noted that whenever this formula occurs in the book it is introduced by a conjunction in MT, but not necessarily in the Greek; in fact, the apodosis is not introduced by καί here.

7:11(21) The translator follows the pattern of v.10 by using the pronoun ἥ as parallel to the ἥτις of v.10, though MT changes to כי; the Byz tradition has changed ἥ to εαν to conform to MT. The person's uncleanness in this verse would come from touching some unclean matter (παντὸς πράγματος ἀκαθάρτου). The word πράγματος has no equivalent in MT, and hex has placed it under the obelus. The source for such uncleanness is given in three ἥ structures, viz. "whether from the uncleanness of a person (ἀνθρώπου) or of unclean quadrupeds or of any unclean abominations." In LXX only the first of these structures, "from the uncleanness of a person," is introduced by ἀπό (modifying ἄψηται). In MT the verb תגע is modified by four ב phrases. The Byz text has also introduced an απο before the first modifier, "any unclean matter," but this has no valid claim to originality.

For the φάγῃ clause see comment at v.10 which has exactly the same modification here, including the relative clause. The penalty is also identical with that of v.10; cf comments ad loc throughout.

7:13(23) Vv.13—17 forbid the consumption of fat and blood. This is addressed not only to the priests, but to the Israelites in general. Specifically all the fat of βοῶν καὶ προβάτων καὶ αἰγῶν is forbidden, presumably because this was intended for the Lord; see 3:9—11,14—16. What is usually intended is the fat of sacrificial animals. In MT these are all singular: "an ox and a sheep and a goat."

7:14(24) The fat of corpses and of those torn by beasts is also unclean. Both נבלה and טרפה are understood as collectives by LXX, and therefore plural nouns are used. In the tradition, both plurals appear in majority A texts as accusative singulars, as θνησιμαιον and θηριαλωτον resp. These are of course not to be taken seriously in spite of their popularity; the genitive plural and the accusative

---

21. As LS sub voce III.4. Also possible is III.5 "with the agent after Pass.Verbs, *by*."

singular forms are homophonic, but only the plural forms are Lev. Actually MT has two bound חלב phrases here, and one O ms indeed has στεαρ θηριαλωτου for the second one, which is obviously recensionally inspired.[22]

In any event, such fat ποιηθήσεται εἰς πᾶν ἔργον "may be used for any purpose," but being unclean "may not be eaten for food." Here εἰς βρῶσιν renders אכל, which the Massoretes vocalized correctly as a free infinitive. The b text has βρωσει, obviously based on an understanding of אכל as a free infinitive. Presumably the translator wanted to parallel the εἰς construction of v.a, but it seems to me to weaken MT's statement: "and it may certainly not be eaten."

7:15(25) MT begins with a כי, which I would take to show cause, i.e. "because any one who eats ..., the person eating shall be excommunicated from his people." The Greek, however, has disregarded כי entirely, and makes an independent statement. In the Greek v.a is a pendant nominative, i.e. "anyone eating fat from cattle from which he is going to bring a sacrifice (κάρπωμα) to the Lord." For κάρπωμα as a rendering for אשה see comment at 2:9. The main clause then identifies the πᾶς ὁ ἔσθων as ἡ ψυχὴ ἐκείνη "that person." "That person" is the translator's rendering for הנפש האכלת "the person eating," which equally identifies the subject with that of v.a. The Byz text has added η εσθιουσα at the end of the verse; ultimately the reading is dependent on MT, but it is not hex, as its placement after λαοῦ αὐτῆς rather than after ψυχή (ἐκείνη) makes clear. The rendering ἡ ψυχὴ ἐκείνη may be a case of leveling with v.17, where MT does have הנפש ההוא. For ἀπολεῖται modified by an ἐκ phrase, see comment at v.20. The B y+ tradition has απο instead of ἐκ, but only ἐκ is correct for the statement. The notion of "destroyed ἐκ τοῦ λαοῦ αὐτῆς" occurs five times in the book (also in vv.10,11,17 23:30 and comp 17:4 19:8 20:6 23:29), and the preposition is never απο, but always ἐκ.

7:16(26) LXX begins asyndetically over against MT. Blood is also forbidden nourishment; comp 3:17. The prohibition locates the consumption of any blood ἐν πάσῃ τῇ κατοικίᾳ ὑμῶν, but in MT the noun is plural, מושבתיכם. This is an idiomatic matter; though ὑμῶν is plural, no one occupies more than one dwelling place at a time, and so the Greek uses the singular. But the Hebrew probably

---

22. See the discussion in THGL 121.

intended "dwelling places," hence, territories, places occupied, settlements, whereas LXX thought in terms of "any dwelling place of yours." In MT two ל phrases modify דם, i.e. "blood of (or from) birds and of cattle." Over against vv.13—15 where the eating of the fat of tetrapods was forbidden, the prohibition of blood as food is made as a general order, i.e. it includes birds as well. The translator took the preposition as indicating source, hence used ἀπό with the postpositive conjunction τε in the first phrase, indicating "both (... and)." Uncertain is the τῇ in the phrase ἐν πάσῃ τῇ κατοικίᾳ ὑμῶν. Its support is limited to A Byz and a few scattered mss, and a compelling majority omit the article; the original reading of B was τη γη, which was entirely omitted by the corrector. The articulated form is the more difficult, and was chosen to represent Lev.

7:17(27) The formulaic penalty, for which see comments at v.10, refers to "every person who consumes blood" as a pendant nominative, which is then referred to as subject by ἡ ψυχὴ ἐκείνη. MT adds כל before דם, and hex has added παν before αἷμα to represent it. For the A B+ variant απο for ἐκ, see comment at v.15.

7:19(29) Vv.19—24 deal with the priests' share of the sacrifice for deliverance. The term זבח שלמיו occurs twice in MT, and in neither case is the suffix rendered, probably since the suffix applies not to the שלמים, but to the זבח שלמים.[23] An αυτου would be misleading. This, however, did not stop Origen from adding αυτου in both cases. A further invasion into the text appears in the case of the first σωτηρίου, where the b text changes the word to των ειρηνικων αυτου, a reading which also recognizes the plural number of the Hebrew noun; this was probably taken from one of The Three; see comment at v.1. Hex has also added an article under the asterisk before θυσίαν to recognize the preposition in את זבח.

The instructions are to be given by Moses to the Israelites, since it is the worshiper whose conduct is being ordered. Moses is commanded καὶ τοῖς υἱοῖς Ἰσραὴλ λαλήσεις; LXX follows the text of Sam, both in the introductory conjunction and in the word order. MT lacks an introductory conjunction, and also has the addressee following the verb. Hex corrects the text by omitting the καί, changing the verb to an imperative λαλησον, and rearranging the order, thereby corresponding word for word to MT's דבר אל בני ישראל.

---

23. So SS 98.

The subject of the instruction is ὁ προσφέρων θυσίαν σωτηρίου κυρίῳ. The majority text has articulated κυρίῳ, which may also be recensional. Hex often used τω (κυριω) to represent the preposition in ליהוה. Why the Byz text should read τω κυριω αυτου is questionable. It is obviously wrong. τω θεω αυτου would be a possible variant, but κύριος as rendering for יהוה can not be modified by a genitive pronoun; it must be understood as a proper noun.

The predicate is οἴσει with the accusative modifier τὸ δῶρον αὐτοῦ. This modifier must refer to those parts of the deliverance sacrifice (ἀπὸ τῆς θυσίας τοῦ σωτηρίου) specifically intended for κυρίῳ, for which see 3:3—5,9—11,14—16. An A B b+ variant text by adding και before "from the sacrifice for deliverance" betrays confusion on this point; this would state that the worshiper was to bring both "his gift" and "some of the deliverance sacrifice" (understanding ἀπό as partitive), which is certainly not what MT nor LXX intended; cf v.20.

7:20(30) This is even clearer in MT from the opening statement: "his hands (i.e. the worshiper's) shall bring Yahweh's sacrifices (אשי יהוה)," which LXX renders by τὰ καρπώματα κυρίῳ, i.e. the sacrifices are to be brought "to the Lord;" in MT they are Yahweh's by right; they are the את אשי יהוה. For καρπώματα/אשי see comment at 2:9. The Lord's portion is then specifically defined as being "the fat which is on the breast, and the lobe of the liver." MT, however, has no reference to "and the lobe of the liver," a detail taken from ch.3 (vv.4,10,15). Why the translator should have singled out this detail is not at all clear. MT then continues with "he shall bring את החזה," but LXX omits את החזה, and since the Lord's portion had both the breast's fat and the liver's lobe, substituted αὐτά to designate both.

The purpose of bringing the Lord's portion was להניף אתו תנופה לפני) יהוה). Precisely what kind of action is involved here is not clear. NRSV translates it by "may be raised as an elevation offering," and NJPS, similarly by "to be elevated as an elevation offering,"[24] while NIV follows an older version, "wave ... as a wave offering," while RSV has "may be waved as a wave offering." All are agreed that some kind of movement is involved, either of raising or of brandishing an offering.[25] Of greater interest is what LXX made of it. That the translator was not overly clear as to its meaning is obvious from the ways in

---

24. As does Milgrom.
25. Harlé-Pralon 42 translates the noun as *balancement*, thus supporting RSV and NIV.

which he translated the cognate expression. Here he used ἐπιθεῖναι δόμα "to place a gift (before the Lord)." δομα occurs only here as a rendering for תנופה. The noun appears 13 times in the book. Six times it is translated by ἐπίθεμα "something put on, something laid down," so "a deposit." Four times it appears as ἀφαίρεμα "something taken away," so possibly then a dedicated portion, a portion set aside. Twice the translator used ἀφόρισμα "something set apart." The verb הניף occurs 10 times, eight of which have the cognate noun as modifier, but unfortunately with no consistency at all. Thus the following combinations occur: ἐπιθήσει ἐπίθεμα (14:24 23:20), ἀφεῖλεν ἐπίθεμα (8:29), ἀφήνεγκεν αφαίρεμα (8:27), ἀφεῖλεν ἀφαίρεμα (9:21), ἀφοριεῖ ἀφόρισμα (14:12), and ἀφόρισμα ἀφορίσαι (10:15).[26] To the translator the verb was described not only by "to put upon, place," but also as "to remove" or "to set aside." In each case some kind of action or movemennt in connection with the sacrifice is demanded.

7:21(31) For ἀνοίσει as a rendering for הקטיר see comment at 2:16. A clear distinction is made here between "the fat" and "the breast." The fat is intended for the Lord, and so it is offered up "on the altar," i.e. it is burned. The breast, however, will be "for Aaron and his sons." In LXX this introduces the breast, which had been omitted in v.20. It now becomes clear why it was omitted in v.20; the breast was food for the priests, and distinct from that which was placed as a gift before the Lord.

In the tradition, the former has been more closely defined on the basis of v.20. "The fat" becomes το στεαρ το επι του στηθινιου in the majority F M text. In the x text the gloss occurs in place of ἐπὶ τὸ θυσιαστήριον.

7:22(32) According to MT "the right thigh you must give to the priest" as a תרומה, which LXX calls an ἀφαίρεμα; see comment at v.4. Actually, MT has a bound phrase שוק הימים "the thigh of the right (side)"; this is of course "the right thigh." LXX, however, has τὸν βραχίονα instead of שוק, i.e. "shoulder," a rendering which is followed throughout the book, and was inherited from the Exodus translator; see Note at Exod 29:22. This is to be taken "from your deliverance sacrifices." The ὑμῶν probably is to be taken as applying to θυσιῶν, or rather to θυσιῶν τοῦ σωτηρίου, and not to σωτηρίου alone, in spite of the suffix

---

26. See THGL 72.

being attached to שלמיו in MT. How else would Hebrew express "your deliverance sacrifice?" Comp comment at v.19. Actually a few mss change the singular to των σωτηριων, which formally equals MT. Similarly the b text has των ειρηνικων, which is clearly recensional.

7:23(33) The priest referred to in v.22 is here identified as "the one offering the blood of the deliverance sacrifice and the fat ἀπὸ τῶν υἱῶν 'Ααρών. The ἀπό phrase obviously does not modify στέαρ, but rather ὁ προσφέρων, though only common sense dictates it; the Masoretes made this clear by placing a *tifcha* as a disjunctive accent on החלב. Oddly the A B b+ text does make the ἀπό phrase refer to στέαρ by placing a το before it; that can only be a thoughtless error.

V.a is set out as a pendant nominative structure, and this is then pronominally referred to in the main clause by αὐτῷ, i.e. "the right shoulder shall be *to him* for a portion." What is meant is that the right shoulder is reserved for the use of the officiating priest.

7:24(34) The γάρ particle shows that the basis for the priestly dues from the deliverance sacrifice is based on the Lord's action. Unfortunately, LXX sheds little light on the distinction between תנופה and תרומה, here rendered by ἐπιθέματος and ἀφαιρέματος resp; see comments at vv.4,20. That the first person referent is to the Lord is clear from v.18, nor is this voided by v.19, since what "you shall say" is a divine word. The use of the perfect εἴληφα is an accurate interpretation of לקחתי; the Lord has taken the breast and the shoulder from the Israelites; these items are further characterized by ἀπὸ τῶν θυσιῶν τοῦ σωτηρίου ὑμῶν, for which see comment at v.22. MT reads שלמיהם which fits contextually with "the Israelites. LXX rendered the Sam tradition of שלמיכם, probably under the influence of v.22 where the second person pronoun fits with תתנו.[27] The coordinate verb is, however, the aorist ἔδωκα. A variant C' n s reading has the perfect δέδωκα, a simplification influenced by the εἴληφα of the preceding clause. The aorist as the default tense is sufficient for the coordinate verb, since the perfect εἴληφα has already set up the context for ἔδωκα.

The νόμιμον αἰώνιον is a second accusative modifier of ἔδωκα. Here it is hardly "an eternal prescription" as suggested at 6:18, but rather a "perpetual

---

27. Kenn 103*,109*,181,200 read שלמיכם as well, and Tar^J also attests to a second person plural suffix with קודשיכון.

custom" (from the Israelites). The Hebrew חק here really means "allotment, due," whereas νόμιμον means "usage, custom." It is often used (19 times)[28] as rendering for חק, especially when combined with עולם.

7:25(35) Unclear is the referent intended by αὕτη, but since τὰ καρπώματα τῷ κυρίῳ is mentioned in v.20, these are probably meant. The feminine singular pronoun takes its inflection from the predicate, ἡ χρῖσις. The usage χρῖσις ... ἀπό is a direct rendering of the Hebrew משחת plus מן. Presumably it is a synecdoche for benefits accruing from unction.[29] I would translate the opening statement: "This is the unction of Aaron and the unction of his sons, even that accruing (to them) from the sacrifices of the Lord." For καρπωμάτων see comment at 2:9. It is, however, clear that the Hebrew משחת here means "portion." This is derived from a homographic root משח, unrelated to משח meaning "anoint." The translator took the word as derived from the better known root.

The temporal clause sets the time for the anointing as ἐν ᾗ ἡμέρᾳ προσηγάγετο αὐτοὺς τοῦ ἱερατεύειν τῷ κυρίῳ. The subject of the verb must be the κυρίου immediately preceding the clause. Since it is modified by the marked infinitive of purpose "to serve as priests," it must mean "brought forward, presented," hence "inducted." The infinitive is modified by τῷ κυρίῳ. The majority text omits the article; Lev is quite inconsistent in its rendering of ליהוה, though more commonly the articulated noun is used. In view of the inconsistency, the reading of A B was chosen to represent Lev.[30]

7:26(36) MT begins with a relative pronoun, for which the antecedent is the general statement of v.25. LXX does well in its rendering καθά (ἐνετείλατο). That the translator intended this clarification is clear from v.28 which also begins with אשר צוה (יהוה), but there for variation he used ὃν τρόπον ἐνετείλατο. The καθά clause makes clear what the odd χρῖσις ... ἀπό of the previous verse really meant; it referred to what the Lord ordered the Israelites to give the priests once they were duly anointed. It is now clear that what they (i.e. the Aaronids) are to receive comes from the Lord's καρπωμάτων, which came to them from the Israelites.

---

28. According to Dos Santos.
29. As suggested by Harlé-Pralon: «prérogatives liées à l'onction.»
30. See THGL 80.

Their divinely appointed allotment is then characterized as a perpetual obligation on the Israelites, i.e. εἰς τὰς γενεὰς αὐτῶν "throughout their generations."

7:27(37) The last two verses of the chapter are a subscription, probably for 6:8—7:26. Note the parallel in 6:9: οὗτος ὁ νόμος τῆς ὁλοκαυτώσεως. It is then a summary recapitulation intended for the Hebrew chh.6 and 7. The verse lists the rituals described: that of τῶν ὁλοκαυτωμάτων "burnt offerings" (6:9—13), θυσίας "the meal offering" (6:14—18), περὶ ἁμαρτίας "the sin offering" (6:25—30), τῆς πλημμελείας "the trespass offering (6:31—40), and τῆς θυσίας τοῦ σωτηρίου "the sacrifice for deliverance" (7:1—24). Inserted after the trespass offering is τῆς τελειώσεως, which seems out of place, since this seems to refer to 8:22—30, where the sacrifice of the κριὸν τελειώσεως is described, which is the ordination sacrifice for the priesthood. In MT the sacrifice is called מלואים, a term used in ch.8 as well as in Exod 29, to denote the sacrifice accompanying the ordination to the priesthood. The Greek term is etymologically determined, since the root מלא means "to be full, to fill," and so "to complete." The τῆς τελειώσεως might then be rendered by "consummation," and the sacrifice would be a consummation, i.e. an ordination, sacrifice. Cf especially 8:33.[31]

7:28(38) For ὃν τρόπον see comment at v.26. The reference to the Lord's having commanded Moses at Mt. Sina is actually only documented for the τελείωσις in Exod 29; see especially vv.9,26,27,31—34. The statement is a general conclusion, and details, such as when the Lord ordered the Israelites to bring their gifts, should not be pressed. Unusual is the rendering ἔναντι κυρίου for ליהוה; in fact, it only occurs elsewhere in the book at 5:19.[32] Presumably, since this was ἐν τῇ ἐρήμῳ Σινά, what was meant by the phrase was "in the tent of testimony," which was part of the desert tradition; see e.g. Exod 33:7—11.

---

31. See the discussion in Harlé-Pralon 41.
32. See THGL 80.

Chapter 8

8:2 For a more detailed statement on the items to be taken along by Moses see Exod 29:1—3. MT orders Moses to take Aaron and his sons אתו, which LXX does not translate, but hex has added μετ αυτου to represent it. Unusual is the rendering καὶ τὰς στολὰς αὐτοῦ for הבגדים. MT refers to the vestments in general, but LXX refers only to the vestments of Aaron, probably because Moses clothed only Aaron before the anointing of the altar and its accoutrements and the tent and its contents. Only then he clothe the sons. The anointing, however, was only for the high priest. Nonetheless the αὐτοῦ is unexpected. The Byz text made an obvious change to αυτων, whereas the hex text, along with popular support, omitted it, thereby equalling MT.[1] Besides the vestments and the anointing oil, there are materials needed for the sacrifices involved in the ordination rites, i.e. the bullock for the sin offering and the two rams and the basket of unleavened bread for the consummation offering; see comment at 7:27, and comp κριὸν τελειώσεως at 8:22.

8:3 The reference "all the assembly" refers to the Israelites. In MT the terms עדה and מועד (in "tent of meeting") are related, but LXX throughout renders the latter as μαρτυρίου "witness." For the term and its meaning see Note at Exod 27:21. The word ἐκκλησιάζω and the compound ἐξεκκλησιάζω are the usual renderings in OT for the Hi of קהל. The modifier ἐπὶ τὴν θύραν designates the place to which Moses is to "summon, call out" the assembly. The door of the tent of testimony is the usual place of assembly for the Israelites on cultic occasions; see comment at 1:3.

8:4 MT has two statements: a) Moses did as the Lord had ordered him; the notion כאשר צוה יהוה את משה recurs throughout the chapter at vv.9,13,17,21,29 and as a relative clause at v.36; LXX renders כאשר as ὃν τρόπον, καθάπερ or καθά. The result was that b) the assembly was summoned to the door of the tent of meeting. LXX has changed the b) part into an active construction: "and he

---

1. See the discussion in THGL 93—94, where Lev is defended as the lectio difficilior.

summoned the assembly ...." The term συναγωγήν "congregation, assembly" is not further defined, i.e. whether this consisted of all the Israelites or simply all the adult males; either is possible. The word is appropriate, since v.a also has an active verb, thus "Moses did ... and he summoned the assembly." It might be noted that LXX now used the compound verb ἐξεκκλησίασεν in contrast to the simplex used in v.2 for the active Hi verb הקהל, but here the Ni obtains.

8:5 Problematic in the verse is the referent for τοῦτο/זה. I suspect that what is intended is a postcedent referent, i.e. the instructions which follow in the chapter.

8:6 The Hi of קרב "to bring near, or forward" can be rendered either by προσφέρω (50 times) or by προσάγω (37 times); there is no discernible semantic difference between the two. Here the B minority text was chosen as Lev, purely on the basis of cod B being the oldest witness, since there seems to be no pattern discernible in the translator's choice.[2] Unusual might seem the articulation of Ἀαρών,[3] since that it is in the accusative is clear from the coordinate καὶ τοὺς υἱοὺς αὐτοῦ, but the τόν stands for the preposition in את אהרן, and this is often rendered by the article.

8:7 Vv.7—9 describe the robing of the high priest. As might be expected, Moses first dressed him with the χιτῶνα, the tunic worn next to the skin. For the word see Note at Exod 28:4. The next step was to gird him with an אבנט "a girdle," which is throughout the Pentatuch rendered by ζώνη; see Exod 28:4. This is followed by the ὑποδύτην, a garment worn underneath the ephod, translating מעיל, a robe worn over the tunic; see Note at Exod 28:27.[4] The term is not inappropriate for מעיל, though its emphasis is different. It refers to it as underneath (the ephod), whereas the Hebrew word calls attention to its being over (the tunic); both are correct in their identification of the garment. MT differentiates in the use of verbs, using יתן for the donning of the tunic, i.e. "he put the tunic on him," but ילבש, for the ὑποδύτην. LXX uses ἐνέδυσεν for both, since in both cases it describes Moses' robing of Aaron. The next verb in MT is again יתן, describing the putting עליו the ephod. Here LXX correctly used ἐπέθηκεν (ἐπ' αὐτόν), i.e.

---

2. See THGL 73.
3. See THGL 81.
4. Aq rendered the word by ἔνδυμα; see Note at Exod, p.459, footnote 34.

"he put the ephod on (or over) it (i.e. the undergarment)." The אֵפֹד is usually translated by ἐπωμίς, first used at Exod 25:6, and fully described at 28:6—14, which constitutes a detailed description of its construction.[5]

According to v.b he then "girded him according to the fabrication of the ephod, and tied him up with it." For the term ποίησιν see Note at Exod 28:8; its Hebrew equivalent is חֵשֶׁב.[6] The Hebrew term is usually rendered here by moderns contextually by something like "skillfully woven waistband" (NIV) or "decorated band" (NJPS, NRSV). The Greek ποίησιν stresses the notion of construction, fabrication, so possibly formation, pattern.[7]

The last clause in MT reads ויאפד לו בו which is ambiguous as to its meaning, depending on the antecedents of the two pronominal suffixes. Both are third masculine singular, one of which refers to Aaron and the other to the חשב האפד, but the problem is to determine which is which. It can mean either "he tied him up with it" or "he tied it around him." In Greek ποίησιν is feminine, and so the translator had to choose between the two interpretations. The text of Lev reads "he tied αὐτὸν ἐν αὐτῇ," i.e. "he tied him up with it," but this is supported by only seven witnesses, A B x+, whereas the overwhelming majority read αυτην εν αυτω "it on him."[8]

8:8 The first clause has Moses putting ἐπ' αὐτόν (i.e. on Aaron) τὸ λόγιον. In the tradition B M y+ read επ αυτην, which reading should not be taken seriously. To place the oracle pouch on the ποίησιν is only barely sensible, and the variant text was probably created under the influence of αὐτῇ at the end of v.7.[9] For a description of the λόγιον see Exod 28:15—26, and for a discussion of the term and of the popular variant λογειον, see Note at Exod 28:15.[10]

The second clause uses the same verb, ἐπέθηκεν, though MT had changed from ויתן to וישם which is then used twice more in v.9. LXX used ἐπέθηκεν throughout, since lexically the two verbs can hardly be distinguished. MT reads

---

5. Aq translated אפד by ἐπένδυμα; see preceding footnote.
6. Schl sub ΠΟΙΗΣΙΣ defines the Hebrew word as: "Vox hebraica quoque *artificium, artifiose excogitatum et elaboratum* notat."
7. Aq translates בחשב by ἐν τῷ διαζώσματι, and Theod Sym, by ἐν τῷ μηχανώματι. Theod and Sym retain τῆς ἐπωμίδος for the next word, but Aq has τοῦ ἐπενδύματος.
8. For the choice adopted for Lev see THGL 99.
9. See THGL 99.
10. See also the detailed discussion in Harlé-Pralon ad loc. Sym read τὸ δόχιον.

"And he put אל the oracle," i.e. "into the oracle"; this makes better sense than ἐπὶ τὸ λόγιον, which follows Sam's על החשן. What he placed on the oracle were τὴν δήλωσιν καὶ τὴν ἀλήθειαν, the problematic renderings for את האורים ואת התמים "the Urim and the Thummim."[11] The Greek terms were inherited by Lev from Exod; see Note at Exod 28:26.[12]

8:9 The term μίτραν for מצנפת "turban" is synonymous with κίδαριν;[13] see Note at Exod 28:4.[14] The golden plate was placed "on the front of it (i.e. of the oracle)"—ἐπὶ τὴν μίτραν κατὰ πρόσωπον αὐτοῦ; see Note at Exod 28:33; it was identified as τὸ καθηγιασμένον ἅγιον "the devoted holy object," which renders נזר הקדש "the holy diadem."[15] Difficult is the αὐτοῦ, since one would expect a reference to the μίτραν, which is feminine. The only possible masculine reference in the context would be τὸ λόγιον, but this does not make any sense. I would suggest that it refers to the high priest, i.e. "in front of him." Being in front of Aaron but on the turban must mean that it was on the man's front side, which was of course the front side of the turban as well.

In the tradition, the accusative in ἐπὶ τὴν μίτραν is supported by A B plus eight other mss, all the others reading the genitive της μιτρας. The genitive is in spite of its popularity secondary, as usage in the book shows. The verb ἐπιτίθημι which the phrase modifies, occurs 64 times in the book; in 61 cases it is modified by an ἐπί phrase, and the preposition always governs the accusative.[16]

The ὃν τρόπον clause probably applies to vv.7—9a, and refers to the injunctions in Exod; comp 36:8—40, and specifically vv.8,12,14,29,34,37 and 40.

8:10—11 V.10 renders only the first clause of v.10 in MT. A rendering of the rest of v.10 is transferred to the end of v.11. Hex has transposed the materials to equal the word order of MT. The opening clause simply states that Moses took

---

11. Aq translates τοὺς φωτισμοὺς καὶ σὺν τὰς τελειώσεις. For a recent review of interpretations of these two Hebrew terms see Milgrom 507—511.
12. For a discussion of these terms in some detail see Harlé-Pralon ad loc.
13. See the detailed discussion of this verse in Harlé-Pralon ad loc.
14. The Three use κίδαριν.
15. Instead of the participle Sym has τὸ ἄθικτον "the untouched, incorruptible, holy." The anonymous ἀφόρισμα is almost certainly Aq; see Note at Exod 29:6, footnote 8.
16. See THGL 121.

some of the anointing oil (the ἀπό is partitive; but MT reads את שמן, not משמן), and then consecrated the altar, all its vessels, the laver and its basin; only after that did he anoint the tent and everything in it, thereby sanctifying it. MT has these in reversed order. Presumably the translator wanted to end with the overall tent and its contents.

In LXX Moses first sprinkled ἀπ' αὐτοῦ, i.e. from the anointing oil, over the altar seven times. An A Byz y+ variant text changed ἀπ' to επ, but this can hardly have been intended, since επ αυτου would then be explicated by ἐπὶ τὸ θυσιαστήριον, with its change to the accusative. Furthermore, ἀπ' αὐτοῦ renders ממנו, i.e. "some of it."

After anointing the altar LXX has καὶ ἁγίασεν αὐτό; this clause has no equivalent in MT, and hex rightly placed it under an obelus. The translator was probably influenced by the repeated "and he sanctified them/it" in the context. It does stress the sanctification of the altar separately from all its vessels and the other furniture in the sanctuary, of which it is also said καὶ ἡγίασεν αὐτά. After all, the altar had been besprinkled seven times!

The verse then concludes with the rendering of part of v.10, viz. "and he anointed the tent and all the τὰ ἐν αὐτῇ and sanctified αὐτήν (i.e. the tent).[17] MT reads ויקדש אתם; in other words, he sanctified not only the tent, but also "all the things in it." A majority variant text has τα σκευη αυτης for τὰ ἐν αὐτῇ, but this does not equal MT, and is due to the influence of πάντα τὰ σκεύη αὐτοῦ earlier in the verse, referring to the altar's vessels. The text of Num must be original.

8:12 The actual act of consecration. This consisted of Moses pouring some of the anointing oil on the head of Aaron,[18] and anointing him and consecrating him. Μωυσῆς is placed under the obelus, since the subject is not named in MT; the subject is fully clear without it. LXX reads for the final clause καὶ ἡγίασεν αὐτόν, though MT has a purposive construction, לקדשו. The translator actually levelled this with the repeated "καὶ ἡγίασεν" plus pronoun rather than using a purposive infinitive. It could, however, be argued that the two coordinate clauses

---

17. For this Aq reads καὶ ἤλειψεν σὺν τὴν σκηνὴν καὶ σύμπαντα τὰ ἐν αὐτῇ καὶ ἡγίασεν αὐτά, whereas Theod has καὶ ἔχρισεν τὴν σκηνὴν καὶ πάντα τὰ ἐν αὐτῇ. Both recensors had this in the MT order at the end of v.10, since in both the beginning of v.11 follows, in Theod: καὶ ἔρανεν, and in Aq: καὶ ἐρράντισεν ἐξ αὐτοῦ εἰς τὸ θυσιαστήριον.

18. The ἀπό is partitive; see SS 161.

of v.b conjointly show the reason for v.a. The pouring of oil on the head of Aaron has as consequence the anointing and the sanctification of the high priest. Only as one anointed, by which he officially and ceremonially becomes high priest, and sanctified, whereby he is put into a state of holiness making it possible for him to serve within the sanctuary precincts does the pouring of oil take on real significance.

8:13 Moses then clothed the Aaronids, but only with χιτῶνας, ζώνας and κιδάρεις.[19] The verb ἔζωσεν is modified by a double accusative: αὐτοὺς ζώνας. Change of the cognate noun to the dative is a popular change to call attention to its instrumental use, but the accusative is fully adequate. Though μίτρα and κίδαρις are synonyms at v.9, the translator used μίτραν at v.9 for מצנפת, but κιδάρεις here for מגבעות. This Hebrew word occurs only three times in MT elsewhere (all in Exodus), and is always rendered by κιδάρεις (28:36 29:9 36:36),[20] and I would suggest that it was chosen to characterize the head bands of the Aaronids in distinction from the high priestly turban. The verb used is περιέθηκεν, well-chosen to represent יחבש which means "to tie on." To tie on the turban means to put it on around the head; see also Exod 29:9. For the καθάπερ clause see comment at v.9.

8:14 Vv.14—17 deal with the sin offering as part of the ordination ceremony. The Greek does not distinguish between the ויקרב of v.13 and the ויגש here, translating both by καὶ προσήγαγεν. It also adds the subject Μωυσῆς as at v.13, but here without MT equivalence, and hex placed it under the obelus. Its omission by the text of F oII b z+ need not be based on the Hebrew, since it is probably merely a case of leveling. The verb is modified by τὸν μόσχον τὸν περὶ τῆς ἁμαρτίας, which renders the bound phrase פר החטאת of MT, i.e. the bullock for the sin offering. Later in the verse the same phrase recurs in MT, but LXX there renders it without περί, i.e. (τοῦ μόσχου) τοῦ τῆς ἁμαρτίας. That περί is not necessary in the former as well is illustrated by its translation at 4:8 by τοῦ μόσχου τοῦ τῆς ἁμαρτίας; cf comment ad loc.

---

19. Instead of χιτῶνας The Three are reported in the Catenae as reading ὑπόδιτος. But this would presuppose מעיל, not כתנת.
20. See Note at Exod 28:36.

The verb in the second clause is ויסמך "and leaned," but LXX chose the popular καὶ ἐπέθηκεν; Lev always renders the verb סמך (14 times) by ἐπιτίθημι, and never makes the subtle distinction between "lean upon" and "put upon." The subject is "Aaron and his sons," but the verb is singular as in MT by attraction to the nearer subject. The verb is modified by τὰς χεῖρας,[21] but most witnesses add αυτων to equal MT's ידיהם. The plus could be hex, though it might simply be added ad sensum.

8:15 MT begins with וישחט ויקח משה, in which משה is probably to be understood as the subject of the coordinate verbs. LXX has added an αυτον after the first verb, by which Moses relation to ἔσφαξεν is made unclear. The subject of the preceding sentence was "Aaron and his sons," and the Greek could be understood as having Aaron as subject, though this was hardly what the translator intended. The αὐτόν is quite correctly placed under the obelus in hex. LXX is, however, much clearer in the modification of the second verb. MT has את הדם, but LXX has a partitive ἀπό construction, i.e. ἀπὸ τοῦ αἵματος, as its parallel at Exod 29:12, where MT indeed as מדם. That LXX is correct in its interpretation is clear from the next clause in which the blood is put on the horns of the altar באצבעו, translated in LXX by an instrumental dative τῷ δακτύλῳ;[22] this could hardly refer to הדם as such, but only to "some of the blood." See also the next two clauses. Most witnesses add αυτου after "finger" to equal MT; see comment on αυτων at v.14. The altar is followed in LXX by κύκλῳ, a word which occurs 16 times in Lev; only at 16:18 does it follow "horns of the altar" as here, and theoretically it could refer either to "horns," or to "altar." Usage in Lev, however, makes it clear that "around the altar" must have been intended, since in only three cases out of the 16 does it not follow the word "altar."

The Hebrew verb in the next clause, the Pi יחטא, is modified by את המזבח. What is meant by this action is the ridding of the altar of uncleanness by means of blood. LXX fully understood this in its translation ἐκαθάρισεν "purify, cleanse."[23] Then Moses poured all the blood into the basin of the altar.

The purpose underlying the rituals with the blood is clear from the last clause "And he sanctified it (i.e. the altar) τοῦ ἐξιλάσασθαι ἐπ᾽ αὐτοῦ. What this

---

21. See SS 96.
22. See SS 119—120.
23. See Daniel 309, note 34.

means is that the altar had to be sanctified, i.e. be made holy, before it could function properly as the place where sacrifices could be sacrificed, where rites of atonement could be performed. The articulated infinitive is purposive; not so clear is the meaning of the prepositional phrase. ἐπί with the genitive most naturally signifies place, thus the structure would mean "to make atonement upon it." The Hebrew equivalent is לכפר עליו, which can mean either "to make atonement upon it" or "for it." But when LXX meant "make atonement for it" it used περί (30 times in the book); in fact, the verb is modified by an ἐπί phrase only twice elsewhere, at 16:10,18, and the latter simply can only mean "upon it," referring to the altar. What the translator intended to say was: "to make atonement on it."

8:16 The parts of the slaughtered animal which Moses offered up on the altar are the same as those for the sacrifice for deliverance in ch.3, and for the sin offering in ch.4, except that the first item refers to all the fat which is τὸ ἐπὶ τῶν ἐνδοσθίων, for which see comment at 4:8, rather than ἐπὶ τῆς κοιλίας as in ch.3. For details see comments at 3:3—4. Slight differences in wording do occur, betraying the translator's love of variation, thus ἀμφοτέρους rather than δύο for the kidneys, and there is no mention here of τὸ ἐπὶ τῶν μηρίων. For ἀνήνεγκεν rendering יקטר see comment at 2:16.

8:17 For a parallel to this verse see 4:11, where, however, עור was rendered by τὸ δέρμα, but here by τὴν βύρσαν "hide" rather than "skin." Furthermore, the μόσχον is also included, along with its hide, its flesh and its dung, all of this syntactically constituting a pendant accusative, which the main clause introduces by the accusative αὐτά modifying the verb κατέκαυσεν.[24] In the tradition, the A B y+ text introduced the verb with και which is not sensible, and is palaeographically motivated.[25] The subject of the verb is unclear. For the previous clause the subject of ἀνήνεγκεν is given as Μωυσῆς, but here this is difficult, particularly in view of the ὃν τρόπον clause in which the modifier of "commanded" is specified by name, τῷ Μυωσῆ. Obviously, the subject must then be unspecified, i.e. indefinite, and the verb is best rendered by a passive. The αὐτά is not supported by MT, and its omission by the b+ text not only equals MT, but it simplifies the

---

24. Aq Sym read ἐνέπρισεν for the verb.
25. See THGL 100.

text by freeing the pendant accusative to serve as straightforward modifier of the verb. The *b* text also adds εν before πυρί, thereby again equalling MT; the dative modifier is obviously instrumental.[26] For the incineration of the μόσχον outside the camp see 4:12,21. For the ὃν τρόπον see comment at v.9.

8:18 Vv.18—21 concern the ram intended for a burnt offering. The bound phrase איל העלה is rendered by τὸν κριὸν τὸν εἰς ὁλοκαύτωμα, which interprets the free element of the phrase as objective in character, i.e. as intended for an עלה.[27] MT does not identify the subject of the verb and may well have intended it to remain indefinite. LXX, however, identifies the subject of προσήγαγεν as Μωυσῆς. In the tradition, Μωυσῆς is placed under the obelus by hex, since it is absent in MT. Incidentally, its omission in Syh betrays an idiosyncratic characteristic of the Leviticus Syh. In the other books of the Pentateuch Syh would retain the word and place it under the obelus, but the parent Greek for Lev must have undergone post-hexaplaric corrections by a scribe who understood the obelus signs, and omitted, at least on several occasions, such passages so as to equal the Hebrew.

For the second clause see comments on v.14b. The two clauses differ, however, in the identification of κεφαλήν; in v.14 it is by τοῦ μόσχου τοῦ τῆς ἁμαρτίας, but here necessarily by τοῦ κριοῦ; furthermore, at v.14 αὐτῶν is absent from Lev, though added by hex.

8:19 MT begins the verse with the same pattern as at v.15, i.e. two coordinate verbs with משה occurring as subject after the second verb. LXX here avoids the ambiguity referred to at v.15, by adding after וישחט Μωυσῆς τὸν κριόν, i.e. "And Moses slaughtered the ram," but also repeating Μωυσῆς after the second verb. Hex placed Μωυσῆν τὸν κριόν under the obelus to show that MT lacked equivalents. The second verb in MT is יזרק "he sprinkled (the blood on the altar round about)." The translator, probably under the influence of the parallel in v.15 where יצק was used, changed "sprinkled" to "poured out," προσέχεεν.

8:20 At 1:6,12 נתח לנתחיו also occurred; there μελιοῦσιν and διελοῦσιν resp were used as verbs, but the prepositional phrase in all three cases was rendered

---

26. See SS 117.
27. See SS 69.

by κατὰ μέλη, i.e. without rendering the suffix.[28] The majority text, which may be recensional in origin, did add an αυτου. The verb used here, ἐκρεανόμησεν, is a hapax legomenon in the OT, but is fully adequate; it means "to divide or cut up meat."[29] The subject is not stated, but the context suggests that it must be Moses. For the parts of the ram offered up by Moses, comp 1:8,12.

8:21 For the washing of the κοιλίαν and the πόδες before being sacrificed on the altar see comment at 1:9, where, however, ἐγκοίλιαν and πόδας are referred to; cf also 1:13. For ἀνήνεγκεν see comment at 2:16.[30] For the offering of the entire ram on the altar see Exod 29:18. The Byz text has ολοκαρπωμα instead of ὁλοκαύτωμα, but these are synonyms. The A B n x y+ text has the relative pronoun o after it, thus reading "a burnt offering which is for a sweet smelling savor as a sacrifice to the Lord." This is certainly secondary, since it is quite impossible to understand MT in this way. The variant is palaeographically explicable.[31] For the εἰς phrase see Note at Exod 29:18. For κάρπωμα as the usual rendering of אשה, see comment at 2:9.[32] For the καθάπερ clause see comment at v.9.

8:22 Vv.22—30 describe the prescribed ritual of the ordination sacrifice. LXX specifies Μωυσῆς as the subject of προσήγαγεν, but this is absent in MT, and hex has placed the word under the obelus. It should be noted that Syh has omitted it, for which see comment at v.18. The second ram is called the κριὸν τελειώσεως "the ram of the consummation sacrifice," for which see comment at 7:27.

V.b is an exact replica of v.18b; see comments ad loc.

8:23 LXX added a pronoun after ישחט as demanded ad sensum, and hex has placed the αὐτόν under the obelus, rightly signalling its absence in MT. For the syntax of the first two clauses see comment at v.15. The ἀπὸ τοῦ αἵματος αὐτοῦ is partitive "some of its blood."[33] This blood he placed on τὸν λοβόν of Aaron's

---

28. See SS 97.
29. The Others have the cognate verb ἐμέλισε.
30. The Others render by ἐθυμίασεν.
31. See the discussion in THGL 107.
32. See also THGL 73—74.
33. See SS 161.

right ear. The term λοβός had occurred earlier for the "lobe" of the liver (3:4,10,15 4:9 6:34 7:20 8:16), as a translation of (הכבד) יתרת, but here the Hebrew has תנוך. This is usually translated by ("ear)lobe." The word occurs eight times in OT (six times in Lev, and twice in Exod), and is always rendered by λοβός, but it is not fully clear what part of the ear it refers to.[34]

Blood was also put on τὸ ἄκρον of the right hand and on τὸ ἄκρον of the right foot. The word ἄκρον translates the Hebrew בהן. The extremity of the hand would be the thumb, and that of the foot, the big toe. Both "hand" and "foot" have suffixes in MT, and majority variant texts add αυτου; the variant texts may well be recensional. The use of blood was symbolic for rendering holy, for removing uncleanness, and so appropriate for the dedication of the priests to a holy service.

8:24 As at v.22 Μωυσῆς is added as subject for προσήγαγεν over against MT, and hex has placed it under the obelus. After the Aaronids are brought forward, the ritual of v.23 is repeated for the sons of Aaron as well. Though MT uses singular nouns throughout: תנוך אזנם, בהן ידם and בהן רגלם, LXX uses the plural. For MT each Aaronid has an ear lobe, thumb and big toe, whereas the translator thinks in terms of the Aaronids having ear lobes, etc. Only for ὤτων has the translator neglected to translate the third masculine plural suffix.[35] The majority text has not unexpectedly added an αυτων. It should be noted, however, that it is by no means certain that the shorter A B x y+ text is original. If the longer text were original, the omission of an αυτων between ὤτων and τῶν (δεξιῶν) would simply be due to homoioteleuton. The only reason for adopting the shorter text is the support of the oldest witnesses, A and B.

After finishing the ritual, Moses προσέχεεν the blood on the altar round about. As in v.19 the Hebrew text has ויזרק, and the translator simply levelled with v.19; see comment ad loc.

8:25 He then took "the fat"; presumably this is the genus, since specific "fats" are listed subsequently. For τὴν ὀσφύν as the regular rendering for אליה see com-

---

34. Sym translated by ἕλικα, which refers to the shell of the ear. Tar^ON have רום which probably refers to the upper ridge (of the ear), whereas Tar^J has חסחום "cartilege." Note that NJPS translated תנוך by "ridge" (of the right ear).
35. See Sollamo, Rep 49.

ment at 3:9.³⁶ For τὸ στέαρ (which was on the κοιλίας) MT has את כל החלב, and hex has added παν before τὸ στέαρ 2° in LXX to equal the Hebrew text. For earlier instances of τὸν λόβον τοῦ ἥπατος see comment at v.23.³⁷ The next case of στέαρ is that on the two kidneys. MT has ואת חלבהן "and their fat," which LXX restates in parallel to "the fat which was on the κοιλίας" as καὶ τὸ στέαρ τὸ ἐπ' αὐτῶν.³⁸ ᾧ ὑ βραχίονα see comment at 7:22.³⁹

8:26 For סל המצות "basket of unleavened bread" LXX has τοῦ κανοῦ τῆς τελειώσεως "basket of the consummation sacrifice," which is a leveling with v.31, where the phrase סל המלאים does occur in MT. For τελειώσεως see comment at 7:27. It does have the advantage of making clear that the sacrifice here detailed is not the one involving the ram τὸν εἰς ὁλοκαύτωμα (v.18), but rather the consummation sacrifice. That this basket should be ἔναντι κυρίου means that it is at the door of the tent of testimony; cf Note at Exod 29:23; see also vv.3 and 4 above. According to MT he took both a חלת מצה and a חלת לחם שמן, both bound phrases. LXX has ἄρτον ἄζυμον "an unleavened bread(loaf)" for the first one, and ἄρτον ἐξ ἐλαίου for the second. Since the translator used ἄρτον to render חלת, and the word לחם only means "bread," he perforce had to coalesce the phrase חלת הלחם "loaf of bread" into a single ἄρτον. The *b* text translated חלת more accurately by κολλυραν,⁴⁰ and for the second one has κολλυραν αρτου, which is obviously recensionally inspired. The ἄρτον ἐξ ἐλαίου probably means "a bread(loaf) made with oil." The term רקיק "thin cake, wafer" is always rendered in OT by λάγανον.

For the second clause LXX has "(and he placed) ἐπὶ τὸ στέαρ καὶ τὸν βραχίονα τὸν δεξιόν." MT, however, has the first noun in the plural, and also repeats the preposition for the second one. Presumably LXX meant τὸ στέαρ in the same sense as τὸ στέαρ 1°, i.e. understood as a collective. Once again the *b* text betrays strong recensional influence by its τα στεατα, which equals MT's החלבים. Hex has added an unnecessary επι before the second noun as well so as to equal MT.

---

36. Aq renders האליה by τὴν κέρκον, and Theod, by τὸ κέρκιον.
37. Aq translates by τὴν περισσίαν τοῦ ἥπατος.
38. See SS 69 and 98.
39. Instead of τὸν βραχίονα τὸν δεξιόν The Others read τὴν κνημῖδα τὴν δεξιάν.
40. The Others also used κολλύραν.

8:27 ἄπαντα equals the את הכל of MT adequately, and could be rendered "all of it together," referring to what Moses took from the basket of the ordination sacrifice in v.26. LXX does not distinguish between כף and יד, correctly taking "palms" as a synecdoche for "hands," hence, χεῖρας.

The second clause has the difficult וינף תנופה structure, which LXX here renders by καὶ ἀνήνεγκεν ... ἀφαίρεμα; for a discussion of how the translator dealt with the cognate Hebrew expression see comments at 7:20.[41]

8:28 LXX uses ἔλαβεν absolutely, though MT does have an אתם modifying the verb, but it occurs after the subject משה. Hex accordingly added αυτα before "from their hands." A popular reading has also added αυτα immediately following the verb. Whether it and the hex reading are related cannot be determined, since the former may have been an ad sensum gloss. The more difficult shorter text must be original.

LXX apparently did not understand the following structure(s) in MT. For ויקטר καὶ ἀνήνεγκεν αὐτά is sensible, with αὐτά supplying the understood object. For the verb in LXX see comment at 2:16. MT then continues with המזבחה על העלה מלאים הם לריח ניחח. The Masoretes placed העלה under the *ethnach*, thus "on the altar along with the burnt offering; these are the ordination sacrifices for a sweet smelling savor." LXX, first of all, must have made the major cut after מלאים, i.e. ἐπὶ τὸ θυσιαστήριον ἐπὶ τὸ ὁλοκαύτωμα τῆς τελειώσεως "on the altar, upon (i.e. over) the burnt offering of the consummation sacrifice." In other words, the translator understood Moses' placement of materials for the ordination ritual, i.e, the ἄπαντα of v.27, on top of the sacrifice described in vv.18—21, viz. the τὸν κριὸν τὸν εἰς ὁλοκαύτωμα. The pronoun is then reinterpreted as a singular relative pronoun ὅ (ἐστιν) which refers not to the "consummation sacrifice" but to τὸ ὁλοκαύτωμα, and then the preposition of לריח is disregarded, and so the clause reads "which is a sweet smelling savor." The translator was trying to clarify exactly what was meant by ἐπὶ τὸ ὁλοκαύτωμα, but in so doing ran into difficulties with הם לריח as well. For κάρπωμα rendering אשה see comment at 2:9. In the tradition, the Byz text has added at the end of the verse καθαπερ ενετειλατο κυριος, which is an ex par gloss.

---

41. Sym apparently read ἐθυμίασεν for the verb (retroverted from Syriac).

8:29 Lev does not usually break up the paratactic clauses through subordination of a verbal idea as a participle, but here καὶ λαβών is used for ויקח to good effect, since thereby the stress is rightly placed on the next clause of MT. The rendering of ויניפהו תנופה here by ἀφεῖλεν αὐτὸ ἐπίθεμα completely disregards the rendering in v.27 where the cognate structure also occurs; see the discussion at 7:20. I would render it "and when Moses had taken the breast), he removed it as a deposit (... from the ram of the consummation sacrifice)." This ἐπίθεμα then becomes Moses' portion.

This also is not what MT says. The translator, in line with his understanding of the previous verse, has taken מאיל המלאים with the preceding clause, whereas the Masoretes divided the verse before it, i.e. the *ethnach* is placed on יהוה 1°. MT begins v.b with מאיל, thus "from the ram of ordination there was a portion for Moses," or more freely: it was Moses' portion from the ram of ordination.

In the tradition, the *C'* *n s* text has αφαιρεμα for ἐπίθεμα; this could have come in under the influence of its use in v.27, or possibly as cognate to the verb ἀφεῖλεν. Hex has transposed ἐγένετο Μωυσῆ to correspond to the word order of MT. The genitive Μωυσῆ for למשה is certainly original, since the dative of "Moses" is always articulated in Lev,[42] though the Byz text did change the word to τω μωυση.

8:30 The opening statement has two clear examples of ἀπό used in a partitive sense, "some of the anointing oil" and "some of the blood;"[43] "the blood" is modified by τοῦ ἐπὶ τοῦ θυσιαστηρίου. This must be understood in the light of v.24; there Moses poured the blood upon the altar κύκλῳ. In other words, blood is not (in fact, never) poured on to the surface of the altar, but only at the base of the altar, or around the altar as in v.24. The translator could well have adopted the syntactic pattern used in v.29 for ויקח, but he reverted to a paratactic rendering which dominates his translation.

For the second clause the verb προσέρρανεν is used absolutely in imitation of MT; of course, what he "sprinkled" was the two partitives of the first clause, some anointing oil and some blood. What he besprinkled (προσέρρανεν ἐπί) was "Aaron and his garments and his sons and the garments of his sons with him."

---

42. See THGL 82.
43. See SS 161.

The verbosity of the statements, which is repeated again in the next clause, is the result of a word for word rendering of the Hebrew. Slight differences between the two do occur in that the first "and" has in its place על in MT. It is possible that the parent text read ועל rather than על.⁴⁴ על also introduces both "his sons" and "the garments of his sons" in MT, but LXX simply reads καί. In both cases majority readings have introduced επι. The clause ends in MT with אתו, which the Masoretes placed under the *ethnach*.

V.b begins with ויקדש, and it is modified by the same modifiers as those for ויז, except that instead of על the preposition את occurs throughout. It should come as no surprise that copyists easily overlooked the entire clause, since both ended with "Aaron and his garments and his sons and the garments of his sons with him." This is a good illustration of the importance of not blindly trusting the evidence of the oldest mss; among those guilty of reading the shorter text are both A and B (along with 20 cursive mss).

8:31 Vv.31—36 detail Moses' subsequent instructions to the newly ordained priests. This is introduced by "and Moses said to Aaron and to his sons"; LXX in the interest of good Greek did not translate the repeated "to," though two mss do insert a πρός; this is, however, unlikely to be recensional.

What Moses said was "Boil the meat ἐν τῇ αὐλῇ of the tent of testimony ἐν τόπῳ ἁγίῳ." MT has no equivalent for the second ἐν phrase, and for the first one it reads פתח. The LXX locative phrases are imported from 6:16,26, where this double designation refers to the place where priests must eat their portions; LXX has thus made a more exact statement; "at the door (of the tent of meeting) means "in the courtyard in a holy place." Hex has dutifully placed ἐν τόπῳ ἁγίῳ under the obelus to show its absence in MT. What is to be eaten is אתו והלחם. LXX has both plural: αὐτά (referring to τὰ κρέα) and τοὺς ἄρτους (because at v.26 it is said that there were two bread loaves taken). For κανοῦ τῆς τελειώσεως see comment at v.26.

The ὃν τρόπον clause in LXX is a pious redaction of MT which said "as צויתי," vocalized by the Masoretes as Pi. The translator, however, changed it to a passive structure, and made it συντέτακταί μοι "he (i.e. the Lord) had commanded me." This shifts the responsibility for the order where it belongs; this is

---

44. As Sam as well as many Hebrew mss did.

the Lord's order, not mine. Actually the majority text adds κυριος, correctly interpreting who the subject must be, though the reading is certainly secondary.

The command given was: "Aaron and his sons יאכלהו," which LXX rendered by φάγονται αὐτά. The difference in number is necessary; the Hebrew לחם is singular, but τοὺς ἄρτους is plural; in fact, the reference is to αὐτὰ καὶ τοὺς ἄρτους.

8:32 The remnants may not be stored. What remained of "meat and bread," both of which are, as expected, plural in Greek, must be burned ἐν πυρί "by fire." The preposition is to be taken as instrumental.[45] The verb in MT, rendered by κατακαυθήσεται, is, however, active and in second plural, תשרפו "you must burn." The majority text is κατακαυσετε, a recensional correction. The singular passive is original, thereby avoiding a direct command to the priests to do the burning, and allowing for the possibility that other sanctuary officials might carry out the incineration.

8:33 Aaron and the Aaronids are to remain in the sanctuary for seven days. For the seven days comprising the ordination ritual, see also Exod 29:30,35. The seven days are defined as lasting ἕως ἡμέρα πληρωθῇ τελειώσεως ὑμῶν "until the ἡμέρα of your consummation (see comment at 7:27) is completed." This is not fully clear, since it might be understood as implying that the actual day of consummation was the last day of the seven day period. The word ἡμέρα, however, means "time" rather than "day," as the final clause of the verse makes clear. MT's text is longer: עד יום מלאת ימי מלאיכם "until the day when the days of your ordination are completed." In the tradition, various attempts to "fix up" the text were made. Since MT has both יום and ימי, ημερων was inserted by one popular text before τελειώσεως, and ἡμέρα πληρωθῇ was changed to ημερας πληρωσεως, which constitutes a substantial rewrite of the text. A better solution is the popular insertion here of ημερα; this would make the text read "until the day is fulfilled, the day of your ordination." This is almost certainly a hex attempt at correcting the text.[46]

The final clause states "For seven days he shall validate your hands." The initial accusative expresses length of time, and τελειώσει τὰς χεῖρας ὑμῶν trans-

---

45. See SS 117.
46. For a fuller discussion of the text history see THGL 105—106.

lates ימלא את ידכם, a Hebrew expression first occurring at Exod 28:37(41);[47] for the Greek translation see Note at Exod 29:9. The term "validate the hand(s)" is a technical term for "ordain to office." The subject is not given, but it is in third person, and can only refer to the Lord. What this means is that the consummation ceremony lasted an entire week, presumably with a daily repetition of the consummation sacrifice, though this is not explicitly stated; comp Exod 29:35.

8:34 The καθάπερ clause refers to what the Lord did today, viz. ordered the ritual of consummation. The subject of the verb is unnamed, but it is obviously the one mentioned in the main clause, κύριος. That what the Lord did was to order the ritual is clear from the verb of the main clause, ἐνετείλατο.

The main clause gives the purpose of all this; it is (τοῦ ποιῆσαι) ὥστε ἐξιλάσασθαι περὶ ὑμῶν. The marked infinitive τοῦ ποιῆσαι complements ἐνετείλατο. Complementary infinitives in Lev are usually unmarked, occurring 45 times, and only 10, marked ones. In the tradition, a few mss (only seven) omit the τοῦ, but the marker is certainly original.[48] Of central importance in the verse is that it is necessary for the priests to have atonement made on their behalf before they can serve as priests. In other words, any guilt, any impurity, must be removed by propitiation before an Aaronid can become a priest. For the meaning of ἐξιλάσασθαι see discussion at 1:4.

8:35 The first clause opens with καὶ ἐπὶ τὴν θύραν (of the tent of testimony). The case of τὴν θύραν is changed to the genitive by n, and to the dative by C′ s, but the accusative is clearly original. Whenever ἐπί governs "door(s)" in Lev (13 times), the noun is always in the accusative case. Since the Hebrew equivalent has no article, and פתח being the bound element in a bound phrase, the omission of τήν by O z may well be hex in origin. What is certainly hex is the transposition of "seven days" after ἡμέραν καὶ νύκτα to fit MT's שבעת ימים יומם ולילה.

The second clause is introduced by καί, which is omitted in the tradition by A B x y+. It is, of course, original, and the omission is probably exegetically induced in view of the ἡμέραν καὶ νύκτα preceding it in Lev.[49] The timer "day and night" would then modify φυλάξεσθε; this makes excellent sense—but it is

---
47. Kenn 9,69,107 used the plural ידיכם instead of the singular ידכם.
48. For the marking of the complementary infinitive see THGL 82.
49. See THGL 100.

not original text. The translator also understood משמרת as a collective, as the plural τὰ φυλάγματα shows, thus "(keep) the charges (of the Lord)."[50] A popular A F text reads the aorist imperative φυλαξασθε instead of the future, but the καί before the verb shows that this can not be original. What is meant by the cognate expression is to guard against any violation of God's commandments.[51] LXX's interpretation of the paratactic ולא תמותו as a ἵνα clause is quite plausible; "and not shall you die" can be either the result or the purpose of guarding the Lord's charges.

The כי clause with which the verse ends has a passive verb, the Pu צויתי, thus "for so I was commanded." Lev has made this active with κύριος as subject and μοι as indirect object. This accords with the oft-repeated formula in the book "as the Lord commanded," thus once again stressing the divine source of the regulations. In the tradition, the A B x y+ text has added o θεος. This not only is not supported by MT, it also never occurs in the 18 cases of the formula in the book. Furthermore, hex has placed κύριος under the obelus, and certainly did not have o θεος in its text.

8:36 A concluding statement that the ordinands carried out all τοὺς λόγους which the Lord ordered τῷ Μωυσῇ. τοὺς λόγους equals הדברים, and refers to the matters spoken, i.e. the orders given. LXX has misinterpreted MT in its dative of indirect object, and thereby overlooked an important point made by the Hebrew. In MT Moses is but the intermediary for the Lord's charges to the ordinands; Yahweh ordered the priests ביד משה, which the b text correctly represents by its εν χειρι μωυση; this must be recensional correction. But LXX missed this by disregarding ביד.

---

50. For φυλάγματα in Lev see Harlé-Pralon ad loc.
51. See Milgrom 541.

Chapter 9

9:1 The use of ἐγενήθη or ἐγένετο plus a timer occurs only here in the book, though it is common elsewhere in the Pentateuch. The change in *b+* to εγενετο is probably merely a stylistic one. The term γερουσίαν "council of elders" occurs only here and at v.3 in the book, and it also occurs in Exod and Num, and is common in Deut. But זקנים only occurs three times in MT of the book (also at 4:15 19:32 where it is translated by πρεσβύτεροι). See also the comment on the term γερουσία at v.3.

9:2 The reference to the eighth day ties this chapter to the preceding one, i.e. after the seven days of the consummation rites have been finished. Now that the priests have been ordained, their work can begin. The Aaronids are now to inaugurate the public cult of sacrifice before the Lord. LXX unnecessarily added Μωυσῆς as subject for εἶπεν, and hex placed it under the obelus, since it had no counterpart in MT. The Hebrew עגל "calf" occurs elsewhere in the book at vv.3,8, and is throughout rendered by the diminutive μοσχάριον, and the appositive בן בקר is well-rendered by ἐκ βοῶν "from the herd" or "from cattle." περὶ ἁμαρτίας distinguishes "sin offering" from ἁμαρτία "sin," though both can render חטאת; see comments at 4:3,8 5:6. Note that περί here represents the same preposition as in לעלה, which, however, becomes εἰς ὁλοκαύτωμα.

In the second clause MT uses הקרב absolutely, whereas LXX has added an αὐτά, referring to μοσχάριον and κριόν, ad sensum. Hex has placed the pronoun under the obelus.

9:3 τῇ γερουσίᾳ is based on Sam's וזקני rather than on the בני of MT. Since in v.1 Moses summoned the priests and the council of elders, the Sam text seems more sensible than MT. LXX then used the imperative, which levels with the λάβε of v.2, rather than the more usual λαλήσεις for תדבר, which, however, is the variant reading in the majority text, but Lev seldom uses λαλησεις (only twice, 7:19 20:2), preferring the imperative.[1]

LXX introduces ἕνα to modify χίμαρον; this has no counterpart in MT, and was introduced by the translator for clarification to contrast with the two animals,

---

1. See THGL 127–128.

μοσχάριον and ἀμνόν, to be taken for the ὁλοκάρπωσιν. Apparently hex omitted ἕνα to equal MT. Obviously, no lexical difference was intended between the ὁλοκάρπωσιν here and the ὁλοκαύτωμα of v.2; both render עלה, and both constitute the burnt offering. But ὁλοκάρπωσιν occurs only here for עלה in Lev, whereas ὁλοκαύτωμα is used 44 times (out of 54). The word, is however, used only for עלה in Gen (seven times), whereas ὁλοκαύτωμα is never used. Presumably ἄμωμα should apply to all three animals, though theoretically it could apply simply to the animals for the burnt offering, but the word in v.2 must apply to both kinds of sacrifice, and this must apply here as well.

9:4 The instructions to the council of elders continue into v.4 with λάβετε of v.3 also governing the coordinate μόσχον καὶ κριόν ... καὶ σεμίδαλον. In MT the bullock and the ram לשלמים לזבח, i.e. "the bullock and the ram for the sacrifice for deliverance to sacrifice (before Yahweh)." LXX simplified this by omitting לזבח entirely, and it simply has εἰς θυσίαν σωτηρίου (ἔναντι κυρίου). A majority F text added εκ βοων after μόσχον under the influence of v.2.

MT then introduces another sacrifice (ומנחה בלולה בשמן) "and a meal sacrifice (mixed with oil)." The translator found this odd; the phrase בלולה בשמן seemed an inappropriate way to describe a meal sacrifice; what was usually mixed with oil was fine flour. By substituting σεμίδαλιν for מנחה a clearer text emerged; furthermore, at 7:2 the θυσίας σωτηρίου included unleavened cakes anointed with oil καὶ σεμίδαλιν πεφυραμένην ἐν ἐλαίῳ, which corresponds exactly with our text. At 6:40, however, "θυσία made up with oil" did occur, but "fine flour mixed with oil" is more common (2:5 14:10 23:13). In Num מנחה (mixed with oil) occurs five times (all in ch.28), whereas "fine flour" occurs 19 times. The Byz text added θυσιαν before σεμίδαλιν, obviously a doublet reading based on the Hebrew.

The verse ends with a ὅτι clause detailing the reason for these instructions: it is "because today the Lord will appear among you." This is not quite what MT has. The verb in MT is modified by אליכם "to you," so "reveal himself to you." The future ὀφθήσεται can equal נראה, though the Masoretes vocalized the verb to be understood as a past tense, but the consonantal text could also be realized as a participle. Since it is modified by היום the participle is likely to have been intended. That the Lord should appear among the elders at the inauguration of the public cult contrasts with the appearance of δόξης κυρίου with which the tent (i.e. the tabernacle) was filled; see Exod 40:28—29, and comments ad loc.

9:5 In MT "they took" has a relative clause as direct modifier, i.e. "they took what Moses had commanded," but LXX has καθό instead of אשר. This would mean that what they took must have been the χίμαρον, μοσχάριον, ἀμνόν, μόσχον, κριόν and the σεμίδαλιν of vv.3—4, and so "they took (them) as Moses commanded." This also makes good sense. It might be noted that the verb ἐντέλλομαι normally has a dative of person as modifier. In fact, only here and at 17:2 does it fail to do so.² MT locates this action אל פני the tent, i.e. "to the front of the tent," which LXX interprets as ἀπέναντι "over against."

The subject in v.b is πᾶσα συναγωγή. In the tradition, the majority text has articulated the noun; it would be difficult to resist the impulse to write ἡ συναγωγη, since that is the usual structure after πᾶσα. The more difficult text is supported inter alia by the oldest witnesses, A and B, and is clearly original.³ In MT העדה is taken as requiring a plural verb, and so ויקרבו and ויעמדו are used. LXX, however, took the first one as a collective singular, προσῆλθεν, but the second one as plural, ἔστησαν. Presumably the congregation as a unit approaches, but they stand as individuals. The latter verb is modified by ἔναντι (κυρίου).⁴ The Byz text "corrected" προσῆλθεν to the plural, thereby equalling MT.

9:6 The word ῥῆμα is modified by a relative clause with εἶπεν, though MT has צוה "commanded," and refers to what had been ordered in vv.2—4. The word εἶπεν had occurred in the opening "And Moses said," which may subconsciously have influenced the translator. Since this issues in an imperative ποιήσατε, εἶπεν practically means "commanded." The *b* text reads συνεταξεν, obviously a recensional change. MT has the future verb תעשו, but contextually a future hardly fits, whereas the imperative must have been intended.⁵

The reward for carrying out this demand is given in the concluding clause: "and the glory of the Lord shall appear among you." For ἐν ὑμῖν rendering אליכם see comment at v.4. This is the first instance of δόξα κυρίου in the book, but the phrase is well-known from Exod; see Notes at Exod 16:10 24:16. The δόξα of

---

2. See THGL 113.
3. See THGL 86.
4. But according to Hesychius Aq read *ante faciem* (probably for ἔναντι προσώπου).
5. See THGL 126.

the Lord refers to the divine presence in a revelatory sense, usually seen in a cloud or fire. It is what can be seen when deity comes into contact with the created world. One cannot see God and live, Exod 33:20, but one can see his glory, his splendor. The term elucidates what was meant by the ὅτι clause in v.4; when the Lord appears to men, it is the δόξα of the Lord that is seen. The term is well-chosen to represent כבוד, since it means "brightness, splendor, radiance," and when referring to God means "glory, majesty, sublimity."[6] In the tradition, most witnesses articulate the word, but this is likely an attempt at stylistic improvement.[7]

9:7 Moses tells Aaron to carry out his high-priestly duties. Principally, these concern his cultic duties at the altar. First of all, he must approach the altar; this is the only occasion on which Aaron is told to do so, since this is the initial occasion. Once having entered the domain of the altar, he has access to it, e.g. v.8. There he must perform his (own) sin offering and his burnt offering. The point of this initial performance is: καὶ ἐξίλασαι περὶ σεαυτοῦ καὶ τοῦ οἴκου σου. MT has for the last noun בעד העם "on behalf of the people." But the atonement on behalf of the people follows in the second part of the verse. Before the priest can make atonement for the people he and his household must be in a pure state themselves; his guilt and that of his house (i.e. his sons) must be removed, and the change of העם to τοῦ οἴκου σου is a sensible restatement or correction on the part of LXX; in fact, it is conceivable that MT is secondary to an original בעדך. The *b* text has added περὶ before τοῦ, which equals MT, and is clearly recensional.

Only after this has been carried out is it appropriate to perform the sacrifices of the people. For τὰ δῶρα MT has the singular קרבן, but number varies in LXX in translating the word;[8] in fact, no rational pattern for change in number is discernible. The purpose of performing the people's sacrifices is to make atonement on their behalf, only possible now that the priest's own offerings have effectively been carried out at the altar. For the meaning of ἐξίλασαι see discussion at 1:4.

The verse concludes with "as the Lord commanded Moses." MT has no equivalent for τῷ Μωυσῇ, though a popular variant text, probably under hex

---

6. According to Bauer sub voce 1a.
7. See THGL 86.
8. See THGL 116.

influence, has omitted it. But usage in the book makes the dative modifier almost certainly original. ἐντέλλομαι only occurs absolutely twice in the book, for which see comment at v.5. Even when צוה occurs without modifier elsewhere (10:15) LXX added τῷ Μωυσῇ;[9] comp also v.21.

9:8 Aaron carried out his first task at the altar, viz. sacrificing the calf which constituted the sin offering, τὸ περὶ τῆς ἁμαρτίας. MT added אשר לו, which recalls the initial instruction to Aaron in v.7 that he was first to perform his own sin offering. That this was in fact understood here as well is clear from his offering up τὸ δῶρον τοῦ λαοῦ later on (v.15). In the tradition, either το αυτου or the simpler αυτου was added by the majority of witnesses, in fact, by all Greek witnesses except A B 121 55 and 319. I suspect that αυτου is simply a variant of an original το αυτου. That the shorter text is almost certainly original is clear; the addition of (το) αυτου is easier to explain (probably as a recensional plus) than its deletion in the tradition.

9:9 The Aaronids, as assistants in the cult, brought the blood of the sin offering to the high priest, who dipped the finger into the blood, and put (it) on the horns of the altar. MT has אצבעו, but LXX consistently omits the suffix of "finger" throughout the book.[10] An αυτου has been added by the F majority text; this may well be recensional (hex?) in origin. For τὰ κέρατα τοῦ θυσιαστηρίου see comments at 4:7, where, however, the altar was the incense altar.

9:10 For the fat and the kidneys and the lobe of the liver as parts of the sin offering, see 4:8—10 and comments ad loc. By contrast the fat is not specifically identified as in ch.4, and presumably all the pertinent fat there mentioned is intended. The majority tradition has added δυο before "kidneys," but this has no support in MT, and is ex par (3:4 4:9 6:34 8:25 9:19). Similarly for "(the lobe) τοῦ ἥπατος," most witnesses have τον επι before τοῦ, which is also ex par (3:4,10 4:9 6:34 8:16 9:19). MT is unique here, since "the lobe" is modified by מן הכבד, which would hardly promote τον επι. The article τοῦ for περὶ τῆς ἁμαρτίας identifies "the sin offering" as genitive, which pertains to the items

---
9. See THGL 113.
10. For Lev's common failure to render such suffixes, especially for parts of the body, see SS ch.8, particularly pp.95—96.

mentioned as belonging to the sin offering. Fo ἀνήνεγκεν rendering הקטיר see comment at 2:16. For the ὃν τρόπον clause comp 7:28.

9:11 The opening καὶ τὰ κρέα καὶ τὴν βύρσαν is a pendant accusative, which then serves as antecedent for αὐτά. The majority F M text, which may well be hex in origin, has omitted αὐτά, and so equals MT. The shorter text is syntactically smoother, since the pendant construction thereby becomes a simple modifier of κατέκαυσεν. The subject of the verb is not explicitly given, but it must be Aaron. For burning the fat and the hide outside the camp, see comment at 8:17, where a similar syntactic pattern obtains, and which may well have influenced the translator here; comp also 4:12,21. The majority F M tradition has changed the verb to the plural; comp comment at 4:12.

9:12 The opening verb ἔσφαξεν has Aaron as subject, i.e. Aaron slaughtered the burnt offering, and the Aaronids brought (προσήνεγκαν οἱ υἱοὶ 'Ααρών) the blood. A majority F M reading has changed the first verb into the plural, εσφαξαν, as well; this would probably mean that the Aaronids both slaughtered ... and brought, though this variant can only be a thoughtless error, since the second verb is modified by πρὸς αὐτόν, i.e. to Aaron, who then poured out, προσέχεεν, the blood. In MT the modifiers of וימצאו follow the named subject as אליו את הדם; LXX has them as τὸ αἷμα πρὸς αὐτόν. Hex has reversed the order of the modifiers to represent the order of MT. It should be noted that LXX levels in its choice of προσήνεγκαν with v.9, even though it is not יקרבו, but ימצאו in MT; cf also vv.13,18. These three instances are the only cases in OT of the Hi of מצא being translated by προσφέρω, a translation which fits the context admirably. In the tradition, a majority M variant text has προς instead of ἐπὶ (τὸ θυσιαστήριον). The variant was created under the influence of the compound verb προσέχεεν which it modified, but MT has על, and the variant is secondary. For προσέχεεν as rendering for יזרק see comment at 6:32. MT reads ויזרקהו, and hex has added an αυτο to represent the pronominal suffix.

9:13 The Aaronids "brought the burnt offering to him (i.e. to Aaron) κατὰ μέλη, αὐτὰ καὶ τὴν κεφαλήν." For the translation of המציאו see comment at v.12. For the meaning of κατὰ μέλη see comment at 1:6. MT reads לנתחיה ואת הראש. The prepositional phrase also occurs at 1:6,12 8:20, and LXX never translates the pronominal suffixes, but here in its slot is the odd αὐτά, which can hardly be taken as related to the suffix. The effect of this is to stress the pieces over against the head, both of which constitute the actual burnt offering, i.e. "these and the head," which contrast with the next verse. For ἐπέθηκεν rendering יקטר, see comment at 2:16; the subject again reverts to Aaron.

9:14 What remains of the burnt offering are τὴν κοιλίαν καὶ τοὺς πόδας, which received special treatment and placement. Before placement Aaron is to wash them with water. The ὕδατι has no counterpart in MT, and is therefore placed under the obelus in hex. These waste pieces are then placed on top of the burnt offering on the altar. For the change to ἐπέθηκεν as rendering for יקטר see comment at 2:16.

9:15 For the offering of τὸ δῶρον of the people, comp v.7, where קרבן is translated by the plural τὰ δῶρα, for which variation see comment ad loc.[11] The B n y+ text read a plural verb, προσηνεγκαν, which is probably a thoughtless error, possibly induced by v.12. It is clearly wrong in a context which is entirely singular.[12] Here it is Aaron who is the officiant, not the Aaronids as at v.2. For the χίμαρον τὸν περὶ τῆς ἁμαρτίας see v.3. τοῦ λαοῦ is a simplification of MT's אשר לעם.

Strange is the translation of יחטאהו "he offered it for a sin offering" by ἐκαθάρισεν αὐτόν. The αὐτόν must refer to the χίμαρον which constituted the sin offering, but "he purified (or cleansed) it" is peculiar, though this rendering for the Pi of חטא is not unique. It also occurs at 8:15 where it is modified by את המזבח; there the cleansing is done by blood. The verb also occurs at Exod 29:36 where Moses is told to purify the altar by making atonement for it. The clue for understanding this lies in the καθὰ καὶ τὸ πρῶτον "as also in the first case."[13] This must refer to vv.3—9, which describe the first sacrificial rite, that for Aaron and his sons. Here the sacrifices are for the people and constitute the second sacrifice. Since the altar and its status are central to the rites in ch.9, it must somehow be involved in the purification referred to. The collocation ἐκαθάρισεν

---

11. See also THGL 116.
12. See also THGL 124.
13. I find the comment of Harlé-Pralon that the verb "est absent du grec" incomprehensible.

αὐτόν must mean "he performed the purification rite with it," i.e. with the χίμαρον of the sin offering. This can only refer to the rite described in v.9, the dipping of the finger in the blood and putting it on the horns of the altar. Note that this is not otherwise ordered in vv.15—21.¹⁴ The use of τὸ πρῶτον is adverbial, and is good Classical usage. The majority variant, τον πρωτον, is a later usage, but the oldest witnesses have the neuter article, and that is to be preferred.

9:16 For ὡς καθήκει "in the usual manner," see comment at 5:10. The n text has a different compound, προσηκει, but this means the same as καθήκει.

9:17 The מנחה had been mentioned at v.4, which undoubtedly gave the impetus for the θυσίαν brought by Aaron, though there LXX changed the meal offering to σεμίδαλιν; cf comment ad loc. The translator might, however, in view of the burnt offering τοῦ πρωινοῦ, have been reminded of the θυσίαν διὰ παντός, half of which was to be offered τὸ πρωί, and half, τὸ δειλινόν, at 6:20.

The second clause has Aaron ἔπλησεν τὰς χεῖρας ἀπ' αὐτῆς (i.e. from the θυσίαν). For χεῖρας as rendering for כפו see comment at 8:27. The structure is to be taken literally, and simply means "to take handfuls" of the meal sacrifice, and is not to be confused with the technical expression at Exod 28:37, where ἐμπλήσεις αὐτῶν τὰς χεῖρας "you shall ordain (or install) them to office";¹⁵ see Note ad loc. Hex has added αυτου to represent the suffix of כפו, which the b text changed to την χειρα αυτου, as another recensional correction. For a fuller statement see 2:2 and comments ad loc. It is obviously a reference to the memorial sacrifice; see discussion on its meaning at 2:2.

For ἐπέθηκεν as rendering for יקטר see comment at 2:16. The meal offering was placed on the altar χωρὶς τοῦ ὁλοκαυτώματος τοῦ πρωινοῦ "apart from (i.e. alongside, in addition to) the morning burnt offering," for which see 6:20, as well as Exod 29:38—42 and Notes ad loc.

9:18 LXX has changed the syntactic pattern of the opening clause. In MT the verb ישחט is modified not only by "the ox and the ram," but also by זבח

---
14. Aq rendered the word וחטאהו by περιημάρτησεν αὐτόν, a neologism obviously based on Lev's rendering of חטאת.
15. As Harlé-Pralon suggest. But this is hardly meaningful here in view of the next clause.

השלמים, thus "he slaughtered the ox and the ram as a sacrifice for deliverance"; LXX has τῆς θυσίας τοῦ σωτηρίου modifying the nominal structure τὸν μόσχον καὶ τὸν κριόν, though it could also be misunderstood as modifying only the second noun; MT's statement is much clearer.

In the next clause the verb προσήνεγκαν levels with the parallel vv.9,12,13, for which see comments at v.12. For both this clause and the last one see comments at v.12 as well, since it has exactly the same wording. Similarly, it recorded the hex plus αυτο after προσέχεεν.

9:19 In LXX the entire verse can be understood as a pendant accusative about fat, which is then brought into the main clause (v.20) by the plural στέατα as a cover term. On the other hand, it could also be taken as a series of coordinates to τὸ αἷμα of v.18, i.e. those parts which the Aaronids brought to Aaron. This would mean that the final clause of v.18 was parenthetical, and could be understood almost like a relative clause. MT begins with ואת החלבים, but LXX disregarded the plural in favor of listing various fatty pieces, considerably beyond the text of MT. In MT "the fat pieces" is modified by two prepositional phrases מן השור ומן האיל; in LXX this becomes τὸ ἀπὸ τοῦ μόσχου καὶ τοῦ κριοῦ, with an introductory τό serving as a relative referring to στέαρ. A majority text has added an απο before τοῦ κριοῦ so as to represent the second מן of MT; the variant is probably hex in origin. For τὴν ὀσφύν rendering האליה see comment at 3:9.

The remaining items in MT are והמכסה והכלית ויתרת הכבד. The first word seems to be a fragment; "that which covers" ought both to have "the fat" as a lost antecedent, as well as some modifier indicating what was being covered. LXX supplied an answer to both of these by adding τὸ στέαρ before τὸ κατακαλύπτον as well as ἐπὶ τῆς κοιλίας after it, thus "(and) the fat which covers (over) the belly." For the latter, comp 3:3,9,14. Both additions were placed under the obelus in hex. LXX has also added δύο before νέφρους, as well as καὶ τὸ στέαρ τὸ ἐπ' αὐτῶν, for which see 3:4 and comp 3:10,15. Both lack equivalents in MT and the second is attested as having been placed under the obelus in hex. The last item is יתרת הכבד, which occurs 10 times in the book. Here it is rendered by τὸν λοβὸν τὸν ἐπὶ τοῦ ἥπατος. The translation for the free element of the phrase fluctuates between a simple genitive, τοῦ ἥπατος, (3:15 7:20 8:25 9:10) and τὸν ἐπὶ τοῦ ἥπατος (also at 3:4,10 4:9 6:34 8:16).

9:20 MT is inconsistent in the number of the verbs in the two clauses, with the first one in the plural, referring to the Aaronids of v.18, and the second one in the singular, referring to Aaron. Sam witnesses to a singular in both clauses, which text LXX follows (as do Pesh and Tar^N). *O b* have "corrected" the ἐπέθηκεν of the first clause to the plural επεθηκαν to equal MT.

The opposite change, i.e. of the second verb ἀνήνεγκεν to the plural ανηνεγκαν occurs in B *b+*; this is a pseudo-correction; it can not be taken seriously in a context where the high priest alone reigns as the officiant at the altar.[16] For the verb rendering יקטר see comment at 2:16.

9:21 The translator here renders החזות by the singular τὸ στηθύνιον, whereas in v.20 he had rendered it by the plural τὰ στηθύνια. In v.20 the reference is to the cut-up pieces of breast meat which were lying on the altar, but here the singular is used, since the whole breast is being dedicated before the Lord. The change to the singular shows an astute translator at work. Specifically Aaron removed the breast and the right shoulder as an ἀφαίρεμα "dedicated portion" before the Lord. For βραχίονα rendering שוק see comment at 7:22. For Lev's rendering of הניף תנופה see discussion at 7:20.

The ὃν τρόπον clause differs considerably from MT, which reads כאשר צוה משה "as Moses had commanded," in favor of the usual formula, as found in Sam: כאשר צוה יהוה את משה.[17] Hex, however, changed κύριος τῷ Μωυσῇ to Μωυσῆς to equal MT; the hex reading actually became popular in the tradition.[18]

9:22 LXX has subordinated the first clause in MT, וישא אהרן את ידו "And Aaron raised his hand(s)" to a participial structure καὶ ἐξάρας ... τὰς χεῖρας, thereby transferring the stress to the main event, blessing the people. The failure to render the suffix of ידו was a common practice of the translator;[19] hex has added αυτου to represent it, as might be expected. LXX has the plural noun, which follows the Qere tradition ידיו. The plural here is certainly correct. Raising the "hands" is the position of prayer, whereas raising the "hand" refers to the swearing of an oath, as in Exod 6:8 and Num 14:30 where the Lord says ἐξέτεινα τὴν

---

16. See THGL 124.
17. And in many Hebrew mss as well.
18. See THGL 113.
19. See SS 96.

χειρά μου. The participle is also modified by a prepositional phrase ἐπὶ τὸν λαόν, which equals Sam's על העם "over the people," rather than MT's "towards the people." The blessing signals the end of the ceremonies on the eighth day, as the day of the consecration of the altar.

In v.b MT has the verb ירד modified by a preposition plus bound infinitive, מעשת, thus "he descended from performing" with the infinitive in turn modified by three coordinate nouns: "the sin offering and the burnt offering and the sacrifice for deliverance." LXX simplifies the prepositional structure by means of a participle, ποιήσας, thus "he went down, having performed ...." This adequately renders the intent of MT. I suspect that the notion of "going down" from the altar is a vestigial recall of the location of the במות, i.e. high places as the place for sacrifice. Technically this would hardly apply to the altar in the tabernacle, but the idiom is an old one, and is here applied to the מזבח as well. The modifiers, however, differ in number. The sin offering is singular, but the next two are plural: τὰ ὁλοκαυτώματα καὶ τὰ τοῦ σωτηρίου. It may be noted that ch.1 does refer to more than one kind of burnt offering, and ch.3 refers likewise to more than one sacrifice for deliverance, and the translator by using the plural created strict consistency, over against MT, which has העלה והשלמים, i.e. a singular word for the sin offering.

9:23 Aaron has now fully performed his first service at the altar, culminating in his blessing the people. It remained for Moses and Aaron symbolically to enter the tent of testimony, and to emerge and jointly bless all the people. LXX imitates the Hebrew in rendering the first verb in the singular, εἰσῆλθεν, by attraction to the nearer member of a compound subject, and thereafter using the plural, ἐξελθόντες εὐλόγησαν. MT does not have an equivalent for πάντα (τὸν λαόν), but in v.b כל העם does occur, and the translator simply levelled the two.

That the second blessing was effective is shown by the divine response: καὶ ὤφθη ἡ δόξα κυρίου παντὶ τῷ λαῷ. This is in response to the divine promise in v.6 that "the glory of the Lord shall appear among you." For the meaning of δόξα κυρίου see comment at v.6.

9:24 A divine theophany was often accompanied by fire; comp e.g. the thunder and lightning in Exod 19:16. The fire symbolized the presence of the divine glory; it "went out from (παρά) the Lord"; MT has "from before" (מלפני). Note especially for the relation of fire to the divine glory Exod 24:17: τὸ δὲ εἶδος τῆς δόξης κυρίου ὡσεὶ πῦρ φλέγον.

Divine acceptance of the installation sacrifices, and thereby of Aaron as high priest of the people, was signalized by the fire from the Lord devouring the sacrifices on the altar, i.e. "the burnt offerings and the pieces of fat"; comp 3Reg 18:38 for a similar event.[20] As in v.22 העלה is rendered by the plural τὰ ὁλοκαυτώματα. "Fire from the Lord" shows that the δόξα κυρίου was operative. Not only did it appear to all the people, but it also exuded fire for the altar, which probably explains why οὐ σβεσθήσεται, and πῦρ διὰ παντὸς καυθήσεται ἐπὶ τὸ θυσιαστήριον, 6:12—13.

V.b describes the people's reaction to the theophanic event. LXX and MT agree exactly on the first clause: "and all the people saw"; what they saw was the sudden devouring of the sacrifices on the altar. For the next clause, MT and LXX differ. MT has וירנו "and they shouted for joy"; the root probably refers to a cultic outcry in response. The verb occurs only once elsewhere in the Pentateuch; the last verse of the Song of Moses (Exod 32:43) calls upon the nations הרנינו, which LXX translates by εὐφράνθητε "rejoice." LXX found such a reaction inappropriate to the appearance of the divine glory revealed in a devouring fire; on the occasion of the Sina theophany when the mountain was smoking διὰ τὸ καταβεβηκέναι τὸν θεὸν ἐπ' αὐτὸ ἐν πυρί the popular reaction was ἐξέστη σφόδρα "confounded, driven out of their mind, utterly amazed" (Exod 19:18).[21] Only in the final clause is the plural of the Hebrew reproduced in the Greek, reflecting the collective nature of πᾶς λαός, hence ἔπεσαν ἐπὶ πρόσωπον. MT has על פניהם, and hex has added an αυτων to represent the suffix. A popular O Byz variant text has the scond aorist επεσον, but the Hellenistic inflection is probably original. The reaction was appropriate after ἐξέστη.

---

20. Hesychius cites Sym as reading *consumere* for האכל (for ἐδαπάνησεν ?).
21. See also Harlé-Pralon 121.

Chapter 10

10:1 LXX subordinates the opening verb יקחו to a participle λαβόντες, and adds an unnecessary δυο before υἱοὶ ᾿Ααρών, "the two sons of Aaron having taken." The second son is called ᾿Αβιούδ, but MT has אביהוא, i.e. without the final dental stop of LXX; see Note at Exod 6:23. The tradition is almost unanimous in supporting the final *delta,* only one ms reading αβιουμ. In the tradition, the other son, ναδάβ, becomes by metathesis ναβαδ, by assimilation ναδαδ, by prefixing a vowel αναδαβ, by aphaeresis αδαβ, and by syncopation νααβ.

In view of the subordination of the opening clause, the main clause follows without an apodotic και; a few scattered witnesses do add και, but the addition is hardly recensional, although it does equal MT. MT has "they put בהן," i.e. referring to the censers, but LXX, in view of the singular reference (ἕκαστος) τὸ πυρεῖον αὐτοῦ, has ἐπ᾿ αὐτό. The majority text has επ αυτα which not only equals MT, but also agrees with the plural verb. The Greek noun means a fire pan, and here it is clearly intended as a censer. ἐπ᾿ αὐτό also appears in the next clause as a modifier of ἐπέβαλον, but there with πῦρ as antecedent. This follows MT's עליה. Sam's text (followed by Pesh) read עליהן, which must be secondary. The πῦρ here should not be confused with the πῦρ of the preceding verse (i.e. the "fire from the Lord"). Here it refers to coals of fire. The incense is not placed on the censers, but on the fire in the censers. Though יתנו and ישימו are synonyms, the Greek indicates the change of root by using ἐπέθηκαν for the first one, but ἐπέβαλον "they cast (the incense on it)" for the second one, an appropriate choice.

V.b characterizes their action as "they brought before the Lord a strange fire." What is meant by this πῦρ ἀλλότριον is unknown, though many commentators have speculated on it; all that is known is that it was something ὃ οὐ προσέταξεν κύριος αὐτοῖς. At Exod 30:9 the term θυμίαμα ἕτερον occurs; this refers to incense other than that made according to specifications given (in vv.34—38), but this occurs in a different context (of what may be offered on the incense altar), and is probably irrelevant here, except that both are unauthorized. The named subject has no support in the relative clause in MT, nor is it necessary, since the subject could only be the κυρίου of the preceding clause.

10:2 Presumably the fire which went out from the Lord contrasts with the "strange fire," which the two Aaronids brought before the Lord. This fire was not a strange fire, but a consuming one: κατέφαγεν αὐτούς. Whether this was the same "fire from the Lord" that consumed the sacrifices on the altar in 9:24 is uncertain, but it is probable. In contrast to their bringing a strange fire ἔναντι κυρίου, they now died ἔναντι κυρίου. Whether ἔναντι κυρίου here refers to the altar or simply to the door of the sanctuary near the altar is not clear; since the same phrase occurs in the two contexts, the location was probably the same, and it may well have been at the altar. In the tradition, the verb has been changed in a majority M text to the Hellenistic inflection, απεθανοσαν, but the Hellenistic inflection is not used in the Pentateuch

10:3 The verb דבר is usually rendered by ἐλάλησεν, but εἶπεν does occur as well; its normal correspondent in MT is אמר. In the tradition, the *b* text has changed the εἶπεν of the relative clause to ελαλησε to equal MT more exactly; the variant text is recensional.

What the Lord is quoted as saying is a couplet. The two parts are in synonymous parallelism, whose synonymity is made even more obvious in LXX. In MT the first hemistich has a verbal modifier to a Ni verb, בקרבי "among those approaching me," where its parallel in the second part is על פני כל העם "before all the people." The translator used ἐν plus the dative for both: thus "in (or among) those approaching me" and "in all the congregation." "Those approaching me" refers to those who may approach the altar. God reveals himself as holy, i.e. deity, which is explanatory for the sudden striking down of Nadab and Abioud. Deity will not be mocked; his cult is sacred, and its performance is not a matter of indifference, but of exact requirements. God is thus sanctified by his fire consuming those who brought the "strange fire" before him. LXX by its συναγωγῇ, rather than by the more usual λαω, puts the glorification in a cultic context, as a better parallel to τοῖς ἐγγίζουσίν μοι. It is in the worshiping congregation assembled at the door of the tabernacle that the Lord is glorified. It is in these contexts that the Lord will reveal himself as God, i.e. as the holy one, and will be acknowledged by the congregation as such, i.e. will be glorified.

Aaron's reaction in MT, ידם "was silent" is graphically rendered by LXX as κατενύχθη "he was stunned, shocked"; see Note at Gen 27:38, where the verb has no counterpart in MT. The verb דמם was translated by κατανύσσομαι three times in the Psalter (4:5 29:13 34:15).[1] Comp the translation of ידמו כאבן at Exod 1:16 by ἀπολιθωθήτωσαν "let them be petrified."

10:4 Proper nouns in the accusative are normally not articulated in Lev, though see comment on τὸν Ἀαρών at 8:6; only if the case is not clear does articulation normally occur. Here both Μισαήλ and Ἐλισαφάν are articulated, since the verb modified is ἐκάλεσεν in the sense of "summoned, called out." Were the names not articulated one would usually understand the nouns to be indirect objects, and so dative. Of course, the υἱούς which follows would eventually clarify the matter.[2] On the other hand, υἱούς is normally articulated (18 times out of 23); here υἱούς occurs twice, but the case is obvious from the appositives, τὸν Μισαήλ and τὸν Ἐλισαφάν,[3] and the lack of a τους is warranted. The second υἱούς is fully otiose, has no basis in MT, and its omission would actually clarify the passage. As it stands Aaron's two cousins are followed by two appositives, "sons of Oziel," and "sons of the brother of the father of Aaron." MT simply identifies Oziel as "the uncle of Aaron."

Moses then said to them: "Approach and carry your kinsmen from before τῶν ἁγίων, outside the camp." MT says "(from before) הקדש)," which is also ambiguous. I would suggest that the plural is used, since the reference is to the tabernacle as a whole, i.e. inclusive of all the areas that are holy, and one might well translate τῶν ἁγίων by "the sanctuary." MT lacks a conjunction between the two imperatives, which is more abrupt in character, with the first verb קרבו used as an invitation to action. I would render the Hebrew: "Come on, carry your kinsmen."

In the tradition Μισαήλ underwent considerable change. The insertion of a *delta* or a *lambda* after the second vowel is due to confusion of the three triangular graphemes in the uncial script: Α Δ Λ, resulting in a large number of misspellings: μισαδαιλ, μισαδαηλ, μισαλεηλ, and along with apocopation: μισαδαι, μεισαδαι, μισαδα, μησαδα, as well as further corruptions: μισαδαν, μιδαδαι and μιδαι. Ἐλισαφάν appears as ελισαφατ in Byz z+, and as shortened forms in:

---

1. Harlé-Pralon translate: "fut frappé au coeur."
2. See THGL 81.
3. See THGL 85.

ελυσφαν, ελισαφ and ελιφαν. Ὀζιήλ also underwent change as οξεηλ, οζηλ, αζιηλ, σοζεηλ (after υἱούς) and οζιηχ.

A problem obtains with respect to the first imperative. It is inflected with the Hellenistic -αν ending, but in the next verse the same verb is inflected with the Classical -ον ending. These are the only relevant forms for the verb in the book, but it would be unlikely that the translator would have inflected differently in successive clauses. In v.4 the majority M text reads the Classical προσέλθετε, whereas in v.5 προσῆλθον occurs as προσηλθαν only in C' b s+. All things considered I would now adopt the Classical inflection throughout, changing the -ατε ending in v.4 to -ετε.

10:5 LXX does not translate the suffix of וישאם "and they carried them," and the majority text witnesses to an αυτους after the verb, which could be original text. Unfortunately the text of B has omitted much of this verse because of homoioteleuton, and it has been restored on the margin, where together with cod A the verb reads absolutely. Unclear is the reference in αὐτῶν. Do the tunics belong to the corpses or to those who are carrying the bodies outside the camp? Either is possible, but the latter is the more sensible; it would also be the more likely grammatically, since the referent would be within the clause, i.e. the subject of προσῆλθον καὶ ἦραν. The corpses would hardly be first undressed and then carried by means of their tunics, whereas the use of their own tunics for carrying the corpses by Misael and Elisaphan makes better sense. After all, priestly χιτῶσιν would be worn next to the skin; see comment at 8:7. For εἶπεν rendering דבר see comment at v.3.

10:6 The two sons of Aaron, Eleazar and Ithamar, are called τοὺς καταλελειμμένους; this has no support in MT, but is a leveling with v.12, where the participle has הנותרים as equivalent in MT. Hex correctly placed it under the obelus to show its absence in MT. What the Aaronids are not permitted to do is show signs of mourning for their dead brothers, i.e. neither תפרעו "unbind, loosen" your heads, nor "tear your garments." Precisely what loosing the head means is not clear; it is usually interpreted either as "do not ruffle your hair" or "do not bare your head." The translator understood it in the latter sense, and created a neologism to render it, ἀποκιδαρώσετε "remove the (priestly) headgear, turban." The verb occurs only here, and at 21:10 in a similar context. The rending of cloof clothing was a common sign of extreme distress, and is amply attested throughout the OT. Such signs of mourning were not permitted priests, under penalty of their own death and of divine wrath for the entire congregation.

Over against this prohibition, "your kinsmen, all the house of Israel" may engage in weeping.[4] Note the contrastive δέ, which A B y+ omit, but it must have been original text.[5] Also in the tradition, the article for οἶκος is omitted by most witnesses. This I would suggest is a case of haplography. οἶκος occurs only 11 times in Lev, and only once, in the phrase "out of the house of bondage" at 26:45, is the article absent.[6]

It should be noted that πᾶς ὁ οἶκος Ἰσραήλ is used here as subject, whereas the penalty for the Aaronids making themselves unclean through the use of mourning rites would affect πᾶσαν τὴν συναγωγήν, i.e. the congregation in front of the sanctuary door(s). What all the house of Israel is to bewail is τὸν ἐμπυρισμὸν ὃν ἐνεπυρίσθησαν ὑπὸ κυρίου. The subject of the passive plural verb is not stated, but presumably it was Nadab and Abioud. The construction is an awkward one indeed, and what is puzzling is the reason for rendering a fully clear Hebrew statement, "the burning which Yahweh kindled," in such a way. I can do no better than to translate it by "the burning (by) which they were burned by the Lord." The translator apparently wanted to make it obvious that this was a reference to the divine fire consuming Nadab and Abioud, and not to the fire consuming the sacrifices on the altar at 9:24.

10:7 Not only may the Aaronids not join in the weeping, they must remain inside the tent of testimony, again under penalty of death. Leaving the sanctuary would apparently void the anointing which they had just experienced (8:30; comp also vv.33—35). It would seem that the period of seven days referred to there, and which had according to 9:1 come to an end, was reinvoked because of the "strange fire" which had been brought, temporarily extending the period of the installation ceremonies until the bewailing for the burning was over. The fact that the anointing oil with which they were anointed was τὸ παρὰ κυρίου put them into a sanctified state; nothing unclean might touch or affect someone in such a

---

4. I would stress the deliberative character of the future inflection here, for which see Porter 424—425.
5. See THGL 100.
6. See THGL 82.

situation. Leaving the sanctuary would put them into a dangerous state, a profane environment.

10:9 Wine and σίκερα may not be drunk when the priests engage in cultic activities. The word σίκερα is a borrowed word from the Aramaic שכרא and means "fermented drink" of some kind. The cognate word in Akkadian means "beer," and it is possible that the Hebrew שכר referred to "beer" rather than to "liquor." The Hebrew cognate שכר occurs here. The verb "(not) shall you drink" is singular in Hebrew by attraction to the nearer subject, אתה, but becomes plural in LXX with the compound subject σὺ καὶ οἱ υἱοί σου μετὰ σοῦ.[7]

The occasion for the prohibition is limited in MT to בבאכם אל אהל מועד "when you enter the tent of meeting," which LXX renders by "ἡνίκα ἂν εἰσπορεύησθε into the tent of testimony." The use of the present subjunctive is rare in Lev; outside of ᾖ the subjunctive occurs 113 times, of which only seven are in the present. These all indicate a type of linear action, and here the clause might be rendered: "whenever you might be entering the tent of testimony."[8] But the Greek adds a correlative, ἢ προσπορευομένων ὑμῶν πρὸς τὸ θυσιαστήριον "or when you would be approaching the altar." This shows how well the translator knew the Biblical regulations. At Exod 30:20 and 38:27 in the context of the priests entering the tent of testimony the correlative ἢ ὅταν προσπορεύωνται πρὸς τὸ θυσιαστήριον λειτουργεῖν occurs. The translator added the correlative as an important corrective to the defective limitation of MT as a single condition for abstinence on the part of priests. Hex has placed the entire correlative structure under the obelus.

The concluding nominal structure also occurs at 6:18 7:26; see particularly the comment at 6:18.

10:10 The verse begins with an infinitive and must modify the nominal structure ending the preceding verse. I would now remove the colon after ὑμῶν at the end of v.9, and would translate: "It is a perpetual obligation throughout your generations to distinguish between holy and profane things and between unclean and clean matters." MT has a *waw* before the marked infinitive, as do Sam and Tar,

---

7. See SS 73.
8. See THGL 125.

which I would render by "even."⁹ Hex has added καί at the beginning of the verse to represent the *waw*.

MT has all the nouns in the singular, but LXX makes them all plural. Since the reference is to distinguishing, the plural is more specific. Rather than differentiating between abstractions, "the holy and the profane" and "the unclean and the clean," the Greek by means of the plural is concrete; one must distinguish between holy and profane things, between unclean and clean things. LXX in good Greek style does not repeat the ἀνὰ μέσον before the second of each pair of nouns, but in the tradition these are supplied, before "the profane things" by Byz, and before "clean things" by the majority text. The terms τῶν βεβήλων/החול occur only here in the Pentateuch. Here it serves as an antonym for τῶν ἁγίων. Since holy things or persons are separated from that which is common or ordinary, and are set aside for sacred use, that which is βεβήλων is not thus consecrated; it is profane, common.

10:11 MT begins with a marked infinitive coordinate with the infinitive with which v.10 begins, ולהורת "and to teach." LXX retains the initial conjunction, but changes the infinitive to a finite, future verb, καὶ συμβιβάσεις "and you must teach, instruct." The majority text has a recensional text of some kind, συμβιβαζειν, probably Byz in origin.¹⁰ The verb is modified by a double accusative, one of person τοὺς υἱοὺς Ἰσραήλ, and one of things πάντα τὰ νόμιμα "all the obligations"; this is the usual rendering for חקות/חקים, particularly in Lev (25 out of 35 times).

These νόμιμα are defined as all those "which the Lord spoke to them (i.e. to the Israelites) through Moses." The final prepositional phrase renders ביד משה of MT, in which ביד simply means "by means of." Presumably what is intended is all the legal materials in the book. Note the frequency of such orders to Moses as "Speak to the Israelites (or Aaron) and say to them," as e.g. 1:2.

10:12 In the opening clause MT states that Moses spoke "to Aaron and to Eleazar and to Ithamar, his sons." For εἶπεν rendering ידבר see comment at v.9. The

---

9. GK's explanation of the verse as "an explanatory addition to the command contained in verse 9b" (114p) is most confusing; probably it was v.9a that was meant. He also adds "but probably the text has been disturbed by a redactor." Why redactors should always write odd Hebrew remains a mystery to me.
10. Aq and Sym(vid) translate by φωτίζειν.

preposition אֶל is repeated for each of the addressees in typical Hebrew fashion. In LXX πρός occurs before Aaron and Eleazar, but not before Ithamar. One would expect only one preposition, and I am sceptical about the originality of the second πρός. The scepticism is enhanced by the fact that Syh has an asterisk before καὶ πρὸς (᾽Ελεαζάρ), and I suspect that the asterisk should be after the καί (in Syh "and to" is wlwt, and the asterisk is on top of the first letter). I would now remove this πρός from the critical text. In the tradition, a popular reading added προς before ᾽Ιθαμάρ; this is probably hex in origin. Also recensional, though not hex, is the change of ᾽Ααρών to αυτου by the majority text, thereby equalling the בניו of MT.

The command given the three is "take the sacrifice which remains of the καρπωμάτων of the Lord." MT has as modifier of the imperative verb אֶת הַמִּנְחָה הַנּוֹתֶרֶת מֵאִשֵּׁי יְהוָה. LXX translates the first three words by τὴν θυσίαν τὴν καταλειφθεῖσαν,[11] an exact rendering of the Hebrew. The preposition which follows, ἀπό for מִן, is partitive,[12] and for καρπωμάτων as translation for אשי see comment at 2:9.[13]

The next clause is coordinate to the preceding one, but with a future verb φάγεσθε for the Hebrew imperative וְאִכְלוּהָ. A variant text adds αυτην, thereby rendering the suffix; the reading is probably hex in origin. A majority M reading changes the verb to the imperative φαγετε. This does equal MT more precisely, but I suspect it is a stylistic change to make it more compatible with the coordinate imperative λάβετε.[14] The verb is modified by the accusative ἄζυμα which probably could refer to the καρπώματα of the preceding clause, i.e. what is to be eaten are (some of) the unleavened καρπώματα. Also possible is a reference to θυσίαν, with incongruent number and gender. Lev does use the neuter, either singular or plural, in cases where no clear antecedent is present.[15] The priestly portion is defined elsewhere as that which remains of the θυσίας at 2:3 6:16, and see also 6:40. That this is to be eaten παρὰ τὸ θυσιαστήριον is said only here; elsewhere it is located "in a holy place," as in v.13. For ἄγια ἁγίων see com-

---

11. Aq translates by τὸ δῶρον τὸ περισσευθέν.
12. See SS 165.
13. Aq has ἀπὸ πυρῶν, whereas Sym has a singular noun πυροῦ (retroverted from Syh). Both apparently think of אשה as a wheat sacrifice.
14. See comment at THGL 128.
15. See Huber 34, where, however, it is thought to refer to the feast of unleavened cakes.

ments at 2:3 and 6:17. In MT this is a כי clause, and hex has placed a οτι under the asterisk to introduce it.

10:13 For the first clause see comments at 6:16; the holy place was already defined in v.12 as being "beside the altar." The reason for this is given in a γάρ clause: "because this is due to you and due to your sons ἀπὸ τῶν καρπωμάτων of the Lord." νομιμόν here means "legal right, due." The unusual position of the subject, τοῦτο, after "your sons" imitates MT. The ἀπό is partitive,[16] and for καρπωμάτων as rendering for אשי see comment at 2:9.[17]

The final clause is another γάρ clause. In MT its equivalent כי clause consists of כן plus a Pu צויתי: "For so I was commanded." LXX has rendered this by an active verb plus μοι, thus "for so he commanded me." Since κυρίου occurs immediately before the phrase "from the sacrifice of the Lord," the subject is obviously the Lord; in fact, most witnesses have added κυριος, although it is quite otiose.[18] The change to an active construction makes clear the source of the command; it is the Lord who gave the orders.

10:14 According to MT the breast of the תנופה and the thigh of the תרומה were also allotted to the priests for food. For תנופה see comment at 7:20.[19] Here it is translated by ἀφόρισμα; the word occurs four times in Lev (also twice in v.15 and at 14:12), and it only renders תנופה. The word itself refers to something set aside. For ἀφαιρέματος see comment at 7:20, as something taken away, a dedicated portion. Precisely what the distinction between the two words, ἀφόρισμα and ἀφαίρεμα, was to the translator is not obvious. I suspect that the two were thought to be synonyms. For βραχίονα translating שוק see comment at 7:22. The place in which the breast and the shoulder were to be eaten is ἐν τόπῳ ἁγίῳ, which is a leveling with v.13; here MT reads במקום טהור, i.e. in a place that is ritually clean. Of course, a holy place would be ritually clean, but every clean place need not be holy. The change in LXX does alter the law by restricting the place where the ἀφόρισμα and the ἀφαίρεμα may be eaten. In MT they may be eaten in any ritually clean place, but not so in LXX. A holy place means at the

---

16. See SS 166.
17. For the translation of אשה in the Pentateuch see Daniel 155—164.
18. See THGL 107.
19. For the variety of its renderings in LXX see THGL 72.

sanctuary, and since the partakers are not limited to priests, presumably it was before the door(s) of the tabernacle. Those who might eat these portions are not only the priests, but include ὁ οἶκός σου μετὰ σοῦ.[20] The reference to "your household" has no support in MT, which has ובנתיך "and your daughters." In the earlier reference to the portions to be assigned from the sacrifice for deliverance, 7:21—24, the recipients are Aaron and his sons; no mention is made either of "daughters" or of "household," and no obvious reason for the change appears. It should be noted that in the next verse "your daughters" does appear in LXX. It is of course possible that καὶ ὁ οἶκός σου had a textual basis, i.e. that instead of ובנתיך the parent text read וביתך, but it is equally possible that the translator simply misread it.

The dues were given from the θυσιῶν τοῦ σωτηρίου. These constituted the זבחי שלמי of the Israelites. τοῦ σωτηρίου is the regular rendering for the plural שלמים. The word שלמים occurs 29 times in the book, and always as the free element in a bound phrase. It is, however, always rendered by the singular word, though here the majority F M text does have των σωτηριων; that this is a secondary text is unquestioned.[21] For the regulations concerning these sacrifices see ch. 4.

10:15 The two parts of the sacrifice mentioned in v.14 recur here, but in reverse order in imitation of MT. The verb is also in third person plural, and its subject is the τῶν υἱῶν Ἰσραήλ at the end of v.14. They must bring these parts besides (ἐπί) the sacrifices of the fat pieces ἀφόρισμα ἀφορίσαι. This translates להניף תנופה, for which phrase see the discussion at 7:20. Hex has transposed the words to equal the order of MT. I would translate the structure as "to set aside a separate portion." The infinitive is purposive, and reflects the reason why the Israelites must bring these portions. The phrase ἐπὶ τῶν καρπωμάτων τῶν στεάτων renders על אשי החלבים, and must mean "besides the sacrifices of the fat pieces."

The next clause has as its verb ἔσται, and the subject is ἀφόρισμα of the preceding clause. The separate portion will be for you, as well as for your sons and daughters with you as a νομιμὸν αἰώνιον, i.e. a perpetual due or obligation. LXX follows the Sam text in reading καὶ τοῖς θυγατράσιν σου. Hex quite cor-

---

20. For φάγεσθε ... σὺ καί .... see SS 72.
21. See the discussion at THGL 117—118.

rectly placed this under the obelus, since it is absent from MT. Incidentally, Syh once again omits the structure to equal MT.

The ὃν τρόπον clause has added an indirect object, τῷ Μωυσῇ, to modify συνέταξεν. It has no counterpart in MT, and is an ad sensum gloss ex par.

10:16 For the "goat of the sin offering" see 9:3,15. The verb דרש is rendered by ἐξεζήτησεν, but the accompanying cognate free infinitive, by the simplex participle ζητῶν. It nonetheless simply serves to intensify the verbal notion of the verb, i.e. "made a thorough search." The structure shows that there is very little semantic difference between the simplex and the compounds here. An ƒ+ variant regularized the construction by unnecessarily changing the verb to the simplex as well, εζητησεν.

In the second clause, ὅδε is used to render הנה. The pronoun refers to τὸν χίμαρον, thus "and this had been burned up."[22] Particularly appropriate in the context is the use of the pluperfect: "it had (already) been burned up."

The subject of ἐθυμώθη is given as Μωυσῆς, though it is absent from MT, since it is quite unnecessary in view of the משה of the preceding clause; hex placed it under the obelus. The anger was directed against Eleazar and Ithamar, with the preposition repeated in MT in accordance with normal Hebrew usage with the second name as well, but not so in the Greek.

10:17 Moses' question is: "Why did you not eat the sin offering ἐν τόπῳ ἁγίῳ"? For the regulation concerning the eating of the sin offering by the priests see 6:26,29. The prepositional phrase is identical with v.13, but MT differs. Here the phrase is a bound phrase במקום הקדש "in the area of the sanctuary." The consonantal text could also be understood as "in the holy place," i.e. the place designated as "the holy place." LXX, however, always translates the phrase as unarticulated (12 times), regardless of the Hebrew; obviously ἐν τόπῳ ἁγίῳ is then a defined place. For the definition of "a holy place," see comment at 6:16, and comp also v.26; in both verses it is located ἐν αὐλῇ τῆς σκηνῆς τοῦ μαρτυρίου. For ἅγιον ἁγίων see comment at 2:3 and comp also 6:17.

Odd is the double translation of כי by ὅτι γάρ, a combination occurring nowhere else in the Pentateuch. The γάρ must be taken as a kind of asseverative which would be quite appropriate here: "For indeed it is very holy."

---

22. Theod and Aq have the usual word for הנה, ἰδού.

MT introduces v.b with ואתה "and it," but the Greek omits the conjunction with its τοῦτο. In the LXX τοῦτο is followed by ἔδωκεν ὑμῖν φαγεῖν. The Hebrew has no equivalent for the infinitive, which the translator added for clarification. In the Hebrew "and it he gave to you" is immediately followed by a marked infinitive showing purpose, לשאת את עון העדה, which is then in turn followed by another marked infinitive, לכפר עליהם לפני יהוה. The relation between the two infinitives is not stated, and I would take the second structure as appositive, thus "to remove ..., i.e. to make atonement." The second structure is more specific, informing the reader "how to remove." LXX renders the first infinitive by a ἵνα clause: "in order that you might remove τὴν ἁμαρτίαν of the congregation." The ἁμαρτίαν refers to the guilt involved in ἁμαρτία, as the Hebrew also indicates by its עון. What is said is that the priests must eat the sin offering in order thereby to expiate the sin, i.e. remove the guilt, of the people.

The second infinitive is rendered by a coordinate clause also governed by the ἵνα particle: "and you might make atonement concerning them before the Lord." By adding καί at the beginning, the two clauses constitute a twofold purpose to the Lord's giving you the sin offering to eat. Neither MT nor LXX give a clue as to how the priests' eating the sin offering effects the removal of the people's guilt, and various speculations obtain among commentators.[23]

10:18 LXX does not render the particle הן, but makes the clause an independent γάρ clause, i.e. "For not was there brought in (any) of its blood into the sanctuary." This differs from MT, which probably means "since there was not brought in ...." The genitive τοῦ αἵματος must be taken as a partitive, and it constitutes the subject of the passive verb. For a parallel construction, see the relative clause at 6:30.

Problematic is the syntactic position of κατὰ πρόσωπον ἔσω "over against, inside." In MT only פנימה occurs, and the Masoretes have put it under an *ethnach*. According to that understanding, the collocation must modify what precedes, i.e. εἰσήχθη. What MT says is: "since none of its blood was brought in inside the sanctuary." But it can also be taken with what follows, i.e. with φάγεσθε, and I consider that to have been intended by the translator. What follows is only a free rendering of MT which reads "you must surely eat it in the sanctuary

---

23. E.g. Milgrom 635–640.

as I commanded." LXX deviates from MT in three further respects; it has disregarded the free infinitive אכול, possibly because of homoiarchon;[24] it has changed בקדש to level with vv.14,17 as ἐν τόπῳ ἁγίῳ, and צויתי has been changed, probably for theological correctness to μοι συνέταξεν κύριος. The stress has been removed from eating by overlooking the free infinitive in favor of the preposed κατὰ πρόσωπον ἔσω. What LXX has done is to amplify the place of eating by adding κατὰ πρόσωπον to ἔσω, i.e. as "opposite," or "over against" inside. By adding κατὰ πρόσωπον LXX localizes the "inside" the sanctuary to that place which is over against where the congregation is assembled in front of the door(s).

In the tradition, a cognate noun has been added before φάγεσθε under the asterisk to represent the free infinitive of MT. In the ὃν τρόπον clause the majority text not only omits κύριος, but also changes the active συνέταξεν to a passive συνεταγη. That the variant text is secondary is clear from the changes made. The μοι was obviously there from the beginning, though it has no actual counterpart in MT. To conform to MT the κύριος had to be omitted, but this required a further change in the voice of the verb.[25]

10:19 The translator has added λέγων to introduce the actual words of Aaron over against MT. Hex has apparently omitted the marker to conform to MT. Aaron's defence before Moses begins with a conditional particle εἰ introducing three clauses, with the apodosis reading μὴ ἀρεστὸν ἔσται κυρίῳ. The first verb is in the indefinite plural, i.e. "if today they have brought." The same indefinite reference occurs in the two cases of αὐτῶν, and must refer to worshipers in general. One might paraphrase the structure by saying "if people have today brought their sin offerings and their guilt offerings before the Lord," i.e. to the sanctuary.

The second condition is in the aorist: καὶ συμβέβηκέν μοι ταῦτα "and these things happened to me." The Hebrew is somewhat different, reading a plural verb with the phrase כאלה serving as subject, thus "things such as these had overtaken me."[26] What ταῦτα refers to is undoubtedly the sudden death of his two sons detailed in vv.1—7. The singular verb of LXX is congruent with the neuter plural subject ταῦτα.

---

24. See THGL 111.
25. See THGL 107.
26. For the number of the verb see SS 197. For a general discussion of the construction of the verb with a neuter plural subject in the Pentateuch see *idem* 189—199.

The third condition is in the future, a future which is relative to the perfect and aorist verbal notions which all took place earlier today. "And I would eat the sin offerings today." Only then does the interrogative apodosis make sense: "would it be pleasing to the Lord?"

It should be noted that MT has vocalized all three references to sacrifices, חטאתם, עלתם and הטאת, as singulars, but the consonantal text would also allow for plural pronunciations. The τά for the sin offerings has in both cases been changed to το with substantial support, and since the usual supporters of hex are part of it, these may well be hex. A majority F M text, including O', has τοιαυτα instead of ταῦτα, which may constitute a hex attempt to render כאלה more closely.

10:20 The Hebrew וייטב בעיניו "And it seemed good in his eyes" is well-rendered by καὶ ἤρεσεν αὐτῷ "and it pleased him," i.e. he was satisfied with Aaron's defence.

Chapter 11

11:1 LXX is shorter than MT. As usual it does not repeat the preposition πρός before the second coordinate noun, 'Ααρών, and hex has added the preposition under the asterisk. MT has an unusual אלהם after לאמר, which LXX does not recognize, and again hex has intervened by adding an equivalent πρὸς αυτους under the asterisk to represent it.

11:2 LXX makes no distinction between החיה, τὰ κτήνη and בהמה, τῶν κτηνῶν. The Greek correctly understood the terms as collectives. The future φάγεσθε is clearly permissive; what is meant is "these are the animals which you may eat." The ἀπό which follows is partitive.[1]

11:3 This verse defines the characteristics of clean animals. MT lacks the generic term for animal (though בבהמה does occur later in the verse), and hex has placed κτῆνος under the obelus to indicate that lack. The first condition is that the animal should have a split hoof, διχηλοῦν ὁπλήν. The second puts this into a more detailed form: ὀνυχιστῆρας ὀνυχίζων δύο χηλῶν "splitting hooves into two claws." Apparently what is meant is that the hoof is not simply split, but that the result is two distinct parts. The word δύο is based on Sam's שתי which BHS lacks.[2] The third condition is that it brings up the cud. MT lacks a conjunction before the third condition, but LXX does have a καί (supported also by Pesh and Vulg). The conditions are followed by ἐν τοῖς κτήνεσιν, which parallels the ἀπὸ πάντων τῶν κτηνῶν τῶν ἐπὶ τῆς γῆς of v.2. MT concludes with אתה תאכלו "it you may eat"; LXX has the pronoun ταῦτα, i.e. a plural ad sensum.

11:4 So too instead of את זה "this one," LXX makes it plural, contextually making it a prepositional phrase in view of the מן construction which follows, thus πλὴν ἀπὸ τούτων "only from these (may you not eat)." The definition of the τούτων has the three conditions repeated in the plural, though in the order 3 - 1 - 2, with the last one shortened to καὶ ὀνυχιζόντων ὀνυχιστῆρας.[3] The text is taken

---

1. See SS 165.
2. But Kenn 157* 185, 193, 382, 411, 416*, 448 and 574 do have שתי. It is also present in the parallel Deut 14:6 passage.
3. That ἀπό is partitive is obvious; see SS 161.

over word for word from its parallel Deut 14:7. The last one, however, has no equivalent in MT, which has only the two, nos. 3 and 1. Admittedly conditions one and two are roughly the same, the second one explaining the first one in greater detail. Hex has placed the last construction under the obelus. It should be noted that the conditions are of two kinds; this is shown by the fine use of ἀπό. What is meant by the verse is: "only from these you may not eat: (either) from those that only bring up the cud, or from those that only split hooves and have the hooves cloven." I have interpreted καί 1° as "or," and added "only" in both phrases. The context demands these, since the animals in the list that follows lack one of the necessary conditions, but have the other one.

The first animal which does not fulfill all the conditions is τὸν κάμηλον. On the positive side τοῦτο is a ruminant.[4] Negatively—note the use of the contrastive δέ—"the hoof he does not split." In MT this is a nominal clause פרסה אינו מפריס, and LXX renders the participle by a present tense διχηλεῖ.

The conclusion is a nominal clause in which the predicate is adjectival, ἀκάθαρτον τοῦτο ὑμῖν.[5] Here too the personal pronoun הוא is rendered by the demonstrative in LXX.

11:5—6 In turn the δασύποδα and the χοιρογρύλλιον are declared unclean in exactly the same terms as for the camel in v.4, except that the contrastive δέ became καί in both verses. MT differs, however, in that the negative clauses in vv.5 and 6 are not nominal, but verbal with a Hi prefix verb as predicate. The LXX rendering, however, does not recognize the distinction, following the pattern laid down in v.4.

For δασύποδα and χοιρογρύλλιον see Note at Deut 14:7, probably the "daman" and the "hare"; here they represent שפן and ארנבת resp., but in the parallel Deut passage ארנבת and שפן resp. One suspects that the Alexandrians were not too certain of their rabbits.[6] The term χοιρογρύλλιον also renders שפן at Ps 103:18 and Prov 30:26, but δασύποδα occurs only here and in the parallel Deut passage.

---

4. For the pronoun as subject see SS 82.
5. See SS 79.
6. Aq has λαγωόν as translation of שפן. The Greek term occurs only once in OT, at Ps 103:18. Possibly the word was avoided so as not to offend the Lagid house; see the discussion in Harlé-Pralon ad loc.

11:7 The pig is unclean for the opposite reason. It both splits the hoof and ὀνυχίζει ὄνυχας ὁπλῆς, "cleaves the claws of the hoof," with which comp the parallel phrase in v.3. Over against this it does not ἀνάγει μηρυκισμόν, though MT has גרה לא יגר, "the cud he does not chew." MT has the cognate verb גרר and inflects it. LXX disregarded the change, simply taking over the structure from v.3 with which it levels. Origen noted that the noun preceded the verb and reordered it as μυρικισμον ουκ αναγει, but made no further change in hex. The pig then is also ἀκάθαρτον ὑμῖν.

11:8 The verse reflects on what their uncleanness involves; it explains this by two prohibitions: a) ἀπὸ τῶν κρεῶν αὐτῶν you may not eat. The ἀπό is partitive,[7] and the αὐτῶν applies to the various tetrapods mentioned which are unclean. τῶν κρεῶν translates בשר, but in the plural, since it is dressed meat which is involved. An *f*+ text has changed the αὐτῶν to the singular αυτου. This would make the prohibition apply only to the pig, which could not have been intended. b) Their carcasses you must not touch, for which see comment at 5:2.

11:9 Vv.9—12 detail the regulations concerning creatures that live in the waters. First, the conditions that describe those that may be eaten are given. MT put this in a preposed singular modifier: את זה, which LXX renders by καὶ ταῦτα. For the conjunction LXX follows Sam;[8] what it says is "and these you may eat ἀπό all those which are en τοῖς ὕδασιν. The A B *n* text has written the final letter of ταῦτα twice, thereby reading ταυτα α; this is simply a case of dittography.[9] The ἀπό is of course a partitive.[10] These necessary characteristics for edible aquatic creatures are πτερύγια "fins" and λεπίδες "scales." The ἐστιν αὐτοῖς illustrates one of the ways in which "to have" is rendered by LXX. The αὐτοῖς is a dative of possession, and reflects the Hebrew use of the resumptive pronoun within a relative clause.[11] The word במים occurs twice in the verse, and is translated by the plural (ἐν) τοῖς ὕδασιν. The noun is sometimes translated by the plural and sometimes by the singular in the book. The plural "waters" is used only with ref-

---

7. See SS 161.
8. Kenn 105ᶜ 129 also read ואת.
9. See THGL 107 for comment.
10. See SS 167; this is also the case in v.10.
11. R.Sollamo's rendering: "All those that are for them" is awkward, and does not communicate what the Greek intends; see Greenspoon—Munnich 48.

erence to the home of aquatic life;[12] otherwise it is always singular. In MT במים is defined by בימים ובנחלים, i.e. "waters" are either "seas" or "streams." The translator, by adding καί before "in the seas," has changed the meaning; aquatic creatures live "in the waters and in seas and in streams." Hex has rightly placed the first καί under the obelus to show its lack of correspondence in MT.

11:10 What is not to be eaten are aquatic creatures without fins and scales. In MT these are located בימים ובנחלים. For the relation between these and במים see the comment at v.9. But LXX follows Sam by having ἐν τοῖς ὕδασιν precede the two as in v.9. The translator, however, made clear the relation between genus and species by introducing "in the seas," not by καί, but by ἤ, thus "in the waters, ἤ in the seas καί in the streams"; i.e. he maintained the distinction discussed for MT at v.9. Hex placed "in the waters" under the obelus, and omitted ἤ. For the secondary nature of the A B x+ text's change to the singular, τω υδατι, see comment at v.9.

For ἀπό 1° see comment at v.9. In MT כל שרץ is nominal, "all swarming things," but the translator took שרץ as a verb, which the consonantal text permits, forcing him to translate by a relative clause ὧν ἐρεύγεται τὰ ὕδατα "which the waters produce." The verb usually has the notion of spouting, belching, and was probably chosen to define the notion of swarming, since שרץ includes not just creatures which live in the waters, but also such creatures as insects which swarm near the waters, and may have been thought to be the product of the waters. The translation is unique in the OT; in fact, this ἐρεύγεται is a hapax legomenon in OT. Whether this verb is related to another ἐρεύγεται meaning "to roar," which does occur a number of times in OT, is uncertain.

Such are not declared unclean, as in v.8, but βδέλυγμά ἐστιν, for which MT has שקץ הם לכם. One might have expected a plural construction in view of the הם, but the translator probably took over the number of the nearer possible reference, ψυχῆς ζώσης "living creature." The addition of καὶ ἀπὸ πάσης ψυχῆς ζώσης as a coordinate to the first ἀπό phrase is intended to cover any aquatic creatures which might not have been covered by the phrase "all those which the waters produce," such as mysterious creatures like sea monsters of some sort. Hex has added υμιν at the end to represent the untranslated לכם.

---

12. See THGL 118.

11:11 The last clause of v.10 in MT is repeated at the beginning, but as a verbal, not as a nominal clause. The difference is reflected in the Greek by καὶ βδελύγματα ἔσονται ὑμῖν, i.e. it is not a simple statement of fact, but it has become a regulation for the future; the reference is now to the πάντων of v.10.[13] The two clauses cover both the present (ἐστιν) and the future (ἔσται), and could be read together, but note the change in number; this means that the second one is regulatory.

What this involves for the people is that they may not eat any of their meat (the ἀπό is partitive[14]), and must abominate their corpses. The verb βδελύσσω as a rendering for the verb שקץ occurs only in Lev (also at vv.13,43 and 20:25), and is always modified by an accusative. The verb "abominate" really means "to treat as a βδέλυγμα."[15]

11:12 This verse is an abbreviated version of v.10, omitting all but the actual statement of principle that everything which lacks fins or scales τῶν ἐν τοῖς ὕδασιν, an abomination τοῦτο is ὑμῖν. The genitive τῶν is used to summarize all things which were detailed in v.10 as being in the waters. Over against v.10 where הם occurred, MT has הוא, which became τοῦτό ἐστιν, and also in contrast to v.10 the לכם was translated here. For details see comments at v.10.

11:13 Vv.13—20 detail a list of unclean πετεινῶν. The verse begins with an accusative καὶ ταῦτα modifying βδελύξασθε. The next two clauses have singular predicates with the ταῦτα as neuter plural subject:[16] "not shall these be eaten (βρωθήσεταί)," and "these are (ἐστιν) an abomination."

With τὸν ἀετόν begins the list of 20 flying creatures (vv.13b—19) all in apposition with ταῦτα. The first three are also the first three in the parallel list of Deut 14:12. In both lists the nouns are articulated. In MT all 20 members of the list are preceded by את, and these in turn are usually preceded by a conjunction. In Deut only ten are preceded by את, and all but one are articulated, only כל ערב lacking an article. In both lists in LXX only the first five are articulated, but in

---

13. See SS 197.
14. See SS 161.
15. Milgrom 656—659 makes the interesting observation that "an abomination" can only defile by ingestion, whereas "an impurity" can also defile by physical contact.
16. See SS 197.

both lists all are connected by conjunctions (καί). For ἀετόν, γρύπα and ἁλιάετον, all vultures of some kind, equalling resp ישר, פרס and עזניה, see Notes at Deut 14:12.

11:14 V.14a is repeated word for word in Deut 14:13, and presumably equals MT of Lev, whereas the Hebrew of Deut has been expanded, and probably corrupted in part. For v.a see Notes at Deut 14:13. I would suggest that MT of Lev is parent text for both Greek texts. As in Deut למינו is translated by καὶ τὰ ὅμοια αὐτῷ; in fact, throughout the list τὰ ὅμοια αὐτῷ is always preceded by the conjunction, for which see Note at Deut 14:13 as well.[17]

V.b has its parallel in Deut 14:14a; see Note ad loc. In MT of both lists כל ערב obtains, but in Deut the verse begins with ואת, and in Leviticus, with את.[18]

11:15 For στρουθόν, γλαῦκα, λάρον as renderings for בת היענה, תחמס, שחף resp. see Notes at Deut 14:14. The word στρουθόν is usually a smaller bird than the ostrich (בת היענה), but how much an urban dweller in Alexandria knew about these birds is quite uncertain. Over against MT, λάρον "a gull(?)" is followed by καὶ τὰ ὅμοια αὐτῷ; this has no correspondent in MT, neither here nor in Deut in both MT and LXX. Hex has put it under the obelus, indicating its absence in MT.

11:16 This verse lists only "the hawk (κόρακα/נץ) and its kind." Its exact equivalent is the last item in Deut 14:14. See Note ad loc.

11:17 From here on the two lists differ considerably. The first bird is the νυκτικόρακα "night-raven," for which the correspondent in MT is הכוס, which appears as the first item in Deut 14:16, where it is rendered by ἐρωδιόν, but it is usually thought to be the "little owl." כוס also occurs at Ps 102:7, where it is also rendered by νυκτικόραξ (dwelling ἐν οἰκοπέδῳ).

The second is καταράκτην, possibly a "cormorant"; at least it is some kind of bird that swoops down. Its equivalent in MT is השלך, which may also mean "cormorant." In Deut 14:16 its correspondent is the קאת or "pelican," whereas השלך in the following verse is rendered by νυκτικόρακα. The last one is ἴβιν,

---

17. For this free rendering throughout, see SS 98.
18. But 12 Kenn mss as well as Sam read ואת.

rendering ינשוף, possibly the large owl. In Deut it renders תנשמת, another kind of owl; see Note at Deut 14:15.

11:18 Three more birds are listed: πορφυρίωνα, πελεκᾶνα, κυκνόν "purple coot, pelican, swan." These represent resp תנשמת of uncertain meaning, possibly a member of the owl family, קאת "pelican," and רחם also uncertain; see Note at Deut 14:15.[19] In Deut all three Greek terms do occur, but their Hebrew equivalents are דוכיפת, חסידה and ינשוף. It is clear that the Alexandrian translators were as confused about these terms as moderns are. Origen transposed πορφυρίωνα and κυκνόν in the hex, but I doubt whether this reflects real ornithological knowledge on his part.

11:19 Four more types of birds are given: 1) ἐρωδιόν "heron" for חסידה "stork"; 2) χαραδριόν occurs in both lists for אנפה, probably some kind of heron; the two terms occur only in these two lists; the χαραδριόν was considered very greedy.[20] 3) ἔποπα "hoopoe" for MT's דוכיפת of uncertain meaning; it was rendered by πορφυρίωνα in Deut, for which see comment at v.18. The ἔποψ also occurs at Zach 5:9 for חסידה. 4) νυκτερίδα "bat" for עטלף "bat," occurring in both lists. The terms also occur at Isa 2:20, and the meaning "bat" is assured.

In the tradition, a fifth is added to the list at the beginning. The A B F+ gloss reads καὶ γλαυκα; it has no support in MT, and is taken from v.14 where it renders תחמס in both lists. In spite of its uncial support it is clearly secondary.[21]

11:20 LXX follows Sam in reading a conjunction at the beginning of the verse, whereas MT does not.[22] Accordingly, hex placed the καί under the obelus. The conjunction is also attested in Tar[JP] and Pesh. The noun שרץ is always rendered by ἕρπετα, except at v.10 where it was understood as a verb; see comment ad loc. Since ἕρπετα is modified by τῶν πετεινῶν, "insects" are probably intended, thus "flying insects." The ἕρπετα are also modified by a relative clause, ἃ πορεύεται ἐπὶ τεσσάρων. Since the verb represents the participle הלך, the present tense indicating usual action is used. The clause occurs in v.21 as well, and in the

---
19. Milgrom 663 suggests "white owl, scops owl, osprey" for the three birds resp.
20. See LS sub χαραδριός.
21. For a discussion of this gloss see THGL 107—108.
22. Kenn 132, 181 do read וכל for כל.

tradition for both verses, A B x+ read the accusative τεσσαρα (or -ερα).²³ The subject of ἐστιν in the last clause must be ἕρπετα, with βδελύγματα as predicate nominative.

11:21 Characteristic of insects which, ἀλλά (however), may be eaten, by way of exception to the rule of v.20. They are described by a relative clause: ἃ ἔχει σκέλη ἀνώτερον τῶν ποδῶν αὐτοῦ πηδᾶν ἐν αὐτοῖς ἐπὶ τῆς γῆς. The verb ἔχει is a free rendering of לא read as לו,²⁴ i.e. "to it there are." σκέλη means "legs," but here it renders כרעים. These are ממעל לרגליו, i.e. "above its feet." The word σκέλη occurs once elsewhere in OT for כרעים; at Am 3:12 reference is made to snatching two σκέλη from the mouth of a lion. "Legs above the feet" must refer to the legs above the knee joints joined to the feet. What is presumably meant is legs in two parts, so probably σκέλη might be translated "jointed legs." The σκέλη is further modified by a purposive infinitive, πηδᾶν ἐν αὐτοῖς "to jump, hop with them," thus "with which to hop."²⁵

In the tradition, τῶν πετεινῶν is preceded by παντων in hex to make up for the כל שרץ of MT. The b t+ text has changed αὐτοῦ to αυτων; this is a rationalizing change, since the reference is to ἑρπετῶν.

11:22 LXX supplies an initial καί, whereas MT continues asyndetically with את אלה. The καί is omitted by n, but this need not be recensional. LXX has the more common order of verb plus prepositional phrase, though MT has מהם תאכלו. Hex has reordered φάγεσθε ἀπ' αὐτῶν to agree with the order of MT.

Four kinds of hopping insects are listed, each one followed by καὶ τὰ ὅμοια αὐτῷ, for which see comment at v.14. The first of these is ארבה, translated by βροῦχον. Both terms refer to some kind of locust. It has been conjectured that ארבה reflects the root רבה, hence locusts which swarm in large numbers.²⁶

The second type is ἀττάκην for the Hebrew סלעם. Both terms are hapax legomena, and all that can be said about these is that they are some kind of locust. This is followed by ἀκρίδα for חרגל. ἀκρίς is the common word for

---

23. For a defence of the genitive as original see the discussion in THGL 121—122.
24. See SS 182; the לא must be a misspelling; in fact, לו is actually the Qere reading.
25. The ἐν is instrumental; see SS 119.
26. Theod and Aq read πολύν, which does reflect an understanding of רבה as source for ארבה. Some s readings suggest Sym and Theod as the ones reading πολύν, but the attributions of M′ are on the whole more trustworthy than those of the s group.

locust, and is the usual translation of ארבה; see above. The Hebrew חרגל is a hapax legomenon; in Syriac the word apparently refers to a wingless locust. The last type is חגב, about which nothing is known, except that it was destructive, and so considered a curse upon the land. It is translated by the hapax legomenon ὀφιομάχην; what kind of locust this referred to is also unknown; the compound consists of two parts: "snake" and "battle;" but how this characterizes grasshoppers is a mystery.

11:23 MT begins with וכל, but LXX, without a conjunction.[27] In the tradition, a popular F M reading did add a και, but the oldest mss do not, and in such cases it seems wise to follow the texts of A B+.[28] The verse is a singular variant of v.20. It also changes the relative clause, as does MT. At v.20 MT read ההלך, which LXX translated by ἃ πορεύεται. Here MT has אשר לו, which the Greek renders by οἷς ἐστιν, with the relative referring to πετεινῶν, rather than as in v.20 to ἕρπετα. A majority variant tradition changed ἐστιν to εισιν; this is a grammatical correction in view of the subject τέσσαρες πόδες, but incongruity in number does occur quite often in Lev.[29]

Of such a ἑρπετόν it is said βδέλυγμα ὑμῖν ἐστιν. For the notion of βδέλυγμα vs ἀκαθαρτός see footnote at v.11. At vv.12,20 Lev read ἐστιν ὑμῖν, but here the order goes against MT's הוא לכם. Hex has changed the order to conform to that of the Hebrew. Incidentally the text of cod B followed the hex order, but this may simply be due to the influence of the more common order.[30]

11:24 LXX begins with (καὶ) ἐν τούτοις which correctly interprets the ולאלה of MT. I would take ἐν to be used instrumentally, i.e. "by these you would defile yourselves." The pronoun is proleptic, and covers the cases which follow in vv.24b—28 (or 40). In the tradition, the b y+ text renders the verb negative by ου. This is based on a failure to realize the proleptic nature of τούτοις, and understanding the pronoun to refer to the four types of locust of v.22.

The first of these is given in v.b: "anyone who touches their carcasses shall be (ritually) unclean until evening." The antecendent of αὐτῶν is the locusts

---

27. Kenn 129, 150 do read וכל for כל.
28. See THGL 100—101.
29. See Huber 37, sect.3.
30. See THGL 103.

referred to in vv.21—23. These may be eaten, but if found dead would render one touching them ἀκάθαρτος. Being ἀκάθαρτος makes one unfit for cultic participation; one is defiled, and such defilement can be communicated to a person by touching something (or someone) unclean. One is thus in a dangerous state, since like a highly communicable disease this can be transmitted to others through contact.

11:25 Another action which renders one cultically impure is carrying any of their carcasses. Again the pronoun refers to the flying insects of vv.21—23. The genitive τῶν θνησιμαίων is partitive, hence the rendering "any of their carcasses."[31] Carrying something which is unclean may well touch one's clothes, hence such a person πλυνεῖ τὰ ἱμάτια. LXX usually does not render the suffix of בגדיו,[32] and a majority F M text, not necessarily, though possibly, hex in origin, has added an αυτου.

11:26 LXX begins with καὶ (ἐν πᾶσιν), though MT's לכל lacks the conjunction. As in the case of v.23 the matter of an initial conjunction is difficult to decide on any exegetical or contextual grounds, and one simply follows the oldest witnesses. Here, as at v.23, a majority reading conforms to MT, by omitting the καί.[33]

The reference in this verse is to κτήνεσιν, for which regulations were outlined in vv.2—8. The word is plural, correctly understanding בהמה as a collective noun. The terms in vv.2—3 referred to tetrapods in general, but here it contrasts with θηρίοις "wild animals" of v.27, and so must refer to domesticated animals, i.e. "cattle." In vv.2—8 cattle which were edible had three characteristics according to v.3. Here "Among all cattle, whatever is διχηλοῦν ὁπλὴν καὶ ὀνυχιστῆρας ὀνυχίζει," both of which are characteristic of edible cattle, and for which see comments at v.3, and lacks the third characteristic, i.e. "does not μαρυκᾶται the cud, they shall be ἀκάθαρτα for you." In vv.3—7 the verb used is ἀνάγει rather than μαρυκᾶται. The verb cognate to μηρυκισμόν occurs only here and at Deut 14:8, though in both cases מעלה obtains, which ἀνάγει would render more accurately. MT differs from LXX in that the second condition is not positive, but

---

31. See SS 161.
32. See SS 97.
33. See THGL 100—101.

negative; i.e. LXX does not translate אינגה; this does make much better sense than MT does.

LXX imitates MT by changing to the plural ἀκάθαρτα ἔσονται ὑμῖν, whereas syntactically it should be singular. The translator does at times display incongruence in number.³⁴

V.b is an exact copy of v.24b; see comment ad loc. From MT it is clear that the translator took over the Greek of v.24, since the בנבלתם of v.24 becomes בהם in v.26. Hex has omitted τῶν θνησιμαίων, thereby equalling MT, but the longer text is original.³⁵ Hex has tried to "correct" the text to equal MT by omitting τῶν θνησιμαίων as well as ἕως ἑσπέρας which also has no counterpart in MT.

11:27 What is here referred to is "everyone that walks on χειρῶν among all wild animals." χειρῶν renders כפיו, and hex has added an αυτου to represent the pronominal suffix. What is meant is wild animals that walk on paws. Such wild animals are also ones which walk ἐπὶ τεσσάρων. In the tradition, A B+ read the accusative τεσσαρα (or -ερα), but the genitive must be original. In the immediately preceding clause ἐπὶ χειρῶν also modified πορεύεται. A translator would hardly have changed cases in the same context in successive relative clauses.³⁶

The last clause is again an exact copy of vv.24b and 26b; see comment at v.24.

11:28 This verse repeats v.25 word for word, but then adds ἀκάθαρτα ταῦτα ὑμῖν ἐστιν as a summary statement for vv.24—28a. The Hebrew is slightly more abrupt than LXX which also adds an ἐστιν at the end; comp similar statements in vv.25,27.

11:29 LXX changes the singular nominal clause which begins the verse to the plural, since it introduces a list of ἑρπετῶν. LXX reads καὶ ταῦτα ὑμῖν ἀκάθαρτα. This does simplify MT's וזה לכם הטמא, in which the predicate adjective is articulated.³⁷ The group to which the ταῦτα refers is described as ἀπὸ τῶν

---

34. See Huber 36, sect.1.a.
35. But Kenn 181, 193, 210 do read בנבלתם for בהם.
36. See THGL 121—122.
37. See THGL 108.

ἑρπετῶν τῶν ἑρπόντων ἐπὶ τῆς γῆς "from the creepers that move about on the ground." The ἀπό represents the preposition ב in MT in the sense of "from." The rendering is fully adequate. Whether the list of unclean ἑρπετῶν is taken "from" or appears "among" makes little difference. These are then listed in v.b and v.30. The first of these is ἡ γαλῆ/החלד "the weasel." This is followed by ὁ μῦς/העכבר "the mouse," and this in turn by ὁ κροκόδιλος ὁ χερσαῖος "the dry land crocodile," probably some kind of large lizard(?). MT has הצב "the lizard." This is followed in MT by למינהו, which is omitted by LXX, and hex added και τα ομοια αυτω to represent it.

11:30 Five more unclean crawlers are listed. Over against MT no initial conjunction obtains in LXX, though the n+ text does begin with a και. In contrast to the three listed in v.29, all five are unarticulated, though MT continues to prefix the article for all in the list. Apparently hex did not attempt to add articles.

The five are 1) μυγαλῆ "field mouse" for the Hebrew האנקה "gecko." Both terms are hapax legomena in OT. 2) χαμαιλέων "chameleon" for הכח which is some type of lizard. 3) καλαβώτης "spotted lizard, gecko." The word also appears as ασκαλαβωτης, which is well-supported in the tradition by C′ Byz s+. The spelling is uncertain. It is a hapax legomenon in OT as is its correspondent in MT, הלטאה, also some kind of lizard. 4) σαύρα "lizard" for החמט, also a member of the lizard family. Both words are hapax legomena in OT. 5) ἀσπάλαξ "blind-rat," a hapax legomenon for התנשמת, hardly to be identified with the תנשמת at v.18, since here it is in the class of שרץ, not of birds. As such it occurs only here, and must be some kind of lizard as well. It should be stressed that for both Hebrew and Greek renderings in English are at best approximations.

Not surprisingly the names of some of these creatures were not fully stable in the language. Thus the Byz text made of μυγαλῆ a compound μυογαλη, as though combining μῦς and γαλῆ of v.29 into a new compound. καλαβώτης gave considerable trouble to copyists, with ασκαλαβωτης favored by the Byz s text, and ακαλαβωτης, by oI. Also unstable was ἀσπάλαξ, with labial variation appearing in ασφαλαξ in C′ s, and aphaeresis producing σπαλαξ in a popular F M text.

11:31 The nominal sentence with which the verse begins is made into a verbal one, either by a popular A F M addition of εστιν after ἀκάθαρτα or by a C′ d εσται, but with demonstrative pronouns זה, זאת or אלה as subject; only once, at 8:5, is the verb "to be" used. The shorter text is almost certainly original here.[38] The ταῦτα refers to the list of unclean creatures presented in vv.29—30. The use of ἀπό (πάντων) may have been occasioned by the מכל of Sam rather than the בכל of MT, but see comment at v.29. LXX defines the ἑρπετῶν as τῶν ἐπὶ τῆς γῆς, possibly under the influence of v.29: (ἑρπετῶν τῶν ἑρπόντων) ἐπὶ τῆς γῆς. In any case, it has no support in MT, and so is placed under the obelus in hex. and omitted by Syh.

V.b is a duplicate of vv.26b,27b, except for the substitution for τῶν θνησιμαίων αὐτῶν by αὐτῶν τεθνηκότων.[39] The majority text, however, changed to των τεθνηκοτων αυτων. The use of the perfect participle here is based on MT's בהם במתם, i.e. "(the one touching) them when they died."

11:32 The principle that touching something unclean renders unclean is explicated further. "Anything on which there has fallen something from them, when they have died, shall be unclean" is the principle to be followed. The preposition in ἀπ' αὐτῶν is understood as partitive.[40] The αὐτῶν is then explicated by τεθνηκότων αὐτῶν. One can compare the translation of במתם in v.31, with that in v.32. In v.31 it was modifying בהם, and in v.32, מהם, but in the latter an extra αὐτῶν appears, and more accurately represents MT by its "from them, they having died."

The πᾶν is then explicated by an ἀπό phrase: "of any wooden vessel or garment or hide or sackcloth." These define that on which something dead has perchance fallen. It will be noted that the list is one of articles made only of organic materials. The term σκεῦος is a calque for the Hebrew כלי, being almost exclusively used to translate כלי (241 out of 250 times).[41] This is further summarized as constituting "any vessel with which work might be done." In MT the Ni verb is modified by בהם. LXX renders this by the singular ἐν αὐτῷ. I would differentiate in translation by rendering כל כלי by "every vessel," which opens the door to being used as referent for a plural pronoun. Furthermore, the Masoretes by placing the בהם under the *ethnach* make the first cut between בהם

---

38. See THGL 108.
39. Theod adopts the LXX text as well.
40. See SS 158, 167.
41. According to the count of Dos Santos.

and יובא; i.e. the structure "any vessel with which work could be performed" is part of v.a, and v.b begins with "it shall be dipped into water." The translator interpreted the text as breaking before כל כלי, i.e. "any vessel with which work would be performed shall be dipped into water." Note also that the ἄν in the relative clause modifying σκεῦος becomes εαν in all the older texts (all the uncials), but this is not original.[42] The verb יובא "shall be brought" is neatly rendered contextually by βαφήσεται "shall be dipped."

The conclusion of the matter is declared as "and it shall be unclean until evening, and (then) it will be clean."

11:33 Unclean clay vessels are to be treated differently. Their uncleanness is occasioned by εἰς ὃ ἂν ἐμπέσῃ ἀπὸ τούτων ἔνδον. The antecedent of the demonstrative is the αὐτῶν of v.32, i.e. "there has fallen inside the vessel something of those things that had died." In the tradition, the verb appears in the simplex form in the A B x+ variant text. The compound verb occurs only here in Lev, but it is original. Throughout this section נפל occurs five times, and in four cases is translated by ἐπιπέσῃ, in each case modified by an ἐπί phrase (for על). But here נפל is modified by אל תוכו, translated by ἔνδον,[43] and so ἐμπέσῃ is used.

Two declarations are made: "whatever (ὅσα) would be inside will be unclean," and "it (αὐτό, i.e. the clay vessel) must be broken." LXX uses the future passive, an adequate translation of the entire construction of the Hebrew "and it you shall break." The future passive verb, συντριβήσεται, is changed to the future middle συντριψεται in Byz, which by itacism appears as συντριψετε in *n*; by coincidence this does equal MT, but this is mere happenstance.

11:34 MT begins with a partitive מן construction, which is oddly, though not incorrectly, translated by a nominative structure, i.e. מכל האכל becomes καὶ πᾶν βρῶμα.[44] This food is defined by two relative clauses, ὃ ἔσθεται "which may be eaten," and εἰς ὃ ἂν ἐπέλθῃ ἐπ' αὐτῷ ὕδωρ. The context is still the clay vessel into which something fell inside at v.33. What is referred to is the context of the clay vessel, i.e. any food which is intended for eating. Water coming upon such food would transmit the impurities. Such food would be unclean.

---

42. See THGD 99—102 for ἄν vs εαν in relative clauses.
43. For a discussion of this reading see THGL 131.
44. See SS 158.

Similarly all liquid (ποτόν) which might be drunk in any (such) ἀγγείῳ is unclean. What is meant is liquid in a clay vessel as over against water from a stream or spring. The change to ἀγγείῳ from σκεύει is simply for variation. Both translate כלי.

11:35 A further elaboration on the fact that corpses render unclean whatever they touch, even if the touching was inadvertent. Then "everything on which anything of their corpses might fall shall be unclean."[45] Though the O b t+ addition of εφ before the relative pronoun is a clarifying gloss, the Hebraic ὅ ... ἐπ' αὐτό is hardly "unintelligible and absurd in its context" as R.Sollamo maintains;[46] the antecedent must be the πᾶν to which ὅ refers. In the tradition, the majority A B F M text has εμπεση instead of ἐπιπέσῃ, a clear case of leveling with v.33.[47]

תנור "oven" is rendered by κλίβανοι "baking pots," a plural word possibly betraying the manner in which food was prepared by the Jews in Alexandria, and כירים, dual in form, thought to be some kind of small hearth, possibly of a size to hold two pots,[48] which is translated by κυθρόποδες "pot-stands," here used metonymically for "pots."[49] Both כירים and κυθρόποδες are hapax legomena in OT. The spelling κυθρ- rather than χυτρ- is Hellenistic, and is probably Ionic in origin.[50] These must be demolished (καθαιρεθήσονται). In MT the verb is singular, which none of the ancient witnesses supports.

LXX imitates MT in using the plural ἀκάθαρτα ταῦτά ἐστιν καὶ ἀκάθαρτα ταῦτα ὑμῖν ἔσονται.[51] The Hebrew equivalent reads טמאים הם וטמאים יהיו לכם. The rendering of the adjective is obvious, but note that in the first clause הם becomes ταῦτά ἐστιν. In the tradition, A B M' plus four cursives support ταῦτα, and all others omit it. For the second clause only A B b x plus three cursives support Lev. Again, the majority of other witnesses omit ταῦτα. But ταῦτα in neither case is a correction; it must be original.[52] The majority text also transposes ὑμῖν ἔσονται; this is a hex correction in word order to equal MT.

---

45. See SS 158.
46. In Greenspoon—Munnich 49.
47. See the discussion in THGL 131.
48. See KB sub כיר.
49. See LS sub χυτρόπους.
50. See LS sub χύτρα.
51. See SS 197.
52. See the discussion in THGL 113.

11:36 The prepositional πλήν phrase serves as subject, i.e. the phrase is nominative. πλήν, of course governs the genitive. The syntax is clearer in Hebrew, since the equivalent to πλήν is אך, a restrictive clause modifier probably best translated by "on the other hand" or "however." The nouns that follow serve as compound subject for יהיה. The first noun is מעין "a spring," to which Sam added מים; the latter must have been the parent reading for LXX's πηγῶν ὑδάτων, understood as a collective, hence plural. I would translate: "except that springs of water and a cistern and a collection of water shall be clean." This differs from MT which has no conjunction before מקום מים. It serves to delimit בור as a cistern with water, rather than a dry pit. LXX makes it a third water source declared clean.

V.b makes the usual statement "but the one touching their corpses shall be unclean," though in slightly different form in that πᾶς is lacking, and a contrastive δέ is used; see comment at v.24. The reference is to the creatures listed in vv.29—30, and comp v.31 as well.

11:37 The subject of ἐπιπέσῃ is the partitive genitive τῶν θνησιμαίων, both here as well as in v.38.[53] The Hebrew equivalent is מנבלתם, and Byz z+ have added απο before τῶν to equal MT, which is probably recensional in character. For σπέρμα σπόριμον "seed grain," see Note at Gen 1:29, where it renders זרע זרע modifying פרי עץ. The Hebrew here is somewhat different, however: "seed sown" rather than "sowing seed," though the intent is the same in both, i.e. not grain for food, but for seed. The σπέρμα is further modified by a relative clause: "which may be sown."

The apodosis is a simple nominal clause טהור הוא, which LXX changes to a verbal clause καθαρὸν ἔσται. The future ἔσται is unusual, and the popular F text which changes the future to εστιν is probably hex in origin, thereby equalling MT.

11:38 ἐπιχυθῇ "should be poured over (or upon)" is a contextual rendering for יתן "should be put (on)." LXX interprets זרע "seed" by πᾶν σπέρμα "any seed." This is not a textual matter, but one of interpretation. For ἐπιπέσῃ τῶν θνησιμαίων αὐτῶν see comment at v.37. Over against v.37 הוא is rendered in the

---

53. See SS 158.

usual way by ἐστιν. For water in vessels rendering unclean, see the discussion at v.34.

11:39 For the partitive genitive τῶν κτηνῶν, see comment at v.37.[54] Such "cattle" is modified by the relative clause ὅ ἐστιν ὑμῖν τοῦτο φαγεῖν "which was meant for you to eat." MT has לאכלה "for food" instead of φαγεῖν. What is meant is cattle which had died rather than being slaughtered. Such cattle might be diseased or torn; in any event, "the one touching their carcasses will be unclean until evening"; cf comment at v.24. The plural pronoun αὐτῶν refers to κτηνῶν in the protasis. This is also clear from the Hebrew, where the suffix is third feminine singular, referring to the feminine בהמה.

11:40 LXX makes a neat distinction by translating מנבלתה by ἀπὸ τῶν θνησιμαίων τούτων, but the נבלתה of v.b by ἀπὸ τῶν θνησιμαίων αὐτῶν. In each case the ἀπό is partitive, and the antecedent of the pronouns is τῶν κτηνῶν of v.39, but the τούτων directs the attention to the fact that one is still referring to the preceding verse. A majority text has voided the distinction by changing τούτων to αυτων; it is obviously a case of secondary leveling. In the second case such a connection is obvious, but the translator added the preposition. The translator by this addition makes it clear that the reference remains the same. The b n+ text has omitted the ἀπό, and thereby equals MT; this may well be due to mediate Hebrew influence. In the tradition, the article is omitted before θνησιμαίων both times. These are simply scribal errors, and should not be taken seriously even when supported by uncials.[55]

Eating such flesh not only renders the offender unclean until evening, but it also demands that one πλυνεῖ τὰ ἱμάτια. For failure to render the suffix of בגדיו both here and in v.b see comment at v.25. In both cases hex has added an αυτου to represent the suffixes.

V.b exacts a further imposition on one who carries "anything of their dead carcasses." Not only shall one remain unclean until evening, and wash (his) clothes, he must also λούσεται ὕδατι. This has no basis in MT, and a popular text, possibly hex in origin, omits it. It is, however, Lev, and represents an

---

54. And see SS 158.
55. See THGL 83.

attempt at leveling with 17:15, where the fuller instructions obtain for one eating such meat is given.

11:41 Syntactically v.a is a pendant nominative, serving as antecedent for τοῦτο of the first clause. Thus about every ἑρπετόν that creeps on the ground it is said that βδέλυγμα τοῦτο ἔσται ὑμῖν, though MT has only שֶׁקֶץ הוּא. For ἑρπετόν see comment at v.20. The verb ἕρπει occurs only four times in Lev (also in vv.42,43,46), and always renders שָׁרַץ. Hex apparently omitted ἔσται, which certainly has no support in MT. The ὑμῖν is ex par, e.g. vv.28,38. A majority reading reads εστιν τουτο instead of τοῦτο ἔσται, but this obviously represents an attempt to correct the tense of the text.[56]

11:42 V.42a is a lengthy pendant nominative, which is then made part of the prohibition through an accusative αὐτό. Note once again that Lev uses a neuter pronoun here, which presumably can be justified in view of the earlier neuter ὅ, which, however, in turn has a masculine antecedent![57] The Byz text has tried to correct the Greek by changing both cases of πᾶς ὁ πορευόμενος to a neuter construction παν ο πορευεται; this is clearly secondary, an attempt to make the Greek conformable to rules of congruence. In the second one, the participle is modified by ἐπὶ τεσσάρων διὰ παντός. The first phrase has ἐπί governing a genitive ("four," i.e. feet). An A B+ text has τεσσερα (or -αρα), but the genitive must be original, since in the coordinate structure, ἐπὶ κοιλίας occurs in a parallel context;[58] a writer would hardly have changed cases in so idiosyncratic a fashion.[59] The second prepositional phrase must have been based on a misunderstanding of עַד as an adverbial meaning "perpetuity," as in the phrase לָעַד, rather than as a preposition "as far as, up to."[60] In MT it governs כֹּל מַרְבֵּה, but the translator understood it as modifying הוֹלֵךְ 2°, i.e. as "everyone going continually on four (feet)."

---

56. See THGL 113.
57. See Huber 110.
58. Aq has στῆθος instead of κοιλίας.
59. See the discussion in THGL 121—122.
60. BDB sub III.עַד I. b. explains the preposition used here as an abbreviation of the מִן עַד ... use, but without the מִן. This would then mean: "upon four (feet) up to all those with many feet."

The ὅ structure constitutes a third element among the inedibles; it refers to "whatever has many feet among all the creeping things that move on the ground." This would refer to such creatures as centipedes or caterpillars, etc.

V.b is the main structure: "you may not eat it, because it is an abomination for you." The αὐτό refers to the ὅ clause as the nearer antecedent, but what is meant is that you may not eat such. MT makes this clearer by the plural suffix in תאכלום. An F C′ n s+ text does change αὐτό to αυτα, but this is hardly recensional, but rather a correction ad sensum. That the singular is intentional on the part of the translator is clear from the ὅτι clause in which the הם of MT is rendered by the singular (ὑμῖν) ἐστιν. The pronoun has no equivalent in the Hebrew, and hex has correctly placed it under the obelus.

11:43 The verse is introduced by καί, whereas MT is asyndetically presented. Syntactically there are three coordinate negative clauses, but the first one is an οὐ μή plus subjunctive clause expressing prohibition, and the next two are simple futures, and probably express purpose, thus "and do not make yourselves an abomination ... that you may not defile yourselves ... and not become unclean."[61] The Pi תשקצו is well-rendered by the transitive βδελύξητε with τὰς ψυχὰς ὑμῶν "your persons" as direct modifier. The verb is further delimited by the prepositional phrase "with all the creeping things that creep on the ground." MT has no equivalent for ἐπὶ τῆς γῆς, which was added ex par, e.g. from v.44, and hex has placed the phrase under the obelus. The addition of the phrase does delimit the ἑρπετοῖς to the creepers on the ground as distinct from the ἑρπετῶν τῶν πετεινῶν of v.21.

Though בהם is merely the long form of בם, the translator distinguished them in the two last clauses by ἐν τούτοις and ἐν αὐτοῖς resp; this is also exegetically fitting, since the demonstrative refers specifically to πᾶσιν τοῖς ἕρπουσιν of the preceding phrase, whereas the last clause is coordinate with the second one, and αὐτοῖς automatically has the same reference as that in the previous clause. The last clause refers to the resultant stage, ἀκάθαρτοι ἔσεσθε, of the verbal process of μιανθήσεσθε. It should also be noted that the translator has carried over the negative of the second clause to the last one, οὐκ ἀκάθαρτοι ἔσεσθε, though MT simply has נטמתם. This adequately renders the intent of MT, how-

---

61. See Huber 79.

ever, which reads "(you may not make yourselves impure with them) and (so) become impure with them."

11:44 Vv.44—45 give the essential basis (ὅτι) for demanding cultic purity of the Israelites. First and foremost is the fact that ἐγώ εἰμι κύριος ὁ θεὸς ὑμῶν. The one who is κύριος is your God. This then sets the Israelites apart from other peoples. That he is your God automatically means that you are his people, with all the demands that this entails. This statement becomes thematic in chh.18—26, it serving as a regularly recurring refrain.

This issues in the demand: ἁγιασθήσεσθε καὶ ἅγιοι ἔσεσθε. The verb in the middle voice involves a separation of the self from all that might render one unclean, in the context of this chapter, with respect to diet. By refraining from eating anything that is ritually unclean one can make oneself holy, and so be holy. The two clauses, though similar, are not identical. The middle form informs the process of making oneself holy by avoiding all things unclean, while the second clause expresses a status of holiness as desirable.

This is in turn grounded in the fact: ἅγιός εἰμι ἐγὼ κύριος ὁ θεὸς ὑμῶν. MT does not identify ἐγώ by "the Lord your God," and it probably is ex par. On the other hand, it does tie the statement: ὅτι ἅγιός εἰμι ἐγώ to the first statement: "I am the Lord your God," which might then be taken to define it. Thus that Israel's God is holy means that he is divine, not human. That this is the basis for the demand that Israel should sanctify themselves and be holy suggests that Israel too must stand apart from the profane, the unclean. Hex has correctly identified κύριος ὁ θεὸς ὑμῶν as having no equivalent in MT by placing the structure under the obelus.

This is restated contextually in the final clause: "and not may you defile your persons with all the creeping things that move about on the ground," actually a restatement of v.43. The ἐν is instrumental, "by means of all the creeping things."

In the tradition, ἅγιοι ἔσεσθε is transposed by hex to equal MT's word order: הייתם קדשים. Hex has treated the two cases of εἰμι differently, omitting the first one, but placing the second one under the obelus; MT simply has a nominal clause for the second one: אני יהוה.

11:45 V.45a is another ὅτι/כי clause giving the reasons for your not defiling your persons (v.44b). This means that vv.43—44a finds its parallel in vv.44b—45.

Practically speaking, this gives a second reason for the Israelites not to defile themselves with any creepers creeping on the land. The reason here is rooted in the fact that "I am κύριος who brought you out of the land of Egypt to be your God." It is not merely that he is κύριος, but he is the Lord who acted redemptively in the Exodus. This is modified by a purposive infinitive "to be your God." This is slightly different from the Hebrew's להית לכם לאלהים. The verb היה plus ל usually means "to become," and it would not be incorrect to translate: "to become your God" or "to become God for you," whereas LXX is simply εἶναι ὑμῶν θεός.

In any event, this makes the second part of the verse particularly relevant. If the Lord is your God, then it is meaningful to demand that "you must be holy, because I, the Lord, am holy." The new dimension that has been added as basis for the demand for holiness upon God's people is the character of God as redeemer of his people; this makes the ὅτι clause take on a new meaning for the people; this redeemer is the holy one, even the Lord. This may also constitute further reason for the translator to have added κύριος, since MT makes the "because" clause shorter as כי קדוש אני. Hex has omitted the κύριος to equal MT. The Byz f+ text, however, has added ο θεος υμων, probably to level with the longer statement in v.44.

11:46—47 The two verses belong together as constituting a subscription to the chapter. It begins with the common formula identifying a set of regulations: οὗτος ὁ νόμος,[62] "this is the rule," which in MT is identified as תורת הבהמה. The bound phrase is neatly rendered by ὁ νόμος περὶ τῶν κτηνῶν "the regulation about the cattle (and birds, etc.)." The preposition governs four genitives "τῶν κτηνῶν καὶ τῶν πετεινῶν καὶ πάσης ψυχῆς which moves about in the water καὶ πάσης ψυχῆς creeping on the ground." The third item in the list represents כל נפש החיה "every living creature." LXX omitted the adjective, probably under the influence of the last item which has נפש without an accompanying החיה, and hex has supplied ζωσης under the asterisk to represent it. Over against the participle in the third item which is articulated, ἑρπούσης is not. The Byz text has added a της, thereby equalling the השרצת of MT. This need not be judged recensional, however, since it could simply be a leveling with τῆς κινουμένης in the previous

---

62. See THGL 108.

item. LXX has levelled the four items as genitives governed by a single περί. MT, however, has changed the final item to a separate prepositional structure by its ולכל נפש. I doubt that any semantic distinction was intended by MT.

V.47 gives the raison d' etre for the νόμος by means of a purposive infinitive; it is "to distinguish between the unclean and (between) the clean ones, and between those engendering the edible and (between) those engendering the inedible."[63] In MT all the nominals are singular, whereas LXX interprets all of them (correctly) as collectives, and so makes them plural.

---

63. Aq renders the second pair of prepositional phrases by ἀνὰ μέσον τῶν ζῴων τῶν ἐσθιόντων καὶ ἀνὰ μέσον τῶν μὴ ἐσθιόντων τῶν ζῴων (retroverted from Syh). The Byz text has also substituted this text for that of Lev.

Chapter 12

12:2 Instead of: "Speak to the Israelites לֵאמֹר," LXX has καὶ ἐρεῖς πρὸς αὐτούς. A majority F M text has added λεγων, whereas hex has merely placed πρὸς αὐτούς under the obelus. This conforms to Origen's usual practice of assessing LXX over against MT in a purely quantitative manner. What Moses is directed to say follows and continues through v.8. The subject of the chapter is neatly stated in v.7b: οὗτος ὁ νόμος τῆς τικτούσης ἄρσεν ἢ θῆλυ.

The protasis is introduced by γυνὴ ἥτις (ἄν), representing אשה כי. This rendering occurs elsewhere in the book only at 15:19, though it does occur for אשה אשר at 20:16. כי is usually rendered by ἐάν, but here the indefinite relative is exactly what the context demands. The first verb in the protasis is a passive adaptation of the Hi תזריע. This does not mean that the translator read the form vocalized as a Ni with Sam,[1] but rather that he adapted the verb sensibly to the context; σπερματισθῇ καὶ τέκῃ simply means "shall become pregnant and bear."

The apodosis is introduced by καί in imitation of the Hebrew, but is marked by the future verb ἔσται, thus "(then) she shall be unclean seven days." The omission of καί by C b f n+ is stylistic; an apodotic καί is not standard Greek. The norm for the seven days is expressed in a separate clause: "she shall be unclean according to τὰς ἡμέρας τοῦ χωρισμοῦ τῆς ἀφέδρου αὐτῆς," i.e. the days of isolation for her menstrual period, for which see 15:19—23. The Hebrew speaks of the days of נדת דותה "her menstrual infirmity." The term נדה is usually rendered by ἄφεδρος, a Hellenistic euphemism, a "sitting apart," but it is also reflected by χωρισμός "isolation."[2] The word דוה means "sick, unwell," hence "infirmity." The form דותה is a Qal bound infinitive with suffix from the root דוה. The translator disregarded this word in favor of a descriptive (or doublet) rendering of נדה.[3] Thus for him the norm for the period of her uncleanness means the period of her being isolated for a

---

1. As Harlé-Pralon suggest.
2. According to Dos Santos נדה is rendered by ἄφεδρος 11 times, and by χωρισμός three times.
3. For נדת דותה Theod and Aq have τοῦ χωρισμοῦ τῆς ὀδύνης <αὐτῆς>, whereas Sym according to Hesychius read *separationis afflictionis* (for τοῦ χωρισμοῦ τοῦ παθήματος <αὐτῆς>?).

menstrual period, which is a sensible interpretation. See also discussion at 15:33.

12:3 In MT ימול is vocalized by the Masoretes as Ni, with "בשר" of his foreskin" as subject. The term σάρκα/בשר probably means "penis," since what is removed by circumcision is not "flesh," but "skin."[4] בשר is regularly employed as a euphemism for the male organ, and σάρξ is the most common rendering for בשר. σάρξ is for all practical purposes a calque for בשר; it occurs 140 times for בשר; 14 times its origin is unclear, twice (in Mic 3) it occurs for שאר, and once at Zach 1:17 for לחום.[5] The translator changed the inflection to an active one, taking advantage of the fact that Greek does not distinguish gender in finite verb forms, and makes "σάρξ of his foreskin" an accusative modifier of the verb. In the Greek rendering the woman can be taken as subject, which is, however, not a possible interpretation of the Ni verb, which is third masculine singular. For the mother performing the rite on her son see Exod 4:25. It could also be understood as having an indefinite subject, which the consonantal ימול would permit, and one should probably take it in this way.

12:4 The initial accusative is one showing extent of time, thus "and for thirty-three days." MT repeats "days" after both "thirty" and "three," but the Greek has it only after the first unit. The verb καθεσθήσεται was chosen both for vv.4 and 5 as translation for תשב, rather than the popular A reading καθήσεται, because the oldest witness supports the rarer verb, though either lexeme would be adequate.[6] The verb used is καθέζομαι, of which the form in Lev is the future, though another future inflection, κατεδοῦνται, is also found at Ezek 26:16. What is meant is "remaining apart," i.e. in isolation. The verb is modified by ἐν αἵματι ἀκαθάρτῳ αὐτῆς. The adjectival phrase translates a Hebrew bound phrase דמי טהרה, but adds a genitive pronoun against MT; the pronoun is an ad sensum addition.[7]

---

4. So Milgrom 748.
5. Acording to HR.
6. See the discussion in THGL 129.
7. The Three render the second noun more precisely by the genitive noun καθαρίσεως.

What this sitting or remaining "in her unclean blood" involves is explained in v.b: "anything holy she may not touch, and into the sanctuary she may not enter." The word ἁγιαστήριον occurs only rarely in OT, and only here in the Pentateuch. מקדש is usually translated either by ἅγιος (45 times) or ἁγιασμός (23 times).[8] Why the translator should choose ἁγιαστήριον here is not clear. It simply means "a holy place." The double prohibition is in turn modified by a ἕως ἄν plus subjunctive verb construction, which translates a prepositional phrase, i.e. עד plus a bound infinitive structure. The subject of ἀναπληρωθῶσιν is αἱ ἡμέραι καθάρσεως αὐτῆς "the days of her purification." The translator realized that this טהרה consisted of טהר plus a suffix, i.e. it is a reference to the period of her impurity.

In the tradition, ἀκαθάρτῳ is changed to καθαρω in O' C' $s+$, which can only be either based on a complete misunderstanding of what is intended or is a thoughtless mistake. Possibly based on the Hebrew is the *b* reading, καθαρισμου, though it too is a wrong translation. Possibly based on Theod/Aq is the omission of αἱ by an F O' C'+ text, whereas the F $s+$ change of καθάρσεως to καθαρισεως is a palaeographically conditioned variant text.

12:5 The rules for bearing a female baby differ; the length of the mother's uncleanness and of her sitting "in her unclean blood" is double that prescribed for delivering a male baby. θῆλυ is an accusative neuter singular nominal, thus "but if she should bear a female (baby)." Note how LXX rendered the dual שבעתים, not by "fourteen," but by δὶς ἑπτὰ (ἡμέρας) "twice seven (days)," thereby calling attention to the fact that the overall period of isolation is double that for a male child. The κατά phrase is much shorter than at v.2. Why κατὰ τὴν ἄφεδρον "according to the menstrual period" should be twice seven days in the case of a female child is baffling, but LXX simply follows MT, except for failing to render the suffix of כנדתה. The majority F M text does add αυτης, but this need not be considered recensional; it is probably merely an ad sensum gloss.[9] The passage has baffled commentators throughout the ages, and the phrase כנדתה is often explained in later Jewish literature as referring to a seven day period; i.e. an ἄφεδρος simply meant a seven day period.

---

8. The count is that of Dos Santos.
9. See SS 96.

V.b is an exact reproduction of v.4a, except that "33" becomes "66."[10]

12:6 LXX translates the preposition plus bound infinitive במלאת by a temporal clause as the protasis of a condition: ὅταν ἀναπληρωθῶσιν. The protasis indicates when the new mother must bring sacrifices, viz. "whenever the days of her purification for a son or a daughter might be completed." In the tradition, the Byz text articulates καθάρσεως as a stylistic improvement. For the variant reading καθαρισεως see comment at v.4.

The apodosis is signalled by the future tense verb προσοίσει. The mother must bring two sacrifices, one εἰς ὁλοκαύτωμα "for a burnt offering," and one περὶ ἁμαρτίας "for a sin offering." Both represent ל phrases in MT. For the burnt offering she must bring "a one-year old spotless lamb." The word ἄμωμον has no basis in MT, and the word has been put under the obelus in hex to indicate that fact. The word ἐνιαύσιον represents בן שנתו, and LXX throughout fails to render the suffix (see also 14:10 23:12).[11] For a sin offering she is to bring either a νοσσὸν περιστερᾶς "young of a pigeon,"[12] or a turtle dove. These are to be presented to the priest at the door of the tent of testimony.

12:7 The subject of προσοίσει is uncertain. Since the subject of the next clause is stated as ὁ ἱερεύς, the normal way to read the passage would be to continue with the subject of the preceding clause, i.e. the mother. On the other hand, there she προσοίσει the sacrifices to the priest. In MT the subject is clearly the priest, and that was probably intended by the translator as well. The αὐτόν must refer to the ἀμνόν, although the plural would be expected, since there are two sacrifices, a lamb and a bird. The variant αυτο of Byz z+ is possible in view of Lev's recurring use of the neuter pronoun when the antecedent is either at a distance or is unclear, but the omission of the pronoun by a popular A B text is highly unlikely to be original. The verb used occurs 70 times in

---

10. For ἀκαθάρτῳ The Three read καθαρίσεως as at v.4. I am sceptical of the attribution of καθαρισμοῦ to Theod in a single *s* ms. More trustworthy in my opinion is the witness of cod M at v.4, where καθαρισμοῦ is listed anonymously.
11. See SS 98.
12. Sym spells the word in the uncontracted form νεοσσόν, as do the majority of witnesses.

Lev, but only twice without a modifier.¹³ The subject of כפר in MT must be הכהן of v.6, since the verb is masculine. In translation its counterpart ἐξιλάσεται has no gender indication, and the addition of ὁ ἱερεύς is made for clarity. Without it a reader might be confused, though the modification of the verb by περὶ αὐτῆς makes it clear that it is not the mother, but the priest that is the subject. The ὁ ἱερεύς has dutifully been placed under the obelus by hex to indicate its formal absence in MT.

The Masoretes have vocalized טהרה as a third feminine singular Qal verb, i.e. "she shall be ritually clean," but the translator understood the word as vocalized as a masculine verb with a third feminine pronominal suffix, i.e. "he shall render her (or probably better, declare her) ritually clean." Either reading of the consonantal text is possible, but having added ὁ ἱερεύς as subject for ἐξιλάσεται, it would make it contextually easier to understand "the priest" as subject for the next verb, καθαριεῖ as well.

V.b is a subscription to vv.1—7a: "this is the regulation for the one bearing a male or female (child)."

12:8 This verse is an addendum alleviating the sacrificial demands on the poverty-stricken mother. The idiom μὴ εὑρίσκῃ ἡ χεὶρ αὐτῆς τὸ ἱκανόν means "her means might not extend to," or "she might not be able to afford (a lamb)." The Greek is a literal rendering of the Hebrew idiom "should her hand not find sufficient."¹⁴

The apodosis is introduced by a καί in imitation of the Hebrew ולקחה. She may thus take (i.e. for presentation as a sacrifice) the cheaper alternative "two turtledoves or two young pigeons," for which see comment at v.6. Two must be brought, "one for a burnt offering, and one for a sin offering."

In MT the final outcome is וטהרה, vocalized by the Masoretes as a Qal, thus "and she shall be ritually clean." The translator has translated this by καθαρισθήσεται, a future passive of the transitive verb καθαρίζω. This is a possible interpretation of the consonantal text, vocalized as a Pual.

---

13. See THGL 113—114.
14. For the idiom see THGL 131.

Chapter 13

13:2 The condition described is that of an οὐλὴ σημασίας τηλαυγής "scar of a spot of brightness." οὐλή is the usual rendering for שאת, except at v.43 where it is translated by ὄψις. What is meant by "brightness" is probably some kind of inflammation; it is an unusual piece of skin that looks scarred but showing a spot of inflammation "in the skin of his flesh."[1] MT reads שאת או ספחת או בהרת "a swelling or a rash(?) or an inflammation." The word ספחת occurs only here and at 14:56 in a similar context, and its meaning is not clear. It also occurs as מספחת at vv.6,7 and 8, and the translator always rendered it by σημασία "mark, spot, blot." It is likely that the translator was also uncertain about the word, and used a relatively neutral word for it. LXX did not translate או, but in the tradition a majority variant text does read η before τηλαυγής; this could be a recensional gloss, though the first או was disregarded.

In the tradition, a popular gloss has added η αυγασμα after τηλαυγής. It is, of course, secondary as its case makes clear, but its possible raison d'etre is interesting. Since copyists realized that this was "leprosy," τηλαυγής was not the best indication of leprosy, and "or whiteness" fitted this much better.

The coordinate condition refers to ἀφὴ λέπρας occurring on the skin of his flesh; this renders נגע צרעת. The term נגע from the root meaning "to touch" means "a stroke, an affliction, infection," and is etymologically rendered by ἀφή, "a touch," hence a stroke, affliction, i.e. something that has touched someone. Modern scholars are quick to point out (correctly) that צרעת is not necessarily leprosy, and refers to any infectious scaly skin disease, but to the translator it was "an infection λέπρας." The term λέπρα is used throughout as a calque for צרעת, a word occurring 51 times in OT and always translated by λέπρα. צרעת can attack people as in this chapter where it represents some kind of scale-like skin disease, but it can also attack garments, as well as houses where it probably intends a kind of deep-seated mildew. The two clauses constituting the protasis are coordinate both in MT and in LXX. Since the first swelling is undefined, and the second is λέπρας, the second clause may well be a development of the first, i.e. the οὐλή may eventuate in the affliction λέπρας. I shall use

---

1. Harlé-Pralon suggest rightly that here σημασία means "a spot" or "blot"; i.e. "Le sens concret de *tache* est une innovation sémantique des LXX" (p.135).

the term "leprosy" throughout when it affects people, in view of the Greek word, but the strictures on it and on the Hebrew צרעת must be borne in mind throughout.

The apodosis is introduced by an unnecessary Hebraic καί. Such a person "must be brought to Aaron the priest or to one of his sons, (who were also) priests." A majority F M reading changed the verb to a self-propelled ελευσεται, but ἀχθήσεται equals MT's הובא, and is read by the oldest witnesses as well; it is original text.

13:3 The priest must serve as expert in the matter; he must look at (i.e. examine) the sore in the skin of his flesh." MT simply has הבשר, and hex has put αὐτοῦ under the obelus.

What the examination might reveal is given in the next two clauses: a) "the hair in the sore should appear white." The word שער is collective, and should be rendered by the plural (or where appropriate by the collective "hair"). Since λευκή is nominative, the verb μεταβάλῃ must here be intransitive, though the C' s $t+$ variant text simplifies by reading the accusative, probably under the influence of v.4.[2] The verb in MT is הפך, i.e. "the hairs in the sore have turned white." A C' gloss adding εἰ before ἡ θρίξ has made it clear that the two clauses are conditional, but common sense dictates that what is meant is "and should the hair ..., and should ..., (then) it is a leprous sore." b) "the appearance of the sore ταπεινὴ[3] ἀπό the skin of the flesh,"[4] is the second condition. The positive adjective plus ἀπό is intended to show comparison, i.e. the surface of the sore "appears deeper than that of the skin" surrounding it,[5] probably because a white spot does seem to be deeper than the darker skin surrounding it. MT has "his skin," and a majority F M text added αυτου to represent the suffix of בשרו. The diagnosis is clear: "it is a leprous sore."

V.b gives the summary statement: "The priest shall examine and declare him infectious." MT has ראהו for the first verb, but LXX follows Sam which has ראה. The verb μιανεῖ must be declarative, and correctly renders the Pi of טמא,

---

2. See THGL 123.
3. Theod Aq translate עמק by κοίλη, but Sym has the more contextually appropriate βαθύτερον.
4. Theod Aq render בשר by κρέατος (retroverted from Syh).
5. See SS 148.

whereas ἀκάθαρτός ἐστιν is the usual translation for the Qal.⁶ What μιαίνω contributes beyond "uncleanness" is that it defiles, it is infectious, contagious.

13:4 Should the conditions for the affliction not exist, i.e. a) "the shiny area should be white in the skin of his flesh"; τηλαυγής means "shiny, conspicuous," so as I had suggested at v.2 it was the inflamed area. This has now turned white, i.e. no longer appears inflamed.⁷ LXX has again failed to render the suffix on בשרו, but a majority F M text does add αυτου. b) its appearance should not be deeper than the skin"; see comment at v.3. c) "its hair did not μετέβαλεν a white hair."⁸ LXX then adds the explanatory comment: αὐτὴ δέ ἐστιν ἀμαυρά "but it is (now) lusterless," i.e. no longer τηλαυγής. This has no equivalent in MT, and hex has placed it under the asterisk; the term is ex par; cf vv.6,21,26,28,56. The shiny character of the inflammation has now become dull, lusterless.

The apodosis is introduced by a καί in imitation of MT; it constitutes v.b which describes the concomitant priestly action: "the priest ἀφοριεῖ τὴν ἀφήν for seven days." The verb was used at 10:15 for להניף, but throughout this chapter it translates הסגיר "shut up, isolate";⁹ it may well be rendered by "quarantine." The use of ἀφήν is of course metonymic for the person with the sore.

13:5 At the end of the provisional period of quarantine, i.e. "on the seventh day," the priest shall examine (ὄψεται) the sore; see comment on ἀφήν at v.4. MT, however, has ראהו "examine him"; obviously what the priest must take a look at is the sore, not the person as a whole; in other words, LXX states more clearly what MT intends. The καὶ ἰδού introduces the diagnosis. MT has concerning the sore עמד בעיניו. NJPS has "has remained unchanged in color"; NRSV has "is checked," and NIV, "is unchanged."¹⁰ The LXX is also unclear: μένει ἐναν-

---

6. Harlé-Pralon 31, fail to take into account the different Hebrew stems as basis for the origin of the distinction between the two Greek renderings.
7. Instead of λευκή Aq has (τηλαυγὲς) λευκόν, whereas Sym has ἔκλαμπρον. The doublet reading in M′ combines two readings; only the λευκόν is Aq, and αὔγασμα of uncertain origin, is probably a gloss on λευκόν.
8. For the transitive character of the verb see THGL 123, but see comment at v.3.
9. Theod translates by συγκλείσει, but Aq and Sym have ἀποκλείσει (retroverted from Syh). I would take the attribution of Syh to be accurate, and that of Barhebraeus, as deficient; cf f.n. at v.11.
10. Tarᴼ has קם כד הוה "stayed as it was," whereas Rashi enlarges on the meaning of בעיניו with במראהו ובשיעורו הראשון.

τίον αὐτοῦ "(the sore) remains before him," i.e. is unchanged; the condition of the ἁφήν remains as before. The prepositional phrase renders בעיניו adequately. The following clause does clarify it: "not has the sore μετέπεσεν in the skin." The verb means "undergone change," which renders פשה "spread."[11]

13:6 For τὸ δεύτερον see comment at v.5. On reexamination on the seventh day, it is clear that the sore ἀμαυρά/כהה. It is no longer τηλαυγής, but it is now dull-colored; the inflammation has disappeared; in fact, "the sore has not undergone change in the skin."[12] In consequence the priest καθαριεῖ αὐτόν, the opposite of the μιανεῖ αὐτόν in v.3, which see. The verb means "shall declare him ritually clean."

MT simply states "it is a מספחת." The translator clearly understood this simply as a variant of ספחת, for which see comment at v.2. He interpreted this in a γάρ clause, i.e. it gives the reason for the priestly declaration. As always, it is translated by "it is (just) a blot."[13] What may be inferred is that it is neither an οὐλή nor a τηλαυγής; see v.2.

13:7 The cognate structure in MT, פשה תפשה, is translated by using two different roots, semantically synonymous: μεταβαλοῦσα μεταπέσῃ, and I would translate: "but should the spot[14] on the skin actually change."[15] The change is probably simply due to the translator's love of variation. He has also changed the אחרי structure of MT. It reads "after he has shown himself (הראתו Ni) to the priest for his purification." LXX reads μετὰ τὸ ἰδεῖν αὐτὸν τὸν ἱερέα τοῦ καθορίσαι αὐτόν. In each case an αὐτόν modifies the infinitive which it follows.

The apodosis, again introduced by an apodotic καί, is rendered correctly, with the Ni נראה translated by ὀφθήσεται "shall show himself."

13:8 The first clause is coordinate with the apodosis of v.7; this is clearly indicated by the use of future verbs in both clauses. MT has no modifier for the verb ראה, though LXX has ὄψεται αὐτόν. A popular variant has omitted the pronoun,

---

11. Theod has διακέχυται, which translates the Hebrew more precisely.
12. Theod again has διακέχυται for פשה as in v.5.
13. Theod gave up on the word and simply transliterated it as μασφααθ; Aq translates by ἐξανάδοσις "a scab," and Sym makes it ἔκβρασμα "a skin eruption."
14. Instead of ἡ σημασία Sym has τὸ ἔκφυμα.
15. Aq has ἐπιδόσει ἐπιδῷ, i.e. uses the same root for both words.

thus equalling the Hebrew. This could well be a hex correction, since mss G-376 Arm Syh, all usually strong supporters of hex, are included in the witnesses to the shorter text.[16]

On this second examination of the spot on the skin,[17] it has changed.[18] The καὶ ἰδού introduces the diagnosis resulting from ὄψεται. Presumably by "it has changed" is meant that the spot has spread, i.e. it did not μένει ἐναντίον αὐτοῦ; see v.6. The conclusion, as usual introduced by καί, accordingly also changes: "the priest shall declare him infectious; it is λέπρα."

13:9 LXX follows Sam in beginning the verse with a conjunction; MT begins asyndetically. For the unusual nominal before the conditional particle ἐάν, see comment at v.2.[19] The verse undoubtedly refers to a new case of leprosy. Both MT and LXX indicate such: LXX by paragraphing; BHS, by a closed section.

The apodosis, introduced by καί in imitation of MT, differs in LXX. MT has a passive verb, הובא, "he shall be brought (to the priest)." The Greek translates by ἥξει, which is active. The translator is being clever at this point. The verb ἄγω is normally transitive. In fact, it occurs 74 times in OT,[20] but it occurs only here for the Ho. Yet here it is used absolutely, and must simply mean "go."[21] By using ἄγω the translator reflects the Hebrew text, but the passive "is brought" is interpreted actively: "he shall go (to the priest)." A majority M text reading makes sure of this understanding by substituting ελευσεται. The Byz text also identifies τὸν ἱερέα by naming him ααρων.

13:10 The priest must make an examination; this statement is coordinate with the preceding clause, both using future verbs. The καὶ ἰδού represents the diagnosis; it describes the condition found in the skin examination. a) The "scar is white on the skin," and b) "it has changed the hair to white"; the antecedent of αὕτη is ἀφή. What is meant is that the skin's hair in the scar, which is normally dark, has turned white. c) "there is some raw, living flesh in the scar."[22] The Greek which

---

16. See THGL 106.
17. Aq translates מחספת by ἐξανάδοσις, and Sym, by ἔκβρασμα.
18. Aq uses the verb ἐπέδωκεν as at v.7; Sym has ὑπερέβη, and Theod, once again has διακεχύται as at vv.5,6.
19. See THGL 74.
20. According to my count in HR.
21. See Bauer sub voce 5.
22. The ἀπό is partitive; see SS 158.

I have translated by "raw" is ὑγιοῦς "healthy," presumably flesh as it would appear without the skin.

13:11 The diagnosis is that it is a נושנת leprosy, i.e. one that has gone to sleep; it is an old or chronic case of leprosy. The translator fully understood it as his παλαιουμένη "of long standing" shows. In fact, "it is in the skin of the flesh," for which see comment at v.2.

For μιανεῖ αὐτόν see comment at v.3. MT then continues in v.b with לא יסגרו plus a כי clause giving the reason for not placing him in isolation, viz. "he is unclean." Possibly what is meant is that he has already been declared unclean. For the placement in isolation see comment at v.4. The translator found the statement contradictory, and simply omitted the לא. What the Greek says is "and he shall shut him up because he is unclean."[23] Obviously, the translator felt that there was a mistake in MT. If one is leprous, one must be isolated, being unclean; after all, it is infectious.

In the tradition, a majority text omits ἐστιν in the second statement "it is in the skin of the flesh." This makes good sense in that it combines two clauses: "it is a case of chronic leprosy in the skin of the flesh," and also equals MT; it may well be hex in origin. This is also probably the case in the addition of αυτου after χρωτός by the majority F M text, since MT has בשרו, though the gloss could be simply ad sensum. An F C' f s+ text has substituted for καὶ (ἀφοριεῖ) a negative particle ου(κ). This is clearly under the influence of MT, probably mediated by one of The Three.

13:12 LXX translates פרוח תפרח in its basic sense, "to bud, sprout," ἐξανθοῦσαι ἐξανθήσῃ: "if the leprosy should sprout out all over on the skin." The participle serves to intensify the action of the verb, hence "all over, throughout." The subject is ἡ λέπρα. The majority M text omits the article, but the articulated form is original, and follows MT. The omission is a clear case of haplography, since the preceding word, ἐξανθήσῃ, ends in eta.[24]

The second clause describes this sprouting more exactly: "And the leprosy should cover all the skin affected by the infection from head to feet." The

---

23. Both Aq and Sym omit the καί; instead of καὶ ἀφοριεῖ Aq has οὐκ ἀποκλείσει, and Sym reads οὐχ ὑπερθήσεται.
24. See THGL 83.

modifier "affected by the infection" represents the genitive τῆς ἀφῆς, the genitive serving to limit the noun it modifies, δέρμα. On the other hand, the genitive could also be understood as metonymic for the one affected by the ἀφή as in v.4 and in v.13. LXX does not translate the suffix of ראשו and רגליו, since these would be otiose in Greek; the leprosy would hardly cover the skin of someone else's head to foot! A majority text, nonetheless, adds αυτου after ποδῶν; the gloss is probably hex. The verb is modified by a καθ' phrase, which might be translated "according to the complete examintion of the priest."

13:13 When the priest makes an examination of the case described in v.12, he finds (καὶ ἰδού) that "the leprosy has covered all the skin of the flesh," but MT has "all בשרו." The addition of τὸ δέρμα is ex par; see e.g. vv.2,3,4,11, and is indeed a correction; the leprosy covers the skin rather than the flesh. The F M majority text has added αυτου to represent the suffix. Whether this is a hex correction or an ad sensum gloss can not be determined.

As a result, "the priest shall declare him clean of the affliction." MT has a shorter text וטהר את הנגע i.e. "and he shall declare the את הנגע pure"; of course, it is the afflicted one that is intended; see comment at v.4. Hex has placed αὐτὸν ὁ ἱερεύς under the obelus, since it has no equivalent in MT. On the face of it this seems a strange instruction; one would think that the spread of the disease over the entire body would certainly involve uncleanness, but this is not the case.

V.b explains why this is not the case, at least in the Greek, which introduces v.b by ὅτι; in MT this is asyndetic. The reason for the absolution given is that "all (i.e. the skin) has become[25] white," and so the judgment is "it is clean." What this probably means is that the scabs have fallen off, and the skin is now a healthy color; it is white. In the Byz tradition, the πᾶν ... λευκόν of the ὅτι phrase has become feminine; it is then not the skin, but the leprosy which has become white, but MT clearly refers to the skin; הוא cannot refer to צרעת. The same confusion appears in the *f n* text reading καθαρος (referring to λέπρα) as well for the neuter καθαρόν.

13:14 This verse helps to explain the judgment of v.13, since it informs how the status of v.13 can change to an unclean state. It reads "and in whatever day live

---

25. Instead of μετέβαλεν Aq has ἔστρεψεν, and Sym has μετεχρώσθη.

flesh (i.e. an open wound) might appear on him, he will become infectious." In other words, when all the skin appears as white, there are no open sores, no "live flesh."

13:15 The translator had distinguished between מחיה and the adjective חי by using ὑγιοῦς for the former, and ζώσης for the latter, but in this verse he uses only ὑγιῆ/ὑγιής to render חי. I have used "living" to render ζώσης, and "raw" for ὑγιῆ, simply to keep them apart. They both mean "live, exposed flesh, not covered by skin." The priest must examine the raw flesh, "and the raw flesh shall render him (i.e. not the priest, but the afflicted person) infectious, because it is unclean; it is leprosy." ἀκαθαρτός could refer to χρῶτα or to αὐτόν; in fact, since the adjective is a diptote, it could even refer to λέπρα. I have taken "it" to refer to χρῶτα as does MT. MT divides the text differently. The Masoretes placed וטמאו under the *ethnach*, which is more sensible. What MT means is "and he shall declare him unclean; the raw flesh is unclean; it is leprosy." The translator had used ὅτι in v.13, and felt compelled once again to state a reason for the raw flesh defiling someone, whereas MT has no support for it. In fact, a majority text has omitted ὅτι, probably due to hex revision.

13:16 MT presents the condition as an alternative, i.e. begins with או, but LXX does not. The translator read וכי rather than או כי; the preceding word is הוא, and the initial letter of או was probably omitted by haplography. The verb ישוב is idiomatically used in coordination with another verb to signify "again," thus here with ונהפך meaning "Or if the raw flesh should again be turned (to white)," i.e. be healed. Here the verb ישוב is rendered by the compound ἀποκατασθῇ "restore, come back." In the tradition, a popular variant simplifies by changing to the passive αποκατασταθη "be restored," but the active is original. What is meant is that the raw flesh should turn back, probably in the sense of "contract, shrink" as a first stage in an eventual return to a healthy white.

The second condition given is καὶ μεταβάλῃ λευκή. The verb is intransitive, and is modified by a predicate nominative. More commonly, the verb governs an εἰς structure, or in any event, an accusative, and both λευκόν and εἰς λευκον are attested by variant popular texts.[26] It should be noted, however, that

---

26. The Others attest to λευκόν.

the old uncials A B F and G all support the more difficult nominative, and it is clearly original.[27]

The last καί introduces the apodosis, as is clear from the future ἐλεύσεται, and the clause is in turn coordinate with the first one of the next verse.

13:17 When he goes to the priest (v.16), the latter must make an examination; LXX follows Sam's וראה. MT has וראהו, and hex has added αυτον after the verb to represent the pronominal suffix of MT.[28]

καὶ ἰδού marks the diagnosis. "The ἀφή has changed to the white"; what is meant by τὸ λευκόν is the skin; the neuter must refer to δέρμα, not to χρώς which is masculine. The open sore has healed over, and the skin is again white. The priestly declaration follows: καθαριεῖ ὁ ἱερεὺς τὴν ἀφὴν καθαρός ἐστιν. Note that τὴν ἀφήν is again metonymic for the person afflicted with the sore; see comment at v.4.

13:18 Vv.18—23 deal with λέπρα as the result of an ulcerous sore. Syntactically v.18 is a protasis which continues with v.19a, with the apodosis appearing in the last clause of v.19 and continuing with the first clause of v.20. The ἐάν clause supposes a ἕλκος "an ulcerous or open sore" appearing in his skin, which heals. The ἐάν clause is preceded by καὶ σάρξ indicating a general subject for which the ἐάν is relevant. One could express this by "and as for flesh, should there be in its skin an open sore."[29] MT locates the שחין "boil" בערו, which must be doublet; the בו refers to the initial בשר.[30] In other words, MT, as well as Tar, preserves a double reading; one must read either בו with Sam, or בערו with LXX Pesh and Vulg. Subsequently ὑγιασθῇ, i.e. the ἕλκος would be healed.

13:19 A further condition is joined to v.18: "and there should obtain in the place of the open sore a white scar or an inflamed spot, growing white or reddening." In other words, the festering sore has seemingly healed, but now in place of it a more dangerous manifestation asserts itself. This differs considerably from MT, according to which either a white swelling obtains, or a reddish-white inflamma-

---

27. See THGL 123.
28. See THGL 106.
29. See THGL 74.
30. Kenn 5,18,176 omit בו, whereas Sam lacks the בערו.

tion. LXX has rationalized on the basis of experience. When a boil appears, there are two stages; first the boil is inflamed and bright red, and in the second stage when a pus sack appears it is whitish. The translator has added a correlative between the two participles: λευκαίνουσα ἢ πορρίζουσα, the two participles reflecting resp. the description of the οὐλή as λευκὴ ἢ τηλαυγής. The critical text ought to have had a comma after τηλαυγής to make the interpretation clear.

In any event, he must show himself to the priest for inspection.

13:20 As in vv.5,6,8,10,13,17 καὶ ἰδού introduces the diagnosis which follows on the priest making an examination. The conditions observed are a) its appearance is lower than the skin, for which see comment at v.4. The Masoretes have vocalized מראה as with a third feminine suffix, referring to שאת or בהרת, which is reflected in the hex plus, αυτης. One ms changed αυτης to αυτου, which would refer to ἕλκους, which could hardly be correct. b) "its (probably referring to οὐλή) hair has changed to white," for which see comment at v.2. The b text has changed εἰς λευκήν to λευκη, for which see comment at v.3.

The apodosis is the priestly judgment: "the priest must declare him infectious." The olfy+ text has αυτην instead of αὐτόν. One can hardly take this seriously; the reference must be to the affected hair, not to the οὐλή. MT states נגע צרעת היא, but LXX, more simply has λεπρα ἐστιν. The majority F M text, however, has αψη λεπρος εστιν, which must be a recensional correction, possibly hex. The verse concludes with "it sprouted in the open sore." The ἕλκος was the seed for the leprosy.

13:21 LXX follows Sam's יראה by its ἴδη, whereas MT has a pronominal suffix, יראהו, with the suffix referring to שאת or בהרת; this also applies to בה in the next clause. LXX has, however, rendered by ἐν αὐτῷ, which has ἕλκους as antecedent. Accordingly, hex has added αυτου after the verb to represent the suffix of יראהו in MT.

The diagnosis is a) "there is no white hair in it" (see above for ἐν αὐτῷ); b) "and it is not lower than the skin of the flesh"; cf comment at v.4. and c) "and αὐτή is lusterless"; for ἀμαυρά see comment at v.4. The pronoun reflects היא, which refers to שאת (or בהרת), and it must refer to οὐλή or τηλαυγής of v.19.

The action to be taken by the priest is that he "must quarantine him for seven days," for which see comment at v.4.[31] The clause is introduced by καί in imitation of MT, though an A B f x y+ text omits the καί as a stylistic improvement.[32]

13:22 "But should it actually spread in the skin" is another possible scenario. In such a case "the priest must declare him infectious." Again the apodosis is introduced by a Hebraic καί. MT concludes with the judgment נגע הוא "it is an infection." LXX enlarges on this by calling it a ἁφὴ λέπρας, and then levels with v.20 by adding ἐν τῷ ἕλκει ἐξήνθησεν, thus "it is an infection of leprosy; it sprouted in the open sore." The Byz text has δερματι rather than ἕλκει, a rationalizing change. After all, the ἕλκος had disappeared; cf v.18. Syh has omitted the last clause, thereby equalling MT. This probably means that the parent hex text translated had the passage under the obelus, giving the Syh translator the impetus to omit it.

13:23 The opposite possibility might occur; "but should the brightness (i.e. the inflammation) stay at the place (i.e. it is stationary) and not spread." The idiom in MT is somewhat differently expressed: תחתיה תעמד "it should stay under itself (i.e. at its place)," but the Greek interprets correctly, except for disregarding the suffix. An F M majority text, probably inspired by hex, has added αυτου after χώραν to make up for it.[33]

The apodosis in MT reads צרבת השחין הוא "it is the scab of the boil." The word צרבת only occurs elsewhere at v.28; it is derived from a root meaning "to scorch, burn." LXX understood it correctly as its οὐλὴ τοῦ ἕλκους ἐστίν "it is the scar of the open sore" shows. Accordingly, "the priest shall declare him ritually clean."

13:24 καὶ σάρξ precedes ἐάν as at v.18,[34] though MT begins with the correlative conjunction. Vv.18—23 dealt with a ἕλκος which either did or did not turn to leprosy; vv.24—28 deal with a κατάκαυμα under similar conditions, and the או is

---

31. Apparently Aq Sym read χωρίσει instead of ἀφοριεῖ.
32. See THGL 101.
33. See Lee 35 for the idiom κατὰ χώραν μείνῃ.
34. See THGL 74.

sensible, since the section begins a new situation, but LXX substitutes the much more common καί. The verse details the conditions, and v.25 gives instructions with regard to those conditions obtaining.

There might appear a κατάκαυμα πυρός "a burning caused by fire" on his skin, with the genitive showing source. The phrase translates מכות אש word for word. What is meant is a burn caused by a burning coal or hot ashes. The second condition speaks of τὸ ὑγιασθὲν τοῦ κατακαύματος which translates מחית המכוה. What is probably meant is the raw flesh of the burn. For the notion that the healthy flesh is the flesh underneath the skin see comment on ὑγιούς at v.10. This raw flesh "appears τηλαυγές reddish-white or quite white." MT has בהרת לבנה אדמדמת או לבנה which is difficult to translate. It seems to say "(and the raw flesh of the burn should become) an inflammation white-reddish or white." LXX has added αὐγάζον "shining bright" (modifying τὸ ὑγιασθέν), which is really a doublet on τηλαυγές.

13:25 The opening verb in MT, ראה, is modified by אתה, which refers to the מחית המכוה or the בהרת, i.e. the affected area, but LXX has αὐτόν, i.e. the priest examines the person with the sore. Should the priestly examination discover (καὶ ἰδού) first that a white hair has appeared in the αὐγάζον. The term appeared with the more usual rendering of בהרת, τηλαυγές, in v.24, and must refer to the inflamed area. The participle, like its Hebrew equivalent, basically refers to something that shines, and refers here to what the burned spot looks like, thus "the shiny spot." For the second condition, "and its appearance is lower than the skin," see comment at v.4.

The conclusion is clear: "it is leprosy; it sprouted in the burn." Since the burn is now exposed flesh "the priest must declare him infectious."

In the tradition, for θρὶξ λευκή the majority F M text reads the accusative τρίχα λευκήν.[35] This is clearly an easier reading, since the verb is μετέβαλεν, which is usually modified either by an accusative or an εἰς phrase. Here the more difficult reading is supported by the oldest extant witnesses, B and A, and is original Lev;[36] for the same pattern see comment at v.3.

---

35. Theod also has τρίχα λευκήν, whereas Sym retains the text of Lev.
36. See THGL 123.

13:26 The opposite diagnosis is also possible. Suppose a white hair does not appear in the area of the shiny spot,[37] nor is it lower than the skin, but it is lusterless, what then? The apodosis, introduced by an apodotic καί, states that the priest must quarantine him for seven days.[38]

In the tradition, hex has corrected Lev by adding αυτην after ἰδῇ; Lev had failed to render the suffix of MT's יראנה, following the יראה of Sam.

13:27 As in similar cases (see vv.4,5; cf also v.21) a week's isolation issues in another priestly examination; this takes place τῇ ἡμέρᾳ τῇ ἑβδόμῃ. In MT this is a prepositional phrase, and hex has introduced the dative structure with εν to equal the Hebrew. Should it (i.e. τὸ ὑγιασθὲν τοῦ κατακαύματος) have actually spread on the skin, then (an apodotic καί) the priest must declare him infectious. For διαχύσει διαχέηται see v.22. MT introduces the collocation with אם, but LXX has ἐὰν δέ; a *d* text omitted δέ; this equals MT, but it is hardly recensional. The Byz text reads και εαν.

The apodosis, introduced by καί, requires that "the priest must declare him infectious." MT ends with the statement: נגע צרעת הוא which LXX does translate, but then adds ἐν τῷ ἕλκει ἐξήνθησεν. As in the case of v.22, the translator has levelled with v.20; cf comment ad loc. It should be noted that Syh again has omitted this; for a possible explanation see comment at v.22.

13:28 By contrast to v.27 should the shiny spot be localized, i.e. "should remain in place ..., it is the scar of the burn." MT has for the opening condition תחתיה תעמד הבהרת. For τὸ αὐγάζον rendering הברהת see comment at v.25.[39] For the reading κατὰ χώραν for החהיה see comment at v.23. For the next clause the verb διαχυθῇ is aorist subjunctive, in contrast to the present subjunctive in v.27. The change in aspect is clear; in v.27 the infection was spreading; here it did not spread. The third clause contains a contrastive δέ, ἀμαυρά contrasting with αὐγάζον. It is no longer inflamed, but is now lusterless. It is identified simply as "the scar of the burn."

Accordingly, the priest must declare him ritually clean. The basis for the priestly declaration (γάρ/כי) is that "it has the distinctive mark of the burn." The

---

37. Sym has τῇ ἐκλάμψει instead of τῷ αὐγάζοντι.
38. Instead of ἀφοριεῖ Sym has τηρήσει, and Theod reads συγκλείσει; cf also v.4.
39. Theod has τὸ τηλαύγημα.

Hebrew calls it צרבת המכוה "the scab of the burn," for which see comment at v.23.

13:29 Vv.29—37 deal with scalp and beard infections. The ἐάν clause is defined by a pair of dative nouns, καὶ ἀνδρὶ καὶ γυναικί.⁴⁰ MT uses the correlative conjunction between the two nouns. The verse only gives the "if." clause.⁴¹ The condition reads: "if there should be ἐν αὐτοῖς ἁφὴ λέπρας on the head or in the beard." MT has the singular pronoun, בו, but the translator noted that it could be "man or woman," and so used the plural αὐτοῖς.⁴² The *C*⁽ ⁾ *n s* text read αὐτῷ which is likely taken from one of The Three. LXX also prejudges the case as an infection of leprosy, while MT leaves the diagnosis to the priest, simply having נגע. The ἁφή is located according to MT בראש או בזקן, "on the head or on the chin." Since the infection can involve either a man or a woman, זקן must here mean "chin," rather than its more usual meaning "beard." The translator, however, uses ἐν τῷ πώγωνι which only means "in the beard." The Hebrew word זקן "beard, chin," occurs 18 times in MT; once LXX has a different text (βραχίονές), and everywhere else it is always translated by πώγων. Similarly πώγων always and only translates זקן. It is therefore a calque, i.e. it takes its meaning from the Hebrew, and should here be translated not by "beard," but by "chin."

13:30 The apodosis, introduced by καί, demands that the priest examine the infection; the examination reveals a) that the infected spot "is deeper than the skin." The translator had rendered עמק in vv.3,4,25 by ταπεινή, but now changes to ἐγκοιλοτέρα (also in v.31), and in vv.32 and 34, back to κοίλη, all with no change in meaning whatsoever; it simply illustrates the Lev translator's love of variation. The syntax is different, however. Since ἐγκοιλοτέρα is a comparative, it is modified by a genitive: "deeper than." κοιλή is a positive degree and is modified by an ἀπό phrase. b) "but the hair in it (i.e. in the infected spot) is yellowed, thin."⁴³

---

40. See THGL 74.
41. The Three differ on the conditional particle: Aq has ὅταν; Theod, ὅτι, and Sym retains the ἐάν of Lev.
42. All The Three read ἐν αὐτῷ.
43. Theod has αὐτῷ instead of αὐτῇ, but this is meaningless without an extant context; or is Theod here imitating the Hebrew בו? Apparently hex also read the masculine pronoun.

The priestly declaration has it that it renders him infectious; cf comment at v.3. The medical diagnosis is: "it is θραῦσμα, i.e. "a scale, scab," for the Hebrew נתק,[44] which is something that can be torn off, and on the skin it would be a scab which is easily scratched off; probably some form of scurf of the scalp is meant. θραῦσμα is further defined as "it is leprosy of the head or leprosy of the chin." MT does not repeat "leprosy" for the second alternative, and Syh has omitted it, illustrating the tendency of the Syriac translator of Lev to correct the text by omitting passages which hex judged to be without counterpart in MT. For the translation πώγwνος see comment at v.29.

13:31 And should the priest examine the scaly infection and discover (καὶ ἰδού; see comment at vv.10,20) that a) it does not appear to be lower than the skin; MT has מראהו, and hex corrects Lev by adding αυτου after ὄψις to render the suffix. b) "and there is no yellowish hair in it" (i.e. in the infection). MT has a different text; it reads שעיר שחר אין בו "there is no black hair in it." The black hair would be normal hair; what is meant is that evidence of normalcy is still not present, and so a period of isolation remains necessary. The translator views it from the perspective of evidence of the infection not being present. And so the priest must then "isolate the one with the scaly infection for seven days"; The term τὴν ἀφὴν τοῦ θραύσματος is, of course, metonymic for the individual with the infection.

13:32 Priestly examination on the seventh day reveals no change: a) "the scaliness has not spread"; b) "and there is no yellowish hair in it." In the tradition, ἐν αὐτῇ is changed to εν αυτω by the Byz text; cf footnote at v.30. MT has בו before שער צהב, and hex has changed the word order to conform to MT. c) "the appearance of the scaliness is not deeper than the skin." Here the positive degree is used for the adjective, κοίλη, with ἀπό to show comparison;[45] cf comment at v.30.

13:33 This verse is the apodosis, but is introduced by καί in imitation of MT. MT distinguishes the stems of גלח in the first two clauses, using the Hithp for the first one, but an active form, the Pi, for the second. LXX uses the future passive

---

44. Aq calls it an ἀπόσπασμα "something torn off, a shred."
45. See SS 148.

for both, i.e. "the skin must be shaved, but the scaly spot must not be shaved." LXX also differs from MT in which the first verb has no subject expressed; LXX has added τὸ δέρμα for good sense along with Tar.⁴⁶ Furthermore, "the priest shall quarantine τὸ θραῦσμα for seven days a second time"; the noun is of course metonymic for the one with the scale. For τὸ δεύτερον see comment at v.5.

13:34 On reexamination after seven days it appears (see comment at vv.10,20 for καὶ ἰδού) that a) "the scaly spot has not spread in the skin after he was shaven." LXX has added μετὰ ξυρηθῆναι αὐτόν, and Syh has omitted it to equal MT; presumably hex had marked it with an obelus, and b) "the appearance of the scaly spot is not deeper than the skin." MT has מראהו "its appearance," but LXX has rendered the suffix by its referent as τοῦ θραύσματος. For κοίλη ἀπό see comment at v.32.

V.b is the apodosis, and exactly reproduces the apodosis of v.6; cf comment ad loc. As at v.6 hex has added an αυτου after ἱμάτια to represent the suffix of בגדיו.

13:35—36 Still another caveat obtains. "Should the scaliness actually be spreading in the skin after he had been declared clean" is a real possibility.

V.36 is the apodosis; as usual it is introduced by an apodotic καί. MT states that the priest ראהו "shall examine him." LXX fails to render the suffix and uses the verb absolutely as at vv.10,13,17,20,21,26. Hex has, however, added αυτον to represent the Hebrew suffix.⁴⁷ The diagnosis (καὶ ἰδού) reveals that "the scaliness has spread in the skin." The use of the perfect διακέχυται neatly contrasts with the present subjunctive of the protasis; "the θραῦσμα has spread."

The conclusion is obvious; he is unclean. It is thus necessary for the priest to search for yellowed hair as evidence. The word for "yellowed" is χανθῆς, which translates צהב. This word also occurred at vv.30,32, where it was translated by the cognate present participle ξανθίζουσα. The majority M text reads χανθιζουσης here, which was undoubtedly due to the influence of vv.30 and 32. The use of the adjective was typically due to the translator's desire to vary the translation.⁴⁸

---

46. The Tar all indicate what is to be shaved: Tarᴼ has סחרני נתקא; Tarᴶ reads שערא ניתקא דחזרגות, and Tarᴺ makes it לניתקא חזור-חזור. Tar all read an active verb as well.
47. See THGL 106.
48. See THGL 73.

The verb used to render the verb בקר "to search out, examine" is ἐπισκέ-ψεται, which occurs here with a περί phrase, thus "to search for."[49] The περί phrase is a good rendering of לשער הצהב.[50] LXX also makes explicit what is probably implicit in the asyndetic טמא הוא by introducing its translation with ὅτι, thereby making the connection between the fact that "he is unclean" and the lack of any need for searching for a yellowish hair in the infected area.

13:37 בעיניו עמד also appeared at v.5, but transposed. There the prepositional phrase was rendered by ἐναντίον αὐτοῦ, but here by an adverbial ἐνώπιον "obviously, clearly." For the ways in which modern versions have understood the Hebrew see comment at v.5. In other words, "but if the scaly spot should obviously remain in place." Hex understood it as a preposition and added αυτου to represent the suffix. On the other hand, it may simply be an ad sensum addition, since the prepositional use of ἐνώπιον is far more common. Hex also placed ἐπὶ χώρας under the obelus, since it has no formal equivalent in MT; it was obviously based on v.23 where κατὰ χώραν occurred. Here it constitutes together with ἐνώπιον a clarifying paraphrase of בעיני. The C' s text has actually stressed this by transposing κατὰ χώρας immediately after ἐνώπιον. A popular variant has attempted similar clarification by reordering the phrase after the verb μείνῃ. A second condition was added: "and a black hair should be sprouting in it"; in other words, evidence of normal growth, a black hair, should appear.

The conclusion is then obvious: "the scaliness has been healed; he is ritually clean." The latter statement must apply to the individual, since καθαρός is used. An A B+ text has καθαρον, which would apply to θραῦσμα. Either would be possible in Hebrew (i.e. הוא could apply to the individual or to הנתק), but only καθαρός is correct. The scaliness could hardly be declared clean. Since he is καθαρός "the priest must declare him clean."

13:38 The ἐάν clause is preceded by καὶ ἀνδρὶ ἢ γυναικί as at v.29,[51] but then τῆς σαρκός in the clause itself is modified by αὐτοῦ, whereas MT read the more logical בשרם. Presumably αὐτοῦ can refer to either ἀνδρὶ ἢ γυναικί in LXX, but

---

49. This was insufficiently exact for Aq who translated it by ζητήσει.
50. But Aq had εἰς τρίχωμα τὸ ξανθόν. For הצהב Theod retained Lev, but Sym had <τῆς> στιλβῆς.
51. See THGL 74.

αυτων would have been more exact. The introductory datives have promoted a majority variant text reading ω before ἐάν, as well as a minority reading ω αν.⁵² What might appear on the skin are αὐγάσματα αὐγάζοντα λευκαθίζοντα "shining white spots," the rendering of MT's בהרת בהרה לבנת. But the Masoretes placed the first cut between the two cases of בהרת, and their text means "shining spots, even shining white spots." LXX found the repetition of בהרת odd, and since its parent text was purely consonantal, it was possible to vocalize the second בהרת as a participle, creating αὐγάζοντα.

13:39 A priestly examination confirms what had been stated in v.38. MT, however, has a different diagnosis: והנה בעור בשרם בהרת כהות לבנת "and behold on the skin of their flesh are dull-white spots." For כהות see vv.21,26,28, where LXX translates by ἀμαυρά/-ρόν. The translator however, simply levelled with v.38, repeating αὐγάσματα αὐγάζοντα λευκαθίζοντα; in other words, he read כהות as a second בהרת. For the intent of αὐτοῦ see comment at v.38.

This is not leprosy, but rather ἀλφός ἐστιν "it is a white rash or scurf."⁵³ The Hebrew it represents is בהק, a hapax legomenon whose exact meaning is uncertain; it obviously was some kind of white looking scale disease. A popular F M variant has omitted the statement καθαρός ἐστιν, which follows the identification of the spot as a white scurf. This may represent a hex correction, since it has no correspondent in MT, and is premature; it is rightly found at the end of the verse.

MT then makes the statement פרח בעור "it has sprouted on the skin." LXX changed the tense to a present ἐξανθεῖ, possibly having understood פרח as a participle. But it has also levelled with v.38 by adding τῆς σαρκὸς αὐτοῦ after δέρματι.

In the tradition, a majority F M variant text has λευκανθιζουσα instead of λευκαθίζοντα. The reading is palaeographically explicable, and the Hebrew לבנת supports Lev.⁵⁴ The omission of τῆν σαρκὸς αὐτοῦ 2° by ms 58 (as well as by Syh) suggests that hex may well have had the structure under the obelus. This ms has undergone post-hexaplaric revision, demonstrated inter alia by its frequent omission of passages under the obelus throughout the Pentateuch.

---

52. See THGL 74.
53. Hardly with LS sub voce *dull-white leprosy*, since the context explicitly states καθαρός ἐστιν.
54. See LS sub λευκαθίζω.

13:40 Vv.40—44 deal with baldness and its possible relation to "leprosy." LXX renders the initial איש "and as for someone" by a dative τινι within the ἐάν structure, which is an appropriate rendering.⁵⁵ The condition described is μαδήσῃ ἡ κεφαλὴ αὐτοῦ "his head has become bald." The Hebrew has the verb מרט "to make smooth, bare," and so in the Ni "to make bald." This is not a disease, but simply φαλακρός/קרח "baldness," and therefore not unclean, or better positively stated καθαρός ἐστιν.

13:41 But "should his head become bald κατὰ πρόσωπον (i.e. on the front side." This is somewhat simpler than MT's מפאת פניו "from the corner of his face." What is probably meant is the forehead and temples. LXX did not render the suffix, and hex has added αυτου to represent it. This is called a גבח/ἀναφάλαντος "a bald forehead." That the Greek term was not well-known is apparent from the tradition, in which αναφαλανδος, αναφαλαφθος as well as αναφανδαλος are attested. As in the case of v.40 this is not a disease, so καθαρός ἐστιν.

13:42 The case is different, however, "if there should be a ἁφὴ λευκὴ πυρρίζοντα in his bald spot or in his bald forehead." MT lacks equivalents for "his" in both phrases, and follows Sam's בקרחתו and בגבחתו. Hex has omitted the second αὐτοῦ to equal MT. MT has נגע לבן אדמדם, which LXX translates correctly by ἀφὴ λευκὴ πυρρίζουσα "a reddening white infection." Almost all witnesses have an η between the two modifiers, but this is simply a case of dittography after λευκή.⁵⁶

This is then identified as "λέπρα ἐξανθοῦσά ἐστιν in his bald spot or in his bald forehead," which renders MT word for word. There is no good reason for considering the A B x+ omission of ἐξανθοῦσα as original text. The shorter text was probably influenced by the common collocation λέπρα ἐστιν.⁵⁷

13:43 MT has אתו as modifier of ראה. This could refer to נגע or to the איש of v.40, whereas Sam has אתה referring to צרעת; LXX has αὐτόν, which can only refer to the person involved. The priestly examination yields the diagnosis (καὶ

---
55. See THGL 116.
56. For a fuller defence of Lev as original text see THGL 101.
57. See THGL 114.

ἰδού): "the appearance of the reddening white infection ... is like the form (εἶδος) of leprosy in the skin of his flesh," in other words, it looks like leprosy. LXX has, however, not rendered MT correctly, but has levelled with other judgments in using ἡ ὄψις (τῆς ἀφῆς), while MT has (הנגע) שאת "the swelling (of the infection)"; see comment at v.2 where the word is rendered by οὐλή, the regular translation of שאת. The term ὄψις had been used throughout the chapter to translate מראה, which occurs in the predicate of the nominal הנה clause as כמראה. The translator could hardly use ὄψις again, so he chose to translate this by ὡς εἶδος, a synonym which I translated by "(like) the form of." The unusual description of צרעת as עור בשר "leprosy of the flesh's skin," LXX simplifies by leveling with ἐν δέρματι τῆς σαρκὸς αὐτοῦ of vv.38,39, and comp also vv.2,3,11. The final αὐτοῦ has been omitted by a popular Byz variant text; this is undoubtedly recensional in character, since MT lacks a suffix for בשר.

13:44 Such a one is declared to be ἄνθρωπος λεπρός "a leprous individual"; the adjective renders צרוע, a passive participle, "one afflicted with צרעת." To this MT has added טמא הוא. The next word is the free infinitive טמא, and the translator's shorter text is based on parablepsis due to homoioteleuton. Hex has corrected Lev by adding ακαθαρτος εστιν.[58]

The priest must then μιάνσει μιανεῖ αὐτόν "declare him fully infectious." The cognate dative represents an attempt at rendering the cognate free infinitive טמא, which adds additional stress on the verbal notion, and the Greek must be taken in the same way. Its omission by an A+ text is an error due to homoiarchon. The verse ends with a nominal clause with "on his head" constituting the predicate for ἡ ἀφὴ αὐτοῦ, thus "his infection is on his head," which renders MT literally.

13:45 This verse and the following describe the conditions under which "the leprous one in whom the infection is must exist. It should be noted that the subject is not the ἄνθρωπος λεπρός of v.44, but is now "ὁ λεπρός in whom ἡ ἀφή is." It is the leprous one in whom infection exists, not with just infection on the head, but generically ἡ ἀφή. The rule applies to anyone suffering from ἡ ἀφή. a) "let his clothing be torn"; Note the Classical usage of congruence between a

---

58. This is also attested for Theod and Sym.

singular verb and a neuter plural subject.[59] In the tradition, an A F M majority text has εσται instead of ἔστω, but the third person imperative must be original.[60] b) "and his head uncovered." MT has a somewhat more vivid picture with its יהיה פרוע "(his head) shall be let loose." What is meant is that his head will not be bound up, and his hair will be allowed to hang loose, dishevelled. The Greek ἀκατακάλυπτος is not incorrect; it is simply unimaginative. Furthermore, the יהיה is not translated. A popular B M variant has the simplex ακαλυπτος; it is palaeographically much more likely that the shorter form is an error, i.e. a *lapsus oculi* from ακα to the second ακα, rather than the addition of ακατ at the beginning. c) "let him cast (something) around his mouth," i.e. let him cover his mouth. MT has על שפם יעטה "let him make a covering over the moustache." LXX has understood this to be metonymic for τὸ στόμα αὐτοῦ. A popular B F M text has the aorist περιβαλεσθω instead of the present; the action involved is something that is to be continuous, and the translator must have intended the present. The variant aorist is then the result of haplography. d) καὶ ἀκάθαρτος κεκλήσεται. MT, however, reads וטמא טמא יקרא "and he must call out: unclean, unclean." LXX has read טמא only once, and understood יקרא as Ni, whereas the Masoretes have vocalized the verb as Qal. An F M+ text has repeated ακαθαρτος, but this is not overly sensible without changing the voice of the verb to an active one.

13:46 The verse begins with an accusative denoting extent of time, i.e. "all the days that the infection might be on him." The ὅσας clause lacks a verb in MT, and the word order also differs. The correction to η αφη επ αυτω equals MT, and is a hex reordering. A *d* reading omits ἧ, but this only by coincidence equals MT; it is a case of haplography (after ἀφή in the hex text).

In MT this all modifies יטמא, which is in turn followed by טמא הוא. These are transposed in LXX which reads ἀκάθαρτος ὤν before ἀκάθαρτος ἔσται. No attempt at reordering these structures was made in the tradition. The Greek may be interpreted as meaning: "since he is unclean he shall (continue to) be unclean."

Furthermore, "set apart he shall dwell; outside the camp shall be his manner of life." MT has בדד to describe how he will dwell, which is well-rendered

---

59. See SS 197.
60. See the comment in THGL 126.

by the perfect passive participle, which does presuppose that the isolation preceded the dwelling, and this results in dwelling in isolation. MT has a noun cognate to ישב at the end of the verse, מושבו "his dwelling place." The translator's love for variation probably promoted his rather fancy αὐτοῦ ἡ διατριβή, which stresses his way of life, manner of existence, at best a free rendering. The correspondence occurs only here in OT; in fact, the word only occurs five times in total (also three times in Prov and once in Jer). The reordering of αὐτοῦ after the noun is probably hex in origin.

13:47 Vv.47—59 concern garments and their possible infection. The ἐάν clause is preceded by a dative ἱματίῳ, which then serves as antecedent for the prepositional phrase within the clause, ἐν αὐτῷ. What might appear in the garment is ἁφή λέπρας. Just what a leprous infection in a garment might be is uncertain, but it probably refers to mildew, i.e. a mold due to dampness, but it is still called "an infection of leprosy" in LXX; obviously λέπρας is hardly "leprosy" here; it would seem sensible to translate the word when it refers to a condition affecting clothing as "mold" or "mildew."

The ἐν αὐτῷ is further explicated by "in a woolen garment or in a στιππυίνῳ garment." The Hebrew term is פשתים more commonly rendered by λινός "linen." The term στιππύινος refers to "tow, oakum," i.e. the flax broken up and readied for spinning.[61] Garments were made almost exclusively either of wool or linen in the ancient Near East; in fact, other types of cloth such as cotton or silk were, if not completely unknown, certainly exceedingly rare.

13:48 This is a continuation of the explication of ἐν αὐτῷ of v.47: "whether in the warp or in the woof, whether in linen or woolen materials, whether in skin or in any skin (i.e. leather) product." LXX introduces each of the six prepositional phrases with the correlative ἤ, whereas MT uses או only for the first and the third pair. The middle pair in the Hebrew read לפשתים ולצמר, i.e. they refer to the first pair. What the Hebrew means is that the infection can be in the warp or woof of either linen or wool, whereas the Greek makes all the phrases not only coordinate, but also levels them to ἐν phrases. It does, however, differentiate the middle pair in two ways: the nouns are in the plural, and they are articulated. Of

---

61. For the word and its various spellings see Walters 78—79.

some interest is the doublet gloss for the middle pair, recensional in character, which appears in two *n* mss: η εις το στιππυον και εις το εριον; I suspect Theod as the source.

13:49 The condition which validates the suspicion of infection is that the ἀφή, here "the infected spot," should become greenish or reddish; LXX uses two present participles to render the Hebrew adjectives. MT then continues with בבגד או בעור "in a garment or in leather (lit. skin)," which LXX transposes: ἐν τῷ δέρματι ἢ ἐν τῷ ἱματίῳ, probably intentionally done so that "either in the warp or in the woof" would follow "clothing" rather than "skin." The translator is consistent in this respect. This is followed in turn by ἢ ἐν παντὶ σκεύει ἐργασίμῳ δέρματος. MT has no equivalent for ἐργασίμῳ, however, which constitutes a leveling with v.48, where מלאכת does occur in MT. Hex has placed the word under the obelus to signal this situation. Hex has also transposed δέρματι and ἱματίῳ to equal the word order of MT.

The apodosis states that "it is a mildew infection," which actually had already been stated as the presupposition being put forward in v.47. MT then continues with והראה את הכהן; the Masoretes vocalized the verb as a Ho, i.e. "and it must be shown to the priest"; LXX renders the Ho by an active verb δείξει, probably in view of the modification by an את phrase, which is usually translated by an accusative or a dative.[62] But there is no subject expressed, and one would have to assume that either the subject is indefinite: "one must show," or that the owner of the infected material is meant.

13:50 The term ἀφήν is used in both clauses; in the first clause it refers to the infected spot, and in the second, to the infected goods. In the second clause the subject ὁ ἱερεύς is repeated, though not in MT,[63] and hex has placed it under the obelus as not present in MT. The infected garment must be quarantined for seven days.

13:51 The results of the priestly reexamination are given in a conditional structure introduced by ἐὰν δέ with the actual apodosis given in v.52, though a declarative judgment intervenes in v.51b. The protasis, introduced by ἐὰν δέ (for

---

62. See GK 121c for the Hebrew construction.
63. But it is present in Kenn 69,111.

Hebrew כי i.e. without a conjunction), presupposes that the infection would be spreading. Note the use of the present tense, rightly understanding פשׂה as a progressive action. LXX had some difficulty with the modifier of בעור, viz. לכל אשר יעשה העור למלאכה, which it rendered by κατὰ πάντα ὅσα ἂν ποιηθῇ δέρματα ἐν τῷ ἐργασίᾳ. It correctly rendered לכל by κατὰ πάντα "according to anything," and did understand the verb as Ni. δέρματα rendered עור as a collective, and is the neuter plural subject of the verb. I would translate the Greek: "in anything for which skins might be worked up in manufacture," in other words, leather products of any kind.

The priestly diagnosis was: "it is chronic mildew," ἔμμονος "continual, persistent, chronic" rendering ממארת. The word occurs only four times in OT, three times of λέπρα (also v.52 14:44) and in Ezek 28:24 in the figure סלון ממאיר וקוץ מכאב describing malicious (?) neighbours of the house of Israel. The ממאיר briars are coordinated with "thorns causing pain," Obviously ממאיר does not mean "chronic," but something like "hurtful, sharp"; in fact, the Greek translates by (σκόλοψ) πικρίας. Moderns are quite uncertain about its meaning. NJPS translates "malignant," and NRSV has "spreading," while NIV makes it "destructive."[64] Since it is λέπρα, it is ἀκάθαρτος "unclean."

13:52 The Greek does not introduce the apodosis with a conjunction, and hex has added a και to represent MT. The subject of κατακαύσει is the priest of v.51. ἱμάτιον is defined by "whether warp or woof in the woolen or in the linen materials."[65] For the plural nouns, see comment at v.48.

It is the next structure that is more problematic. In MT it is clear from the prepositions that "the garment" and "every vessel of skin" are coordinate, since both are governed by את. But the translator has used ἐν which makes ἐν παντὶ σκεύει δερματίνῳ coordinate with "in woolen or in linen materials," which is difficult. Only the relative clause modifying σκεύει rescues it from misunderstanding. Common sense dictates that it must modify κατακαύσει, even though κατα-

---

64. Vulg supports LXX with its *perseverans*, and see also Tar^JN מחלטא, and Tar^O מחזרא.
65. SS 123 in my opinion is wrong in the statement "In Lev 13:52 hat der Übersetzer wohl den Text nicht verstanden und das ב mit ἐν wiedergegeben, obgleich die Übersetzung keinen Sinn ergibt." The ב is not, as the writer suggests, a ב of material, but simply of location. The warp or the woof is in the materials.

καίω ἐν is abnormal Greek. The translator was apparently momentarily inattentive, and continued with an ἐν structure instead of the normal accusative.

The reason for the destruction is given in a ὅτι/כי clause: λέπρα ἔμμονός ἐστιν. For ἔμμονος see comment at v.51. It is chronic leprosy, it must be burned up by fire.[66]

13:53 LXX has failed to render הנה in the usual fashion by ἰδού; actually this makes no lexical difference, since והנה after "but if the priest should make an examination" merely informs what he saw, i.e. it constitutes the diagnosis. In this case, it is noted that the infected spot had not spread in the garment ... or in the leather vessel.

13:54 The apodosis states that "the priest must give orders καὶ πλυνεῖ (that) on which the infection would be." MT more sensibly has וכבסו with indefinite plural subject, i.e. "the priest shall order that they wash ...;" in LXX the subject must be an indefinite singular; one might translate: "the priest must order that the object be washed." The Greek is hardly luminous, and it seems to say that the priest himself shall do the washing. The *n* text has corrected the verb to πλυνουσιν, obviously a recensional variant. Highly unusual is πλυνεῖ ἐφ', since the verb is normally modified by an accusative. MT has את אשר בו הנגע as modifier of כבסו "and they shall wash that on which the infection obtains." The Greek has tried to render it word for word by ἐφ' οὗ (ἂν ᾖ) ἐπ' αὐτοῦ ἡ ἀφή. The *n* text has an even more literal rendering, substituting for the prepositional structures εν ω and εν αυτω resp; these may well represent Theod.

The final clause states "and the priest shall isolate the infection for seven days a second time." For τὸ δεύτερον see comment at v.5. MT does not name the subject,[67] and hex has accordingly placed ὁ ἱερεύς under the obelus. Nor does MT support τὴν ἀφήν; rather it has a pronominal suffix to the verb: הסגירו, and hex has added αυτο after ἀφοριεῖ. It should be noted that both G and Syh have omitted τὴν ἀφήν, i.e. have substituted αυτο for the nominal, thereby equally MT exactly. This may well represent what hex actually did.

---

66. The ἐν (πυρί) is instrumental; see SS 117.
67. But Kenn 9,110,152 add הכהן after והסגירו.

13:55 The priest shall make an examination μετὰ τὸ πλυθῆναι τὴν ἀφήν. The subject of the passive infinitive is τὴν ἀφήν, thus "after the infected (spot) has been washed." In the tradition, a B+ gloss has added αυτο after the infinitive, and an A F b+ text has glossed it with αυτου. Neither can be considered original, since the infinitive is not active, i.e. it cannot be understood as "after his having washed the infected spot."[68]

The following clause is introduced in highly unusual fashion by καὶ ἥδε for והנה. The pronoun has wide and varied usage, however, and is not incorrect as a rendering for הנה. Apparently Lev simply varied the translation. That the itacistic ιδε of the d+ text technically equals MT as the apparatus in Lev indicates is only formally correct; ἥδε can also equal MT. Within the הנה clause MT has הפך modified by את עינו. LXX has understood this by its translation τὴν ὄψις "appearance," though hex has added αυτης to represent the suffix, the feminine pronoun referring to ἀφή.[69] One would expect the mildewed area to have been washed clean, and therefore to have altered (its) appearance. The declaration ἀκάθαρτόν ἐστιν must apply to ἱματίῳ and/or σκεύει of v.58. An n x+ variant text reads ακαθαρτος εστιν, an obvious attempt at simplification, i.e. making it apply to ἀφή, but the more difficult neuter must be original.

The third clause uses a present tense, διαχεῖται "is spreading." The point being made is that even though the infection is not spreading, it had not changed appearance, and it is thus unclean, and must be burned with fire.

The final statement explains all of this clearly in LXX: "it has been firmly set in the garment, either in the warp or the woof." The perfect passive verb ἐστήρικται represents a nominal construction in MT: פחתת הוא.[70] Unfortunately the hapax legomenon פחתת is completely unknown, and one can only guess at its meaning, as LXX did. Neither the ancients nor moderns know the word. It is modified by בקרחתו או בגבחתו "in its baldness or in its forehead baldness," often interpreted as referring to the bald spot towards the back or towards the front." but this is all quite uncertain. For the terms see vv.40—42. The translator, I suspect, also did not understand the clause, and did what a good translator should do in such a situation, i.e. make a contextual translation. This made fine sense,

---

68. See THGL 108; it might be noted that some witnesses add αυτω, but this is merely an itacistic spelling of the B text.
69. See SS 97.
70. See SS 81.

though I doubt whether that is what MT meant.[71] In the tradition, A B M G n+ read εστηριοται instead of ἐστήρικται. The older form attested by Lev is Attic, whereas the -σται inflection is only first found in NT.[72]

13:56 LXX, as at v.53 where the initial verb is also ἴδῃ, does not translate הנה as designating the diagnosis, but has only καί. This stated that the infected object would be lusterless μετὰ τὸ πλυθῆναι αὐτό "after it was washed." The αὐτό, however, cannot refer to ἀφή, but must be to the ἱματίῳ mentioned in v.56.

MT as usual introduces the apodosis with a conjunction, but LXX does not. This is unique for this chapter,[73] and Byz z add a και to represent it, which must be recensional. "He (i.e. the priest) must tear it (the infected spot) from the garment." αὐτό 2° must refer to the infected spot, even though ἀφήν is feminine. Lev often used the neuter where the antecedent was vague; furthermore, since αὐτό referring to ἱμάτιον had just occurred, it easily led to another neuter, i.e. the infected part of the garment as opposed to the garment as a whole from which it was to be torn.[74] In MT this is followed by "or from the skin or from the warp or from the woof." Lev follows this exactly, but I do not believe this to be original. The position of ἢ ἀπὸ τοῦ δέρματος in the majority M text is at the end of the verse. The consecution "either from the warp or from the woof" is consistently placed so as to refer to "the garment"; cf comment at v.49. I would now take ἢ ἀπὸ τοῦ δέρματος to have been moved to the position immediately after "garment" by hex in order to conform to the order of MT. Note that support for the hex order includes inter alia O Arm Syh, i.e. all the chief supporters of the hex recension.[75] The fact that A B F all support this shows that the hex text had wide influence and support.

---

71. Moderns have rendered the hapax legomenon plus its modifiers in various ways: NJPS has "it is a fret, whether on its inner side or on its outer side"; NRSV translates "whether the leprous spot is on the inside or on the outside," and NIV renders "whether the mildew has affected one side or the other." The ancients did no better. Pesh reads *mḥwt' hy bḥdtwth 'w bblywth* "whether the infection is fresh or old, i.e. chronic." Vulg renders paraphrastically by *eo quod infusa sit in superficia vestimenti vel per totum lepra*. Tar⁰ has תברא היא בשחיקותה או בחדתותה; Tarᴶ reads שקיעא היא ברדדיה או בלבדיה, and Tarᴺ has פחיתא היא בכליותה או בחדתותה.
72. For a detailed analysis see THGL 123—124.
73. See THGL 101.
74. See Huber 34—35.
75. My comments at THGL 103 incorrectly evaluate the evidence, placing overly much credence in the evidence of the old uncials.

13:57 "But if it still appears in the garment ...." The apodosis reads "λέπρα ἐξανθοῦσά ἐστιν." The subject must be ἡ ἀφή of v.56, though in MT the verb cannot refer to נגע which is masculine, and תראה is feminine, and probably refers to the פחתת of v.55. The translator's rendering is sensible, since the Hebrew word is not understood; see discussion at v.55. MT simply has פרחת הוא "it is sprouting." The translator identified this as "sprouting mildew," and hex has placed λέπρα under the obelus, it being absent from MT.

The subject of the last structure is ἐν ᾧ ἐστιν ἡ ἀφή, i.e. "that in which the infection resides"; this must be burned by fire.

13:58 This verse begins with an extended nominative pendant structure: "As for a garment, either the warp or the woof, or any leather vessel, which will have been washed and the infection will have disappeared from it." MT has a second person singular verb תכבס for the first verb, i.e. "which you might wash." The instructions are introduced by καί: "(and) it shall be washed a second time and it will be clean."

13:59 The subscription to vv.47—58. It declares this to be the rule (ὁ νόμος) concerning a mildew infection of a woolen or linen garment ... εἰς τὸ καθαρίσει αὐτὸ ἢ μιᾶναι αὐτό. The two cases of αὐτό refer to any of the possibilities given: "garment woolen or linen, either warp or woof, or any leather vessel."

The stress rests on the εἰς structure. In other words, what is important is how one knows on what basis the priest is to declare such material ritually clean or defiling. For the notion of defiling see comment at v.3.

Chapter 14

14:2 The superscription for regulations concerning the cleansing of the one afflicted with a scaly skin affliction, which are contained in vv.3—32. In MT this is put into the future, but LXX simply has a nominal clause: οὗτος ὁ νόμος. Hex has inserted εσται after the pronoun to represent the יהיה of the Hebrew. The use of יהיה in this formula is unique in the book. LXX has followed the usual pattern as in 6:9,14,25,31 7:1,27 11:46 12:7 13:59 14:32,54 15:3. The term λεπρός is the agentive corresponding to λέπρα; in MT it represents מצרע, a Pu participle, i.e. the one afflicted with מצרעת, for which see comment at 13:2.

The timer is expressed in MT by ביום plus a noun טהרתו, which in turn is coordinated to a verbal structure. LXX has represented these by ᾗ ἂν ἡμέρᾳ plus two coordinated verbals, only the second corresponding morphologically to MT. For טהרתו LXX has the passive καθαρισθῇ, thus "he might be declared ritually clean."[1] The coordinate verbal does, however, modify the timer, but is the apodosis, as the future passive verb indicates. What the Greek means is "at the time that he would be declared clean, he shall be brought to the priest"; this follows the pattern of 13:2, and comp v.9. The interpretation of LXX is fully possible, since MT does not make clear whether והובא is the apodosis, or is simply coordinate to טהרתו. In MT this does constitute v.b, with טהרתו accented with an *ethnach*.

14:3 Since the individual is still unclean, "the priest must go outside the camp." After all, one that is unclean may not enter the sanctuary. The priestly examination reveals (for καὶ ἰδού; see comment at 13:10,17) that "the scaly affliction is removed (literally has been healed) from the leprous one." More idiomatically put, "the scaly one has been healed of the scaly affliction." The phrase ἡ ἁφὴ τῆς λέπρας is unusual in that both nouns are articulated; except for v.32 and here it is always without articles.[2] In other words, it occurs only in the οὗτος ὁ νόμος formula in the chapter.

---

1. See SS 98.
2. See THGL 84.

14:4 προστάξει is used absolutely, "shall give orders"; this then is followed by καὶ λήμψονται, which accords with Sam's ולקחו rather than with the singular of MT. The plural is a simplification, since the indefinite subject is usually put in the plural in Hebrew. The singular λήψεται is attested in z+, but this is not necessarily recensional; it may simply be due to the influence of the coordinate προστάξει. For the pattern προστάξει ὁ ἱερεὺς καί plus a plural coordinate verb, see v.5 as well. The dative perfect passive participle is a dative of advantage, i.e. "for the one who has been declared clean."

Four things are to be gathered for the one involved: a) two, live, clean, small birds. For "clean bird" see Deut 14:11. The term ὀρνίθιον occurs only in this chapter, and always renders צפור (13 times). Elsewhere in OT צפור is usually translated by ὄρνεον. b) ξύλον κέδρινον "cedar wood" occurs here in the Pentateuch for the first time. It may well have been considered appropriate by reason of its red color.³ c) κεκλωσμένον κόκκινον "red thread." The participle is from κλώθω "to spin," hence "that which has been spun, a thread."⁴ See the Note at Exod 25:4, and d) ὕσσωπον. The "hyssop" also occurred in the Passover story in Exod 12:22, where a bunch of hyssop was used to paint the lintels with blood. The term ὕσσωπος is a calque for the Hebrew אזוב, which it always and only translates in OT.

14:5 "The priest must give orders that they should kill the one bird." As in v.4 the second verb is inflected in the indefinite plural, following Sam over against MT; see comment at v.4. The slaughter is to be done "over fresh water." The term actually means "living" water, and it probably intends "running water" as opposed to still or stagnant water. Furthermore, it is to be done "in a clay vessel," which would presumably be broken after use, since it was contaminated by the blood.

14:6 LXX follows Sam in beginning the verse with καί, over against MT.⁵ The verse begins with a pendant accusative: τὸ ὀρνίθιον τὸ ζῶν, which is then brought into the verbal clause by an αὐτό, thus "as for the living bird, he shall take it." The subject is singular, and must be the priest. For the nominals coordinate with

---
3. So Milgrom 835.
4. Sym has διπλοῦν κόκκινον (retroverted from Syh).
5. But Kenn 69,81*,84,95*,602 do change את to ואת as well.

αὐτό see v.4; instead of κεκλωσμένον there, v.6 reads κλωστόν with the same meaning. In the tradition, A b n+ read the participle, undoubtedly under the influence of v.4. The αὐτά must refer to the coordinate nominals only, since καὶ τὸ ὀρνίθιον τὸ ζῶν follows. All these as well as the living bird he must then dip in the blood of the slaughtered bird. The final phrase, ἐφ' ὕδατι ζῶντι, modifies the participle σφαγέντος; this is clear from v.5 where the phrase modifies σφάξουσιν.

In the tradition, τὸν (ὕσσωπον) appears as την in the F M majority text. The gender of the word is quite obscure, and Lev's τόν simply follows the oldest witnesses, B and A.[6]

14:7 Then "he shall sprinkle about over the one declared clean of the scaly infection seven times," after which "he (i.e. the one declared clean) shall be ritually clean." MT, however, has a Pi verb with suffix: "he shall declare him clean." LXX is a case of leveling with the popular statement וטהר/καὶ καθαρὸς ἔσται, which occurs elsewhere, e.g. vv.8,9. In fact, it may even have been intended to avoid an oxymoron. Since the afflicted one is already τὸν καθαρισθέντα one can hardly declare him clean once again; rather "he shall be clean." The Byz text has revised the statement to και καθαρισει αυτον to equal MT, and may well be recensional. Instead of εἰς (τὸ πεδίον) MT has על פני. It is possible, though unlikely, that the reading επι of ms 72 (an oII ms) is recensional. πεδίον is used in the sense of the "open field," rendering שדה, which is more commonly rendered by ἀγρός, "field" in the sense of "the sown" as over against the "unsown."

14:8 The candidate must undergo an intermediate ritual of cleansing: "wash his garments," "shave off all his hair, and wash himself with water."[7] In the tradition, the future passive ξυρηθήσεται is changed to the middle form ξυρησεται by a popular F text, but with no change in meaning.[8] The passive (and middle) are used here with active meaning, as their modification by an accusative shows. The order of αὐτοῦ πᾶσαν τὴν τρίχα is changed by hex to conform to the MT order, i.e. with αὐτοῦ at the end.

---

6. See the discussion in THGL 119.
7. The ἐν is instrumental; see SS 118.
8. Sym also used ξυρήσεται.

Though he is now said to be ritually clean, on entering the camp he may still not dwell in his house, but must διατρίψει outside it for seven days. MT has ישב, but the translator has him "pass the time, reside." It only occurs here for ישב, but comp 13:46 διατριβή and comment ad loc. It would appear that to be fully καθαρός involved stages of purification.

14:9 The use of ἔσται plus τῇ ἡμέρᾳ plus an asyndetic verbal is unique for the book, as is its counterpart in MT. The cleansing rituals of v.8 are to be repeated, but are outlined here in much greater detail. Listed first is ξυρηθήσεται, for which see comment at v.8, but instead of simply "all his hair" as in v.8, this is detailed appositively as "his head, and τὸν πώγωνα καὶ τὰς ὀφρύας." MT has זקנו ואת גבת עיניו. ὀφρύας is the rendering for the bound phrase "brow of his eyes."[9] LXX disregards the suffixes in both cases as otiose. Since κεφαλήν was modified by αὐτοῦ, the repetition of the pronoun would be unidiomatic in Greek. Hex has, however, added αυτου after πώγωνα, and οφθαλμων αυτου after the second noun, in order to represent MT more exactly. The importance of the shaving of all his hair is stressed in that the order "he must shave all his hair" is an envelope statement, which both introduces and concludes the various areas of hair listed for shaving. Similarly LXX says "and he must wash τα ἱμάτια," to which most witnesses, possibly also hex in origin, have added αυτου as well. Over against v.8's "he must wash himself ἐν ὕδατι," here λούσεται τὸ σῶμα αὐτοῦ ὕδατι obtains. The lack of ἐν is of no consequence; ὕδατι and ἐν ὕδατι both mean the same, and the designation of the reflexive as τὸ σῶμα αὐτοῦ is a further detailing in exact fashion as was the case with the shaving.

14:10 The subject is still ὁ καθαρισθείς of v.8. According to MT, on the eighth day he is to take two male lambs and one female lamb, but LXX renders כבשים by ἀμνούς, and כבשה by πρόβατον. Since all are one year olds according to LXX, it is difficult to understand what distinction was intended by the translator. Actually, MT does not designate the כבשים as one year olds at all, which makes the text of LXX even more puzzling. Hex has placed ἐνιαυσίους, which followed the בני שנה of Sam, under the obelus to show its lack of equivalent in MT. The

---

9. See SS 69.

ἕν modifying πρόβατον, which does have an MT basis in אחת, is omitted by a B V x y+ text, but the next word is ἐνιαύσιον, and the shorter text is simply a matter of haplography.[10]

The structure τρία δέκατα σεμιδάλεως is an odd one, since one expects some kind of measure after "three-tenths," but LXX follows the Hebrew exactly. NRSV and NIV add "an ephah of" before "fine flour," and NJPS has "a measure of." This is "for a sacrifice." πεφυραμένης modifies σεμιδάλεως; it is the fine flour that is mixed with oil. It should be noted that this differs from MT, where בלולה modifies מנחה rather than סלת, i.e. "a sacrifice mixed (with oil)."[11] Also modifying λήμψεται, i.e. to be taken along with the fine flour, is "one κοτύλην of oil." This is a liquid measure of cir. one cup or a half-pint. This is somewhat less than the Hebrew לג, which is thought to be about two-thirds of a pint.

In the tradition, the V f n x+ text has πεφυραμενην instead of the genitive. This is a careless copyist error by attraction to the case of the immediately preceding θυσίαν. But it is the flour, not the sacrificial animals, which is mixed with oil.

14:11 The use of two present participles correctly differentiate the two cases of המטהר, the first being vocalized by the Masoretes as a Pi, thus active: "the one cleansing," and the second, as a Hithp: "the one seeking cleaning for himself." The Greek also distinguishes by voice, the first one being active, and the second, middle. They are in the present tense, since process is involved. The priest is the one engaging in the action of pronouncing cleansed, whereas the one who must be set before the Lord is the one who is seen to be seeking cleansing as a process.

Not only the one being cleansed is to be set before the Lord, but also ταῦτα, which refers to the lambs, the sheep, the fine flour and the oil of v.10. The phrase "before the Lord" is further defined as being located "at the door of the tent of witness."

14:12 The priest must bring forward the one lamb τῆς πλημμελείας, which translates לאשם. προσάξει would normally be modified by a second accusative, but πλημμελείας in the sense of a type of sacrifice is always in the genitive so as to distinguish it from its usual meaning of "trespass." For the genitive πλημ-

---

10. See THGL 114.
11. See Daniel 207.

μελείας as "trespasss offering," see comment at 5:15. At times the preposition is translated by περί, and a popular Byz text added a περι. Also to be brought is the κοτύλην of oil, for which see comment at v.10.

V.b identifies the ordered sacrificial action as ἀφοριεῖ αὐτὸ ἀφόρισμα, for which see comment at 10:15. "He shall set it aside as a separate portion" translates הניף אתם תנופה, for which see discussion at 7:20. The rendering of אתם by αὐτό is unusual; in fact, the majority of witnesses have "corrected" to αυτα.[12] The reference must be to τὸν ἀμνόν and τὴν κοτύλην, a masculine and a feminine. The translator voided the difficulty by using a neuter singular pronoun as a collective.[13]

14:13 LXX renders the singular verb שחט "he (i.e. the priest) must slaughter" by the indefinite plural σφάξουσιν. This is more sensible for the next verb ישחט where LXX uses the present tense σφάζουσιν, following the plural of Sam rather than MT. But that LXX avoids having the priest perform the slaughtering of the lamb is surprising, particularly since in the rest of the ceremony detailed in vv.14—20 the priest is the sole officiant. I suspect that the plural was used to place the major stress on the change in tense. After all, the indefinite plural does not exclude the priest. The future is a deliberate one,[14] whereas the present signifies customary action, thus "they shall sacrifice ... where they customarily sacrifice."

The coordinate modifiers of σφάζουσιν are τὰ ὁλοκαυτώματα καὶ τὰ περὶ ἁμαρτίας "the burnt offerings and the sin offerings." LXX has rightly understood the singulars of MT as collectives, but it has transposed the two. Hex has not only reordered the two but has also "corrected" the burnt offerings as a singular: τα περι αμαρτιας και το ολοκαυτωμα,[15] but left the sin offerings in the plural. This is a possible understanding of the consonantal text of MT; though החטאת can be read as a plural, העלה can not; it is a singular. These are to be offered במקום קדש; the bound phrase is correctly rendered by an adjectival one ἐν τόπῳ ἁγίῳ,[16] though the article of הקדש would expect an articulated phrase in translation. The כי clause is rendered by a γάρ structure, and details the reason

---

12. See Huber 35.
13. See THGL 97.
14. See Porter 424—425.
15. For חטאת as sin-offering see THGL 117.
16. See SS 65.

for sacrificing the two in a holy place, both belonging to the priests; see 6:36—37, and comments ad loc. I would translate: "For the sin offering is just like the trespass offering; it belongs to the priest." For the meaning of ἅγια ἁγίων ἐστιν see comment at 2:3. The plural ἅγια refers to the two types of sacrifice.

14:14 The priest must take ἀπό the αἵματος τοῦ of the trespass offering. The ἀπό is partitive.[17] The omission of τοῦ by C' s x+ does equal MT, but the recapitulive article occurs throughout the chapter and is original.[18] LXX unnecessarily repeats ὁ ἱερεύς for the second clause, in which it follows MT. The omission of the second הכהן in Sam and by the b+ text is a stylistic improvement, but is not LXX. For the placing of some blood on extremities of the right ear, right thumb, right big toe, see comments at 8:23. LXX idiomatically does not render the suffixes of ידו and רגלו, but the majority of witnesses, probably hex inspired, adds αυτου to both nouns. A meaningful variant obtains in an n+ text, reading κεκαθαρισμενου instead of the present participle of LXX, but the recipient is not yet fully cleansed; he is in the process of being cleansed, and the present tense is original.

14:15 The first clause in MT is reduced to a participial structure, λαβών, thereby placing the stress on the verb ἐπιχεεῖ. λαβων ... ἀπό means "taking some oil from." For κοτύλης see comment at v.10. The verb ἐπιχεεῖ is used absolutely, but what he is to pour out must be oil. The repetition of "the priest" modifying χεῖρα is in imitation of MT, and serves the useful purpose of assuring that the reference is not to the hand of the one being cleansed, but of the priest himself.

14:16 For the unusual modification of βάψει by an ἀπό phrase and its interpretation, see comment at 4:17; see also Note at Exod 12:22. The verb is usually modified by εἰς or ἐν phrases, e.g. v.6. The notion of "dipping from" also makes sense, since he must sprinkle the oil retained by the finger seven times before the Lord. MT has a pronominal suffix in both cases of "finger," but Greek avoids rendering it, since the reference could only be to his own finger.[19] Similarly, "hand" represents ידי in MT. Hex has in all three cases added αυτου to represent

---

17. See SS 161.
18. See the discussion in THGL 83.
19. See SS 96.

the suffixes. The Greek does not state what he is to sprinkle, whereas MT has מן השמן immediately after the verb. The מן is obviously partitive, and so is the απο of the popular hex gloss, απο του ελαιου, representing the untranslated phrase of MT. It might well be understood that the priest repeatedly dipped the right finger, since he must sprinkle seven times; obviously he would have to dip his finger each time in order to sprinkle the oil. This is even clearer in MT which has מן השמן repeated with והזה as well (as with וטבל).

14:17 The bound phrase יתר הדם is neatly rendered by an attributive participial phrase τὸ (δὲ) καταλειφθὲν ἔλαιον "the oil that was left," with a δέ added to show contrast with the sprinkled blood in v.16, but LXX has failed to render the partitive מן of מיתר, which contrasts with v.18. The LXX has thereby created an apparent oxymoron by dealing with τὸ καταλειφθὲν ἔλαιον in two different ways; see comment at v.18 for understanding the apparent contradiction. Obviously, here the oil that was left is not entirely used up by the daubing of the extremities. For the placement of the blood see v.14, which is repeated exactly here. Since these extremities had already had blood applied in v.14, this time it is to be put ἐπὶ τὸν τόπον τοῦ αἵματος τοῦ τῆς πλημμελείας. MT has no equivalent for τὸν τόπον, but the translator made excellent sense by leveling with the parallel passage in v.28.[20] Hex has omitted the nominal so as to conform to MT. MT also has no equivalent for the recapitulating τοῦ (before τῆς), and it has been omitted by an F O b n+ text. This may also be a hex correction, but the τοῦ is certainly original.[21]

14:18 The opening accusative structure is the same as in v.17, but the Hebrew represents a different syntagm והנותר בשמן "but that which is left of the oil." In view of the opening syntagm of v.17, the collocation must then mean "but that which is still left over of the oil." The Hebrew by its מיתר in v.17 and the הנותר here is much clearer than the Greek. ἔλαιον is modified by "that which is on the hand of the priest," which is then followed by the verb ἐπιθήσει plus an otiose ὁ ἱερεύς given as subject. Hex correctly placed the named subject under the obelus, since MT did not have it. Lev was probably influenced by v.17, where the named subject might well have been expected.

---

20. As was also done by Tar^J and Pesh.
21. As is argued in THGL 83—84.

This oil is to be placed on the head τοῦ καθαρισθέντος. At the beginning of the ceremony (v.11) the candidate was called τὸν καθαριζόμενον, but here the aorist passive participle is used to translate המטהר, also vocalized by the Masoretes as a Hithp. Since in v.19 the translator returns to the present middle participle, I suspect that this is once again illustrative of the translator's love of variety; it is obvious that the aorist participle intends no differentiation from that of the present middle.

For ἐξιλάσεται see the discussions at 1:4 and 4:20. The propitiation by the priest on behalf of the καθαρισθέντος is to take place in the sanctuary, i.e. ἔναντι τοῦ κυρίου.

14:19 Since חטאת here means "sin offering" rather than "sin," LXX places περί before it; so החטאת is rendered by περὶ τῆς ἁμαρτίας. The word is governed by את, and to make an accusative modifier out of the περί phrase a τό is placed before it.[22]

The second clause serves throughout the book as a concomitant to a sacrifice (see especially chh.4 and 5). Once the priest has offered up some kind of sacrifice, in this case a sin offering, he "shall make atonement for the one seeking cleansing from his sin." This differs from MT in the final prepositional phrase. To the translator the sin offering serves to cleanse one "from his sin." To MT the atonement applies to the "one seeking to cleanse himself from his uncleanness," מטמאתו. Each can be logically defended, but the two represent different points of view. LXX understands the sin offering as ridding the worshiper of his sin. In this context, however, MT views the sin offering in the context of the one afflicted by the scaly infection, which constitutes an impurity which needs removal before he can once again resume a normal place in Israelite society. It might be noted that an A B V x+ text has attempted to bridge the two interpretations by adding the gloss του ακαθαρτου in front of τοῦ καθαριζομένου. This indicates an early reflection of unease with calling λέπρα "his sin." LXX repeats the subject ὁ ἱερεύς for each of the three clauses; MT more economically has הכהן only for the first one. Hex has placed the third case of ὁ ἱερεύς under the obelus, and apparently omitted the second one.

---

22. See the discussion in THGL 117.

The adverbial אחר is translated by μετὰ τοῦτο. It refers to the offering of the περὶ τῆς ἁμαρτίας. The slaughter of the burnt offering occurs after the sacrifice for sin has been offered.

14:20 The verb ἀνοίσει occurs only here in Lev as a translation for the verb העלה, but העלה only occurs elsewhere in MT twice, at 17:8 where LXX follows the יעשה of Sam, and at 24:2 where no sacrifice is involved. The priest is to offer up both the burnt offering and the sacrifice on the altar. For the θυσίαν, which represents the meal offering, see ch.2, especially vv.3—10. Here, however, the θυσίαν is to be offered up completely on the altar along with the ὁλοκαύτωμα. LXX adds the common phrase ἔναντι κυρίου after θυσιαστήριον; the altar is, after all, in the sanctuary, thus "before the Lord." Hex apparently omitted the phrase to equal MT.

For ἐξιλάσεται see comment at 4:20. The concluding statement, καὶ καθαρισθήσεται, might at first blush seem ambiguous, but common sense dictates that the subject has changed; it is not ὁ ἱερεύς, but (περὶ) αὐτοῦ that is the one who shall be cleansed. The important result is that the one seeking cleansing now finally "shall be cleansed." At earlier stages of the procedure, vv.8 and 9, it was said ἔσται καθαρός, but now the process is complete; there is no more to be done; he shall be (fully and finally) cleansed.

14:21 Vv.21—31 deal with those afflicted with scaly infections who are too poor to afford such sacrifices. In this verse the protasis consists of two nominal clauses: דל הוא ואין ידו משגת, which LXX interprets as verbal clauses. For the first one, LXX uses πένηται absolutely to render the adjective,[23] and disregards the pronoun, which then becomes otiose. In the tradition, the majority text, possibly hex in origin, has πενης η, a reading which represents MT more exactly, i.e. uses an adjective to render דל, and η for הוא. For the second clause it follows the usual pattern of rendering a participial predicate by a present tense. The Hi verb השיג literally means "to reach," and "his hand does not reach" means "he cannot afford." The participle is here used absolutely as well; what is meant is "he cannot afford so much (NRSV)," i.e. as demanded in vv.10—20. This was rendered in LXX by εὑρίσκη, thus "his hand could not find," which renders the Hebrew well.

---

23. See SS 81.

The sacrifice demanded of the poor is given in the remainder of this verse and v.22a. It is to consist of a) one lamb, defined in MT as אשם לתנופה "(as) a trespass offering for תנופה," for which see comment at 7:20. LXX had some difficulty with אשם, and paraphrased it with εἰς ὃ ἐπλημμέλησεν; the translator's problem lay in not recognizing אשם as a noun, but taking it as a verb, which he then paraphrased as "for what he had transgressed." For εἰς ἀφαίρεμα "for a dedicated portion," see comment at 9:21.[24] Apparently the sacrifice of a quadruped was a sine qua non for an אשם sacrifice. For ἐξιλάσασθαι see comment at 1:4 and 4:20. b) "a tenth (measure) of fine flour mixed with oil for the meal offering," for which see the discussion at v.10. c) κοτύλην ἐλαίου μίαν, which levels with v.10. MT has no equivalent for μίαν, and hex has appropriately placed it under the obelus.

14:22 He shall also take (λήμψεται v.21) "two turtle doves or two young pigeons"; for τρυγόνον see comment at 1:14, and for νοσσοὺς περιστερῶν see comment at 12:6. This is defined as ὅσα εὗρεν ἡ χεὶρ αὐτοῦ, for which idiom see comment at v.21. Presumably what LXX means is "what was available," whereas MT offers the choice whichever "he could afford." Unexpected is the rendering of תשיג by an aorist, thus "whatever his hand found." In the tradition, the Byz text has changed it to αν ευρη, probably a recensional correction. That in such a case one should be intended for a sin offering and the other for a burnt offering had also been stated at 5:7; see comment ad loc, and comp 12:6.

14:23 The pronoun αὐτά refers to the items of the offering listed in vv.21—22a. These he (i.e. the poor candidate) "must bring εἰς τὸ καθαρίσαι αὐτόν to the priest." MT has לטהרתו "for his cleansing, purification." The translator took this noun to be a marked infinitive, though he did nominalize it by means of an article. αὐτόν is the objective modifier, thus "for rendering him clean." The Byz text misunderstood the syntax of αὐτόν, and took it as the subject of the infinitive, necessitating a change of the infinitive to the passive καθαρισθῆναι.

The items are to be presented "at the door of the tent of testimony ἔναντι κυρίου." Since "before the Lord" also means "in the sanctuary," it is a doublet to "at the door of the tent of testimony"; in fact, the doublet only occurs once elsewhere in the book (4:4), but LXX simply translated MT in both cases.

---

24. See also THGL 72.

14:24 As in v.15 the translator subordinated the first clause to a participial modifier; see comment at v.15. The bound phrase כבש האשם is translated by ἀμνὸν τὸν τῆς πλημμελείας "the lamb which was (for) the trespass offering." An A B V *b d f*+ text has omitted τόν, which formally equals MT. I have argued earlier that the omission is secondary, possibly recensional,[26] and the evidence there assembled I believe to be convincing.

The main clause is introduced without a και (which would be bizarre Greek), but hex does add a και to represent the apodotic conjunction of והניף. For the various ways in which the cognate structure הניף תנופה is rendered in Lev see the discussion at 7:20. Here LXX has ἐπιθήσει ... ἐπίθεμα, i.e. "he shall place (them) as a deposit." The pronoun αὐτά, rendering אתם, is neuter; since its antecedents are ἀμνόν (masculine) καὶ τὴν κοτύλην (feminine), the neuter is the correct compromise. For ἔναντι κυρίου see comment at v.23. MT repeats הכהן as the subject for the second clause, but LXX, because it had rendered the first clause by a subordinate participle, perforce omitted it. Hex, however, added ο ιερευς after αὐτά to represent it. Incidentally, Sam also omitted the הכהן as unnecessary, but the shorter text need not have been parent text for Lev.

14:25 For the variant A B V+ omission of the recapitulative article after ἀμνόν, see the comment at v.24, which is equally applicable here. Note that the τοῦ after αἵματος is also omitted by *b d*+, but this too is secondary, even though it equals MT.

In the second clause ἀπό is partitive: "the priest shall take some of the blood of the trespass offering."[27]

For the third clause see the comments at v.14, which, except for the addition of the stated subject ὁ ἱερεύς, is exactly the same. As in v.14 hex has added αυτου after both χειρός and ποδός to represent the suffixes of ידו and רגלו resp.[28]

14:26 The instruction given is essentially the same as that in v.15, except that it begins more simply with "and from the oil the priest shall pour" rather than "and

---

26. In THGL 83.
27. See SS 161.
28. See SS 96.

the priest having taken from the measure of oil, he shall pour." For the rest see comment at v.15.

14:27 Detailed information on the sprinkling ritual. He is to sprinkle "with the right finger." MT has באצבעו, and hex has added αυτου to represent the suffix. What he is to sprinkle is "ἀπὸ τοῦ ἐλαίου which is in his left hand." The ἀπό is clearly partitive.[28] The Byz text has glossed the recapitulative article τοῦ by the participle οντος; this simply makes explicit what is already implicit. The Byz text also changed the εν phrase "in the left hand" to an επι with the genitive phrase. Since MT has the preposition על this could be recensional, but is probably due to v.28, which see. The text also insists that the sprinkling is to be done in the sanctuary; it is ἔναντι κυρίου.

14:28 Here the daubing of extremities with oil is introduced by "and the priest shall put some (ἀπό) of the oil which is in his hand" instead of "the oil left, that which was in the hand, the priest put" of v.17, but for the rest of the verse it is exactly the same as v.17, except that here αὐτοῦ is present for both χειρός and ποδός. See comments at v.14. MT differs only in that the parent text for τὸν τόπον obtains here, but is lacking in v.17; see comment ad loc.

14:29 This verse is identical with v.18 with two exceptions: it adds the participle ὄν after ἔλαιον τό, and it lacks ὁ ἱερεύς as expressed subject after ἐπιθήσει. See comments at v.18.[29] MT has מן השמן, whereas Sam has בשמן as at v.18. It seems clear that the translator had his own v.18 in mind.

The translator has levelled with the last clause of v.18. MT has a marked infinitival construction showing the purpose underlying the placing of the remaining oil on the head of the one declared clean: לכפר עליו לפני יהוה, but LXX has the coordinate clause of v.18 of Lev instead.

14:30 MT has three cases of מן; the first two are rendered by ἀπό, i.e. "one from the turtledoves or from the young pigeons." These are obviously hebraically inspired, since their deletion would result in much better Greek. In fact, a popu-

---

28. See SS 161.
29. Instead of (τὸ δὲ καταλειφθὲν) ἔλαιον Sym reads τοῦ ἐλαίου, whereas Theod retained ἔλαιον.

lar A B V text omits the first ἀπό, though not the second one. No translator would, in my opinion, omit the first one, but retain the second. He would either leave both cases without a preposition, or both with it.[30]

The third מן occurs with the relative pronoun as מאשר. What that does in MT is show that the מאשר clause is at the same syntactic level as the first two מן structures; the clause might be paraphrased: "namely, from what his hand found (i.e. could afford)." LXX approached it somewhat differently by rendering it as a καθότι clause "according to what he could afford." Actually the reworked clause is more elegant than an ἀπό rendering would have been. Hex reordered αὐτοῦ ἡ χείρ as η χειρ αυτου to represent ידו more exactly.

14:31 MT begins with את אשר תשיג ידו, an obvious doublet (in fact, simply a variant), to מאשר תשיג ידו immediately before it. LXX omitted it, either consciously viewing it as a dittograph, or by parablepsis due to homoioteleuton. Hex restored it by its οσα ευρεν η χειρ αυτου.

LXX picks up on the μίαν of v.30, and thereby defines the distinction between the two, viz., "the μίαν for a sin offering and the μίαν for a burnt offering," for which see v.22. To this is added "alongside the meal offering."

For ἐξιλάσεται see comments at 1:4 and 4:20. LXX reverts to the middle participle to render מטהר, vocalized by the Masoretes as a Hithp., for which see comment at v.11. Oddly enough, no statement about a final stage, i.e. that he will be cleansed, is made; comp v.20.

14:32 The subscription to vv.1—31 in general, and for vv.21—31 in particular. In MT תורת is the bound element of a bound construction in which the free element is two אשר clauses: thus "the rule for anyone in whom there is a leprous infection, even one whose hand has not found (i.e. cannot afford) for his cleansing." What is meant is one who cannot afford the usual offerings for his cleansing.

Over against MT the Greek has joined the two clauses by καί. The free elements are realized by a) a relative clause: ἐν ᾧ ἐστιν ἡ ἀφὴ τῆς λέπρας "for the one in whom the infection of leprosy exists," and b) a genitive construction modifying νόμος, i.e. (the rule) "for the one not finding in the hand for his clean-

---

30. See THGL 114.

sing," i.e. for the individual who cannot afford sufficient for his cleansing. The use of the genitive is an intentional change of construction from that in a). By this device he has neatly shown that a) must be included within νόμος and τοῦ μὴ εὑρίσκοντες; in other words, the subscription is not to vv.21—31, but to vv.1—31. Hex has added αυτου after χειρί to represent the suffix of ידו.

14:33 LXX did not repeat the preposition πρός before Ἀαρών, since it is otiose in Greek. Hex has, however, added προς to represent MT exactly.[31]

14:34 The protasis is introduced by ὡς ἄν, which only occurs three times in Lev; in 22:27 it occurs for כי, and in 27:14, for כאשר. Here it renders כי, probably intentionally chosen to avoid ἐάν. After all, that the Israelites would enter the land of the Canaanites was not problematic; it was simply a matter of "when." Why the Promised Land should be called τὴν γῆν τῶν Χαναναίων is unknown. Actually כנען only occurs three times in the book; at 18:3 and 25:38 it becomes Χανάαν.

That it is the land of promise is clear from the relative clause ἣν ἐγὼ δίδωμι ὑμῖν ἐν κτήσει. The pronoun plus present tense is the usual rendering for the nominal clause: pronoun plus participle. The term אחזה "possession" (literally "something seized," so a possession acquired by force) occurs twice in this verse, and elsewhere it occurs only in chh.25 and 27 (18 times; usually rendered by κατάσχεσις).[32] κτῆσις also occurs at 20:24, but for לרשת. The word was known from Gen (49:30,32 50:13). The second case of אחזה obtains at the end of the verse in the collocation ארץ אחזתכם "land of your possesion," which LXX rendered by τὴν γῆν τοῦ ἐγκήτου ὑμῖν "the land possessed by you." ἔγκητος also occurs at 22:11, and elsewhere in OT only at Num 31:9. The suffixed noun is here reinterpreted by using a dative pronoun instead of a subjective genitive. I would understand the Greek as "land which you possess," or better "land possessed by you."[33]

The second clause states "I shall put ἀφὴν λέπρας in the houses of the land possessed by you." It is by now fully obvious that λέπρας does not mean "leprosy," but a kind of green mold or mildew attacking the plaster in stone

---

31. The Others do read πρὸς Μωυσῆν καὶ πρὸς Ἀαρὼν λέγων.
32. The Others read the more usual εἰς κατάσχεσιν.
33. See SS 98.

houses. The matter of a mildew infection is not mere happenstance; it is the Lord who says δώσω ... ἐν ταῖς οἰκίαις. In fact, the translator has taken this as the apodosis, introduced by a καί reflecting the conjunction in MT. In other words, once you are in the Promised Land I will put a mildew infection into your houses.[34] This probably differs from MT in which v.b is part of the כי clause, and the next verse begins the apodosis. It is, however, possible to interpret MT as LXX has done. The preposition ἐν shows the Hellenistic confusion between ἐν and εἰς. One might have expected εἰς with an accusative, but ἐν in the sense of movement in or into is common.[35]

In the tradition, a popular reading has εν κληρω instead of ἐν κλήσει. The two nouns are synonyms, but κλῆρος is more common as a translation of נחלה, which term is particularly characteristic of Deuteronomy; in Lev it obtains only at 16:8—10 for גורל. The Byz text has υμων for the ὑμῖν at the end of the verse. It represents the suffix of אחזתכם, and is probably a recensional reading.

14:35 The subject of ἥξει is τίνος αὐτοῦ ἡ οἰκία, translating אשר לו הבית. The לו is understood as indicating possession, thus "the one of whom the house is," i.e. the owner of the house. The Byz text has attempted to make this clearer by adding εστιν before (or after) ἡ οἰκία.

The owner must inform the priest with the statement: ὥσπερ ἀφὴ ἑώραταί μου ἐν τῇ οἰκίᾳ "something like an infection has appeared in my house." The collocation ὥσπερ ἀφή is a nominal which renders MT's כנגע correctly; it constitutes the subject of the quoted speech. This is a simplification of what MT says. MT has נראה לי בבית "has appeared to me in the house." The Ni verb נראה plus ל means "appeared to"; the translator has taken the prepositional phrase as modifying "house" rather than the verb. That copyists realized that ἑώραται is usually modified by a dative of person is clear from the popular change of μου to μοι, though this could be a hex correction; in any event μοι could hardly lead to "in my house," nor should לי be so construed.

14:36 LXX has rendered the consecution of וצוה and ופנו economically by making the indefinite plural verb a complementary infinitive; this neatly inter-

---

34. This is hardly evidence for the translator not really knowing what he was doing, as SS 34 seems to suggest.
35. See SS 136.

prets what MT meant: "the priest shall give orders to clear out the house." This is in turn modified by a πρό construction. The preposition governs τοῦ ἰδεῖν. The subject of the infinitive is τὸν ἱερέα, which is modified by a participle, thus "before the priest on entering sees (the infected spot)." The word order in MT differs somewhat. It has טרם יבא הכהן followed by לראות הנגע, thus "before the priest enters to see the infected spot." LXX has τὸν ἱερέα after ἰδεῖν, and hex has transposed these to equal MT. The construction also differs in that the participle εἰσελθόντα modifies the subject, and the preposition governs the marked infinitive. The perspective of LXX is slightly different from that of MT; in LXX the stress is on the infinitives, whereas in MT it is on בא with לראות as a purposive infinitive. In the tradition, a popular A B F text has changed ἀφήν to οικιαν, but this is an error based on the occurrence of οἰκίαν earlier in the verse.

The point of the evacuation of the contents is given in the next clause: "and not shall whatever might be in the house become unclean." What this implies is that the mildew is not contagious, and the uncleanness is only communicable to the contents of the house after the priestly inspection; before this, nothing has been affected by the infection. In MT the subject of יטמא is כל אשר בבית, and a recensional correction rendering the כל has been preserved by n s^{mg}+.

Lev does not really distinguish between μετὰ ταῦτα and μετὰ τοῦτο. At v.19 μετὰ τοῦτο rendered אחר, but at v.8 and 15:28 אחר is translated by μετὰ ταῦτα. Actually the singular occurs elsewhere only at 5:3, where it has no adequate equivalent in MT; see comment ad loc. μετὰ ταῦτα occurs here for אחר כן, but note that Sam has אחרי כן. At 16:26,28 it occurs for אחרי כן. The phrase also occurs without MT correspondence at 26:21.

Once the house is cleared the priest shall enter "καταμαθεῖν the house." MT has לראות, which had also occurred in v.a as complement to יבא, and was translated by ἰδεῖν; once again Lev prefers to vary the translation, and that in excellent fashion, since καταμαθεῖν fits especially well in the context, for it means "to examine closely, to inspect."

14:37 MT begins with וראה את הנגע והנה הנגע, and the translator has made a lapsus oculi by jumping from one הנגע to the second one. LXX reads καὶ ὄψεται τὴν ἀφὴν (ἐν τοῖς τοίχοις). Most witnesses have added και ιδου η αφη, probably hex in origin, and it might be argued that this is original text, but this is not the case, since the modifier κοιλάδας would then have to be in the nominative; in fact, the Byz text not only added the hex plus και ιδου η αφη, but also made the further correction κοιλαδες χλωριζουσαι η πυρριζουσαι. In Lev the accusative is a second modifier of ὄψεται: "he shall see the infected spot in the walls of the house as greenish or reddish depresssions." The term κοιλάδας renders the hapax legomenon שקערורת.[37] What is meant is that the colors in the infected spots have penetrated the stones.

That this was probably intended is clear from the final clause: "and their appearance is deeper than the walls." The comparative degree with the genitive (for the comparative מן) occurs only four times (also as ταπεινοτέρα at 13:20, and as κοιλοτέρα at 13:30,31).[38] MT has the singular הקיר, but this can be taken as a collective.

In the tradition, most witnesses add ο ιερευς as subject for ὄψεται, but this is overly repetitive, nor is it present in MT, though it does occur in Sam.

14:38 LXX makes a single syntagm out of the verse by subordinating the first verb as a participle, ἐξελθών, but retaining the καί before the main verb ἀφοριεῖ. Possibly one might translate this odd Greek by a "when ... then" construction. The Byz text has changed the participle to εξελευσεται to equal MT; this might be due to mediate Hebrew influence (one of The Three?), though it could also be taken as a correction due to the καί introducing the main clause. The ἐπί plus accusative must mean "to," since it follows an ἐκ phrase. And then at the door "ὁ ιερεύς shall quarantine the house for seven days." MT does not repeat the subject, and hex has placed ὁ ιερεύς under the obelus to show that it was not present in MT.

14:39 The use of ἐπανήξει is rare in the OT, occurring elsewhere only in Wisdom Literature. It occurs for שוב at Prov 3:28 and at 7:20 for בוא (and obtains twice in Sir).[39] It is, however, appropriate in this context, i.e. "shall come back."

In MT, the priest shall make an examination, i.e. ראה is used absolutely, whereas LXX has ὄψεται τὴν οἰκίαν. The interpretation is not incorrect, but hex rightly placed τὴν οἰκίαν under the obelus, since it was not represented in MT.

---

37. For various interpretations of the word see Milgrom 870—871. Pesh has *qlp'* "scales," and Vulg reads *valliculas*. LXX's κοιλάδας is as good a guess as any.
38. See SS 148.
39. According to HR.

The diagnosis (καὶ ἰδού; see comment at 13:5,10) is that "the infection had spread in the walls of the house." In the tradition, the A B x y+ text has ου before διεχύθη, which negates the verb, i.e. the infection has not spread. This is obviously an error, a dittograph after ἰδού, and should be dismissed as a careless error.[40]

14:40 In contrast to v.36, which see, the translator renders the paratactic indefinite plural verb literally; what is meant is that "the priest shall give orders to remove," rather than "... and they shall remove." In the tradition, the Byz text has changed ἐξελοῦσιν to εξαρουσιν "they shall lift out," a freer and less adequate rendering of חלצו than that of Lev.

Another clause with an indefinite plural verb is coordinate to the ἐξελοῦσιν clause, and is also part of the priestly orders: "They must throw them (i.e. the infected stones) outside the city into an unclean place."[41] Since houses are now involved, the illusion of dwelling in a camp is abandoned (see also in vv.41,45,53) in favor of "houses," though at v.8 "outside his house" did occur, but it is explicitly stated that the camp had been reentered. The word ἔξω occurs twice adverbially (17:4 18:9), but for the rest of Lev throughout it serves as a preposition with a genitive: 13 times with τῆς παρεμβολῆς, three times with της πόλεως, and once with τοῦ οἴκου. Since MT reads אל מחוץ hex added προς before ἔξω under the asterisk to represent אל.[42]

14:41 LXX follows the plural יקצעו of the Sam text.[43] The Masoretes vocalized יקצע as a Hi. What MT says is "he (i.e. the priest) shall cause the house to be scraped inside round about." Then the next clause has a plural verb שפכו "they shall pour out." LXX (and Sam) has a simpler text with both verbs in the plural. It is possible to interpret the plurals as based on an understanding of the Hebrew verb as causative, i.e. "cause (people) to scrape," which is then made explicit in the coordinate plural שכפו. MT had also begun with the modifier before the verb: ואת הבית יקצע, which LXX transposed. The majority of witnesses follows hex in

---

40. See THGL 109.
41. Milgrom 872 makes the interesting observation that reference to "an impure place" occurs only in this section (also in vv.41,45) in all of the Hebrew Scriptures.
42. Retroverted from Syh.
43. As do Tar^JO and Pesh, but Tar^N reads the singular יקלף with MT. Vulg uses a complementary infinitive, probably presupposing a plural verb as parent text.

transposing the text to agree with MT. Stern measures are to be taken: "they must scrape off (i.e. the walls) inside round about, and pour out the dust outside the city into an unclean place." What is undoubtedly meant by τὸν χοῦν is the plaster dust. In MT, the dust is defined as אשר הקצו "which they caused to cut off." Hex has added ον απεξυσαν under the asterisk to represent the relative clause, presupposing, however, the verb הקצעו. It should be said that the Hi of קצה also appears in v.43, which see.

14:42 As replacement for the stones that were scraped, removed and cast outside the city, MT states "they shall take other stones," but LXX has "other ἀπεξυσμένους stones." Why the new stones should be scraped is not clear; the translator was probably influenced by v.41, but there the scraping was due to the infected character of the stones, which would at first sight be inappropriate for the replacement stones. The translator probably rationalized that the mildew actually only penetrated the plaster rather than the actual stones. Thus there would be an opportunity to reuse the stones (rather than throwing them away in an unclean place) as long as they were fully scraped, i.e. that all the plaster had been completely removed. Furthermore, it recurs as an infinitive in v.43. In any event, hex placed the participle under the obelus, since it had no correspondent in MT. Syh omitted the word, and in this way approximated the Hebrew.

They are also to take other χοῦν and plaster the house. This simplifies MT, which read the verbs as singular: יקח וטח, as in Sam and in 4QLev-Num^b.[43] But the LXX reading need not be textually based. The χοῦν must be wet, and the word should be translated as "mud," or better still, as "plaster." In the tradition, hex has supplied προς under the asterisk before ἀντί; this is intended to render the אל in תחת אל. Some uncertainty is evident in the tradition with regards to ἐξαλείψουσιν; b+ has the επ- compound, and the Byz text has the simplex. But ἐπαλείφω never occurs in OT, and the simplex only obtains for טוח in Ezek. All the oldest texts, A B F M V, use the ἐξ- compound, and it must be original.

14:43 But should the infection come again and sprout in the house. This verse elaborates on this possibility. The conjunction used is a contrastive δέ; it contrasts with the attempts to repair the damaged house in v.42. LXX has added πάλιν

---

43. See DJD XII 157–158.

after the verb for clarification; the translator probably intended ἐπέλθῃ πάλιν as equivalent for ישוב. The subject is ἡ ἀφή, and although the oldest witnesses, B and A, along with *ol C'* z+, omit the article, it must be original. Note that MT reads הנגע.[44]

The clause is triply modified by μετά plus articulated infinitives: a) μετὰ τὸ ἐξελθεῖν "after the removing," reflecting the first action ordered in v.40. The Masoretes vocalized the word, not as an infinitive, but as an inflected tense form. The translator has understood each of the verbal forms in the three structures as bound infinitives, which is possible in a purely consonantal text. b) μετὰ τὸ ἀποξυσθῆναι τὴν οἰκίαν "after the house was scraped." As in MT of v.41 the Hi of קצה occurs, but here as an infinitive. The translator made no distinction between the two Hi roots הקציע and הקצה, translating both by the verb ἀποξύω. The second μετά structure reflects v.41a. c) μετὰ τὸ ἐξαλειφθῆναι "after the being (re)plastered," which reflects v.42b. It is a translation of the Ni bound infinitive of טוח. I would translate the three structures by "after removing the stones and after the house was scraped and after it was replastered."

In the tradition, the majority F M V text has εξελθειν instead of ἐξελεῖν; this is obviously an old palaeographic error based on the confusion between the uncials E and Θ, and promoted by the frequency of εξελθειν in the OT. The second infinitive also suffered in this way in that *C'* has αποξυρισθηναι; admittedly ἀποξύω is a rare word, but what a shaven or scalped house is supposed to represent is puzzling; it is simply a careless copyist error.

14:44 After the initial "and the priest shall enter and make an examination," MT continues with the usual והנה to indicate a diagnosis. Oddly enough, the translator misread this as הן, which in Aramaic means "if"; hence "if the infection has spread." In the context a conditional makes good sense: "if the infection has spread in the house, it is a chronic mildew in the house." For ἔμμενος see comment at 13:51.

14:45 LXX follows Sam in the use of the indefinite plural as in vv.40—42. The verse has two verbal clauses, but it is not clear with which verb all but the first accusative modifiers belong. It is obvious that τὴν οἰκίαν modifies καθελοῦσιν

---

44. See THGL 84.

"and they shall tear down the house." This is followed by three accusatives "and its timbers, and its stones, and all the dust (plaster)." MT makes the basic cut after the fourth modifier, so that the והוציא begins v.b "And he shall bring out to the outside of the city to an unclean place." In the critical text I have placed a comma after οἰκίαν. I felt that the component parts of the house were "its timbers, stone and plaster," and these modified the second verb ἐξοίσουσιν "they shall bring out." Note that MT has a singular verb as well, whereas LXX again follows Sam in reading a plural verb. The autographon had, of course, no punctuation, and the comma is editorial, but it seems to be a better cut than that of the Masoretes who ended v.a with עפר הבית, particularly since LXX read no conjunction before הוציא. LXX omitted הבית, and most witnesses added τῆς οἰκίας, which is probably recensional. Also over against MT is the order "and all its timbers" and "and all its stones." Hex has transposed the two structures to equal MT. Also recensional is the addition of καὶ before ἐξοίσουσιν by the Byz text, since MT has והוציא. Also hex is the addition of πρός under the asterisk before ἔξω to represent the אל of אל מחוץ of MT.[45] For εἰς τόπον ἀκάθαρτον see comment at v.40.

14:46 The subject is ὁ εἰσπορευόμενος and the predicate is ἀκάθαρτος ἔσται; in other words, the uncleanness of the infected house is contagious; everyone who enters the house during the quarantine period will become unclean as well. The timer πάσας τὰς ἡμέρας is modified by a relative clause ἃς ἀφωρισμένη ἐστίν, which makes good sense, but the participle uniquely represents the Hi verb הסגיר. MT has the timer כל ימי הסגיר אתו. The free element of the bound phrase is הסגיר אתו "he has quarantined it" with the subject being "the priest" of v.44, and with אתו referring to the οἰκίαν. LXX has simplified this considerably by its "it has been isolated," i.e. "all the days in which it has been quarantined."

14:47 The verse has two statements, identical except for a change in subject. The first one concerns "the one lying down (i.e. sleeps) in the house," and the second one, "the one eating in the house." In MT, the regulation in both cases is "he shall wash his garments." LXX adds a second rule in both cases, which levels with v.46, viz. "(and) he shall be unclean until evening." The glosses are not

---

45. Retroverted from Syh.

incorrect, since the strictures imposed in v.46 concerned mere entrance into the infected house; here activities in the house are added, and so only the extra imposition of laundering clothing is specified in MT. Hex has placed both of these extra clauses under the obelus, since they are not represented in MT. It should be noted that C′ s z+, and including Syh, have omitted both of these clauses, thereby equaling MT; the omission must be recensional.

14:48 The cognate free infinitive structure, בא יבא, has been translated by LXX by a non-cognate nominative participle plus verb, παραγενόμενος εἰσέλθῃ, presumably for variation's sake, although possibly the translator intentionally made a distinction "having arrived, he should enter." The added stress by these structures marks a turning point in the regulations; from here on what is discussed is what happens if the inspection yields a favorable diagnosis. The usual formula ἴδη καὶ ἰδού denoting examination and diagnosis follows. The diagnosis is that the infection has not spread at all. Over against MT LXX adds διαχύσει before οὐ διαχεῖται, which only occurs elsewhere at 13:22,27,35; it presumes a parent text with a cognate free infinitive as at 13:22,27,35, or at least the translator was influenced by these verses. What is presupposed is that it reflects the status μετὰ τὸ ἐξαλειφθῆναι τὴν οἰκίαν "after the house was replastered."

The apodosis is introduced by an apodotic καί, imitating MT's וטהר. The ritual declaration of cleanness is to be made by the priest, "because the infection has been healed." For ἰάθη see comment on ἰᾶται at v.3.

14:49 The subject of λήμψεται is ὁ ἱερεύς of v.48, though presumably the materials would be supplied by the owner of the house. For the "two live clean birds and cedar wood and red thread and hyssop," see comments at v.4, from which the expansion in LXX "live, clean" is borrowed. At v.4 exactly the same list obtains in the Greek, but here MT is shorter. Hex has omitted ζῶντα καθαρά to equal MT. The reason for the priestly collection is ἀφαγνίσει τὴν οἰκίαν "to purify the house." The verb occurs here for the first time, and see also v.52; it translates the Pi of חטא, a technical term for performing a rite of purification, a rite for ridding someone or something of sin or uncleanness, i.e. a rite of decontamination, and ἀφαγνίσει is used here in that same cultic sense.[47]

---

47. The Others translate by a neologism based on the Hebrew root, περιαμαρτίσαι; cf Note at Exod 29:36, f.n.32.

14:50 For the rite described see comments at the parallel v.5. Here, however, it is the priest who must slaughter the one bird, not the indefinite "they" of v.5 who are ordered by the priest to do the slaughtering. The only other difference is in the rendering of כלי "vessel." Instead of the ἀγγεῖον of v.5, here the more common σκεῦος is used, but they both mean "vessel."

14:51 Comp the parallel description of v.6, and see comments ad loc for details. LXX follows Sam in the order of καὶ τὸ κεκλωσμένον κόκκινον καὶ τὸν ὕσσωπον. Hex has transposed the two structures to equal the order of MT. For the gender of (τὸν) ὕσσωπον see comment at v.6.[48] Most witnesses read την, but the oldest witnesses, B and A, read τόν. These same witnesses change αὐτά to αυτο, but this is an unthinking mistake.[49] Not only does MT have אתם, but in the next clause the same referent occurs in ἐν αὐτοῖς. This is, however, not changed to αυτω, which would be required if the αυτο were intended. In LXX the priest is to "dip them in the blood of the slaughtered bird and in the living water," whereas LXX has the same text as at v.6, viz. ἐφ' ὕδατι ζῶντι. The double dipping is attested only here, and it is not clear why these articles should also be dipped in running water. I would suggest that LXX here represents a better tradition.

The priest is then to "sprinkle ἐν αὐτοῖς the house seven times." MT has no equivalent for the prepositional phrase, and hex has rightly placed it under the obelus. The Lev gloss makes explicit (viz. that "they" are the instruments for the sprinkling) what is only explicit in MT. MT has the verb modified by an אל phrase, which is uncommon, על being used normally. LXX has ἐπὶ (τὴν οἰκίαν) which might presuppose the על of a Qumran text, though not necessarily.[50]

14:52 For ἀφαγνιεῖ as rendering for חטא Pi, see comment at v.49. The purification ritual for the house is to be executed by a series of instruments of purification shown by ἐν phrases.[51] These are listed as: the blood of the bird, the running water, the living bird, the cedar wood, the hyssop, the red string, and they correspond exactly to MT's list. For the gender of τῷ ὑσσώπῳ see comment at v.6.

---

48. See also the discussion in THGL 119.
49. See THGL 97.
50. 4QLev-Num^b; see DJD XII 158.
51. See SS 122.

14:53 For the first clause see the parallel passage at v.7b, and comments ad loc. Since MT has אל מחוץ hex judged ἔξω insufficient and added πρός under the asterisk before ἔξω.⁵² Over against v.7 "outside the city" is added. This is sensible, since "house" implies a permanent dwelling, and not a camp.

V.b states that "he shall make atonement concerning the house, and it shall be ritually clean." To make atonement for a house seems strange, but it is simply a summary statement. All the rites have been correctly performed; this is atonement, as the concluding statement verifies: "it shall be clean." The Byz text elaborates on that conclusion by its καθαρισθησεται και καθαρα εσται, but this is a doublet gloss.

14:54 Vv.54—57 constitute the subscription to the chapters on λέπρας (chh.13—14). It begins with the usual οὗτος ὁ νόμος,⁵³ which is modified by κατὰ πᾶσαν ἀφήν "concerning every infection."⁵⁴ The structure πᾶσαν ἀφήν is then modified by a series of genitive lexemes extending through v.56. The first one is λέπρας, which represents הצרעת. Note that the word is unarticulated in LXX; this is unique in the book for the articulated Hebrew noun,⁵⁵ but it must be original; no witness articulates it, and it is coordinated with θραύσματος. Its equivalent לנתק is also vocalized by the Masoretes as an articulated noun. The first infection refers to 13:1—28, and the second one, θραύσματος, to 13:29—37.

14:55—56 A continuation of genitives modifying the ἀφήν of v.54. The first one is τῆς λέπρας ἱματίου καὶ οἰκίας, representing 13:47—58 and 14:33—53 resp. MT has לצרעת הבגד ולבית. LXX rightly interprets the second prepositional phrase as an abbreviation for ולצרעת הבית, and simply renders it as a second genitive modifier of τῆς λέπρας.

V.56 reflects the οὐλὴ σημασίας τηλαυγής of 13:2; see comments ad loc. That αὐγάζοντος is a synonym for τηλαυγής is clear from 13:24—28, and the renderings of בהרת there. In v.24 it is rendered by αὐγάζον τηλαυγές, but in vv.25,26 and 28 without τηλαυγές. It refers there to the appearance of a burn; cf comments ad loc.

---

52. Retroverted from Syh.
53. See THGL 108.
54. Sym read the preposition περί (retroverted from Syh).
55. See THGL 83.

14:57 MT begins with the marked infinitive להורת "to teach, determine." LXX introduces the articulated infinitive τοῦ ἐξηγήσασθαι with καί; I would take this in the sense of "even," thus "even to expound, determine."[56] In MT what is to be determined is ביום הטמא וביום הטהר "when there is the unclean and when there is the clean," in other words, the νόμος is to determine when a given case is ritually unclean and when it is ritually clean. LXX translates the two differently. ביום in both cases becomes ᾗ ἡμέρᾳ "in which day." הטמא is translated by ἀκάθαρτον for which the subject must be an indefinite neuter, but הטהר becomes καθαρισθήσεται. What is said in v.a is "even to interpret on which day something is unclean, and on which day it will be declared ritually clean."

The concluding subscription is a general one: "this is the rule for λέπρας."

---

56. Kenn 9,81,136,153 all have an initial *waw*. Pesh also begins with a conjunction.

Chapter 15

15:2 According to v.1 the Lord spoke to Moses and Aaron, but what he commanded is put in the singular in LXX, possibly on the understanding that only one of them would actually address the Israelites. Hex has changed λάλησον ... ἐρεῖς to the plural λαλήσατε ... ερειτε to correspond to MT.[1] What is said in MT is איש איש כי יהיה זב מבשרו. The repetition of איש probably means "any, or every, man."[2] LXX translates this by ἀνδρὶ ἀνδρί, which would make no sense to a monolingual Greek speaker; it is a pure Hebraism. The כי clause, as representing the conditional or protasis element, is translated by ᾧ ἂν γένηται ῥύσις ἐκ τοῦ σώματος αὐτοῦ. בשר does not mean "body" here, but rather refers to the male genital organ, the penis, and a זב is one who (involuntary) discharges semen. But σῶμα does not mean the male organ in Greek, and it is here an obvious calque for בשר. I would translate the Greek as "As for any man to whom there might be a discharge from his member." This differs somewhat from MT in which זב as a participle refers to the man who has the discharge, i.e. "as for any man who might be one who discharges from his penis, his discharge is unclean." LXX interprets the participle as though it were זוב, both being rendered by ῥύσις. An anonymous marginal s reading corrects the first ῥύσις to ρεων.

The apodosis is straightforward: "his discharge is unclean." In the tradition, the verb is changed to the future εσται by A b+; this is a stylistic change, conforming to the common pattern in which the future characterizes the apodosis. One might also note that ἐρεῖς is modified by πρὸς αὐτούς, but the A B V O x+ text reads αυτοις. But ἐρεῖς is always modified by a πρός construction in Lev, and πρὸς αὐτούς must be original.[3] A popular variant omits one ἀνδρί, an omission which is inspired either by haplography or by stylistic considerations; it certainly makes for better Greek.

15:3 LXX begins with "and this is the rule for his uncleanness," which makes of MT's "and this shall be his uncleanness" a regulation. LXX commonly introduces a set of rules by οὗτος ὁ νόμος (15 times), and the translator may have been

---
1. The Others also read λαλήσατε τοῖς υἱοῖς Ἰσραὴλ καὶ ἐρεῖτε αὐτοῖς.
2. See GK 123c.
3. See THGL 79–80.

influenced by four occurrences in chapter 14 (vv.2,32,54,57). Since LXX is relatively free in this verse, it is hardly necessary to presuppose that its parent text read תורת instead of תהיה. Such a variant text would be difficult to justify palaeographically. In any event, it makes an excellent introduction to this section. MT adds בזובו to the clause, i.e. "his uncleanness in his discharge." LXX takes this with the next word רר, a hapax legomenon in Hebrew related to the noun ריר "slime, spittle." LXX paraphrases בזובו רר as though the text read זב רר; cf comment at v.1 on ῥύσις 1°. It reads ῥέων γόνον "flowing sperm," i.e. a seminal discharge. This is modified by ἐκ σώματος αὐτοῦ ἐκ τῆς ῥύσεως "from his member from the discharge."[4] Hex has added αυτου after ῥύσεως to represent the suffix of זובו.[5] All of this refers to the running flow of sperm.

This contrasts with ἢ συνέστησεν τὸ σῶμα αὐτοῦ διὰ τῆς ῥύσεως αὐτοῦ,[6] a rendering of MT's או החתים בשרו מזובו "or his member has blocked up from its discharge." The verb has been rendered by συνέστησεν "has come together, become constricted." Here it contrasts with ῥέων γόνον, and probably refers to what happens after the sperm ejaculation has stopped and the γόνον has dried up, i.e. constricted on the male member.[7] Instead of ἢ the vast majority of witnesses, including all the uncial texts, read ης. Since the next word, συνέστησεν,[8] begins with *sigma* the origin of the variant text is clear; it is a dittograph. That only ἢ could be original is immediately clear from the Hebrew או.[9]

The text of LXX is much longer than that of MT, and is probably dependent on Sam which has טמא הוא instead of טמאתו היא, and then adds כל ימי זב היא בשרו או החתים בשרו מזובו טמאתו היא. LXX begins with αὕτη ἡ ἀκαθαρσία αὐτοῦ ἐν αὐτῷ. The ἐν αὐτῷ is an explanatory gloss, somewhat unnecessary, but making the point that his uncleanness resides "in him."[10]

The addition is simply a doublet, except that a timer is added: πᾶσαι αἱ ἡμέραι. The point that is being made is that the impurity lasts during the entire

---

4. Sym has ἐκ σώματος αὐτοῦ ἐν ῥύσει αὐτοῦ (retroverted from Syh).
5. See SS 96.
6. Sym has ἢ περιπήγνυται τὸ σῶμα αὐτοῦ ἀπὸ ῥύσεως αὐτοῦ (retroverted from Syh).
7. Schl interprets as *Sermo enim ibi est de remissione fluxis seminis.*
8. Aq renders החתים by ἐσφραγίσθη, and Theod preferred ἐσφράγικεν.
9. Harlé-Pralon try to make sense out of ης by their rendering "par lequel son corps a été constitué," but admit that sense can only be gained "au prix d'anomalies grammaticales telles que deux verbe *sunistánai* avec *diá* et non *ek*"(p.146). But the Hebrew is decisive. See also the discussion in THGL 129—130.
10. Also attested by a בו in 11Q Lev; see D.N.Freedman, CBQ 36(1974),528—529.

period involved. Again there is the contrast between the ῥύσεως of his member ἤ his member has dried up through the flow.¹¹ The contrast intended is between the discharge when still slimy and when it was dried up on the male member. The doublet concludes with a literal rendering of the concluding phrase of MT: טמאתו היא as ἀκαθαρσία αὐτοῦ ἐστιν.

In the tradition, Syh omits both the ἐν αὐτῷ as well as the rest of the verse. This equals MT, and is obviously recensional, i.e. based on a hex parent text with an obelus marking the non-MT text.

15:4 In the relative clause modifying המשכב, the subject of the verb is given as הזב, an articulated participle. This is translated by ὁ γονορρυής,¹² a neologism created to designate one suffering from γονόρροια "spermatorrhea," not to be confused with the derived term "gonorrhea," an infectious sexual disease. The term refers rathers to the involuntary discharge of semen, and I would suggest that the neologism be rendered by another neologism "spermatorrheic." Though the relative clause is properly introduced by ἐφ' ᾖ, the verb is modified by an otiose ἐπ' αὐτῆς, a Hebraic reproduction of עליו. The judgment in such a case is that it (i.e. the bed) "shall be unclean." The future ἔσται has a majority variant ἐστιν, supported inter alia by all the uncials. But ἔσται plus adjective translates יטמא which occurs 51 times in the book, and is never rendered by ἐστιν plus the adjective; in 48 cases it occurs as ἔσται plus adjective, and here ἔσται, as well as in the parallel v.b, is original Lev.¹³

V.b is, except for an introductory καί, an exact parallel to v.a, even in repeating the subject of the verb in the relative clause, ὁ γονορρυής, which has no equivalent in MT, and is therefore placed under the obelus in hex. Incidentally, the Byz text may show recensional characteristics in that it omits the subject, thereby equalling MT; on the other hand, its omission may simply be stylistic, since it is otiose.

15:5 The subject of the verbs πλυνεῖ, λούσεται and ἔσται is "a person who might touch τῆς κοίτης αὐτοῦ." איש is here translated by ἄνθρωπος rather than by

---

11. For ᾖ rather than the majority ἧς see the discussion in the earlier paragraph, as well as THGL 129—130.
12. The Others read ὁ ῥέων.
13. See the discussion in THGL 126.

ἀνήρ; see v.2. The choice is a good one, since ἄνθρωπος need not be male, though common sense tells us that the antecedent of αὐτοῦ must be the spermatorrheic of v.4. λούσεται is modified by an instrumental dative, ὕδατι;[14] MT has במים, but in the 19 times that λούσεται obtains in Lev, only once is it modified by ἐν ὕδατι (at 14:8 though even here the ἐν is omitted by F Byz+), and in 18 times, simply by ὕδατι. The state of uncleanness is, however, short, lasting only ἕως ἑσπέρας.

15:6 Precisely the same judgment is made for ὁ καθήμενος ἐπὶ τοῦ σκεύους ἐφ᾽ ὃ ἂν καθίσῃ ἐπ᾽ αὐτὸ ὁ γονορρυής.[15] Once again, the impurity is contagious, and any object on which the spermatorrheic might have been sitting transfers the resultant impurity to the one sitting on it. Note how the Hebraic ἐπ᾽ αὐτό recurs, though the Greek would certainly be improved if it were omitted. In fact, an A B V *b f y*+ variant text does precisely that, which is a stylistic change, and not original.[16] If one would read the entire chapter, this peculiar Hebraism would show up ten times, and not once does Lev omit the otiose prepositional phrase.

15:7 This verse concerns "the man who touches τοῦ χρωτός of the spermatorrheic." MT has בשר, which was used to denote the male genital organ, but here the reference is to the body. This was recognized by the translator who rendered בשר by χρώς "skin." The judgment given in vv.5—6 is repeated here with one exception; here he is to wash τὰ ἱμάτια, i.e. without rendering the suffix of בגדיו.[17] As one might expect, the majority text has added αυτου, a gloss either hex in origin or a case of leveling with the preceding two verses. An M *C′ b s*+ text has added το σωμα αυτου after λούσεται. This has no basis in MT, nor is it necessary; the verb is already reflexive, and means "wash oneself, bathe." If one examines the usage of λούσεται in Lev, it appears that it occurs without the accusative modifier, τὸ σῶμα (αὐτοῦ), eight times, five of which occur in vv.5—10. Beginning with v.11 it always has this modifier (nine times), except at 17:15. There seems to be no particular reason in the parent text, either for the absence or the presence of בשרו.

---

14. See SS 118.
15. The Others translate הזב by ὁ ῥέων.
16. See the discussion in THGL 114—115.
17. See SS 97.

15:8 The hapax legomenon ירק, from רקק, means "to expectorate, spit" as the noun רק "spittle" makes clear. It is translated by a Greek hapax legomenon, προσσιελίσῃ, but the simplex, either as σιελίζω or σιαλίζω is known in the sense of "to salivate, foam."[18] τὸν καθαρόν refers to a person who is ritually clean.

The judgment given in v.7 is repeated word for word here. The subject is τὸν καθαρόν, not ὁ γονορρυής. As in v.7 a majority F M V text has added αυτου after ἱμάτια, for which see comment ad loc.

15:9 MT's subject is כל המרכב "every means used for riding," hence "saddle." LXX makes sure that this be not misunderstood, and adds ὄνου, i.e. "every ass's saddle"; after all, the common means of transportation was the ass. A popular F M variant text does omit ὄνου, but this is apparently not a hex correction. Its source was probably one of The Three; note the marginal reading of cod M: κάθισμα for ἐπίσαγμα ὄνου. This is modified by a relative clause: ἐφ᾽ ὃ ἂν ἐπιβῇ ἐπ᾽ αὐτὸ ὁ γονορρυής. For ἐπ᾽ αὐτό see comment at v.6.

Over against MT LXX has ἕως ἑσπέρας after "shall be unclean," under the influence of the oft-recurring "shall be unclean until evening" throughout the chapter. Its popular omission is probably hex in origin. What makes this gloss unusual in the present context is that the uncleanness of the saddle also only lasts until evening; all other instances of such uncleanness ending must undergo ritual cleansing and only then remain unclean until evening.

15:10 This verse is divided into two parts; the first part deals with everyone who touches anything which might be under αὐτοῦ; this in v.7 referred to the ἐπίσαγμα, but here it is an undefined plural πάντων, i.e. "anything," not just a saddle but any other kinds of objects on which one might sit as well. An A B x+ text omits ἀπὸ πάντων, but this cannot be original, since without the phrase, ἁπτόμενος would be modified by the accusative ὅσα. The verb is always modified, either by an ἀπό phrase (twice) or by a genitive (26 times), but never by an accusative.[19] The judgment is abbreviated from the usual triple one to the single "shall be unclean until evening."

---

18. Aq uses the better known verb προσπτύσῃ.
19. See THGL 115.

V.b refers to ὁ αἴρων αὐτά, with the pronoun referring to the πάντων ὅσα ἂν ᾖ ὑποκάτω αὐτοῦ of the preceding clause. What is meant is "the one who carries these things," e.g. whoever unsaddles the ass on which the spermatorrheic had ridden. For such contaminated people the usual judgment is given; they must launder their clothes and bathe in water, and then remain unclean until evening. For the b+ gloss το σωμα after λούσεται see comment at v.8.

15:11 The use of the plural ὅσων is unexpected as the object of ἅψηται, though MT does have כל אשר. In fact, one ms plus Syh add παντων before ὅσων; this could be hex, though this is quite uncertain, since the plural ὅσων can be taken as a fully adequate translation. In any event, it concerns anyone whom the spermatorrheic might touch καὶ τὰς χεῖρας οὐ νένιπται, i.e. "without having rinsed the hands." The verb νίζω differs from λούω in that the latter refers to bathing the entire body, whereas νίζω only refers to a part of the body, hence the use of "rinse."[20] MT has וידיו לא שטף במים. An F M V majority text adds αυτου after "hands," thereby representing the suffix of ידיו. Similarly an F M V majority reading has added υδατι after the verse to equal MT. Whether these are recensional or simply ad sensum glosses cannot be determined.

Though ὅσων is plural, the judgment is given in the singular, which is a good ad sensum adjustment. The translator followed Sam in lacking an apodotic conjunction. Both Pesh and Vulg concur in the shorter text. In the judgment, λούσεται is modified by τὸ σῶμα, which has no equivalent in MT, but presumably the parent text had a בשרו, as in v.13; see comment ad loc.

15:12 For the breaking of unclean clay vessels see 6:28 and 11:33 and comments ad loc. For v.b MT begins with וכל כלי, but LXX follows Sam in omitting כל; hex has added παν before σκεῦος to equal MT.[21] Which reading is earlier cannot be determined, since כל was either added as a dittograph before כלי, or omitted by haplography; the parent text for LXX was, however, the shorter text. In contrast to clay vessels, those made of wood were not destroyed, but were only to be

---

20. Harlé-Pralon (p.147) make an interesting observation concerning the three verbs used for "washing." νίπτειν refers to rinsing, πλύνειν means to wash "per agitation dans l'eau," and λούειν "to bathe." Greek distinguished "selon les modes opératoires," whereas Hebrew distinguished largely "selon les objets." See also Lee 39—40.
21. The Others also read πᾶν σκεῦος.

rinsed with water. Instead of the passive νιφθήσεται an A B F V x+ text has the middle νιφήσεται,[22] but the middle is not attested for BCE times, nor is it particularly fitting here. It is simply a copyist error palaeographically inspired.

LXX has also added the judgment concerning the rinsed-off wooden vessel, καὶ καθαρὸν ἔσται, which is lacking in MT. Hex has duly marked it with an obelus to indicate that fact. The clause is clearly ex par; see 11:32,36,37 13:13,58.

15:13 Finally, the purificatory rites for the individual suffering from the discharge are dealt with. The protasis must be the first clause, since the next clause, though introduced by καί in imitation of the Hebrew, is in the future. The condition reads: "but if the spermatorrheic should have become cleansed from his discharge." Since he is not καθαρός until he has washed his clothing and bathed his body, the verb can hardly mean "be ritually cleansed"; all that is probably meant is that he is now physically clean from his discharge; the dried remnants of the discharge have disappeared.

Nonetheless he must count off for himself (i.e. silently?) seven days for τὸν καθαρισμὸν αὐτοῦ; this must mean "his ritual purification," since it involves washing his garments and bathing the body in water, after which καθαρὸς ἔσται. LXX does not insist that the bathing be done במים חיים "in running water," as MT does. Such "living" or fresh water contrasts with stored or stagnant waters. The F M V majority text has "corrected" the text of Lev by adding ζωντι after ὕδατι; this is probably hex in origin, as may also be the case for a similarly attested majority reading adding αυτου after σῶμα to represent the suffix of בשרו.

15:14 But mere ablutions are not sufficient. On the eighth day he must take "two turtledoves or two young pigeons," for which see comment at 1:14, and comp 14:21—23. According to MT ובא לפני יהוה ..., and give them to the priest, but LXX levels with v.29, changing ובא to καὶ οἴσει αὐτά.[23] Milgrom[24] makes the interesting point in defence of MT that the verb ונתנם intervenes here, i.e. "come ... and give them to the priest," whereas at v.29 the text reads "and he shall bring them to the priest." The LXX is, however, equally valid; the worshiper

---

22. Though also read by Theod.
23. As do Tar^J and Pesh.
24. P.925.

brings them to the sanctuary and gives them to the priest. The two actions are hardly contradictory. This is to be done in the sanctuary, i.e. "before the Lord at the doors of the tent of testimony." The double designation "before the Lord" and "at the doors of the tent of testimony" does occur elsewhere, though a single designation is more common; see 3:13 4:4 14:11,23 16:7 17:6 and comp 17:5 19:21; see also comment at 3:13. The preposition for the second one, however, often occurs as παρά rather than ἐπί. For "doors" as rendering for פתח see discussion at 3:2.

15:15 For "one for a sin offering and one for a burnt offering" see 14:31, as well as 12:8 where the two are transposed. For ἐξιλάσεται see comment at 4:20. For its modification by an ἀπό phrase see comment at 4:26; it probably means "because of his discharge."

15:16 The verse begins with a nominative: καὶ ἄνθρωπος, which acts as a pendant for the relative clause "for whom there might go out from him κοίτη σπέρματος"; this constitutes the condition, with the apodosis following in a καὶ λούσεται structure, for which ἄνθρωπος serves as subject. The term κοίτη can only be understood as a calque for the Hebrew (זרע) שכבת. The root שכב means "to lie down," but the noun שכבה when combined with זרע is a technical term for "an emission of semen," But κοίτη normally means "bed, a lying down," and was chosen by the translator to represent the root שכב. Here it must take on the meaning of the Hebrew, hence "an emission of semen." I suspect that the use of κοίτη may imply that the emission was nocturnal, i.e. while lying on a κοίτη, but see also v.18.

What is required is introduced by καί in imitation of MT; it demands washing "all his body with water." The use of "πᾶν/כל his body" is intentional, since בשר could refer simply to the penis. The demand here is for a full bath.

15:17 πᾶν ἱμάτιον καὶ πᾶν δέρμα refer to the κοίτη on which one slept. During sleep an involuntary emission of semen might ᾖ ἐπ' αὐτό. The prepositional phrase is Hebraic, since the clause is already introduced by ἐφ' ὅ.

The Greek is much improved by the b+ omission of καί 3°, which introduces the main verb πλυθήσεται in imitation of MT's וכבס; the passive future correctly represents the Pu vocalization of כבס. The garment and leather on which the semen had spilled must be washed with water, and shall be (remain) unclean until evening. A cI b n+ text has ακαθαρτος instead of ἀκαθαρτόν. This is hardly to be taken seriously. V.16 had already said that the man would remain unclean until evening; here it is ἱμάτιον and δέρμα that remain so.

15:18 καὶ γυνή is a pendant nominative, which then was grammatically brought into the protasis by the prepositional phrase μετ' αὐτῆς. The relative clause is a peculiar construction in that κοιμηθῇ is modified by a cognate accusative structure κοίτην σπέρματος, for which term see comment at v.16. In this verse, however, the κοίτην is hardly involuntary; it refers to sexual intercourse, including the normal sexual discharge, i.e. it refers to copulation.

Sexual intercourse results in the uncleanness of both partners, and both "must bathe themselves in water, and remain unclean until evening." The verse is unusual in that it serves as a transition between male impurities (vv.2—17) and female impurities (vv.19—30).

15:19 The initial noun plus the relative clause constitute a nominative pendant, which is then brought into the main clause by αὐτῆς. The indefinite relative pronoun renders כי of MT.[25] The use of the dative αἵματι modifying ῥέουσα, though good Greek, is unique, the accusative being usually used throughout the OT.[26] The construction ᾗ ῥέουσα imitates the verb plus participle structure of MT, but the participle in MT has a direct modifier, דם. The pendant might be rendered: "And as for a woman who would be discharging blood."

In unusual fashion the three clauses that follow are all asyndetic. An M V majority text has added a και before the first one of these, probably leveling with vv.16 and 17. Since the oldest witnesses do not have the και, nor is it supported by MT, the Lev text must be original. This first statement has it that "her discharge shall be ἐν τῷ σώματι αὐτῆς. For τῷ σώματι comp comment at v.2; here it refers to the female genitalia. The preposition differs from that of v.2, since the discharge is from inside the body, i.e. through the vagina.

This is explained in the next clause, which is introduced by an accusative of extent of time: "for seven days shall she be (remain) ἐν τῇ ἀφέδρῳ αὐτῆς.[27] The

---

25. See THGL 74.
26. See THGL 122.
27. Sym renders the noun etymologically by ἐν χωρισμῷ <αὐτῆς> (retroverted from Syh).

term ἄφεδρος also occurs at 12:2,5, and is regularly used to render נדה "menstrual period." The term focuses on the isolation which the menstruant must undergo; it is a "sitting away from," an isolation. This is clear from v.b which is also introduced asyndetically over against MT, and hex has added a καὶ to represent the conjunction of וכל. In contrast to her seven days that she must remain in her ἀφέδρῳ, "anyone touching her shall (only) remain unclean until evening."

15:20 The two clauses refer resp to anything on which the menstruant might be lying, and on which she sat. Highly unusual is the use of a present subjunctive verb in the first clause, κοιτάζηται, whereas the second one has an aorist subjunctive, ἐπικαθίσῃ. Throughout the book the aorist is the default, thus the use of the present calls attention to linear action.[28] The menstruant must lie down for rest, whereas "sitting" is by her choice. Only the former indicates a process, i.e. "anything on which she would be lying down ἐπ᾽ αὐτό." The recapitulative prepositional phrase occurs in both clauses; it is otiose in Greek, and simply imitates the Hebrew.

15:21 Touching her bedding also involves uncleanness until evening. It is clear that this refers to a male; it concerns πᾶς, and he must wash his clothing and bathe his body in water in consequence. τὸ σῶμα αὐτοῦ has no equivalent in MT, and the *oII f z+* text omits the structure. This could be a hex correction, since Syh also omits it.

15:22 The rule given in v.21 also applies to anyone touching any object on which a menstruant sat. Again LXX presupposes a male subject to whom the rule applies. In the tradition, ἐφ᾽ ὅ become ου in an A B F V *x+* text. This is probably a case of leveling with v.23 where σκεύους is modified by an οὗ clause. But Lev continues the pattern established in vv.4,9,17,20, and continued in v.26, and is original.[29]

---

28. See the discussion on 2:8 in THGL 125.
29. See THGL 94.

15:23 MT is unclear in the opening statement. It reads ואם על המשכב הוא; what is not clear is what הוא refers to.[30] LXX follows Sam which reads היא, and translates by ἐὰν δὲ ἐν τῇ κοίτῃ αὐτῆς οὔσης. The genitive absolute construction gives the condition for "when he touches her."[31] What LXX is saying in the protasis is "but if while she is in her bed or on the vessel (i.e. seat, chair) on which she might be sitting."

The accentuation in Lev of κάθηται is incorrect. Relative clauses introduced by οὗ ἄν take the subjunctive, and not the indicative. The verb should be changed to καθῆται.[32] This is then another case where the rarely used present subjunctive occurs in Lev;[33] see comment at v.20.

In MT the basis for "he shall be unclean until evening" is given in בנגעו "when he touches it," the "it" being the הוא of the opening statement. If the reference of הוא is as often suggested to "any object" of v.22 it would mean that touching the object would by contagion render unclean. Sam retains בנגעו, but LXX in the interest of consistency renders the phrase by ἐν τῷ ἅπτεσθαι αὐτὸν αὐτῆς "when he touches her," but this had already been said in v.19b.

In the tradition, the Byz text has ετι επι της κοιτης instead of ἐν τῇ κοίτῃ; this constitutes an attempt at clarification; MT has no equivalent for ετι, though an επι construction does represent the על of MT more exactly. The *x* text has a curious variant in its rewrite of αὐτὸν αὐτῆς as αυτην αυτου, i.e. "when she touches him"; this is obviously a thoughtless mistake on the part of a copyist.

15:24 The protasis means "but if someone should actually lie with her"; what is meant is "have sexual intercourse with her." The cognate structure κοίτῃ κοιμηθῇ represents the Hebrew cognate free infinitive plus verb, which is used to put particular stress on the verbal idea, and the cognate dative noun is a common LXX choice for rendering this Hebrew construction, hence the rendering "should actually lie with her."

The next clause has a present subjunctive verb; it is part of the protasis, and constitutes a factor concomitant to intercourse with a menstruant; "and her

---

30. Milgrom (928—939) gives five possibilities, but opts for כל כלי of v.22, as others have done as well; cf especially the references in Gispen ad loc.
31. See SS 76.
32. See Mayser II.1.261—267 for usage in Egyptian papyri; only the subjunctive is attested.
33. See THGL 125 for other occurrences.

impurity (i.e. the menstrual blood) should be on him." In MT it is uncertain where the apodosis begins, although the LXX's interpretation is likely to have been intended.³⁴

The judgment is that "he will be impure for seven days." ἑπτὰ ἡμέρας is an accusative showing extent of time. The seven days correspond to the seven days of the woman's menstrual period; cf.v.19.

The man's resultant impurity is also transferable to any bed on which he might subsequently lie; it too will be unclean.

In the tradition, the order of τις κοιμηθῇ is transposed in a popular text; presumably the transposition was inspired by hex, since MT reads ישכב איש.

15:25 With v.25 the rule concerns a woman's abnormal discharge, i.e. outside her normal menstrual cycle. That a new section begins is clear from the initial nominative καὶ γυνή preceding the conditional ἐάν.³⁵ The verb ῥέῃ is modified by a cognate accusative ῥύσιν, thus "if she should flow a flow of blood." Hex has added αυτης, since MT has דמה. An A B+ text reads a dative ρυσει instead of the accusative, but LXX normally prefers the accusative.³⁶ The flow lasts ἡμέρας πλείους "more days," which is explained by οὐκ ἐν καιρῷ τῆς ἀφέδρου αὐτῆς, i.e. "outside the time of her period."

MT continues with a second כי clause introduced by the correlative conjunction או. LXX has a postpositive καί instead, i.e. ἐὰν καί, in which the καί serves in an adverbial sense.³⁷ It further defines the first ἐάν clause, thus "even if it flows after her period," i.e. as a continuation of the flow beyond the normal seven days. MT then goes on to say "all the days of the discharge of her impurity she shall be like the time of the menstrual period." Hex has added αυτης to render the suffix of נדתה. LXX renders this as a nominal clause, and does not recognize a תהיה, which is indeed rather difficult.³⁸ By omitting תהיה entirely, the translator has made καθάπερ αἱ ἡμέραι τῆς ἀφέδρου the predicate, thus "all the days of the discharge of her impurity are like the days of the menstrual period."

---

34. Milgrom 940—941 opts for the second clause; i.e. "her menstrual impurity is transmitted to him" is part of the apodosis.
35. See also THGL 74.
36. See THGL 122.
37. See Bauer sub voce II.2.
38. See SS 74.

The majority F M text has added αυτης at the end to equal the suffix of נדתה; this may well be hex in origin.

The conclusion in LXX is straightforward: ἀκάθαρτος ἔσται "she shall be unclean," but MT has הוא טמאה תהיה, and hex has both transposed the words as εσται ακαθαρτος and then added εστιν under the asterisk to equal MT. So the hex text might be rendered "as the days of her menstrual period shall be, she remains unclean."

15:26 The Greek begins with καί, whereas MT begins asyndetically.[39] Pesh and Tar[J] also begin with a conjunction. As is the case with a woman's normal period, both any bed or seat she might have used will be unclean as well; see v.20 and comments ad loc. The translator in good Greek style did not translate the suffixes of זובה and of נדתה 1° and 2°, being otiose in Greek. The references could only be to "her" discharge, "her" period. In all three cases the majority text has added αυτης. These are probably all recensional, possibly hex in origin.[40] He did, however, add the recapitulative prepositional phrases, ἐπ' αὐτῆς and ἐπ' αὐτό, as he did in v.20, in spite of the introductory ἐφ' ἥν and ἐφ' ὅ introducing the relative clauses. These are, of course, pure Hebraisms, imitiating the syntax of MT.

The accusative of time, πάσας τὰς ἡμέρας τῆς ῥύσεως, could modify either what precedes or what follows. I had placed a comma after the structure on the understanding that what the translator intended was "on which she might lie all the time of (her) discharge," and this seems to me preferable. The Masoretes took it in this way as well, as the *zaqeph qaton* on זובה makes clear.

In the tradition, the A B b text read πασαν κοιτην instead of the nominative. πᾶσα κοίτη must, however, be correct, since it is the subject of ἔσται. The accusative is a case of mistaken assimilation to the ἐφ' ἥν which follows.[41]

15:27 MT begins with וכל, but LXX has no conjunction.[42] This verse is similar to the last clause in v.19b, which see, except that in the case of a woman with abnormal discharge, the one touching her also "must wash garments and bathe the body with water." MT, however, differs in that it reads "everyone touching

---

39. Though Kenn 199,200,615 read וכל for כל.
40. See SS 96.
41. See THGL 122.
42. Kenn 5 does read כל as well.

בם," rather than αὐτῆς. The suffix in MT must refer to כל המשכב and כל הכלי of v.26.[43] Some scattered mss do read αυτων instead of αὐτῆς, which must represent an intrusion from one of The Three into the LXX tradition. MT has בגדיו for τὰ ἱμάτια, and hex has added αυτου to represent the suffix.[44] MT, on the other hand, reads ורחץ במים, i.e. has no equivalent for τὸ σῶμα; the translator has levelled with vv.11,13; comp also vv.16,21. Accordingly, hex has placed τὸ σῶμα under the obelus to indicate the shorter text of MT. It might be noted that Syh has omitted it; once again it appears that the Syh translator of Lev correctly understood the meaning of the obelus of his parent hex text, and so omitted the nominal.

15:28 The Greek uses the verb καθαρίζω in two different senses, as does MT with its Qal verb טהר. In the protasis καθαρισθῇ must mean cleansed in the sense of physically free from the discharge. MT has "from her discharge," and the majority F M text has added αυτης to represent the suffix. But at the end of the verse LXX says "and afterwards καθαρισθήσεται," by which is meant "she will be ritually cleansed." The apodosis begins with an apodotic καί based on MT. For "she shall count off for herself seven days" see the parallel v.13.

15:29 On the eighth day the woman is to take her offerings to the priest. For two turtledoves or two young pigeons, see 5:7 12:6. Instead of ἑαυτῇ B cl x+ read αυτη, but the contracted form is not used by Lev. For the meaning of the verse see comments on the parallel v.14.

15:30 The priest must then offer one of the pair for a sin offering and the other one for a burnt offering, for which see comments at 14:31 as well as at 12:8 where the two are transposed. The verb which I have translated "offer" is ποιήσει "to do, make, effect." To effect a sacrifice is to offer it. This technical usage occurs frequently in the book; see also 4:20 5:10 14:19,30 15:15 and 16:24.

For ἐξιλάσεται see comment at 4:20. The ἀπό phrase gives the reason for the need for atonement; it is "because of the discharge of her uncleanness," i.e. her unclean discharge. For this usage of ἀπό see comment at 4:26.

---

43. Though Kenn 84,136,176*,200*,248 also read בה.
44. See SS 97.

15:31 MT begins with a second person plural verb, i.e. the Lord is addressing Moses and Aaron; cf v.1. The verb is an unusual one, הזרתם, the Hi of נזר, and means "to keep apart, separate, isolated," thus "you shall keep the Israelites separate from their impurities." LXX found this difficult to translate, and used a paraphrastic construction, εὐλαβεῖς ποιήσετε. The adjective means "holding on to," hence "discreet, cautious," and then in a derived sense "reverent, awe-stricken, pious." Here it probably means "you shall make the Israelites discreet over against their impurities."[45] That הזיר is difficult is clear from the fact that it occurs elsewhere only five times, all in Num 6, but is never translated in the same way: ἀφαγνίσασθαι (v.2), ἁγνισθήσεται (v.3), ηὔξατο (v.5), εὐχῆς (v.6), and ἡγιάσθη (v.12).[46]

V.b is paratactically expressed, but the change to third person plural makes the καὶ οὐκ plus future a warning. I would translate "that they should not die." Moses and Aaron are to instill a sense of caution among the Israelites; otherwise they might die "because of their uncleanness when they defile my tent which is among them." Nothing that is unclean may enter the tabernacle (i.e. my tent), and that which is holy would be rendered profane by the presence of anything unclean. Since the σκηνήν belongs to the Lord who is still the speaker (v.1), defiling it is a direct affront to him; such uncleanness constitutes desecration, and it must somehow first be removed. This is the underlying raison d'etre for the laws of purification in ch.15.

15:32—33 The nominal clause οὗτος ὁ νόμος occurs 15 times in Lev, either as an opening or a closing statement for sections containing a body of rules or regulations, i.e. instructions for the Israelites in various cultic affairs. The subscription calls this "the νόμος of the spermatorrheic." In MT this is followed by a paratactic relative clause, but LXX renders this by a condition, i.e. by a καὶ ἐάν structure: "and for someone (τινι) when an emission of semen should go out from him, so that he would be defiled by it." The syntax of these verses is odd. It begins with "this is the rule τοῦ γονορρυοῦς," i.e. with a genitive modifier. Then there follow three dative modifiers, all of which define the νόμος τοῦ

---

45. Harlé-Pralon render the collocation well with their "tenez les fils d'Israël on garde contre leurs impuretés."
46. Milgrom 945 wrongly suggests that LXX followed Sam's הזהרתם. εὐλαβεῖς never renders הזיר in OT; such uncleanness constitutes desecration; it must be cancelled out in some way.

γονορρυοῦς, with a peculiar interruptive clause "and the spermatorrheic in his discharge," followed by a pair of datives "for male or for female," after which comes the third and last dative modifier. The first dative is τινι, i.e. "even (καί) should there go out an emission of semen for someone, so that he would be defiled by it."

The second modifier is τῇ αἱμορροούσῃ ἐν τῇ ἀφέδρῳ αὐτῆς "to the one who is haemoraging in her menstrual period." This is not quite what MT says with הדוה בנדתה "the one who is unwell in her menstrual period." LXX interprets דוה "being sick" as "losing blood."

What I have called an interruption is difficult syntactically, a difficulty also experienced by copyists. It reads "and the spermatorrheic in his discharge for male or for female." It is grammatically divorced from its context, a kind of summary statement applying the notion of the νόμος τοῦ γονορρυοῦς to both male and female, since both suffer from a form of ῥύσει. A popular Byz revision changed the nominative ὁ γονορρυής to the dative τω γονορρυει; this would make the structure another modifier, i.e. "to the spermatorrheic in his discharge."

τῷ ἄρσενι ἢ τῇ θηλείᾳ can only make sense as an explicative or apposite structure to ῥύσει, i.e. the discharge pertains to both the male and the female. Actually a popular Byz text changes the ἢ to και, which may be recensional, since it does equal MT. This fits in with the earlier revision of the nominative to the dative τω γονορρυει. Both changes are intended to clarify the structure, and make it fit into its context, but overlook the fact that this is interruptive. I would place the entire καί 2° structure within parentheses. Provisionally I would render it paraphrastically as "(the pattern of) the spermatorrheic in his discharge (applying equally) to male or female."

MT is much simpler; it has a paratactic והזב את זובו, followed by לזכר ולנקבה, thus "and the one who flows with his discharge for male and for female," or more simply with NIV "for a man or a woman with a discharge."

The final modifier of νόμος is "and to the man who lies down (i.e. has intercourse) μετὰ ἀποκαθημένης. The noun means "she who sits apart," and is a rather delicate way of referring to a woman who must be isolated because of her ἄφεδρος, either menstrual or an abnormal loss of blood. MT is much blunter: עם טמאה "with an unclean woman." [47]

---

47. Theod and Sym translate the noun literally by ἀκαθαρτοῦ (retroverted from Syh).

Chapter 16

16:1 Understandably the Lord only speaks to Moses, since he is told to speak in turn to Aaron. The time of speaking is given as "after the two sons of Aaron died ἐν τῷ προσάγειν αὐτοὺς πῦρ ἀλλότριον before the Lord καὶ ἐτελεύτησαν." Though the final clause is paratactic, it obviously must show result; after all, the text had already said that they had died. MT differs in the prepositional structure. It simply has בקרבתם "when they approached." The translator knew the occasion as detailed at 10:1—2; cf comments ad loc, and comp also Num 3:4. The two sons, Nadab and Abioud, had brought strange fire before the Lord and a fire from the Lord "consumed them and they died before the Lord." The translator found their mere approach an incomplete and unclear statement, and gave the full explanation. The text is unusual, and modern translations show this: NRSV renders by "when they drew near"; NIV has "when they approached," and NJP makes it "when they drew too close," which is similar to Milgrom's "when they encroached upon."[1] What makes this text odd is that the Aaronids are accused of coming near before the Lord, but this is precisely what priests are supposed to do. Actually the Hebrew is also somewhat unusual in that קרב is not ordinarily modified by לפני, but rather by אל, though it does occur at Exod 16:9 and Num 9:6.[2] Hex has placed πῦρ ἀλλότριον under the obelus, since it is not present in MT. In the tradition, the majority F M text has προσφέρειν rather than προσάγειν. Either of these roots presupposes the Hi stem rather than the Qal of MT.

16:2 Moses is to give Aaron all the rules for his conduct for the day of atonement (vv.2—34a). The rules begin with a general warning: "at no time may he enter the holy place inside the veil into the presence of the propitiatory." What I have translated by "at no time" is πᾶσαν ὥραν. What is really meant is "(not) at any time." The time for entering adytum is specified later on in the chapter. The term τὸ ἅγιον here refers to the holiest place, the adytum, as the modifier ἐσώτερον

---

1. P.1008. Of the ancient translations, all but Tar[N] witness to a transitive verb plus the modifier "a strange fire," and this might well be the better reading.
2. Milgrom 1012 suggests that "with the Lord as object, the implied anthropomorphism is softened by the use of *lipnê* ..., in other words, not in direct contact with divinity, but in his presence."

τοῦ καταπετάσματος indicates. Throughout this chapter the term is uniquely used to designate the adytum. For the "veil" see Notes at Exod 26:31—34. For ἱλαστήριον see Note at Exod 25:16. It regularly renders כפרת (20 times; only once at 1Chr 28:11 is it rendered by ἐξιλασμός, probably understanding כפרים). The word also renders עזרה four times in Ezek 43, but is otherwise limited to translating כפרת, which does not mean "propitiatory" at all; for its description see Exod 25:16—21; see Notes ad loc. כפרת is rendered by "cover" in NJPS, as "mercy-seat" in NRSV, and rather oddly as "atonement cover" in NIV,[3] but to the Alexandrian it was a propitiatory, the so-called "mercy-seat" where the Lord appeared, and propitiation could be made for the sins of the people on the day of atonement.

It was located ἐπὶ τῆς κιβωτοῦ τοῦ μαρτυρίου "on the ark of the testimony," and since the root may mean "to cover," the rendering "cover" is not implausible. MT simply has "on the ark," but no equivalent for τοῦ μαρτυρίου, which is, however, attested in Tar^P; it is marked by an obelus in hex. For the term μαρτυρίου used to designate the ark see Note at Exod 16:34. For the first use of κιβωτὸν μαρτυρίου (uniquely without an article) see Exod 25:9 and Note ad loc.

Such entrance on Aaron's part would be lethal; he must not do so καὶ οὐκ ἀποθανεῖται. The reason for this is given in a γάρ clause: "for in a cloud I will appear (ὀφθήσομαι) on the propitiatory." Divine appearances in clouds are common in theophanies, but these were normally not lethal; cf Exod 40:28—32 where the cloud filled the tabernacle; in fact, Moses was in consequence unable to enter it. At Exod 25:21 the Lord says to Moses "I will speak to you ἄνωθεν τοῦ ἱλαστηρίου ἀνὰ μέσον τῶν δύο χερουβὶμ τῶν ὄντων ἐπὶ τῆς κιβωτοῦ τοῦ μαρτυρίου." Another understanding of "a cloud" is that it might refer to the cloud of incense,[4] but this is most unlikely, since it is only after entering the adytum that Aaron ἐπιθήσει τὸ θυμίαμα ἐπὶ τὸ πῦρ ἔναντι κυρίου. In the tradition, the b f+ text read θυσιαστηριον instead of ἱλαστηρίου at the end of the verse, but this is simply a careless copyist error.

16:3 MT begins with בזאת, which means "in this (manner)," which LXX fully understood by its οὕτως. Clearly the advice to Aaron not to enter the adytum was

---
3. For a recent statement on its possible meaning and function see Milgrom 1014.
4. An interpretation which Milgrom 1014—1015 prefers.

not absolute. He must enter with sacrificial animals, a bullock from the cattle for a sin offering and a ram for a burnt offering. For these see 8:14—21, and comments ad loc.

16:4 LXX follows Sam in beginning with a conjunction, as does Pesh. Aaron must put on a sanctified linen garment. The participle ἡγιασμένον translates קדש, and the translator thought of a "holy garment" as a garment that had undergone some process of purification; it had been made holy, thus dedicated to sacral use.

Furthermore, linen breeches must be on his skin. The use of χρωτός rather than σῶμα for בשר is a refinement; it marks a greater precision. The περισκελές are not on the skin in MT, but on the body. בשר could here actually be a euphemism for genitals as Milgrom maintains;[5] the translator rendered it by χρωτὸς αὐτοῦ, which presumably could be so understood as well. In any event the περισκελές were intended to hide a priest's private parts, for which see Note at Exod 28:38. Also made of linen were the girdle and the turban which he was to wear. The stress in the verse seems to be placed on the fact that all the garments were made of linen, the ordinary cloth worn by Israelites. It is expressly stated that ἱμάτια ἅγιά ἐστιν "they are holy garments"; this is in distinction from the χιτῶνα which was specifically sanctified; i.e. all were holy, but the cloak was rendered such by some process.

The last two clauses state "and he must bathe all his body with water, and put them (the garments) on." Since the verse begins with "he must put on a cloak," the last clause shows that the dressing of Aaron is subsequent to his bathing. The Greek specifies "all" his body, following the text of Sam, but MT lacks an "all." Hex has "corrected" the text by omitting πᾶν. Here בשר means "body," as the Greek fully understood.

16:5 The term עדת occurs twelve times in the book, and is throughout rendered by συναγωγή "community." The term also translates קהל, but only five times. The community of the Israelites must supply two kids from the goats as well as one ram. Instead of χιμάρους a C' n s+ reading has τράγους, but the latter never renders שעיר in OT, whereas χίμαρος is the usual translation.[6] As usual, when two types of quadrupeds are taken for sacrifice, the first is for a sin of-

---

5. P.1017.
6. The Others also read χιμάρους here as well as in v.7.

fering and the other for a burnt offering. Only at 12:6,8 are the two reversed, whereas the usual order is attested nine times in the book.

16:6 προσάξει, like its Hebrew counterpart הקריב, means "to offer up" in the context of sacrifice. The bullock which is brought for sacrifice is a sin offering τὸν ἑαυτοῦ "which is his own." ἑαυτοῦ is original rather than the short form attested by A B M *b n x*+.[7]

The second clause, though paratactically presented, is the reason for what is said in the first one. The sin offering is offered in order to make atonement for him and his house. For ἐξιλάσεται see comment at 4:20. One might well have expected (περὶ) εαυτου, i.e. "for himself and his house," and a popular V text does read εαυτου, but the textual evidence is too strong in support of αὐτοῦ. I would, however, suggest that the "spiritus" of Lev be changed to "asper," i.e. to αὐτοῦ. The atonement is then on his own behalf and on that of the Aaronids (τοῦ οἴκου αὐτοῦ).

16:7 Aaron is then to take the two kids referred to in v.5, and set them before the Lord. LXX renders העמיד by στήσει, which can be either transitive or intransitive, but must here be transitive. The majority text has the compound παραστησει; this is secondary, being influenced by the παρα phrase which modifies it. MT has no preposition for the phrase at all, and LXX interprets intelligently that the kids are to be stationed παρά "at" or "near" the door of the sanctuary. Here τὴν θύραν is singular, which makes better sense than the Byz variant text τας θυρας, but there is no discovered rhyme or reason for the varying number of the word in Lev; see the discussion at 3:2. Here the παρά phrase is necessary, since ἔναντι κυρίου could be misinterpreted as being in the adytum. The παρά structure ensures that the sacrifices are placed within the holy place near the sanctuary door.

16:8 LXX renders the opening clause literally as "and he shall place upon the two kids lots." The verb does not mean "cast," but "put, place" lots. This is fully clear from the unique use of נתן modified by גורלות in MT. What is intended is a placing of the lot on the head of the animals, one lot reading τῷ κυρίῳ and the

---

7. See THGL 96.

other τῷ ἀποπομπαίῳ.⁸ Instead of χιμάρους C´⁾ n s+ read τράγους,⁹ but for its secondary character see the discussion at v.5.

The designations for the two kids concern their disposition.¹⁰ The Hebrew word עזאזל has been variously interpreted, but is most commonly thought to be a proper name, paralleled by, but over against, יהוה. It is then taken to be the name of a desert demon.¹¹ The translator in my opinion did not know what it meant, but from the ritual it was clear that this kid was sent away into the desert; see v.10. And so he contextualized it by a neologism, an adjectival ἀποπομπαίῳ "the one sent off."¹² See the further discussion at v.10 below.

In the tradition, the A B V f x+ text has omitted κλήρους. Since the word before it also ends in -ρους, the omission is due to homoioteleuton. It is merely a palaeographically inspired error, and should not be considered seriously.¹³

16:9 Aaron must then bring forward (προσάξει) the kid, which is described as ἐφ᾽ ὃν ἐπῆλθεν ἐπ᾽ αὐτὸν ὁ κλῆρος τῷ κυρίῳ. The lot is called "(belonging) to the Lord," i.e. the Lord's. The verb has been changed to "came upon," and represents עלה. It is no longer the priestly action, ἐπιθήσει/נתן, that is stressed, but simply the effect; the lot came upon him; one might say "on whom the lot fell." The high priest must offer this one as a sin offering, which becomes περὶ ἁμαρτίας; this does not mean "concerning sin," but simply "a sin offering" throughout the book. MT has ועשהו חטאת, and the Greek correctly understood עשה to mean "to offer, sacrifice," though it failed to render the suffix. The Byz text, represented here only by the *t* group, added αυτον, as did Syh; this could be hex in origin.

16:10 The verse begins with the pendant accusative καὶ τὸν χίμαρον ἐφ᾽ ὃν ἐπῆλθεν ἐπ᾽ αὐτὸν ὁ κλῆρος τοῦ ἀποπομπαίου. The structure is an exact parallel

---

8. Sym has a different understanding: παλεῖ ᾽Ααρὼν ἐπὶ δύο τράγους κλήρους (retroverted from Syh). Aaron is actually to cast lots over the two animals.
9. The Others, i.e. all but Sym, read χιμάρους.
10. Sym has κλῆρον ἕνα εἰς κύριον καὶ κλῆρον ἕνα εἰς τράγον ἀπερχόμενον. Aq's reading is only extant for the second one: κλῆρον ἕνα εἰς κεκραταιωμένον "one lot to a fortified place." Sym read לעזאזל as לעז אזל, whereas Aq presupposes the root עזז.
11. See especially the fine summary of opinions in Gispen ad loc.
12. I find puzzling the rendering in Harlé-Pralon "l'éliminateur," though the lengthy discussion of the word is not uninteresting.
13. See THGL 115.

to the modifier of προσάξει in v.9, except that "the lot" is modified by a genitive. This supports the interpretation in v.9 of τῷ κυρίῳ as representing a dative of possession. Here the κλῆρος is "of the one sent off."[14] The pendant is brought into the main clause by the pronoun αὐτόν modifying στήσει, i.e. "he (i.e. Aaron) shall set him." This differs from MT's יעמד, which the Masoretes vocalized as a Ho "he shall be set." LXX makes explicit that the high priest is to be the actor in the setting of the second kid. The pattern of active verb with accusative pronoun as modifier follows the pattern of v.7: στήσει αὐτούς; the Ho vocalization of the Masoretes is made necessary by the lack of a pronominal modifier. In contrast to the first kid this one is ζῶντα. The purpose of setting the second kid alive before the Lord is τοῦ ἐξιλάσασθαι ἐπ' αὐτοῦ. For the infinitive see comment at 4:20. Here the atonement ritual involves ἐπ' αὐτοῦ. Making atonement "upon" or "over him" is explicated later on in vv.21—22; see discussion ad loc. Making atonement over him involves a symbolic transfer of guilt from the people to the head of the animal being sent out into the desert. Here the infinitival notion is explicated by a ὥστε plus an infinitive construction showing probable result of the atonement ritual: "so as to send it (i.e. the kid) off εἰς τὴν ἀποπομπήν."

Since the translator thought of עזאזל in v.8 as well as in v.10a as "the one sent off," its recurrence in v.b as modifier of ἐξαποστεῖλαι (αὐτόν) created difficulties; it could hardly be translated by the nominalized adjective, and so he chose the cognate abstract noun ἀποπομπήν "(to the) sending off," probably in the sense of "for letting (it) go off or free."[15]

In MT לעזאזל is followed by המדברה "to the desert." This probably meant "to Azazel into the desert." The translator was now in further difficulties. He had solved the problem of לשלח אתו לעזאזל by using ἀποπομπήν, but the further modifier המדברה made little sense after εἰς τὴν ἀποπομπήν. This necessitated the introduction of a new verb which εἰς τὴν ἔρημον might then modify, and so he introduced ἀφήσει αὐτόν "he sent him away." Hex showed this to be an addition by placing the two words under the obelus. I would translate v.b as "to let him go off into the wilds (literally, the sending off); he must send him away into the desert."

---

14. Sym has εἰς τράγον ἀφιέμενον instead of the genitive nominal.
15. Aq has εἰς τράγον ἀπολελυμένον, and Sym translated by εἰς τράγον ἐπερχόμενον, for which see v.8, f.n.6. Aq also omits ἀφήσει αὐτόν, continuing immediately with εἰς τὴν ἔρημον. I imagine that Sym did so as well, but this is not extant.

In the tradition, the majority M V text has added v.22a at the end of the verse, as an exegetical gloss; actually three mss, M 127 344, placed this gloss mistakenly under the asterisk. It should be noted that the O group does not support the gloss.

16:11 V.a is an exact repetition of v.6; cf comments ad loc. As at v.6 the phrase περὶ αὐτοῦ should be changed in the critical text to read περὶ αὑτοῦ; cf comments at v.6.

V.b then directs Aaron to slaughter "the bullock intended for the sin offering, which was his own." In the tradition, the final ἑαυτοῦ becomes αυτου in the A B V O b x+ text, but the full form is expected.

16:12 MT has the high priest take (גחלי אש) מלא המחתה, but LXX sensibly transposes with τὸ πυρεῖον πλῆρες, i.e. "the fire pan full of coals of fire.[16] Most witnesses follow the Hebrew order, which is probably due to hex. Those coals are to be taken from the altar τοῦ ἀπέναντι κυρίου, which renders מלפני יהוה. An F+ text omits the τοῦ, but this is probably due to homoioteleuton after θυσιαστηρίου, rather than a recensional change based on the Hebrew.

For θυμιάματος συνθέσεως see discussion at 4:7. The compound is λεπτῆς, i.e. ground fine; thus a high-grade incense is required. The officiant is to fill the hands with it; LXX does not translate the suffix of חפניו, and hex has supplied an αυτου to represent it. The high priest is then to enter the adytum, described as ἐσώτερον τοῦ καταπετάσματος, for which see comment at v.2.

16:13 The priest must place the incense on the fire in the presence of the Lord. The exact mechanics of the priestly action of vv.12—13 are not fully clear. He takes the fire censer filled with coals of fire, then he must fill (his) hands with incense and enter the adytum. He is also to "place the incense on the fire before the Lord." Does he place the incense on the fire in the censer before going inside the veil, i.e. arrive with the ἀτμίς of the incense billowing before him, or does he perform this within the adytum? In any event, the ענן "cloud" is here not translated by the usual νεφέλη (75 times in OT),[17] but by ἀτμίς. This equivalence only occurs elsewhere at Ezek 8:11, where it is used of seventy elders,

---

16. See SS 66.
17. According to the count of Dos Santos.

each with a censer in his hand, standing before the idols depicted on the wall, and ἡ ἀτμὶς τοῦ θυμιάματος ἀνέβαινεν. I suspect that the translator intentionally used the Lev phrase to stress the idolatrous parallel to the day of atonement ritual. An ἀτμίς is hardly a cloud; it is at best a mist or a vapour, and it might cover the propitiatory, but hardly hide it from priestly view. The LXX translator knew ענן to be a νεφέλη, since he had used it in v.2, where the "cloud" was the context in which the Lord revealed himself. But here the context is not one of divine self-revelation, but one of atonement through the atonement ritual. It is then not a νεφέλη of incense, but an ἀτμίς. This vaporous mist will cover the propitiatory τὸ ἐπὶ τῶν μαρτυρίων "that which is over the testimonies," which is metonymic for ἐπὶ τῆς κιβωτοῦ τῶν μαρτυρίων as at Exod 30:6; cf Note ad loc. The plural noun refers to τὰ μαρτύρια which the ark housed; these were the tablets containing the Ten Words; see Note at Exod 25:15. Usually it is singular as at Exod 25:21, but at 30:36 ἀπέναντι τῶν μαρτυρίων occurs, exactly the same usage as here.

16:14 The ἀπό modifying λήμψεται is partitive;[18] the priest is to take some of the bullock's blood. He must then perform two actions. 1) He must sprinkle τῷ δακτύλῳ[19] upon the propitiatory eastwards." κατά is used here in the sense of "over against,"[20] presumably with a downward motion. What is meant is that facing east, i.e. over against the east, he sprinkles blood on the propitiatory. 2) He must also sprinkle (some of the blood with the finger) seven times κατὰ πρόσωπον τοῦ ἱλαστηρίου, i.e. "over against the front of the propitiatory." What needs purification is the adytum as a whole, the area in front of the propitiatory. For both cases of sprinkling τῷ δακτύλῳ is used, though MT has באצבעתו. Hex has in both cases added an αυτου to represent the unrepresented suffix.[21] Also in the tradition, an O C' s text has added και before the second ῥανεῖ. This is a careless mistake based on καὶ ῥανεῖ introducing the second clause, but here a και is out of place; furthermore, it would be quite impossible to interpret MT's יזה in this way.

---

18. See SS 161.
19. The dative is instrumental; see SS 120.
20. See LS sub voce B.I.3.
21. See SS 96.

16:15 The first clause in LXX has amplified MT by adding ἔναντι κυρίου, and hex has placed it under the obelus to indicate its absence in MT. Only at 4:4 is the priestly slaughter said to occur "before the Lord." The phrase is, however, exceedingly common throughout Lev, and need not presuppose an actual parent text with לפני יהוה. That priestly slaughter of the sin offering was done in the Lord's presence is implicit; the gloss simply makes it explicit. The sin offering, as usual designated in the book as (τὸν) περὶ τῆς ἁμαρτίας, is the kid which is intended περὶ τοῦ λαοῦ "on behalf of the people."

The second clause begins with καὶ εἰσοίσει τοῦ αἵματος αὐτοῦ (i.e. of the slaughtered kid). εἰσφέρω normally takes an accusative, and the Hebrew הביא את דמו, if literally rendered, would have been το αιμα αυτου. MT says "he must bring its blood (inside the veil)." The use of a genitive modifier constitutes the translator's rationalization that the writer would hardly have meant what he said; surely only some of the blood should be brought into the adytum, and the genitive is intended as a partitive. The A B+ variant addition of an απο before the genitive is making explicit what was implicit in Lev.[22]

The point is then to deal with its blood (ποιήσει τὸ αἷμα αὐτοῦ, probably best rendered as "he must manipulate its blood") as he had done in the case of the bullock; see v.14. This is then explicated in the final clause, which is a shortened version of the parallel ritual referred to in the ὃν τρόπον clause, i.e. in v.14. In MT the double sprinkling is preserved: "and he shall sprinkle it (i.e. the blood) on the propitiatory and before the propitiatory." For the double sprinkling see comment at v.14. LXX, however, abbreviates even more, and thereby creates confusion. It has eliminated "and," so that it reads "and he must sprinkle its blood (rather than "it" as in MT) upon the propitiatory κατὰ πρόσωπον the propitiatory, i.e. both the ἐπί and the κατά phrases modify the verb. I must admit that an original και κατα would make better contextual sense. After all, an original και κατα could easily change to κατα by haplography. I would have adopted this as original Lev, except that there is not even one witness for such a και. What the translator has done is to describe the sprinkling of blood as a single sprinkling action upon the propitiatory, over the face of the propitiatory.[23] It must

---

22. See THGL 104.
23. Harlé-Pralon without comment render the clause: "et il fere aspersion de son sang sur la propitiatoire, sur la face du propitiatoire."

be admitted that the Greek is not fully consistent; ὃν τρόπον ἐποίησεν in v.14 made the manipulation of the blood a double action, not a single one.

16:16 ἐξιλάσεται occurs here with an accusative modifier for the first time in Lev. This also occurs at v.33 (twice; τὸ ἅγιον, τὸ θυσιαστήριον), and in v.32 it is used absolutely. The usual modification is with a περί phrase (27 times), and once with ἐν (6:37) and once with επ (16:18). In Lev if the object is personal, περί is used, but if it is an object (such as sanctuary or altar) an accusative obtains. A variant text supported by n s+, adds a περι before the accusative; this is probably taken from one of The Three, since MT has (הקדש) על. The verb is further modified by an ἀπό phrase, i.e. "the making atonement from ..." means that atonement involves cleansing, purification, i.e. getting rid of the ἀκαθαρσιῶν of the Israelites, and of their unrighteous actions. Note that ἀδικημάτων is not as strong a term as MT's פשעיהם "their willful transgressions."

Not fully clear is the syntax of the περί phrase which follows. Its equivalent in MT also has a different preposition. The first two are both מן phrases, but this one is לכל חטאתם "concerning all their sins." In MT this probably is a coverall which refers to both טמאת and פשעיתם, and means "whatever sins they might be." The translator also understood it in this way, and chose περί, thus "(as) concerning all their sins."

V.b requires the same action τῇ σκηνῇ τοῦ μαρτυρίου τῇ ἐκτισμένῃ ἐν αὐτοῖς. This is a rendition of MT's לאהל מועד השכן אתם. Note that the tent of meeting is personified; it is "the one dwelling with them." The tent is differentiated from the קדש by which the adytum is intended throughout this chapter, and so it must refer to the holy place. The translator was troubled by this personification of the tent, and chose a unique translation, the perfect passive participle of κτίζω "to form, produce, build," and in the passive " plant, found." By NT times the verb meant "to create." Here I would suggest "built, set (among them in the midst of their uncleanness)." The term has the suggestion of permanence about it, i.e. it has been set, founded by divine command; see Exod chh.25—30, and was chosen to indicate its origins by God's own orders. The irony of this setting ἐν μέσῳ τῆς ἀκαθαρσίας αὐτῶν should not be overlooked. Instead of τῆς ἀκαθαρσίας the Byz text has the plural των ακαθαρσιων, which might be recensional, since the Masoretes vocalized טמאתם as a plural noun as well.

16:17 For the meaning of σκηνῇ τοῦ μαρτυρίου over against τῷ ἁγίῳ see comment at v.16. The genitive absolute construction "when he (i.e. the high priest) enters the adytum" details the condition for the first clause "and there shall be no one (i.e. no priest) in the tent of testimony until he leaves." What is meant is that as long as the high priest is performing the ritual of atonement, there may be no one present in the holy place until he appears outside, i.e. when he has left the holy place.

V.b states for whom atonement is to be made: "for αὑτοῦ and his house and for all the community of Israelites." As at vv.6,11 περὶ αὑτοῦ should be read rather than περὶ αὐτοῦ; the pronoun is reflexive. The repetition of περί occurs only for the first and third nouns. As usual, when a preposition recurs in MT, the second one is omitted in LXX.[24] Here קהל rather than עדה obtains, but συναγωγῆς is used; see discussion at v.5. LXX actually has "community υἱῶν of Israel." The majority F V text omits the υἱῶν, which conforms to MT; the omission may well be hex. An s^mg y+ variant text articulates the υἱῶν as well, but the evidence is too sparse to be taken seriously.[25]

16:18 That אל can be rendered by ἐπί is clear from ἐξελεύσεται ἐπί, i.e. ἐπί simply means "to (the altar)." In MT "altar" is modified by a relative clause, which LXX renders by an attributive participle, τὸ ὄν "the one being (before the Lord)"; this refers to the altar of burnt offering which was placed in the αὐλή, the outer courtyard; see Exod 40:6. The Byz text has shortened this by omitting the participle ὄν, but this does not change the meaning; it is still "the one before the Lord." Here the high priest was to make atonement on the altar; for this he was to take some of the blood of the bullock and of the kid, i.e. the sin offerings for the high priest and his family and that for the people resp (see vv.5,6), and to put (it) on the horns of the altar round about. In the tradition the C^ɔ n s+ text has τράγου instead of χιμάρου; though both words mean "he-goat," τράγος never translates שעיר in OT; in fact, it never occurs at all in Lev. In the Pentateuch it usually renders עתוד.[26]

The placing of blood on the horns of the altar is a case of pars pro toto; the extremities of the altar are cleansed by the blood, which then means that the altar as a whole has been purged of impurities; see also 4:7,18,25,30,34 8:15 9:9.

---

24. See THGL 104.
25. For LXX usage on articulation of υἱῶν see THGL 85.
26. The Others read χιμάρου with Lev.

16:19 The phrase ἐπ' αὐτό refers to the altar of v.18, which is to be besprinkled. An A B+ text has επ αυτου, which would also make sense, but whenever ῥανεῖ is modified by ἐπί the preposition governs the accusative.[27] He is to sprinkle some of the blood[28] with the finger.[29] Most witnesses add αυτου after "finger," which represents MT, and is probably recensional.

The two verbs, καθαριεῖ and ἁγιάσει, are not synonyms. The former means to render ritually clean, and is regularly used throughout the book to this end. The word ἁγιάζω means to make holy, i.e. to set aside for the realm of the holy, the consecrated. It then means that the altar has been sanctified for sacred purposes; it has been removed from the realm of the profane, the ordinary, and has been set aside for "holy" ends. And this follows καθαριεῖ, i.e. ridding the altar "of the uncleannesses of the Israelites," thereby making them a holy people. It should be noted that though the verbs are not synonyms, their actions are closely intertwined.

16:20 MT begins with וכלה modified by מכפר, i.e. מן with a Pi bound infinitive. LXX has made of this συντελέσει plus a nominative singular participle, i.e. "and he shall finish making atonement for." Note that the participle ἐξιλασκόμενος is modified by accusative nominals, demonstrating that atonement is a matter of purgation, of ritual cleansing. This begins the first of three clauses presented paratactically, but the last clause details what comes after the first two. One might translate the pattern by "when he shall have finished ... and cleansed ..., then he shall bring forward the living kid." The ritual dealing with the second kid can only take place after the ritual dealing with the first kid is finished. According to LXX, rituals voiding impurities attached to τὸ ἅγιον "the adytum," τὴν σκηνὴν τοῦ μαρτυρίου "the tent of testimony," τὸ θυσιαστήριον "the altar," and the περὶ τῶν ἱερέων "matters concerning the priests," must be over and done with before the presentation of the living kid.

MT only mentions the first three; the second clause, καὶ περὶ τῶν ἱερέων καθαριεῖ, has no counterpart in MT. The immediate stimulus is probably v.33 where καὶ περὶ τῶν ἱερέων καὶ περὶ πάσης συναγωγῆς ἐξιλάσεται follows the statement that "he shall make atonement for the holiest place, and for the tent of

---

27. See THGL 99.
28. The ἀπό is partitive; see SS 161.
29. The dative is instrumental; see SS 120.

testimony and the altar he shall make atonement." Furthermore, at v.11 Aaron brings forward his own sin offering and makes atonement, not only for himself, but also τοῦ οἴκου αὐτοῦ, i.e. for the priests. The translator apparently felt MT to be incomplete. The priests, though not the people, had to be cleansed before the ritual of the second kid was performed. That the people were not included is well-reasoned. All their lawless actions, their unjust deeds, and all their sins were to be transferred in the next ritual to the head of the second kid (v.21). The clause is placed under the obelus in hex, since it has no equivalent in MT; it is also omitted by Syh, which is another instance of post-hexaplaric revision.

16:21 Aaron must place his hands on the head of the living kid. MT has "his two hands," and a popular hex text has added δυο to represent the שתי of MT. The point of this action is clear from the next two clauses. With his hands on the head of the animal he must "make known (i.e. confess) over it all the ἀνομίας of the Israelites and all their ἀδικίας and all their ἁμαρτίας, and (then) place them on the head of the living kid." MT omits the adjective, and hex has placed τοῦ ζῶντος under the obelus. The act of placing is one of symbolic transfer. The verb ἐπιθήσει occurs twice in the verse; here it translates נתן, and is expected, but in the first clause it renders סמך "to lean upon." LXX does not distinguish the two, since in both contexts the priests "puts ... on the head (of the animal)." What is transferred are "lawless acts," "unrighteous matters," and "sins" of the people. One might note that "uncleanness," or "impurities" are not mentioned; these were removed by the sacrifice of the first kid as a sin offering for the people, v.15. The Greek distinguishes three kinds of wrongdoings to which guilt is attached: ἀνομίας for עונת, ἀδικίας for פשעי "transgressions," and ἁμαρτίας for חטאת, but MT does not array them in coordinate fashion; the first two are introduced by את, but the last one, by ל. The last one is a summary statement, i.e. "he shall confess ... all the iniquities ... and all their transgressions, even for all their sins." In other words, their sins are of two kinds, עונת and פשעים.

Finally, "he must send (it) away by the hand of a man prepared into the desert." The "man prepared" translates איש עתי. The term עתי is a hapax legomenon, but is usually taken to be related to עת.[30] The term ἀνθρώπου ἑτοίμου probably means "an individual ready (for the task)," possibly then someone judged fit to carry out the sending away of the animal.

---

30. The Tar all render by some form of זמן.

16:22 V.a states that "the kid shall take on himself τὰς ἀδικίας αὐτῶν into an ἄβατον land." According to MT what the kid takes on are את כל עונתם. Hex added πασας before the nominal to represent the כל of MT.³¹ The translator had distinguished between ἀνομίας and ἀδικίας in v.21, but here MT has only עונת, which in v.21 had been rendered by ἀνομίας. LXX chose "unrighteous actions" as a preferable term to cover the various types of sin transferred to the head of the kid. The translation of ארץ גזרה "a cut-off land" by γῆν ἄβατον "a desolate land" is a good approximation.³²

V.b has a different subject, though it is not named. Common sense demands that "and he shall send the kid into the desert" must revert to the high priest as subject. The clause more or less repeats what had already been said at the end of v.21.

16:23 The ritual of the "sending away" being completed, Aaron "must go into the tent of testimony (i.e. the holy place)," and remove his priestly garment. This "linen garment" is described as ἣν ἐνεδεδύκει εἰσπορευομένου αὐτοῦ εἰς τὸ ἅγιον. The majority B F M text has changed the verb to the perfect ενδεδυκει, but the pluperfect is correct; he had donned the linen garment earlier. The structure εἰσπορευομένου αὐτοῦ is a badly conceived genitive absolute, since the αὐτοῦ refers to the subject of the verb. The n text "corrected" it to a simple εισπορευομενος. It undoubtedly means "when he entered (the adytum)." The garment he must leave there, i.e. in the tent of testimony.

16:24 After having removed his linen outer garment, the high priest must bathe and put on his robe again before performing the sacrifice of the burnt offering. Whether this is the same garment which he had taken off or another στολήν is not said, but it would seem to be the same one. This performance is introduced by a subordinate participle ἐξελθών followed by ποιήσει τὸ ὁλοκάρπωμα αὐτοῦ και τὸ ὁλοκάρπωμα τοῦ λαοῦ. Highly problematic is the use of ὁλοκάρπωμα by the translator for translating עלה, both for himself and for the people. The word only

---

31. Theod and Sym also read πάσας τὰς ἀδικίας αὐτῶν.
32. Tar⁰ makes it ארעא דלא יתבא, i.e. "without inhabitant"; Tarᴶ calls it a צדיא land, i.e. "ravaged, laid waste," whereas Tarᴺ renders גזרה literally by מפסקה "cut off, isolated."

occurs once elsewhere (Wis 3:6). The usual rendering for עלה is ὁλοκαύτωμα; in fact, it occurs 34 times in Lev as well as 12 times in the plural. The simplex, κάρπωμα, does occur for עלה, but only in ch.1 (vv.4,9,13,14, 18), and otherwise it is used (14 times) as translation for אשה, for which see comment at 2:9. But why choose this neologism here, when in vv.3,5 the burnt offering was designated a ὁλοκαύτωμα? Admittedly, the word is popularly changed in both cases to ολοκαυτωμα (or -ματα), but this is under the influence of the more common word. There must have been some reason for avoiding the usual word in translating עלה. The word is clearly a synonym for ὁλοκαύτωμα; it too was wholly sacrificed. The basic element -καυτωμα stresses the consumption of the sacrifice by fire, whereas the element -καρπωμα refers to "fruit," and the verb καρπόω not only means "to bear fruit," but also "to enjoy the fruit of," and even simply "to enjoy." Was the compound possibly chosen, it being the last reference to the burnt offering in the day of atonement account, to show that the עלה was wholly dedicated to the Lord's enjoyment?

The final clause has the high priest making atonement "on behalf of himself and his house, and on behalf of the people as on behalf of the priests." MT has no equivalent for καὶ τοῦ οἴκου αὐτοῦ nor for ὡς περὶ τῶν ἱερέων, and hex has placed both under the obelus to indicate that fact. A popular B M variant text has added περι before the τοῦ οἴκου, but this is demonstrably secondary.[33] The addition of "and of his house" is a case of leveling with vv.6,17, and for the other gloss see comment at v.20 on καὶ περὶ τῶν ἱερέων καθαριεῖ. The translator apparently felt that Aarons's making atonement for himself and for the people had omitted an essential element, viz. the priests. This he then supplied in double fashion, first by adding "and his house" after "himself," but then also after "for the people," though, since he had already added the Aaronids, only a reference to the Aaronids in a comparison phrase seemed appropriate.

16:25 The bound structure חלב החטאת is rendered by a noun plus an articulated περί phrase, thus "the fat which is for the sin offering." The Masoretes vocalized חטאת as a singular, but the translator, being conscious not only of Aaron but also of his house and of the people, logically made the sacrifice plural, περὶ τῶν ἁμαρτιῶν. For ἀνοίσει as rendering for יקטיר see comment at 2:16.

---

33. See THGL 104.

16:26 In MT the subject throughout is המשלח את השעיר לעזאל "the one sending away the kid to Azazel." Presumably this is a roundabout way of referring to the high priest, though it could be thought to be the איש עתי of v.21 who was instrumental in the sending off of the animal into the desert. But in v.21 the subject of שלח is אהרן. LXX had no trouble with "the one sending away the χίμαρον, but the prepositional phrase is translated by an articulated participle plus prepositional phrase: τὸν διεσταλμένον εἰς ἄφεσιν "the one set apart (i.e. separated) for release."[34] The term ἄφεσιν means "release," i.e. release into the desert, though at least as early as the second century BCE it also had the secondary notion of remission (i.e. of debt).[35] Admittedly the sins of the people had been transferred to the head of the live goat, but the goat does not symbolize pardon; it is destined to be sent off into the wasteland; he is set apart in order to be released.

Obviously the high priest's role as officiant is finished; it remains for him to "wash the garments, and bathe his body with water," after which he may enter the camp. In the tradition, the F M majority text added αυτου after ἱμάτια. This may be hex in origin, added to represent the suffix of בגדיו.

16:27 The verse begins with a lengthy pendant accusative: "the bullock which is for the sin offering and the kid which is for the sin offering whose blood had been brought in to make atonement into the adytum"; the reference is to v.15. This is then referred to in the next two clauses by αὐτά, specifically to μόσχον and χίμαρον. The choice of a neuter pronoun was made because of the distance from the antecedents. One would certainly have expected the masculine pronoun αυτους.[36] The relative clause has as its subject in MT את דמם. Lev reads (ὧν) τὸ αἷμα. Only the three mss A B 58 and Arm lack the recapitulative genitive pronoun, and I would now add the otiose αὐτῶν after αἷμα, read by all other witnesses except for three mss reading αυτου (which is a thoughtless error for αὐτῶν). The recapitulative pronoun almost invariably appears in the book, whereas the A B+ reading is a stylistic improvement. Lev also reordered הובא את דמם as τὸ

---
34. The anonymous rendering ὁ ἐξαποστελλόμενος ἅμα τῷ χιμάρῳ εἰς ἀζαζήλ is almost certainly Aq.
35. See LS sub voce 2.a.
36. Probably as Huber 35 suggests, wrongly influenced by the τὰ δέρματα ... καὶ τὰ κρέα αὐτῶν later in the verse.

αἷμα (αὐτῶν) εἰσηνέχθη which hex transposed as εισηνεχθη το αιμα αυτων to equal MT.

The verbs in the main clause no longer have the high priest as subject; they are now in the indefinite plural, and might well be translated by a passive construct. I would render: "they must be brought outside the camp, and they (αὐτά; see comment above) and their skins and their flesh and their excrement must be burned by five.[37]

16:28 The individual who actually burned them (αὐτά now refers to coordinated modifiers of κατακαύσουσιν of v.27) was rendered unclean by his handling of the materials mentioned in v.27, and so must wash (his) garments and bathe himself, and only aferwards "might enter the camp." This is an exact replica of the instructions for the one sending away the kid in v.26, including the failure to render the suffix of בגדיו, which, however, was made up for by the majority text adding αυτου, undoubtedly recensional in origin; see comments at v.26.

16:29 Vv.29—34 constitute the conclusion to vv.1—28, the instructions concerning the day of atonement. It begins with καὶ ἔσται τοῦτο ὑμῖν νόμιμον αἰώνιον. MT lacks an equivalent for τοῦτο, which hex accordingly placed under the obelus. The translator simply levelled with v.34, where exactly the same words begin the verse; there MT does have זאת. It should be noted that this is no longer part of the instructions transmitted by Moses to Aaron (v.2), but the people are now addressed; the ordinance is ὑμῖν.

On the prescribed date, the tenth day of the seventh month, the people are told "ταπεινώσετε τὰς ψυχὰς ὑμῶν "you must humble yourselves." This is a literal translation of MT: תענו את נפשתיכם, and is usually considered to mean "you must fast," as e.g. reflected in Ps 35:13 עניתי בצום נפשי, and this interpretation is still followed on Yom Kippur throughout the Jewish community. Presumably the Alexandrian community carried out their self-denial in this way as well. An A B t+ text reads ταπεινωσατε, i.e. an aorist imperative. But the translator does not translate prefix inflections in this way; תענו requires a future.[38]

---

37. The ἐν of ἐν πυρί is instrumental; see SS 117.
38. See THGL 127.

Also demanded is πᾶν ἔργον οὐ ποιήσετε. This day of atonement is to be observed, along with the Sabbath, as a day on which no work may be done. This applies both to the native born, ὁ αὐτόχθων, and the resident alien, ὁ προσήλυτος. Both are in the nominative, since they are in apposition to the subject of the verbs. In MT the גר is described as הגר בתוככם "the one residing in your midst." LXX does not use a cognate participle, but has "ὁ προσκείμενος ἐν ὑμῖν "the one settled among you." This also occurs, however, elsewhere in the book, in describing the גרים; see 17:8,10,12,13 25:6,[39] in all of which cases the participle προσκείμενος was used by LXX.

16:30 No subject is given for ἐξιλάσεται, though the last reference to ἐξιλάσεται was modified inter alia by περὶ τοῦ λαοῦ, and the subject was the high priest. This was in v.24, and far removed. Presumably here the subject could be taken as indefinite, and one might render it by a passive construction, i.e. "atonement shall be made for you." It is, however, true that the one making atonement is to be the regnant high priest as v.33 makes clear. The verb is modified by a complementary infinitive καθαρίσαι ὑμᾶς "to render you ritually clean"; in fact, the cleansing is "from all your sins before the Lord." Both prepositional phrases modify the infinitive. This differs from MT where these phrases modify תטהרו, and constitute v.b; thus: "from all your sins you shall be rendered clean before the Lord." LXX, however, has a καί before the verb, thereby making a separate clause: "and you shall be rendered clean." Hex has omitted καί so as to equal MT. It is difficult to find a reason for adding καί here, and I imagine the parent text may well have read ותטהרו, but there is no Hebrew textual evidence for such a reading.

16:31 LXX begins with σάββατα σαββάτων ἀνάπαυσις αὕτη ἔσται ὑμῖν, whereas MT has שבת שבתון היא לכם; in other words, שבתון seems to have two equivalents. The phrase σάββατα σαββάτων occurs only twice in OT, here and at 23:32. The Hebrew שבתון also occurs three times in Exod, twice following שבת as here (21:15 25:4) where it became ἀνάπαυσις in LXX, and once before שבת; at 16:23 שבתון שבת appears as σάββατα ἀνάπαυσις in LXX, presumably having transposed the two Hebrew words; for the term σάββατα see Note at Exod

---

39. See THGL 130.

16:23. At Lev 23:32 MT reads שבת שבתון הוא לכם, for which LXX has σάββατα σαββάτων ἔσται ὑμῖν. At 25:4 שבת שבתון also occurs, but becomes σάββατα ἀνάπαυσις. From all this it is clear that שבתון is either transliterated, or translated by ἀνάπαυσις. The word also occurs separately at 23:24 and twice at 23:39, and in all three cases is translated by ἀνάπαυσις.

Our verse with its double rendering of the word is unique. Furthermore, היא also has a double rendering in αὕτη ἔσται. The clause must mean either "this rest shall be for you a sabbath rest" or "this rest shall be for you a sabbath of sabbaths," in other words, a very special day, possibly meaning "a sabbath of complete rest."[40]

For the next clause see comments at v.29. I would take νόμιμον αἰώνιον as a separate clause: "(it is) a permanent ordinance."

16:32 LXX follows Sam's יכפר rather than the וכפר of MT; it has ἐξιλάσεται. The verb is used absolutely, but is then introduced with modifiers in the next verse. This priest is the one in succession, which is described as "whom they will anoint (him) and whom they will ordain to serve as priest after his father." The verbs are both plural, a simplification of MT where both verbs are singular, "one will anoint," "one will ordain." The rendering "will ordain" represents a Hebrew idiom ימלא את ידו "will fill his hand." The Greek τελειώσωσιν τὰς χείρας αὐτοῦ "they will validate his hands" is a calque, and must be understood in the Hebrew sense. For the use of τελειόω in this sense see Note at Exod 29:9, as well as the comment at 8:33. The plural rendering for ידו is insignificant; the translator seems to have paid little attention to the number of the word יד. In the tradition, τελειώσωσιν becomes indicative in an A B F V f+ text, but this text does not omit ἄν, and therefore must be secondary.[41] An n reading has the singular, τελειωσει, and could be recensional, since MT also has the singular.

As mark of his high priestly status the successor priest must according to MT don בגדי הקדש את בגדי הבד. Both bound phrases are rendered by adjectival structures, the first one articulated as τὴν στολὴν τὴν λινῆν to show the את preposition, and the second one reinterpreted entirely as an unarticulated adjectival phrase, στολὴν ἅγιαν. The Hebrew has a bound phrase בגדי הקדש which means "garments of (i.e. for) the adytum," a reference to the garments to be

---

40. As Milgrom 1057 suggests for the Hebrew equivalent.
41. See the discussion in THGL 128.

worn by the priest on the day of atonement. The translator obviously did not understand the phrase in accordance with the meaning of קדש in this chapter. A popular M text does add an article before ἅγιαν, but this peculiar Greek really does not constitute a rendering of MT, except formally.

16:33 A full statement outlining the objects of atonement. The first of these is set off in a separate clause, viz. τὸ ἅγιον τοῦ ἁγίου; this is unique in the book as is its Hebrew counterpart את מקדש הקדש; in fact, this occurs nowhere else in OT. I would render this "the most holy place"; it refers in singular fashion to the adytum. It should be noted that הקדש no longer refers to the adytum by itself, but a new nominal structure is used to describe it in unique fashion. The Byz *f* text has changed the genitive nominal to the more usual plural των αγιων, but the translator knew what he was doing in choosing the unique τοῦ ἁγίου.

The next clause has two preposed modifiers to the verb, viz. "the tent of testimony and the altar." The last clause is similarly patterned with περὶ τῶν ἱερέων and περὶ πάσης συναγωγῆς as preposed modifiers to a repeated ἐξιλάσεται. The last modifier represents על כל עם הקהל in MT, i.e. "concerning all the people of the community." The translator presumably felt no need for rendering עם, since the קהל could only be composed of עם.

16:34 The opening structure is exactly the same as in v.29, but here the τοῦτο has a counterpart in MT; see comments at v.29 for details. Since the νόμιμον is a lasting one (αἰώνιον), the complementary infinitive is a present inflection, appropriate since it represents an ongoing process; it is to be carried out annually. Not at all surprising is the fact that a popular variant text should have changed ἐξιλάσκεσθαι to the default aorist εξιλασασθαι.[42] I would render the structure as "a permanent ordinance for making atonement." MT has אחת בשנה modifying the infinitive, but LXX has changed the text considerably. MT has the *ethnach* on בשנה, with v.b beginning with ויעש "and he did," referring to Aaron, as is clear from the כאשר clause referring to vv.1—2. But the translator made the major cut in the verse before ἅπαξ, and changed ויעש to ποιηθήσεται, thus "once per year shall it be done." LXX makes the annual performance of the ritual part of the instructions. The καθάπερ clause then refers to v.2.

---

42. As did Aq; The Others, however, retained the present infinitive of LXX.

Chapter 17

17:2 λάλησον is modified by three πρός phrases, the last one being πρὸς πάντας τοὺς υἱοὺς Ἰσραήλ. The accusative plural υἱούς is normally articulated; in fact, only twice does it occur without an article (both in 10:4), and the B G V+ text omitting τούς must be secondary.¹ The address has changed from previous chapters in that Moses is to speak not only to Aaron (as in ch.16), but also to the Aaronids and the Israelites. The instructions are of general interest and concern.

For the formula "this is the word which the Lord commanded," see 8:5. Quite unusual is the absolute use of ἐνετείλατο; in fact, it occurs elsewhere only at 9:5. Normally it is accompanied by a dative of person.²

17:3 This verse along with v.4a constitutes the protasis, for which the apodosis obtains in v.4b. Actually the construction of the protasis is peculiar in that relative clauses modifying "anyone of the Israelites" constitute the protasis, i.e. "whatever individual of the Israelites would ..., (that individual) shall be guilty ...)." איש איש occurs ten times in Leviticus, and eight times it is rendered as here by ἄνθρωπος ἄνθρωπος.³ It simply means "anyone." This is followed in MT by מבית ישראל, but LXX translates by the genitive τῶν υἱῶν Ἰσραήλ. מבית ישראל only occurs four times in the book (also at vv.8,10 22:18), but is always interpreted as τῶν υἱῶν Ἰσραήλ. It occurs without the preposition only once (10:6), where it is translated by ὁ οἶκος Ἰσραήλ; comp also comment at v.13. An A B F M popular variant text has added η των προσηλυτων των προσκειμενων εν υμιν, but this has no equivalent in MT and is an intrusion from v.10, and comp vv.8,13.⁴

The potential action of the subject is that he "might slaughter a bullock or a sheep or a goat in the camp καί who might slaughter outside the camp." MT has a correlative או instead of καί, which is smoother. The Hebrew for μόσχον is, however, not פר as in ch.16, but שור. The פר is a younger version of the שור, but LXX makes no distinction between the two. The same distinction obtains between the שעיר and the עז, but LXX does distinguish by χίμαρος vs αἴξ.

---

1. See THGL 84—85.
2. See THGL 113.
3. See THGL 122.
4. See also THGL 109.

17:4 The second condition. MT has a much shorter text than LXX which follows Sam. Sam begins with ואל פתח אהל מועד לא הביאו לעשות אתו עלה או שלמים ליהוה לרצונכם לריח ניחח וישחטהו בחוץ, which is absent from MT, but is fully supported by 4QLev^d.[5] Both MT and Sam read the rest of the verse as in MT. The present MT text may have been the result of parablepsis due to homoiarchon.[6] The longer text was parent text for LXX, and it was placed under the obelus in hex (though the actual text is marked at a different juncture) to indicate the large amount of text not present in MT.

LXX did not render the suffix of הביאו (Sam 1°), and hex has added αυτο to represent it. The worshiper had failed to sacrifice it (ὥστε ποιῆσαι αὐτό) for a burnt offering, for which see ch.1, or for a sacrifice for deliverance, for which see ch.3. A popular variant text has added an εἰς before σωτήριον under the influence of the coordinate εἰς ὁλοκαύτωμα. Such sacrifices to the Lord are δεκτὸν εἰς ὀσμὴν εὐωδίας "acceptable for a smell of sweet fragrance." δεκτόν is the usual rendering for (ל)רצון. It occurs at 1:3 for לרצנו. The prepositional phrase occurs with second masculine plural pronominal suffix four times in MT (19:5 22:19,29 23:11) and is throughout rendered by this adjective, though with ὑμῖν (but as ὑμῶν at 19:5) following. The לרצינכם of Sam is probably the parent text for LXX, although in view of LXX the parent text may well have been לרצון. For the εἰς phrase, which is a calque for לריח ניהה, see comment at 1:9. For καὶ ὃς ἂν σφάξῃ ἔξω see the last clause of v.3. Here its parent text is probably Sam's וישחטהו בחוץ, though failing to translate the suffix. The remainder of the condition renders v.1 of MT adequately, but the condition in LXX refers specifically to the one "who would slaughter outside."

This raises the question: To what do the preceding conditions which equal the longer text of Sam apply? They follow the final clause of v.3 "and who would slaughter outside the camp," but that makes the next part seem like a doublet. Obviously some disruption of text has occurred. I would suggest that it is precisely this final clause of v.3 that is interruptive, since the section not present in MT most logically applies to the one who would slaughter ἐν τῇ παρεμβολῇ. Note also that the ὥστε clause differs considerably from that in the first part.

---

5. The shorter text is supported by 11QpaleoLev; for both see DJD XII 194—195.
6. Daniel 193 seems to have overlooked the fact that the shorter text is clearly secondary.

There it was "to sacrifice it for a burnt offering or for a sacrifice for deliverance," but here it is "to bring forward a δῶρον for the Lord before the tent of the Lord." δῶρον translates קרבן which in large part refers to the meal offerings of ch.2; see there vv.1,4,5,7,12,13. Thus understood, the conditions for the one offering within the camp and those for the one sacrificing outside the camp are fully distinct, the former for burnt offerings or sacrifices for deliverance, and the latter for δῶρα, i.e. for meal offerings.

This is the first occurrence of the bound phrase משכן יהוה in the Pentateuch; it also occurs five times in Num (16:9 17:28 19:13 31:30,47), and only three times in the rest of the OT. Its translation by σκηνῆς κυρίου is expected. LXX uses σκηνή for both אהל and משכן, and only makes a distinction when they come together. This only happens in Exod; see Notes at 26:7—13, 35:10 and 40:2, but particularly at 26:7. In the tradition, A B 121 add a μη before προσενέγκαι, but this is otiose in view of μὴ ἐνέγκῃ αὐτό introducing the ὥστε clause.[7]

The apodosis is a twofold one: a) "And there shall be reckoned to that man αἷμα." MT does not witness to an initial conjunction, and the majority M V text omits the καί; this may well constitute a hex correction. Hex has also reordered the text. MT begins with דם, whereas αἷμα is at the end in LXX; hex has transposed αἷμα to the beginning to equal MT. The next clause explains what the reckoning of αἷμα means; it means "he has shed αἷμα." This would make the first αἷμα refer to "bloodshed." I would understand αἷμα ἐξέχεεν as constituting a comment on the first αἷμα which the translator had already reordered to the end of the a) clause, so that αἷμα ἐξέχεεν would immediately follow the first αἷμα. On the other hand, it also gives a basis for the judgment of b) "ἡ ψυχὴ ἐκείνη shall be destroyed from his people." MT does not read הנפש ההיא but האיש ההוא. The Lev text is ex par, since "that ψυχή shall be cut off from (the midst of) its people" is formulaic; see 7:20,21,25,27 19:8 22:3 as well as Exod 12:15,19 31:14 Num 9:13 15:30,31 19:13,20. The parent text has נכרת plus מקרב, i.e. "shall be cut off from the midst of," i.e. that person will be excommunicated from the community. The translator fully appreciated that this meant "death, destruction," hence ἐξολεθρευθήσεται.

17:5 This verse, beginning with a ὅπως ἄν construction, gives the raison d'etre for the ῥῆμα commanded in vv.3—4. That "word" was given in order that the

---

7. See THGL 109.

17:5 This verse, beginning with a ὅπως ἄν construction, gives the raison d'etre for the ῥῆμα commanded in vv.3—4. That "word" was given in order that the Israelites might sacrifice correctly. ὅπως renders למען אשר. The combination למען אשר occurs only 12 times in OT, five occurring in the Pentateuch (also Gen 18:19 Num 17:5[16:40] Deut 20:18 27:3). It is apparently simply a variant of למען, and in the Pentateuch is also rendered by ὅπως in Gen and Num, but in Deut by either ἵνα or ὡς; in all cases an ἄν follows. Here the verb is the rarely used present subjunctive φέρωσιν,[8] used to indicate a constant process; the default would be the aorist. Incidentally, ἄν φέρωσιν was misread by A B 121 as αναφερωσιν, but the Hi of בוא is never translated by ἀναφέρω; it is simply a copyist error.[9]

The sacrifices which the Israelites might bring are described by the limiting ὅσας clause: ὅσας ἄν αὐτοὶ σφάξωσιν ἐν τοῖς πεδίοις "which they would slaughter in the open fields." The αὐτοί is otiose in the context, but it represents the subject of a nominal clause in MT: הם זבחים. The translator could hardly follow his usual pattern of translating such a nominal clause by a pronoun plus a present indicative verb, since the ὅσας clause is subordinate to a ὅπως plus subjunctive clause. Since the predicate had to express a potential notion, he used the default aorist subjunctive,[10] plus the pronoun to show the הם of MT, a rather clever rendering.

Note that LXX continues using σφάζω, even though MT changes to זבחים, and the verb θύω might have been expected. But the translator distinguishes between the slaughtering in the fields and the θύσουσιν θυσίαν in the last clause. The translator used the plural πεδίοις to render the singular שדה; either number would have been adequate in Greek.

LXX makes the first cut in the verse at this point, whereas MT divides the verse after הכהן, which it placed under the *ethnach*. This is clear from the change in mood to the indicative. This is no longer part of the ὅπως construction, but constitutes demands on the Israelites. I would take the καίs introducing the last two clauses as a "both ... and" construction. The Israelites must both "bring (them) to the doors of the tent of testimony to the priest, and sacrifice them as a sarifice for deliverance to the Lord." The Greek does not translate the suffix of

---

8. See THGL 125.
9. See THGL 132.
10. See THGL 95.

הביאם, and the majority F M text has added αυτα after οἴσουσιν; this may well be hex in origin. Note also that the plural τὰς θύρας is used to translate פתח. The use of the plural "doors" of the tent of testimony is arbitrary;[11] at times the singular, and at times the plural, obtain with no pattern that I can discover. The verb θύσουσιν is modified by two accusatives, θυσίαν σωτηρίου and αὐτά. MT has the plural זבחי שלמים which agrees with the other modifier אותם, but the singular simply designates the class of sacrifice, and is fully adequate.[12] The f text does change to the plural θυσιας, but this need not be recensional, since the change of final nu to sigma may simply be by attraction to the opening sibilant of the next word, σωτηρίου. The pronoun αὐτά is unexpected, since its most natural antecedent would be θυσίας, but Lev often uses the neuter when the antecedent is vague; note the possible references to μόσχον ἢ πρόβατον ἢ αἶγα of v.3 and to δῶρον of v.4.[13]

17:6 According to MT the priest must pour out the blood upon מזבח יהוה. This is the first occurrence of "altar of Yahweh"; it also occurs five times in Deut, and for the rest of the OT: three times in Jos and 1Kgs resp, six times in 2Chr, and once each in 2Kgs, Mal and Neh. Lev avoided translating it directly. θυσιαστήριον was modified by κύκλῳ ex par; actually κύκλῳ follows θυσιαστήριον in the context of pouring blood 11 times in the book. But after κύκλῳ has been added to θυσιαστήριον, the free element of the MT bound phrase needs contextualization; again usage came to the rescue. The phrase "before the Lord" occurs 59 times in Lev, usually as ἔναντι κυρίου, but occasionally the compound ἀπέναντι occurs (see 16:12,18). Since κύκλῳ ἀπέναντι has no counterpart in MT, hex has placed the words under the obelus. For the plural τὰς θύρας see comment at v.5. In MT פתח designates place, but LXX renders this by a παρά phrase; see 3:13 16:7 where the prepositional phrase also occurs after "before the Lord," and comp 3:2,8 4:4,14 19:21.

The second clause demands that he shall offer up the fat εἰς ὀσμὴν εὐωδίας to the Lord. For ἀνοίσει as a rendering for הקטיר see discussion at 2:16.

---

11. For the usage see THGL 73.
12. See Daniel 278—281.
13. See Huber 33—36.

that they have been idolatrous in the past. In MT they are not to sacrifice לשעירם. The word שעיר means "he-goat," and is so used in the previous chapter, where it was rendered by χίμαρος throughout. It is related to the word שער "hair." The goat is a shaggy creature, and so is called "the shaggy one." Here, however, "the hairy ones" are objects of worship, and the term is usually regarded as referring to a kind of goat demon or satyr, which inhabits the desert regions; comp Isa 13:21 34:14. The translator chose a nominalized adjective, ματαίοις, to translate the word; they are "the empty, vain ones," ones who amount to nothing, are worthless beings.[14] The translator probably chose the word to contrast with τῷ κυρίῳ, the true object of cult as seen in the verses preceding this one. At 2Chr 11:15 the word also occurs in the context "And he established for himself priests for במות both for לשעירים and לעגלים." The Greek renders these two ל phrases by καὶ τοῖς εἰδώλοις καὶ τοῖς ματαίοις and τοῖς μόσχοις, i.e. לשעירים is rendered by a doublet: "to idols and to vanities." The adjective occurs in the Pentateuch only once in the plural, but five times in the singular (always for שוא). The word is obviously intended as a judgment, a term of derision; the שעירם are worthless non-entities, vain things.[15]

These ματαίοις are then characterized by a relative clause: οἷς αὐτοὶ ἐκπορνεύουσιν ὀπίσω αὐτῶν "after whom they were going for illicit ends." The verb means "to fornicate, engage in illicit sexual relations. It is in the present tense, since it represents the participial predicate of a nominal clause with הם/αὐτοί as subject. Sollamo finds the use of οἷς ... ὀπίσω αὐτῶν confusing,[16] but I fail to see the difficulty. οἷς is of course dative by attraction to its antecedent τοῖς ματαίοις, and common sense indicates that the antecedent for αὐτῶν must be the same, hence the above rendering.

The subscription to this section in MT reads "This will be a lasting ordinance for them throughout their generations." Why the translator failed to translate זאת is puzzling; the Greek reads "a permanent ordinance shall be to you throughout your generations." Hex has added τουτο before ἔσται to make up for it. The translator has also made the clause one of direct address to the Israelites instead of the third person used by MT; the third person is consistent with the

---

14. See the word study in Harlé-Pralon for general OT usage.
15. Aq translated the word literally by τοῖς τριχιοῦσιν "the hairy ones," and Sym transliterated by τοῖς σεειρειμ. Tar[J] makes them טעיון "idols," but Tar[O] has שדין and Tar[N], שדיה "demons."
16. In Greenspoon-Munnich 49.

section as a whole, though a second person referent in the subscription is equally sensible.

17:8—9 These verses constitute a similar warning to that of vv.3—4, but it is not limited to the Israelites, since it also includes the class of proselytes, i.e. resident aliens, who must also present their sacrifices at the tent of testimony for implementation. LXX has transposed אלהם תאמר to the more usual order ἐρεῖς πρὸς αὐτούς, and hex has rearranged the order to equal that of MT.

For ἄνθρωπος ἄνθρωπος τῶν υἱῶν Ἰσραήλ see comment at v.3. Coordinate with "Israelites" is καὶ ἀπὸ τῶν υἱῶν τῶν προσηλύτων τῶν προσκειμένων ἐν ὑμῖν "and from the sons of the resident aliens who abide among you." MT has a different text: ומן הגר אשר יגור בתוכם "and from the resident alien who abides among them." The amplification of הגר אשר יגור stems first of all from the מן; as a partitive this would logically expect a plural noun. But the addition of τῶν υἱῶν is not justified by this. I suspect that it is due to the pressure of the coordinate τῶν υἱῶν (Ἰσραήλ) which renders a מן structure מבית ישראל.[17] In other words, just as "the sons of Israel" means the class of Israelites, so "the sons of proselytes" means the class of resident aliens. I would render the structure "and of the resident aliens who dwell among you." Furthermore, the suffix of תוך is a third plural masculine pronoun, which LXX changed to second person.[18] It should be noted that this is exactly what the translator did in the last clause of v.7 as well. He has changed this quite intentionally to direct address.[19]

The relative clause which follows modifies the opening subject ἄνθρωπος. It reads: "who might perform a burnt offering or a sacrifice." MT uses the verb יעלה "offer up," but ποιήσῃ follows the יעשה of Sam.

The second part of the protasis begins as in v.4 with "and at the door of the tent of testimony he would not bring." The verb is then modified by a purposive infinitival construction: ποιῆσαι αὐτὸ τῷ κυρίῳ "to execute it to the Lord," which is considerably shorter than v.4. The penalty is, however, the same: "that man shall be destroyed from his people." The reference is to ἄνθρωπος rather than to

---

17. But see THGL 109, which discussion I no longer find adequate.
18. But Kenn 84 does read בתוככם rather than בתוכם.
19. I do not find the explanation in SS 31 at all convincing. It reads: "der Kontakt ist nur dermassen schwach geworden, dass der Übersetzer sich der vorausgehenden *Konstruktion* nicht mehr bewusst war."

the ψυχή of v.4, but excommunication is again interpreted as destruction, ἐξολεθρευθήσεται; see comment at v.4.

17:10 Vv.10—12 deal with the prohibition against eating blood. For καὶ ἄνθρωπος ἄνθρωπος τῶν υἱῶν Ἰσραήλ see comment at v.3. For "or from the resident aliens who are abiding among you," see v.8, and especially its comment on ἐν ὑμῖν for בתוכם. LXX has ἤ instead of the καί of v.8, but MT supports καί with its ומן. Either conjunction makes sense, and no particular reason for the change to ἤ need be given except that of free choice. The condition is simply expressed: ὃς ἂν φάγῃ πᾶν αἷμα.

The apodosis consists of two clauses, and is introduced by καί in imitation of the Hebrew. ἐπιστήσω is an unexpected rendering for נתתי. Except for Isa 3:4 the equation occurs only in this book; it also occurs at 20:3,6 26:17, and each time is modified by τὸ πρόσωπόν μου ἐπί plus an accusative, i.e. as "I will set my face against." Here the preposition governs τὴν ψυχὴν τὴν ἔσθουσαν τὸ αἷμα "the person who eats blood." In the second clause LXX has ἀπολῶ for הכרתי, rather than ἐξολεθρευσήσεται as at vv.4,9,13, but it is a synonym used simply for variety.

In the tradition, the V O x+ text has the simplex στησω instead of ἐπιστήσω. This may well be a recensional change, since ἵστημι is a much more common rendering for נתן. But most of the same witnesses mistakenly have την ψυχην instead of τὸ πρόσωπον; this is an error created under the influence of the following prepositional phrase ἐπὶ τὴν ψυχήν; it is quite bazarre, and is never predicated of God; even in the sense of a reflexive it can only apply to creatures, never to the creator. Clearly hex is the addition of μεσου before τοῦ λαοῦ to represent the Hebrew מ)קרב).

17:11 The first כי/γάρ clause gives the reason for the prohibition of v.10. The Greek ψυχή is simply a calque for נפש, as its frequency of use shows. Out of 732 cases of נפש, 695 become ψυχή in Greek, and in five, the reflexive pronoun σεαυτοῦ.[20] נפש basically means "self," i.e. person, and the Greek ψυχή is usually best rendered by "person, individual" or as a reflexive pronoun. Here, however, reference is made to the ψυχὴ πάσης σαρκός, also attested by a Qumran ms,[21] of

---

20. According to the count of Dos Santos.
21. By כול בשר in QLev^d; see DJD XII 195. This reading is almost certainly the parent text for LXX.

which it is said αἷμα αὐτοῦ ἐστιν; MT lacks the suffix, having בדם.²² נפש/ψυχή is here best translated by "life," thus "the life of all flesh is its blood." This is not quite the same as MT which says "the life of all flesh is in the blood"; in other words, MT finds the source of נפש to be in the blood, whereas LXX makes the two equal to each other. The addition of αὐτοῦ could be a textual matter, since 4QLevᵈ reads בדמו; on the other hand, this may well be a simple case of leveling with v.14 where MT reads דמו.

The next clause is paratactically given. The ἐγώ is the Lord; "it is I who have given it (i.e. the blood) to you to be making atonement on your behalf on the altar." The phrase ἐπὶ τοῦ θυσιαστηρίου is placed immediately after ὑμῖν in imitation of MT, but good sense dictates that it must modify the purposive infinitive ἐξιλάσκεσθαι, which the translator has astutely put in the present tense; it is a process which is repeatable, and the present tense is appropriate.

It is now clear that the blood spoken of in the opening clause refers specifically to the blood of animals for sacrifice. After all, what is being discussed is the rationale for the prohibition of the eating of blood. I would also suggest that the plural in (περὶ) τῶν ψυχῶν ὑμῶν is best rendered simply by "on your behalf."

In the tradition, a popular text has εδωκα instead of δέδωκα. The two are often confused, but exegetical considerations, as well as support by all the uncial texts, make the perfect the preferred reading; God has given it to you, and it remains a lasting effect; blood is a divine gift which continues to serve to make atonement for you. A C⁽ˀ⁾ s+ text adds μου after θυσιαστηρίου, but this pious gloss has no support in MT or elsewhere.

A כי/γάρ clause also ends the verse, but the two versions differ. MT says "because it is the blood (which) makes atonement בנפש." LXX says "because its blood shall make atonement on behalf of the person (ἀντὶ τῆς ψυχῆς)." The αὐτοῦ modifying αἷμα has no equivalent in MT;²³ on the other hand, LXX paid no attention to הוא. Or did the translator take הדם הוא as "the blood of him," which would be a highly unusual, though apparently not an impossible, understanding of the structure? Also unusual is the free rendering of בנפש by an ἀντί phrase,²⁴ though in my opinion it does give the sense of what MT intended.²⁵ What ἀντί contributes is a notion of exchange; what "its blood," i.e.

---

22. Theod, Aq have ἐν αἵματι, and Sym has σὺν αἵματι (retroverted from Syh).
23. See SS 74.
24. See SS 125.
25. I am sceptical of Gispen's explanation as ב instrumenti.

the blood of the sacrificial animal, does is to substitute atonement for the life; comp Gen 9:5 which gives the reason for not eating κρέας ἐν αἵματι ψυχῆς.²⁶

17:12 Again it is deity speaking: "Therefore I said to the Israelites." What is said is repeated, first with "every person among you" as subject, and then with "the proselyte who is abiding among you." For both it is said οὐ φάγεται αἷμα "he may not eat blood."

17:13 The subject is an exact repetition of the subject in v.10, except for the conjunction (καί rather than ἤ); it is "anyone of the Israelites and of the resident aliens abiding among you." For "Israelites" rendering מבית ישראל see comment at v.3. It should be said, however, that the majority F M text has η rather than καί, as in v.10, but Lev follows MT with its καί. The regulation concerns ὃς ἂν θηρεύσῃ θήρευμα "who might hunt game," or "who might engage in hunting." The objects are θηρίον ἢ πετεινόν.²⁷ Syntactically these are in apposition to θηρευμα, since the verb does not ordinarily take a double accusative. I would suggest that the cognate accusative is used simply as a grammatical catchbasin for what the hunter is hunting, here "wild animal or bird," thus "who might engage in hunting wild animal or fowl." The hunt is not for sport, but for ὃ ἔσθεται "what may be eaten," i.e. legitimate for food, for which see ch.11.

The apodosis, introduced in Hebraic fashion by καί, insists that "he must pour out the blood and cover it with earth." Most witnesses follow the A F M text in adding αυτου after τὸ αἷμα to agree with את דמו of MT;²⁸ the addition may well be recensional. The Hebrew counterpart to τῇ γῇ is בעפר; the dative is instrumental.²⁹ Since what עפר intends is "ground, soil," one would have expected a more specific term such as χούς or χῶμα, but γῆ is the most common rendering for עפר according to Dos Santos.³⁰ Blood not covered by soil could be misunderstood as spilt blood, which lying out in the open would demand some kind of retribution; comp Ezek 24:7–8.

---

26. For further elaboration on ἀντί see Harlé-Pralon ad loc. Their paraphrastic rendering gives the correct sense of the clause: "car c'est son sang tenent lieu de l'âme qui fera l'apaisement."
27. Since θηρίον stands for חיה, Aq translates by ζῷον.
28. See THGL 92 concerning cod A and its relation to cod B.
29. See SS 122.
30. Instead of τῇ γῇ Aq Sym have τῷ χοΐ, whereas Theod read <τῷ> χώματι.

expected a more specific term such as χούς or χῶμα, but γῆ is the most common rendering for עָפָר according to Dos Santos.³⁰ Blood not covered by soil could be misunderstood as spilt blood, which lying out in the open would demand some kind of retribution; comp Ezek 24:7—8.

17:14 The γάρ clause is an exact copy of the opening clause of v.11; cf comments ad loc. MT, however, follows this with הוא בנפשו. The Masoretes have made good sense out of this by making דמו the subject with בנפשו הוא as predicate, i.e. "its blood is in its life"; see comment at v.12. The נפש כל בשר is then a pendant structure: "(for) as for the life of all flesh, its blood is in its life." The translator has simplified all this by omitting הוא בנפשו entirely, and leveling with v.11. See also the final clause of our verse. Hex has added εν ψυχη αυτου under the asterisk, but has not supplied an equivalent for הוא.

A divine statement (καὶ εἶπα τοῖς υἱοῖς Ἰσραήλ) summarizes the prohibition, along with the reason for it: "you may not eat the blood of any flesh, because the life (ψυχή) of all flesh is its blood."³¹ The "because" clause is identical with the opening γάρ clause, except that ὅτι is used rather than γάρ. The closing statement is odd in MT, since the subject אכליו is plural but the predicate יכרת is singular.³² The translator simplified this by making the subject singular, πᾶς ὁ ἔσθων, as does Sam with אכלו. Instead of εἶπα the n text witnesses to the Classical second aorist ειπον; But this should be discounted as secondary, since the n text consistently uses ειπον.

17:15 A rule is given for "any person who eats something that died or something torn by wild animals, whether among the native born or among resident aliens." The term ψυχή now reverts to its usual sense of "person, individual." For θνησιμαῖον ἢ θηριάλωτον see 7:14. LXX interprets the nouns אזרח and גר correctly as collectives, and makes them plural. The Hebrew has "and" rather than "or," but the two are often interchanged. The ἐν phrases of course modify ψυχή as good sense demands. MT then introduces the predicate by a conjunction, which is odd indeed. This made it possible for the Masoretes to have also made

---

30. Instead of τῇ γῇ Aq Sym have τῷ χοΐ, whereas Theod read <τῷ> χώματι.
31. For αἷμα ἐστιν αὐτοῦ Sym has τῷ αἵματι αὐτῆς ἥνωται "it is united with its blood."
32. Other examples in MT are found listed in GK 145l.

the first cut between the subject and the predicate, placing ובגר under the *ethnach*. LXX wisely omitted the conjunction.

The predicate consists of four verbals in future tense: "must wash his garments and bathe with water and remain unclean until evening and (then) be clean." Only here in the book does the fourfold verbal pattern obtain. A triple pattern does occur: at 14:8,9 and 15:13 all but no.3 are demanded, and at 15:6— 8,10,11,16,21,22,27 all but no.4 obtain. Most unusual is the combination of nos.3 and 4, but see 11:32. In the tradition, copyists tended to add a modifier after λούσεται, either the popular το σωμα or the fuller το σωμα αυτου in *n z+*, but Lev equals MT.

17:16 But suppose the persons of v.15 should neglect the ritual cleansing by not washing the garments nor bathing the body, what then? For the "if" clause MT has no equivalent for τὰ ἱμάτια, and hex has placed it under the obelus. Most witnesses have added an αυτου under the influence of the common nominal "his garments." On the other hand, instead of τὸ σῶμα MT has בשרו, and the majority F M text has also added an αυτου, but this need not be recensional. MT also has no equivalent for ὕδατι, and hex has duly placed it under the obelus.

The penalty for non-obsevance is καὶ λήμψεται ἀνόμημα αὐτοῦ; note the usual otiose apodotic καί. In MT at 5:1 and 7:28 the same clause obtains, i.e. ונשא עונו, where, however, עונו is rendered by τὴν ἁμαρτίαν; cf comments ad loc. The noun ἀνόμημα means that which breaks the law, but like its counterpart in MT עון, can also mean the guilt associated with it. I would translate: "he shall bear his guilt." An F *n+* reading has the reflexive εαυτου instead of αὐτοῦ, a correct interpretation, though not the original text.

Chapter 18

18:1 LXX has εἶπεν, which is unusual for "and the Lord said/spoke to Moses" in introducing a new section; in fact, it only occurs four times (also at 16:2 21:1 23:1). This is expected at 16:2 21:1 since MT has ויאמר, but here and at 23:1 it has וידבר. In both cases a popular M ol C' d f s t z+ reading witnesses to ελαλησεν, presumably a recensional correction. The formula with ἐλάλησεν κύριος occurs 36 times in the book, but here the divergent εἶπεν appears to be original.

18:2 What Moses is to say to the Israelites on behalf of the Lord begins with the self-identification formula: ἐγὼ κύριος ὁ θεὸς ὑμῶν. This formulaic statement, either with or without εἰμι after ἐγώ, occurs 26 times in chh.18—26. Slight variations occur twice more (22:9 26:44), and without ὁ θεὸς ὑμῶν, i.e. either as ἐγὼ κύριος or as ἐγώ εἰμι κύριος, the formula occurs 15 times. It is obvious that the formula sets this section off as a distinct entity within the book, a unit in which the Lord gives personal instructions to his people. The more common long form of the formula insists that κύριος is the God of the people, their own God who has peculiar rights to make his demands for conduct, both within the cult or outside it, upon his people. The formula is of central importance, particularly in the context of the holocaust, in a world in which the Jewish community lived. Over against the Hellenic notion of a chief or a high God stands the self-identification of the Lord, i.e. of Yahweh, not as God of all peoples, but as ὁ θεὸς ὑμῶν.[1]

Presumably the placement of these formulae serves in some way to structure the materials, but this is not by any means always clear. In fact, sometimes they occur beteween two laws which seem closely related; e.g. why should the formula be placed between the φυλάξεσθε clause in v.4 and the φυλάξεσθε clause opening v.5? But at times the occurrence of the formula makes structural sense, e.g. the short formula occurs at the end of v.6 which is an introductory statement forbidding incest in general terms, but within the section vv.7—18 which constitute detailed prohibited incestual relations no such formulae obtain.

---

1. For a particularly fine discussion of precisely this point see Robert Hanhart, "Der status confessionis Israels in hellenistischer Zeit," Zeitschrift für Theologie u. Kirche 92(1995), 315—328.

18:3 As the Lord's people they must avoid the practices of other peoples, among whom they might reside. LXX chose exactly the right word in ἐπιτηδεύματα to render the collective מעשה. This is first used of the land of Egypt, which is described as ἐν ᾗ κατῳκήσατε ἐπ' αὐτῆς. The verb is popular in the Pentateuch as the translation for the root ישב. A majority F M variant text reads παρωκησατε, but this cannot be original. Lev never uses παροικέω at all, and it is extremely rarely used for ישב elsewhere.[2] The variant is exegetically inspired, suggesting that the Israelites' stay in Egypt was a sojourn, a temporary residence, but that is not what either MT or LXX meant to say.[3] Similarly ἐπ' αὐτῆς is original text, and not the επ αυτη of B+, nor the Byz εν αυτη which is a recensional text reflecting the בה of MT. Whenever κατοικέω is modified by an ἐπί phrase in the Pentateuch, it always, with but one exception (Dt 25:5 in which the idiom ἐπὶ τὸ αὐτό occurs), governs the genitive.[4]

The second context for ἐπιτηδεύματα is projected into the future, retaining thereby the notion of the people in transit between Egypt and the promised land of Canaan. This was characterized as εἰς ἣν ἐγὼ εἰσάγω ὑμᾶς ἐκεῖ. The ἐγώ is hardly necessary; in MT the relative clause was nominal with אני as subject and מביא as participial predicate. This pattern was commonly rendered by a pronoun plus an inflected present tense verb. The ἐγώ betrays its origin in the Hebrew pattern.[5] For both κατά structures the divine command states οὐ ποιήσετε "you may not eat."

Furthermore, τοῖς νομίμοις αὐτῶν οὐ πορεύσεσθε "in their ordinances you may not walk." The genitive pronoun has no expressed antecedent, but the context makes it clear that the peoples of (Egypt and) Canaan are intended. The Masoretes made the first cut after the first clause, which would mean that the suffix of בחקתיהם would be understood to refer to כנען, but in LXX both lands may be considered anaphorically. LXX did not translate the preposition, and the A *b* tradition inserted εν before the dative nominal, but this is hardly recensional; it is merely stylistic. The dative modifying πορεύομαι is a metaphorical extension of a dative of place, i.e. it signifies the realm where one goes, i.e. "to act according to."[6] To walk in such a realm is forbidden; their ordinances follow heathen

---

2. According to Dos Santos only eight times in the OT.
3. See THGL 130.
4. See THGL 99.
5. See SS 82.
6. See especially Harlé-Pralon ad loc.

norms, and "you may not walk in the ordinances" of such people. A popular variant text has the present tense verb πορευεσθε, but this is palaeographically explicable; the consecution ΣΕΣ easily became ΕΣ by haplography. Only the future is sensible.

18:4 The positive counterpart to v.3. "My judgments you must execute, and my statutes (חקתי) you must be careful to walk in them." (as well as in v.5). The noun, either as חק or חקה occurs 35 times in the book and is normally rendered by νόμιμος (23 times; see e.g.v.3), and by πρόσταγμα six times, three times by νόμος, once each by δικαιώματα and κρίματα, and once (26:15) it is represented by the pronoun αὐτοῖς. The complementary present infinitive πορεύεσθαι is unarticulated, but MT has the infinitive marker ל governing it, ללכת, and hex has accordingly added a του to represent it.[7] The present infinitive is appropriate, since "to walk in them" is a continuous process. Variant popular traditions have changed the infinitive to a coordinate inflected form, either as a future και πορευσεσθε or a present imperative και πορευεσθε.[8]

The formulaic "I am the Lord your God" concludes the verse, and gives added solemnity to the demands to follow the Lord's directions (his κρίματα and προστάγματα).

18:5 The first two clauses are a restatement of v.4a, with the nouns reversed, but with πάντα added to modify each of the two nouns over against MT. Only the first πάντα is attested in the tradition as placed under the obelus in hex. Similarly the verbs are in reverse order, though only φυλάξεσθε governs both nominals: "and you shall guard all my statutes and all my judgements," and ποιήσετε is used simply in a coordinate "and you shall do them." But this clause is not attested in MT; it represents an attempt to include everything that v.4 had said here as well. In the tradition, d and Syh omit the clause, an omission which is probably recensional. An A F M C' d+ text attests to the aorist imperative φυλαξασθε, and an F C' s+ text has the aorist imperative ποιησατε, instead of future indicatives, but only the future tense forms can be taken as Lev text.

The relative clause, however, adds something new. In MT this reads אשר יעשה אתם האדם וחי בהם "which mankind shall do and live by them." LXX sub-

---

7. So too Aq read τοῦ πορεύεσθαι.
8. Theod also attests to καὶ πορεύεσθε.

ordinates the verb יעשה to a participle, ποιήσας, thereby placing the stress on ζήσεται ἐν αὐτοῖς;⁹ the ἐν is to be taken as instrumental. That "he shall live by them" implies that "not living by them" would involve death.¹⁰ LXX did not translate אתם as modifying ποιήσας, though the ἐν αὐτοῖς modifying ζήσεται may well reflect it, i.e. by downsizing יעשה to a participle, the "them" might then be transferred to the main verb. The popular text witnesses to the addition of αυτα after the participle. This is probabaly recensional, though it is also attested in a NT citation (Gal 3:12).

In MT the short formula of divine self-identification, אני יהוה, ends the verse. LXX, however, levels with v.4 in its ἐγὼ κύριος ὁ θεὸς ὑμῶν. Here the formula is an appropriate conclusion to the general call to obey the divine instructions, before proceding to the specific laws concerning incest.

18:6 Vv.6—18 deal with the laws of incest. V.6 is a general prohibition against sexual intercourse with family relatives. For ἄνθρωπος ἄνθρωπος see comment at 17:3. The term for family relative is οἰκεῖα σαρκός, a rendering of שאר בשר. The term שאר usually means "flesh," but in Lev 18—25 it has the specialized sense of a near relative. The term occurs only in Lev (vv.6,12,13,27 20:19 21:2 25:49), and is translated throughout as a form of the adjective οἰκεῖος, except at 20:19 where the derivative οἰκειότητα is used.

What is forbidden is that one προσελεύσεται ἀποκαλύψαι ἀσχημοσύνην. The idiom "to uncover shame" means "to engage in sexual intercourse." The term ἀσχημοσύνη is a euphemism for the privy parts of either male or female, so what is meant is to uncover the privy parts and engage in sexual relations.

The concluding short formula ἐγὼ κύριος puts the rules concerning incest in the proper perspective. The one delivering the rules on incest is the Lord, and the people are his own covenant people; cf 19:2. Its occurrence here is appropriate both to end the general prohibition of incest and to set the tone for the catalogue of possible incestuous relations that follow.

18:7 "The shame of your father" is not separate from "the shame of your mother," and the καί ought to be translated by "even." What this involves is the

---

9. Aq attests to ἃς ποιήσει αὐτὰς ἄνθρωπος ...," and Theod translates as ὅσα ποιήσει αὐτὰ ὁ ἄνθρωπος καὶ ζήσεται, a word for word rendering of MT. In Aq the pronoun probably refers to κρίσεις, whereas in Theod αὐτά probably presupposes κρίματα.
10. See the interesting discussion in Harlé-Pralon ad loc.

belief that the shame of the mother belongs only to the father; it is his shame. That this is what is intended is clear from the γάρ clause. It says nothing about the father, since only the mother is involved; see also v.8. In MT there is no equivalent for γάρ; it is exegetically correct, but it is original to LXX.[11] In the tradition, both πατρός and μητρός are articulated by the majority of witnesses, but modifiers of ασχημοσύνην are never articulated in this section.[12]

MT introduces the last clause asyndetically, and this is the pattern throughout the entire section on incest, vv.6—18, though see v.14. Lev has introduced the clause by καί, and I would now take this to be secondary. It is an early careless error continued in A B V b+, whereas all other witnesses lack καί. The pattern is clear in LXX; clauses are not joined by καί throughout this section, and the καί before οὐκ should be deleted from the Lev text.

18:8 This verse presupposes polygamy, i.e. "the wife of your father" is not your mother. Relations with her had already been prohibited in v.7. The shame of your father's wife is the property of the father: ἀσχημοσύνη πατρός σού ἐστιν. For an instance of such incest see the Note at Gen 49:4 where Reuben's incestuous relations with Balla, his father's concubine (35:21), is condemned not only as an act of hybris, but also as one of defilement (ἐμίανας τὴν στρώμνην).

18:9 "The shame of your half-sister, whether agnate or cognate, you may not uncover." The following structure explains the matter of the half-sister. One who was ἐνδογενοῦς was probably an agnate, since one born within the home would be the daughter of another wife, i.e. not of one's mother, but sharing a common father. If, however, she were γεγεννημένης ἔξω, she would be a cognate half-sister, i.e. sharing a mother, but not the father, thus of an earlier marriage of the mother, here characterized as "born ouside."

The syntactic pattern is that of an initial pendant accusative, ἀσχημοσύνην, which is then brought into the S—P structure by repeating τὴν ἀσχημοσύνην αὐτῆς as modifier of the verb. Thus "as for the shame of your sister ..., not may you uncover her shame."

In the tradition, most witnesses, including all the uncial texts, articulate ἀδελφῆς. That this is, nonetheless, secondary is clear from the pattern of the

---

11. See THGL 115.
12. See THGL 87.

incest laws. The genitival noun modifying ἀσχημοσύνην is throughout never articulated; the original text is retained only by $C^{\prime}$ Byz+, all others adding the secondary της. The opposite is true of ἀσχημοσύνην when in modifying ἀποκαλύψεις it follows the verb; then it is always articulated, and the omission of τήν by A B x+ is secondary.[13]

18:10 Also forbidden are sexual relations with a granddaughter, either born of son or daughter. The reason is that your granddaughter is σὴ ἀσχημοσύνη. An A B+ text omitted σή, but this can only be a thoughtless error. Not only does MT support the pronoun; it is also the regular pattern in Lev. Only in v.6 in the general prohibition against sexual relations with close relatives is the absolute use of the norm warranted.[14] The pronoun in the כי clause of MT is plural, הנה, but LXX renders it by the singular copula ἐστιν. The singular refers to ἀσχημοσύνην, whereas the antecedent of הנה is to either granddaughter; both possibilities are intended by הנה.

18:11 Relations with an agnate half-sister are forbidden. LXX has quite a different syntactic pattern from that of MT, which cuts the verse with הוא under the *ethnach*. Its pattern is a pendant structure "the nakedness of the daughter of your father's wife," followed by the bound structure "offspring of your father," which is an appositive of בת, followed by a nominal clause with הוא the subject referring to בת, and the predicate as "your sister." V.b then continues: "you may not uncover her nakedness."

LXX interprets by means of three distinct clauses. By adding οὐκ ἀποκαλύψεις to MT's first unit, the clause reads: "the shame of the daughter of your father's wife you may not uncover." Syh omits οὐκ ἀποκαλύψεις, from which fact one may conclude that its parent (hex) text had this under the obelus to show its absence from MT. The next clause reads ὁμοπατρία ἀδελφή σού ἐστιν. The choice of the compound ὁμοπατρία to render the bound phrase (מולדת אבי(ך is especially apt, particularly in view of the fact that this is rarely done.[15] The final clause renders v.b of MT literally. In spite of the syntactic freedom shown by the translator, LXX correctly interprets MT's text.

---

13. See THGL 87.
14. See THGL 115.
15. See SS 70.

18:12—13 The two verses are strictly parallel, forbidding sexual relations with agnate or cognate aunts. In each case a γάρ clause follows, detailing the reason for the prohibition, in the former "because she is your father's οἰκεία," in the latter "because she is your mother's οἰκεία. For the notion of שאר and its rendering see comment at v.6. The word also occurred in the general prohibition of incest at v.6 with σαρκός as modifier, and the structure was rendered as "family relative." The terms means "household," hence "family." MT has no equivalent for the γάρ in v.12,[16] though it is obviously implied.[17]

Incidentally, the *b* text combines the two verses into one by adding η αδελφη μητρος σου after σου, and η μητρος σου after σού in v.12, and then deleting v.13 entirely. Apparently the parent scribe of the tradition found the incest list tediously repetitive.

18:14 This verse begins unusually (but see v.7) with ἀσχημοσύνην of a male. The first clause reads: "the shame of your agnate uncle you may not uncover." This, however, is not a ban on homosexual behaviour, as the next clause makes clear: "and to his wife you may not go in," i.e. to have sexual intercourse. This is a Hebraism representing the common use of בוא in the sense "to enter in to a woman," and is idiomatic for "having sexual relations." What is unusual here, however, is that MT does not have בוא at all, but הקרב. What MT says is "you may not approach, come near to his wife." The rendering of the root קרב by εἰσέρχομαι is unique for OT, whereas εἰσέρχομαι occurs 578 times for בוא and the simplex 759 times. Other frequent renderings include ἥκω (189 times), εἰσπορεύομαι (119), παραγίνομαι (108), and ἐπέρχομαι (46).[18] As already explained at v.7 a woman's privy parts were considered the possession of her husband, hence the reference to the "shame of your agnate uncle." MT does not introduce the clause with a conjunction, but LXX follows Sam which reads ואל.[19] The Tar^JN Pesh and Vulg all support the καί as well. The use of a πρός phrase modifying an εισ- compound verb, which normally governs an εἰς phrase, is

---

16. But Kenn 3(vid),173,665 do add כי. Pesh and Vulg also attest to the causal particle.
17. See THGL 115.
18. Acording to the count of Dos Santos.
19. And so do Kenn 1,4,9,17,18,132,136,181,193 and 665.

unexpected.[20] The b n+ variant text reading προσελευση was probably conditioned by the πρός phrase.

In the tradition, the unarticulated πατρός is articulated by the A B M V majority text, but genitive modifiers of ἀσχημοσύνη are never articulated within this section on incest, and the unarticulated πατρός must also be original.[21]

LXX again has a γάρ clause, though this is only implied in MT.[22] MT states the obvious: "she is your aunt," your דדתך. LXX has συγγενὴς (γὰρ) σού ἐστιν, i.e. "she is your kinswoman," she belongs to your family, your clan. Obviously the translator either misread דדתך as, or actually read, דדתך, i.e. a feminine word based on דוד. This makes excellent sense contextually; in fact it is a synonym of οἰκεία, for which see vv.6,12, and comment at vv.12—13.

18:15 Intercourse with one's daughter-in-law is also forbidden. The reason is given in a γάρ clause: "for she is the wife of your son." Once again MT only implies a כי; it simply states: "she is your son's wife." In the tradition, γάρ is omitted by the majority text; whether this is recensional or not is not clear, but in view of the fact that γάρ clauses commonly occur throughout this section, it is probably original.[23]

18:16 In the case of the sister-in-law, sexual relations are also prohibited, but the appended nominal clause of MT, ערות אחיך הוא, is not rendered by a γάρ clause, but follows MT. The clause is, however, different. All the γάρ clauses identified the person as a relative of some kind, but here the predicate of the nominal clause is the ערות of your brother, not the wife of your brother. What is meant is that the sister-in-law's shame is the property of your brother. The A 84 text does add γαρ after ἀσχημοσύνην, but this is ex par, not original text.

18:17 Also prohibited is intercourse with a woman and her daughter; presumably what is meant is to have a woman and her daughter as wives. The reference is to a wife and a step-daughter, i.e. the בת is from a previous marriage. The same rule applies to a granddaughter, i.e. actually a step-granddaughter; whether the

---

20. See THGL 77.
21. See THGL 87.
22. See THGL 115.
23. See THGL 115.

offspring of a son or a daughter is immaterial; both are prohibited. What is meant in each case is that the γυναικός is a first wife, and the daughter or granddaughter would be a second wife. That it is marriage which is contemplated is clear from οὐ λήμψῃ ἀποκαλύψαι; "not may you take" means "not take as wife." MT has with respect to the granddaughter "you may not take so as to uncover ערותה. The singular suffix is quite intentional, since only one granddaughter is involved. But the reference to the granddaughter reads "the daughter of her son and the daughter of her daughter," and one might misunderstand the translation τὴν ἀσχημοσύνην αὐτῶν as referring to the two granddaughters. The αὐτῶν, however, refers rather to "woman and granddaughter"; it is not a triple, but a double marriage.

A γάρ clause follows, though MT only implies the causal relation. Only three Greek mss, A B and 121, as well as five of the versions, witness to the γάρ, all the others omitting it, thereby equalling MT. But the γάρ is probably original,[24] as in vv.12,13,14. The clause reads οἰκεῖαι γάρ σού (εἰσιν) "for they are your relatives."[25] The Hebrew word is שארה, which the Masoretes vocalized as a feminine noun, not as שאר plus a third feminine singular pronominal suffix. It is, however, synonymous with שאר. Since the feminine noun is a hapax legomenon, the possibility of the final hê having resulted from a misread final kaph is a possibility, since LXX translated by οἰκεῖται σου. What makes the suggestion plausible is that whenever שאר was rendered by οἰκεῖα, LXX always followed with a genitive; cf vv.6,17,18 25:49.

The verse ends with זמה הוא "it is a wicked, scandalous act." The Greek calls it ἀσέβημα "a profane, sacrilegious act." The Greek term is somewhat stronger than the Hebrew, and puts it in the realm of the irreligious, of ungodliness.[26]

18:18 MT begins the verse asyndetically, whereas LXX begins with καί. MT divides the verse after תקח, i.e. "and a woman you may not take alongside her sister." This is followed by לצרר which is somewhat unclear, but probably means

---

24. See THGL 115.
25. Aq has λίμμα αὐτῆς ἐστιν.
26. Sym translates the term by μῦσος "defilement," and Theod simply transliterates it with ζεμμα.

"so as to promote rivalry," i.e. to make a צר of her.²⁷ In any event, two sisters would, like Leah and Rachel, vie for the attention of their common husband.

V.b then means "to promote rivalry by having sexual relations with her (the sister), in her (the first wife's) lifetime," i.e. while she is still living.

LXX renders לצרר by the noun ἀντίζηλον "rival"; it is a hapax legomenon in the Pentateuch, and the translator has taken the infinitive as a noun, making it a second accusative modifying λήμψῃ, thus "do not take a woman along with her sister as a rival." In other words, for the Greek the first cut comes after ἀντίζηλον. The remainder of the verse is a purposive infinitival construction: "so as to uncover her shame alongside her (the first wife) while she (the first wife) is still living." What the infinitive expresses is what happens in the case of marriage with sisters—the rivalry is stimulated by the husband having sexual relations with the sister while the first wife is still alive, a certain formula for trouble in the household. Since ζώσης αὐτῆς is a genitive absolute referring to the first wife, the reference in ἐπ᾽ αὐτῇ is confusing. The succession of αὐτῆς ἐπ᾽ αὐτῇ ... αὐτῆς is as bewildering as MT is which has a third feminine suffix repeated in ערותה עליה בחייה. Modern translators void the problem by disregarding עליה completely. I would take the first αὐτῆς as referring to the second wife, and the other two pronouns to wife number one. I would translate v.b: "by uncovering her (i.e. the sister's) nakedness alongside her (the first wife) while she is still living."

18:19 Relations with a woman during her menstrual period are forbidden. This is described as ἐν χωρισμῷ ἀκαθαρσίας αὐτῆς, a literal rendering of בנדת טמאתה. For χωρισμῷ see 12:2; the more common term for נדה is ἄφεδρος; see comment at 12:2. I would take ἀκαθαρσίας as a genitive of origin, i.e. an isolation due to her impure state. Actually the text uses οὐ προσελεύσῃ "you may not approach." An ol z+ variant states it more baldly: ουκ εισελευση.

18:20 The collocation δώσεις κοίτην σπέρματός σου means "to produce an ejaculation of your semen," interpreting the Hebrew תתן שכבתך לזרע. For the meaning of the collocation see the discussion at 15:16. The transposition of σπέρματός σου by V 426+ is probably a hex correction to equal MT. Also found

---

27. Gispen translates "om jaloers te maken," understanding the verb to mean "to be jealous." Rashi explains לעשות את זו צרה לזו, which is probably what is intended.

in the tradition is the F M V majority text which articulates the infinitive ἐκμιανθῆναι. This represents a tendency in later Greek, and is almost certainly secondary.[28] The use of πρὸς αὐτήν modifying ἐκμιανθῆναι to render לטמאה בה is unexpected, but the preposition merely represents a relation between two parties.[29] It can probably be best understood as "to defile yourself with her."

18:21 The verse begins with a partitive ἀπό; ἀπὸ τοῦ σπέρματός σου means "anyone of your seed, i.e, your children."[30] What is forbidden in MT is מזרעך לא תתן להעביר למלך "not may you let any of your seed pass over to Molech." The Hi of עבר is used to indicate a pagan sacrifice of children by having them pass through the fire. For the god Molech see Bible Dictionaries.

LXX apparently read להעביר as להעביד with Sam; it has λατρεύειν, which in Exod occurred frequently for עבד, but occurs only here in Lev, and refers particularly to cultic service. The translator also did not recognize מלך as the pagan god, and translated it by ἄρχοντι. מלך occurs only as designating the pagan god Moloch in the book (see also 20:2—5), but it was well-known as the word for "king." The translator did not use βασιλεύς, the usual word for "king," but rather ἄρχων "ruler." This would probably be safer than βασιλεύς in an Egyptian context in the third century BCE. Furthermore, in an Alexandrian context this was sensible. The Egyptians, after all, did consider the Pharaoh to be divine; in fact, when the Pharaoh died he was thought to become Osiris, the god of the underworld. The Ptolemies also considered themselves divine, as heirs of the deified Alexander. Actually the fourth Antiochus even called himself Epiphanes. The translator in this context felt free to translate להעביד למלך by λατρεύειν ἄρχοντι "to serve a ruler cultically."[31]

The second clause is presented paratactically in imitation of the Hebrew, but obviously explicates the first one. λατρεύειν ἄρχοντι would indeed be a case of defiling the holy name, would thus be idol worship. MT, however, does not

---

28. See THGL 82. Schwyzer II. 368 says with reference to the articulation of the infinitive "Doch gehört der Artikel beim Infinitiv an einer chronologisch jüngeren Schicht des Artikelgebrauchs und ist teilweise selbständig aus vorbereitendem Demonstrativ hervorgegangen."
29. What Johannessohn, Gebrauch 269 calls "Bezeichnung der Gesinnung und der Beziehung zwischen zwei Partei."
30. See SS 161.
31. Aq, Sym and Theod all translated by παραβιβάσαι τῷ Μολοχ.

refer to "the holy name," but to את שם לאלהיך "the name of your God." The interpretation is not incorrect. The name of your God is יהוה, which is the holy name, for which see 20:3 22:2,32. It remains an unusual translation, however, and the translator may well have had the שם קדשי of 20:3 22:2,32 in mind. The rendering of a bound phrase by an adjectival phrase is not all that unusual.[32] The short formula of divine self-identification closes this verse, probably because a reference to "the name" had just occurred.

18:22 Male homosexuality is forbidden. What is prohibited is κοιμηθήσῃ κοίτην γυναικός with a male, usually rendered by "you may (not) lie as with a woman." This translates משכבי אשה, but only A B F support the Lev text; others support κοίτην γυναικείαν, which probably arose as an explanatory gloss added to avoid a possible conflict between γυναικός and ἄρσενος; but the phrase also occurs at 20:13 with unanimous support in the tradition.[33]

The prohibition ends with a γάρ clause. The γάρ has no equivalent in MT, which simply makes the statement תועבה הוא,[34] i.e. βδέλυγμα γάρ ἐστιν. βδέλυγμα is the most common rendering for תועבה (68 out of 131 cases.[35] It refers to something as loathsome, an abomination, and is an excellent rendering of the Hebrew noun.

18:23 Neither males nor females may have sexual relations with tetrapods. In the first clause the Hebrew שכבתך is rendered correctly by τὴν κοίτην σου, but the translator added in explanation εἰς σπερματισμόν, which is a hapax legomenon in OT. The word normally means "for production of seed" for plant life. Its use for human seed is a neologism created by the translator. The addition was made by the translator to ensure the understanding of κοίτην in the same sense as in v.20. Hex recognized that the phrase had no equivalent, and omitted it to equal MT. For πρός modifying ἐκμιανθῆναι see comment at v.20.[36]

"And a woman may not στήσεται πρὸς πᾶν τετράπουν βιβασθῆναι." I would render this by "set herself in position towards a tetrapod so as to be

---

32. See SS 65.
33. See THGL 130.
34. See THGL 115.
35. According to the count of Dos Santos.
36. According to Hesychius of Jerusalem Sym read *succumbere* (possibly for κοιμηθῆναι) instead of ἐκμιανθῆναι.

defiled." The subject of the infinitive is γυνή. What is meant is to have sexual intercourse with an animal. The infinitive has as counterpart in MT לרבעה, which also occurs at 20:16 in a similar context. It is quite uncertain what the word means; what is clear is that sexual relations are referred to. The translator probably was also unclear about the word and rendered it contextually; see also 20:16. MT has no equivalent for πᾶν, but LXX levelled with v.a.

The reason for the prohibition, presumably applying to both male and female, is given in a γάρ clause: μυσερὸν γάρ ἐστιν. "for it is loathsome." The adjective translates תבל "a confusion" (i.e. of what God intended).[37] MT has no counterpart to γάρ, and a popular M text omits it, thereby equalling MT. Whether this omission is recensional or not is not certain, since O has the word, though Syh does not.[38] The majority text reads the Classical spelling μυσαρον, but the oldest mss read the Hellenistic form, which was therefore chosen as Lev. The translation is not literal, but it does provide a parallel to the final statement in v.22.

18:24 A general warning to avoid practicing any of the aforementioned aberrations. The warning is presented asyndetically as in MT, but the Byz text has placed a και before it.

Both MT and LXX give a reason for the warning not to defile themselves, viz. ἐν πᾶσιν γὰρ τούτοις ἐμιάνθησαν τὰ ἔθνη. The verb occurs twice: as a present middle in the initial warning, appropriate in a general prohibition which will be continually valid. But in the γάρ clause the aorist passive is used, i.e. "in all these (practices) the nations were defiled." These nations are characterized as ἃ ἐγὼ ἐξαποστέλλω πρὸ προσώπου ὑμῶν "which I am sending away before you (literally before your face)." An A V d t+ text has a future verb, which in the desert journey context that the text presupposes would seem to be sensible. But the Hebrew has a nominal clause אני משלח. LXX normally renders such a construction by a pronoun plus an inflected present tense verb. The form εξαποστελω is simply the result of haplography.[39] In the tradition, the n+ text

---
37. Theod simply transliterated the word as θεβελ. Aq translated by ἀπειρημένον "forbidden," and Sym has ἄρρητον "unspoken," i.e. something so unnatural that it cannot be said.
38. See THGL 115.
39. See THGL 95.

read the singular εμιανθη instead of the plural, i.e. the Classical understanding of the neuter plural, ἔθνη, as a collective noun taking a singular verb as predicate.[40]

18:25 This verse follows logically on v.24. "The nations defiled themselves ... and the land was defiled." MT continues with "and I visited its iniquity upon it," with third person personal pronouns referring to "land." But LXX has quite a different message. It reads καὶ ἀνταπέδωκα ἀδικίαν αὐτοῖς δι' αὐτήν "and I repaid unrightness to them (referring to ἔθνη) on its account (i.e. the land's account)." The verb ἀνταποδίδωμι occurs only here for פקד. The Qal of פקד occurs 184 times in OT, of which ἐπισκέπτω is the rendering 100 times, ἐκδικέω 20, and ἐπισκοπή 18 times, and the remainder scattered among 23 different equivalences.[41] Instead of עונה "its iniquity" LXX has ἀδικίαν αὐτοῖς with the pronoun referring to the "nations."[42] עליה in isolation could be rendered by δι' αὐτήν, but not in the context of MT.[43] The tradition had much trouble with this passage. Instead of αὐτοῖς n+ read αυτης, which is probably a case of itacism, since both η and οι were pronounced as /i/. The *b* text made it dative αυτη, i.e. changed αὐτοῖς to the singular, whereas the A text changed the case to the genitive, αυτων. The Lev text is, however, so strongly based in the tradition that it must be considered original. δι' αὐτήν was also affected; *b* changed it to δι αυτους, whereas *n* had a different preposition, επ αυτην, which could be a recensional change.

MT in v.b reads "the land spewed out (תקא) its inhabitants." LXX has an odd translation for the verb: προσώχθισεν "was angry (with those who dwelt ἐπ' αὐτῆς)" or better "became weary."[44] It does occur in Lev for this verb four times (also twice in v.28 and once at 20:22), but it is never found elsewhere in OT. I would render the clause: "and the land became vexed with those who dwelt in it." The rendering of ישביה by τοῖς ἐγκαθημένοις ἐπ' αὐτῆς is also unusual, since the prepositional phrase is an amplification.[45]

---

40. See SS 197.
41. According to Dos Santos. Some of these equations are extremely dubious, however.
42. Daniel 311 in note 48 suggests that the reason for ἀδικίαν being used is: "c'est sans doute afin de présenter l'autre aspect de ces fautes, l'aspect religieux étant suffisamment évoqué par la phrase 'et le pays est devenu impur.'"
43. Instead of αὐτοῖς δι' αὐτήν The Others read αὐτῆς ἐπ' αὐτήν, which equals MT.
44. Aq translates the verb by ἐξῆρεν; Theod, by ἀπέβαλεν, and Sym has ἐξήμεσεν "vomited."
45. Both Theod and Aq simply have τοὺς ἐνοικοῦντας.

18:26 MT has the pronoun אתם after שמרתם, which is quite otiose, and LXX has omitted it, nor is there any recensional attempt to add a υμεις after φυλάξεσθε attested anywhere.[46] The accusative modifiers νόμιμόν μου and προστάγματά μου represent חקתי and משפטי resp. νόμιμον translates only חק or חקה in Lev, but προστάγματα translates five different Hebrew words in Lev; see discussion at v.4. Most common (six times) is חקה, followed by three cases of משפט, two of מצוה and one each of משמרת and פה. The translator took משפט to be a rather non-specific word for legal requirements; for the notion of משפט see footnote at 4:2. The translator certainly insisted by his "my ordinances" and "my statutes" that these were divine regulations for conduct given to God's people. In the tradition, the future φυλάξεσθε is popularly changed to the aorist imperative, φυλαξασθε, but Lev normally renders the contextual suffixal inflection by the future. Over against MT the translator added πάντα in modification for both nouns. The second πάντα is popularly omitted, though not by O witnesses; on the other hand, Syh does omit it, which suggests that its parent hex text had placed it under the obelus.

In the paratactic second clause ποιήσετε is modified by a partitive ἀπό phrase, thus "you may not do any of all these abominations.[47] The clause is the negative counterpart to the first one. The subject is explicated by two nouns, ἐγχώριος and προσήλυτος. The former renders אזרח (also at 24:22), but is not as common as αὐτόχθων, which occurs five times in Lev as translation of אזרח (and once for עם, at 20:4). Both are satisfactory, though ἐγχώριος, one who is at home in the area, is not as literal as αὐτόχθων, an indigenous, a native-born.

The proselyte is defined in MT as הגר הגר (בתוככם) "the resident alien who resides in your midst." This becomes ὁ προσγενόμενος προσήλυτος (ἐν ὑμῖν). Hex has transposed participle and noun to equal the word order of MT. προσγενόμενος "one who has been added (to)," probably in the sense of one who has joined, is an unusual rendering for the participle גר, but Lev has no standard rendering.[48]

---

46. See SS 74. It should be added that Kenn 150 does omit אתם.
47. See SS 161.
48. See THGL 130.

18:27 A historical analogy making the injunctions of v.26 valid; the verse is interruptive. It is set up as a γάρ statement as equivalent to כי, though the statement is hardly a causal one. But γάρ is really a calque for כי, which need not be causal at all. Here it might well be understood as a weak asseverative, thus "indeed all these abominations ...." "All these abominations" refers to the practices forbidden in vv.6—23. The subject is "all the people (ἄνθρωποι) of the land who were before you," presumably the inhabitants of Canaan. This does not quite fit the assumed pre-invasion desert locale for the divine orders that the book presupposes, since the verb ἐποίησαν is aorist, but the illusion is rather difficult to carry through consistently.

The result of these practices is given in the last clause: "and the land was defiled," for which see comment at v.25.

18:28 That v.27 was an interruption is clear from the structure of this verse, which in spite of the introductory καί, relates to v.26, i.e. "guard ... and do not do ..., lest the land προσοχθίσῃ against you when you defile it." The verb means "be vexed toward, be angry with"; see comment at v.25. The γῆ is personified, and I would suggest translating "lest the land be vexed with you." In the tradition, hex has placed ὑμῖν after the subject ἡ γῆ to equal the order הארץ אתכם of MT. It should be noted that LXX tends to place pronominal modifiers next to the verb. For the verb as translating תקיא see comment at v.25.

The verb recurs in the ὃν τρόπον clause: "as it was vexed with the nations who were before you." MT has the singular את הגוי, in which it is supported among ancient witnesses only by Sam, Tar^J and Vulg. The plural is the simpler reading in that it agrees with v.24, but I suspect that את הגוי is original, it being the more difficult reading. τοῖς πρὸ ὑμῖν translates the relative clause אשר לפניכם, which also occurs in v.27, but was translated by οἱ ὄντες πρότερον ὑμῶν. The change in translation is simply for variation; the Lev translator loved variation.[49] The verb is here in the aorist indicative, the default tense.[50]

18:29 A dire warning is put into a ὅτι/כי clause, which begins with a pendant nominative relative clause: "as for everyone who might do any of all these

---

49. See THGL 72—75 but especially p.72.
50. Aq read either ἐξήρασεν or ἐξῆρεν, for which also see f.n. at v.25; Sym translated ἐξήμεσεν, and Theod, ἀπέβαλεν.

abominations." In contrast to v.28 כי is here rendered by ὅτι; both are intended as causal particles, and the verse is meant as the reason for carrying out what has been ordered in vv.24—28. For ποιήσῃ ἀπό see comment at v.26. This is then referred to in the main clause as αἱ ψυχαὶ αἱ ποιοῦσαι, which serves as subject for the verbal predicate ἐξολεθρευθήσονται ἐκ τοῦ λαοῦ αὐτῶν. In MT this predicate is נכרתו מקרב עמם. This excommunication from the clan becomes destruction; see comment at 17:8—9. The change from the singular of the pendant to the plural in the main clause simply explicates the sense of πᾶς ὅς; they are the persons practicing (all these abominations). The Byz tradition has changed πᾶς to πας ανθρωπος, in which the gloss is not incorrect, but is quite unnecessary. It should also be noted that a majority F M tradition supports the recensional (probably hex) addition of μεσου after ἐκ to equal MT's מקרב.

18:30 One might have expected the cognate structure שמרתם את משמרתי to have been translated by a similar cognate in LXX, but it has φυλάξετε τὰ προστάγματά μου, for which see comment at v.26. Actually a recensional change, possibly hex in origin, does read τα φυλαγματα μου; this is attested in ms 376 *b n+*.

לבלתי plus the bound infinitive עשות is correctly translated by ὅπως μὴ ποιήσητε "lest you should do." In the tradition, a popular F text has ποιητε, i.e. a rare present subjunctive. The present is inappropriate here, and is probably an error due to homoioteleuton; note the recurring *eta*.[51]

For ποιήσῃ ἀπό see comment at v.26. Unexpected is the use of the participle ἐβδελυγμένων to render the noun תועבת. But for the Greek to render the free noun of the bound phrase חקות התועבת as a noun would be awkward, whereas an attributive participle gives the correct sense. In fact, the bound phrase has troubled translators considerably. NRSV has "detestible customs"; NJPS reads "abhorrent practices," whereas NIV simplifies by "abominations." LXX makes it "abominable customs."

The relative clause ἃ γέγονεν πρὸ τοῦ ὑμᾶς modifies νομίμων. The πρό structure represents the Hebrew לפניכם. The τοῦ is an elipsis, i.e. it is an article before some elided infinitive such as προσγένεσθαι or εἰσελθεῖν. Actually the Byz text added εισελθειν εκει, whereas *ol s z+* glossed with εισελθειν ενταυθα,

---

51. See THGL 125.

and two unclassified mss added γενεσθαι. What is meant is "which happened before you (arrived)."

The next clause is a summarizing injunction: "and not may you defile yourselves with them"; the αὐτοῖς refers to the abominable νομίμων of the ὅπως clause.

The verse (and the chapter) ends appropriately with the divine self-identification formula as a ὅτι clause, though MT has no causal particle at all. The ὅτι may well have had a textual basis in a parent כי, since the Qumran text 11QLev has it.[52] The prohibitions, the warnings, the dire threats, are all relevant to the Israelites because ἐγὼ κύριος ὁ θεὸς ὑμῶν. This becomes especially clear from the contrast between the practices of the "nations which were before you," i.e. the πάντων τῶν νομίμων τῶν ἐβδελυγμένων, and those demanded of the Lord's people, i.e. τὰ προστάγματά μου.

---

52. See Freedman 530.

Chapter 19

19:2 Over against MT the Greek reads τῇ συναγωγῇ, omitting the כל of כל עדת.[1] The majority hex text added πάσῃ before it to represent the כל, which reading in turn led to the omission of τῇ due to homoioteleuton.

What is to be said to the community of the Israelites is ἅγιοι ἔσεσθε ὅτι ἐγὼ ἅγιος κύριος ὁ θεὸς ὑμῶν. MT has the adjective in first place in the ὅτι clause as well, whereas the Greek uses an a:b::b´:a´ pattern. Hex has, however, transposed ἐγὼ ἅγιος so as to correspond to MT.

For the notion of holiness both as applied to the Lord as well as to the demand on the Israelites to be holy, see the discussion at 11:44. The stress is on the separateness of God's people from all that is profane, either in material or in conduct. The basis for holy living lies in the nature of the Lord your God. He is holy, i.e. he is divine, and therefore separated from all that is profane. It is that separateness that is demanded in the order ἅγιοι ἔσεσθε. How the Israelites are to live holy is detailed in the rest of the chapter. The details describing holy living consist of both negative and positive regulations.

In the tradition, the omission of τῶν by O Byz+ could well be recensional, i.e. could be an attempt to equal בני more exactly.[2] Also found in the tradition is the amplification by an *s* marginal reading of ἐγώ to εγω ειμι.

19:3 MT has the unusual איש modifying the subject of תיראו, i.e. "let each one of you fear." LXX voids the problem by using φοβείσθω, the third singular present imperative: "let each one be fearing." The *n* text shows recensional change by its φοβηθησεσθε. The variant text then has the odd pattern εκαστος ... φοβηθησεσθε; the recensor obviously paid no attention to the context, but treated the verb in isolation, but see the Hebrew. MT has as modifier אמו ואביו, which order LXX changes to πατέρα αὐτοῦ καὶ μητέρα αὐτοῦ, the more common order. The same change is attested by Pesh and Vulg, the latter also following the φοβείσθω of the Greek. That LXX should change the order to place "his father" before "his mother" may well be a case of (unconscious?) male prejudice, though it is probably simply due to the influence of the more

---

1. Kenn 69,84,136,184 omit כל עדת, i.e. reading simply אל בני ישראל.
2. See THGL 85.

usual order, especially in the well-known Decalogue's "honor your father and your mother." Hex duly changed the order of the nouns to conform to MT.

The second clause follows MT in its second plural verb, φυλάξεσθε. The popular A variant text, which changes the future to the aorist imperative, φυλάξασθε, is secondary; see comment at 18:26. Guarding τὰ σάββατά μου is ordered here for the first time in the book, though see 16:31. It is, of course, enshrined in the Decalogue. The word is a transliteration of the Aramaic שבתא, and refers to the seventh day interpreted as a necessary day of rest. Once the word was taken into Greek, it was easily understood as a presumed neuter plural noun, and the singular σάββατον, was created. The Pentateuch and the Latter Prophets use only the plural (except for σάββατον ἐκ σαββάτων at Isa 66:23), but the singular becomes the dominant form in the Former Prophets and the Writings. Possibly this fact might be of some help in dating the various translations.

The verse ends with the long form of the formula for the Lord's self-identification. This use is particularly frequent in this chapter where it occurs 13 times (also at vv.4,10,12,14,16,25,28,31,32,34,36,37), and the short form at vv.18,30; in MT it is the short form that is attested for vv.12,14,16,28, 32,37, but LXX has levelled in all these cases to the long form of the formula. The formula serves not only to remind the Israelites that the Lord is particularly their patron, but also that the demands made in this chapter are clearly the Lord's demands. Moses may well be the medium for the message, but he is only a medium. It is the Lord who is speaking, especially in this chapter. From the point of view of the original composition the formula circumscribes small sections, but these sections do not necessarily have a common theme. If they were intended as structural boundaries, it is often difficult to recover that original intent.

19:4 MT begins with אל תפנו אל "do not turn towards (האלילים)." LXX interprets "turning towards" as ἐπακολουθήσετε "follow." This verb is also used in other contexts in Lev, occurring at v.31 and 20:6, where the verb is modified by ἐγγαστριμύθοις; see comment at v.31. This equation is found only in Lev; elsewhere the verb occurs mainly to translate the root אחר. האלילים is a term meaning worthless things, and is commonly used as a pejorative term for idols. The translator understood this well, and translates by εἰδώλοις.

The coordinate clause that follows, elaborates the same theme. "You may not make for yourselves molten gods." MT has a bound phrase אלהי מסכה "gods of molten metal," and the adjectival phrase is precisely what is intended by the Hebrew.

For the recurring formula ending the verse see the discussion at v.3. It should be mentioned that it serves to mark the end of the first section; in other words, it serves to limit a structural unit.

19:5 Vv.5—8 deal with rules about the eating of the sacrifice for deliverance. For the θυσίαν σωτηρίου see not only ch.3, but more particularly ch.7. V.5 states the general rule: "and if you should sacrifice a sacrifice for deliverance to the Lord, δεκτὴν ὑμῶν you must sacrifice." MT has לרצונכם "in a manner acceptable for you." What is meant is that the sacrifice must be effected so that it will be acceptable on your behalf; it must be done properly. LXX's text is an attempt to say precisely that.[3] For "you must sacrifice" MT has הזבחהו, but LXX did not translate the suffix. Only ms 767 has added αυτην; since this ms occasionally has hex readings, the pronoun could be hex.

The adjective δεκτήν describes θυσίαν; the sacrifice must be acceptable for you. Copyists had trouble with the word; *C'* read δεκτον; *b* has δεκτας, *n* reads δεκτα, and A B F *x+* actually have δεκατην. This last-named is, of course, wrong, and is an error based on δεκτήν, which is the only form that can be considered as original.

19:6 MT begins with ביום זבחכם "on the day of your sacrifice"; the Masoretes have vocalized זבח as a noun, but LXX interprets it as though it were a bound infinitive, an understanding which the consonantal text permits; it reads ᾗ ἂν ἡμέρᾳ θύσητε "on whatever day you might sacrifice.[4] In the *f* tradition, θύσητε becomes a present indicative θυετε, or it is changed to a future θυσετε in a popular F text, but after ἄν a subjunctive would be expected. On that same day βρωθήσεται "it shall be eaten (καὶ τῇ αὔριον)." The καί coordinates ᾗ ἡμέρᾳ with τῇ αὔριον, thus: "and on the next day." αὔριον is an adverb nominalized as a dative.

---

3. Aq has translated the ל phrase by τῇ εὐδοκίᾳ ὑμῶν, Theod has preserved the LXX text, but placed εἰς before it, while Sym has εἰς τὸ εὐδοκηθῆναι ὑμῖν.
4. See THGL 73.

MT then continues in v.b: "That which is left (והנותר)," which LXX makes into a coordinate (καί) ἐάν clause, precisely like the first clause. It contrasts what is to be done the following day with v.a, i.e. with today and tomorrow, and concerns something which might be left up to the third day. This would no longer be edible; "ἐν πυρί it must be burned up."[5] The κατα- compound is used to indicate complete consumption by fire, hence "burned up."

19:7 The Hebrew Ni structure האכל יאכל is rendered by βρωθῇ preceded by a cognate noun in the dative, βρώσει, and must be interpreted as a syntactic calque of the Hebrew. I would translate the protasis by "But if it is actually eaten on the third day."

The apodosis brands such eating as ἄθυτον, "unfit as sacrificial food." The adjective is derived from θύω, "to sacrifice" with an *alpha* privative prefix, hence unfit for sacrifice.[6] It translates פגול "something foul, refuse." At 7:8(18) it was rendered by μίασμα "stain, defilement."[7] There the statement on what eating the sacrifice for deliverance on the third day entails is given in somewhat more detail, and it should be read together with comments ad loc. οὐ δεχθήσεται is defined as αὐτῷ τῷ προσφέροντι αὐτό, οὐ λογεσθήσεται αὐτῷ. In other words, the one who was offering this sacrifice voids any benefits from it by his eating on the third day.

19:8 The opening clause in MT is peculiar in that the subject אכליו is plural, but the predicate ישא (עונו) is singular. The translator followed Sam in making the subject singular as well, as he did at 17:14; see comment ad loc. The predicate in LXX is ἁμαρτίαν λήψεται. The noun renders עונו of MT, which can mean either "iniquity" or the "guilt" associated with it; similarly ἁμαρτίαν must here be understood not as sin, but as the guilt asssociated with sin. What is meant is that the one who eats αὐτό (i.e. the ἄθυτον) on the third

---

5. The ἐν is instrumental; see SS 117.
6. Schl defines the word as *quod sacrificii loco offerri non potest, insacrificabile, profanum.*
7. Theod simply transliterates as φεγγουλ, and Aq translates as ἀπόβλητον "something to be thrown away, worthless," and Sym has ἀργόν, negative of ἔργον, thus "something that is not done, unworked." Sym's translation for the following לא ירצה is also extant as οὐκ εὐδοκηθήσεται.

day shall take on himself guilt for what he has done. That eating sacrificial food on the third day can be called ἁμαρτίαν or עון is typical of the book. LXX disregarded the suffix of עונו, since the referent was obvious.⁸

The reason for this being ἁμαρτίαν is a cultic one: τὰ ἅγια κυρίου ἐβεβήλωσιν. The translator renders את קדש "that which is holy" by the neuter plural, thereby generalizing the sin. In MT the singular specifically refers to the θυσίαν σωτηρίου; of course, this is not excluded by τὰ ἅγια, but the plural is much broader; in fact, it thereby sets up a general rule about holy things. The verb, like its Hebrew counterpart חלל means "to profane," i.e. to remove it from the realm of that which is set aside as holy, and bring it into profane, i.e. common, use.

That the use of τὰ ἅγια generalizes is clear from the concluding statement. MT says "that person shall be cut off from his people." LXX makes it plural, αἱ ψυχαί, but then adds the limiting modifier αἱ ἔσθουσαι, which has no basis in MT; "the persons who eat these shall be destroyed from their people."

19:9 Vv.9—10 constitute a pair of verses detailing the need to leave gleanings in fields and vineyards for the needy. In v.9 MT presents the protasis by means of ב plus a bound infinitive, i.e. by בקצרכם "when you harvest." The translator renders this by an apparent genitive absolute, ἐκθεριζόντων ὑμῶν. It is not really an absolute, since the subject of the main clause agrees with ὑμῶν, and should thus be taken as an appositive for it. It reads "when you reap the harvest of your land, οὐ συντελέσετε your harvest of the field ἐκθερίσαι," or possibly " you must not ... the field, during your reaping ...." What is meant is "you must not make a total cropping in harvesting your land." This is a free translation of the Hebrew which says: לא תכלה פאת שדך לקצר. MT has suddenly changed to the singular, but LXX continues with the plural of the opening genitive; the Greek only changes to the singular in the next clause. The word פאת refers to the edges or corners (of the field). The translator disregards the notion of sides or corners entirely. I would translate the Greek: "you must not completely crop off your harvest of the field."⁹ Somewhat prob-

---

8. See SS 97.
9. The anonymous reading τὸ φααθ τοῦ ἀγροῦ σου is obviously from Theod; it stands for פאת שדך.

lematic is what ὑμῶν 2° modifies. It can refer to θερισμόν which it follows, or to τοῦ ἀγροῦ which it precedes, for which see the שׂדך of MT. But the natural way of reading it is as "your harvest of the field." This is how readers understood it; I suspect this is also how Origen understood it, since the addition of σου after ἀγροῦ by the majority A B F V text must be hex. Accordingly, the sparsely supported omission of ὑμῶν could reflect hex as well; at least mss 58-72 which omit the pronoun commonly support the hex text. Origen apparently understood it in this fashion, since he changed θερισμὸν ὑμῶν τοῦ ἀγροῦ to θερισμον του αγρου σου to agree completely with MT.

The next clause is much clearer; it reads "and those (stalks) that fall off from your reaping you must not collect." The participle τὰ ἀποπίπτοντα and the verb συλλέξεις represent a cognate collocation in the parent text: ... לקט תלקט, thus "the gleanings ... you may (not) glean." The Greek correctly describes the intent of the Hebrew collocation, without attempting to make an artificial cognate structure.

19:10 The verb ἐπανατρυγήσεις is a neologism which occurs only here and at Deut 24:21. It means "to glean the fruit," and it only translates תעולל. What the text says is "you must not second-harvest your vineyard." The coordinate clause parallels the second clause of v.9: "nor may you collect the grapes of your vineyard." The word ῥῶγας refers to the individual grapes, i.e. those that remain on the vine after the clusters have been stripped off. Here it is masculine, though it also occurs as feminine, and a number of mss including the entire *b* text group changed τούς to τας.

The gleanings are to be left τῷ πτωχῷ καὶ τῷ προσηλύτῳ. The poor and the resident alien are here representative of the downtrodden; more common as symbols of the helpless are the widow and the orphan; see Note at Dt 10:18. The pronoun referring to τοὺς ῥῶγας is, however, the neuter plural, αὐτά, which the translator often uses without regard to the gender of the antecedent.[10]

For the divine self-identification formula see discussion at v.3. Here it has the variant ἐγώ εἰμι instead of ἐγώ.[11] The majority tradition omits εἰμι,

---

10. See Huber 35.
11. See SS 79.

which may well be hex; at any event the support includes O' and Syh. The formula serves a formal purpose in that it delineates the section on gleanings. It also serves an exegetical end in that the regard for the poor and the proselyte is linked to the divine self-identification as "your God." The covenantal relation demands compassion for the disadvantaged in Israelite society.

19:11 Vv.11—14 constitute a series of apodictic commandments reminiscent of the Decalogue. For οὐ κλέψετε see Exod 20:14. With οὐ ψεύσεσθε "not shall you cheat, deceive," the verb renders תכחשו precisely, but MT presents this order, as well as the third one, syndetically. In the tradition, most witnesses have και ου in both cases, but the και is almost certainly secondary, possibly hex in origin. The translator follows the pattern of the Decalogue.[12]

The third order is reminiscent of Exod 20:16, which see; it is, however, cast into quite a different form. The Exodus order forbids bringing false witness, whereas the Hebrew has the verb תשקרו "speak falsehoods, (a man against his fellow)," but LXX uses συκοφαντήσει (ἕκαστος τὸν πλησίον) "not shall anyone berate a neighbour." The translation is unique; in fact, the verb occurs only once elsewhere in the Pentateuch; at Gen 43:18 it renders the difficult להתגלל; see Note ad loc. Elsewhere it is used in OT only for the root עשק. Its use here may well have been colored by the ψεύσεσθε in the second clause. LXX changes the second plural verb to the third singular to agree with ἕκαστος. πλησίον is also presented absolutely, i.e. without a genitive pronoun.[13] The $b+$ text does add αυτου, which equals MT, but I suspect its origin is stylistic, and not recensional.

19:12 A different version of the commandment in the Decalogue, Exod 20:7. It interprets the commandment in a clear manner. Thus "to take up the name of the Lord your God ἐπ' ματαίῳ" becomes ὀμεῖσθε τῷ ὀνόματί μου ἐπ' ἀδίκῳ "swear by my name falsely." Forbidden is "swearing an oath by means of (i.e. by using) the divine name to false or unjust ends. The word שקר is commonly rendered in OT by the root αδικ- (49 times), almost equal in number to the use of the ψευδ- root (53 times).[14]

---

12. See THGL 101—102
13. See SS 97.
14. According to the count of Dos Santos.

MT switches to the singular at the second clause, whereas LXX delays switching to the next verse. The clause is introduced by καὶ οὐ, whereas MT does not repeat the negative of the first clause. What MT's conjunction means is "that" or "lest," thus "lest you should profane the name of your God." LXX makes it a second commandment: "and you must not profane ...." The Greek by repeating the negative particle makes the second clause parallel to the first one, whereas MT makes it the purpose (or result) of the first one, i.e. of swearing by my name falsely." The Greek text was probably fostered by misunderstanding the relation between the two clauses in MT.

The verse concludes with the long divine self-identification formula, for which see discussion at v.3. MT has the short formula: אני יהוה, but the long one is more frequent in the chapter, (though not in MT, in which the long form occurs eight times, and the short one, eight times as well) and the translator levelled with it; see e.g. vv.10 and 14. Hex has placed εἰμι under the obelus as having no equivalent in MT.

19:13 LXX interprets תעשק by the more general term ἀδικήσεις "deal unjustly," as at 6:2,4; cf comment at 6:2. As often, רעך is translated simply by πλησίον, since the reference to "your" neighbour is obvious; it would hardly be to someone else's neighbour.[15] Hex, however, makes the implicit explicit by adding σου to represent the suffix. The coordinate καὶ οὐχ ἁρπάσεις is presented absolutely, but what is meant is "nor may you despoil (him, i.e. your neighbour)"; the πλησίον/רעך is carried over from the preceding verbal structure.

V.b represents Sam rather than MT by its καί.[16] The A B 121 text mistakenly read the double negative ου μη instead of οὐ, but the verb is future, and the usage of μή plus the future indicative is highly dubious.[17] MT refers to פעלת שכיר "the wages of a hireling," which LXX renders by a cognate structure: ὁ μισθὸς τοῦ μισθωτοῦ; this "may not lie with you until morning." What is meant is that wages must be paid immediately; the payment may not be delayed.

---

15. See SS 97.
16. Though many Kenn mss also read ולא.
17. See THGL 115—116.

19:14 The translator realized full well that תקלל means "curse," see 24:11,14,15,23, but he uses κακῶς ἐρεῖς to translate the verb. He uses καταράσσω only of cursing God, whereas for cursing human beings, he uses "to speak evilly"; see also 20:9 (twice). But he uses an accusative modifier, κωφόν "one who is deaf," to represent חרש. I would suggest the rendering "you may not revile a deaf person." The occasional copyist was troubled by the accusative, and changed it to κωφῷ: "speak evilly to a deaf person," but the accusative, which represents the direct modifier חרש of MT, is original.

LXX follows the chiasmus of MT in changing the order of syntagms in the next clause: "and before a blind person you may not place a stumbling block." The term σκάνδαλον occurs only here in the Pentateuch, but twice elsewhere also for מכשל. It is used more commonly for מוקש "a trap," particularly in Reg and Pss. In the tradition, the B F M V majority text read προσθήσεις instead of προθήσεις, but "you may not add" is a palaeographically inspired error for "you may not place before." The variant was influenced by the similarity of Θ-Σ in Greek.[18]

It is the opposite which is enjoined! "And (i.e. but) you must fear the Lord your God." To "fear the Lord" means to live the life of the Yahwist. It is a summary statement which covers all the injunctions of vv.11—14. MT does not have an equivalent for κύριον, simply having "be in awe of (i.e. fear) your God." Note that MT has a prepositional phrase מאלהיך modifying the verb יראת; see also v.32. The Greek does not distinguish between "to fear" and "to be in awe of," probably rightly so.

As at v.12 the Greek ends with the long self-identification formula instead of אני יהוה; see comment ad loc. Hex has placed both εἰμι and ὁ θεὸς ὑμῶν under the obelus, since these have no counterparts in MT.

19:15 Vv.15—18 are all in the singular, except for the first clause in which both MT and LXX have a plural verb: תעשו/ποιήσετε. The plural is used to indicate the theme of the verse, and the singulars which follow illustrate this theme. Actually, the not doing ἄδικον remains thematic through v.18. V.15 deals with legal matters. The first command is a general one: "You may not act unrighteously in judgment." The translator used the same word ἄδικον as

---

18. See THGL 130.

he had used in v.12, but here it renders עול rather than שקר. The equation is unusual, and occurs elsewhere in the Pentateuch only at Dt 25:16. The Greek puts it thus: "you must not do anything unrighteous in a judgment."

This is then explained illustratively in the next two clauses; "to lift up the face" means "to show partiality"; it is similar to "$\theta\alpha\upsilon\mu\acute{\alpha}\sigma\epsilon\iota\varsigma\ \pi\rho\acute{o}\sigma\omega\pi o\nu$" "to show favoritism."[19] To show partiality to the poor probably means to "curry favor with the poor"; comp Absalom's actions described in 2Reg 15:2—6. In judging a case a judge may favor neither the poor nor the powerful ($\delta\upsilon\nu\acute{\alpha}\sigma\tau o\upsilon$), but must dispense judgment impartially to the weak and the strong, to the poor and the rich, alike. In other words, "$\dot{\epsilon}\nu\ \delta\iota\kappa\alpha\iota o\sigma\acute{\upsilon}\nu\eta$ you must judge your neighbour." In contrast to vv.11—13 רעך is translated as $\pi\lambda\eta\sigma\acute{\iota}o\nu\ \sigma o\upsilon$, i.e. with the suffix also rendered; cf also vv.16,17,18 as well as 25:14. The suffix is not translated nine times in Lev. I can see no reason for the distinction; either with or without $\sigma o\upsilon$ is an acceptable rendering. The final clause is the positive counterpart to the three negative clauses in v.a.

19:16 LXX translates לא תלך רכיל "do not go about slandering" by $o\dot{\upsilon}$ $\pi o\rho\epsilon\acute{\upsilon}\sigma\eta\ \delta\acute{o}\lambda\omega$ "do not go about deceitfully." The term רכיל "slander" occurs only six times in MT, and is never translated by the same word more than once. The root means "to go about," hence "to engage in trade," and also "in talk." The noun is used only in that latter sense, i.e. as a "gossip," or a "slanderer." MT follows with בעמיך, but LXX with its singular $\dot{\epsilon}\nu\ \tau\hat{\omega}\ \check{\epsilon}\theta\nu\epsilon\iota$ $\sigma o\upsilon$ follows Sam.[20] I would translate: "deceitfully among your people."

The next clause is difficult; in fact, MT's text is quite unclear. The collocation לא תעמד על דם "not stand against blood" has been variously understood. NJPS has "do not profit by the blood," which is similar to that of NRSV: "you shall not profit by the blood." NIV has "do not do anything that endangers the life." ZürB translates "sollst nicht wider das Leben ... auftreten." LXX interprets as $o\dot{\upsilon}\kappa\ \dot{\epsilon}\pi\iota\sigma\upsilon\sigma\tau\acute{\eta}\sigma\eta$ ($\dot{\epsilon}\phi'\ \alpha\hat{\iota}\mu\alpha$ of your neighbour) "not may you conspire or combine against." The verb has the notion of conspiracy about it. I would then take $\alpha\hat{\iota}\mu\alpha$ in the sense of lifeblood, and so $\dot{\epsilon}\phi\ \alpha\hat{\iota}\mu\alpha$ to mean "against the life (of your neighbour)." An A B V+ variant text has simplified the verb as $\epsilon\pi\iota\sigma\tau\eta\sigma\eta$ "stand (up) against," but the more difficult F M

---

19. For a thorough study of these idioms see Harlé-Pralon ad loc.
20. Many Hebrew mss also read the singular בעמך.

majority text, which also occurs at 26:16, is to be preferred. It is much easier to understand copyists changing from ἐπισυστήσῃ to επιστηση (due to homoioteleuton) than the reverse.[21]

For the long form of the self-identification formula see comment at v.12. The omission of εἰμι by a popular O' text may well be hex, since it has no equivalent in MT. Also hex is the placement of ὁ θεὸς ὑμῶν under the obelus, since MT has the short formula. Why the formula should occur in the middle of this section is not clear; I can see no structural reason for its occurrence.

19:17 LXX translates בלבבך by τῇ διανοίᾳ σου. No conclusions can be drawn from this except that hatred is presumably rooted in one's διανοίᾳ. The noun occurs only three times, but at 26:36,41 where the context is one of divine punishment, καρδία is used to translate לבב. The dative is locatively intended. One may not harbor hatred inwardly, i.e. in one's mind.

V.b requires that ἐλεγμῷ ἐλέγξεις τὸν πλησίον σου. For the use of a cognate dative noun, see remarks at v.7. What is meant is "you must really reprove your neighbour." The last clause, though paratactically presented, is the raison d'etre for the need to reprove your neighbour.[22] λήμψῃ ἁμαρτίαν means "take on guilt." חטא/ἁμαρτίαν mean not only "sin," but also the guilt resulting from sin. Since ἁμαρτία basically means "missing the target," the term is particularly appropriate here, since contextually it refers to the guilt attached to one's failure to reprove one's clansman.

19:18 LXX elaborates on the opening clause לא תקם "you may not take vengeance" by changing the subject to σου ἡ χείρ. No exegetical reason occurs to me for the change, except that taking vengeance is an action, not just a state of mind as "hating your brother" in v.17. Possibly what the Greek then intends to convey is "you may not actively exact vengeance." LXX also begins the verse with καί, but MT has no conjunction.

MT then goes on with ולא תטר "you may not hold, keep"; what is meant is correctly understood by LXX which reads "καὶ οὐ μηνιεῖς "nor may you be

---

21. Harlé-Pralon prefer the variant text, which they then translate "tu ne te dresseras pas contre la sang de ton prochain."
22. See Harlé-Pralon 57.

angry." What may not be held or kept is a lasting anger, a grudge. את בני עמך is literally translated by τοῖς υἱοῖς τοῦ λαοῦ σου, "your fellow kinsmen."

The obverse of these prohibitions is the positive commandment "And (i.e. but) you must love your neighbour as yourself." This commandment was taken over by the NT as the summation of the whole law, Rom 13:9 Gal 5:14. It is quoted as the royal law in Jam 2:8, and is given as the last law following the second table of the Decalogue by Jesus at Mt 19:19. When asked which of the commandments were the most important he cited both Dt 6:5 and this one as the second, as the summary of all the law in Mt 22:37—39 Mk 12:30—31. Mark adds "There is no commandment greater than these," whereas Matthew states that "all the Law and the Prophets depend on these two commandments (22:40).[23]

The verse concludes with the short self-identification formula ἐγώ εἰμι κύριος. Hex has omitted εἰμι, since it has no counterpart in MT.

19:19 חקת is not usually translated by νόμος in Lev, but it does occur at v.37 as well; cf also 6:22(15) where it translates חק. Here as in v.37 it is a summary statement of "my statutes" which "you must guard," defined by the Greek as "my instruction, law." That the opening clause is a summary statement is clear from the use of a plural verb in a singular context: φυλάξεσθε/תשמרו. An A M C'+ text reads the aorist imperative φυλαξασθε, but the future is the normal rendering for the prefix inflection of Hebrew.

The individual orders concern כלאים; the dual formation means "of two species." The first forbids cross breeding of animals. MT uses לא תרביע "not shall you make crouch," a reference to the act of mating. For this the translator used a neologism based on the Classical ὀχεύω "to cover," i.e. in the course of breeding, the compound κατοχεύσεις, modified by ἑτεροζύγῳ, thus "you shall not make (your cattle) mate with a different species."[24] The word כלאים occurs three times in the verse; here it is translated by a dative ἑτεροζύγῳ. The term means "differently yoked," thus "different breed or species."

---

23. One might add that Rashi quotes Rabbi Aqiba as saying זה כלל גדול בתורה.
24. Sym reads (οὐχ) ὑποβαλεῖς ἀνομοιοφύλῳ. For the meaning of ἑτεροζύγῳ see Lee 97.

The next prohibition concerns "your vineyard." The initial καί has no equivalent in MT. The order is more specific than MT which has שדך "your field." The translation is simply an error. ἀμπελών is a calque for כרם throughout the OT; in fact, it did so twice at v.10, and elsewhere it always represents כרם, except possibly at Jer 5:17 where גפן "vine" occurs in MT. On the other hand, שדה is almost invariably rendered by ἀγρός (210 times out of 222 occurrences).[25] Whether the translator actually had כרמך as at v.10 in his parent text or was inattentive at this point cannot be verified. Here כלאים refers to seed, and LXX uses διάφορον, thus "you may not sow mixed seeds," i.e. seeds of different kinds; cf Note at Dt 22:9.

And finally, the same principle is applied to cloth. It concerns ἱμάτιον ἐκ δύο ὑφασμένον κίβδηλον. MT has בגד כלאים שעטנז. For שעטנז see Note at Dt 22:11. Here the spurious nature (κίβδηλον) of the garment is defined as "woven out of two," i.e. of two kinds of thread.[26] This is clearer in the parallel Dt passage where the κίβδηλον consists of ἔρια καὶ λίνον.[27]

19:20 The initial ואיש כי of MT is reordered simply as καὶ ἐάν τις. Fortunately, no revisor attempted to reorder this to equal MT. For κοίτην σπέρματος see discussion at 15:16. For κοιμηθῇ modified by an accusative see comment at 15:18. The woman is further defined in the protasis by two conditions: a) she is a household slave, an οἰκέτις, διαπεφυλαγμένη ἀνθρώπῳ "held in reserve (i.e. promised to, intended for) a man." This would then mean a slave betrothed, or at least promised to, someone. This renders נחרפת לאיש. The participle is a hapax legomenon and probably means "designated for,"[28] though some maintain that the participle means "acquired," i.e. as concubine;[29] and b) "she has not been ransomed at all nor has freedom been given her." The use of λύτροις with the cognate λελύτρωται represents a Hebrew idiom in which a cognate free infinitive precedes a verb, thereby placing unusual stress on the verbal idea. Somewhat unusual is the change in stem with

---

25. According to the count in Dos Santos.
26. For כלאים Sym (not Theod as mss 130 128 have it; σ' and θ' are easily confused) translates by ἀνόμοιον; see f.n. on כלאים 1°.
27. Hesychius records Theod as transliterating שעטנז as *satanae*, which is a spelling error in the tradition for *satanaz* = σατανας.
28. See KB sub I חרף.
29. See BDB sub חרף IV. This interpretation is also preferred by Gispen.

the Ho infinitive occurring with the Ni verb, but this is attested for MT.[30] Actually both Ni and Ho are rare in OT, and no lexical distinction between the two can be verified.

The apodosis states: ἐπισκοπὴ ἔσται αὐταῖς. The pronoun is put under the obelus in hex, since MT has only בקרת תהיה. The word בקרת is a hapax legomenon, and its meaning is uncertain,[31] though the root בקר "inquire, seek" would make the notion of "an inquiry" of a judicial nature (as NIV) more likely than "punishment (NRSV) or "indemnity" (with NJSP). LXX makes it a "visitation," but adds that it will be for both, not just for the woman.

In any event, "they will not be put to death because she had not been freed." In the tradition, ἀπηλευθερώθη appears in the simplex form in the majority of witnesses, but the old uncials all have the compound, and it was likely original.

19:21 For πλημμελείας see comment at 5:15. The trespass offering was to be presented at the door of the tent of testimony. For the details concerning the κριὸν πλημμελείας also see 5:15.

19:22 See also the parallel at 5:16b and the discussion ad loc. For ἐξιλάσεται see comment at 4:20. Its occurrence is the final one in the book, where it obtains 33 times. The notion of atonement is obviously one of central importance to Lev; as a priestly ritual it somehow healed the rift between the Lord and the worshiper(s) by means of cultic action. The verb is normally modified by a περί phrase, but here it is uniquely modified by two such, περὶ αὐτοῦ and περὶ τῆς ἁμαρτίας,[32] the second one rendering על חטאתו. As often, the translator did not translate the suffix,[33] though the majority F M text did add αυτου, which was undoubtedly recensional. The verb is also modified by an instrumental ἐν construction: "by the ram of the trespass offering.[34] For ἀφεθήσεται see comment at 4:20. What is to be pardoned is ἡ ἁμαρτία which

---

30. See GK 113w for various possibilities noted.
31. Tar^N has מרדו אנון חייבין; Tar^J elaborates with "there must be a judicial examination for determining punishment should she be guilty."
32. See THGL 112.
33. Se SS 97.
34. See SS 119—120.

represents מחטאתו. The preposition is disregarded by the translator, but see 4:35, and so is the suffix. Hex has, however, added αυτου to represent it. The modification of נסלח by a מן phrase is unique. In Lev elsewhere it is always modified by a dative of person, and only once (5:26) by a further על clause, rendered by "περί concerning one of all things which he did." נסלח also occurs three times in Num (15:25,26,28), modified each time only by a ל clause as well. Disregarding it by LXX was a simplification of the problem.

19:23 The ὅταν introduces two clauses: "you should enter the land ... and you should plant ...." The B+ variant text changes the subjunctive καταφυτεύσητε to the future indicative καταφυτευσετε,[35] but this is unlikely to have been intended either by MT or by Lev.[36] The planting of any fruit tree is part of the condition described; it is not part of the apodosis.[37] The translator has identified the land which you are to enter by a gloss as ἣν κύριος ὁ θεὸς ὑμῶν δίδωσιν ὑμῖν; hex placed it under the obelus to indicate its lack of an equivalent in MT; in turn, Syh interpreted the obelus correctly, and omitted it, as did ms 58 which often also engaged in this type of post-hexaplaric activity. The relative clause is a common designation of the promised land, and its origin is ex par; the clause is a correct statement, but it is otiose.

The apodosis is introduced by καί, imitating MT. In MT this reads "you must circumcise its foreskin, namely its fruit." It then continues with "for three years it (i.e. its fruit) shall be foreskins to you, and it may not be eaten." Modern translations avoid the notion of circumcisions and foreskins. Typical is that of NJSP: "you shall regard its fruit as forbidden. Three years it shall be forbidden for you." But this is hardly translation; it is exegesis. In fact, I would suggest that the notion of מול, as would that of its common translation περιτέμνω, in the context of fruit trees means "to prune," and that which is pruned is the fruit grown in the first three years of its life.

---

35. For the compound being used in the same sense as the simplex φυτεύω see Lee 57—58.
36. See THL 128.
37. The fact that the cod B reading was adopted by Ra misled SS 34: "In langen Perioden kommt der Indikativ bisweilen schon zu früh vor ... und das bestätigt wieder, dass die Übersetzer sie nicht immer beherrschen konnten." In general, I am sceptical of this observation as characterizing the Pentateuch translators.

The translator looked at the text differently. First of all, he divided between ערלתו and את פריו. This left the original statement of the apodosis ending with ערלתו, which he, not unreasonably, interpreted by τὴν ἀκαθαρσίαν αὐτοῦ "its impurity." This then led to understanding the verb as necessarily meaning a form of purification. That he understood מול is clear from the περι- compound he chose: περικαθαριεῖτε, a neologism formed by the translator to represent the notion of circumcising the fruit trees. So it then reads "then you must purify its impurity."

The את פריו is treated as the subject of what remains, viz. an explanation of what purifying its (i.e. the fruit tree's) impurity means. "Its fruit shall be impure (ἀπερικάθαρτος) to you for three years; not may it be eaten." The translator exercised some freedom in disregarding the preposition את, and making the subject ὁ καρπὸς αὐτοῦ. He has really gotten around the revolting Hebrew figure of ערלים, which לא יאכל. Note also the use of the singular verb with a plural subject.

19:24 "And in the fourth year all its fruit shall be ἅγιος αἰνετὸς τῷ κυρίῳ." That the fruit should be holy means that it has been set apart for sacred use, presumably for the use of the priests. αἰνετός translates הלולים; the word only occurs twice in MT (also in Jdg 9:27). The root means "to praise," hence the translation αἰνετός. In the Jdg passage the word is rendered in the A text by χορούς "dances"; the B text transliterates as ελλουλιμ. I would suggest the translation: "as a laudation (to the Lord)."

19:25 The initial *waw* of MT is here rendered by δέ, and indicates that the verse is contrastive over against vv.23—24. "But in the fifth year you may eat the fruit." The Greek fails to render the suffix of פריו,[38] and the majority text adds an αυτου to represent it; this is obviously recensional, possibly hex.

MT continues with a purposive infinitive, להוסיף לכם תבואתו "so as to increase for you its yield."[39] LXX translates the infinitive in an unusual fashion. One would expect the usual προστίθημι (possibly as προσθεῖναι; see Exod 10:28 Num 32:15), but Lev has πρόσθεμα "addition, increase," a noun occurring only twice in OT (also at Ezek 41:7 where the parent text is obscure).

---

38. See SS 96.
39. Sym translates this freely by ἀνάγοντες τὸ γένημα αὐτοῦ.

The nominal clause is probably best interpreted with τὰ γενήματα αὐτοῦ as subject. I would translate: "its products (will be) a supplement for you."

For the long self-identification formula see discussion at v.3. Hex has omitted εἰμι, since this is not reflected in MT.

19:26 Vv.26—28 forbid engaging in non-Israelite, i.e. pagan, cultic practices. The first is "do not eat upon the mountains." This prohibition refers to "partaking of sacrifices on the high places which had been declared illegal by the D reform."[40] MT's text reads לא תאכלו על הדם. Obviously the translator read הרם "mountains" rather than "the blood." A reference to eating on mountains also occurs at Ezek 18:11,15 22:9. The translator probably knew the Ezek passage, and after על found "mountains" more meaningful in the context than "the blood." Either reading makes sense. The prohibition of eating with the blood does occur at 3:17 7:16,17 17:10,12,14. He obviously misread the *daleth* as a *resh*.

Also prohibited are two forms of divination, οἰωνιεῖσθε and ὀρνιθοσκοπήσεσθε. Both initially had to do with birds, the first referring to their flight patterns, whereas the second involves the actual inspection of birds, probably of their insides. Their Hebrew counterparts are תנחשו and תעוננו resp. Since the nouns נחש "serpent" and ענן "clouds" are well-known, possibly serpent- and cloud-divinations were originally intended. The verb נחש occurs in nine passages, and only once is it not rendered by the verb οἰωνίζω; at 2Paral 33:6 φαρμακεύω is used. LXX simply followed the usage of Gen; see 30:27 44:5,15, and see Note at Gen 30:27. The verb is obviously simply used in the general sense of "practice divination." ὀρνιθοσκοπέω is a hapax legomenon in the OT.[41] The first prohibition is introduced by καί following Sam; hex placed the καί under the obelus to agree with MT.

In the tradition, a popular reading has οιωνεισθε instead of οἰωνιεῖσθε, thereby presupposing a contract verb rather than οἰωνίζομαι.

19:27 The verb תקפו from נקף "go around," in the Hi probably means "to trim," or "to make round." The translator rendered this by ποιήσετε σισόην.

---

40. J.W.Wevers, Ezekiel. The Century Bible: New Series. (London, 1969), comment on 18:6, p.141.
41. For οὐκ οἰωνιεῖσθε The Others read οὐ κληδονισθήσεσθε.

The noun is a hapax legomenon, and is otherwise unknown.[42] It is usually thought to be "a curl (of hair)," though this is quite uncertain, and is really based on the notion of "making round" of the Hebrew stem. So possibly "you may make a curl out of the hair of your head."[43]

The second clause states οὐδὲ φθερεῖτε τὴν ὄψιν τοῦ πώγωνος ὑμῶν "nor may you destroy the shape of your beard." LXX follows the Sam text in continuing with the plural, whereas MT reads the singular תשחית and זקנך. The change to the singular in MT is odd, since it is imbedded in a plural context extending from v.23 to v.28.[44] The term τὴν ὄψιν is a stylistic adaptation of פאת "edges (of the beard)."[45]

19:28 MT says "and you may not put (תתנו) on your flesh שרט לנפש." A שרט is a cut or incision; it occurs only here in OT, though the feminine equivalent שרטת occurs (also uniquely) at 21:5. The latter passage helps to understand this one. The context is that of mourning, and the נפש "person" is dead; see נפשת מת at 21:11. What is meant is "you may not cut into your flesh for a person (who is dead)." LXX renders the structure by ἐντομίδας ἐπὶ ψυχῇ "gashings for a person." I understand ἐπί with the dative to mean occasion or cause.[46] That the person or individual is no longer alive, only the context can determine. The translator correctly understood שרט as a collective.[47]

Similarly prohibited are making "γράμματα στικτά on you."[48] This represents the Hebrew כתבת קעקע usually understood as "tattoo marks," as does the Greek, though קעקע is a hapax legomenon, and its meaning is not certain.[49]

---

42. Schl defines as *cincinnum* vel *nodam capillorum (facio) in occipitio, reliqua capillitie in orbem circumtonsa*. The word may well be related to the Hebrew ציצת.
43. Aq renders the clause by οὐ περικυκλώσει τὸ κλῆμα τῆς κεφαλῆς σου. Sym has οὐ περιξυρήσετε κύκλῳ τὴν πρόσοψιν τῆς κεφαλῆς ὑμῶν, and Theod reads οὐ κυκλώσετε τὸ φααθ τῆς κεφαλῆς <ὑμῶν>.
44. Aq follows the singular of MT, but translates תשחית by ξυρήσεται. Presumably he intended "the edge ... shall not be shaven."
45. The transliteration τὸ φααθ must derive from Theod.
46. See LS sub ἐπί III.1.
47. Sym has for καὶ ἐντομίδας ἐπὶ ψυχῇ the reading οὐδὲ σπαραγμὸν ἐπὶ ψυχῇ.
48. For the use of ἐν with a verb of movement, i.e. in the sense of εἰς see SS 136.
49. Tar^O has רושמין חריתין "traces etched," which probably does mean tattoo marks. Tar^N has כתב חקיק, to which Tar^J adds in explanation לרשם חרית ציורא.

Once again LXX has the long self-identification formula to end the verse, for which see v.3, though MT has the short one, אני יהוה. Hex has omitted εἰμι, which has no equivalent in MT, but there is no extant evidence for its designation of ὁ θεὸς ὑμῶν under the obelus.

19:29 This verse is necessarily in the singular. MT has אל תחלל את בתך להזנותה "do not defile your daughter so as to make her a harlot." LXX has rendered this literally, except for the initial negative command, which has been translated by οὐ plus a future, "you may or shall not defile."

V.b has two clauses paratactically presented, though what is meant are result clauses. I would translate "and the land would not become harlotous and be filled with lawlessness." ἀνομίας translates זמה here as well as at 20:14. At 18:17 the word was translated by ἀσέβημα; cf comment ad loc. Elsewhere in the book ἀνομία renders עון.

19:30 This verse recurs at 26:2. For "my sabbaths observe," see comment at v.3. MT then says "be in awe of my sanctuary," i.e. venerate it. The translator vocalized מקדשי differently, understanding the initial *mem* as the preposition מן, and so translates by ἀπὸ τῶν ἁγίων μου φοβηθήσεσθε, "be afraid of (be fearful, be chary of) my holy things." What is meant is to be reverent over against the holy things of God.

The short form of the divine self-identification formula follows, but hex omits εἰμι as not being represented by אני יהוה.

19:31 For ἐπακολουθήσετε see comment at v.4. MT has two אל prohibitions, i.e. negative imperatives, which LXX interprets as לא structures, i.e. οὐκ plus future verbs. The word אבת remains uncertain; it is often thought to refer to spirits of the dead, e.g. of Samuel in the witch of Endor narrative in 1Sam 28:3,6—9. LXX translates "you may not follow ἐγγαστριμύθοις," i.e. ventriloquists; see Note at Dt 18:11.

The second prohibition in MT reads: "and for the wizards do not search," i.e. do not consult the wizards (or soothsayers)." The ידענים are people who were presumed to know the hidden things of the future. LXX translates by ἐπαοιδοῖς "charmers, enchanters," for which see Note at Dt 18:11. Unique is Lev's interpretation of the verb תבקשו by προσκολληθήσεσθε, since προσκολλάω is usually reserved for translating the root דבק throughout OT. Instead of "seek out, search for," the Greek has "attach yourselves." What Lev says is "to the charmers you may not attach yourselves." Lev warns against habitual association with those who recite charms or incantations, whereas MT forbids seeking out those who pretend to special knowledge of what is hidden from ordinary mortals. The verb is modified by an infinitive showing the result of such attachment: "so as to be defiled by them." Association with ventriloquists and charmers, since they presume to foretell the future known to the Lord alone, is said to render unclean.

The omission of εἰμι in the long self-identification formula by the popular M variant text is probably hex in origin, since it lacks a counterpart in MT.

19:32 Respect for one's elders is enjoined. This is ordered in three clauses: "before a greybeard you must rise, and you must honor the elder, and you must fear your God." This third is not really out of character. Showing deference to the greybeard and the elder is not only expressive of the fear of God, it is also a matter of degree. God is the eternal one, to whom full deference must be accorded. MT does not have a direct modifier of the verb תיראו, but rather מאלהיך. For a מן phrase modifying תיראו see comment at v.30. In the tradition, τὸν θεόν σου is defined by an F b y z+ text as κυριον, which is theologically correct, but textually secondary.

The long self-identification formula levels with its frequent occurrences in the chapter, since MT has only אני יהוה. As usual a popular reading, hex inspired, omits εἰμι, and hex has also placed ὁ θεὸς ὑμῶν under the obelus.

19:33 The verb יגור is rendered by various words in Lev, but always by an attributive participle, except here; in fact, only here is the root προσέρχομαι used, though it is particularly appropriate with גר, i.e. as προσελθῇ προσήλυτος.[50] The plural ὑμῖν follows the אתכם of Sam rather than the אתך of MT; in fact, all the early witnesses have the plural, even including Tar⁰. Incidentally, that MT is an oddity with its אתך becomes especially clear, since it is followed by בארצכם (גר). The ἐν phrase modifies the active verb προσελθῇ in the sense of "come into."[51]

---

50. See THGL 130.
51. See SS 137—138.

The apodosis is unambiguous: "you may not afflict him," which accurately renders the verb תונו, the Hi of ינה "to oppress, afflict." In the tradition, the majority M text has transposed προσήλυτος ὑμῖν; this reflects the order of MT, and is probably recensional, though this is by no means certain. The tendency in the Pentateuch generally is to place modifying pronouns next to the verb in favor of a subject noun. The translator here kept the related words προσελθῇ προσήλυτος together as cognates, showing a fine feeling for style.

19:34 MT begins with כאזרח מכם "as one of your native-born," in which the מן is clearly partitive. The translator could hardly render this by ἀπό, and wisely chose ἐν ὑμῖν, thus "as a native-born among you."[52] The ὡς structure modifies ἔσται, of which the subject is "the resident alien who comes to you." Here an attributive participle is used to represent הגר; the verb differs from προσελθῇ translating יגור in v.33, probably merely for variety's sake.[53] The prepositional phrase modifying the participle, πρὸς ὑμᾶς, has as its counterpart in MT אתכם, vocalized by the Masoretes to mean "with you." But the participle προσπορευόμενος favors a πρός phrase as modifier, and the rendering is determined by Greek stylistic considerations.

For the next clause see comments at v.18; the one whom you must love, αὐτόν, refers to the resident alien, as he too is τὸν πλησίον σου. Here the order to love has an added ὅτι clause to give a reason for the order: it is "because you were resident aliens ἐν γῇ Αἰγύπτῳ," i.e. "in Egypt land." The phrase בארץ מצרים occurs only here in Leviticus, but is almost always translated thus throughout the Pentateuch, i.e. with Αἰγύπτῳ, in Exod (15 times) as well as in Dt (12 times).[54] It is also the usual rendering in Gen (nine out of ten times; Αἰγύπτου obtains at 41:48), and in Num the dative occurs twice, and the genitive, once.

For the long self-identification formula see discussion at v.3. Hex omitted εἰμι after ἐγώ to equal MT. The *n* text added υμιν after ἔσται; this equals MT's יהיה לכם, and the plus is undoubtedly based on the Hebrew,

---

52. See SS 165—166.
53. But see THGL 130.
54. But see the strictures on Exod usage in Note at Exod 12:30, and comp also THGE 201, sub 12:1.

probably mediated by one of The Three. The translator omitted it as otiose. The Byz text used παροικοι instead of προσήλυτοι. Its source is also likely to have been one of The Three; note the anonymous πάροικοι on the margins of M´.

19:35 "You may not make use of wrong (or false) standards in measures and in weights and in balances." The opening οὐ ποιήσετε ἄδικον ἐν κρίσει literally "you may not do an unrighteous act in judgment" also occurs at v.15; see comment ad loc. In the present context it refers to the use of false standards used in selling. The areas of possible injustice reflect standards used in trade. The translator understood each of the Hebrew terms, מדה, משקל and משורה, resp referring to length, weight and quantity, as collectives, and used plural nouns. The Greek terms reflect measures of a different era and culture, though the general demand for honest trade is correctly reflected. μέτρον is a common word for "measure," but it does contrast with στάθμιον which clearly refers to weights. The last one, ζυγόν, really means a yoke, but in the plural may refer to balances used to weigh metals used in trade.

The three ἐν phrases are joined by καί throughout, i.e. the pattern used is a + b + c. The *b* text does omit the first καί, but though this equals the MT pattern, I suspect that this is a stylistic variant, not a recensional one.

19:36 ζύγα is here used for מאזני; the word מאזנים is never translated in any other way; both are balances; see comment at v.35 where, however, it renders משורה. The bound phrase has צדק as its free element; this is quite correctly rendered by the adjective δίκαια.[55] MT has three more such measures which are described as צדק, viz. אבני צדק followed by איפת צדק which LXX omits, and הין צדק. The pattern followed is a b c + d. LXX joins each of its three members by καί, as was done in v.35.

The second phrase "accurate stones" refers to the weights used to weigh goods, usually in the balances. These are translated by στάθμια, for which see comment at v.35. Both of these are correctly rendered by plural nouns. The next two are in the singular. The איפה was a measure of about 18 liters or half a bushel, and it consisted of six הין, so the latter was c. three liters. The omis-

---

55. See SS 65.

sion of the third phrase was almost certainly inspired by homoioteleuton—note the recurring צדק; it would hardly have been intentional. Hex made up for the phrase by adding (και) οιφι δικαιον, reflecting the singular of MT correctly. Another correction towards the Hebrew is reflected by Byz which added και μετρα after στάθμια, whereas the *b* text added και μετρα δικαια in the correct slot as number three, though these "corrections" are wrongly put into the plural, presumably through attraction to ζυγά and στάθμια.

The last one is translated by χοῦς, also a measure of capacity. The size varies from place to place, and may vary anywhere between 2.5 and 4 liters. Since a הין is c. three liters, χοῦς is a good approximation to it.[56] Elsewhere (23:13) it is also transliterated as ἵν. הין is also transliterated in Exod (three times) and 11 times in Num.

The verse concludes with the long self-identification formula, amplified by an identification of ὁ θεὸς ὑμῶν as the redeemer God: "the one bringing you out of the land of Egypt." The articulated participle renders אשר הוצאתי. The participle is, however, timeless, and could be understood as a constant reality, but since the default aorist is used it is unlikely to have been intended by the translator in that sense. The popular hex text has omitted εἰμι to represent its absence from MT.

19:37 The chapter ends with a general order to "observe (φυλάξεσθε) all my law and all my statutes," along with yet another long self-identification formula, with a popular hex text omitting εἰμι to correspond exactly to MT. MT, however, has only אני יהוה, and the same popular text has omitted ὁ θεὸς ὑμῶν, again probably hex in origin.

LXX has used νόμον μου and προστάγματά μου to render חקתי and משפטי resp. The use of νόμον μου was probably intentional as an overall characterization of ch.19. At 18:26 almost the same text occurs except that τὰ νόμιμά μου occurs instead of τὸν νόμον μου; there too προστάγματά μου was used to render משפטי, which may well have influenced the translator.

In the tradition, the *b*+ text actually has τα νομιμα instead of τὸν νόμον, almost certainly under the influence of 18:26. The verb φυλάξεσθε has also suffered considerably in the tradition; an A *d*+ text has changed it to

---

56. The Others transliterated as ἵν (retroverted from Syh).

φυλαξασθε, the aorist imperative; a popular F V text has changed the form to the active φυλαξετε, and another popular reading has an aorist active imperative φυλαξατε, but the B+ text is nonetheless original Lev.

Chapter 20

20:2 λαλήσεις reflects the תדבר of Sam rather than the תאמר of MT. This is also attested in 11QLev.[1] MT has a long antecedent for אשר, beginning with איש איש מבני ישראל, i.e. "anyone from the Israelites (and from the resident aliens who reside in Israel)." LXX simplifies this considerably by making the איש איש construction an ἐάν τις one.[2] The different syntactic pattern interprets correctly what is intended by MT, thus "if someone ...." The ἀπό governing "the Israelites or the residing resident aliens" is clearly partitive.[3] The ἤ makes good contextual sense, though MT has ומן. LXX also does not repeat the preposition. The τῶν προσγεγημένων προσηλύτων[4] represents הגר הגר, with the articulated participle following the noun. Hex has changed the word order to fit that of MT by placing προσηλύτων before the articulated participle. In MT the הגר הגר is governed by מן which Lev disregarded; see comment on ἤ above. Hex has apparently added απο before it to equal MT.[5]

Within the relative clause δῷ is modified by a genitive which must also be partitive, thus "who might give one of his seed."[6] For ἄρχοντι see the discussion at 18:21.[7] To give one of his seed to a ruler must refer to the devotion of offspring (possibly a firstborn?) to an idol called "Ruler." This can hardly refer to a human ruler, since the penalties are destruction from one's people (v.3). It involves defilement of God's holy things, a profanation of the name of ἡγιασμένων to God (see v.3). But the object of such devotion can be plural; see ἐκπορνεύειν αὐτοὺς εἰς τοὺς ἄρχοντας ἐκ τοῦ λαοῦ αὐτῶν in v.5; see comment at v.5. The translator must have realized that מלך was a pagan deity called מלך, i.e. ἄρχων, and one might have expected a transliteration.

The apodosis translates מות יומת which is formulaic, as is its translation, though occasionally יומת is rendered by τελευτάτω; see Note at Exod 21:12. It may be translated by "he will most certainly be put to death."

---

1. See Freedman 530.
2. See THGL 122.
3. See SS 167.
4. See THGL 130.
5. See THGL 104.
6. See SS 161.
7. Aq did recognize the name מלך as a transcription, and rendered the phrase here and in v.3 by τῷ Μολοχ. The Others understood it as a genitive τοῦ Μολοχ.

The manner of his death is described in the last clause: "the people who are on the land shall stone him ἐν λίθοις," The ἐν is instrumental.⁸ τὸ ἔθνος τὸ ἐπὶ τῆς γῆς translates a bound phrase עַם הָאָרֶץ, a phrase designating the ordinary folk, the people of the land as over against the priests and rulers. The translator apparently thought of those people rather differently, as those belonging to the land, i.e. the native-born; see comment at v.4.

20:3 The unnecessary pronoun ἐγὼ (ἐπιστήσω) is in imitation of MT. It constitutes an important discourse signal that the subject has changed to first person, i.e. to stress its contrast with the third plural of the last clause of v.2. That God should set his "face against that man" expresses adamancy of determination. The first two clauses are reminiscent of 17:10; cf discussion ad loc; see also 20:6. The reference in ἄνθρωπον ἐκεῖνον is to the τις of v.2. For the ὅτι clause see the discussion of the relative clause in v.2. It gives the reason for the judgment: "because he gave some of his seed to Ruler."

The ἵνα clause normally expresses purpose when used with the subjunctive, but that seems inappropriate here, where it must show result. Possibly, as in the case of לְמַעַן which it translates, it is a case of hyperbole.⁹ The ἵνα clause has two parts: a) μιάνῃ τὰ ἅγιά μου "to defile my holy things." MT has מִקְדָּשִׁי "my sanctuary," but Lev has disregarded the initial consonant (or took the *mem* as a partitive מִן as at 19:30). The translation is not really fully sensible, since it refers to the ὅτι clause. To speak of giving one's seed to the ruler in order to defile God's holy things is somewhat obscure, but the Greek simply translates MT word for word. What is, however, fully possible is that the plural noun might refer to the two parts of the sanctuary; comp 21:12 and comments ad loc.

On the other hand, b) is luminous, though it too misrepresents MT. MT says "and profane my holy name." The translator renders (אֶת) שֵׁם קָדְשִׁי as a bound phrase in which the second element would be vocalized as a plural noun with suffix, and so renders it by τὸ ὄνομα τῶν ἡγιασμένων μοι "the name of those who have been sanctified for me," i.e. "the sanctified ones" have been set aside specifically "for me," of which that man's "giving offspring to the ruler" is a complete profanation. In the tradition, ms 376 must represent hex by its το αγιον μου which equals MT exactly.

---

8. See SS 119—120.
9. Which BDB and KB both call an ironic use; see sub voce.

20:4 The protasis in MT begins with "and if the people of the land should actually hide their eyes from that man." LXX uses a contrastive δέ instead of "and," since the situation of v.4 is in contrast to that demanded in v.2. LXX interprets the cognate verbal structure of MT, as commonly, e.g. see 19:17, by a cognate dative noun plus a finite verb; it translates as "should actually overlook with their eyes," i.e. disregard "that man when he gives some of his seed to the ruler."[10] The rendering of בתתו reproduces the Hebrew structure exactly by ἐν τῷ δοῦναι αὐτόν, i.e. a preposition governing an articulated infinitive with an accusative pronoun as its subject: "when he gives." For the collocation and its meaning see discussion at v.2. The penalty exacted in v.3 was death by stoning by the people "who were on the land." Disregarding it means τοῦ μὴ ἀποκτεῖναι αὐτόν, "so as not to kill him." Here עם הארץ is interpreted as οἱ αὐτόχθονες τῆς γῆς "the native-born of the land." This serves to explain what τὸ ἔθνος τὸ ἐπὶ τὴν γῆς in v.2 meant to the translator as well.

Odd is the intent of ἀπό, since the prepositional phrase must modify ὑπερίδωσιν, and it must be judged as a rather unthinking reflection of מן modifying יעלימו; "to hide from" makes good sense, but "to overlook from" is as odd in Greek as it is in English.[11]

20:5 V.5 is the apodosis to v.4. If the land's inhabitants overlook a man's giving of his seed to a ruler, God will not. For the first clause, see comment at v.3 and 17:10. In contrast to v.3 the otiose אני is not translated in Lev.[12] Included with "that man" is τὴν συγγένειαν αὐτοῦ, i.e. his משפחתו "his clan." Apparently the translator intended by συγγένειαν not so much his physical kinsmen, as those who were akin to him in attitude, as the next clause makes clear.

Fo ἀπολῶ rendering הכרתי see comment at 17:10. MT defines those who were במשפחתו as ואת כל הזנים אחריו לזנות אחרי המלך "and all those prostituting themselves after him so as to prostitute themselves after Molech." The translator neatly avoids the repetitiousness of הזנים ... לזנות by rendering the participle by τοὺς ὁμονοῦντας (αὐτῷ), and then continuing with ὥστε ἐκπορνεύειν αὐτοὺς εἰς τοὺς ἄρχοντας, thus "and all those likeminded to him so as to prostitute them-

---

10. Aq again has τῷ Μολοχ.
11. See SS 31.
12. See SS 74.

selves to the Rulers." The αὐτούς becomes singular in A B+, but this can not be taken seriously. It was probably the influence of the singular pronouns in the verse, αὐτοῦ, αὐτόν and αὐτῷ, but only the plural makes sense here.[13] The phrase εἰς τοὺς ἄρχοντας is unexpected; presumably the plural is due to the αὐτούς, as each of them would relate to a ruler. Did the translator think of the plural in terms of each individual having his own idolatrous ἄρχων? The C′ n s text has the singular τον αρχοντα, which is what one would expect.[14]

The concluding ἐκ phrase modifies ἀπολῶ. It represents מקרב עמו, and the plural αὐτῶν is necessary because of its reference to "him and those likeminded to him." The קרב is not translated, and the Byz text has supplied μεσου before τοῦ to represent it.

20:6 The whole of v.a is a pendant nominative, which is then incorporated into the clause by means of τὴν ψυχὴν ἐκείνην and αὐτήν. For the relative clause, ἣ ἂν ἐπακολουθήσῃ ἐγγαστριμύθοις ἢ ἐπαοιδοῖς, see comments at 19:31a. This is then followed by a ὥστε clause showing probable result: "so as to prostitute themselves after them (i.e. after the ventriloquists and charmers)." For the main clause see the comments on v.3. It differs from v.3a in omitting καὶ ἐγώ and having τὴν ψυχὴν ἐκείνην instead of "that man," as well as feminine pronouns instead of masculine in the second clause. MT differs in having masculine pronouns, אתו and עמו, which bypass v.a entirely and find their antecedents in האיש of v.6, but LXX follows Sam which has הנפש as referent; this is the simpler and the expected anaphoric referent.

20:7 LXX follows Sam in omitting והתקדשתם, possibly due to homoiarchon. Hex has added και αγιασθησεσθε at the beginning to represent it. On the other hand, the omission could be construed as a case of harmonizing with v.8 where κύριος is described as ὁ ἁγιάζων ὑμᾶς; thus if it is the Lord who sanctifies you, how can "you make yourselves holy"? For the demand καὶ ἔσεσθε ἅγιοι, see the discussion at 11:44 and 19:2.

LXX has levelled with v.26 (and 19:2) in adding ἅγιος as a predicate adjective within the ὅτι clause. MT roots the demand "you must be holy" in the fact that אני יהוה אלהיכם. Since the Lord who demands that you be set apart,

---

13. See THGL 97–98.
14. Aq has ὀπίσω τοῦ Μολοχ, a literal rendering of the Hebrew אחרי המלך.

separated from all that is profane, is your God, he has the right to make this basic demand on you, his people. LXX, however, changes this by making κύριος ὁ θεὸς ὑμῶν an apposite to ἐγώ the subject, with the adjective ἅγιος as predicate. The demand upon Israel to be holy is rooted in the holiness of the Lord your God. See the discussion at 11:44.

In the tradition, a popular variant text transposes ἅγιος ἐγώ, but all the uncial texts have the Lev order.[15]

20:8 Both verbs correctly interpret MT as future. The Catena text makes both verbs aorist imperative, φυλαξασθε ... ποιησατε, but these variants are palaeographically inspired and secondary. Lev consistently renders contextual suffixal verb forms by the future. For the translation of חקתי by τὰ προστάγματά μου see comment at 18:4.

The verse ends with a nominal clause ἐγὼ κύριος ὁ ἁγιάζων ὑμᾶς. As in MT it is asyndetically presented, though the Byz text makes it a οτι construction, probably under the influence of v.7; this does make good sense, and may well express correctly the relation between the coordinate verbal clauses and the nominal. In other words, precisely because I am the Lord who sanctifies you, you must guard my statutes and do them. This is obviously closely related to v.7. Guarding the Lord's statutes and keeping them is the way in which the separateness of Israel is demonstrated, and the separateness of Israel is by divine appointment. Their covenant God, κύριος, is the one who sets them apart, puts them into a sanctified state; also comp comment at v.7.

In the tradition, copyists amplified the κύριος. A popular variant added ο θεος, whereas the A d+ text added the fuller ο θεος υμων. But MT has the short self-identification formula אני יהוה plus the participle מקדשכם modifying יהוה, and LXX translated this correctly.

20:9 MT begins with כי to introduce a protasis, i.e. "if there is someone who would curse his father and his mother, מות יומת." The translator found the syntax somewhat awkward, i.e. the relative pronoun within a כי construction was odd, and so he simplified it by disregarding the כי; so it becomes a straightforward: "let anyone who ... be surely put to death." Note the occurrence of the third per-

---

15. But Kenn 80,109 do read קדוש after אני.

son imperative of θανατόω used throughout this section on incest rather than the future tense. Hex has added εαν at the beginning to represent the כי. As might be expected, $d\ n+$ have by haplography only one ἄνθρωπος, but Lev usually (eight out of 10 times) rendered איש איש by the double ἄνθρωπος.[16] Lev is probably leveling with ἄνθρωπος ἄνθρωπος ... ὅς of 17:3,8,10,13 22:18.

For κακῶς εἴπῃ/εἶπεν see discussion at 19:14. LXX uses the correlative conjunction ἤ for the waw of MT. MT describes the bad-mouthing as directed against both his parents, whereas LXX, against either parent. Modern translations tend to follow th LXX's interpretation by using "or."[17]

The penalty is death. For the formulaic θανάτῳ θανατούσθω see comment at v.2. The appended judgment is "his father or his mother he badmouthed (or berated); ἔνοχος ἔσται," i.e. "he shall be liable, guilty." This interprets the Hebrew idiom דמיו בו "his blood (shall be) on him."[18] Clearly LXX had the Lev text as parent text rather than Sam's דמו, since the plural noun is used of shed blood, but the singular is not.

In the tradition, hex has corrected both cases of ἤ joining "his father" and "his mother" to καί. The Byz variant εστιν for εσται is not original, though it may well be closer to the intent of MT, and could be a recensional change towards MT.

20:10 MT reads "and let anyone who shall commit adultery with the wife of someone who shall commit adultery with the wife of his neighbour (be certainly put to death)." Not surprisingly the suggestion is sometimes made that MT was the result of dittography, איש אשר ינאף את אשת having been copied twice. If this was the case, it must have predated both Sam and LXX. LXX made sense out of it by adding ἤ before the second relative pronoun.[19] It then read "anyone who might commit adultery with the wife of someone (ἀνδρός) or who might commit adultery with the wife of a neighbour." The translator has not translated the suffix of רעהו, since it would be otiose in Greek. Hex has, however, added αυτου to represent it. Since the second relative clause specifies the ἀνδρός as τοῦ πλησίον,

---

16. See THGL 122.
17. But NJPS translates by "or" in the first instance, but then continues with "he has insulted his father *and* his mother."
18. An anonymous marginal reading has αἷμα αὐτοῦ ἐν αὐτῷ; the source could be anyone of The Three.
19. Kenn 109,181,199,244 and 615 do read ואשר instead of אשר 2°.

the repetition may be justified as one of greater specificity. The sense of the second clause would then be "I mean: who would commit adultery with the wife of the neighbour."

Over against v.9 MT and LXX do not repeat איש/ἄνθρωπος, but most Greek witnesses do repeat ἄνθρωπος, undoubtedly under the influence of v.9. The Byz text has also added a και to introduce the verse; this is undoubtedly recensional, since MT reads ואיש. The Byz text has also omitted ὃς ἂν μοιχεύσηται γυναῖκα ἀνδρὸς ἤ. This does simplify the text, but it is not original; the omission is due to homoioteleuton.

LXX has articulated πλησίον, i.e. it has γυναῖκα ἀνδρός in the first relative clause, but γυναῖκα τοῦ πλησίον in the second. This seems to give plausibility to the above suggestion about specificity, i.e. "a man's wife ... the neighbour's wife." In the tradition, the majority F text has also articulated γυναῖκα, obviously a stylistic change.

In the apodosis, MT uses a singular verb: "the adulterer shall certainly be put to death (יומת), and (i.e. as well as) the adulteress." LXX has the plural verb, θανατούσθωσαν, in view of the coordinate subject. The majority text has changed this to the singular; admittedly, this equals MT, but that this reading is recensional is questionable in view of the fact that the singular had occurred in the preceding verse.

20:11 The verse begins with καὶ (ἐάν), which codd A B omit. But MT does have waw. Furthermore, whenever Lev begins with ἐάν it almost always has either καί or δέ with it (only three exceptions). The καί must be original.[20] So is the ἐάν τις, for which MT has איש אשר, i.e. LXX has made this into a conditional, rather than a "whoever" structure. The n text has changed ἐάν τις to ανθρωπος ος, which equals MT, and this must be a recensional change mediated by one of The Three.

For the form of incest involved see comments at 18:8. Sexual relations with one's stepmother mean that he has "uncovered the shame of his father." This is a capital crime; "let both certainly be put to death." For ἔνοχοί εἰσιν see comment at v.9.

---

20. See THGL 102.

20:12 For καὶ ἐάν τις rendering ואיש אשר see comments at v.11. Sexual relations with one's daughter-in-law are also a capital offence. For the apodosis see comment at v.11. LXX gives a reason for the death penalty in a γάρ structure: ἠσεβήκασεν γάρ "for they have acted impiously." MT has a simple statement: תבל עשו "they have committed a perversion"; תבל is a confusion of nature, something perverse.²¹ Making this a γάρ statement explicitly makes the impious actions the basis for the penalty. For ἔνοχοί εἰσιν see comment at v.9.²²

20:13 LXX does not translate איש before אשר, and the Byz text has supplied an ανθρωπος to represent it; this is clearly recensional. The failure to render איש is lexically taken care of in Greek by the masculine singular relative pronoun ὅς. What is forbidden is male homosexuality, lying with a male κοίτην γυναικός. For the latter structure see comment at 18:22.²³ Such conduct is called a βδέλυγμα, an "abomination" on the part of both male partners, and the death penalty is invoked for both. For ἔνοχοί εἰσιν see comment at v.9.

20:14 For failure to render איש see comment at v.13. Here too the Byz text inserts ανθρωπος to represent the absent איש. What is prohibited is that one "should take a woman and her mother." Polygamy is not forbidden, but relations with both daughter and mother are. This is described as ἀνόμημα "an unlawful act," which translates זמה "wickedness." The word occurs again in the last clause, where it is rendered by ἀνομία, merely for variety's sake.²⁴ That copyists should have either written ανομια in both cases (as n+), or ανομημα (as A Byz+) is hardly surprising; they are similar in sound and are synonyms as well.

Instead of the usual formula, the penalty is "ἐν πυρὶ κατακαύσουσιν him and them"; note that the verb used in the penalty is now in the future. After that radical solution Lev can safely say καὶ οὐκ ἔσται ἀνομία ἐν ὑμῖν. The change of ἔσται to εστιν in x+ is of course a thoughtless copyist error; only the future is sensible; it is only true after the ἀνόμημα is removed as the תהיה of MT also demands.

---

21. Theod (not Aq as ms 344 has it) transcribes תבל by θαβελ plus the verb ἐποίησαν.
22. See SS 98.
23. See also THGL 130.
24. The anonymous transcription ζεμμα is almost certainly Theod.

20:15 For failure to render איש see comment at v.13; again the Byz text added ανθρωπος to equal MT. As at 18:23 what is forbidden are sexual relations with a quadruped. MT calls this giving שכבה "copulation." At 18:23 this was translated by τὴν κοίτην, but here a hapax legomenon was coined, κοιτασίαν, presumably a synonym created for the sake of variety.[25] The condition is graphically described: "whoever might put his discharge in a tetrapod." The ἐν is used here with a verb of movement, i.e. in the sense of εἰς.[26]

For the formulaic penalty see comment at v.2. Furthermore, "you must kill the quadruped." The variant spelling in numerous scattered mss, αποκτεινεται, is not a "real" variant at all; it is an itacistic spelling of ἀποκτείνετε.

20:16 The verse begins with a long pendant nominative consisting of γυνή plus a relative clause; this is then incorporated into the main clause by the accusative τὴν γυναῖκα καὶ τὸ κτῆνος. The pendant may be translated: "And whatever woman will approach any animal so that she may be defiled by it." Comp the similar statement in 18:23, and see comment ad loc. The Hebrew reads as counterpart to the infinitival structure, לרבעה אתה "to impregnate her"; this LXX interprets as βιβασθῆναι αὐτὴν ὑπ' αὐτοῦ; in other words, attention is drawn to what happens to the woman rather than to the action of the animal.

For the penalty to be imposed on both woman and animal see comment at v.15, and for ἔνοχοί εἰσιν see comment at v.9.

20:17 The initial ואיש is disregarded by Lev, but the Byz text supplied και ανθρωπος to represent it. Sexual relations with a half-sister, either agnate or cognate, are forbidden. The syntax is quite loose; apparently, the predicate is ὄνειδός ἐστιν, and all that comes before it is subject, i.e. "whoever takes his half-sister ... and sees her shame, and she sees his shame." ὄνειδος "reproach" is a literal rendering of חסד; the latter word occurs only here in the Pentateuch; in fact, it occurs only once elsewhere (at Prov 14:34); here the translator simply contextualized, using ἐλασσονοῦσι contrast with ὑψοῖ.[27]

---

25. I am sceptical about the statement in Harlé-Pralon: Il renforce ici la gravité du cas rapport à 18,23 où figurait le simple *koité*.
26. See LS sub voce I.8.
27. I am sceptical of the note in BHS "frt l וחסר." It is of course possible that the translator thought of חסר instead of חסד, but in view of the freedom with which he worked, it is dangerous to suggest an emendation on such a basis.

The penalty for this offence is ἐξολεθρευθήσονται ἐνώπιον υἱῶν γένους αὐτῶν. In MT this is introduced by a conjunction, and hex has added a καὶ so as to equal the Hebrew. A marginal s reading has added ἀμφότεροι as subject after the verb, but this is ex par; see vv.11—13. The ἐνώπιον phrase "before their kinsfolk" means that the penalty will be publicly carried out.

In MT the final clause, עונו ישא "he shall bear his guilt," is tied to the preceding clause; it is the consequence of the man's having uncovered the nakedness of his half-sister. LXX has tried to make the final clause fit in with the penalty, which applies to both: "they shall be destroyed in the presence of their kinsfolk," and so makes it plural: ἁμαρτίαν κομιοῦνται "they shall bear guilt." In other words, both parties share the guilt. Hex has added an αυτου to represent the suffix of עונו, but in view of the plural verb a popular reading has made this αυτων. Furthermore, the majority F text reads λημψεται. I suspect this to be a hex correction, both to the singular, and as a more literal rendering of ישא.

20:18 For γυναικὸς ἀποκαθημένης "a woman set apart," see the comment at 15:32—33. The participle refers to a woman, isolated because of her monthly flux. To make doubly clear that sexual intercourse with a menstruating woman is meant, this is stated in coordinate clauses: "who would lie with ... and would uncover her shame."

In such a case, both have done wrong. According to MT, the man את מקרה הערה "her source he has laid bare," and the woman has revealed את מקור דמיה "the source of her (spilt) blood." In both cases the word מקור occurs. The translator tried to make all of this clear. First of all, he used the same verb, ἀπεκάλυψεν, in both clauses, i.e. הערה and גלתה are not distinguished. But he did distinguish between the two instances of מקור. The man "uncovered τὴν πηγὴν αὐτῆς, but what she uncovered was τὴν ῥύσιν τοῦ αἵματος αὐτῆς. The word πηγή means "spring, source," and the source is the female genital organ; this is what the man uncovered. But what the woman uncovered was "the flow of her blood," i.e. the impure discharge.

The penalty is shared by both: "they shall be destroyed from their kinsfolk." The word for "kinsfolk" is τοῦ γένους. The F M V majority text, however, has της γενεας. Though the two are synonyms, γενεά is used almost exclusively in the OT to render דור, and never עם, whereas γένος is used to render various words, including עם ten times in the Pentateuch. Obviously τοῦ γένους is original text.

20:19 Forbidden are sexual relations with agnate and cognate aunts. LXX follows the order of Sam, but MT reverses the two as אחות אמך ואחות אביך. Hex has transposed πατρός and μητρός to correspond to the order of MT.

The γάρ clause gives the raison d'etre for the prohibition; in such a case, he (would have) uncovered a near relative. The use of the aorist shows the resultant situation obtaining from the offence. The structure τὴν οἰκειότητα ἀπεκάλυψεν is metonymic for "uncovered the shame of a near relative."[28]

The concluding עונו ישאו or its singular equivalent also occurred at v.17 and 19:8. In each case, Lev used a different verb. At 19:8 the normal λήμψεται was used, and at 20:17 it was κομιοῦνται; here the translator used ἀποίσονται "carry off." It is unlikely that the translator was trying to make distinctions; he simply enjoyed variation.[29] ἁμαρτίαν appears without a genitive pronoun, but the Byz text has added αυτων to represent the suffix of עונם. The Byz text has also added ατεκνοι αποθανουνται, but the gloss is taken from v.20, which see.

20:20 MT begins with ואיש, which LXX disregards entirely; it begins with ὅς, but hex has added και ανηρ at the beginning to equal the ואיש of MT. The verse refers to the offence of having relations with דדתו; this would mean that he had uncovered the nakedness of דדו. A דד is an agnate uncle, the brother of one's father. Obviously then the דדה would be his wife. The translator found this difficult to translate, since Greek does not make a distinction between an agnate and a cognate uncle. So he translated דדתו by a more general term, τῆς συγγενοῦς. By making the adjectival noun feminine, he makes reference to having relations "with a female near of kin." This leaves the problem of דדו. He could have used θείου, but this can refer to either agnate or cognate uncle. To avoid that he used τῆς συγγενείας "near of kin," which can be either male or female, but the context demands that it refer to the husband of τῆς συγγενοῦς. The two terms are synonyms. συγγενής also occurs at 18:14 for דודה, but at 25:45 it renders משפחה. συγγένεια also occurs for משפחה at 20:5. Obviously the translator is using the two cognate synonyms to make a contextual distinction.

MT has a double penalty: חטאם ישאו ערירים ימתו. Lev has only the second one: ἄτεκνοι ἀποθανοῦνται "they shall die childless." Why the translator should

---

28. Aq translates כי את שארו by ὅτι τὸ λίμμα αὐτοῦ.
29. See THGL 72—74, where this characteristic is amply illustrated.

shorten the text is not clear; all I can suggest is carelessness, though this is unusual for the translator. Possibly he was influenced by v.21 where the single penalty of childlessness also occurs, but there MT also lacks חטאם ישאו. Hex has represented the first clause by αμαρτιαν αυτων αποισονται, whereas the Byz text has added αμαρτιαν αυτων ληψονται. For the use of the two verbs to render נשא see comment at v.19.

20:21 As at v.21, which see, MT begins with ואיש, which LXX omits, proceding directly to ὅς. A majority F M text has added και ανηρ before ὅς. This is undoubtedly recensional, but apparently it is not hex. The offence castigated is having relations with the wife of one's brother. The ὅς clause is a pendant construction of which it is said: ἀκαθαρσία ἐστιν "it is an impurity." The syntax of the Greek is somewhat loose, since one hardly expects one who commits a sexual offence to be an impurity, though syntactically that is what it seems to represent.

The penalty is the same as in v.20: "they shall die childless."

20:22 Vv.20—26 are an extended homily urging the keeping of all τὰ προστάγματά μου and τὰ κρίματά μου, and avoiding all evil influence. Instead of φυλάξεσθε the A B C' f+ text has the aorist imperative, φυλαξασθε, which is not original text. Imperatives in such contexts are hardly ever to be found in Lev.[30] The b text has the active future φυλαξετε, which is even rarer. For προστάγματά μου as translation of חקתי see comment at 18:4. In v.b MT's תקיא אתכם "shall spit you out" is rendered by LXX in odd fashion by προσοχθίσῃ ὑμῖν "be angry with you." For this translation see comment at 18:25.[31]

The subject, ἡ γῆ, is modified by an εἰς ἥν clause. The clause translates אני מביא by the usual pattern of pronoun plus a present tense verb, ἐγὼ εἰσάγω.[32] The ἐκεῖ, representing שמה, is recapitulative, but is common after an εἰς ἥν construction. The verb is modified by an unarticulated purposive infinitive, κατοικεῖν (ἐπ' αὐτῆς). The Byz text makes its purposive nature clearer by articulating the infinitive, του κατοικειν. The subject of the infinitive is ὑμᾶς.

---

30. See THGL 127.
31. Theod translates by ἀποβάλῃ ὑμᾶς. Sym translates the verb by ἐξεμέσῃ; cf also f.n. at 18:25.
32. See THGL 95.

20:23 "And not πορεύσεσθε τοῖς νομίμοις τῶν ἐθνῶν." The A B V *d f*+ text has the present imperative, πορευεσθε, but this is an error palaeographically inspired, i.e. ΣΕΣ becoming ΕΣ.³³ The modifier of the verb in MT is בחקת הגוי, but LXX follows the הגוים of Sam.³⁴ By taking הגוי as a collective the verse becomes consistently plural; note the plural ἐποίησαν and the pronoun αὐτούς. ἐθνῶν is in turn modified by a relative clause, οὓς ἐξαποστέλλω ἀφ' ὑμῶν. The Hebrew has אשר אני משלח מפניכם. The failure to render אני by εγω is highly unusual, possibly an oversight on the part of the translator; cf comment at v.22 for the usual pattern.³⁵ The pronoun is admittedly unnecessary, since the verb is inflected in the first person singular, but its absence does break with the normal pattern. Also unusual is the failure to render the פני element in מפניכם.³⁶

V.b can be understood as an independent construction, as the punctuation of the critical text intends. The ὅτι clause gives the reason for the final clause, which is introduced by an otiose καί in imitation of MT. The ὅτι clause reads "because ταῦτα πάντα they did." MT has את כל אלה, and hex has transposed the Greek to agree with the word order of the Hebrew. The apodosis "(and) I abominated them" renders MT literally. V.b might then be rendered: "because they did all these things, I loathed them."

In the tradition, the Byz text has added εν before τοις νομίμοις; this is probably a recensional correction, since MT read בחקת. Hex has added εγω before ἐξαποστέλλω to represent the אני of MT. The A *z*+ reading εξαποστελω is a copyist error through haplography. The future is not used to render the participial predicate of a nominal clause.

20:24 As at 17:14 the *n* text read the Classical second aorist ειπον instead of the Hellenistic εἶπα. In contrast to the pattern: pronoun plus present tense verb rendering the nominal clause, when the Hebrew has a pronoun plus a prefix verbal inflection, LXX represents both literally, i.e. pronoun plus future inflection, thus ὑμεῖς κληρονομήσετε as well as the contrasting ἐγὼ δώσω. The pronouns are discourse markers, and must not be omitted in translation, thus "as for you" ...

---

33. See also THGL 127 for the future as the normal rendering.
34. Theod translated the text of MT literally by ἐν τοῖς ἠκριβασμένοις τοῦ ἔθνους.
35. See also THGL 95.
36. Hesychius cites The Others as reading *quas ejicio ego a facie vestra* (probably translating οὓς ἐξάγω ἐγὼ ἀπὸ προσώπου ὑμῶν).

"as for me." A popular B variant text has the aorist imperative for the first one, κληρονομησατε, but this is secondary.[37]

After "and as for me, I will give it to you as an inheritance," LXX has an interruptive nominative structure, i.e. γῆ ἥτις ἐστὶν ῥέουσα γάλα καὶ μέλι "it is a land which is flowing with milk and honey." The two nouns are used as symbols for productivity of the land. The clause represents a common idiom in the Pentateuch, though this is its only occurrence in Lev. It occurs four times in Exod; see Note at Exod 3:8. That the clause does not fit rhetorically and syntactically into its context easily led to a change to an accusative construction attested in the A B V b n x+ text as γην ρεουσαν instead of γῆ ἥτις ἐστὶν ῥέουσα;[38] in fact, this is precisely how it occurs in the Exod passages.

The long self-identification formula follows, here without an otiose ειμι,[39] but with a relative clause modifier in which the Lord describes himself as "διώρισα you from παντων the nations." MT has no equivalent for πάντων, which was probably added to strengthen Israel's distinctiveness over against other nations. The verb used means to draw a dividing line between, thus to separate from. In the tradition, the Byz text has changed the relative pronoun plus verb to an articulated participle, ο διορισας.

20:25 MT begins with והבדלתם בין "and you shall make a distinction (or divide) between," using the same verb as in the relative clause ending v.24. LXX has an unusual rendering in that it adds an accusative pronoun to the verb, καὶ ἀφοριεῖτε αὐτοὺς ἀνὰ μέσον, and what is meant is not fully clear. First of all, the use of ἀφορίζω to render the Hi of בדל is unusual for Lev. It only occurs twice in this verse, and once in v.26. Elsewhere the verb usually renders the Hi of סגר (nine times). The verb with accusative of person means "to separate, set apart," thus "and you shall set them aside," with ἀνὰ μέσον then being understood as "(separating) between." What the translator has apparently done is to think of הבדלתם in its two senses, that of "separate, set aside," and that of "distinguish (between)." So I would translate "and you shall separate them (i.e. distinguishing) between pure cattle and (between) impure cattle, and between pure and impure birds." MT has "pure" and "impure" in reverse order, and hex has in turn

---

37. See THGL 127.
38. See THGL 122.
39. See THGL 79.

reversed them to agree with MT. MT also has a shorter text, לטמאה, than LXX's καὶ ἀνὰ μέσον τῶν κτηνῶν τῶν ἀκαθάρτων.

The other possible way of understanding ἀφοριεῖτε αὐτοὺς ἀνὰ μέσον is the way many copyists understood it; the F M V b z+ text read εαυτους instead of αὐτούς, whereas the Byz text went a step further towards simplification by the dative εαυτοις. This would probably presuppose that αὐτούς was read as αὑτούς, i.e. as a reflexive pronoun. It would then mean: "And you shall separate for yourselves between." I suspect that the translator intended the first understanding, i.e. with the modifier αὐτούς; it certainly is the more difficult reading.

V.b then goes on to say: "and not must you make yourselves (τὰς ψυχὰς ὑμῶν) loathsome by animals and by birds and by all those things that creep on the ground." The verb βδελύξετε is transitive, as the accusative modifier τὰς ψυχὰς ὑμῶν "your persons (i.e. yourselves)" shows. The ἐν phrases express means or instrument.[40]

The relative clause ending the verse is introduced by a neuter plural accusative pronoun ἅ. Theoretically this should refer to ἑρπετοῖς, which is neuter, though actually all three nouns, κτήνεσιν, πετεινοῖς and ἑρπετοῖς are intended. The neuter was probably chosen to agree with the nearest referent, though the Lev translator did tend to use the neuter when no particular antecedent was intended.[41]

The clause renders הבדלתי by ἐγὼ ἀφώρισα; the hex recension omitted ἐγώ, since it had no correspondent in MT, but the translator probably added it to lay stress on the subject over against ὑμῖν. Once again the verb ἀφορίζω is used, but in the aorist ἀφώρισα; what is being separated, set aside, are the animals, birds and creeping things. MT has a complementary infinitive לטמא, i.e. God has "set these aside for you to treat as unclean," but LXX probably followed the לטמאה of Sam, i.e. as ἐν ἀκαθαρσίᾳ "in uncleanness." The ἐν is probably locative; it states that God set these aside for you in the realm of uncleannness. By such a setting aside, the avoidance of making your person loathsome is circumscribed.

20:26 V.a is similar to 19:2, but differs in the opening καὶ ἔσεσθέ μοι ἅγιοι which follows MT exactly: והייתם לי קדשים; at 19:2 the text reads ἅγιοι ἔσεσθε.

---

40. See SS pp.116—130 on the translation of instrumental ב in the Greek Pentateuch.
41. See Huber on Congruence, pp.33—38, especially p.36.

The addition of μοι stresses the personal relations between God and people, and gives added point to the ὅτι clause; thus even as I, the Lord your God, am separate from all that is profane, i.e., am holy, so you must be separate from all that can defile, all the nations, as well as all uncleanness in creatures "for me." LXX has levelled with 19:2 for the first part of the ὅτι clause, and has actually taken over the entire clause. Over against MT ἐγὼ ἅγιος is transposed, and also taken over from 19:2 is ὁ θεὸς ὑμῶν after κύριος, which has no support in the Hebrew. In the tradition, ἐγώ εἰμι has fared badly, not only in transposing the two words to equal MT, which was certainly recensionally inspired, probably by hex, but also by adding ειμι in various positions; an A F M x+ text has simply added ειμι at the end. Other readings are the popular αγιος ειμι εγω of the Byz text, and the n text's αγιος εγω ειμι.

Unusual over against other examples of ὅτι clauses following a divine self-identification formula is the attributive modifier ὁ ἀφορίσας ὑμᾶς ἀπὸ πάντων τῶν ἐθνῶν εἶναι ἐμοί. Here the root ἀφορίζω comes to its climactic use; the Lord your God is the one who has separated you (i.e. Israel as God's people) from all the nations in order to be his own. Israel is different from all others; she has been chosen to be God's own, and to that end he has set Israel apart. God himself has distinguished Israel from all other people. The Hebrew text had stated this by a coordinate clause, i.e. the articulated participle of LXX has as counterpart in MT ואבדל "and I separated."

20:27 This verse seems oddly displaced, since it is a single statute pertaining to אוב או ידעני. As a conclusion to the section, chapters 18—20, it is inappropriate. The verse begins with "and a man or a woman," which in MT continues with כי יהיה בהם אוב או ידעני "should there be a medium or a wizard among you." For the terms אוב and ידעני, as well as for their translation "ventriloquist (or) charmer," see comments at 19:31. The Greek has made of the כי clause a relative one.[42] For בהם the translator used a genitive αὐτῶν, which with γένηται would be partitive, thus "who would be of them a ventriloquist or a charmer," or more idiomatically "among whom one would be a ventriloquist or a charmer."

The penalty is formulaically expressed, for which see Note at Exod 21:12. The subject ἀμφότεροι has no correspondent in MT; it was probably added

---

42. See THGL 74.

because the verb of the formula יומתו was plural; it could refer to ἀνὴρ ἢ γυνή, which would be difficult to express pronominally, and he levelled with vv.11—13,18 where two individuals were involved. What is meant is "both man or woman," or more idiomatically "either" of the two.[43]

The penalty is described more specifally by λίθοις λιθοβολήσετε αὐτούς. The dative is one of means.[44] In MT the verb is in third person, ירגמו, but LXX follows the second person of Sam. Only two f witnesses actually read λιθοβολισθητωσαν, which would equal MT. A popular A B M variant text has an aorist imperative λιθοβολησατε. Imperatives are rarely used in Lev, and then not at all for prefix inflection verbs, and it must be judged secondary.[45] For ἔνοχοί εἰσιν see comment at v.9.

---

43. Harlé-Pralon render this by "tous les deux."
44. See SS 119—120.
45. See THGL 126—127.

Chapter 21

21:1 The usual formula for introducing a chapter or section is "And the Lord spoke to Moses saying," but here εἶπεν occurs, following MT's ויאמר. The λέγων has no equivalent in MT, and is ex par. But I do not now believe that it is original LXX, even though all the uncial texts support it. λέγων is used throughout to introduce direct speech in the same way that לאמר is used. But εἶπον τοῖς κ.τ.λ. is not really what the Lord wanted to convey. The real message comes in what is to be said to the priests, and follows πρὸς αὐτούς. The majority text also omits the λέγων, and if one examines the mss which omit the word no picture of recensional activity emerges; note the odd combination oII C' f s x+; the omission is not hex, nor is it Byz, neither of which support the shorter text. I would now consider λέγων to be a secondary gloss.

The command to Moses that follows is repetitious: "say to the priests ... and you shall say to them," but this follows MT exactly, which uses the root אמר three times.

Those who are to receive the instructions are τοῖς ἱερεῦσιν τοῖς υἱοῖς Ἀαρών, i.e. the Aaronid priests. In the tradition, an F V majority text omits the second article, but the article must be original.[1] The Byz text transposes "the priests" after "the Aaronids," as the more usual order, but Lev follows MT and is original text. The order to the priests is at first blush strange. It reads ἐν ταῖς ψυχαῖς οὐ μιανθήσονται ἐν τῷ ἔθνει αὐτῶν; I would take the first ἐν as instrumental, and the second one as locative. Furthermore, the section makes it clear that the individuals (or persons) involved are according to v.11 ψυχῇ τετελευτηκυίᾳ. What is meant then is that the Aaronid priests "may not be defiled by dead persons among their people." MT has the order in the singular לנפש לא יטמא בעמיו, though the noun עמיו is plural, which is odd, and the ancient witnesses including Sam Tar^ON and Pesh all attest to עמו. The LXX's plural αὐτῶν is based on the antecedent τοῖς ἱερεῦσιν τοῖς υἱοῖς Ἀαρών. This is clear from the contrast which follows in vv.2–3.

21:2–3 Here the ψυχαῖς with whom the Aaronid priests might defile themselves are listed; these are defined as (ἀλλ' ἢ) ἐν τῷ οἰκείῳ τῷ ἔγγιστα αὐτῶν "with the

---
1. See THGL 84.

relative who is the nearest of them," αὐτῶν referring to the Aaronid priests. This is inconsistent throughout these verses, since in v.3 the singular obtains both in αὐτῷ and the verb μιανθήσεται, but common sense dictates that the relative is of an Aaronid, just as in v.3. The plural αὐτῶν can hardly refer to ψυχαῖς. The introductory conjunction ἀλλ' ἤ indicates contrast, listing exceptions to the general rule about not allowing oneself to be defiled by contact with a corpse. These concern the following: father, mother, sons, daughters, brother and virgin sister. In MT all are introduced by the preposition ל, and then are all joined by conjunctions. Thus "with mother and with father and with sons, etc." LXX does not render the ל by ἐν as was done for לנפש in v.1 and לשארו in v.2, but by ἐπί, and omits the preposition if the conjunction was translated; in other words, never does και επι occur, but either the one or the other does; ἐπί occurs only before the first item identifying οἰκείῳ and before "brother."[2] Furthermore, the first two are transposed; instead of לאמו ולאביו LXX reads ἐπὶ πατρὶ καὶ μητρί. Hex has transposed the two to agree with MT. It should also be noted that each member in the list has the third masculine singular suffix in the Hebrew, all of which are unrepresented in LXX.[3] Hex has in every case but ἀδελφῷ added αυτου to represent the suffix. In each case hex has seen to it that και επ(ι) precedes each member of the list (except of course the first one which would have no και before it).

The "virgin sister," which ends the list, is further described as τῇ ἐγγιζούσῃ αὐτῷ τῇ μὴ ἐκδεδομένῃ ἀνδρί "the one who is near to him, not having been given to a man." The sister remained in the father's household as long as she remained unmarried; once she has been married she is no longer ἐγγιζούσῃ αὐτῷ; she belongs to the household of her husband.

Finally, the rule is given: ἐπὶ τούτοις μιανθήσεται "for these he may be defiled."[4] In MT the prepositional phrase applies only to the sister: לה, "for her (he may be defiled)." LXX has made it apply to the entire list. Actually the Hebrew does intend this as well. The כי אם of v.2 may be translated by "except for," i.e. the list in v.2 is excepted. But v.3 deals only with the unmarried sister, and so v.3b is made to apply only to the sister.

---

2. See THGL 104.
3. See SS 96.
4. For the potential nature of the future tense see Porter, ch.9 "The Future Form: Tense, Aspect or Mood," especially pp.411–426.

21:4 MT says "he shall not defile himself בעל בעמיו להחל". The term בעל means "master" or "husband," but here its meaning is quite uncertain, since it is used absolutely.⁵ The infinitive is a Ni of חלל with the suffix referring to בעל, i.e. to the same referent as in עמיו.⁶ The translator also found בעל difficult; he has in its slot the adverb ἐξάπινα "suddenly, unexpectedly," possibly reading something like (כ)בלע "as a swallowing," occurring at Num 4:20, which the Greek also translates by ἐξάπινα. The root בלע "to swallow, engulf" does have the notion of "suddenness, momentariness" about it, and may have been in the mind of the translator. He also read בעמיו as a singular noun: ἐν τῷ λαῷ αὐτοῦ with Sam. As for the infinitive "that he should be rendered profane," LXX created a neologism βεβήλωσιν "profanation." What is meant by ἐξάπινα is something accidental, which would in other situations lead to his profanation. It is not his own fault; it was unexpected, accidental, and so did not result in a change in his devoted status, i.e. he does not become profane; comp v.6.

21:5 LXX follows Sam in beginning the verse with καί. MT has the verse in third person plural, which is consistent with its context, but LXX makes the first clause second person plural; the Byz text changes the verb to ξυρησονται to equal MT. MT has its verb modified by a cognate noun, קרחה, and a prepositional phrase, בראשם, i.e. "not may they (i.e. the priests) shave a bald spot on their head." LXX understood "shaving a bald spot" to refer to the practice spoken of in Dt 14:1 οὐκ ἐπιθήσεται φαλάκρωμα ἀνὰ μέσον τῶν ὀφθαλμῶν ὑμῶν ἐπὶ νεκρῷ, adding the ἐπὶ νεκρῷ from the Dt passage against MT at the end of the clause as an explanatory gloss for shaving the head by making a bald spot for a dead person. The translator may well have had the prohibition of Dt 14:1: ולא תשימו קרחה בין עיניכם למת in mind, particularly the למת. This notion was naturally propelled by vv.1—4, which referred to impurity created by involvement with dead relatives.

With the second clause the translator reverted to third person. For τὴν ὄψιν τοῦ πώγωνος rendering פאת זקנים see comment at 19:27. Hex has added αυτων to represent the untranslated suffix of MT.⁷

---

5. Tar^J understood it in the sense of "husband": לא יסתאב בעלא לאיתתיה. Rashi explains the passage in a similar way, i.e. as לא יטמא לאשתו פסולה, i.e. "for a disqualified wife."
6. See GK 67t.
7. The anonymous reading τὸ φααθ to represent פאת must be that of Theod; see f.n. at 19:27.

The last clause forbids cutting "gashes in their flesh." For understanding this passage see the discussion at 19:28. MT has a cognate structure: ישרטו שרטת, presumably reading the noun as plural. The translator disregarded the cognates in favor of the clear statement κατατεμοῦσιν ἐντομίδας.

21:6 That the priests "must be holy to their God" is to be understood in the context of mourning rituals for the dead (vv.1—5). The rules for remaining pure are to ensure that they will remain holy, i.e. set aside for the cultic activities in the service of their God, and avoid anything which might lead εἰς βεβήλωσιν, v.4.

Negatively put, "they may not profane the name of their God." By "the name" is meant "the reputation." So what this intends is that the priests must avoid any action which would reflect unfavorably on their God's reputation, both within Israel and among the nations. That reputation must remain holy, may not be rendered common, either by action or by speech; comp Exod 20:7 Dt 5:11.

That these rules involve the priests in their cultic activities is clear from the γάρ clause. For θυσίας as a translation for אשי see comments at 1:9. The nominal clause הם מקריבם is translated by the usual Greek pattern of pronoun plus a present tense verb, αὐτοὶ προσφέρουσιν.[8] Here the present tense as showing a continual process is particularly appropriate in showing the usual activity of the priests: "because they are sacrificing the sacrifices of the Lord as δῶρα of their God." The term δῶρα "gifts" has לחם "food" as its counterpart in MT. The same rendering occurs at vv.8,17,21,22 and 22:25.[9] At 3:11 לחם as a reference to sacrifice was rendered by ὀσμὴν εὐωδίας. The term לחם also occurs (as part of a sacrifice) at 3:16 where it is apparently omitted, i.e. κάρπωμα appears for לחם אשה in LXX. At 7:13(3) and 8:26 the term is omitted by LXX. The word ἄρτον does appear twice at 8:26, but as a rendering for חלת. The word also occurs at 23:17,20, but there the word means "loaves," and is translated by the plural ἄρτων/ἄρτους. It is clear that Lev avoided assiduously the notion of a sacrifice being designated as food, i.e. bread, for God. The term δῶρα is completely neutral; sacrifices are "gifts" for God; they are not food for God, which in an Egyptian context would be a dangerous notion. The term δῶρα occurs in Lev (and Num) as the usual rendering for קרבן, also a general, neutral term for all kinds of sacrifices.

---

8. For the pattern see THGL 95.
9. For a discussion of God's לחם see Daniel 139—141.

Whether the final word ἅγιοι reflects a parent קדש with MT, or קדשים with Sam cannot be determined, After all, how else would LXX render וֹהיו קדש?

21:7 Priests may not marry a "harlotrous and defiled woman" nor "a woman cast out (i.e. divorced) by her husband." MT repeats לא יקחו after "her husband" as well; this is clearer, since what I rendered by "nor" is actually καί/ו. Hex has supplied ου λήψονται so as to equal MT. The participle ἐκβεβλημένην is modified by a ὑπό of personal agent structure, "by her husband." An A B Byz+ text has changed the preposition to απο. MT has מאישה, and the απο is a crass literalism, an unfortunate recensional correction.[10]

This is followed by a ὅτι clause detailing the raison d'etre for the prohibition; it is "because he (i.e. such a one, a priest) is holy to the Lord his God." Actually an A B M V x+ text omits the ὅτι, but this could not be original text. The Lev translator may at times add ὅτι or γάρ to make explicit a relation between two clauses only implicit in Hebrew, but he does not normally reverse the process, i.e. make implicit such a relation which is explicitly expressed in MT.[11] Also in the tradition is the variant articulation of κυρίῳ, either by transposition of κυρίῳ τῷ as in A B+, or by prefixing an article to κυρίῳ as in F V+. The former could not be original text, since an unarticulated θεῷ never occurs in Lev, whereas the latter's support is too ephemeral to be seriously considered.[12] MT does not even support κυρίῳ, simply reading לאלהיו. It should be mentioned, however, that κυρίῳ is supported by all witnesses in the tradition.

21:8 MT reads וקדשתו "and you must treat him as holy," which LXX changes to third person καὶ ἁγιάσει αὐτόν. The majority text has changed the verb to αγιασεις, but this can not be original; rather it is a recensional change. For Lev it is not the people (i.e. those who are being addressed), as in MT, but the subject in LXX is the Lord.[13] MT retains the second masculine singular throughout up to the final כי clause in which the suffix of the participle is second masculine plural. LXX has the third singular here, but changes the pronoun in the final clause to the plural αὐτούς. LXX simply levels with the context, since, except for the first

---
10. See THGL 78.
11. See THGL 115.
12. See THGL 80.
13. For a fuller discussion of the LXX over against MT see THGL 124—125.

clause in v.5, it is consistently third person. The change to a consistent third person reference also avoids the possible misunderstanding that the people would sanctify the priest; of course, MT did not intend that interpretation, but rather as "consider as holy." In LXX it is God who sanctifies the priest.

MT follows the initial וקדשתו with a כי clause, i.e. "because he offers up the food of your God." LXX does not translate the כי at all, rendering the clause as τὰ δῶρα κυρίου τοῦ θεοῦ ὑμῶν οὗτος προσφέρει.[14] For δῶρα see comment at v.6. MT has no correspondent to κυρίου, and the b text omits it, probably under the influence of one of The Three. LXX does change to second plural with its ὑμῶν modifying θεοῦ, whereas MT has אלהיך.

MT follows this with קדש יהיה לך, of which LXX only translates the first two words, thereby avoiding a second person reference. Hex added σοι to represent the לך;[15] this makes for an odd text indeed; note the consecution: ὑμῶν ... σοι ... αὐτούς; Origen paid little attention to context, but simply applied a quantitative norm; since לך had no equivalent in Lev he added σοι, even though this did not fit in the context. The basis for "he must be holy" is given in a ὅτι clause: "because I, the Lord who sanctifies them, am holy." MT has a second instead of a third person pronoun, but LXX follows the מקדשם of Sam, which is also supported by 11QLev.[16]

21:9 The verse is introduced by a pendant nominative, καὶ θυγάτηρ ἀνθρώπου ἱερέως, thus "and as for the daughter of a priest." The ἀνθρώπου represents איש; neither is necessary for sense; it is similar in usage to the indefinite article in English, hence "of a priest." The conditional structure then follows in a general condition in present time, i.e. the protasis consists of ἐάν plus a subjunctive, and the apodosis has its verb in the present tense. The subjunctive is modified by an articulated infinitive showing what the verbal notion of the subjunctive consisted of. The protasis may be rendered: "if she should be defiled through acting as a prostitute."

The apodosis translates a nominal clause היא מחללת in the usual way by a pronoun plus a present tense: αὕτη βεβηλοῖ. The Hebrew preposes a modifier את

---

14. According to Hesychius, The Others read *quia panes dei tui ipse offeret* (sic!), which would probably represent ὅτι ἄρτους τοῦ θεοῦ σου οὗτος προσφέρει (surely not future!).
15. As did The Others.
16. See Freedman 531.

אביה "her father," which LXX modified by inserting "the name of," i.e. τὸ ὄνομα τοῦ πατρὸς αὐτῆς. This specifies in greater detail how she has defiled her father; it is not the father whom she is defiling, but rather it's his reputation that she has besmirched, and so the penalty "ἐπὶ πυρός she shall be burned." The preposition is instrumental.[17]

21:10 Vv.10—15 consist of regulations for the high priest. The use of an adjective plus מן is the most common way by which Hebrew expresses the comparative degree. The construction הכהן הגדול מאחיו means "the priest who is greater than his brothers," a descriptive way of referring to the high priest. The translator has translated this by ὁ ἱερεὺς ὁ μέγας ἀπὸ τῶν ἀδελφῶν αὐτοῦ, but this simply means "the priest who is great among his brothers,[18] which serves as a nominative pendant. The αὐτοῦ is then described as τοῦ ἐπικεχυμένου ἐπὶ τὴν κεφαλὴν τοῦ ἐλαίου τοῦ χριστοῦ (καὶ τετελειωμένου).[19] This serves as a pseudo genitive absolute costruction, thus "on whose head the oil of anointing had been poured, and who been ordained ...." LXX did not render the suffix of ראשו, which is taken for granted as the suggested translation indicates; but the Byz text supplied an αυτου; this is clearly a recensional correction. Syntactically the genitive singular participles are in apposition to αὐτοῦ.

The second participle, τετελειωμένου, is a free rendering of מלא את ידו, "has filled his hand," a Hebrew idiom for "was ordained,"[20] and for the participle see the translation in the preceding paragraph. The translator concentrated on the root מלא, not rendering את ידו by itself; it is this idiom which is rendered by the participle. Hex has added τας χειρας αυτου to represent the modifier separately. For the underlying notion see the comment on τελειώσεως rendering למלואים at 7:27(37). The participle is modified by a complementary infinitive, ἐνδύσασθαι, thus "ordained to don the garments." By τὰ ἱμάτια are meant the high-priestly garments referred to in 8:7—9.

With reference to his attire, "he may not remove the turban from the head and his garments he may not tear," for which orders see comments at 10:6. For ἀποκιδαρώσει as rendering for יפרע also see comment at 10:6.

---

17. See SS 117.
18. See SS 148—149.
19. Aq read ᾧ ἐπεχύθη ἐπὶ κεφαλὴν αὐτοῦ ἔλαιον ἀλείμματος (retroverted from Syh).
20. See SS 88.

In the tradition, the majority M V text has substituted αγια for ἱμάτια 1°, possibly on the understanding that the high priest put on more than ἱμάτια, but also the ephod, the breastpiece, turban and the diadem; cf 8:7—9, thus "ordained to wear the holy things," but the Hebrew has הבגדים. On the other hand, the ατια of ἱμάτια could easily be misread as αγια, since T-Γ are easily confused. Hex also added αυτου to τὴν κεφαλήν 2°, since MT has את ראשו. The second τὰ ἱμάτια represents בגדיו, and accordingly, hex has added αυτου here as well to translate the suffix.

21:11 LXX states "he (i.e. the high priest) may not enter ἐπὶ πάσῃ ψυχῇ τετελευτηκυίᾳ, i.e. "to any person that has died." MT has a plural noun נפשת, but the singular is an improvement, and must be what MT also intended. Obviously the priest could not enter in to all dead people, and the translator astutely made this clear. The regulation makes the prohibition absolute as over against the Aaronid priests; cf vv.2—5.

In practical terms this means "not may he be defiled with his father nor with his mother." For the use of ἐπί governing the dative to translate ל to express "contact with," see comment at vv.2—3.

21:12 MT states "and from the sanctuary he shall not go out." What is meant is that the high priest must remain in the sanctuary in the context of a death; he might profane it. This is clear from the next clause: "and he shall not profane the sanctuary of his God." The translator avoids translating the two cases of מקדש in the same way, but he does it in strange fashion. At 20:3 he had translated מקדשי "my sanctuary" by τὰ ἅγιά μου, and here he uses the same word "καὶ ἐκ τῶν ἁγίων he may not go out." Presumably the translator has in mind the two parts of the sanctuary, the holy place and the adytum, hence the plural noun, "the holy places." It must then refer to the sanctuary as a whole, i.e. "the holy (areas)."

The second reference to מקדש is rendered by τὸ ἡγιασμένον in the context of "and not may he profane τὸ ἡγιασμένον of his God." Note that in a similar context at 20:3 reference is made to "profane the name of קדשי," which LXX translated by τῶν ἡγιασμένων μοι; cf comments ad loc. Here, however, the passive participle is neuter singular, i.e. "the sanctified place"; it too refers to the sanctuary. What is not said is by what agency the place has been sanctified; this is described in the concluding verses of Exod; see 40:28—32. The translator may well have read מקדש as a passive participle.

The basis for this isolation of the high priest is given in a ὅτι/כי clause. The Hebrew states that "the נזר of the anointing oil of his God is on him." The word means "consecration," and the cognate verb means "to dedicate, consecrate, separate."[21] It denotes something distinctive; the anointing oil has placed the high priest separate from all that might defile. It is this then that justifies the LXX's interpretation of the word by the attribute ἅγιον, in τὸ ἅγιον ἔλαιον τὸ χριστόν "the holy anointing oil." This oil is holy, i.e. it is set apart, dedicated to a special use. The rendering of נזר by ἅγιοι only occurs once elsewhere in OT in the obscure λίθοι ἅγιοι κυλίονται ἐπὶ τῆς γῆς αὐτοῦ at Zech 9:16, where MT has אבני נזר מתנוססות על אדמתו. The anointing oil had the effect of isolating the high priest from all that might defile.[22] The verse ends with ἐγὼ κύριος, to which the Byz text has added the gloss ο θεος.

21:13 MT begins paratactically, but LXX does not. Hex has apparently added και to introduce the verse, thereby equalling MT. The verse details whom the high priest may marry. MT simply has אשה בבתוליה "a woman in her virginity," which LXX simplifies by γυναῖκα παρθένον. LXX has amplified this in turn by ἐκ τοῦ γένους αὐτοῦ, which was factually correct, since the phrase does occur in v.14 with which it levels; there the legitimate candidate is called בתולה מעמיו. Hex has correctly placed the ἐκ phrase under the obelus to indicate its absence from MT.

21:14 MT begins asyndetically, but LXX uses a contrastive δέ. V.13 had stated whom he might marry; this verse lists those whom he may not marry, and the δέ is appropriate. These are χήραν "a widow," ἐκβεβλημένην "a divorcee"—cf comment at v.7, βεβηλωμένην "one who is defiled," and πόρνην "a harlot." MT has no "and," but LXX follows Sam's וזנה. ταύτας is recapitulatory, referring to the list, which he may not take (in marriage). At v.7 the last two items are also joined, though in reverse order. They differ in that βεβηλωμένην refers to a virgin who has been defiled, i.e. has had her virginity destroyed, possibly through rape, whereas the πόρνην is a prostitute, one who trades her wares for gain.

---

21. See the extensive word study in Harlé-Pralon on this word.
22. For the ὅτι clause Aq has ὅτι ἀφόρισμα ἔλαιον ἀλείμματος θεοῦ αὐτοῦ ἐπ' αὐτῷ. Sym translates ὅτι ἄθικτον ἔλαιον τοῦ χρίσματος τοῦ θεοῦ αὐτοῦ ἐπ' αὐτῷ, and Theod renders ὅτι τὸ ναζερ ἔλαιον τὸ χριστὸν παρὰ θεοῦ αὐτοῦ ἐπ' αὐτῷ.

V.b is adversative; "but a virgin from his clan (γένους) he may take as wife." MT has מעמיו, and presumably LXX read מעמו of Sam as parent text, but the choice of γένους is intentionally limiting; the translator was probably aware of the tradition that the bride of a high priest was not to be any Israelite woman; she had to be of priestly descent, i.e. of his tribe, and so not εθνους, or λαου as in B x+, but γένους.

21:15 The high priest "may not defile his seed among his people," which, were he to marry one of the prohibited candidates for marriage, would happen. After all, the male seed of the high priest would be priests in turn, and priests born of such a marriage would be cultically illegitimate. In MT this prohibition is rooted in the fact that God is יהוה מקדשו. The translator rendered this as an independent clause. The Byz text did translate the כי by adding οτι before ἐγώ; the οτι is probably recensional in origin. To MT the high priest may not defile his seed "because I am Yahweh, the one sanctifying him." LXX treats the self-identification formula in the popular fashion. In chh.18—26 the formula occurs 49 times, but only eight times is it in a ὅτι clause; 41 times it is given asyndetically. I doubt that LXX omitted כי intentionally; it is simply a case of ex par. What is important about the formula here is that the Lord calls himself ὁ ἁγιάζων αὐτόν. The Lord has sanctified the high priest, set him aside to a separate rank in which he must be holy, because the Lord himself is holy.

21:17 V.16 had said "and the Lord spoke to Moses saying," and then continues in v.17 with דבר אל אהרן לאמר, but LXX simply has εἶπον 'Ααρών "say to Aaron." More commonly דבר would be rendered by λαλησον. This is the only instance where the dative 'Ααρών is not articulated in the book,[23] but comp 22:2. Hex has added λεγων to represent לאמר, as well as inserted προς before 'Ααρών, thereby equalling MT.

The subject ἄνθρωπος is modified by a partitive ἐκ phrase,[24] ἐκ τοῦ γένους σου "out of your tribe," which renders מזרעך "from your seed." זרע is usually rendered by σπέρμα (198 times), and by γένος only eight times,[25] but it is fitting here, since the reference is to the priestly tribe. This is followed by εἰς τὰς

---

23. See THGL 81.
24. See SS 167.
25. The count is that of Dos Santos.

γενεὰς ὑμῶν, which is peculiar, since the pronoun is now plural. The σου had referred to ἄνθρωπος, but ὑμῶν is barely sensible. It may well be based on a careless reading of לדרתם as לדרתכם. It is more likely, however, that it is ex par. Exactly the same phrase occurs nine times elsewhere in Lev (3:17 6:18 10:9 17:7 22:3 23:14,21,41 24:3). The V 72 text has changed it to αυτων, which equals MT. This may, however, not be recensional at all, but a change simply based on good sense. In Lev ὑμῶν must be a reference to γένους, i.e. as though not just ἄνθρωπος but the entire tribe is being addressed.

The important modifier is, however, the relative clause: τίνι ἐὰν ᾖ ἐν αὐτῷ μῶμος "to someone in whom there might be a blemish." What is meant is, should there be some priestly descendant in the future who has some kind of blemish on his body; such a one "may not approach to sacrifice τὰ δῶρα of his God." "To approach" means to come near to the altar where the sacrifices are offered. For "gifts" rendering לחם see discussion at v.6.[26]

In the tradition, the n text has stylistically improved the odd τίνι ἐὰν ᾖ by ος εχει. Also stylistically motivated is the M oI C' s+ text reading ωτινι for τινι.

21:18—20 What is meant by having a μῶμος is illustratively defined. The prohibition is restated, i.e. "no person in whom there is a blemish may approach"; in MT this is introduced by כי, and hex has added οτι under the asterisk before πᾶς to represent it. Its omission by LXX may have been due to a failure to see what כי could mean. If it means "because," it is not overly sensible. After all, it simply restates what v.17 had said, viz. that any member of the priestly class who had a bodily blemish may not serve at the altar. I would suggest that the כי should here be understood as an emphatic particle, asseverative in meaning. It restates the rule, and then gives a list of blemished individuals who may not serve at the altar. Note the Hebraism by which the ᾧ clause contains ἐν αὐτῷ to reproduce the בו of MT.

The rule is followed by twelve such types. The first four are ἄνθρωπος χωλός or τυφλός or κολοβόριν or ὠτότμητος "a lame person, or blind, or one with a slit nose, or with an ear slit." These do not correspond exactly to MT. The first two are transposed, and the majority F V M text has retransposed them to

---

26. The Others read τοὺς ἄρτους.

equal the order of MT; this is probably a hex correction. The third word in MT is חרם, a passive participle which means "mutilated or slit." It is not limited to the nose, but may refer to ears or lips as well. It is, however, a hapax legomenon. The fourth is שׂרוע of uncertain meaning. It is thought to be from a root meaning "to extend," hence one with an extended or overly long limb, but this is quite uncertain. See also 22:23. The translator apparently did not know the word either, and contextualized, making the third one with a mutilated nose, and this one with a mutilated ear.

V.19 lists two more who are unfit for service at the altar. These are individuals with a fractured hand or foot. The word for "individuals" is the general word ἄνθρωπος rather than ἀνήρ both here and in v.18. In MT איש occurs. The terms are simply used for class designation, and in English are best omitted entirely or simply rendered by "an individual." MT has יהיה as verb in the relative clause, i.e. "a man in whom there would be ...." LXX has ᾧ ἐστιν, and hex corrects the verb to εσται. Most witnesses, however, witness to η, a stylistic change to the subjunctive "in whom there might be." The Byz text adds εν before the relative ᾧ, but then retains ἐν αὐτῷ, i.e. makes only a partial improvement in the Greek. Hex also corrects the order of the two, i.e. transposes χειρός and ποδός to equal the Hebrew order.

V.20 lists the remaining defects. The first one, גבן, is a hapax legomenon, usually understood to mean "hunch-backed," as is its translation, κυρτός. The second is דק, an adjective meaning "thin, fine," so probably "withered," possibly referring to someone unnaturally thin. LXX has ἔφειλος which refers to some eye disease in which white specks appear, resulting in blurred vision.[27] The third defective is תבלל (בעינו). The word appears only here, but may be related to תבל "confusion," for which see comment at 18:23. It is in the eye, and must mean bad vision of some kind, possibly blurred vision. LXX has πτίλος τοὺς ὀφθαλμούς, an inflamation with respect to the eyes.[28]

V.b lists three more defects: גרב או ילפת או מרוח אשך. For גרב translated by ψώρα ἀγρία "wild or severe itch," see Note at Dt 28:27, where גרב is translated by the same phrase in the dative. Since the adjectival phrase renders a single word in the Hebrew hex has placed ἀγρία under the obelus. This is followed by ילפת, which occurs only here and at 22:22, and is a skin disease of some kind.

---

27. Aq had a similar understanding: ὑπόχυμα "cataract."
28. The Others have λεύκωμα ἐν ὀφθαλμοῖς; cf LXX's ἔφειλος for the previous defect.

Lev translates by λειχήν. The word means "lichen," so here presumably a lichen-like eruption on the skin. Note the Vulg's *impetiginem in corpore*. The last defect concerns the testicles. מרוח is a hapax legomenon, and its meaning is not certain. The root מרח means "to rub," thus a rubbing, i.e. a crushing(?) of the testicles. LXX interprets by μόνορχις "having a single testicle."

21:21 V.21 restates the rule as a summary statement, i.e. "no one in whom there is a blemish from Aaron the priest's seed may come near to offer τὰς θυσίας τῷ θεῷ σου."[29] MT reads אשי יהוה. For τὰς θυσίας translating אשי see comment at 1:9. Since MT begins with כל איש hex has added ανθρωπος after πᾶς. The substitution of τῷ θεῷ σου for יהוה is unexpected. The majority text, inspired by hex, substitutes κυριω. What is puzzling is who is intended by σου. It can hardly be Aaron, since he is referred to in third person. The translator apparently addresses Israel as a people, but this too is unusual, since the entire section is in third person; in fact, I can find no convincing explanation for the switch to second person singular in the middle of a prohibition for a priest with a physical defect to serve at the altar "to your God." But the text must be original, since no reviser would change an original κυριω to a contextually inappropriate τῷ θεῷ σου.

The next clause is introduced by ὅτι, i.e. "because there is a blemish in him." MT has no equivalent to ὅτι, simply stating: מום בו. The addition of ὅτι merely makes explicit the implicit relations within the text. MT makes the first cut in the verse before מום, i.e. יהוה is marked by an *ethnach*. The ὅτι clause is also to be taken with what follows rather than with v.a, thus "because there is a blemish on him, the δῶρα τοῦ θεοῦ he may not approach to sacrifice." The infinitive details the purpose of the approach. For δῶρα as interpretation of לחם, see discussion at v.6. LXX does not translate the suffix of אלהיו,[30] but hex has supplied an αυτου.

21:22 For τὰ δῶρα see discussion at v.6. LXX does not render the suffix of אלהיו, but as in v.21, which see, hex has added αυτου to represent it. In MT "the food of his God" is modified by two partitive coordinate מן phrases.[31] What Lev says is quite different from MT. Lev breaks up the verse into two separate,

---

29. Instead of πᾶς ᾧ ἐστιν The Others read πᾶς ἀνὴρ ᾧ ἐστιν.
30. See SS 97.
31. See SS 165—166.

though coordinate, clauses. V.a becomes a nominal clause which identifies the gifts (MT: food) of God as being most holy; then v.b becomes a verbal clause. Lev states that "the gifts of God are most holy, and he may eat (only) the holy things," i.e. the gifts of God are sacrifices; these he may not eat, but of the holy things which belong to the priests he may eat. After all, the δῶρα of their God priests must sacrifice (vv.6,8,21); LXX has tried to rationalize what the priests may eat, by excluding the לחם אלהיו. Actually priests were allowed to eat the very holy sacrifices, but the δῶρα of God in LXX when rendering לחם is never allowed as priestly food. In the tradition, the majority F M text has added αυτου after θεοῦ; this is probably hex in origin since MT has אלהיו.

21:23 Though he may eat of the priestly portions he may not perform cultic duties; "he may neither go to the curtain, nor approach the altar, because μῶμον ἔχει." LXX here renders מום בו in good Greek: "he has a blemish."[32]

V.b in MT says "and not may he profane את מקדשי," i.e. "my sanctuaries." LXX interprets this as τὸ ἅγιον τοῦ θεοῦ αυτοῦ.[33] The translator avoids any notion of plural sanctuaries by translating the noun as τὸ ἅγιον "the holy (place)," and used "of his God," as at v.12.

The raison d'etre for thse prohibitions is given in a ὅτι clause; it is "because I am the Lord who sanctifies them." In MT the suffix of מקדשם refers to the plural מקדשי; in LXX this is no longer possible, since αὐτούς can not refer to τὸ ἅγιον; it must refer to those Aaronids who have blemishes.

In the tradition, the hex text has omitted εἰμι, since it has no express counterpart in MT.

21:24 The content of this verse is usually at the beginning of a section, but here it is apparently a subscription, probably to chh.17—21; it is, however, not the Lord who is speaking, but Moses; cf 17:2. There Moses had been commanded to speak to the three: Aaron, his sons and all the Israelites. This verse is appropriate in saying that Moses had now carried out that initial command. In MT וידבר is modified by three אל phrases, "to Aaron, and to his sons, and to all the Israelites." The Greek does not repeat πρός for the middle one. The *b* text,

---

32. See SS 185 for the use of ἔχει.
33. The Others read τὸ ἁγίασμά <μου>. It should be noted that they read מקדשי as a singular noun.

however, adds προς there as well to equal MT, and this was probably mediated through one of The Three.

τοὺς υἱούς occurs twice in the verse, and a number of mss, including cod B, omit the article for the second instance. Usually the accusative plural of υἱός is articulated; in fact, out of 23 cases of υἱούς in Lev, only twice (both in 10:4) does the unarticulated noun appear. The remaining three have τούς in the majority text, and the articulated noun must be original here as well.[34]

---

34. For a detailed study of the articulation of the plural υἱοί see THGL 84—85.

Chapter 22

22:2 In imitation of 21:17 LXX reads εἶπον (Ἀαρών), though MT reads דבר. Since MT reads אל אהרן, hex has added πρός under the asterisk before "Aaron." The Aaronids are directed to deal carefully. The verb is προσεχέτωσαν, which occurs only here in OT as a rendering for ינזרו (Ni), but this is probably what the Hebrew intends; after all, the root נזר does not occur often in MT (only four times in Ni, and six, in Hi). It is usually understood in the sense of "to separate" in a cultic sense, so in the Ni "to separate oneself." What is unusual is modification of προσέχω by an ἀπό phrase, but this is well-attested in the sense of "be on one's guard against," e.g. Mt 7:15 Lk 20:46 and comp 12:1.[1] It was undoubtedly chosen to represent the מן of MT. So LXX warns against the possible misuse of the holy things of the Israelites; the holy things are the sacrifices which the Israelites bring to the Lord. Presumably meant by the warning is the eating of the sacrifices devoted to the Lord. The warning is then explicated in the verses that follow (vv.3—16; for the priests more particularly, vv.3—9).

The verb in the second clause is future, and not third person imperative as in the first clause. This change is intended to relate the two clauses, so that the second one shows the reason for the first one. The priests are warned not to misuse the holy things ..., "and so they will not profane my holy name." What is meant is that by not misusing the sacrifices, the priests will avoid profaning the Lord's holy name. The adjectival phrase renders a bound phrase of MT: שם קדשי.[2] An M V O cII s+ text actually has the genitive του αγιου instead of τὸ ἅγιον, which would be a more literal rendering, but I suspect this is merely a leveling with v.32 where the phrase occurs in a similar context.

The relative clause which follows represents a nominal clause in MT, which LXX, as usual, renders by a pronoun αὐτοί plus a present tense verb ἁγιάζουσιν; what is relatively unusual in such a construction is the third person.[3] The ὅσα refers to τῶν ἁγίων, i.e. the holy sacrifices "which they dedicate to me." The short self-identification formula which concludes the verse authenticates what has been said.

---

1. See Bauer sub voce 1.b, and Bl-D 149, f.n.2.
2. See SS 65.
3. See THGL 95.

22:3 Vv.3—9 interpret v.2 as it concerns the Aaronids. Its importance is made clear by the introductory εἶπον αὐτοῖς. What Moses is to say is a dire warning: "throughout your generations any person ἀπό your seed who might approach the holy things which the Israelites ἁγιάζωσιν to the Lord, and his impurity is on him, that individual will be destroyed from me." The ἀπό is clearly partitive.[4] The use of a present subjunctive in the relative clause is rare. Since the aorist subjunctive is the default, when the present occurs it is intended in a linear sense.[5] I would translate "which the Israelites might be consecrating to the Lord."

What is meant by "his impurity is on him" is explicated in the verses that follow.

MT introduces the penalty by a conjunction, which the translator (fortunately) disregarded. Hex, however, added και before ἐξολεθρευθήσεται to represent it. Instead of ἀπ' ἐμοῦ the Byz text has απο προσωπου μου, which must be recensional, since MT has מלפני. The verse ends with the long form of the self-identification formula, though MT simply has אני יהוה. Hex is probably the source of the popular omission of ὁ θεὸς ὑμῶν. The formula authenticates the penalty; that person will be destroyed ἀπ ἐμοῦ. One might have expected "before me," but the ἀπό renders the *mem* of מלפני. The modification of ἐξολεθρευθήσεται by an ἀπό phrase is unique in OT; it is only modified by ἐκ phrases; see Gen 17:14 Exod 12:15,19 30:33 31:14 Lev 17:4,9 23:29 Num 9:13 15:30 19:20.

22:4 MT begins with איש איש מזרע, which LXX renders by καὶ ἄνθρωπος ἐκ τοῦ σπέρματος.[6] איש איש occurs 10 times in the book; only here is it rendered by a single ἄνθρωπος (and once by τις, at 20:2), but eight times it is rendered by ἄνθρωπος ἄνθρωπος. O Syh add another ανθρωπος here, i.e. it is a hex correction.[7]

The limiting clause has it that that one λεπρᾷ ἢ γονορρυής "has leprosy or is a spermatorrheic."[8] For an understanding of the former see comment at 13:2; for the latter, see comment at 15:4. Why the translator should have chosen the verb λεπράω rather than the usual adjective λεπρός is not clear. This is its only

---

4. See SS 166.
5. See THGL 125.
6. Sym adopts the text of LXX, but Theod and Aq read ανὴρ ἀνὴρ ἀπὸ σπέρματος.
7. See THGL 122.
8. Theod Aq have λεπρὸς ἢ ῥέων; Sym has λεπρὸς ἢ γονορρυής.

occurrence in the OT for the Qal of the root צרע. The verb also occurs twice at Num 12:10 for the Pu participle מצרעת where it describes Miriam's condition. In any event, in neither state may he eat of the holy things (i.e. the portions reserved from the sacrifices for the priests) until he were purified. A popular A text, supported by the fourth century papyrus 931, actually reads λεπρος instead of λεπρᾷ.

V.b together with v.5 describes other forms of impurities, and vv.6—7 detail how such impurities are to be dealt with. Two such are described in v.b: "and the one touching any impurity ψυχῆς, or a person from whom a seminal discharge erupts (ἐξ αὐτοῦ)." The term ψυχῆς renders נפש, which is usually translated here as "of a corpse," for which see 21:11, and that may be what was intended,[9] though ψυχή normally means "animate being." As for the ἐξ it is partitive.[10]

The second example of impurity is a person who is unclean because of a κοίτη σπέρματος, for which term see the discussion at 15:16.

22:5 For איש אשר LXX has ὅστις, which is idiomatically correct. Two further possibilities for defilement are given. One might either touch a) "any unclean creeping thing, which would defile him," or b) "a person who would defile him according to all his uncleanness," i.e. whatever this uncleanness might be. Both cases modify ἅψηται, though the second one is not an expected genitive, but an ἐπ' phrase, in which the dative ἀνθρώπῳ is modified by a relative clause; this is governed by ᾧ, the case of which is dative by attraction to the dative antecedent pronoun; the pronoun is, however, the subject of the clause, thus "a person who would defile him" (referring to the introductory ὅστις). MT simply has שרץ, but Sam, as well as 4QLev[ell][11] has שרץ טמא, and this reading is parent for LXX's ἑρπετοῦ ἀκαθάρτου. The future μιανεῖ (occurring twice) expresses potential, i.e. timeless or conditional action, and could equally well have been expressed by a subjunctive.[12]

---

9. But Harlé-Pralon have rendered it by "d'un être vivant," which is not to be discounted.
10. See SS 167.
11. See DJD XII 200.
12. See Porter 421—424.

22:6 The subject of the opening clause is ψυχὴ ἥτις ἂν ἅψηται αὐτῶν "whatever person might touch αὐτῶν." In the C'' n s+ tradition η ψυχη is read, but Lev never articulates ψυχή without an accompanying δέ. Only the unarticulated noun can be original.[13] The plural pronoun refers to the four cases of vv.4b—5. In MT the verb is modified by בו, i.e. a singular pronoun referring to אדם of v.5, but the translator makes it plural; this intuition is quite correct; a touching making unclean can be of ἑρπετοῦ or of ἀνθρώπῳ, or of a corpse or a spermatorrheic, and the plural is sensible. The singular αυτου is, however, the majority reading, and is also read by 931, a fourth century fragment from Mt.Sinai, and the plural can be questioned, which, however, does fit the overall context better than the singular.[14] The αυτου must be a recensional correction.

Uncleanness due to touch makes one unclean "until evening." Furthermore, he may not eat[15] ἀπὸ τῶν ἁγίων, i.e. any of the holy portions assigned to priests for food,[16] "unless he would have washed his flesh with water." For the need to wash one's body when one is unclean see 11:40 14:8,9 ch.15 passim 16:4,26,28 17:15.

22:7 The first clause has the verb in the subjunctive, δύῃ, and must be part of the ἐάν clause with which v.6 ends, i.e. "unless he would have washed ..., and the sun have set." The apodosis begins with καὶ καθαρὸς ἔσται as the change to the future makes clear. The apodotic καί imitates MT, and I would translate "he shall be clean, and then he may eat τῶν ἁγίων." The genitive here must be partitive, i.e. he may eat of (or from) the holy things.[17] The majority text reads an απο before it, which is probably recensional in view of the מן of MT.

22:8 For θνησιμαῖον and θηριάλωτον making unclean see comments at 17:15. οὐ φάγεται is modified by an infinitive which shows probable result, i.e. "so as to be defiled." The αὐτόν is the subject of the infinitive. In MT the infinitive is modified by בה "by it," but as in v.6 where αὐτῶν was used rather than a singular as in MT, so here ἐν αὐτοῖς serves as a clarification. There are two things that

---

13. See THGL 86.
14. See THGL 98.
15. Aq has οὐ φάγεται, but Theod and Sym retain the οὐκ ἔδεται of LXX. The two can hardly be distinguished semantically. The Aq reading is Attic.
16. The ἀπό is partitive; see SS 161.
17. See SS 161.

could defile, θνησιμαῖον καὶ θηριάλωτον. Of course, from MT's point of view that which defiles is not the two together, but one or the other, hence the singular. The *b* text "corrects" αὐτοῖς to the singular.

Since v.8 ends the specifics on avoiding defilement, the formula ἐγὼ κύριος puts the divine seal on what has been said.

22:9 In accordance with the plural addressees (see v.3), the general orders are in the plural: "and they (the Aaronids) must keep my charges." As at 8:35 משמרתי is taken as a collective, and translated by the plural. In Lev μου precedes τὰ φυλάγματα, but hex has reordered to the Hebrew order.[18]

LXX correctly understood the coordinate second and third clauses as expressing purpose, hence ἵνα with the subjunctives: "lest they should incur guilt (ἁμαρτίαν) on their account, and should die because of them." The pronouns are, of course, plural, αὐτά referring to φυλάγματα.

In MT these are followed by כי יחללהו "because they would have profaned it." The reference in the masculine suffix is uncertain. In fact, MT is difficult, since its pronominal reference in בו, עליו and the suffix in יחללהו are all unexpected as third masculine singular. LXX has understood them as referring to φυλάγματα, but משמרת is feminine. Possibly the logical antecedent is קדש, except that this could only be inferred contextually.[19] LXX makes good sense, but this is hardly what MT says. A procedent referent rather than an antecedent is highly unusual. One would have expected a feminine suffix referring to משמרתי. The translator has indeed made the suffix refer to φυλάγματα, and he has interpreted כי not as a causal particle, but a conditional one, thus "if he should have defiled them."

The self-identification formula ends the section, but for אני יהוה it reads ἐγὼ κύριος ὁ θεός. Hex has "corrected" this by omitting ὁ θεός. In ὁ ἁγιάζων αὐτούς the pronoun refers to the Aaronid priests.

22:10 LXX uses ἀλλογενής "foreigner" to translate זר. Such a one may not eat ἅγια. Nor may a priest's πάροικος or μισθωτός. A πάροικος is a sojourner. For its use as translation of תושב see Note at Gen 23:4. Here the term probably

---
18. See THGL 103.
19. Vulg has *ut non subiaceant peccato et moriantur in sanctuario cum polluerint illud.*

means no more than the temporary guest of the priest. So neither the temporary guest nor a hireling may eat of the priestly portions.

In the tradition, φάγεται becomes εδεται in the majority of witnesses. Since the two are exact synonyms only the tradition can give guidance as to the original text. All the oldest witnesses, A B F V 931, support the Attic φάγεται, and so it was chosen as original text. Over against ἤ MT reads waw, and the Byz text changes ἤ to και to agree with it.

22:11 THe initial וכהן כי is rearranged by Lev in good Greek style as ἐὰν δὲ ἱερεύς. The protasis has the priest purchasing a person (ψυχήν) bought by money. For the term ἔγκτητον see comment at 14:34. It renders קנין "a purchase." MT has כספו "his money," but Lev does not render the suffix;[20] hex has supplied αυτου under the asterisk to represent it. I would take ἔγκτητον as a second accusative modifier, i.e. "a person as purchased by money."

The apodosis refers to that ψυχήν by οὗτος in which it follows MT. When נפש refers to males the pronoun הוא can be used.[21] And Lev does tend to use masculine referents if ψυχή refers to a person.[22] In contrast to those referred to in v.10, οὗτος may eat τῶν ἄρτων αὐτοῦ, which identifies the בו as food. Codd A B+ add εκ before the article, but this is secondary. The structure occurs in exactly the same form in v.b where, however, MT has בלחמו.[23] The plural rightly interprets לחם as ἄρτων; the plural is generic for "food."

V.b begins with καὶ οἱ οἰκογενεῖς αὐτοῦ, possibly following the plural ילידי of Sam rather than the יליד of MT, though יליד may well be taken as a collective. These are the ones who are born in the household, i.e. offspring of the ψυχὴν ἔγκτητον of v.a. "Also these may eat of his food."[24]

22:12 The structure θυγάτηρ ἀνθρώπου ἱερέως levels with 21:9, where בת איש כהן occurs in MT; here MT has בת כהן. Nowhere else in the book does the combination occur, and I am not sure what ἀνθρώπου is supposed to mean. In 21:9 the איש acts much like an indefinite article, i.e. "daughter of a priest," and I

---

20. See SS 97—98.
21. See GK 145t.
22. See Huber 33.
23. See the discussion in THGL 104—105.
24. Instead of φάγονται τῶν ἄρτων αὐτοῦ Aq and Sym have φάγονται τῆς τροφῆς αὐτοῦ, whereas Theod has φάγονται ἐν τοῖς ἄρτοις αὐτοῦ.

presume that here it is also to be taken as a Hebraism. This is conditioned by "should she belong to a foreigner (ἀνδρὶ ἀλλογενεῖ)." The apodosis states that under that condition "she may not eat of the holy first-fruits." The translation of תרומת by τῶν ἀπαρχῶν occurs only here in the book. תרומה is otherwise translated by ἀφαίρεμα, which is a more literal rendering, "a raising up" (7:4,22,24 10:14,15). The rendering by ἀπαρχή does occur five times in Exod, where the word is probably to be understood as a synonym of ἀφαίρεμα, "something taken up," or "taken away." See Note at Exod 25:2—3. The term ἀπαρχῶν may be justified as the first things removed, viz, the holy portions reserved for the priests, hence "the holy (i.e. the dedicated) first fruits (of the sacrifices)." Possibly problematic is the syntax of αὐτή; it could be taken as the subject of φάγεται or of γένηται. The critical text, by placing a comma before it rather than after it, has decided for the latter. This choice is based on the Masoretic interpretation which placed זו under the *ethnach*. The original text of Lev of course had no punctuation, and the Lev text is the interpretation (probably correct) of the editor.

22:13 A stipulation similarly induced applies to a priest's daughter who is a widow or a divorcee without offspring; she may return to the paternal home as in her youth. The Greek follows the format of MT by placing θυγάτηρ ἱερέως outside the protasis, and only then proceeding with ἐάν. LXX interprets the *waw* connecting אלמנה וגרושה as a correlative, ἤ, which is clearer than MT; the daughter is not both a "widow" and "one cast out"; she is the one or the other. The δέ clause speaks of seed μὴ ᾖ αὐτῇ, i.e. to the divorcee. In the tradition, an A B b x+ text has ην for ᾖ, but the imperfect can only be a mistake; μή requires a subjunctive form. The ην is palaeographically inspired; the uncial text reading MHHI can easily be misread as MHHN; it is certainly an error.[25]

The adjectival structure τὸν οἶκον τὸν πατρικόν renders the bound phrase בית אביה "house of her father"; it is a free, but correct rendering.[26] A majority text added αυτης to represent the suffix, but this need not be recensional; it may represent a stylistic gloss.

The apodosis grants that she may eat ἀπὸ τῶν ἄρτων of her father. The ἀπό is typically partitive, as is the ἀπ' of ἀπ' αὐτῶν in the next clause.[27] MT reads

---

25. See THGL 126.
26. See SS 98.
27. See SS 161.

מלחם, and the plural is used to indicate food in general, i.e. לחם is understood as a collective; see comment at v.11. The rationale for the permission does not differ from that for the denial in v.12. What is determinative is the relation to the household of the father. A married woman no longer belongs to that household, but on her return to it she is again a member of it, and thus has a member's rights.

The last clause restates v.10a, substituting ἀπ' αὐτῶν for ἅγια; cf comment ad loc.

22:14 The initial ואיש כי is here rendered by καὶ ἄνθρωπος plus a relative pronoun ὅς (ἄν); this also occurs at v.21 24:17 27:14.[28] "Whatever man might eat ἅγια unwittingly"; here קדש is still taken as a collective; someone may have eaten of the holy portions in ignorance. For κατὰ ἄγνοιαν as translation for בשגגה see comment at 5:18.

The apodosis is introduced by καί in imitation of MT. He must add one fifth of it to it, and give τὸ ἅγιον to the priest. The αὐτοῦ and αὐτό refer to a single portion of τὰ ἅγια, i.e. to τὸ ἅγιον which he must give to the priest. For the penalty see 5:16 and comment ad loc. Here הקדש is translated by the singular; it is a specific holy portion. In v.a קדש was rendered by the plural, since the reference is general, i.e. to the holy portions reserved for the priests. An interesting tradition is preserved as a marginal reading in M s. Instead of ἅγιον, αργυριον is read; the repayment can hardly be ἅγιον which he ate, so he must pay money instead!

22:15 Vv.15—16 are addressed to the priests. "They may not profane τὰ ἅγια of the Israelites which they are setting aside to the Lord." The ἅγια must refer to the sacrifices which are described as being holy, i.e. the holy sacrifices. That these are indeed holy is emphasized by the verb in the relative clause, ἀφαιροῦσιν, which basically means "to remove" (see 6:10,15), so here "to set aside." These are holy, set apart, devoted to the Lord. Unexpected is the construction αὐτοὶ ἀφαιροῦσιν. The pattern is normally reserved to translate the nominal structure of pronoun plus participial predicate, but here MT has ירימו. The prefix inflection is, however, well-rendered by the present tense, since the

---

28. See THGL 74, and comp 116.

relative clause follows a clause in the future. But the pronoun is not explained thereby; its special function seems to me to make certain that the subject of ἀφαιροῦσιν is not the "Israelites," but the priests, i.e. the same as the subject of βεβηλώσουσιν.

In the tradition, copyists did not always fully understand the use of ἀφαιροῦσιν. One might well expect a verb in the sense of "offer up," and the C⁾ Byz+ text actually substituted αναφερουσιν, and an A s^mg+ reading has προσφερουσιν, while the ol n text read αφοριουσιν.

22:16 This verse is closely connected to v.15, since it shows what would happen should the priests profane the holy sacrifices of the Israelites. LXX says "and they would bring upon themselves ἀνομίαν πλημμελείας, when they (the priests) eat their (the Israelites') sacrifices." This is, however, not what MT says. It begins with והשיאו אותם "and they would make them bear (עון אשמה)." The subject of השיאו is the priests, and אותם refers to the Israelites. The term אשמה is an infinitive meaning "wrong doing, a trespass." In MT the guilt incurred by the priests' profanation of the holy sacrifices is laid on the Israelites who were the source of the ἅγια. But in v.9 the disobedience of the priests (not keeping the Lord's charges) would result in their incurring guilt themselves, καὶ ἀποθάνωσιν δί αὐτά. The translator interpreted MT in accordance with v.9. The noun אשם is regularly translated by πλημμελείας, for which see the discussion at 5:15. The term ἀνομία "something lawless" is often used to render עון "iniquity." The structure ἀνομίαν πλημμελείας then means "an illegal offence."

The reason for the statement of vv.15—16 is given in the ὅτι clause; it is "because I am the Lord ὁ ἁγιάζων αὐτούς." For the latter see comment at v.9.

22:18 Moses is commanded to "speak Ἀαρών and to his sons and πάσῃ συναγωγῇ of Israel." Hebrew uses the preposition אל for all three addressees, and hex has added πρός before Ἀαρών under the asterisk to represent it. LXX used the dative case to show the addressees, but Ἀαρών, being indeclinable, did not make that fact explicit. MT lacks an equivalent for συναγωγῇ; in its stead it simply has בני, i.e. "and to all the Israelites." A few scattered mss add the article τη before συναγωγῇ, but Lev never articulates this noun when it is modified by "all."[29]

---

29. See THGL 87.

The subject referred to in what is to be said is "any man ἀπὸ τῶν υἱῶν of Israel ἤ τῶν προσηλύτων τῶν προσκειμένων πρὸς αὐτούς in Israel." The ἀπό is clearly partitive, as is the genitive after ἤ.[30] MT has מבית for ἀπὸ τῶν υἱῶν, for which see comment at 17:3. MT joins the two structures governed by ἀπό by a *waw*, but the correlative is what is intended. That second structure is much shorter in MT which simply reads ומן הגר בישראל. That גר is understood as a collective is clear, and the addition of the attributive participle presupposes Sam's (ומן הגר הגר בישראל), also attested in 4QLev^b,[31] as in MT at 16:29 17:10,12,13 18:26 19:34 20:2.[32] The πρὸς αὐτούς after προσκειμένων has no counterpart in MT, and a popular text does omit it, though the omission does not appear to be recensional. The verb προσκεῖμαι is often modified by a πρός phrase, as e.g. at 25:6. I would translate the structure as "or of the resident aliens who are attached to them in Israel."

In the tradition, hex added an απο before "the resident aliens" to represent the repeated מן of MT. A popular B V 931 text added των υιων before it, but this was probably added under the influence of the coordinate τῶν υἱῶν Ἰσραήλ; in any event, it can not be original in spite of fourth century support.[33] The subject is further defined by a relative clause: "who might offer his gifts in accord with any agreed on offering or any offering of choice which they might offer to God for a burnt offering." The Hebrew has נדר and נדבה. The two offerings also occur at 7:6(16) where נדר "vow" is rendered by the usual (52 times) εὐχή, and נדבה "voluntary offering," by ἑκούσιον, also its usual translation. Here נדר becomes ὁμολογίαν "agreement, compact," thus an offering agreed upon earlier. This is unique in the Pentateuch; in fact it only occurs elsewhere twice (in Jer). נדבה is translated by αἵρεσιν which also occurs at v.21. It also occurs at Gen 49:5, but not for נדבה. It simply means "choice," so an offering of choice, of free will. Both offerings have αὐτῶν as modifiers. The plural continues into the second relative clause. The change in number follows that of MT. The rationale for it is straightforward; the singular is obvious: "anyone who might offer his gifts." The plural is broader than the individuals. Vows and voluntary sacrifices are made by Israelites. In LXX such sacrifices are offered τῷ θεῷ, though MT

---

30. See SS 167.
31. See DJD XII 182—183.
32. Kenn 4,69,109,129 also read הגר after הגר.
33. See THGL 109.

has ליהוה. θεῷ was chosen as original text purely on the basis of its support by A B F, and its support is, except for the x group, scattered. I am no longer as confident as formerly that the critical text should read θεῷ rather than κυρίῳ which most witnesses read. I know of no reason why the translator should have used θεῷ for יהוה, and I now suspect that it was a copyist error, i.e. rooted in the misreading of K͞Ω͞I as Θ͞Ω͞I.

22:19 This must be read as a continuation of v.18; it states what such a burnt offering must consist of. The phrase לרצנכם "for acceptance on your behalf" is freely rendered by δεκτὰ ὑμῖν, for which see also v.29 23:11.[34] In the tradition, an F M V 931 popular reading has υμων instead of ὑμῖν. The genitive does occur as δεκτὴν ὑμῶν at 19:5, but otherwise the pronominal modifier is always dative; see e.g. v.29 and comp v.20. The translator makes no distinction between לרצון לכם and לרצנכם. δεκτά is accusative neuter plural, since its antecedent is apparently ὅσα; it describes ἄρσενα, which is plural being modified by three ἐκ phrases, i.e. males of cattle, and of sheep, and of goats. The word ἄρσενα is followed by ἄμωμα for MT's תמים זכר. Hex has transposed the two words to equal MT. The hex text is supported by A B V and 931, but it is nonetheless secondary. Lev always has ἄμωμος following the noun it modifies, never before it.[35] I would translate "to be acceptable on your behalf (they must be) males, blameless, of cattle, etc."

22:20 Particular attention is here drawn to the ἄμωμα requirement. The modifier of the verb προσάξουσιν is "everything ὅσα ἂν ἐχῇ μῶμον ἐν αὐτῷ."[36] The use of the present subjunctive, outside of ᾖ, is rare, and when it occurs it stresses something which is a general situation.[37] The Hebrew has אשר בו מום, but only the b text transposes μῶμον and the ἐν phrases; this is probably due to the influence of one of The Three. The main verb in MT is תקריבו, but LXX translates it by a third person verb, προσάξουσιν, modified by κυρίῳ; the dative modifier has no counterpart in MT, and is accordingly placed under the obelus in hex. The change to third person is probably due to leveling with προσενέγκωσιν

---

34. See SS 98.
35. See THGL 103.
36. For the use of the verb ἔχω in LXX see SS 181—188, as well as 58—59.
37. See THGL 125.

of v.18. Both refer to the indefinite plural; for the reasoning underlying the plural in v.18 see comment ad loc. The reason for the prohibition is given in the διότι/כי clause; "it would not be acceptable for you." δεκτόν is neuter, with no particular antecedent, something which this translator often uses.[38] For its use in translating רצון see comment at v.19.

22:21 For כי the Greek has ὃς ἄν, a not uncommon rendering in Lev.[39] The syntax of most of this verse is loose. The entire ὅς structure is pendant, and the main clause, ἄμωμον ἔσται εἰς δεκτόν, has no actual antecedent; the neuter refers vaguely to a sacrifice which one might make, see comment at v.20. The ὅς clause refers to ἄνθρωπος, i.e. the man who might offer a sacrifice for deliverance, for which see discussion at 3:1. This is modified in MT by a marked infinitive, לפלא, in turn modified by נדר או לנדבה. This is an idiom, also occurring at Num 15:3,8, meaning "for discharging a voluntary sacrifice" of some kind, but see comment at 27:2. For this Lev has διαστείλας εὐχὴν κατὰ αἵρεσιν ἢ ἐν ταῖς ἑορταῖς ὑμῶν. This text, however, cannot stand as original. All mss, except A B* 29 b 610 121 and 68′ have ἤ before κατά, and that must be read;[40] comp also Num 15:3. The participle does mean "discharge," thus "in the discharge of a vow or in accord with a voluntary offering or in your feasts." The vow is quite separate from the αἵρεσιν, and those in turn should be kept distinct from ταῖς ἑορταῖς. MT does not have the third modifier, and hex has taken note of that by omitting ἢ ἐν ταῖς ἑορταῖς ὑμῶν. θυσίαν σωτηρίου is also modified by two ἐκ phrases showing the source for the sacrifice as "from cattle or from sheep."

The main clause then reads "it must be flawless for acceptability." As in v.20 the emphasis is on the need for sacrifices to be without blemish. In fact, to make this doubly clear, a final clause states "there may be no blemish in it," with the αὐτῷ having the same referent as ἄμωμον, which see.

22:22 Possible blemishes are listed; these all modify the verb προσάξουσιν. These refer to something "blind or broken" or חרוץ "mutilated," translated by γλωσσότμητον "with a cut tongue." The fourth is יבלת, a hapax legomenon probably meaning "a running sore," translated by μυρμηκιῶντα, also a hapax

---
38. See Huber 34—35.
39. See THGL 74.
40. As Harlé-Pralon quite rightly insist.

legomenon in OT; it apparently means "afflicted with warts." The fifth is גרב "an itch," translated by ψωραγριῶντα, another hapax legomenon meaning "having a bad itch." The last member in the list is ילפת, for which see 21:20. Its translation is "having λειχῆνας," for which see comment at 21:20 on λειχήν.[41] The addition of ἔχοντα at the end of the list probably refers to the sacrifices which are illegitimate as including animals "having a lichen-like skin disease." It is not the disease which is illegitimate but the sacrifices having the disease that are intended. The list is syntactically an accusative pendant which is brought into the clause by an αὐτά. The verb is again in third person rather than the second person of MT, תקריבו, as in v.20. As in v.18 I now would take θεῷ as secondary, and would take κυρίῳ to be original. For a justification for this change see comment at v.18.[42] The reading κυρίῳ is actually supported by all the oldest witnesses, A B F and 931. In the tradition, αὐτά is changed to ταυτα in a popular B M V 931 text, but this must be a Hebraizing correction towards the Hebrew אלה, and therefore secondary.[43]

In the second clause the ἀπ' of ἀπ' αὐτῶν is partitive,[44] thus "you may not put any of them." κάρπωσιν occurs only here in Lev for אשׁ; it is simply a variant for the usual κάρπωμα, for which see comment at 2:9. What is forbidden is putting "any of them for a sacrifice to the Lord on the altar."

22:23 The accusative pendant refers to "a bullock or a sheep with a cut ear or a shortened tail." For ὠτότμητον and its Hebrew counterpart, שׂרוע see comment at 21:18. κολοβόκερκον is a real hapax legomenon, but its component parts make its meaning clear. Its correspondent in MT, קלוט, is also a hapax legomenon, and its meaning is uncertain; the LXX's rendering may well be correct, though note how Tar⁰ hedges its bets.[45] LXX interprets the *waw* joining the two nouns as well as the two adjectives as correlatives, i.e. as ἤ, which is sensible.

The pendant is brought into the main clause by the pronoun αὐτά (referring to both μόσχον ἤ πρόβατον) in "you may use them as sacrifices (σφάγια) for yourself, but for your vow it will not be acceptable." MT has for the first clause

---

41. For the use of ἔχοντα see SS 185.
42. I would now take the comment at THGL 130 to be faulty.
43. See THGL 96.
44. See SS 161.
45. Tar⁰ renders the two words by יתיר וחסיר roughly translated as "too long or too short."

נדבה תעשה אתו "you may use it as a voluntary sacrifice." MT singles the sacrifice out, whereas LXX generalizes by using plural nominals, αὐτά and σφάγια. Unique is the rendering of נדבה by σφάγια. The term σφάγιον is a Classical term for a sacrificial victim, an offering, and occurs only here in the Pentateuch. In fact, it only occurs five times in OT (once in Amos, and three times in Ezek), but only here as a free interpretation of נדבה. One can conclude from its contrast with εὐχήν that it is a voluntary sacrifice, but the Greek does not say so. Lev had some trouble with the word נדבה.[46] It occurs five times in Lev; twice the usual (nine times) translation ἑκούσιος occurs (7:6 23:38), whereas earlier in our chapter (vv.18,21) the word αἵρεσις (limited to Lev) was used. Since it falls outside the usual group of prescribed sacrifices, its cultic observance was not firmly defined, and some ambiguity was felt. This is not the case with εὐχή/נדר. The "vow" was also not prescribed, but it was something undertaken, a promised sacrifice, and its execution could follow a regular pattern; cf 27:2.

22:24 Again an accusative pendant list precedes the clause, and αὐτά is used to bring the list into the clause. Lev follows the Sam text in beginning the list asyndetically.[47] The list has four members: 1) θλαδίαν "a eunuch" for מעוך a passive participle meaning "castrated"; 2) ἐκτεθλιμμένον "squeezed out" for כתות "beaten, crushed," both with reference to the testicles; 3) ἐκτομίαν "castrated" for נתוק "torn," and 4) ἀπεσπασμένον "drawn off" for כרות "cut." The four terms all refer to various means of castration: by crushing, bruising, tearing, extracting, and the renderings are only approximate, both for the Greek and for the Hebrew. This is also clear from their usage in OT. θλαδίαν occurs only twice, also at Dt 23:1; ἐκθλίβω is not uncommon, but occurs uniquely for כתת. ἐκτομίας is a hapax legomenon in OT, and ἀποσπάω, though occurring 10 times in OT, is unique as a rendering for כרת.

In any event, "οὐ προσάξετε αὐτά to the Lord"; sacrifices of such a kind are animals with a blemish, and not fit to be brought as sacrifices to the Lord; see v.20. In MT there is no equivalent for αὐτά, and the initial list constitutes modifiers of the verb; in other words, there is no pendant construction. Hex has "corrected" Lev by omitting the pronoun so as to equal MT.

---

46. But see Daniel 251, note 50.
47. Vulg also lacks an initial conjunction.

The second clause might present a problem of interpretation if read in isolation, but it becomes clear when read as a contrast to v.25, where offering of (such) sacrifices from strangers are forbidden. Here the Israelites are banned from performing (such blemished sacrifices) ἐπὶ τῆς γῆς ὑμῶν. Such animals could be used for other purposes on the land, e.g. a μόσχος as a beast of burden, but it might not be sacrificed.

22:25 Also forbidden is offering τὰ δῶρα of your God from the hand ἀλλογενούς. For τὰ δῶρα as rendering for לחם see discussion at 21:6. The term בן נכר specifically refers to a non-Israelite, and the rendering αλλογενούς is exactly correct; it is someone from another race or tribe. The gifts of your God you may not take are ἀπὸ πάντων τούτων. The ἀπό is partitive; it means "any of all these."[48] The pronoun refers to the list of blemished animals unfit for sacrifice given in v.24.

A ὅτι clause explains why the above is the case by φθάρματά ἐστιν ἐν αὐτοῖς, μῶμος ἐν αὐτοῖς. MT reads for the first word משחתם "their corruption," but LXX omits the suffix, an omission which the tradition fails to correct. To the translator the suffix may well have been intentionally omitted for good sense;[49] after all, it is followed by a doublet statement in which the noun μῶμος is also used absolutely. The term φθάρματα is a hapax legomenon in OT; the word is non-Classical; the word is rare, and its meaning revolves around the notion of destructiveness; cf φθαρματός "perishable," and φθαρματικός "destructive." It was probably intended here as an equivalent for משחת.

Since these damaged animals constitute φθάρμα or μῶμος, οὐ δεχθήσεται ταῦτα ὑμῖν "these may not be accepted for you" (i.e. considered acceptable on your behalf). Note the Classical use of a singular verb with a neuter plural subject.[50]

22:27 The subject is given before the condition, thus "as for a bullock or a sheep or a goat, when it is born, it must be under the mother for seven days." The apodosis is introduced by καί in imitation of MT; it is signalled by a change to

---
48. See SS 165.
49. See SS 97 as well.
50. See SS 197. On the other hand, 11QLev also omits the subject as well as the preposition in בהם. Its reading is הם משחאתים; see Freedman 531.

the future tense. LXX does not translate the suffix of אמו, since it could hardly refer to someone else's mother. Hex is probably the source for the majority text addition of αυτου to represent the suffix.

The next clause is rendered by a δέ structure, since it is contrastive: "but on the eighth day and beyond, it will be acceptable εἰς δῶρα." The Masoretes vocalized קרבן as a bound form, but LXX did not understand it in this way; κάρπωμα is merely an appositive for δῶρα. The plural renders the singular קרבן, which is usually translated by a singular; actually the plural of קרבן only occurs once (at 7:38); this is out of 40 occurrences in the book. In fact, δῶρον/δῶρα is a calque for קרבן, but the plural occurs only eight times as its equivalent. Here the translator probably thought of the list preposed—a bullock or a sheep or a goat—which might be presented εἰς δῶρα,[51] though it modifies the singular verb ἔσται. The b text "corrects" to the singular δωρον; this is obviously based on the Hebrew text. For κάρπωμα as a rendering for אשה see comment at 2:9.

22:28 The preposed pendant accusative, καὶ μόσχον καὶ πρόβατον, is based on Sam; MT joins the two nouns by או; comp v.23. The variant text of A B O b+ reading η in its stead is a hex correction.[52] That the intent is correlative is clear from the αὐτήν which brings the μόσχον and the πρόβατον into the clause as modifying σφάξεις. The feminine αὐτήν is intentionally chosen, since it is the cow and/or the ewe that is meant. What is forbidden is that you should slaughter both "her and her offspring" ἐν ἡμέρᾳ μίᾳ. By the phrase "in one day" what is meant is "in the same day."[53]

There is an odd change in number involved in the statement. MT has a plural verb תשחטו which LXX changes to the singular σφάξεις, while the word for "her offspring" is singular in MT, בנו, but becomes plural in LXX, τὰ παιδία αὐτῆς. The plural παιδία might be defended as a generalization, but I see no rationale for the change in number of the verb to the singular. The τὰ παιδία is, however, changed by the majority text to the singular παιδιον, a change which is certainly recensional, possibly hex in origin. That the plural is original seems assured from its support by A B and 931, our oldest Greek witnesses. That the

---

51. See THGL 116.
52. See THGL 102.
53. See SS 110.

plural verb of MT is original is clear from the context. The section, vv.26—33, is throughout addressed in the second plural.

22:29 The translator continues with the singular second person for the protasis, but then switches to the plural for the apodosis, and continues with the plural of MT for the rest of the chapter. MT is consistently plural throughout the verse. The verb θύσῃς in the protasis has a double accusative modifier, θυσίαν as a cognate, and εὐχὴν χαρμοσύνης, thus "if you (singular) should sacrifice as a sacrifice a vow of delight (or gladness)." The Hebrew refers to זבח תודה "a sacrifice of thanksgiving," but the translator renders תודה as "a vow of gladness." The term χαρμοσύνης occurs only here in the Pentateuch, and never translates תודה elsewhere in this way. It is usually translated by αἴνεσις; see for the thank (offering) rendering by περὶ αἰνέσεως 7:2 and the discussion ad loc. This unique interpretation may well be an understanding of the thank offering as the result of a vow (which it may be) not so much of praise, but as praise stimulated by χαρμοσύνης.

The apodosis appears in the plural, i.e. follows MT which has לרצנכם תזבחו. LXX translates freely by εἰς δεκτὸν ὑμῖν θύσετε αὐτό. The dative pronoun does make good sense.[54] The αὐτό has no equivalent in MT, but reflects the Sam text, תזבחהו.[55] The αὐτό is another case of Lev's use of the neuter pronoun when no obvious antecedent obtains.[56]

22:30 The verse begins with τῇ ἡμέρᾳ ἐκείνῃ, but an A B V majority text prefixes this with αυτη. There is no basis for this in MT which has ביום ההוא, and it is an error rooted in a partial dittograph of the preceding word αὐτό (ending v.29.)[57] What the text says with respect to the "vow of gladness" is that "it must be eaten on that (same) day."

Negatively stated, "you may not leave ἀπὸ τῶν κρεῶν to the morning." The ἀπό is partitive,[58] and τῶν κρεῶν interprets the pronoun of MT, ממנו, as meaning

---

54. See SS 98, as well as 68.
55. According to a marginal reading of ms 344 The Others read αὐτὸ αὐτήν instead of αὐτό. I am highly sceptical of this tradition, and suspect that it represents the beginning of v.30, which see. Kenn 80*,107,136 read תזבחהו, and Kenn 129 has תזבחוהו.
56. See Huber 34—35.
57. See THGL 109.
58. See SS 161.

"the flesh." The interpretation is probably correct in view of the reference to μόσχον and πρόβατον (and αἶγα) in vv.27—28.

Since this verse ends the section beginning with v.26, the self-identification formula ἐγώ εἰμι κύριος is used. The εἰμι is omitted by C' f+; this could be thought to reflect the absence of an equivalent in MT, but it is more likely a case of leveling with the more frequent form ἐγὼ κύριος, e.g. in vv.2,3,8,9,16, where ειμι never appears.

22:31 Vv.31—33 constitute a general conclusion to the chapter exhorting the Israelites to be faithful in following its dictates and recognizing their covenant God who redeemed them.

The general order to "guard my commandments and execute them"[59] is followed in MT by אני יהוה, which Lev, following the text of 4QLev[b60] and Sam, omits. The majority text does add εγω κυριος, but it is probably not original in view of the support of the shorter text by A B 931, i.e. all the oldest witnesses. The majority text is an early recensional text, probably hex in origin.

In the tradition, φυλάξετε is changed extensively. A popular text reads the middle form, φυλαξεσθε; the C' d+ variant has gone a step further to the aorist imperative, φαλαξασθε, but Lev is supported by all the uncials as well as 931, and must be original.

22:32 For the first clause comp v.2. Here the command is in second person plural: "not may you profane." Instead of τὸ ὄνομα τοῦ ἁγίου v.2 had το ονομα το αγιον μου, though in both cases MT read את שם קדשי. Here the genitive is used to render the free element of a bound phrase, and the suffix is not rendered.[61] The genitive is, however, adequate to render the קדש; it means "the holy name." The Byz text revises on the basis of MT by including μου, but then is forced to change the genitive to το αγιον as well; on the other hand, this may well have been effected under the influence of v.2. The "holy name" is, of course, "the Lord," representing the tetragrammaton.

The second clause is presented, as in MT, paratactically, though it is actually the purpose for the first clause, thus "you must not profane ..., that I

---

59. Aq and Sym keep the φυλάξετε of LXX, but Theod reads φυλάξεσθε.
60. See DJD XII 182—183.
61. See SS 65.

may be sanctified in the midst of Israel." The short self-identification formula is modified by ὁ ἁγιάζων ὑμᾶς, for which see discussion at 20:8. Here, however, it is related to clause two, particularly through the verb ἁγιασθήσομαι. Thus I, who am the one sanctifying you, will also myself be sanctified within Israel.

22:33 A second modifier to the formula in v.32. "The one bringing you out of the land of Egypt" also occurs at 19:36; see also 25:38 26:13. Not only did κύριος set you aside, i.e. consecrated you, he was also the redeemer God revealed in the redemptive act of the Exodus. The participles, both in MT's המוציא as well as LXX's ἐξαγαγών, are particularly appropriate, since as nominals they are timeless. The redemptive act is not something that happened back there in history, but it is a constant reality with a covenantal purpose: "to be your God." The chapter ends with ἐγὼ κύριος.

Chapter 23

23:1 For καὶ εἶπεν used for וידבר, and the recensional correction to και ελαλησεν, see discussion at 18:1.

23:2 What "you must say to them" concerns "the feasts of the Lord which you must call as sacred convocations." This serves as the pendant for αὗται which is the subject of the main clause: "these are my feasts." The word ἑορταί means "feasts," and is not an exact equivalent for MT's מועדי "set, appointed occasions." As such they may be called feasts, but the Hebrew stresses that the feasts are set in the calendar. The entire chapter is devoted to a description of the regulations for the various fixed occasions which the Israelites are called upon to celebrate. The festivals are described as ἃς καλέσετε αὐτάς, which is cumbersome Greek but represents אשר תקראו אתם word for word; the αὐτάς is otiose in Greek, though it does serve as anaphoric referent for κλητὰς ἀγίας.[1] The term κλητάς occurs only for מקרא or קרא, and is the usual rendering for מקרא (12 out of a possible 17 times).[2] It is probably best rendered by "convocations"; the Lord's feasts are thus holy convocations, and must be observed with full seriousness.

The main clause states: "These are my feasts." ἑορταί is in both cases articulated in LXX, though in both instances the article is omitted in a number of witnesses, in fact in the second instance by a majority A B 931 text. Since αι and ε were both pronounced as /ε/ in Hellenistic Greek, the loss of /hε/ before /hεortε/ is simply a case of haplography, and is not to be taken seriously.[3]

23:3 The first of the appointed occasions is the Sabbath day. The Sabbath commandment in the Decalogue was well-known to all Israelites, as well as to later copyists, and certainly influenced the tradition, as will appear below. The Masoretic tradition vocalized תעשה in the opening command as Ni, with מלאכה as its subject; thus "for six days work may be done." It is not surprising that LXX read this as a second masculine singular Qal: "Six days may you do work,"

---

1. See THGL 102.
2. According to Dos Santos.
3. See THGL 85.

since both the Exod 20 and Dt 5 versions read תעבד ועשית. The Byz text has the plural verb ποιησετε, a case of leveling with the plural for the entire verse. For the use of the plural ἔργα see Note at Exod 20:9.

The next clause begins "καὶ τῇ seventh day," but the majority text reads τη δε. The clause is indeed contrastive, but the majority text is nonetheless secondary. The Lev text is supported inter alia by A B F V 931, and the smoother δε construction has entered the tradition from the Decalogue, both versions reading δέ.[4] For σάββατα see comment at 16:31. שבתון is translated by ἀνάπαυσις here, but at v.32 it is transliterated as σαββάτων. For a full discussion of both renderings see the discussion at 16:31. The Sabbath is also called a κλητὴ ἅγια τῷ κυρίῳ "a sacred convocation to the Lord." For κλητή see the discussion at v.2. The dative has no equivalent in MT, and Syh omits the phrase, from which I would conclude that the parent hex text used by the Syh translator had τῷ κυρίῳ under the obelus.

The next clause reads "no work ποιήσεις," followed by the raison d'etre for the prohibition: "it is a Sabbath to the Lord in all κατοικίᾳ ὑμῶν." מלאכה is not translated by εργα, but by the singular; for this contrast see Note at Exod 20:9. MT has consistent plurals in תעשו and מושבתיכם. ποιήσεις is supported by A B V 931 x y+, and the rest of the witnesses read the plural. It should be added that A and B also add υμων after "to the Lord," from which I would conclude that the evidence of the two uncials in this context is not to be trusted. I would now take ποιήσεις to be a secondary adaptation to the ποιήσεις/תעשה of the Decalogue (both in Exod and Dt). One would not expect the translator to change a consistent ποιήσετε ... ὑμῶν to ποιησεις ... ὑμῶν; the text should read ποιήσετε.

23:4 Vv.4—8 deal with the Passover feast, V.4 is a general introduction which differentiates the annual feasts from the weekly Sabbath. It reads: "These are the feasts of the Lord, and they are sacred convocations which you must summon in their καιροῖς." The term καιρός is well-chosen, since it means "an appropriate occasion." For ἑορταί as rendering for מועדי see comment at v.2. In distinction from v.2 the feasts are τῷ κυρίῳ, rather than του κυριου which the bound phrase מועדי יהוה might be thought to promote.[5]

---

4. See THGL 102.
5. See THGL 80 and well as 68.

367

The second clause identifies the feasts to the Lord as sacred convocations. Over against MT it is introduced by καὶ αὗται. MT has מקראי קדש in apposition to מועדי יהוה, but the translator is intent on contrasting with the κλητὰς ἁγίας of v.2. There the structure modifies αὐτάς within the relative clause, for which see comment ad loc, but here it is outside the clause as both position and case show. LXX says two things: "these are the Lord's feasts" and "these are sacred convocations which you must summon at their fixed times," i.e. there are two contrasting foci: the feasts belong to the Lord, but you must summon the holy occasions. καιροῖς is a good rendering for מועד. The same word in the plural was rendered by ἑορταί (vv.2 and 4a), but this would be inappropriate here, where מועד refers to the time appointed, and καιρός is what is meant. The plural is used since αὐτάς/אתם immediately preceded the word במועדם. Either the singular or the plural would be a possible translation. The Byz text has actually substituted εν ταις εορταις αυτων, which is not overly sensible.

23:5 Designations of time are usually made in MT by ב phrases, thus בחדש and בארבעה עשר. LXX follows this pattern as well with ἐν phrases. The feast is πάσχα, which is the Aramaic equivalent of the Hebrew פסח, traditionally called "Passover," for which comp Exod 12:11—12; it recalls the night of deliverance when the Lord "passed over" the dwellings of the Israelites. The "Pesach" or "Passover to the Lord" is to be in the first month on the fourteenth ἡμέρᾳ of the month." The word "day" does not occur in MT, but it does in Sam; it is of course understood. Hex has placed ἡμέρᾳ under the obelus to show its absence in MT. ἐν τῷ πρώτῳ μηνί renders בחדש הראשון, and hex has changed the order to εν τω μηνι τω πρωτω to correspond to MT exactly. The specific designation of time in MT is בין הערבים, a phrase which is variously interpreted. Literally it means "between the two evenings." The phrase occurred five times in Exod; twice (12:6 16:12) it is translated by πρὸς ἑσπέραν; twice (29:39,41) it becomes τὸ δειλινόν, and once (30:8) it is interpreted by ὀψέ. To the Exod translator it obviously meant "at eventide, at vespers." Lev simply translates the phrase word for word as ἀνὰ μέσον τῶν ἑσπερινῶν "between the vespers," and just what LXX meant by this is hard to say; presumably it meant בין הערבים!

23:6 "And on the fifteenth day of this month" according to MT חג המצות (ליהוה), which LXX renders by ἑορτὴ τῶν ἀζύμων. The translator used the same word both for מועדים and for חג, except that for חג the singular is necessarily used; see also v.34, whereas when the plural occurs it is throughout the chapter מועדי, with the translator using the noun ἑορτή for both, but reserving the singular for חג and the plural for מועדי (see also vv.2,3,37,44). In fact, the singular מועד, except for מועדם in v.4, always occurs in the phrase אהל מועד, and is rendered consistently by σκηνὴ τοῦ μαρτυρίου. המצות is rendered literally by τῶν ἀζύμων "of the unleavened." Syntactically the timer is the preposed predicate of a nominal clause, thus "on the fifteenth day of this month is the feast of the unleavened (loaves) to the Lord." A C' s+ text has changed τούτου to τοῦ αὐτοῦ, i.e. "of the same (day)," which is an attempt to elucidate the pronoun.

The accusative phrase ἑπτὰ ἡμέρας designates length of time, i.e. "for seven days," and modifies the verb ἔδεσθε. During that period ἄζυμα ἔδεσθε "you must eat unleavened (bread)." A popular M V text reads φαγεσθε instead of ἔδεσθε.[6] Since the two are synonyms, one can only decide on the original text by the support of the oldest witnesses, A B 931.

23:7 MT begins the verse asyndetically with the time designation ביום הראשון, but LXX reads καὶ ἡ ἡμέρα ἡ πρώτη, presupposing a parent והיום הראשון. What is meant is the first day of the feast of the unleavened; "this is to be a sacred convocation; you may do no ἔργον λατρευτόν," i.e. service work. This translates מלאכה עבדה, a phrase which refers to regular work, working at one's job; cf Note at Exod 12:16. The phrase occurs six times (also at vv.8,21,25,35,36) as well as six times in Num, and it always renders the same Hebrew idiom.[7] What is meant is that on such "special days" one must abstain from all kinds of service work, and engage in "Sabbath rest."

23:8 For the translation of אשה by ὁλοκαυτώματα see comment at 1:9. The noun occurs for אשה also at vv.25,27,36(twice), but אשה also occurs at vv.13,18 (as θυσία) and at v.37 (as καρπώματα). The word is obviously a general term for sacrifice. An F b+ text reads the singular, but throughout the chapter the number of this noun is chosen according to a pattern. The variant is palaeographically conditioned; paraplepsis has occurred from -ματα to -μα. The singular is used to

---

6. As do Theod Aq, whereas Sym retains the text of Lev.
7. See SS 66.

indicate holocausts for specific days, but when it is for more than one day the plural is used.⁸

"The seventh day must be a sacred convocation for you." For κλητὴ ἄγια see the discussion at v.2. An old A B V 931 x+ variant text reads η εβδομα ημερα instead of ἡ ἡμέρα ἡ ἑβδόμη, but ordinals with ἡμέρα between first and tenth always follow the noun throughout the Pentateuch.⁹ As at v.7 LXX has a conjunction plus a nominative adjectival phrase, though MT has ביום השביעי. I suspect that the translator levelled with v.7. For the concluding clause see comment at v.7.

23:10 Moses had said in formulaic terms "Say to the Israelites and say to them"; comp vv.2,24,34 for slight variations. The initial εἶπον occurs here for דבר, for which see comment at 22:2. The *n* text changed the imperative to λαλησον, which equals MT. This verse introduces the section on the firstfruits (vv.10—14).

The כי is well-rendered by the temporal particle ὅταν, thus "whenever you should enter the land ... and you should harvest its harvest." This constitutes the temporal protasis, which is what MT presupposes as well. The relative clause in MT is a nominal clause with אני as subject and the participle נתן as predicate. As usual, LXX translates this by a pronoun plus a present tense. An M V Byz+ variant text has changed θερίζητε to θεριζετε. The present indicative is highly unusual; either it is an error for θερίζητε or for the future θερισετε. The latter would then signal the onset of the apodosis.

The apodosis is signalized by the change of verbal inflection to the future. The initial καί reflects the Hebrew pattern. What is commanded is "you must bring δράγμα ἀπαρχὴν τοῦ θερισμοῦ ὑμῶν to the priest." The Hebrew has את עמר ראשית קצירכם. עמר is a bound element in a bound structure, and one might well have expected ἀπαρχήν to have been in the genitive. LXX has, however, the accusative. The word עמר is usually rendered "sheaf," thus "the sheaf of the firstfruits of your harvest." Syntactically ἀπαρχὴν τοῦ θερισμοῦ is an appositive explicative of δράγμα. δράγμα actually means "handful," thus an amount of grain stalks which the hand could envelop; it would not be unwarranted to render it by "sheaf," thus a sheaf consisting of the firstfruits of the harvest. One might

---

8. See THGL 118—119.
9. See THGL 103, where it is suggested that the variant text may have been influenced by the phrase ἑπτὰ ἡμέρας occurring in the immediate context.

then render the apodosis by "then you must bring a sheaf as the firstfruit of your harvest to the priest."

23:11 The verb הניף occurs 11 times in Lev, and is rendered in a variety of ways, by ἐπιτίθημι (7:20 14:24 23:20), by ἀφαιρέω (8:29 9:21), by ἀφορίζω (10:15 14:12), by φέρω at 23:12, and by ἀναφέρω here (twice) and 8:27. For a fuller discussion of the cognate expression הניף תנופה and its translation see discussion at 7:20(30). In context Lev says: "And he shall offer up the sheaf before the Lord to be acceptable on your behalf." For δεκτὸν ὑμῖν see comment at 22:19, and comp v.29.[10] The second clause states "τῇ ἐπαύριον τῆς πρώτης the priest shall offer it up." ἐπαύριον means "tomorrow," so here the phrase must mean "in the morning after the first (day)." MT has השבת as counterpart of τῆς πρώτης. Since the Sabbath is the last day of the week the morning of the first day would be the "tomorrow of the Sabbath," Possibly this odd way of putting it simply betrays his love for variation.

23:12 The verse changes to second plural, "and you must sacrifice (ποιήσετε) on the day on which φέρετε the sheaf," i.e. the Israelites (see v.10) are now directly addressed. The Byz text continues the third person singular with ποιησει and αφοριζηται. This makes the priest of v.11 the subject. That this reflects an exegetical change intended as a correction is clear from the change from φέρετε, referring to lay activity, to αφοριζηται which refers to a setting aside as a priestly function. The subjunctive is a present subjunctive which calls attention to a process or linear action, thus "on which you would be offering the sheaf."[11]

What you are to sacrifice is a כבש תמים בן שנתו. The בן שנתו is freely rendered by an adjective ἐνιαύσιον, thus "a year-old sheep without blemish" (πρόβατον ἄμωμον).[12]

23:13 The recipe for its sacrifice. This is coordinate with the preceding clause, thus in the accusative as a modifier of ποιήσετε, and coordinate with πρόβατον which was εἰς ὁλοκαύτωμα. θυσίαν renders מנחה, for which see ch.2; cf comment on 2:1. The αὐτοῦ must refer to δράγμα, i.e. the sheaf which constitutes

---

10. See SS 98.
11. See THGL 125.
12. See SS 98.

the firstfruits. The grain sacrifice is defined as consisting of two-tenths of fine flour prepared in oil. The measure is not given, but presumably intended was two-tenths of an ephah. The participle ἀναπεποιημένης renders בלולה "mixed," and becomes the regular equivalent in Num (24 times), but in Lev it is used only three times (also 6:40 7:2). Lev also used φυράω "mix," a more literal rendering (five times).

A nominative structure interrupts the instructions. It defines the previous sacrifices in "(it is) a sacrifice to the Lord, a sweet-smelling savour to the Lord." The word θυσία translates אשה this time. The translator makes no distinction between מנחה and אשה; both are rendered by θυσία. For אשה as θυσία see comment at 1:9. In the tradition, the majority F M text read εις οσμην instead of ὀσμή, but θυσία is not changed to the accusative, and the parenthetical character of the two structures is original.[13] Its syntactic independence has been shown in Lev by colons both before and after the structure.

Also modifying ποιήσετε is καὶ σπονδὴν αὐτοῦ "and its libation." This consists of τὸ τέταρτον τοῦ ἱν οἴνου "a fourth of a hin of wine." MT has יין רביעת ההן, and hex rearranges the word order by transposing οἴνου before τό to equal the Hebrew order. One quarter of a hin would equal slightly less than a liter/quart.

23:14 A further instruction: "and bread and roasted fresh ears you may not eat ἕως αὐτὴν τὴν ἡμέραν ταύτην." The use of the two pronouns modifying ἡμέραν is an attempt to render the Hebrew idiom עצם היום הזה "this very day." For πεφρυγμένα χίδρα νέα see comment at 2:14.[14] MT of 2:14 is, however, longer: קלוי באש גרש כרמל; here MT has וקלי וכרמל, but LXX disregarded the conjunction. A second ἕως structure defines what is meant by "this very day": ἕως ἂν προσενέγκητε ὑμεῖς τὰ δῶρα τῷ θεῷ ὑμῶν "until you have offered the gifts to your God." By τὰ δῶρα are meant the offerings of the firstfruits. Though it renders a singular קרבן it takes on the plural from the context.[15] The translator has added ὑμεῖς, presumably for emphasis, since it has no counterpart in MT. Hex has omitted the pronoun to equal MT. MT has קרבן אלהיכם, but LXX rendered "your God" in the dative; this makes "your God" modify the verb

---

13. See THGL 120.
14. For χίδρα νέα The Others read ἁπαλά.
15. See THGL 116.

rather than the noun. The majority A text has changed τῷ θεῷ to του θεου; this could be a recensional change, though not necessarily so.

For the last clause see comments at 3:17a with which this clause is identical, except for reading (νόμιμον) αἰώνιον instead of εις τὸν αἰῶνα.

23:15 Vv.15—22 deal with the feast of weeks. MT says "and you shall count לכם," i.e. for yourselves, but LXX uses the nominative ὑμεῖς, for which comp v.14. Most witnesses change ὑμεῖς to υμιν, which equals MT. The text is, however, by no means certain. It was chosen on the basis of support by codd A and B, along with b x+, but it could well be a secondary adaption to the pattern of v.14. ἀπὸ ἐπαύριον τῶν σαββάτων means "from the morning following the Sabbath day";comp comment at v.11. This is further defined as being "from the day which you would bring τὸ δράγμα τοῦ ἐπιθέματος." An ἐπίθεμα is a deposit, so "a deposit sacrifice"; see comment at 14:24. For the varied translations of תנופה and its meaning, see discussion at 7:20. Why the sheaf should be called "the sheaf of the deposit" is not clear. Possibly the idea is that the firstfruits are an offering deposited by the subject, or it might refer to the notion that this is an addition to the usual sacrifices which worshipers were accustomed to bringing. What is to be counted are seven full weeks, from which the designation "feast of weeks" is derived. The Hebrew word for "weeks" is שבתות, a feminine plural formation on שבת "Sabbath," which LXX rightly rendered by ἐβδομάδας, plural of ἐβδομάς "a period of seven days," i.e. a week. In MT this is followed by תהיינה, and hex has added εσονται υμιν. The υμιν suggests that the text of Origen read תהיינה לכם. The majority text, however, added αριθμησεις, probably under the influence of the parallel passage in Dt 16:9a which, however has εξαριθμήσεις σεαυτῷ.

23:16 This is part of the construction of v.15, i.e. "you must count from ... until the morning after the last week you shall count fifty days." The use of τῆς ἐσχάτης is exegetically correct, but the Hebrew has השביעת "the seventh." Since the feast starts with a Sabbath, a count from the next day through the last (or seventh) Sabbath adds 49 days, i.e. a total of 50 days. Comp the designation of this feast in Tob 2:1 as ἐν τῇ πεντηκοστῇ ἑορτῇ, eventually leading to the feast called Pentecost in the Christian tradition; cf Acts 2:1.

The coordinate clause instructs the Israelites to offer a θυσίαν νέαν to the Lord. The νέα sacrifice in this context means "a new grain sacrifice," as is the case of the Hebrew מנחה חדשה.

23:17 "From τῆς κατοικίας ὑμῶν you must bring loaves ἐπίθεμα." The Hebrew has a plural noun מושבתיכם, as well as at vv.3,14,21,31 and 3:17 7:26(16), but it is throughout rendered by a singular noun, except at v.31 where LXX does render it by the plural ἐν πάσαις κατοικίαις ὑμῶν. It is of course obvious that no Israelite would have more than a household, which is probably the rationale for the use of the singular noun. For ἐπίθεμα see comment at v.15. LXX follows Sam's חלות in its "(two) loaves." Hex omits "loaves", thereby equalling MT. MT's text is equally possible though one would expect שתי for שתים, and to be transposed before לחם. For the composition of the two loaves comp the fuller recipe of v.13. LXX also follows Sam's משני by its ἐκ δυό.[16] "Leavened they must be baked, from the firstfruits of the Lord." The genitive πρωτογενημάτων must designate source or origin. One might then render the clause freely as "Since they are the firstfruits for the Lord, they must be baked as leavened (loaves)."

In the tradition, the Byz text has the genitive επιθεματος for ἐπίθεμα. Since לחם תנופה could be taken as a bound phrase this might be recensional. A majority F M text has εσται ο αρτος ο εις instead of ἔσονται, clearly based on 24:5.

23:18 The loaves are insufficient; along with these "you must bring seven unblemished year-old lambs and one bullock from the herd and two unblemished rams." Hex has transposed ἕνα after "herd" to agree with the word order of MT. At v.12 Lev rendered כבש by πρόβατον, but here the plural is translated by ἀμνούς. In both cases they must be a year old, but an ἀμνός is supposed to be under a year old. The urban translator was apparently not all that knowledgeable about sheep, and possibly unaware of the distinction between ἀμνός and πρόβατον. MT does not state that the two rams must be תמימם; since sacrificial rams per se had to be without blemish, this is implicit. LXX makes this explicit by its ἀμώμους, which is based on the אילם שנים תמימם of Sam. Hex placed this word under the obelus to show its absence from MT.

---

16. As do Pesh and Vulg.

The next clause states that these animals shall be ὁλοκαύτωμα to the Lord. Scattered mss change to the plural, probaby because there are a number of animals, but the singular equals MT, and is Lev.[17]

The concluding clause is a nominal construction with αἱ θυσίαι αὐτῶν καὶ αἱ σπονδαὶ αὐτῶν as subject, and the remainder of the verse constituting the predicate. This is clearer in MT where θυσίαι represents מנחה and θυσία renders אשה. What the clause means is "both their sacrifices and their libations (constitute) a sacrifice, a sweet-smelling savor for the Lord"; this is similarly expressed in the parenthetical statement in v.13, which see.

23:19 The Israelites are also commanded to sacrifice both a sin offering and a sacrifice for deliverance along with the loaves of the firstfruit. The order is as usual in second person, ποιήσετε. In the tradition, an A B x+ text reads ποιησουσιν, which does not make a great deal of sense. It may have been stimulated by the double occurrence of αὐτῶν in the preceding clauses, but it is wrong.[18] For a χίμαρον ἐξ αἰγῶν see comment at 4:23. This is to be brought περὶ ἁμαρτίας, i.e. as a sin offering. For περὶ ἁμαρτίας see comment at 4:3.

The second offering is to consist ot two year-old lambs. For ἀμνοὺς ἐνιαυσίους see comment at v.18. For θυσίαν σωτηρίου see comment at 3:1. σωτηρίου is the standard translation of שלמים. Though the Hebrew is plural, Lev never renders the term in any other way but σωτηρίου. The Byz text does read ειρηνικων, which is well-attested as a reading from The Three;[19] see the anonymous reading on the margins of M′ 344. The last prepositional phrase, μετὰ τῶν ἄρτων τοῦ πρωτογενήματος, has no counterpart in MT, and is taken over from v.20. Hex omits the phrase to equal MT.

23:20 For הניף modified by תנופה and the various ways in which it was translated by Lev see discussion at 7:20; for ἐπιθήσει ... ἐπίθεμα also see 14:24. It might be noted that ἐπιθήσει occurs here without an ἐπί phrase, a rare usage in the book (only three times out of 64 cases of ἐπιτίθημι).[20] הבכורים was translated by the plural πρωτογενημάτων in v.17, but here (and perforce in its copy in v.19) by

---

17. See THGL 118—119.
18. See THGL 125.
19. See THGL 118.
20. See THGL 98 and 121.

the singular. But in v.17 the word stands by itself and unarticulated, whereas here it modifies ἄρτων, thus loaves of the firstfruit. Both in vv.19 and 20 the loaves are part of a sacrifice, the firstfruit offering, and therefore singular. These are to be placed ἔναντι κυρίου, i.e. in the sanctuary along with the two lambs.

There is a problem with αὐτά 1° and its reference, as well as with the Hebrew אתם. It seems to refer to all the sacrifices mentioned in vv.18,19. Or could it refer simply to the two year-old lambs intended as a sacrifice for deliverance in v.19? The fact that αὐτά is neuter is not decisive, since Lev often used the neuter pronoun when the reference was vague.[21]

MT concludes rather strangely with קדש יהיו ליהוה לכהן "holy shall they be to Yahweh, to the priest." This could easily be misinterpreted to mean that Yahweh was the priest, which is obviously to be avoided. The translator made sense of this by adding τῷ προσφέροντι αὐτὰ αὐτῷ ἔσται "to the priest, the one who presented them, his shall they be." The repetition of αὐτά does not help to identify the antecedent, which must be the same as for v.a. Note the fluctuation in number; the ἅγια ἔσονται, and αὐτά ...ἔσται.[22] The subject is in both cases that which the priest shall place as a deposit sacrifice.

23:21 The syntax of the opening clause(s) is not clear. It begins with וקראתם בעצם היום הזה and this is followed by מקרא קדש יהיה לכם. Where does the break come? Is קראתם used absolutely, or does מקרא קדש modify it, and if so, is יהיה לכם a modifier of מקרא, i.e. "a sacred convocation which shall be to you"? The Masoretes placed a *rabia*ᶜ on הזה, thereby taking וקראתם absolutely. LXX is also problematic; it has divided after מקרא, contrary to the Masoretes which joined מקרא and קדש by a *maqqeph*. LXX has understood מקרא to be the modifier of קראתם by its κλητήν, thus "and you shall call a convocation; holy shall it be to you." A popular A F reading has κλητή, i.e. the cut comes between הזה and מקרא. The Byz text has adopted both, reading κλητήν κλητή. I now would understand the Lev text as the least likely to be original. The collocation מקרא קדש is an oft-recurring structure; its first occurrence is at Exod 12:16, and in our chapter it occurs eight times (and once in the plural מקראי at v.23), and it is rendered as κλητὴ ἅγια throughout except here. Incidentally מקרא קדש also occurs in Num (six times), and only once is κλητὴ ἅγια used; in five cases it is

---

21. See Huber 34—35.
22. See SS 197.

rendered by ἐπίκλητος ἅγια. Never did translators consider the structure as anything but an adjectival one. I would suggest that the original reading is the A reading, i.e. κλητή. This would then involve moving the colon as well. I would now read ἡμέραν· κλητή, and translate "And you shall make a proclamation on that very day; it shall be a sacred convocation for you."[23]

At v.14 עצם היום הזה (עד) was translated by αὐτὴν τὴν ἡμέραν ταύτην, but here where it is governed by ב, it becomes ταύτην τὴν ἡμέραν. The tradition was not overly satisfied with this, some witnesses changing ταύτην to αυτην, and others transposing it to the end. The odd order is an attempt to allow for the עצם, which has no real equivalent in Greek.

For the clause "no service work may you do in it," see comment at v.7. The ἐν αὐτῇ has no correspondent in MT (nor in v.7), and hex has placed it under the obelus to indicate that absence. The phrase simply makes explicit what is already implicit. The last clause is identical with that ending v.14, which see. It is a case of leveling, however, in that MT has transposed the last two prepositional phrases, whereas LXX has simply taken over the Greek of v.14. Hex has "corrected" the Greek by transposing the two clauses.

23:22 This verse is paralleled in 19:9—10, with which it is identical in the Hebrew, except for reading בקצרך instead of לקצר, and omitting v.10a, i.e. the reference to vineyards.[24] LXX, however, translated the Hebrew of our verse; the two Greek versions are substantially different.

LXX translates the opening ובקצרכם, i.e. a pronoun plus bound infinitive, by a temporal clause structure, καὶ ὅταν θερίζητε "and whenever you might harvest." A marginal reading of s mss substitutes εκθεριζοντων for ὅταν θερίζητε, i.e. the reading from 19:9.

The apodosis realizes פאת שדך quite differently as well. At 19:9 LXX had τὸν θερισμὸν ὑμῶν τοῦ ἀγροῦ, but here it becomes more descriptive: τὸ λοιπὸν τοῦ θερισμοῦ τοῦ ἀγροῦ σου. What is meant is "you may not finish off the harvest of your field completely," i.e. leave your field completely clean.[25] But what is particularly odd about LXX's rendering is the συντελέσετε, i.e. it continues the

---
23. This is also the reading adopted by Harlé-Pralon.
24. Gispen suggests that v.10a was omitted by parablepsis due to homoioteleuton, both vv.9 and 10a ending with תלקט, which is a reasonable suggestion.
25. As at 19:9 the anonymous reading τὸ φααθ must be from Theod.

plural of the protasis, but changes to the singular immediately thereafter, which together with MT it continues for the remainder of the verse. It thus reads "*you may not finish off the rest of the harvest of thy field ....*" MT changed to the singular for the entire clause, i.e. it read תכלה (not תכלו).

The coordinate clause is identical in the two versions; for its interpretation, see comments at 19:9. V.b is also like that of 19:10b, with two exceptions; instead of the verb καταλείψεις our text has ὑπολείψῃ; the two are, however, synonyms, and secondly, in the long self-identification formula 19:10b has an unnecessary εἰμι after ἐγώ; see comments ad loc. In the tradition, a majority V text levels with 19:10 by reading καταλείψεις; the reading is clearly secondary.

23:23—24 Vv.23—25 constitute a separate section introduced by "and the Lord spoke to Moses, saying"; the Israelites are told that "the seventh month, on the first of the month there shall be for you an ἀνάπαυσις." This renders שבתון; for a full discussion see comment at 16:31. This "rest" is called a μνημοσύνην σαλπίγγων "a memorial of trumpets." MT has זכרון תרועה. The term תרועה refers to some kind of cultic blast of sound; since at 25:9 reference is made to שופר תרועה, the translation of σαλπίγγων is a reasonable interpretation; it is a "memorial of trumpet blasts." In post-exilic Judaism this trumpet blast signalled the beginning of the year, and this festival became known as ראש השנה "New Year's Day." The translation "on the first (for μιᾷ) of the month" is not literal; it represents באחד, i.e. "on (day) one," but this is the way Hebrew expresses "on the first of," and it, along with its Greek rendering, must be idiomatically translated into English by "on the first of."

"A sacred convocation ἔσται ὑμῖν" also occurs at v.7, which see; see also the discussion on κλητὴ ἅγια at v.21. MT lacks the לכם יהיה of v.7 here, and hex has rightly placed ἔσται ὑμῖν under the obelus.

23:25 For the first clause see comments at v.7. The אשה sacrifice is here translated by ὁλοκαύτωμα; for אשה as a general term for sacrifice, see the discussion at 1:9. A popular V text reads the plural ολοκαυτωματα, but here a single burnt offering is intended, and the plural is secondary.[26]

---

26. See THGL 118.

23:27 Vv.27–32 concern the day of atonement. In contrast to vv.1–2, 9–10, 23–24, 33–34 this section does not have the Lord's order "speak/say to the Israelites ...," as part of what the Lord communicated to Moses; the regulations follow immediately on "and the Lord spoke to Moses, saying." The feast is to take place "on the tenth of this seventh month." In MT this is introduced by אַךְ, a particle which calls special attention to what follows. LXX simply has καί. The pronoun τούτου, as well as its counterpart הזה, calls attention to the fact that it is the same seventh month as the feast of the memorial trumpets (v.24), but nine days later. The subject of this nominal clause is ἡμέρα ἐξιλασμοῦ, for which MT has יום הכפרים הוא. The failure to render הוא is remarkable; in fact, only here and at 25:33 is that the case. Usually it is rendered by ἐστιν (89 times) or by οὗτος (19 times), and rarely by both.[27] Hex has added εστιν under the asterisk to represent the הוא. The noun ἐξιλασμοῦ occurs only here and in v.28, though the simplex also occurs once (25:9). The term, like its Hebrew counterpart כפרים, means "propitiation, expiation, atonement," and always involves a sacrifice. Precisely how this was done has been much discussed, but the basic idea must remain that of removing obstacles between the worshiper and deity; a reconciliation is in some way being attempted. For the verbal notion see comment at 1:4.

Atonement must consist of at least two parts: a) "you must humble yourselves." Precisely how this humiliation of the person (ψυχή) is to be effected is not said, but it is commonly thought to involve fasting as a form of self-denial,[28] as well as confession of sin, and b) "you must bring a burnt offering to the Lord"; this is an exact repetition of the last clause in v.25; cf comments ad loc. Here too, a popular variant text reads the plural ολοκαυτωματα, but only a single sacrifice is intended.[29]

23:28 LXX does not begin with a coordinate conjunction as MT does, but just begins with πᾶν ἔργον. It is not ἔργον λατρευτόν work that is forbidden, but ἔργον, which simply follows MT. The distinction between the prohibition for this feast and the Sabbath and that of the other feasts is undoubtedly important. On the day of atonement complete cessation of work activity is demanded. This gives added impetus to the understanding of "humbling yourselves" in v.28 that this

---

27. See THGL 112.
28. See νηστεύσατε, the anonymous reading on the margin of M'.
29. See THGL 118.

might involve fasting; see also v.30. For the rendering of בעצם היום הזה, see comment at v.14.

The reason for the abstention from all work is given in the γάρ/כי clauses. It is "because this is a day of atonement for you," followed by a purposive infinitive "ἐξιλάσασθαι on your behalf before the Lord your God." For the infinitive see comment at 4:20. The clause translates MT word for word, except that MT has no correspondent for ὑμῖν "for you." Of course, ὑμῖν is easily added even where MT lacks an equivalent, as e.g. at vv.8,24.

23:29 MT begins this verse with כי which is not sensible as a causal particle, even though NRSV begins its translation with "For." NJPS has sensibly taken it as an asseverative, and translates "Indeed," whereas NIV simply disregards it, as does LXX. In the tradition, hex has added γαρ to represent it. The use of μή plus a future tense is "of dubious usage,"[30] though here found in a ἥτις clause. For ἐν αὐτῇ τῇ ἡμέρᾳ ταύτῃ see v.28. The penalty for disobedience is destruction from the people. Oddly enough, whenever the verb כרת occurs in a penalty statement, either as הכרתי of God, or נכרתה of a person (נפש) and is modified by מן plus עם, the noun is plural as here, מעמיה (ten times), but LXX always renders it by a singular noun (ἐκ τοῦ λαοῦ).

23:30 A similar fate awaits anyone who does any work on the day of atonement. V.a is a pendant construction which defines the subject ἡ ψυχὴ ἐκείνη. In MT the pendant is coordinated with what follows, but fortunately LXX does not introduce the subject with καί. Syh does represent the waw, and this may be a hex correction. The verb differs (from that of v.29); it is here ἀπολεῖται, but the Hebrew has also changed from נכרתה to האבדתי. The Hebrew has "I shall cause that person to perish"; the Lord himself will kill that נפש, whereas LXX uses exactly the same pattern as in v.29 with a passive transform using "that person" as subject. It is significant that only vv.29–30 record any penalty for non-observance in the entire chapter, but the translator goes a step further than MT by voiding divine involvement in carrying out the death sentence. In the tradition, the O b text has changed the verb ἀπολεῖται to αποθανειται.

---

30. According to LS sub μή A.3.

23:31 For the first prohibition see comment at v.28. The second statement also occurs at vv.14,21 and 3:17 (with εἰς τὸν αἰῶνα for αἰώνιον), but here בכל משבתיכם is not translated by a singular noun, but literally by the plural, ἐν πάσαις κατοικίαις ὑμῶν. The b text levels with the other occurrences by its παση κατοικια. I see no reason for the difference in number, except to illustrate the translator's love for variation.

23:32 σάββατα σαββάτων occurs elsewhere in the book only at 16:31; there the structure is followed by ἀνάπαυσις as a doublet explaining what the word means; cf comment ad loc. The next clause is a repetition of v.27; cf comment ad loc.

MT dates the feast as "on the ninth of the month in the evening." This is followed by "from evening to evening," i.e. one full day. LXX has shortened this by changing the opening preposition ב to ἀπό, and omitting בערב "in the evening," thus "from the ninth of the month, from evening to evening." The rendering is somewhat more economical in that בערב is otiose, and the time is more simply communicated by the Greek. Hex has tried to "correct" this by rendering בערב by εσπερας, and inserting it after "month"; this must be taken as a genitive of time within which something occurs, which does not fit well in the context.

During this time σαββατιεῖτε τὰ σάββατα ὑμῶν which renders MT adequately. The verb was created by the Exod translator at 16:30 as a denominative verb taken from the noun σάββατα, an Aramaic loanword taken into Greek by the Jews of Alexandria. It was then taken to be a neuter plural noun, resulting in a new singular σάββατον, which, however, never appears in the Pentateuch. The sense of the Greek is best rendered by "you must sabbatize your Sabbath."

23:34 Vv.33—36 plus 39—43 concern the feast of tabernacles. The section has the full introduction "and the Lord spoke to Moses saying: speak to the Israelites saying." The time of the feast is given as "on the fifteen of this seventh month." For τούτου see comment at v.27. MT defines the fifteenth as יום, and hex has added ημερα to represent it. The feast is called ἑορτὴ σκηνῶν. For ἑορτή as translation for חג see discussion at v.6. The Hebrew סכות is usually rendered by σκηνῶν, particularly when it designates the ἑορτή. The feast is to continue for ἑπτὰ ἡμέρας, the accusative indicating extent of time.

23:35 The verse begins asyndetically in MT, but LXX begins with καί. MT begins with a prepositional phrase ביום הראשון, thus "on the first day (there will be) a sacred convocation." LXX reworks this by changing the phrase to the subject ἡ ἡμερα ἡ πρώτη, i.e. "the first day is a sacred convocation." This too is a day on which no service work is permitted. The prohibition is an exact replica of v.7, for which see comment ad loc.

23:36 The word אשה "sacrifice" occurs twice in the verse; the first time it is taken as a collective and rendered by ὁλοκαυτώματα, and the second time as a singular. For the translation of אשה see comment at 1:9. The first time the word refers to bringing sacrifices ἑπτὰ ἡμέρας, and so it can be plural. The singular in MT means a sacrifice for each of the seven days. The second case is valid for ἡ ἡμέρα ἡ ὀγδόη, and therefore must be singular. In the tradition, a popular B V text has, however, changed the word to the plural ολοκαυτωματα, which can only be secondary. Similarly ὁλοκαυτώματα was changed to the singular by a popular A M V text, but it too is not original.[31]

For the second clause LXX follows the conjunction of Sam's וביום rather than the ביום of MT. LXX, however, changes the construction to the nominative, i.e. to the subject, following the pattern of v.35, rather than a predicatival prepositional phrase as in MT; like the first day, v.35, the eighth day is a sacred convocation. It is called an ἐξόδιον, a word occurring here for the first time in the Pentateuch (it also occurs at Num 29:35 Dt 16:8). It only translates עצרת, a word of uncertain meaning, though except for Jer 9:1b, it always occurs in the context of some festival or festivals. In the Pentateuch it is used only for the final day of a festival lasting a full week. Modern versions differ: NIV translated by the traditional "solemn assembly"; NJPS has "a solemn gathering," and NRSV makes it "a closing assembly." Since ἐξόδιον in Classical Greek refers specifically to the finale or conclusion of a dramatic production, usually, though not necessarily, of a tragedy, the word is not ill-chosen; the feast of tabernacles can be thought of as a dramatic festival, of which the eighth day is an ἐχόδιον; see also 2Par 7:9 2Esdr 18:18.[32] For the last clause see comment at v.7.

---

31. See THGL 118—119.
32. See also Harlé-Pralon ad loc.

23:37 Vv.37—38 are a concluding summary of the festivals interrupting the section on the feast of tabernacles. One might well have expected these verses to come after v.43. MT begins with a nominal clause, אלה מועדי יהוה, which LXX renders without a linking verb, closely following MT, αὗται αἱ ἑορταὶ (τῷ κυρίῳ). The free element of the bound phrase is not rendered by an expected genitive κυρίου, but by an articulated dative, which the translator does use occasionally as a dative of possession.[33] Actually Lev is weakly supported both in the articulated dative and in the omission of the article by B M C′ʼ x+, and the F V majority text reads κυρίου, which may constitute a recensional correction. Lev, however, far more often articulates the dative in rendering ליהוה (73 out of 93 cases), and the article is likely to be original here as well.

The relative clause which follows modifies ἑορταί. ἅς is an atypically idiomatic rendering for אשר plus אתם. The translator usually would have used ας ... αυτας, i.e. in Hebraic fashion rendering אתם by a recapitulative pronoun; in fact, a majority F M text actually added αυτας after καλέσετε, presumably as a recensional correction.

The verb καλέσετε is modified by a ὥστε plus infinitive structure, indicating the probable result of calling sacred convocations, viz. "so as to present to the Lord sacrifices, burnt offerings and their (grain) sacrifices and their libations day by day." For καρπώματα as a rendering for אשה see discussion at 2:9. The Byz text has changed καρπώματα to the singular, which may well be a recensional change in view of the singular אשה. ὁλοκαυτώματα correctly renders עלה, which can only be a collective in this context.[34] The "burnt offerings" were referred to in vv.12,18.

MT follows עלה by ומנחה זבח ונסכים "and grain sacrifices, sacrifices and libations." LXX omits זבח entirely, and adds αὐτῶν to both θυσίας and σπονδάς. θυσίας rendering מנחה occurred in vv.13,16,18, whereas the pair σπονδας/נסכים is found in vv.13,18. The two cases of αὐτῶν have no basis in MT, but probably constitute instances of leveling with v.18. It is not at all clear to what the pronouns refer. It could hardly be to the ὁλοκαυτώματα; burnt offerings do not consist of grain sacrifices and libations. Probably intended as antecedent were the ἑορταί, which is more likely as a referent than κλητάς or καρπώματα. In the

---

33. See THGL 80, and also SS 68.
34. See THGL 118—119.

tradition, only the second one has been removed recensionally.³⁵ The accusative phrase τὸ καθ' ἡμέραν εἰς ἡμέραν is one indicating extent of time, thus "day by day." The construction appears elsewhere only at Exod 16:5 where it renders יום יום. MT has דבר יום ביומו here; "the matter of a day in its day" is an idiom for "daily," and is correctly interpreted by the adverbial collocation of LXX. See also Note at Exod 16:5.

23:38 The list of sacrifices referred to in v.37 excludes four items, which are listed in four πλήν structures; in other words, v.38 is syntactically part of the preceding verse. The first exclusion is (πλὴν) τῶν σαββάτων κυρίου, which in sense differs from the next three in that observance of the Sabbaths is legislated (cf v.3), and the other three, τῶν δομάτων, πασῶν τῶν εὐχῶν and τῶν ἑκουσίων, in each case modified by ὑμῶν, are all voluntary. This means that the concluding relative clause can only refer to these three; these are ἃ ἂν δῶτε τῷ κυρίῳ "which you might give to the Lord." The pronoun is neuter, since it has no single antecedent; in such cases Lev often employs the neuter.³⁶ LXX follows MT except that MT also has a כל before "your voluntary offerings." In the tradition, ms 376 and b do add πάντων before τῶν ἑκουσίων, which is probably recensional in character. After all, ms 376 is an important member of the O group which usually represents the hex recension.

23:39 With v.39 the regulations concerning the feast of tabernacles resume. It begins by repeating parts of vv.34—36. For the time of the feast see comments at v.34. That the translator was influenced by v.34 is clear from the inclusion of τούτου which has no counterpart in MT here, but does obtain in v.34. For אך rendered by καί see comment at v.27. A new bit of information is given by the ὅταν structure defining the time of the feast as the time "whenever you have finished (harvesting) the products of the land," i.e. whenever you have finished the harvest. MT makes this clearer by its ב plus the bound infinitive אספכם, i.e. "when you have gathered." LXX uses the verb συντελέσητε "you have finished, completed"; of course, what is meant is "finished gathering." The feast then comes at the end of the harvest season.

---

35. See THGL 93—94.
36. See Huber 33—36.

The apodosis to the ὅταν clause is signalled by the future ἑορτάσετε "you must make a feast to the Lord for seven days." MT has a cognate expression, (תחגו את חג יהוה), which LXX has nicely coalesced in the single verb ἑορτάσετε. MT has a bound phrase חג יהוה "feast of Yahweh," which is shortened in LXX to τῷ κυρίῳ. The dative was necessitated by the failure to render חג. Not surprisingly hex has added under the asterisk τὴν εορτην to represent the cognate noun, but has not changed the dative to κυριου. Lev has τῷ κυρίῳ modifying the verb along with the accusative of extent of time, "seven days." Instead of the future verb a B *oII n y+* variant has the aorist imperative, but Lev normally issues apodoses in the future tense, and the B reading must be judged secondary.

Vv.35—36 had ordered for the first and eighth day of the feast that "you may not do any service work," which v.39 states more economically by the single word ἀνάπαυσις/שבתון as the subject of two nominal clauses, with preposed datives of time when (first/eighth day) as respective predicates. The term שבתון is always rendered by ἀνάπαυσις. It usually follows שבת, only occurring without it at v.24 and here; for a full discussion of the words see comment at 16:31.

23:40 Detailed regulations for the celebration. The Israelites are commanded to take various things on the first day; in MT these are פרי עץ הדר כפת תמרים וענף עץ עבת וערבי נחל. For the first item the word הדר means "splendor," hence a tree of splendor; the item is translated by καρπὸν ξύλου ὡραῖον in which הדר is translated by an adjective, "fine (i.e. ripe) fruit of a tree." The second item[37] is adequately translated by κάλλυνθρα φοινίκων "dusters, i.e. leaves, of palm trees." The next item probably means "branches of leafy trees" which was adequately rendered by κλάδους ξύλου δασεῖς "bushy branches of trees."

The last item creates some difficulty. It seems to mean "poplars(?) of the wady." Lev has in its place ἰτέας καὶ ἄγνου κλάδους ἐκ χειμάρρου "branches of the willow and of the *agnos* tree near the river." The term ἄγνος means "chaste, pure." but here it refers to a type of tree, botanically defined as "agnus castus,"[38] thus a "chaste-tree"(?) The Hebrew has a bound phrase, but Lev renders the sec-

---

37. The anonymous reading καφφω, error for καφφω<τ> undoubtedly comes from Theod.
38. LS s.v. equates it with λύγος. Apparently its branches were strewn by women on their beds at the Thesmophoria. Obviously the translator did not know exactly what the ערבי of the wady was, and used two terms to describe it.

ond element by an ἐκ phrase. The trees must have commonly bordered streams, receiving their nourishment "out of the river."[39]

MT continues with a clause coordinate with the καὶ λήμψεσθε one, viz. ושמחתם, which the Greek rendered by a purposive infinitive, εὐφρανθῆναι.[40] Undoubtedly, the second clause of MT does express the point of the gathering of fruit, leaves and branches of various trees. The feast is to be one of rejoicing, but this is to be cultic in nature; the rejoicing is to be done לפני יהוה אלהיכם.[41]

In the tradition, ξύλου 2° was changed to the plural by A Byz+, but this is probably due to the plural context: κλάδους ... δασεῖς, and is secondary. Of more importance is the recognition by hex that the Greek text for the last item in the list is longer than the parent Hebrew; hex has placed καὶ ἄγνου κλάδους under the obelus to show that it has no Hebrew equivalent. Furthermore, the majority M text reads και ευφρανθησεσθε instead of the infinitive. Since O' and Syh both attest to this text, the revision is almost certainly hex in origin. The change by the C' t+ text of ἄγνου to αγνους was probably due to the influence of κλάδους which follows; it is a senseless error.

23:41 V.40 in MT ended with ימים. V.41 continues with וחגתם אתו חג ליהוה שבעת ימים (בשנה) "and you shall celebrate it as a feast for Yahweh seven days per year." LXX only attests to the last word by its τοῦ ἐνιαυτοῦ, which perforce must then go with v.40 to make sense. The translator simply made a mistake, his eye jumping from the first ימים to the next ימים; it is a case of parablepsis due to homoioteleuton. Hex has added και εορτασατε αυτην εορτην τω κυριω επτα ημερας under the asterisk before τοῦ ἐνιαυτοῦ (of v.40) to make up for the omission.[42]

---

39. Aq rendered the bound phrase by ἰτέας χειμάρρου; Theod and Sym have ἰτέαν χειμάρρου.
40. Aq, Sym and Theod read καὶ εὐφρανθήσεσθε.
41. Aq translates εἰς πρόσωπον κυρίου τοῦ θεοῦ ὑμῶν; Sym reads ἔμπροσθεν κυρίου τοῦ θεοῦ ὑμῶν, while Theod retains the text of Lev.
42. Theod and Aq have καὶ ἑορτάσατε (-σετε Aq) αὐτὴν ἑορτὴν τῷ κυρίῳ ἑπτὰ ἡμέρας, whereas Sym has καὶ πανηγυρίσετε αὐτὴν πανήγυριν τῷ κυρίῳ ἑπτὰ ἡμέρας. Instead of τοῦ ἐνιαυτοῦ Aq has <ἐν> ἐνιαυτῷ; Theod read ἐν τῷ ἐνιαυτῷ, while Sym retained LXX.

LXX begins with νομιμὸν αἰώνιον which is a second accusative modifier to the verb ἑορτάσετε; it also has αὐτήν, thus "you shall celebrate it as an eternal prescription."[43] This prescription or usage is to continue εἰς τὰς γενεὰς ὑμῶν.[44]

23:42 After the order ἐν σκηναῖς κατοικήσετε ἑπτὰ ἡμέρας, the text makes reference to πᾶς ὁ αὐτόχθων in Israel, i.e. "everyone native-born in Israel." In MT the predicate reads ישבו בסכת. Since the term האזרח is modified by כל the word is readily understood by a plural verb. The Greek has the collective noun as a singular, and the predicate is singular as well: κατοικήσει (ἐν σκηναῖς).[45] Sam also reads a singular: ישב. In spite of the πᾶς ὁ αὐτόχθων, a majority text does read a plural verb as well; the change is almost certainly recensional.

23:43 The divine purpose underlying the order to dwell in tents during this feast was an instructive one. It was "in order that your generations εἴδωσιν that I made the Israelites dwell ἐν σκηναῖς." Instead of εἴδωσιν the A B M V majority text reads ιδωσιν, an itacistic variant which, however, means "see" from εἴδω rather than εἴδωσιν from οἶδα "to know." Since in Hellenistic and Byzantine times the two words were homophonous, copyists easily confused the two, but the Hebrew has ידעו, which no copyist could confuse with יראו, and only εἴδωσιν can be from the translator.[46] Since κατῴκισα is a transitive verb, one might expect modification by an εἰς phrase, but in Hellenistic times ἐν and εἰς were often confused.[47] A popular F variant text added αν after ὅπως. This in no way changes the intent of the passage.[48]

The divine author effected this "when I brought them out from the land of Egypt," for which see comment at 19:36. The feast will then serve to remind the

---

43. Aq makes this an ἀκρίβεια αἰῶνος; Sym reads πρόσταγμα αἰώνιον, and Theod retains LXX.
44. Which Sym also adopts, but Aq has ταῖς γενεαῖς ὑμῶν.
45. This, of course, would not do for The Three. Aq has for the verb καθίσονται; Sym translates by μενοῦσιν, and Theod makes it κατοικήσουσιν. Aq also changes ἐν σκηναῖς, which Sym retains, to ἐν συσκιασμοῖς.
46. See Walters 197—204.
47. See SS 136.
48. According to Bauer sub ὅπως 2.a.β, the αν particle occurs with the aorist subjunctive. But here it occurs with εἴδωσιν which is present tense. But, of course, the popular itacistic variant ιδωσιν is aorist.

Israelites of the great redemptive act of the Exodus by reliving their manner of dwelling at the time of deliverance from the land of bondage.

This concludes the regulations for the feasts, and appropriately it ends with the long formula for divine self-identification, which authenticates the instructions for their celebration.

23:44 The final verse is peculiarly out of place: "And Moses made known (lit., spoke) the feasts of the Lord to the Israelites." The accusative τὰς ἑορτάς is a synecdoche for "regulations for the feasts." The *b* copyist was apparently bothered by the harshness of the figure "(speak) feasts," and substituted ευτολας ταυτας. In the tradition, the majority F text added του θεου after κυρίου, but the Hebrew simply has יהוה; the variant text is ex par.

Chapter 24

24:2 The text of MT is, except for צו instead of ואתה תצוה, exactly the same as Exod 27:20, but LXX differs considerably. What the Israelites are ordered to do is "let them take for you (i.e. for Moses) pure beaten olive oil εἰς φῶς." In the tradition, an A B F+ text has μοι instead of σοι, but this is a mistake. The people are not to take the oil to the Lord but to Moses, as in MT. The error is easily understood, since in the context of a divine command that the Lord would have the people take something for him in the practice of the cult is readily understood. The parallel passage in Exod also reads λαβέτωσάν σοι. The phrase εἰς φῶς "for light" renders למאור "for a light bearer"; the word has the instrumental prefix ma-, hence something that makes light. It is not to be confused here with נר "a lamp," and LXX has carefully distinguished between φῶς "light" and λύχνον "lamp."

This is followed by a purposive infinitive with λύχνον as accusative subject, thus "that a lamp might burn διὰ παντός," The Byz text has changed the structure to a ινα clause, ινα καιηται λυχνος, which is borrowed from Exod 27:20.

24:3 The verse begins with ἔξωθεν τοῦ καταπετάσματος ἐν τῇ σκηνῇ τοῦ μαρτυρίου. This belongs with v.2b, and modifies the infinitive καῦσαι, giving the location for the perpetually burning lamp; it is "outside the veil in the tent of testimony." In the parallel Exod 27:21 passage the two phrases are transposed, which the *b* text also follows.

LXX continues with a syndetic clause: "καὶ καύσουσιν αὐτόν (i.e. the λύχνον) Aaron and his sons." What the verb here means is "they shall make (it) burn." The verb καίω can be intransitive (see v.2) as well as transitive. The priests are to see to it that the lamp should not go out, but it must burn "from evening to morning before the Lord (i.e. in the sanctuary) continually." The Hebrew does not introduce this clause with a conjunction, and B *b*+ omit the καί. But this is neither original nor recensional. It precedes καύσουσιν, and the shorter text is simply a case of haplography.[1] In MT the veil is characterized as the פרכת העדת, and hex has added του μαρτυριου to render העדת. In MT the

---

1. See THGL 102.

pronominal modifier אתו must refer to נר; it is the lamp that must be tended. LXX agrees by rendering this by αὐτόν. In the tradition, a popular A variant text has αυτο rather than αὐτόν. This would mean that Aaron and his sons were to make the φῶς burn rather than the λύχνον. The verb καύσουσιν interprets the Hebrew יערך. MT has Aaron responsible for "arranging, tending" אתו. יערך in this context must mean to see to the care of the light, but LXX thinks in terms of the result—if one has tended and cared for the lamp it will burn ἐνδελεχῶς. MT has תמיד, which in v.2 had been rendered by διὰ παντός. For still a third interpretation see v.4. καὶ οἱ υἱοὶ αὐτοῦ follows the Sam text rather than MT.[2] Hex has placed the text under the obelus, since it was absent from MT. The responsibility for the perpetually burning lamp is not only Aaron's; it is shared by the Aaronids as well.

For the concluding nominal clause, see comment at 23:41, where exactly the same text obtains.

24:4 MT has the verse in third person singular: "on the pure lampstand יערך the lamps before Yahweh תמיד." LXX has the verb in second person plural, and again uses καίω, i.e. καύσετε; presumably the Lord's instructions are now directed to Aaron and his sons. The *b* text has changed it to καυσουσιν, which is consistent with, and probably leveling with, v.3.

The translator's love for variation becomes particularly apparent in his translation of תמיד by ἕως τὸ πρωί, for which most witnesses insert εις after ἕως, and the A *b n*+ text levels with v.3 in which the lamp is to be burning from evening ἕως πρωί before the Lord ἐνδελεχῶς, i.e. it omits τό. But "until morning" is hardly תמיד. On the other hand, the lamps do not burn continually, but only until the morning. It is possible to understand the διὰ παντός in v.2 as meaning always have plenty of oil in readiness, whereas the ἐνδελεχῶς is similarly limited by "from evening until morning"; here the phrase stands by itself absolutely, i.e. the translator "corrects" תמיד to what it actually means, i.e. the light must always burn until the morning.[3]

24:5 Vv.5—9 deal with the bread set before the Lord. The bread is to be made of fine flour. The directions are throughout given in second person plural, i.e.

---

2. Though Kenn 4,14,69,109,129,136,153,199 and 242 do add ובניו.
3. Daniel 267, note 41 makes it "pour plus de clarté."

Aaron and his sons are ordered to prepare the bread. In MT the orders in these verses are in the singular, i.e. Moses is addressed; or could Aaron possibly be the intended addressee?—see v.3 and the comment ad loc. In any event, the verbs are in the second singular. LXX is consistent throughout this section in involving Aaron and his sons, though in v.9 they are admittedly referred to in third person. The persistent plural in these verses is due to the plural of vv.3 and 4.

They are ordered to make "twelve bread loaves." In MT these are more precisely defined as חלות "loaves," (and החלה resp), but LXX uses ἄρτους, the regular translation for לחם. Since these are referred to as "twelve" and "one" resp. they perforce refer to units of bread, i.e. to loaves. These bread loaves are more fully described in Exod 25:29 as ἄρτους ἐνωπίους translating לחם פנים "bread of the presence," or at 39:18 as τοὺς ἄρτους τοὺς προκειμένους "the bread loaves placed in front." See Note at Exod 25:29(30).

Each loaf is to consist of "two-tenths (of an ephah)." The measure is not given; this was unnecessary, since only "of an ephah" makes sense; see comment at 23:13.

24:6 The priests are to "place them (i.e. the loaves) as two deposits (θέματα), six bread loaves as the one deposit." The noun refers literally to something placed, and could simply mean "heaps"; the term says nothing about how these were arranged; it is neutral and is best rendered "deposit." In MT these are two מערכות "two arrangements, orders," often interpreted as "two rows," though this is more precise than the Hebrew permits. The notion of ערך הלחם also occurs in Exod 40:23 where the phrase is translated by ἄρτους τῆς προθέσεως "the bread loaves of the setting forth (before Yahweh)." MT lacks an equivalent for τὸ ἓν θέμα, and simply has "you shall set them in two arrangements, six per arrangement." Hex has placed τὸ ἓν θέμα under the obelus to indicate their lack of correspondents in MT.[4] LXX, as well as modern translators, simply added this to make sense; the gloss correctly interprets the rather cryptic Hebrew.

Two prepositional phrases modifying ἐπιθήσετε indicate where the loaves are to be placed. They are to be placed ἐπὶ τὴν τράπεζαν τὴν καθαρόν. What is meant by "the pure table" is clear from the more detailed description in Exod 25:22(23) τράπεζαν χρυσίου καθαροῦ "table of pure gold," Furthermore, it is within the sanctuary, i.e. ἔναντι κυρίου.

24:7 The priests are also ordered to put on the deposit "pure frankincense and salt." The "and salt" has no basis in MT here, and is based on 2:13 where the Israelites are told to season every δῶρον θυσίας ὑμῶν with salt; they may not "withhold the salt of the Lord's covenant." The translator realized that the grain sacrifice had to be seasoned; see discussion at 2:13.⁵ Hex correctly placed καὶ ἅλα under the obelus. For the variant αλας in *f n z+* see comment at 2:13. For frankincense on sacrifice see 2:1.

The next clause in MT is in the singular, since it refers only to לבנה, but since LXX has added "salt," it is in the plural ἔσονται, which in turn is modified by two εἰς phrases: a) "for the bread loaves," i.e. the ἄρτους had frankincense and salt added, and b) εἰς ἀνάμνησιν "for a memorial sacrifice." The latter represents לאזכרה.⁶ Elsewhere the word אזכרה is always translated by μνημοσύνη; see the discussion of the difficult term at 2:2. In MT the clause concludes with אשה ליהוה "as a sacrifice to Yahweh," but LXX has in its place προκείμενα τῷ κυρίῳ "set before the Lord." The participle is neuter plural, which would seem to make the antecedent "frankincense and salt," but common sense would dictate a reference to ἄρτους, which is masculine. For ἄρτους as προκειμένους see Exod 39:18 and Note ad loc. I suspect that the use of the neuter is again evidence of the translator's use of the neuter in places where the antecedent is vague; probably intended by the neuter was bread plus frankincense and salt.⁷ In the tradition, a popular F M variant text simplifies matters by making the participle masculine, προκειμενοι, thus referring to ἄρτους.

24:8 MT begins with the distributive ביום השבת ביום השבת,⁸ which LXX simplifies by rendering a single "on the day of the Sabbath" by a dative of time in which, τῇ ἡμέρᾳ τῶν σαββάτων.⁹ The translator also changed the transitive verb plus suffix, יערכנו, "one (presumably Aaron?) shall arrange it," to a passive transform with subject unstated, προθήσεται (ἔναντι κυρίου) "shall be placed

---

5. Harlé-Pralon comment: "Cette glose témoigne sans doute aussi d'une pratique ancienne consistent à saler l'encens avant de d'exposer avec les pains." See also the discussion in Daniel 159, and for the verse as a whole, pp.159—161.
6. For a fuller discussion of the term ἀνάμνησις see Daniel 235—236.
7. See Huber 34—35.
8. See GK 134q.
9. See SS 110. Kenn 107,129,181 witness to a single ביום השבת as well.

before the Lord." The subject must be the ἀνάμνησιν; it is the memorial sacrifice consisting of the twelve loaves of bread that is to be set before the Lord every Sabbath day. And this is to be done διὰ παντός "regularly," i.e. without fail.

The prepositional phrase παρὰ τῶν υἱῶν Ἰσραήλ modifies the verb, i.e. "it shall be placed ... (taken) from the Israelites." The preposition means that their committment came from the Israelites. The διαθήκην αἰώνιον is then an adverbial accusative.[10] I would translate the verse: "On the Sabbath day it shall be set before the Lord without fail on behalf of (i.e. coming from) the Israelites as an eternal covenant." The covenant is then shown by the part that Israelites play in providing for the regular provisions of the bread set before the Lord.

In the tradition, an A B x+ text has simplified the predicate by changing παρά to ενωπιον, a preposition not favored by Lev (it only occurs seven times in the book). Here the change is influenced by the context in which ἔναντι κυρίου had occurred. But MT reads מאת, which παρά represents correctly; the more difficult text with παρά is original.[11] Also in the tradition is the gloss αυτα read by V O b+ after the verb. This may well be a hex correction intended to represent the suffix of יערכנו, necessarily in the plural because of the context.

24:9 V.a states that it "ἔσται for Aaron and his sons, and they shall eat αὐτά in a holy place,"[12] which at 6:26 is located ἐν αὐλῇ τῆς σκηνῆς τοῦ μαρτυρίου. The subject of ἔσται is the διαθήκην of v.8, which is synecdochic for the loaves of the covenant, as is clear from αὐτά. For the use of the neuter see the comment at v.7 on προκείμενα; it refers to the combination of bread, frankincense and salt.

The γάρ clause gives the reason for what is said in v.a. These loaves are set aside as very holy, i.e. intended solely for priestly consumption; cf the discussion at 2:3. This is followed by "this shall be for him (i.e. for Aaron) an eternal prescription from the things being sacrificed to the Lord." The critical text would make better sense if the comma after κυρίῳ were transposed after ἁγίων. The translation of מאשי by ἀπὸ τῶν θυσιαζομένων is unique; for the more usual renderings of אשה see the discussion at 1:9. Furthermore, the participle is a present participle and means "those things being sacrificed." Since what is being dis-

---

10. The Sym reading on the margin of M reads θήκην, but it almost certainly is short for συνθήκην, as HR sub συνθήκη makes likely.
11. See THGL 77.
12. Aq has ἐν τόπῳ ἡγιασμένῳ instead of ἐν τόπῳ ἁγίῳ; Theod and Sym retain the Lev text.

cussed here are the loaves of bread proferred to the Lord on a weekly basis, the term אשי might not seem overly appropriate as κάρπωμα or even θυσία, whereas the participle generalizes; it would include anything being offered to the Lord.[13]

24:10 Vv.10—23 describe an incident of a blasphemer in the camp, with vv.14—22 constituting the Lord's instructions on the matter. The case concerns "a son of an Israelite woman, and he was the son of an Egyptian," MT has בן איש מצרי, and hex has added ανδρος under the asterisk before Αἰγυπτίου to equal איש. Actually, the ανδρος is quite unnecessary, since Αἰγυπτίου is inflected as a masculine nominal. The verb ἦν has no counterpart in MT, but was added for good sense. This individual went out ἐν τοῖς υἱοῖς ᾽Ισραήλ, an obvious case of ἐν being used in the sense of εις,[14] since movement is implied. The ἐν was probably used because the Hebrew has בתוך "in the midst of."

The next clause states that "ὁ ἐκ τῆς ᾽Ισραηλίτιδος and the Israelite man had a fight." MT has בן הישראלית, but LXX has ἐκ instead of בן,[15] which could also have been expressed simply by ο της ισραηλιτης; the article was necessarily used for the coordinate structure, and stylistically the articulation is expected here as well. It is, however, also attested in Qumran texts.[16]

24:11 The translator understood ויקב either as from קבב "to curse," or from the "Nebenform" נקב; see v.16 where נקב presupposes the latter. He subordinated the first clause as an attributive participle to κατηράσατο, which rendered the second clause ויקלל, and so he chose ἐπονόμασας "pronouncing," thus: "And the son of the Israelite woman by pronouncing the name, cursed." Presumably for a half-breed, and thus not a true Israelite, to pronounce the sacred name was itself a curse. Actually, three mss do add the name κυριου after ὄνομα. The translator clearly understood it, as v.16 shows, as meaning that the cursing involved pronouncing the sacred name by someone who was not a true Israelite. What made this a judicial affair was that he κατηράσατο.[17]

---

13. Aq translated v.b by ὅτι ἡγιασμένον ἡγιασμένων ἐστὶν αὐτῷ ἀπὸ πυρῶν κυρίῳ ἀκριβασμὸς αἰῶνος. Theod reads ὅτι ἅγια ἁγίων ἐστὶν αὐτῷ ἀπὸ τῶν τοῦ πυρὸς κυρίου νόμμον αἰώνιον, whereas Sym has ὅτι ἅγιον ἁγίων ἐστὶν αὐτῷ ἀπὸ τῶν καρπωμάτων κυρίου σύνταξις αἰώνιος.
14. See SS 138.
15. See SS 69.
16. Both by 4QLev^b and 11QpaleoLev^a; see DJD XII 185—186.
17. Sym makes the crime clear by his ἐβλασφήμησεν.

The subject of ἤγαγον/יביאו is not stated; it is the indefinite "they." The man's name is never given, but the mother's name, since she was an Israelite, is given as Σαλωμίθ. The name suffered greatly in the tradition. Disregarding all instances of itacistic spelling, there remain: ω to α as in σαλαμειθ, σαλαμιθ, σαλαμηθ; by aphaeresis in αλαμιθ, αλαμηθ; by syncopation in σαλμιθ; θ to ν in σαλαμειν, and by apocopation in σαλαμη and σαλαμει. The tradition had much greater difficulty with the name Δαβρί. The following list illustrates how badly an unknown name can fare: δεβρι, λαβρει, λαβρη, διαβρη, δαβαρει, δαφρη, ζαμβρι, δεβρην, δαβειρ, λαβειρ, λαβιρ, δαβριθ, θαβριθ, δαφριθ and δαβαιθ.

24:12 Again no subject is specified for ἀπέθεντο, thus "they put him away (in custody)." When an indefinite plural subject is used, it might be preferable to render it by a passive transform: "he was put away." MT adds a marked infinitival structure לפרש להם "to make clear to them," together with the norm for clarification, על פי יהוה "according to the mouth (i.e. the word) of Yahweh." The LXX has a different statement; for לפרש להם it has διακρῖναι αὐτόν "to make a decision with respect to him," i.e. to make a judgment in his case; the norm to be used is διὰ προστάγματος κυρίου "through a statute of the Lord."[18] This shows a somewhat different understanding of the judicial process. It is not so much the accusers who seek instruction in what to do through a divine word. For LXX a new word of the Lord is unnecessary, since the Torah has been given. Thus one can readily consult a "statute of the Lord"; one can make a judicial decision through the application of a προστάγματος.

24:14 Moses is ordered to "bring out the one who cursed outside the camp."[19] In MT the equivalent for "outside" is אל מחוץ, and hex has pedantically corrected the text by adding προς under the asterisk before ἔξω. In the second clause סמכו is rendered by the usual, but more colorless, ἐπιθήσουσιν; the Hebrew word means "to lean upon." The word χείρ is often translated without a genitive pronoun, but here χεῖρας αὐτῶν occurs.[20]

---

18. The Others have διαστεῖλαι αὐτοῖς ἐπὶ στόματος κυρίου.
19. Sym substitutes τὸν βλασφημόν for τὸν καταρασάμενον.
20. For the rendering of suffixes with יד see SS 95—96.

The capital punishment is death by stoning, carried out by πᾶσα ἡ συναγωνή. The noun is articulated when preceded by "all" only if the noun is not limited by a genitive modifier, as e.g. πᾶσα συναγωνὴ Ἰσραήλ, at v.16.[21]

24:15 MT reads "and to the Israelites תדבר לאמר," which is an unusual collocation, appearing elsewhere in the Pentateuch only at 9:3 Exod 30:31 and Num 27:8, and always with a preposed "and to the Israelites" as here. LXX renders the verb by an imperative as at 9:3, and continues with καὶ ἐρεῖς πρὸς αὐτούς; this pattern occurs 13 times in Lev, though in two cases with αὐτοῖς, and in two others with εἶπον; the LXX text here is clearly the result of leveling with this common pattern.[22] A popular F M text has changed λάλησον to λαλήσεις, which happens to equal MT, but is probably not recensional, since the future is the dominant inflection for commands throughout the book. In fact, hex has added λεγων after λάλησον and placed καὶ ἐρεῖς πρὸς αὐτούς under the obelus, thereby reflecting the Hebrew text.

What Moses is to say is introduced by ἄνθρωπος ἄνθρωπος introducing a condition. A popular A B text reads ανθρωπος ος, but this cannot be taken as original. MT has איש איש which is never rendered by ανθρωπος ος, but normally by a repeated ἄνθρωπος. Only twice does LXX not render it by a repeated "man"; at 22:4 it has a single ἄνθρωπος, and at 20:2 it reads τις. The repeated איש occurs ten times in the book. It should be noted that ος was simply a dittograph from ἄνθρωπος.[23]

The protasis reads "if he should curse θεόν," for which MT has אלהיו, and hex has added an αυτου to represent the suffix.[24] Here the failure to render the suffix may well have been intentional. After all, the half-breed involved need not have claimed Israel's God as his own.

As usual, the apodosis is in the future ἁμαρτίαν λήμψεται "he shall take on guilt." In MT the apodosis reads ונשא חטאו. LXX has not only transposed the two words, but in the interests of good Greek style disregarded both the initial conjunction and the suffix to the noun. The transposition does place the emphasis on the ἁμαρτίαν involved. Hex has added an αυτου under the asterisk after the

---

21. See SS 87.
22. See THGL 128.
23. See THGL 122.
24. According to Hesychius Sym read *homo qui detraxerit deo suo*, whereas Aq made it *vir quando blasphemaverit deum suum*.

noun, and also transposed the verb before the noun, thus reading λημψεται αμαρτιαν αυτου.²⁵

24:16 For ὀνομάζων as a rendering for נקב see comment at v.11. The root נקב is a variant of קבב. The initial conjunction is translated by δέ, contrasting with the condition of the preceding verse. The clause says "but let the one pronouncing the name of the Lord surely be put to death."²⁶ The second clause describes the manner of execution: "with stones let the entire community of Israel stone him." The dative noun λίθοις interprets the cognate free infinitive רגום which is intended to place further emphasis on the verbal idea of stoning. The noun is simply a dative of means.²⁷ In the tradition the Byz text reads λιθοβολια instead of λίθοις, obviously mediated through one of The Three. It represents a more literal rendering of רגום. As was the case with the first clause, the prefix inflection, usually rendered by a future, is translated by a third person imperative. The inflection is in the singular, grammatically agreeing with the subject συναγωγή. The subject in MT is also singular, העדה, but the predicate is in the plural ירגמו. עדה is, of course, a community, and so it can take either a singular or a plural predicate. The Hebrew כל העדה has πᾶσα συναγωγὴ Ἰσραήλ as an expanded subject. Hex has omitted Ἰσραήλ to equal MT, and has also added the article before συναγωγή. The pattern of articulation of a noun modified by "all" depends on whether the noun is followed by a genitive modifier, in which case the noun is unarticulated.²⁸ The addition of Ἰσραήλ is quite unnecessary; the entire congregation could only be that of Israel; the gloss merely makes explicit what is implicit.

V.b insists on no exception to the previous statement. It is now no longer an ad hoc decision applying only to the son of Salomith, but is made to apply to anyone in Israel. This gives a further basis for the LXX interpretation of v.12b as well; see comment ad loc. כגר כאזרח "whether resident alien or native-born"²⁹ is idiomatically translated by an ἐάν τε ... ἐάν τε structure. This is set up as a nominative pendant, to be taken up by αὐτόν as subject of an infinitive, thus

---

25. According to Hesychius Aq read *et acceperit iniquitatem sibi* for the apodosis.
26. According to Hesychius Aq read *et denominans nomen domini morte moriatur*.
27. See THGL 105.
28. See THGL 86—87.
29. BDB sub ב 2 defines the repeated preposition as "to signify the completeness of the correspondency between two objects (peculiar to Hebrew)."

"whether ... or ..., when he pronounces the name of the Lord, let him die." The Hebrew word is יומת, which in the first clause was rendered by θανατούσθω, but here by τελευτάτω. τελευτάω means "to come to an end, to finish," and so to die. MT simply has שם, whereas LXX has τὸ ὄνομα κυρίου. Hex has placed κυρίου under the obelus to show that it was absent from MT. LXX has given the offence greater precision by its identification of τὸ ὄνομα; it is of course already implicit as v.11 shows.

24:17 The formulaic introduction to casuistic law, ואיש כי, is here rendered by καὶ ἄνθρωπος ὅς, which also occurs at 15:16 20:9 22:14,21 and 27:14.[30] The protasis in MT reads כי יכה כל נפש אדם. LXX does not render the כל, and hex has added πασαν before ψυχην. LXX has also added a second condition at the end, καὶ ἀποθάνῃ, thereby leveling with vv.18,21. Hex has taken note of this as an addition by placing it under the obelus. The phrase ψυχὴν ἀνθρώπῳ seems somewhat tautologous, but it equals the נפש אדם of MT, and probably means "(smiting) a man to the quick," i.e. the καὶ ἀποθάνῃ is superfluous; if one's ψυχή is struck, it is fatal, but see comment at v.18.

24:18 That "to smite the ψυχή" means καὶ ἀποθάνῃ seems clear from this verse. MT has as subject מכה נפש בהמה "the one smiting the נפש of an animal," i.e. to the quick—see comment at v.17, and the translator fully understood this. He does not translate נפש as such, ὃς ἂν πατάξῃ κτῆνος, but then does add καὶ ἀποθάνῃ, which hex omitted on the mistaken notion that MT lacked it.[31] Again this shows how Origen operated using a purely quantitative yardstick; there was nothing corresponding to the καὶ ἀποθάνῃ slot, and therefore there was no correspondent in MT.

The apodosis reads ἀποτεισάτω ψυχὴν ἀντὶ ψυχῆς "let him repay life for life," i.e. the lex talionis is to be applied. MT has a pronominal suffix to the verb, ישלמנה. Hex added αυτο under the asterisk, the pronoun correctly referring to κτῆνος. The suffix is not necessary to the sense; it is already implicit.

24:19 LXX begins the protasis by καὶ ἐάν τις. This is unusual on two counts. ἐάν τις for כי איש is unusual, and only occurs elsewhere at 19:20.[32] Also unusual

---
30. See THGL 116, and comp 74.
31. But this could be textual; Kenn 128,178 as well as Vulg also omit נפש.
32. See THGL 74.

is καὶ ἐάν. The b text has changed this to εαν δε, which is the usual conjunction with ἐάν in Lev. In fact, it occurs 85 times, whereas καὶ ἐάν obtains only 11 times. The b variant is obviously secondary.[33] The protasis reads "if someone should injure (δῷ μῶμον) a neighbour."[34] MT has בעמיתו "his neighbour." Lev often leaves the suffix untranslated when it is unnecessary to the sense. Obviously τῷ πλησίον will be "his" neighbour, not someone else's. Nonetheless, hex has added αυτου to represent the suffix.

The apodosis applies the law of the talion clearly: "as he did to him, so will it be done in return to him." MT has no correspondent to the dative pronoun in the "as" clause, but only Arm omits it; in theory this could be recensional, but that is highly doubtful. The pronoun was simply added ad sensum; the referent is to πλησίον.

24:20 The actual lex talionis: "fracture for fracture, an eye for an eye, a tooth for a tooth." Other forms of the lex talionis are found at Exod 21:24 Dt 19:21. Unique to the Lev form is the first element, σύντριμμα ἀντὶ συντρίμματος; in fact, no two forms of the law are exactly alike, though all three include "eye" and "tooth." The principle of retribution underlying the law is clearly stated in v.b: "as he δῷ μῶμον to a man, so δοθήσεται to him." Again this is μῶμος for μῶμος, injury for injury. I would translate this as "As he injured a man, so shall he be injured."

In the tradition, ἀνθρώπῳ has been changed to πλησιον in the b text under the influence of v.19 where someone injured τῷ πλησίον. The Masoretes vocalized באדם as articulated, and LXX followed that tradition. That the majority text should omit τῷ is not surprising, since ἀνθρώπῳ had not been defined. But the more difficult τῷ is to be preferred. An interesting variant is that shown by t. The καθότι clause has no expressed subject, but has an indirect object τῷ ἀνθρώπῳ. By changing this to ανθρωπος the clause becomes: "as a person might injure." It is of course secondary, and "person" is better suited as the indirect object, since stating the subject is quite unnecessary.

It is difficult to interpret two well-supported variants to δοθήσεται. An F V popular variant has δωσετε; in other words, it is incumbent on the Israelites to apply the lex talionis. On the other hand, an M f+ text has δωσεται. Almost

---

33. See THGL 102.
34. For δῷ μῶμον Sym has ποιήσει σίνος.

certainly these two readings, being homophonous, are in origin a single variant. I suspect that δωσεται is simply a misspelling of δωσετε, but the reverse is equally possible.

24:21 MT has two clauses, both beginning with ומכה. The translator skipped the first clause, a mistake promoted by homoiarchon. Hex has added a translation of the missing clause under the asterisk: και ο τυπτων κτηνος αποτεισατω αυτο.

The text of LXX is a shorter version of v.17, omitting its καὶ ἄνθρωπος and reading ἄνθρωπον instead of ψυχὴν ἀνθρώπου. Note that v.21 also includes the καὶ ἀποθάνῃ, which, as in v.17, has no basis in MT. As at v.17 hex has placed it under the obelus. Here the clause is important; it places a stricture on מכה; one might strike someone a non-fatal blow, and the Hebrew does not exclude such a case from capital punishment, but LXX does.

24:22 LXX uniquely uses δικαίωσις, a hapax legomenon in OT, to render משפט, whereas one might have expected κρίμα.[35] The term is appropriate, however; it means a judgment as to the rightness of a matter. The translator has simplified MT by changing v.a into a single clause: "there shall be one (i.e. a common) judgment, whether resident alien or native-born." MT has two clauses (which modern translators tend to disregard) in v.a. It has "there must be one judgment; it shall be alike for proselyte and native born." For the Hebrew phrase כגר כאזרח see comment at v.16. Hex did supply a υμιν to represent the לכם of MT.

The reason for this evenhanded justice is given in v.b, a ὅτι clause; it is based on who God is; thus "because I am the Lord your God." What is implied is that Israel's God is evenhanded in justice, and so his people who are holy, as their God is holy, must also be evenhanded in meting out justice. Most witnesses follow hex in omitting εἰμι, since MT simply represents ἐγώ.

24:23 Vv.13–22 had interrupted the narrative about the half-breed Israelite blasphemer, and this verse concludes that narrative of vv.10–12. On Moses' orders the Israelites brought out the one who had cursed ἔξω the camp and stoned him λίθοις. MT has אל מחוץ as at v.14, and hex has again added an unnecessary πρός under the asterisk before ἔξω to represent the אל. λίθοις equals אבן in MT.

---

35. The Others translated as κρίσις.

An A B b+ variant text has added εν before the noun, but this is secondary. The dative is simply one of means, and no preposition is necessary, nor is there justification for it in MT.[36]

The chapter ends with the statement that the Israelites obeyed the instructions; they "did as the Lord συνέταξεν to Moses." An ol n z+ text substituted ενετειλατο for the verb, but this is a synonym. Either verb can translate צוה, though ἐντέλλομαι is more frequently used than συντάσσω (341 times vs 79).[37] That συνέταξεν is original text here is unquestioned.

---

36. See THGL 105.
37. According to the count in Dos Santos.

Chapter 25

25:1 The Lord speaking to Moses is localized as ἐν τῷ ὄρει Σινά. In MT this mountain is called סיני, and the *n* text read σιναι, which was probably mediated through one of The Three. The *n* text is, however, quite consistent in reading σιναι throughout.

25:2 What Moses is to say to the Israelites refers to the time when they are to enter Canaan. The time is introduced by ἐάν in the sense of "when" or "whenever."[1] In fact, the majority F M text has substituted οταν for ἐάν as an easier reading. Since the temporal use of ἐάν is infrequent, the variant text ensures that the reader will read it in this sense, but ἐάν as the more difficult reading is original. The protasis reads "When you enter the land ἣν ἐγὼ δίδωμι ὑμῖν. The ἐγὼ δίδωμι is the usual pattern by which LXX renders a nominal clause with אני as subject and a participle as predicate.[2]

The apodosis is introduced by an apodotic καί in imitation of MT's ושבתה, and is signalled by a future tense ἀναπαύσεται. In MT its subject is הארץ, but LXX adds to its translation ἡ γῆ the same relative clause modifier as that identifying τὴν γῆν, i.e. a second ἣν ἐγὼ δίδωμι ὑμῖν, which is placed under the obelus to show its absence from MT. It is clearly taken over from the protasis; though it is hardly necessary, it does serve to stress that the land they are to occupy is a gift from the Lord, although that had already been said. I suspect that the translator made a mistake. It unnecessarily interrupts the cognate שבת שבתה of MT. The verb is modified by an accusative, which is quite possible, since ἀναπαύω is basically a transitive verb meaning "to stop, finish, make to cease" or "to rest." With σάββατα it would probably mean "the land must enjoy a sabbath rest for the Lord." It is, however, unique; nowhere else in OT is this verb modified by σάββατα. The cognate structure in MT would be well rendered by "the land shall sabbatize a sabbath for Yahweh," i.e. it will celebrate a sabbath rest.[3]

---

1. See Bauer sub ἐάν 1.d. where a number of examples are given.
2. See THGL 95.
3. Aq translated the apodosis by σαββατιεῖ ἡ γῆ σάββατον τῷ κυρίῳ.

25:3 Normal agricultural activities may be performed for six years. This means that "you may sow your field," and "cut (i.e. prune) your vines," and "gather its fruit." Unusual is the translation of כרם "vineyard" by ἄμπελον here and in v.4. The translator makes the agricultural judgment that it is the "vines," taking ἄμπελον as a collective, that are pruned, rather than the vineyard. Actually כרם is only rendered by ἄμπελος three times in the Pentateuch (also in Num 6:4), and only once elsewhere, whereas ἀμπελών translates כרם 79 times.[4] Also rare is the rendering of תבואתה by καρπὸν αὐτῆς. תבואה is normally translated by γενήματα in Lev.[5] Nowhere else in the Pentateuch does καρπός occur for this word. In fact, it only occurs elsewhere once in 2Esdr (19:36) and three times in Prov (10:16 15:6 18:20). The choice of καρπόν here is probably due to the context; since the preceding clause spoke of trimming vines, the notion that vines produce καρπόν rather than γενήματα does make sense.

25:4 MT begins with *waw*, which LXX renders by δέ, since the verse contrasts with v.3. The preposition of ובשנה is not translated, but the dative τῷ δὲ ἔτει is quite sufficient to represent time when. A popular M text does add εν, reading εν δε τω, which could be recensional in origin, though probably not hex. For σάββατα ἀνάπαυσις as rendering for שבת שבתון see discussion at 16:31. A Sabbath for the Lord is not for its own sake, i.e. intended to preserve its fertility through having it lie fallow for a year, but it is a Sabbath in honor of the Lord, a mark of respect for the Lord's gift of the land to his people.

For v.5, which constitutes the negative of what was allowed for the six years of the hebdomadal cycle, see comments ad loc.

25:5 LXX follows Sam's ואת rather than the את of MT in beginning the verse with καί, as does Pesh. Whether τὰ αὐτόματα τὰ ἀναβαίνοντα which is neuter plural translates the ספיחי of Sam or the ספיח of MT is difficult to determine, since at v.11 the same collective occurs for the plural noun in MT. The use of the plural does not mean that its parent text was necessarily Sam's ספיחי, since the plural is dependent on the sense; after all, ספיח is a collective, referring to that which grows without having been specifically sown. In the course of the harvest of ripe grain some grains will inadvertently fall and serve as seed. What then

---

4. According to the count of Dos Santos.
5. See THGL 119.

grows from these is "that which comes up by itself." This you may not harvest during the Sabbatical year. In the tradition, the B F V popular text omits τά 2°, but this is obviously a case of haplography after αὐτόματα; the article modifies an attributive adjective, and that must agree in articulation with its headword.[6] The Byz text reads αμητου instead of ἀγροῦ, but ἀμητός never renders שדה in OT, whereas ἀγρός is the standard word used (210 times) for its translation.[7]

In the tradition, the A B F x+ text reads εκθερισεις for ἐκθεριεῖς. LXX as a third century BCE product still retains the Attic future inflections,[8] whereas by NT times the Hellenistic sigmatic forms had taken over almost entirely.[9] Obviously, the witness of the old uncials is not to be trusted in the matter of Classical vs Hellenistic inflections uncritically.

Nor may "you gather the grape clusters τοῦ ἁγιάσματός σου." The genitive noun translates נזיר, which is usually understood as referring to that which is untended, thus "of your untended vines." The translator, however, approached the word differently. Since the root נזר means "to dedicate, consecrate," a passive nominal would mean "something dedicated." I would understand the σου as a subjective genitive, and thus translate: "the grape clusters of that (i.e. of the vines) which you dedicated"; in this case the vines also undergo a σάββατα τῷ κυρίῳ; they have been uncultivated, untrimmed, i.e. subject to complete neglect, a rest devoted to the Lord. It must, after all, be a שבת שבתון, an ἐνιαυτὸς ἀναπαύσεως for the land.

25:6 The terms σάββατα/שבת are synecdochic for the products of the Sabbath year. The products of unsown fields, and dedicated vines "will constitute food for you and your male and female servants and for your hireling and τῷ παροίκῳ τῷ προσκειμένῳ πρὸς σέ." The structure in MT reads ולתושבך הגרים עמך תושב must here be understood as a collective, since the attributive participle modifying it is in the plural, i.e. the plural is used ad sensum.[10] The translator has solved this in the opposite way, by changing הגרים to a singular modifier.[11] For the use

---

6. See THGL 85.
7. The count is that of Dos Santos.
8. See Thack 228—231 for a fuller discussion of the Attic future.
9. See Bl-D 74.1.
10. See GK 132g.
11. For various ways in which Lev translated the root גור see THGL 130.

of πάροικος to translate תושב see Note at Gen 23:4. What LXX says is "to the stranger who is attached to you."

In the tradition, the Byz text has added υμων after γῆς. This must be a further change of the addition of σου in hex in order to equal MT's לכם more exactly. The Byz text had also changed the plural βρώματα to the singular βρωμα, but this may have originated simply as a copyist's error. Hex had added σου as consistent in number and case to the six cases of second singular nominal suffixes which follow in the verse. Hex also "corrected" Lev, which had not translated the suffix of תושבך, and added σου to make up for it.

25:7 Non-human beneficiaries of the Sabbath year. These are both "domesticated cattle (τοῖς κτήνεσίν σου) and wild beasts (τοῖς θηρίοις)"; the plural nouns correctly render the singular collective nouns of MT. The θηρίοις are τοῖς ἐν τῇ γῇ σου which represents a relative clause in MT. An F C′ b s+ text has simplified this by its της γης σου. The subject is πᾶν τὸ γένημα αὐτοῦ, with the αὐτοῦ referring to ἐνιαυτός of v.5. The Hebrew equivalent is תבואתה, with the feminine suffix probably referring to בארצך, and hex has corrected αὐτοῦ to αυτης. Lev, however, is not an impossible error, since שנת of v.5 is also feminine, i.e. the antecedent could be construed as ἐνιαυτός. It should also be noted that the singular translation of the word is unique, since elsewhere throughout Lev the noun is always translated by the plural.[12]

25:8 The remainder of the chapter deals with the year of release; for the term see v.10 below. Vv.8—12 deal with the determination of the year of release, and its observance. MT begins with "and you must count for yourself seven שבתת שנים "Sabbaths of years," i.e. Sabbatical years. LXX has translated שבתת by ἀναπαύσεις (ἐτῶν). Throughout the rest of Lev the term is reserved for rendering שבתון, for which see the discussion at 16:31. Here it renders the plural of שבת uniquely, and the word (together with ἐτῶν) hardly admits of literal translation, and I would suggest "Sabbatical year-periods" as a translation.[13] That this is what is meant is clear from the rest of the verse: "seven years seven times; and they shall be for you seven weeks of years, forty-nine years." In MT "seven weeks" is preceded by ימי. What MT means is "the period of seven weeks," i.e. the amount,

---

12. See THGL 119.
13. The Others substitute σάββατα for ἀναπαύσεις.

the time expended (by seven weeks). This constitutes the subject of היו. Lev had omitted the word, since it was unnecessary to the sense, by making ἑβδομάδες "weeks" the subject, but hex added ημεραι under the asterisk before "seven weeks" to represent it. Since hex did not change (ἑπτὰ) ἑβδομάδες to the genitive the ημεραι is bizarrely intrusive.

25:9 MT begins with והעברת שופר תרועה which word for word equals "and you shall make the horn to pass through with a sound," i.e. you shall sound aloud the horn. This is correctly understood by Lev with its διαγγελεῖτε σάλπιγγος φωνῇ "you must proclaim with the sound of the trumpet," except that the verb is put into the plural. MT changed to the plural only with v.b, but Lev has levelled the entire verse to the plural. By making σάλπιγγος the genitive modifier of φωνῇ it has shown the right semantic relations of the Hebrew bound phrase. This sounding of the trumpet is to take place ἐν πάσῃ τῇ γῇ ὑμῶν which has no counterpart in MT, and is "borrowed" from its occurrence in v.b, where it also modifies the verb διαγγελεῖτε as a locative phrase. Hex has quite rightly placed the phrase under the obelus. The date is given as "in the seventh month, on the tenth of the month," for which see 23:27.

V.b identifies this particular day as ביום הכפרים, which LXX translates by a dative, again without rendering the preposition.[14] For this "day of atonement" see comment at 23:27. In the tradition, an A B x y+ text reads εξιλασμου for the simplex under the influence of its occurrence in the compound form in 23:27,28; similarly, the verb occurs 50 times in the book, but always in the compound form. I would argue that it is much more difficult for an ἐξιλασμοῦ to become ἱλασμοῦ than the reverse, and that the simplex is original here.[15] The command of v.a is virtually repeated with the date now identified as the "day of atonement," and with the change of σάλπιγγος φωνῇ to σάλπιγγι. Also in the tradition, a B+ text added εν before τῷ μηνί; this happens to equal the בחדש of MT, but the reading is hardly recensional; rather the preposition has entered the text under the influence of the prepositional phrase immediately preceding it.

25:10 The first clause calls on the Israelites to "sanctify the fiftieth year for a year." ἐνιαυτόν is then an adverbial accusative answering the question "how

---

14. See SS 110.
15. See THGL 132.

long?" What is meant is that the entire fiftieth year is to be set aside as a Sabbatical year. In the tradition, an A B+ text has changed the verb to an aorist imperative, αγιασατε, for ἁγιάσετε; this is a common error, but the future inflection is what Lev normally uses; in fact, the imperative in such a context is extremely rare. Another variant text, that of F V cI+, changes the second τό to τον, thus reading το ετος τον πεντηκοστον ενιαυτον "the year, the fiftieth year." This is not to be taken seriously, as a glance at MT's שנת החמשים שנה shows; the bound phrase ties "fifty" to the preceding "year," not to the following.

The sanctification of the Sabbatical year involves your proclamation of "release" for the land to all those inhabiting it. The term ἄφεσιν also occurred at 16:26 for עזאזל; there it clearly means "release"; cf comment ad loc. Here it occurs for דרור "freedom, liberty," which is usually rendered by ἄφεσις (seven times out of eight). But דרור occurs only here in the Pentateuch, and then appears in Jer five times translated by ἄφεσις. By the second century BCE it also took on the notion of remission of debt, which has led some to prefer the notion of remission here as well. ἄφεσις occurs commonly in Lev as a rendering for יובל both in this chapter and in ch.27, and elsewhere only at Num 36:4. The term refers specifically in these cases to the "year of the Jubilee" with which the entire ch.25 is concerned.[16]

V.b begins in MT with יובל הוא. The term first occurs at Exod 19:13 in the phrase במשך היבל "when the horn sounds." The word refers to the ram's horn which was used as an instrument for proclamation, a calling to attention. The lexeme is used here for the first time to designate every fiftieth year set aside for "release," the terms of which are described in this chapter. When יובל is used in this sense it is commonly called "the jubilee" or "the year of the Jubilee." The translator did not have a clear rendering for it, so he expanded it descriptively by ἐνιαυτὸς ἀφέσεως σημασία αὕτη[17] ἐστιν ὑμῖν) "as a year of release will this signal be for you."[18] The translator continues his uncertainty in vv.11—13 by

---

16. E.g. Harlé-Pralon who translate by "remission" for what to me is for the wrong reason. They translate it thus: "en vue de son riche réemploi dans les ecrits néotestamentaires et patristiques (=rémission des peches)." But reading NT notions back into the LXX is methodologically questionable. The more neutral "release" is attested earlier, and must be preferable.
17. Theod renders יובל by ιωβηλ, whereas Aq renders it by παραφέρων.
18. Harlé-Pralon renders this differently: "pour un an ce sera pour vous le signal de la rémission." This in my opinion is a fine paraphrase, but it is not quite what Lev says, since ἐνιαυτός is nominative, not accusative.

rendering the word by ἀφέσεως σημασία, but from v.28 to the end of the book the single term ἄφεσις is consistently used to render יובל.

The jubilee year is to be a year of return. ἕκαστος shall return to his possession, and you shall return, each to his πατρίαν. MT has a second person plural verb in both clauses, but the Greek retains this only for the second one, ἀπελεύσεσθε, and has the same verb in third singular, ἀπελεύσεται, for the first one. This may simply be the translator's love for variation being expressed. It should be noted that a b d+ text reads απελευσεσθε for the first verb as well; though this equals MT, it must be secondary. An A B x y+ text has added εις "one" before ἕκαστος, but this is probably influenced by the preposition εἰς which follows ἕκαστος. In any event, εις εκαστος never occurs in OT, and it is secondary.[19] πατριάν is an accurate rendering for משפחה "clan, sept." In the tradition, an A B F C+ variant reads πατριδα, but only πατριάν reflects משפחה, whereas πατρίς is secondary; it really means "fatherland, country."[20]

25:11 יובל הוא is rendered paraphrastically by ἀφέσεως σημασία αὕτη "this signal of release."[21] The paraphrase is obviously taken from v.10, where ἀφέσεως also comes before σημασία αὕτη. I would translate the final clause: "this signal of release, even the fiftieth year, shall be a year for you." What is meant is that it will be a full year for you.

Forbidden for this year are sowing, for which see v.4, reaping that which comes up by itself, for which see v.5, and gathering τὰ ἡγιασμένα αὐτῆς. For the participle see comment at v.5. The pronoun αὐτῆς in both cases refers to γῆς. In the tradition, most witnesses follow F M in adding εν υμιν after αὕτη, but this is clearly taken over from v.10. The τά modifying ἀναβαίνοντα is omitted by a popular A B F V text, but as in v.5 this is an error of haplography. See comment ad loc.

25:12 The prohibitions of v.11b are rationized by a ὅτι structure: you may not sow, reap, gather, because it is a signal of release. This again renders יובל הוא, though rendering הוא here by ἐστιν rather than by αὕτη. An x text substitutes

---
19. See THGL 109—110.
20. See Walters 310—311, referred to in THGL 130.
21. Theod and Sym have ιωβηλ. Aq again has παραφέρων (retroverted from Syh) as in v.10.

αυτη for ἐστιν, obviously under the influence of the preceding two verses. For the rendering of יובל הוא see comments at vv.10 and 11.

Accordingly, it will be holy for you. The subject is neuter, and it must be ἔτος, i.e. the fiftieth year of v.11. Understanding השדה as a collective singular is sensible, since the Israelites made "fields" not a field.[22] MT refers to תבואתה in which the suffix must refer to ארץ of v.10, rather than to השדה which is masculine. LXX's αὐτῆς, as in v.11, refers to γῆς of v.10.

25:13 MT begins with a clear statement: בשנת היובל הזאת תשבו "in this year of the jubilee you shall return,"[23] but the translator, still enamored of his earlier paraphrase of vv.10—12, attempts a further explanation. He begins quite well with ἐν τῷ ἔτει ἀφέσεως "in the year of release," but then instead of an expected τούτῳ for הזאת, has σημασίᾳ αὐτῆς "with its signal," in which the αὐτῆς must refer to ἀφέσεως. The majority M V text has the genitive σημασιας instead of the dative, which is apparently rooted in an attempt to clarify the text. Though O′ Syh also support the text it is not a normal hex correction, and I suspect it to be an early prehexaplaric attempt at improving the text. The change of the verb to a third singular verb is easily explicable, since it goes on naming the subject and verbal modifier by ἕκαστος εἰς τὴν κτῆσιν αὐτοῦ. The verb is thus in agreement with its subject ἕκαστος. In the tradition, the F M V majority text read εγκτησιν (or the assimilated spelling εκτησιν) for κτῆσιν. But only κτῆσιν "possession" is fitting here.

25:14 LXX follows the singular of Sam תמכר rather than the plural of MT, as do all the ancient versions. The plural is at odds with the rest of the verse in which עמיתך, i.e. with a singular suffix, recurs. The variant text of b n y+ reading the active αποδως is unexpected. The notion "to sell" is more commonly put in the middle voice. The verse has coordinate protases: "If you should make a sale (i.e. of land) to your neighbour, and if (ἐὰν καί) you should buy from your neighbour." That the transaction involves land is clear from vv.15—16. The term πλησίον σου twice renders עמיתך, a term which refers to a countryman, here then to a fellow-Israelite. At the end of the verse the same noun is used to translate

---

22. Lee 58 notes the LXX use of πεδίον in the sense of "land ... appropriated for pasture or tillage." LS recognizes only the notion of "plain."
23. Sym has ἐν τῷ ἔτει τοῦ ιωβηλ τούτῳ ἐπίστρεψον (retroverted from Syh).

אחיו, but for this one the suffix is not translated.[24] The failure to render a suffix with את is uncharacteristic for Lev. אחיו only occurs three times in the book, and only here is the suffix disregarded. Note also that for אחיך which occurs nine times in the book, Lev always has σου after "brother." Hex has, however, added an αυτου to make up for it.

LXX signalled the coordinate conditions by ἐὰν δέ ... ἐὰν καί. The second one is unusual, and hex apparently transposed them. Copyists had trouble with the structure, some omitting the one, and some, the other one, while the Byz text inserted δε. Actually MT had the much more appropriate correlative או, a reading which only the Bohairic reflects correctly. Why the translator avoided using ἤ, but adopted the rare ἐὰν καί is baffling. The translator rightly understood the use of קנה as a contextual free infinitive, and translated it by κτήσῃ, a second singular aorist subjunctive, i.e. contextually parallel with ἀποδῷ.

The apodosis in MT reads אל תונו איש את אחיו; LXX preferred to render the second plural verb by the third person singular θλιβέτω to agree with the subject ἄνθρωπος. The verb is well-chosen, since θλίβω means "to squeeze, constrict," i.e. a man should not take advantage of (his) neighbour in transferring property. The verb is commonly used in the general sense of "oppress, afflict." The present tense is apt, since a process is involved.[25]

25:15 The price of transactions shall be rated proportionally according to the distance from the jubilee year. The verse is divided in two parts; the first part deals with the purchase price, and the second, with that of selling. The buying price is determined "according to the number of years after τὴν σημασίαν." The Hebrew reads "after היובל," i.e. the jubilee year. Only here is the ἀφέσεως σημασία of vv.10—12 as an expanded rendering of היובל abbreviated to σημασίαν, and what "after the sign" means is "after the sign of release," i.e. the jubilee year; see the discussion at v.10b, as well as the comment at v.11. From this point on the translator uses only ἄφεσις as translation for יובל. παρὰ τοῦ πλησίον renders מאת עמיתך. For עמית see comment at v.14. Hex has added σου to represent the

---

24. See SS 97.
25. Sym also has the verse (except for ἐὰν δέ). It is only extant in Syh. It reads mzbn ʾnt bzbyntʾ lhw dmn ʿmʾ dylk ʾw zbn ʾnt mn hw dmn ʿmʾ dylk dlʾ {lʾ} mṣʾ klḥd lʾhwhy. For Sym at vv.14—16 (as well as at v.52) the text is only known from Syh, and I have refrained from retroverting the text into Greek as an overly speculative procedure; accordingly its evidence has been presented in transcription.

untranslated suffix.[26] The term עמיתך occurs five times in the book, and the suffix is always rendered except here (18:20 19:15,17 25:14), but comp v.17.

V.b deals with the determination of the selling price. Again it is determined κατὰ ἀριθμῶν, but the number concerns the number of "years of produce (remaining)." From this it becomes clear what is actually bought and sold; it is not the land as such, but what it produces that is in question. What this constititutes in modern terms is a contracted lease of land which extends up to the onset of the jubilee year. The main clause of v.b reads ἀποδώσεταί σοι "he shall sell to you," which renders MT exactly.[27]

25:16 This verse sets forth the general principle underlying the determination of price for buying and selling property. "According to the increase in years you must increase τὴν ἔγκτησιν αὐτοῦ, and according to the decrease in years you must decrease τὴν ἔγκτησιν αὐτοῦ." This renders מקנתו "its purchase price." The noun ἔγκτησις is well-chosen, since it refers to "land tenure," and then secondarily to "acquisition," but in the context it must mean the cost or price of acquiring property. It is then the "acquisition price," or more exactly, the price for holding the land, i.e. for its tenure.[28] The αὐτοῦ refers to the seller, i.e. the ἄνθρωπος of v.14.

The raison d'etre for the regulation is given in a ὅτι clause. It is "because the number of crops αὐτὸς ἀποδώσεταί σοι." In MT the subject is הוא, and the predicate is a participle מכר. The occurrence of the pattern in third person is relatively rare, but when it occurs the predicate is usually represented by a present tense verb, but here the verb is in the future, which is unique in the book.[29] The use of the future is unexpected, and must have been chosen to indicate timeless or omnitemporal occurrence.[30] I would translate freely by "he can only sell you the number of crops."

In the tradition, the pronoun has undergone some change. For the pattern rendering Hebrew nominal clauses one expects either αὐτός or οὗτος, and a y+

---

26. See SS 97.
27. As for v.14, Sym is extant in v.15 only in Syh, which, however, is badly transmitted by the copyist. What remains reads *lpwt mnyn' d'llt' dšny' nzbn lk*. But this equals only v.b. The original note undoubtedly included a translation of v.a as well, but the copyist's eye skipped from the first *lpwt mnyn'* to the second.
28. See LS sub ἔγκτησις.
29. See THGL 95.
30. See Porter 421—424.

text does read ουτος instead of the αὐτός of Lev. ουτος is used far more frequently by Lev (19 times), but mainly (15 times) for זאת in the collocation "this is the rule for ...." In four cases it renders הוא, three times as subject of a nominal clause. αὐτός occurs only five times, once without Hebrew equivalent so as to give emphasis to a verb (6:38), once also without Hebrew counterpart at 26:28 in αὐτὸς πορεύσομαι. At v.54 it occurs for הוא in "αὐτός and his sons with him," and also for הוא at 5:18 in "and αὐτός did not know." Through homophony this has become ουτως in the V b x+ text, which in turn has been blended to αυτου ουτως in A B 121. Both words are errors; αυτου makes no sense, since a reference to ἔγκτησιν would have to be αυτης, which is read by F n+. The pronoun adopted for Lev is likely to be original.[31] It is then clear that only the produce is bought; the land reverts to the original owner in the jubilee year.[32]

25:17 The first clause in LXX is identical with the last clause of v.14: "let a man not take advantage of a neighbour." See comment at v.14. MT, however, has עמיתו instead of אחיו, but both texts are translated by πλησίον. As at v.14 hex has added αυτου to represent the untranslated suffix.

The second clause is coordinate: "And you must fear the Lord your God." MT has no equivalent for "the Lord," reading יראת מאלהיך as at vv.36,43, and see comment at 19:14. Hex has omitted κύριον, so as to equal MT.

In MT this is followed by the long self-identification formula present as a כי clause. LXX disregarded the כי, and hex added οτι at the onset to represent it. Hex also omitted εἰμι as not in MT, since it simply had אני, which is adequately rendered by ἐγώ. Presumably the formula authenticates the section, vv.13–17, and brings it to a close.

25:18 An injunction to obey God's laws. What the Lord orders is "And you must execute all my ordinances (δικαιώματα) and all my judgments (κρίσεις), and guard and execute them." MT has no "and" before "guard." Thus the second clause reads ואת משפטי תשמרו, which is a more balanced construction. Hex has "corrected" the text by omitting the καί. MT also has no "all" in either of the

---

31. See THGL 99.
32. The text of Sym is again extant only in Syh. It reads lpwt sg'wt' dšny' tsg' lzbynt' dylk wlpwt z'wrwt' dšny' tz'r lzbynth mnyn' gr d'llt' hw mzbn lk.

indicate that fact. An A B+ text has changed φυλάξεσθε to the aorist imperative φυλαξασθε, but this is secondary. The waw plus suffix inflected verb is with remarkable consistency rendered by καί plus future verbs, and φυλάξεσθε must be original. Also found is a popular F text in the active form φυλαξετε, but the middle is far and away the dominant form in Lev.[33]

The resultant reward for this obedience is καὶ κατοικήσετε ἐπὶ τῆς γῆς πεποιθότες. The perfect participle "with confidence" represents the adverbial phrase לבטח "safely, securely." לבטח occurs only three times in the book; at v.19 it is rendered as here, but at 26:5 it becomes μετὰ ἀσφαλαίας "with safety, security."

25:19 The reward for faithful observance of God's demands is given in three coordinate clauses. The first one is agricultural plenty: "and the land will yield פריה." This is well-interpreted by ἐκφόρια αὐτῆς "its products," that which is borne out of the land; in this context this is more fitting than the usual κάρπος. The b text has changed the noun to γενηματα, which is a synonym. This is logically followed by καὶ φάγεσθε εἰς πλησμονήν "and you shall eat to satiety." For the last clause, see comment at v.18. The αὐτῆς refers to the γῆ of the first clause.

25:20 A hypothetical question (ἐὰν δὲ λέγητε): "What are we going to eat in this seventh year, if we may not sow nor gather our produce"? MT has no counterpart to "this," and hex has omitted τούτῳ to equal MT. The δέ is used to indicate contrast. In the tradition, an M Byz+ reading has the present subjunctive συναγωμεν instead of the aorist συναγάγωμεν of Lev. The coordinate verb is σπείρωμεν, which could be either present or aorist subjunctive. Since the default tense is aorist, I would suggest that the aorist is original LXX here. There is no good reason for using the present subjunctive, which would indicate a process, such as "keep sowing, keep on gathering," and συναγωμεν must be judged secondary, and may well be a case of haplography, i.e. reading αγαγ as αγ. μήδε is a fine rendering for ולא, though the και μη of the M *ol f*+ text would also be adequate. But all the other uncials support μήδε, and it must be original. Also secondary is the simpler και of the Byz text.

---

33. See THGL 127.

25:21 The reply to the hypothetical question raised in v.20 is introduced by καί in imitation of MT. MT has God say וצויתי "and I will command," which LXX interprets contextually by ἀποστελῶ "I will send," which is appropriate with τὴν εὐλογίαν μου, thus "I will send my blessing (for you)"; one modern version, NIV, actually does the same thing; it reads "I will send you such a blessing ...." The second clause details the result of God's sending his blessing. That blessing will increase its yield for the sixth year sufficient for three years. For τὰ γενήματα αὐτῆς MT has no equivalent for the pronoun. LXX rendered the Sam text which reads את תבואתה rather than MT's את התבואה. The αὐτῆς refers to ἡ γῆ of v.19. The *b* text has changed this to αυτου, in which case it would refer to τῷ ἔτει of the preceding clause. The Byz text has changed the subject of ποιήσει by adding η γη after the verb.[34]

25:22 The accusative τὸ ἔτος shows extent of time, i.e. "during the (eighth) year." Both this clause and the next are paratactically presented in imitation of MT. The first clause obviously states the time during which the second one is valid. Thus "while you will be sowing ..., you may eat." The loss of a year of seeding and harvesting is to be made up for by the extra yields referred to in v.21. What you may eat is ἀπὸ γενημάτων παλαιά. The ἀπό is partitive, i.e. "from the products."[35] The adjective παλαιά is accusative neuter plural, and modifies φάγεσθε, thus " you may eat from the products the old (produce)," or idiomatically put "you may eat of the old products," i.e. from the produce that remains from the sixth year's abundance.

I would now begin v.b with the second ἕως clause; αὐτῆς must still refer to ἡ γῆ of v.19 as it did in v.21. This would involve removing the colon after παλαιά, and changing the comma after ἐνάτου to a colon within the critical text. This also disagrees with the accentuation of the Masoretes, who made the first cut after ישן 1°, which was placed under the *ethnach*. The text then reads more sensibly: "you shall eat of the old produce until the nineth year," i.e. until the beginning of the nineth. Then v.b reads "until its produce comes you may eat παλαιὰ παλαιῶν." The "its" now refers, not to the nineth year, but to the eighth, which is what the legislation must intend.

---
34. As did Tar[N]: ותעבד ארעא פי עללתה.
35. See SS 161.

The term παλαιὰ παλαιῶν is a case of leveling with 26:10. The leveling also rationalizes the text. The food for the year will be the product of the past two years. For the structure see comment at 26:10. In the tradition, τὰ γενήματα is changed to the singular by the A B V *b n x+* text, but Lev consistently renders תבואה by the plural.[36]

25:23 "The land may not be sold εἰς βεβαίωσιν." The noun occurs only once elsewhere in OT (Sap 6:18) in προσοχὴ δὲ νόμων βεβαίωσις ἀφθαρσίας "the observance of the laws (i.e. of wisdom) is the assurance of imortality." The word means "consideration, validity," and in the context here means "with legal validity." What is meant is that all sales are provisional, since in the year of release the land will return to the former owner; in fact, vv.24—34 make clear how temporary all land transfers in Israel are. Hebrew has לצמתת which occurs elsewhere only at v.30, but the root is well-known as "to put an end to, exterminate, annihilate." i.e. for all time, in perpetuity. The translator understood this; such sales are not final.[37]

The γάρ clause helps to understand the phrase; it is so "because the land is mine." A second כי clause is rendered by a διότι structure. In MT this reads כי גרים ותושבים אתם עמדי "because you are (but) resident aliens and strangers with me." The difference between the two is that a גר is a landed immigrant, probably a permanent resident with defined rights, whereas a תושב is a temporary resident. The statement seems surprising in view of the central claim of Israel as the people of the covenant, but the point that is being made is that the land of promise is not yours absolutely; it belongs to God, and over against the land, you have only alien or temporary rights. The translator rendered the prepositional phrase by ἐναντίον μου, and translated the nouns by προσήλυτοι καὶ πάροικοι, which are consistently the equivalents resp in Lev for the corresponding Hebrew words.

25:24 The initial prepositional phrase בכל ארץ אחזתכם is translated by κατά plus accusative which I would translate "for all the land which you possess," rather than the "in" or "within" of MT. What is ordered is "you must provide a ransom for the land." How this provision for a λύτρα/גאלה is to be attained is then

---

36. The Others also read τὸ γένημα; see for Lev THGL 119.
37. Aq translates by παγκτησίαν "full ownership," and Sym uses ἀλύτρωτον "unredeemable."

described in the following vv.25—28. This use of the notion of "ransom" gives added clarification to the comment on ownership at v.23.

25:25 LXX translates ימוך "depressed, downcast," and hence "be impoverished" by πένηται, which is contextually apt in view of the second clause "and must sell some of his possession."[38] The subject ὁ ἀδελφός σου is modified by the appositional structure ὁ μετὰ σοῦ which has no counterpart in MT, and hex accordingly placed it under the obelus. עמך does follow אחיך, however, in vv.36,39, which see; these vv. undoubtedly are the source which influenced the translator. Here, however, the appositive is not particularly apt. The ἀπό of the second clause is a clear case of a partitive; it must mean "some of his possession."[39]

The third clause is a further part of the protasis in LXX, since ἔλθῃ is an aorist subjunctive, whereas λυτρώσεται is a future and is an apodosis; the first clause is a further condition, thus "and when ὁ ἀγχιστεύων ... comes, he must redeem ...." The actual apodosis in Lev is the last clause. This differs from the Masoretic interpretation, which divides the verse at the end of the second clause, placing מאחזתו under the *ethnach*. This would mean that the apodosis consists of clauses three and four. In MT what must happen is that the גאל must come ... and ransom.

In LXX, clause three states as a third condition that ὁ ἀγχιστεύων ὁ ἔγγιστα αὐτοῦ should come. The participle renders גאלו. The reference is to "the next of kin." The term is a technical term in Hebrew for the next of kin who has certain responsibilities, one of which is set out in this verse. He is principally concerned in carrying out the lex talionis in the event of his kin being killed or hurt. The verb is usually translated either formally by ἀγχιστεύω or more functionally by λυτρόω. Here the term is further defined in the former sense by הקרב אליו, translated by ὁ ἔγγιστα αὐτοῦ "the one nearest to him," i.e. his closest relative. In the tradition, both ἔγγιστα and αὐτοῦ are changed. A majority F M text reads εγγιζων for the noun, and an F M V majority text changed αὐτοῦ to αυτω. The popular ο εγγιζων αυτω seems likely to be an attempt at greater literalism. At 21:2 the same text occurs in MT, and it is rendered by τῷ ἔγγιστα αὐτῶν. The popular text is undoubtedly mediated through one of The Three.[40]

---

38. Aq renders the verb by ἐκπέσῃ, and Sym, by ταπεινωθῇ. That the Hebrew is better rendered by Lev is clear from the common rendering of Tar: יתמסכן.
39. See SS 161.
40. See THGL 110.

Actually the text of A B cannot be trusted in this verse as their support for the variant text αποδωσεται instead of ἀποδῶται shows. This would make clause two the apodosis for clause one, which cannot be correct. It should be noted as well that LXX did not translate the suffix of גאלו; hex has added αυτω to represent it.

What the next of kin is to do is λυτρώσεται τὴν πρᾶσιν τοῦ ἀδελφοῦ αὐτοῦ "he must redeem the sale of his kinsman." In other words, he must buy back what has been sold. The πρᾶσιν refers to the ἀπὸ τῆς κατασχέσεως αὐτοῦ of the second clause. The sold land is "some of his possession," and must now be redeemed by the ἀγχιστεύων.

25:26 But suppose such an individual has no ἀγχιστεύων, what then? This condition is represented in Lev as "but if μὴ ᾖ τινι the next of kin," i.e. if there should not be to someone a next of kin. In MT איש "someone" stands at the beginning before כי, and the majority of witnesses transpose τινι before μή, possibly a correction towards MT.[41] Note that Lev has rendered the initial *waw* by δέ, thereby showing that v.25 contrasts with the situation of v.24.

The verse procedes to two further possible conditions, for which v.27 then serves as the apodosis. Suppose then that εὐπορηθῷ τῷ χειρί and εὑρεθῷ αὐτῷ τὸ ἱκανὸν λύτρα αὐτοῦ. The first clause represents a Hebrew idiom השיגה ידו "his hand should reach," i.e. his fortunes change; he becomes prosperous. The Greek may be translated "and he should have plenty in hand."[42] LXX does not translate the suffix of ידו, it being otiose in Greek,[43] but hex has dutifully supplied an αυτου.

The last clause renders מצא by εὑρεθῇ αὐτῷ; the αὐτῷ is an ad sensum addition, and is needed for good sense. The verb has two accusative modifiers τὸ ἱκανόν and λύτρα αὐτοῦ, i.e. "sufficient as his ransom." This renders a bound phrase of MT כדי גאלתו, but is a good rendering. The Byz text has substituted λυτρωσιν for λύτρα, thus "the right of redemption"; see comment at v.29.

25:27 This is the apodosis for the hypothetical query of v.26. The poor man whose fortunes have turned must now "compute the years of his sale," i.e. the years since he had sold the property. Thereupon "he shall return what remains to

---

41. See THGL 74.
42. See THGL 131.
43. See SS 96.

the man to whom he sold it." ὃ ὑπερέχει refers to what time or number of years remain up to the year of release. The repurchase is based on a proportional assessment of the value of the crops for what remains of the period of possession, since the sales contract lasted only to the fiftieth year of the jubilee cycle. The αὐτό is neuter, since its antecedent is not readily apparent; when the antecedent is vague Lev tends to use the neuter pronoun as a kind of default pronoun.[44] Failure to recognize this peculiar use of the neuter pronoun in this odd fashion would obviously bother any grammarian, since a specific neuter antecedent is not to be found in the context.[45] Since מָכַר in MT is used absolutely, hex has omitted the pronoun as having no basis in MT. In the tradition, the pronoun has been changed by the A F M oI+ text to αυτον; a change to the feminine αυτην might have been justified with κατασχέσεως of v.25 as referent, but the masculine is simply a thoughtless error, or might this be read as the contracted form of εαυτον as in B? It should be noted, however, that this text also changed αὐτῷ to εαυτω, which makes it even more confusing. The B x+ text has changed the pronoun to εαυτον; this arose from a misunderstanding of what was sold. But the poor man did not sell himself, but only some of his property.[46] The αὐτῷ which follows is a recapitulative pronoun, a slavish rendering of MT's לו, where it is fitting. It can only be left out in translation, thus "to whom he had sold it."

Only then may the original owner return to his possession. A majority M variant has επανελευσεται instead of ἀπελεύσεται. The double compound occurs only rarely in OT, but here it has been introduced on the basis of v.13 where it occurs in the context of ἕκαστος εἰς τὴν κτῆσιν αὐτοῦ.

25:28 But suppose the poor man's fortunes do not change, i.e. "if his hand should not find sufficient to repay him." Instead of εὕρῃ the majority F M V text reads ευπορηθη, passive of εὐπορέω. But the accusative modifier τὸ ἱκανόν simply can not fit as a modifier to this passive verb. In the passive the verb is intransitive, and only εὕρῃ can be original here.[47] The variant text has intruded under the influence of v.26. Furthermore, the notion of one's hand finding is a

---

44. See Huber 34—35.
45. See R.Sollamo in Greenspoon—Munnich 49—50.
46. See THGL 96—97.
47. Harlé-Pralon follow Ra in reading ευπορηθη and translate "si sa main n'a pas été chanceuse pour avoir assez de quoi restituer à l'homme," which is a fine idea, but it cannot be Lev.

common idiom amply documented for Lev,⁴⁸ and מצאה simply does not mean ευπορηθη.

The apodosis is introduced by καί in imitation of MT. "ἡ πρᾶσις shall belong to the one who bought αὐτά until the year of release." MT reads ממכרו, but LXX does not render the suffix.⁴⁹ Hex has supplied an αυτου to represent it. The αὐτά modifying the participle must refer to τὰ ἔτη (τῆς πράσεως αὐτοῦ) of v.27. What LXX correctly understands is that a buyer can only buy the lease of land for a number of years; what would be due would be the value of the crops after the sale remaining to the year of release, i.e. he must buy back the lease. In MT the pronoun is אתו which apparently refers to ממכר; in any event, it is singular. The *b* text has changed αὐτά to αυτον which does equal MT. The Byz text has changed it to αυτην, which is apparently an attempt to correct the text by making it refer to the κατάσχεσιν of v.27.

The purchase is thus to remain valid until τοῦ ἔτους τῆς ἀφέσεως, i.e. שנת היובל.⁵⁰ A popular A B V gloss has added εκτου before ἔτους. I suspect this is rooted in a careless misreading of ἔτους as εκτου; it is, however, quite wrong. The jubilee year is preceded not by a sixth year, but by a forty-nineth. In spite of its impressive ms support, it is quite wrong, and may be dismissed as unworthy of serious consideration. One wonders how readers of "the sixth year of the release" might have understood what was read.⁵¹

In the last two clauses no subjects are expressed, but the subject of ἐξελεύσεται must be the property in question, whereas the subject of ἀπελεύσεται must be the poor man who originally owned it. I would translate: "and it shall revert in the (year of) release, and he shall return to his possession." MT has ביובל which LXX rendered by the dative τῇ ἀφέσει; the term is clearly synecdochic for the year of release. Most witnesses have the structure governed by εν, which may well be recensional. The verb ἀπελεύσεται becomes επανελευσεται, for which see comment at v.27.

---

48. See THGL 130—131.
49. See SS 98.
50. Sym read τοῦ ιωβηλ for היובל.
51. See THGL 110. Harlé-Pralon recognize that the word "sixth" is here "supranent. Il pourrait provenir d'une confusion entre année sabbatique et année jubilaire." But they retain it in their text: "jusqu'à la sixième année de la remission"!

25:29 Vv.29—34 deal with the ransom for dwellings. MT begins the protasis with ואיש כי which Lev renders idiomatically by ἐὰν δέ τις "should someone." What someone might sell is an "οἰκίαν οἰκητήν in a walled city." MT has בית מושב "a dwelling," which LXX has interpreted as "a residential house." In MT עיר is tied to מושב as the free element of a bound structure, but LXX has rendered this by an ἐν phrase, which is probably what MT intended.

The apodosis reads καὶ ἔσται ἡ λύτρωσις αὐτῆς "and there shall remain the right of its redemption." Here גאלתו is rendered, not by λύτρα αὐτοῦ as in v.26, but by λύτρωσις αὐτῆς. The Hebrew term is used in a somewhat different sense from that of vv.24,26. It is not the ransom itself, but the right of redemption that is intended. This difference was recognized by Lev who chose the abstract λύτρωσις; cf also v.48.

The apodosis is then amplified by declaring a term limit. LXX reads "until a year of days (i.e. a full year) is fulfilled there will remain the right of its redemption." MT has a somewhat different text; it has "until the completion of שנת ממכרו ימים the right of its redemption shall remain." The intent of תם שנת is to ensure a full year of (i.e. after) its sale. Obviously LXX disregarded ממכרו completely, and joined שנת ימים; "a year of days" means a full year. The omission has not really changed the interpretation. For both MT and Lev the right of redemption continues for a full year—obviously after the sale. Hex has added πρασεως αυτης after ἐνιαυτός to represent ממכרו. This left ἡμερῶν, which was then changed to the adverb ημερολεγδον "by day count" to make sense.

25:30 But should such redemption not be effected (λυτρωθῇ) "until an entire year has elapsed" is another possibility. In MT מלאת is followed by לו which has no exact counterpart in LXX; hex has addded αυτη after πληρωθῇ to represent it. This was subsequently corrupted to αυτης in modification of ἐνιαυτός which followed it in the A B F x+ text, but it is obviously not original, even though it formed a sensible text.[52]

The apodosis is not introduced by a καί even though MT reads וקם. The verb קם means "to stand," so here "remain fast," which the Greek interprets by κυρωθήσεται "be established, confirmed." The verb is modified by the adverb βεβαίως, thus "be confirmed with legal validity," as legally binding, for which

---

52. See THGL 110.

see comment at v.23. Its subject is "the house ἡ οὖσα ἐν πόλει τῇ ἐχούσῃ τεῖχος." In the parent text this is represented by two relative clauses, אשר בעיר which in turn is modified by אשר לו חמה. MT has לא rather than לו, but the לו of 11QLev[53] and Sam is parent to LXX; in fact, only MT among the ancient witnesses attests to the negative. The prepositional phrase is rendered by the participle ἐχούσῃ, since the pronoun ל indicates possession.[54] In the tradition, the majority F text articulates πόλει under the influence of τῇ ἐχούσῃ modifying it, but the unarticulated form is intended by Lev. It refers to "a city which has a wall," which is exactly what the parent text had.

The verb κυρωθήσεται is modified by a dative showing indirect object "to the one buying it," and the prepositional phrase εἰς τὰς γενεὰς αὐτοῦ "to his generations," i.e. to his descendants. The conclusion as far as ownership is concerned is that the jubilee year will not affect it; "and he (i.e. the buyer) shall not leave (it) in the release."

25:31 MT begins with a plural subject בתי החצרים, but has a singular verb יחשב. MT continues with singular structures for v.b as well. Obviously, the Hebrew writer is thinking of בתי החצרים as a collective group or whole. Sam has an inconsistent text; it does read a plural verb, יחשבו, but v.b is entirely in the singular. LXX follows the יחשבו of 11QLev[55] and Sam, as do Tar and Pesh. LXX then continues for the rest of the verse in the plural as well. The translator simplified by using the plural throughout.

The translator begins the verse with a δέ construction, which is sensible since the subject contrasts with that of v.30, where houses within walled cities were discussed. Here the houses are αἱ ἐν ἐπαύλεσιν; this renders a bound phrase in MT: "the houses of villages." The term ἔπαυλοι simply means "enclosures" here.[56] Its meaning is clearly defined by a relative clause αἷς οὐκ ἔστιν αὐταῖς τεῖχος κύκλῳ "to which there is no wall about." What is meant is unwalled villages. A B F b+ variant text mistakenly added εν before αὐταῖς which would be self-contradictory; there was no wall around it, so "in them" is not sensible.[57]

---

53. See Freedman 532.
54. See SS 58 as well as 182.
55. See Freedman 532.
56. But see Harlé-Pralon who speak of the term as of uncertain meaning.
57. See THGL 105.

The point that is being made, however, is that the houses in unwalled villages are to be considered as belonging πρὸς τὸν ἀγρὸν τῆς γῆς "to the open country."

V.b continues logically in the plural; after all, this also concerns the houses of the unwalled villages. αὗται shall always be redeemable, and shall go out in the jubilee. The first clause is a free rendering in the plural of MT's גאלה תהיה לו, though except for the διὰ παντός it does represent MT fairly. Hex has placed διὰ παντός under the obelus as having no counterpart in MT. The gloss is an exegetical plus, making explicit what is only implicit in MT. It was, however, probably added under the influence of v.32. An A B V b n x+ text has omitted αὗται, but this serves to show that the subject is still αἱ οἰκίαι.[58] The contrast with v.30 is clear; the houses outside walled cities are always redeemable, but they are also subject to release, i.e. return to the original owner in the jubilee year.[59]

25:32 The verse begins with a lengthy subject: καὶ αἱ πόλεις τῶν Λευιτῶν, οἰκίαι τῶν πόλεων αὐτῶν κατασχέσεως "and the cities of the Levites, the houses of the cities of their possession."[60] The predicate is ἔσονται, which governs a predicate nominative λυτρωταί. Both διὰ παντός and the dative modify the verb. The majority F M text has transposed αὐτῶν κατασχέσεως; this represents אחזתם and is likely a hex correction in origin. In MT this is a pendant construction: "As for the cities ...."

In MT's v.b the pendant of v.a becomes relevant in the mention of the Levites: "The Levites will always have the right of redemption." Thus the prepositional phrase ללוים alone relates the pendant to the main clause, for which גאלת עולם is the subject. MT and LXX are structured quite differently, though it should be said that LXX does render the sense of the Hebrew.

25:33 The opening relative structure is a pendant one: "And as for whoever from the Levites is one who has redeemed." This nominal structure has been simplified in the majority M tradition by changing the participial λυτρωσάμενος to a finite

---

58. See THGL 116.
59. Sym has for v.b: σὺν ἀγρῷ τῆς γῆς λογισθήσονται. λυτρωταὶ ἔσονται ἐν τῷ ιωβηλ ἐξελεύσονται (retroverted from Syh).
60. Sym has for καί—πόλεων a shorter version: αἱ δὲ οἰκίαι τῶν Λευιτῶν πόλεων (retroverted from Syh).

verbal form λυτρωσηται; this easier reading also reflects MT more exactly, and I suspect it to be Byz in origin.[61]

The actual clause of v.a begins with καί 2°: "Even their sale of houses πόλεως of their possession shall go out in the release," i.e. when a Levite sells a house it will return to the Levite in the jubilee year. The word πόλεως is a genitive of source; the houses are from the Levitical cities. The first αὐτῶν "their" has no equivalent in MT and the majority M text has omitted it. The omission is almost certainly a hex correction.[62] The text of MT is not fully certain in that it reads ממכר בית ועיר אחזתו "the sale of a house and the city of its possession." Modern translators agree that it must mean "a house sold in a city which they hold (or possess)." The translator has done his best by a plural statement through which a general principle is enunciated which probably is close to what MT intended.

V.b is fully clear; it is a nominal statement in which הוא, usually translated by ἐστιν, is in unusual fashion omitted;[63] in fact, only twice is it omitted in the book (also at 23:27), and hex has added αυτη η under the asterisk before κατάσχεσις to represent it.[64] The clause is a ὅτι clause giving the basis for their return to their Levitical owners in the jubilee; it is because "the houses of the cities of the Levites are their possession in the midst of the Israelites."

25:34 This verse speaks about the שדה מגרש of their cities. The term מגרש is a difficult one; it refers to land which is around some kind of special area such as a sanctuary or around Levitical cities, which serves as land for which the inhabitants have usage rights. OT translators tended in two directions; some emphasized the fact that it surrounded something: thus περισπόριον, περιπόλιον, περίχωρος, or προάστιον "suburb," and others stressed that it was set apart for something. Our translator followed the latter course: these are οἱ ἀγροὶ οἱ ἀφωρισμένοι (ταῖς πόλεσιν) "fields set apart for the cities." LXX interpreted שדה as a collective, again making of the singular a general rule, viz. "they may not be sold." The reason for this rule is "because an eternal possession τοῦτο αὐτῶν ἐστιν." LXX understands להם as expressing possession, "this (is) theirs."

---

61. According to Hesychius Sym and Aq rendered this by *quicunque affinis est de Levitis*.
62. See THGL 93—94.
63. See SS 80.
64. See THGL 112.

The τοῦτο is neuter without a specific antecedent; it rather states a general rule. A C'+ text has αυτοις instead of αὐτῶν, probably a reading coming from one of The Three, since it renders להם more literally.

25:35 Vv.35—38 are rules concerning the impoverished brother. The protasis of v.35 speaks of your brother being poor καὶ ἀδυνατήσῃ ταῖς χερσὶν παρὰ σοί "and he should become weak in strength (literally in hands) near you," What is meant is that he has fallen into straightened circumstances. The Hebrew has a colorful statement ומטה ידו עמך "and his hand should shake near you." The verb מוט occurs commonly as a figure for feebleness and insecurity. The meaning of MT is not overly clear, but it probably intends that he has become dependent on you; the Greek seems to imply this as well by its παρὰ σοί. LXX uses the plural ταῖς χερσίν without rendering the suffix,[65] the genitive pronoun being otiose in Greek. In the tradition, the majority F M text has added ο μετα σου after the subject, which is taken over from v.25.

For the apodosis LXX says "ἀντιλήμψῃ him[66] like a resident alien and stranger, and your brother shall live with you." The verb means "to help, assist, treat well." Its Hebrew counterpart is והחזקת "you shall hold on (to him)," and the Greek correctly interpreted what MT intended. The גר and the תושב had to be well-treated. The Greek has made the case as showing how one must help the poor brother, and has introduced the comparison by ὡς; though MT does not have an equivalent, the interpretation is correct.

The last clause does not mean that your brother will become a member of your household, but that he will remain alive with you, i.e. he will not perish, because of your help. Hebrew simply has וחי עמך, i.e. ὁ ἀδελφός σου has no equivalent in MT. It is probably a case of leveling with v.36 where אחיך does occur. Hex has rightly placed it under the obelus.

25:36 Forbidden is your taking from your brother τόκον οὐδὲ ἐπὶ πλήθει. τόκον is the usual rendering for נשך (12 of 17 times). The Greek word refers to what is produced, thus may refer to childbirth, and then by extension to any product brought forth, and as a rendering for נשך refers to that which lent money brings

---

65. See SS 96.
66. According to Hesychius Aq read for the protasis plus ἀντιλήμψῃ αὐτοῦ, *si exciderit frater tuus et culpaverit manus eius tecum auxiliari ei*.

forth, viz. interest. The second term has similar connotations, but refers to increase. It is a paraphrastic rendering for תרבית, more commonly rendered by πλεονασμός, for which see v.37. I suspect that the distinction intended by the Greek is between interest on money lent, with the second one referring to increase in capital lent as an added payment.[67] For translation I would keep the more general terms "interest" and "increase."[68]

For the next clause see comment at 19:14 where MT reads ויראת מאלהיך אני יהוה; our Greek text disregards the preposition, probably rightly so. MT does not have an equivalent for ἐγὼ κύριος here, and hex correctly placed it under the obelus. The formula is anticipatory of the longer form at the end of the section in v.38. For the last clause see comment at v.35.

25:37 Here the prohibitions are more specific. "Your money you may not give him for interest, and for increase you may not give him your food." In both cases the Greek uses ἐπί with a dative to translate Hebrew ב phrases. The ἐπί with dative indicates price, thus "at the cost of interest," "at the cost of increase."[69] An M ol f z+ text has changed the first ἐπί to εν, but not the second. I doubt that this was due to recensional activity; it is simply a stylistic change. Somewhat uncertain is the parent of πλεονασμῷ. The noun occurs only six times in OT, and otherwise translates only תרבית. Since Sam reads תרבית rather than מרבית, I suspect that Sam's text may well have been parent for πλεονασμῷ here as well.

25:38 The self-identification formula in its long form is used to conclude this section, accompanied by an apposite statement identifying the Lord your God as the one who effected the redemptive exodus from the land of Egypt "in order to give you the land of Canaan ὥστε εἶναι ὑμῶν θεός." The b text has a different form for the formula: εγω ειμι κυριος ο θεος, but the Lev text represents MT correctly. The majority F M variant making δοῦναι an articular infinitive was created by dittography. The του repeats the ending of the preceding Αἰγύπτου.[70] The purpose of the divine redemptive actions is that the Lord may "be your God." MT

---

67. Harlé-Pralon have quite a different understanding of the second term, making it refer to long-term loans: "(interêt) même à longue échéance."
68. For the second item The Others read οὐδὲ διπλασίασμα "nor doubling (i.e. of the capital)."
69. See LS sub ἐπί B.III.4.
70. See THGL 82.

has להיות לכם לאלהים "to become (or be) for you God." The pattern היה ל often means "become," i.e. the divine redemptive activity of the Exodus and gift of land had as its purpose that God may become, i.e. be recognized as God for them. The translator has adopted a simpler understanding: "to be your God," so what God demands is recognition by his people of his relation to them.

25:39—40 As at v.35 LXX renders וכי by ἐὰν δέ, showing thereby contrast to what had preceded. In MT v.39 opens as at v.35 with כי ימוך אחיך, but the verb מוך "be depressed, become poor" is here not translated by πένηται but by ταπεινωθῇ "is humbled, abased," hence "has fallen into straightened circumstances." The παρὰ σοί modifies ἀδελφός, thus "your brother (who is) with you." The result is that "he should be sold to you."

In such a case he may not serve you with the service of a household slave. In MT the equivalent for σοι is an instrumental בו, i.e. "you may not work with him the work of a slave," i.e. you may not impose on him the work of a slave. The δουλεύσει σοι is a free rendering, but not as direct a prohibition on the employer. The translator has softened the command by transferring the focus on to the indentured fellow-Israelites.

V.40 gives the positive statement, but as in the parent text, without a contrastive particle. MT begins with two כ phrases which LXX correctly interprets by ὡς μισθωτὸς ἢ πάροικος "as a hireling or a stranger (he shall be to you)," i.e. neither as the hireling who worked for his pay day by day nor as the πάροικος. For this term as a translation of תושב see comment at 22:10, and more particularly the Note at Gen 23:4. Here it refers to temporary non-native help.

In the last clause the verb יעבד occurs, but here it is not translated by δουλεύσει as in v.39, but by ἐργᾶται. "Until the year of the release he will work along with you." A rather fine point is made by this change in translation. The verb עבד can be understood in the sense of "do the work of an עבד" a household slave, or in the sense of "work," as e.g. by a hireling, but not one of inferior status. He is a fellow-Israelite, "your brother," who must work with you, but only up to the jubilee year.

25:41 Instead of MT's "(and he shall go out) מעמך" LXX reads τῇ ἀφέσει, i.e. "he will go out at the release." The substitution of τῇ ἀφέσει is explanatory in nature. It ensures that the departure is not arbitrary, but as inferred from the preceding verse was occasioned by the jubilee. Hex recognized that this was not in MT and placed the dative structure under the obelus, and then added ἀπο σου to represent מעמך. MT then adds הוא ובניו עמו. The translator omitted the הוא, i.e. has only καὶ τὰ τέκνα αὐτοῦ μετ' αὐτοῦ. Hex also repairs this by adding αυτος before the καί.⁷¹ I can see no good reason for LXX's failure to render מעמך הוא. The addition of τῇ ἀφέσει hardly justifies it, though admittedly the omission does not change the sense of the passage.

V.b consists of two clauses. The first one translates MT word for word: "and he shall return to his γενεάν," i.e. to משפחתו "his clan, his family." But not only will he be reunited with his people, εἰς τὴν κατάσχεσιν τὴν πατρικὴν ἀπεδραμεῖται. The adjectival structure "the paternal possession" refers to the hereditary land, which presumably he had sold to meet his debts. The hereditary nature of this possession is clear from the Hebrew bound phrase which it translates: אחזת אבתיו "the possession of his fathers."⁷² Hex has added an αυτου to represent the suffix of אבתיו. The verb is the future of ἀποδιδράσκω "to flee from, escape." Here then "he shall go freely to his paternal possession." It should be noted that MT also introduced the last clause syndetically. The F M majority text also added a και, which must be based on the Hebrew, though the usual representatives of the hex text do not add the και. It probably came through the Byz text from one of The Three.

25:42 MT makes the entire verse plural: "because they are my servants ... not may they be sold ...." LXX follows the plural of MT for v.a: "because these are my οἰκέται whom I brought out from the land of Egypt." οἰκέται occurs in Lev only in this chapter (four times, also in vv.39,55) for עבד. The term "household slaves" describes a relationship valid for Israel only over against the Lord (vv.42,55) but is always invalid as a relation between fellow-Israelites (vv.39,42). Furthermore, they are the Lord's οἰκέται by virtue of the great act of redemption in the exodus, i.e. having freed them from oppression, they are now the Lord's personal servants, his οἰκέται.

LXX puts v.b in the singular. In other words, because the Israelites are my servants, he (ὁ ἀδελφός σου of v.39) may not be sold ἐν πράσει οἰκέτου "with the sale of a household slave." In other words, he may not be sold like a slave

---

71. See SS 74.
72. For the adjectival structure translating a bound phrase see SS 66 and 98.

(possibly on the open market, publicly?), i.e. MT makes a general statement, whereas LXX specifies the case presented in vv.39—41. Accordingly, MT makes this all plural, the variant b+ text changing the verb to πραθησονται may well be a recensional (hex?) change.

25:43 For v.a MT reads לא תרדה בו בפרך "do not rule over him with severity." LXX has a colorful rendering: "not shall you κατατενεῖς him ἐν τῷ μόχθῳ." The verb means "to stretch, render taut," so "do not make him tense with toil, hardship," in other words, do not overwork him. This is a fine interpretation of MT.[73]

For the second clause see comment at 19:14. MT has no equivalent for κύριον, and hex has omitted the word to equal MT. Implied by the demand to fear the Lord your God is that overworking a fellow-Israelite would be at odds with the life of the true Yahwist. A true follower of the Lord would not do such a thing.

25:44 Vv.44—46 deal with slaves as property. MT makes the first cut in the verse after לך, i.e. "As for your man-servant and your maid-servant which are yours." This is then a pendant construction, and one continues with "from the nations which ... from them you may buy ...." The translator probably understood the syntax of the verse somewhat differently. In view of the מהם, which seems somewhat otiose in MT if understood as the Masoretes did, LXX made the break later. The reference made is to "both man-servant and maid-servant which you might have from the nations which are around you." In other words, ἀπὸ τῶν ἐθνῶν modifies γένωνται, not κτήσεσθε. This too might then be taken as a pendant construction, and the main clause brings only the ἐθνῶν into the structure by its ἀπ' αὐτῶν, i.e. "from them you may buy a male slave and a female slave." The translator was trying to interpret this statement and still allow for some master-servant relationships among Israelites. Though MT uses עבד and אמה in both v.a and v.b LXX translates them differently. In v.a he renders καὶ παῖς καὶ παιδίσκη, disregarding the pronominal suffixes of the parent text, ועבדך ואמתך; hex added σου after both nouns to make up for them; these terms I have rendered

---

[73]. Lee 21—22 suggests "to overwork, strain," which he maintains differs from the Hebrew רדה.

as "male-servant and maid-servant." in v.b LXX uses δοῦλον καὶ δούλην, i.e. "male slave and female slave." I would suggest that LXX by using different terms in v.b also changes the nature of עבד and אמה. In v.a the master-servant relation is a present reality; in v.b the terms are products of the market, and the relation is that of buyer and bought, hence "slaves" rather than "servants."

It should be added, however, that it is quite possible to understand LXX as making the first cut in the same way as the Masoretes did, and to make this possibility apparent, I would now place a comma after σοι in the critical text as well. After all, the autographa had no punctuation marks of any kind as far as we know, and punctuation is the product of the modern editor, meant to aid the reader to make correct syntactic judgments.

25:45 Not just from the surrounding nations, but also "from the υἱῶν τῶν παροίκων τῶν ὄντων ἐν ὑμῖν" was it legitimate to purchase slaves.[74] The term υἱῶν, like the Hebrew בני, simply means "members of." For παροίκων translating תושבים see Note at Gen 23:4. τῶν ὄντων translates the participle הגרים. This root is variously translated throughout Lev, but only here by ὄντων.[75] Admittedly "those who reside (הגרים) among you" are τῶν ὄντων ἐν ὑμῖν, i.e. "those who are among you," but this does lose the notion of resident alienship which the root גור has. Note that this structure is a pendant one, and only the τούτων reference brings the structure into the clause. Not only may you purchase slaves from strangers, but also "from their relatives (συγγενῶν αὐτῶν) ὅσον ἂν γένωνται ἐν τῇ γῇ ὑμῶν" i.e. who might be born in your land." The introductory καί joins what follows with τούτων. This relative clause is preceded by another clause אשר עמכם which the translator overlooked because of homoioteleuton, the next word being אשר as well. Hex has supplied των μεθ υμων to represent the omitted clause, whereas a C′ s z+ text has supplied των εν υμιν, which is either a variant text developed from hex or created through another recensor (one of The Three?).

The important matter is expressed in the concluding statement ἔστωσαν ὑμῖν εἰς κατάσχεσιν "let them become a possession for you," i.e. your property, something which would never be allowed for a fellow Israelite.

---

74. According to Hesychius Theod and Sym read *a filiis inquilinorum qui habitant in vobis*.
75. See THGL 130.

25:46 For התנחלתם "you may will inherited property (to someone)," LXX has κατομεριεῖτε "you may distribute." This is the first use of this verb in the Pentateuch, but it occurs for the Hithp of נחל again in Num 32:18. One might have expected the more explicit verb κατακληρονομέω. In any event, slaves as defined in vv.44—45 may be passed on to one's heirs. MT follows with לרשת אחזה לעלם "to inherit as a possession forever," which LXX makes into a separate clause: "and they shall be for you κατόχιμοι forever." The word is a hapax legomenon in OT, and means "can be held in possession," which makes excellent sense in the context, and stresses the fact that the year of release is not applicable in their case. This is followed in MT by בהם תעבדו "you may enslave them," but this is omitted by LXX, possibly as not quite fitting in the context. After all, the verse speaks of passing such on as an inheritance to one's children, and the clause seems intrusive. It is also possible that the translator overlooked the clause, since בהם תעבדו is followed by a coordinate ב phrase ובאחיכם, i.e. it may have been a simple case of parablepsis. Hex has added αυτους καταδουλωσεσθε to represent it; it can then serve as a contrast to what follows, which, however, is not how the Masoretes took it; they placed תעבדו under the *ethnach*.

V.b is contrastive, which is aptly shown by δέ. Its omission by the A B C+ text is a mistake, probably a partial haplograph based on the occurrence of ΔΕ in the next word ἀδελφῶν. In any event, the δέ is contextually correct, since the case of what may happen with bought slaves contrasts with "but among the Israelites no one may overwork his brother." For the idiom κατατενεῖ ἐν τοῖς μόχθοις see comment at v.43. MT uses a second singular verb תרדה, which undoubtedly influenced the Masoretes to separate the clause from the בהם תעבדו which preceded it; cf above. LXX, however, uses third person which is congruent with its subject ἕκαστος.

25:47 This verse is the protasis, and the apodosis follows in vv.48—53. The condition described is that of a prosperous resident alien or stranger over against an Israelite who has fallen on evil days, who sells himself to the wealthy alien or stranger or to the offspring of the resident alien. The Hebrew idiom for becoming prosperous used is יד תשיג "the hand overtakes, reaches." This idiom occurs frequently in Lev, and the translation here εὕρῃ ἡ χείρ is usual;[76] see comment at

---

76. See THGL 131.

14:21. What "if the hand of the resident alien or of the stranger who is with you should find" means is "if the resident alien ... should prosper." The Byz text has changed εὕρῃ to the present subjunctive, but this is secondary; the default aorist tense is fully adequate here.

The second condition concerns the Israelite, ὁ ἀδελφός σου. MT has two clauses" a) ומך אחיך עמו "your brother with you is impoverished." LXX subordinates the verb to a participle ἀπορηθείς and omits עמו, thus "being impoverished". Hex has added μετ αυτου under the asterisk after σου to render the prepositional phrase. b) ונמכר לגר תושב עמך או לעקר משפחת גר. LXX follows Sam in reading ותושב instead of תושב.⁷⁷ Its text is straightforward: πραθῇ τῷ προσηλύτῳ ἢ τῷ παροίκῳ τῷ παρὰ σοὶ ἢ ἐκ γενετῆς προσηλύτῳ. It translates the Hebrew clearly at least up to the last conjunction. The Hebrew עקר is a hapax legomenon, and is usually understood to mean "offspring," though this is but an educated guess.⁷⁸ The Hebrew then means "or to the offspring of the family of a resident alien." This is rendered economically in LXX by "or to the resident alien by ancestry" (i.e. by birth).⁷⁹ In the tradition, an A B V n x+ text has omitted the ἤ, but this is due to an auditory error,⁸⁰ i.e. after σοι, pronounced /si/ before ἤ, pronounced /i/, thus /si i/.

25:48 MT begins with אחרי נמכר "after he has sold himself," which LXX renders by an infinitival construction μετὰ τὸ πραθῆναι αὐτῷ. This puzzled Origen, and so hex placed αὐτῷ under the obelus. In the tradition, a V ol b+ text "corrected" αὐτῷ by its αυτον. For λύτρωσις ἔσται αὐτῷ see comment at v.29. In the tradition, ἔσται αὐτῷ suffered considerably. The n text has αυτου εσται; an F V O y+ text reads εσται αυτου, and the Byz text has αυτω εσται. But Lev rendered תהיה לו correctly. What it says is that the right to redemption shall remain to him. Change to the genitive is a stylistic change; it remains his. Since the right of redemption remains, εἷς τῶν ἀδελφῶν αὐτοῦ must redeem him. The

---

77. As do Kenn 17,18,109,151,196 and 252.
78. As the Tar illustrate: Tar⁰ has (זרעית גיורא) ארמי "the heathen offspring of the גר." Tar^N simply takes over the Hebrew לעקר followed by זרעית גיור, while Tar^J explains the word as לשריש פולחנא נוכראה למשמשא.
79. Sym translated by ἡ ῥίζη (or ῥίζης) συγγενείας προσηλύτου. I am unsure how Sym understood עקר, possibly "or from the root of the alien's family"? See the rendering of Tar^J in the previous f.n.
80. See THGL 116.

genitive translates a partitive מן expression in MT: מאחיו.⁸¹ Presumably it is the ἀγχιστεύων who is referred to as "one of his brothers."

25:49 MT begins with a correlative conjunction which LXX omits. MT makes those referred to in v.49 alternatives to אחד מאחיו, whereas in LXX v.49 identifies who "one of his brothers" might well be. A z+ reading does add η at the beginning, but this need not be taken as recensional; it could simply be an ad sensum gloss.

Three possible redeemers are given. First, either an agnate uncle or agnate cousin might redeem him. MT calls them דדו או בן דדו, and LXX disregards the suffix in both cases as being otiose—that these should be his own uncle or cousin is obvious. Nonetheless hex has supplied an αυτου for both to equal MT.⁸² The word דד is one of the few Hebrew words which require two Greek words for its translation: ἀδελφὸς πατρός.

The second possibility is "someone of his blood relatives (οἰκείων τῶν σαρκῶν) from his tribe might redeem him." The use of the plural σαρκῶν is fine Classical usage, and is hardly to be distinguished from the singular in meaning, i.e. "of his flesh," those related by blood. Nonetheless an F+ text did change to της σαρκος. I have rendered the ἀπό phrase as partitive, "someone of,"⁸³ which in turn explains why τῶν οἰκείων should be plural. Actually, the collocation שאר בשרו is rather tautologous, both words meaning "flesh," and LXX's τῶν οἰκείων τῶν σαρκῶν only makes a slight differentiation, i.e. "(some) of his relatives related by blood." The further modifier ἐκ (τῆς φυλῆς αὐτοῦ) also represents a partitive מן.⁸⁴

The third possibility reads או השיגה ידו וגאל "or his hand has reached (i.e. he has prospered) and he can redeem himself." LXX has idiomatically changed או השיגה to ἐὰν δὲ εὐπορηθείς (ταῖς χερσίν). The verb השיג in the idiom is more commonly rendered by the verb εὑρίσκω as at v.47, and for which see comment at 14:21. In fact, it occurs elsewhere only at v.26, which see, while εὑρίσκω occurs 12 times.⁸⁵ The δέ is clearly contrastive: "but should he become prosperous, he may redeem himself." ταῖς χερσίν disregards the suffix of ידו,

---

81. See SS 166—167.
82. See THGL 92.
83. See SS 158.
84. See SS 165.
85. According to Dos Santos.

but this is not uncommon in Lev.[86] Unusual is the plural χερσίν for ידו, but the number of the word יד is not rigidly rendered by LXX at all. Hex has placed ἑαυτόν under the obelus; it is true that MT has no separate reflexive pronoun, but the Ni נגאל is either passive or reflexive. Once again the use of the obelus shows how mechanically Origen tended to work. After all, the translator wanted to make certain that the Ni be properly understood in this context as reflexive.

25:50 The determination of the amount of service sold is to be jointly settled: καὶ συλλογιεῖται πρὸς τὸν κεκτημένον αὐτόν "and he shall reckon together with the one who had bought him."[87] The C' s+ text has the aorist participle κτησαμενον instead of the more appropriate perfect.

The general reckoning is clear; it is to extend "from the year of his selling himself to him up to the year of release." In other words, the standard employed for determining the cost is the number of years remaining up to the jubilee year.

The definition of what "the money of his sale" is to be is ordered differently in LXX and MT. The Hebrew reads במספר שנים כימי שכיר יהיה עמו "in number of years, like the days of a hireling it shall be with him," i.e. the price will be determined by the number of years; it will remain with him like a hireling's wages. LXX has rearranged and shortened this in order to make clear the rather ambiguous Hebrew. It reads "like a salary; per year shall it be with him." LXX has made good sense, and probably says what MT intended. Hex was quite disturbed by this free rendering, and has rewritten it as follows: ετος εξ ετους ως ημεραι μισθιου εσται μετ αυτου. It should be noted that of the usual witnesses to the hex text only Syh has the plural ημεραι, all the others having lost the final iota.

25:51 The Hebrew begins asyndetically, whereas LXX begins as usual with ἐὰν δέ. Hex seems to have omitted the δέ to conform to MT. The protasis in LXX reads "but if there should remain more years to someone." LXX does not translate עוד, and actually has τινι in its slot, but LXX adequately renders the sense of MT. An $O\ C'$ s+ variant has τι, which must be secondary. The only possible recensional change is ετι πλειω for πλεῖον as an n reading, but this may well be a

---

86. See SS 96.
87. According to Hesychius Theod had *tractabit cum eo qui acquisivit eum*, and Aq read *supputabit cum eo qui possedit eum*.

change within the Byz reading εpi πλειω. Since *iota* and *pi* are similar in shape it is easily possible to confuse ετι and επι, and one could argue the priority of either one as the original Byz text.

The apodosis is clear: "πρὸς ταῦτα (referring to ἐτῶν) he shall pay his ransom from the money of his sale." The prepositional phrase designates the scale to be used for the amount of the ransom to be paid, i.e. "according to these." This is exactly what לפיהם of MT means.

25:52 The protasis contrasts with that of v.51: "but if a few should remain of the years to the year of release," i.e. ὀλίγον obtains instead of πλεῖον. Instead of εἰς the Byz text reads εως εις, which may be recensional in view of MT's עד.

The apodosis is introduced by καί in imitation of MT. It is simply put in LXX in two clauses: "and one shall reckon to him according to his years (i.e. those that are left to the jubilee), and he shall repay his ransom." The next phrase, ὡς μισθωτός, is part of this verse, but as in MT it really belongs in sense with v.53, and it has been punctuated accordingly in the critical text. MT has divided v.52 differently, placing לו under the *ethnach*; i.e. "and it should be reckoned to him" belongs to v.a. The next clause is then introduced asyndetically. The *n* text has omitted καί 2°, which agrees with MT, and this omission was probably mediated through one of The Three. I am not sure why the Masoretes divided the verse as they did, since וחשב לו seems so obviously part of the apodosis.[88]

25:53 The ὡς μισθωτός ending v.52 must be read as in MT with v.53, thus "as a hireling shall it be with him year by year."[89]

For the second clause see discussion at v.43. It differs, however, in adding ἐνώπιόν σου at the end, which is tautological in view of the mistranslation of ירדנו as a second person verb. Oddly enough no Greek witness has changed κατατενεῖς to third person, or omitted the prepositional phrase. What κατατενεῖ must have meant to a reader is "not shall you allow someone to overwork him in your presence."

---

88. Sym translated the apodosis by n'bd ḥwšbn' lwth ayk mlt' dylhyn dšny' ntl pwrqn' dylh.
89. Sym adopts Lev except for reading πρὸς αυτόν (retroverted from Syh) for μετ' αὐτοῦ.

25:54 In contrast to the various ways of ransom given in the preceding verse, suppose that one should find no redeemer, i.e. "he would not be redeemed κατὰ ταῦτα." MT has באלה "by these," and LXX interprets by "according to these."[90] The ταῦτα refers to ἐτῶν, i.e. according to the years that remain up to the year of release.

Since there has been no redemption in this case, there remains the certain end to his period of service: "He will go out in the year of release," in fact, not only he, but "he and his children with him." The verb is singular, which is induced by the αὐτός, the nearer of the compound subject.[91]

In MT the apodosis is introduced by *waw*, but the translator wisely did not translate it. A majority M text has, however, added a και to make up for it. This must be a recensional change, possibly introduced by the Byz text. Also in the tradition, κατὰ ταῦτα has been changed by the A B b+ text to μετα ταυτα; this is particularly unfortunate, since it completely changes the meaning. The phrase usually occurs simply in the sense of "afterwards," which would be quite inappropriate.

25:55 The ὅτι structure concludes the chapter with a statement giving the reason for the detailed instructions concerning anything related to the jubilee phenomenon. It is given in two parts: a) "because the Israelites are household servants (οἰκέται) to me." The notion that the Israelites are God's household servants is a bold and unusual statement. But the term is reserved for Israel's relation to the Lord; it cannot refer to the relation of an Israelite to a fellow-Israelite; see comments at vv.39,42. The relationship is that of one who works as a house servant; the Israelites are not slaves, but God's house servants.

This is further defined by b) "they are my servants (παῖδες) whom I brought out of the land of Egypt." The term παῖς was the preferred rendering for עבד in Gen, but is used in Lev only three times (also in vv.6,44 where the term is used coordinate with παιδίσκη in the sense of man-servant and maid-servant); see comment at v.44. The plural occur only here in the book, and may well have been chosen not only to contrast with οἰκέται which translates the same word, but also to stress the relationship between master and servant as an intimate one;

---

90. See SS 124—125.
91. See SS 72.

Israel is in service as a παῖς to the master. MT's הם is translated by οὗτοί εἰσιν. Origen wanted to show that Hebrew had only one word, and placed an obelus in the text, but it is not certain which word was placed under the sign. The extant tradition gives a confusing picture, with Syh placing both under the obelus, and ms G only οὗτος. It would seem that the metobelus was wrongly placed in Syh; in other words, it was intended to place only οὗτος under the obelus.

Chapter 26

26:1 The chapter begins with the long self-identification formula, which in MT ends the preceding verse. It is more usual to use this as a subscription than as a superscription. Since the verse is a prohibition against any form of idol worship, the verse also ends with the same formula, i.e. it is surrounded by the reminder that "I am the Lord your God."

The prohibitions of the verse deal with the first two prohibitions of the Ten Words, forbidding not only having other gods besides the Lord, but also various representations of God in worship. It is fitting then that the verse should begin and end with the divine reminder "I am the Lord your God." The second instance includes εἰμι after ἐγώ, which hex omits as not represented in MT. In the Hebrew the end formula is introduced by כי, which LXX, supported by all Greek witnesses, omits. This may be a stylistic matter, i.e. made to parallel the opening clause as a true inclusio.

The prohibitions are three in number. The first forbids the making of χειροποίητα or γλυπτά, i.e. "hand-crafted or carved (objects of worship)." χειροποίητα renders אלילם, normallly interpreted as "worthless objects" as contrasted with אלים "powerful ones, gods." LXX stresses their irreality by its χειροποίητα; they have no independent existence, but are made by human hands. The equation was adopted by Isa where it occurs five times; cf especially 31:7, where such handcrafted idols are both of silver and gold; comp the scathing denunciation of such hand-crafted objects in Isa 44:9—20. At v.30 below, reference is made to the divine annihilation of τὰ ξύλινα χειροποίητα ὑμῶν; cf ad loc. For γλυπτά as the usual rendering for פסל see Note at Dt 4:16.

The second prohibition is that of setting up στήλην or מצבה. A מצבה was in origin a neutral word, and like στήλη, might simply be a pillar set up as a kind of memorial, but in OT it is more often used of sacred pillars or stones, and eventually became associated with the pagan cult, and something which "the Lord God hates"; see Dt 16:22.

The third prohibition is that of putting "λίθον σκοπόν in your land so as to worship it." The Hebrew term is אבן משכית. Precisely what kind of stone was intended by משכית is not clear. The word apparently means "figure, imagination," and so a stone which has been imaginatively hewn or figured; comp the abomination described in Ezek 8:12, where each one is בחדרי משכיתו, which is rendered in the Greek by ἐν τῷ κοιτῶνι τῷ κρυπτῷ (αὐτῶν). The phrase is rendered by λίθον σκοπόν, probably "a distinctive stone," i.e. one which calls attention to itself." The phrase is a hapax legomenon in OT. Since it is potentially an object of worship, it must be a special stone of some kind.¹

In the tradition, the ὑμῖν αὐτοῖς for לכם led to some confusion. A majority M reading has changed αὐτοῖς to the reflexive εαυτοις, so as to stress the reflexive nature of ὑμῖν modifying a second plural verb. Hex, on the other hand, omitted αὐτοῖς as having no equivalent in MT. Both χειροποίητα and γλυπτά are changed to the singular in *b n*, but *O* only changed γλυπτά to γλυπτον, which equals MT's פסל and is probably hex in origin. A popular M text has changed θήσετε to στησετε, but this was probably palaeographically inspired. An *O* Byz+ text has changed αὐτῷ to the Classical αυτον as modifier of προσκυνῆσαι, but the dative modifier is dominant in OT.

26:2 This verse is an exact copy of 19:30; cf comments ad loc. Hex has omitted εἰμι as having no equivalent in MT. The Byz text has added ο θεος υμων to the short self-identification formula, but the short form equals MT, and is original text.

26:3 This verse is the protasis for which vv.4–12(13) are the apodosis. The protasis has three clauses, the first two of which have preposed modifiers to a present subjunctive verb, πορεύησθε and φυλάσσησθε resp. These are sensible, since what is intended is the process of continual walking in and guarding the statutes/commandments of the Lord. The third clause, however, uses the default aorist, and has the pronominal modifier (αὐτάς referring to ἐντολάς) following the verb. Oddly enough, the present subjunctive of ποιέω is avoided throughout Lev, probably for semantic reasons, i.e. "doing" viewed as a single action rather than a continuing process.²

In the tradition, the Byz *f*+ text has added εν before τοῖς προστάγμασίν μου. Since MT has read בחקתי this may be a recensional plus to represent the Hebrew preposition.

---

1. Harlé-Pralon translate by "pierre repère," but see their discussion for another possible understanding of the phrase, viz. a "pierre protectrice."
2. See THGL 125.

26:4 The onset of the apodosis is introduced by καί in imitation of MT; its omission by O+ might be a hex correction, though it could also be taken as a stylistic improvement. The first clause promises "ὑετὸν ὑμῖν (in its season)." This is a somewhat free rendering for גשמיכם "your rains." But ὑετός occurs throughout OT only in the singular (except in wisdom literature at Job 37:6 Prov 25:14 and twice in Sap). Qumran ms 801 has [τ]ης γης υμων instead of ὑμῖν, which could possibly have been influenced by Dt 28:12,24 τῇ γῇ σου.³

The second blessing is that "the land shall yield its produce." τὰ γενήματα translates יבול as at Dt 32:22. MT, however, has the verb before the subject, i.e. ונתנה הארץ, and hex has transposed ἡ γῆ and δώσει to equal MT.

The last clause in MT reads ועץ השדה יתן פריו "and the tree of the field shall yield its fruit." That עץ is to be taken collectively in view of the bound structure with השדה is sensible, and LXX reads both words as collectives, i.e. καὶ τὰ ξύλα τῶν πεδίων ἀποδώσει τὸν καρπὸν αὐτῶν. If השדה is to be taken as a collective, i.e. as τῶν πεδίων, it follows that the plural τὰ ξύλα is mandatory. This nicely contrasts with τὸ ξύλον τοῦ ἀγροῦ of v.20. The Qumran ms 801 has a broken text which reads τον ξυλινον κα..., and it has been suggested that this should read καρπον; comp 27:30: "every tenth ... τοῦ καρποῦ τοῦ ξυλίνου belongs to the Lord," where presumably the adjective is to be understood nominally, i.e. as "fruit of the tree." The adjective occurs elsewhere for עץ only twice in the book; both at 11:32 and 15:12 it is used adjectivally in "wooden vessel." If 801 did read τον ξυλινον καρπον it would mean "the wooden fruit," and then by extension fruit wooden in source, i.e. "tree fruit."⁴ It will be noted that in the second clause the verb יתן was rendered by δώσει, but here by ἀποδώσει; this simply reflects the translator's delight in variation.

---

3. Ulrich 53 considers this "either a legitimate, free translation of the same Hebrew or a literal reflection of a slightly different Hebrew *Vorlage.*" I am, however, as a general rule, chary of retroversions without any extant remains.
4. Ulrich 54 believes 801 to represent the original Greek based on a different Hebrew parent. This is of course possible, but it remains highly speculative. That it is further removed from MT than Lev is obvious, but I am not ready to accept the text of Lev as a revision of a Hebrew for which there is no extant evidence at all. Ulrich restores some such text as "the land will give its produce and its arboreal fruit," which is textually very different from MT.

26:5 The Hebrew noun דוש is a hapax legomenon, though the root is well-known as meaning "to thresh." Lev has ἀλόητος, but it should be noted that A B both support αμητος, as does Philo. I am not clear why I adopted the majority ἀλόητος as original text, since ἄμητος seems to me to be LXX, and ἀλόητος a revision towards the notion of "threshing." The word ἄμητος is an acceptable rendering for "threshing" as any grain or dairy farmer would know.[5] The growth will be so phenomenal that "the grain harvesting will overtake the grape harvest, and the grape harvest (in turn) will overtake the seeding."

For eating bread εἰς πλησμονήν see Exod 16:8. To dwell לבטח also occurred at 25:18,19, where it was rendered by πεποιθότες; cf comment plus f.n. at 25:18. Its translation by μετὰ ἀσφαλείας is equally valid. For this see Note at Dt 12:10.

The last clause "and war shall not go through your land" does not have an equivalent here, but it occurs as וחרב לא יעבר בארצכם at the end of v.6, the translator correctly understanding the metaphor of חרב "sword" as πόλεμος. In fact, hex has transposed the clause there to equal MT. It would appear that the bilingual copyist of 801 made the same correction. Jewish copyists of the LXX text undoubtedly knew their Hebrew text by heart, probably much better than its Greek translation, and would easily make corrections almost subconsciously in the course of copying the Greek.[6] The transposition of the clause to follow "and you shall dwell in safety on your land" was probably an attempt on the part of LXX at a more logical consecution of clauses. It does fit better in this position than after "and I will destroy evil beasts out of your land."

26:6 For ἐν τῇ γῇ O reads επι της γης, while n reads επι την γην, but the literal rendering of בארץ of Lev is original. Over against MT Lev adds ὑμῶν for good sense, but hex has placed it under the obelus to show its lack of equivalent in MT. The structure "your land" occurs in the preceding clause as well as at the end of the verse.

The second and third clauses represent a common promise of peace: "you will lie down and there will be no one making you afraid." The latter clause is

---
5. Ulrich 54—56 suggests that ἄμητος might well be original, and I am grateful to him for rousing me to reassess the evidence.
6. For a discussion of bilingual scribes see J.W.Wevers, The Earliest Witness to the LXX Deuteronomy, Catholic Biblical Quarterly 39(1977), 240—244. See also the extensive statement on The Text of 848 in THGD 646—85.

nominal in MT: ואין מחריד. Participial predicates are usually rendered by the present tense in Lev, but the future ἔσται plus a participle is demanded by the context. The ὑμᾶς is an ad sensum addition modifying the participle ἐκφοβῶν. Again, the pronoun is placed under the obelus by hex to show its absence in MT.

In the final clause ἀπολῶ is used to represent the Hi השבתי. This is unique in the Pentateuch, in fact it only occurs elsewhere in the three Major Prophets; it does make better sense, however, with θηρία πονηρά than the more usual καταπαύω or καταλύω. Once again, the translator has added ὑμῶν at the end for good sense, and once again, hex has placed it under the obelus because of its absence in MT. At the end of the verse a majority A F M text has added καὶ πολεμος ου διελευσεται δια της γης υμων; see comment at v.5, where the clause also occurs, though hex had transposed it to the end of v.6, where MT also has the clause. The variant text has it in both positions, which in spite of its strong support can hardly be original Lev.; see comment at v.5.

26:7 Victory over the enemy is promised. In fact, "they will fall before you by slaughter." φόνῳ is an unusual rendering for לחרב "by the sword"; it occurs only three times in OT (also at Exod 5:3 Dt 28:22); see Note at Exod 5:3. V.8, where the same phrase occurs in MT, renders it by μαχαίρᾳ, which is the more usual rendering (167 times in OT[7]).

26:8 The Qumran 801 text uniquely reads πεντε υμων for ἐξ ὑμῶν πέντε. What is surprising is that more copyists did not do so, since it is an obvious improvement in style over Lev. In fact, only the larger context makes clear that it is not "five-hundred of you that will pursue," but rather that "five will pursue a hundred" that is intended. Lev, however, simply followed the מכם חמשה of MT, which has the partitive מן, here rendered by ἐξ,[8] whereas in the next clause the מכם is rendered by a simple genitive. In the second clause מאה מכם becomes ἑκατὸν ὑμῶν, which probably influenced the copyist of 801 as well. Here the Byz text has changed ὑμῶν to ἐξ ὑμῶν under the influence of the first clause; this does equal MT, but is probably not recensional. In MT this is followed by רבבה ירדפו, but LXX has διώξονται μυριάδας. Hex has transposed the two words, so as to equal the word order of MT. For μαχαίρᾳ see comment at v.7.

---

7. According to my count from HR.
8. See SS 166—167.

26:9 The verse consists of four paratactic future clauses, all divine promises of grace to the obedient Israelites. The opening clause uses ἐπιβλέψω "I shall look upon" to render פניתי "I shall turn towards," and ἐπιβλέπω is used to render פנה (31 times) in OT. The Qal of פנה is rendered by a large number of different verbs, but ἐπιβλέπω is the most common, followed by ἐπιστρέφω (22), βλέπω and ἀποστρέφω (10 each), ἐκκλίνω (4), etc. For the coordination of αὐξάνω and πληθυνῶ see Note at Gen 17:20 as well as at Gen 1:22 where the pair first occurs.

For στήσω τὴν διαθήκην μου see Gen 6:18 9:11 17:7,21, and see Note at Gen 6:18. In Gen this is in turn modified by a πρός phrase, but here more literally by μεθ' ὑμῶν rendering אתכם; this reflects the much more isolate type of translation found in Lev. Instead of τὴν διαθήκην μου ms 801 has [μο]υ την διαθηκην. The difference in word order is common in Hellenistic Greek, but in the Greek of LXX it is much more unusual. The change is probably stylistic. In 801 this is apparently followed by εν υμιν, though only the *epsilon* is certain. The origin of this reading is v.11, where an early A B text read διαθηκην instead of σκηνήν (μου); this is followed by ἐν ὑμῖν, which text probably influenced the copyist of 801.[9]

26:10 The term παλαιά refers to the old year's grain, and renders ישן, which contrasts with נושן; this must refer to that which had already been rendered old, i.e. the harvest of the year before last year's. The translator had a neat rendering for נושן, παλαιὰ παλαιῶν, i.e. the old year's grain of the old year's grain, i.e. that which was παλαιά last year. So what you will be eating is the harvest of the past two years. Origen did not understand that παλαιὰ παλαιῶν was the rendering for נושן. Since Hebrew had two words, one of the three was in his mind an extra, and so mistakenly παλαιά 1° was placed under the obelus. Another witness has παλαιῶν under the obelus, and it is not certain which obelus is original, though the general intent of hex is clear.

So plentiful will the harvests have been that παλαιὰ ἐκ προσώπου νέων ἐξοίσετε "you must bring out the old before the new," i.e. you will have to put away the old grain to make room for the new. Instead of ἐκ προσώπου νέων 801 reads μετα των νεω[ν]. Unfortunately the text breaks off here, and what precedes

---

9. There is no need for speculating about a possible Hebrew parent בתוככם as in Ulrich 58.

it is not decipherable. This text seems to interpret the difficulty of "bring out ἐκ προσώπου" differently. It means "bring out the old together with the new." I suspect that the copyist was trying to improve the text.

26:11 The opening clause promises "I will place my tent in you." An early A B n x y+ text read διαθηκην instead of σκηνήν. The notion that God should place his "tent" in Israel is fully sensible, but the proximity of v.9 with its στήσω τὴν διαθήκην μου μεθ᾽ ὑμῶν obviously influenced an ancient copyist to change "tent" to "covenant." The structure θήσω τὴν διαθήκην μου was well-known from Gen 17:7,19 (and comp 17:2). In fact, even the verb was affected by v.9, since the Byz text substituted στησω for θήσω. Cf also comment at v.9 on μεθ᾽ ὑμῶν as εν υμιν.

The second clause changes the subject from "I" to ἡ ψυχή μου. This is, however, simply a substitute for "I," i.e. my ψυχή means "my person, my self." Again, the bilingual copyist of 801 was unconsciously influenced by his knowledge of the parent text, and changed βδελύξεται ἡ ψυχή μου to βδελυξομαι, which means the same. This also makes this clause more clearly parallel to vv.6,9,11a and 12a. The verb געל is rendered by βδελύσσω only here. Somewhat more appropriate would have been προσοχθίζω which occurs for this verb at vv.15,20,43,44.

26:12 The verb ἐμπεριπατέω obtains only for התהלך in OT, but occurs a mere five times in all. This is its first occurrence, but see also Dt 23:14 for the notion of God walking about in Israel's camp. The verb is appropriate here, and is closely allied to the notion in the previous verse of God's placing his tent ἐν ὑμῖν.

The remainder of the verse repeats the common covenantal formula, which is closely connected to the deliverance from Egypt, for which see Note at Exod 6:7.[10] Covenants involved at least two parties; on the one hand, "I will be your God," and on the other, "you will be my people." In both clauses the genitive pronoun renders a ל phrase of the parent text. That "God to you" is correctly understood by ὑμῶν θεός is clear, though υμιν is attested by B ol d+, and could be original text. Similarly, μοι appears for μου in the majority F M V text, and is also read by 801. I suspect that μοι is original, and I would now read μοι rather

---

10. See Harlé-Pralon for a fuller statement on the covenant formula.

than μου. This does not necessarily mean that υμιν would also be read for ὑμῶν; it is sufficient to say that the ὑμῶν is not certain in Lev. Unfortunately, λαός can also be called into question, since 801 reads εθν[ος]. MT reads עַם, which is rendered elsewhere in the book by λαός six times, but by ἔθνος five times (though three times referring to foreign nations). Either is acceptable, but since 801 is so much older its reading ought to be adopted, all other matters being equal. I would now read ἔθνος.[11]

26:13 The verse begins with the long self-identification formula; hex has omitted εἰμι to conform more closely to MT. As an apposite to κύριος ὁ θεὸς ὑμῶν the text continues with "the one bringing ὑμᾶς out of the land of Egypt." The genitive absolute which follows describes the conditions under which ὑμᾶς were at the time: ὄντων ὑμῶν δούλων "while you were slaves." The construction is not fully Classical, since ὑμᾶς is repeated in ὑμῶν. The term δοῦλος had occurred at 25:44 for the first time in the Pentateuch, but only here as a term describing the Israelites while they were in Egypt. LXX did not translate להם which modifies היות in MT; oddly enough, hex did not add an αυτοις to equal MT, as might have been expected.

The next two clauses describe the deliverance. First of all, "I broke מטת עלכם (the bonds of your yoke)." Lev rendered מטת in the singular, which the consonantal text allows, i.e. as τὸν δεσμὸν (τοῦ ζυγοῦ). Ms 801 has τον ζυγον τ[... in its place, which presumably represents τον ζυγον του δεσμου of the Byz text. This kind of transposition of nouns often happens in the text tradition. Here it does make perfectly good sense, which would also promote this kind of copyist error, but a glance at the Hebrew informs us which must be original.

The last clause reads "and I brought you (out) μετὰ παρρησίας (i.e. openly)." The phrase occurs only here in the Pentateuch, and represents the hapax legomenon קוממיות, usually understood as "with head held high, walking erectly." The LXX text is a free rendering, but may reflect a corrrect understanding of the Hebrew word.

26:14 Vv.14—15 constitute a general protasis to the lengthy set of threats found in vv.16—39. It is introduced by ἐὰν δέ, thereby showing contrast to the section

---

11. As suggested by Ulrich 75.

preceding it. This protasis is the reverse to that of v.3. It puts it negatively; it states "if you do not obey me, nor perform these my statutes." The tradition had a great deal of trouble with the final nominal. MT has a somewhat different text; it reads את כל המצות האלה, i.e. it has no equivalent for μου, but it has "commandments" modified by "all." The Byz text has supplied παντα to introduce the nominal; this is clearly a revision of the text based on MT. The omission of μου by ms 426 may well be hex in origin; it does equal MT. A number of scattered witnesses has omitted ταῦτα; ordinarily this would have little significance, since this type of omission occurs frequently, except that 801 also omits the pronoun. To suggest, however, that the shorter text is therefore original is overly daring in my opinion. Precisely this kind of error in copying I have met so frequently that, in spite of the age of the ms, I would not adopt the shorter text. It is exactly the same error in copying that occurred in the unrelated mss 321,121 and 126.[12]

26:15 MT makes this verse coordinate with v.14 by its ואם. Since v.15 is the obverse of v.14, stating positively what the disobedient Israelites would do, the use of ἀλλά is particularly fitting. In fact, LXX restates the initial "if" clause entirely. MT reads ואם בחקתי תמאסו "and if my statutes you should reject," but LXX freely interprets by ἀλλὰ ἀπειθήσητε αὐτοῖς "but you should disobey them," the αὐτοῖς referring to the προστάγματά μου of v.14. Having translated המצות in v.14 by τὰ προστάγματά μου, the translator could hardly now use that structure to render בחקתי, so he simply used the pronoun,[13] which has that structure as its referent.

The second clause reads καὶ τοῖς κρίμασίν μου προσοχθίσῃ ἡ ψυχὴ ὑμῶν, while MT has ואם את משפטי תגעל נפשכם. Since for the first clause LXX had used ἀλλά, it became clear that the translator could only use καί here. The use of κρίμα to render משפט is not unexpected; in fact, κρίμα is only used in Lev to render משפט. The rendering would be unquestioned, except for the fact that 801

---

12. Ulrich 62 makes the value judgment that "the scroll reads well without ταυτα, and there is no reason to suggest that it was unintentionally or accidentally omitted." Of course it was not intentionally omitted, but to state that "the word seems superfluous in" the critical edition is to forget that LXX is a translation of the Hebrew, and MT has האלה.
13. According to Hesychius Aq and Theod read *si subtilitates meas renueritis*, and Sym had *si constituta mea reprobaveritis*.

has ...]γμασι μου here, which must be for προσταγμασι μου. In view of the discussion of the first clause above, and its problem with בחקתי, and the use of τὰ προστάγματά μου for rendering המצות in v.14, one should be extremely sceptical about the appearance of the word here, particularly in view of its being a unique reading. To my mind, this is merely a careless mistake on the part of the copyist of 801.[14] For ἡ ψυχὴ ὑμῶν see comment at v.11.

The verse concludes with two ὥστε plus infinitival structures which can best be taken successively, i.e. with the second one dependent on the first one. The first one represents a לבלתי plus infinitive in MT, correctly rendered by "ὥστε ὑμᾶς μὴ ποιεῖν all my commandments." This constitutes the probable result of your disobedience of the divine statutes and your rejecting God's judgments. This results in negative action, viz. in not performing πάσας τὰς ἐντολάς μου.

This in turn leads to ultimate betrayal: ὥστε διασκεδάσαι τὴν διαθήκην μου "so as to shatter my covenant." The infinitive is a good rendering for להפר, the Hi marked bound infinitive of פרר "to break up." Oddly enough, LXX has added ὑμᾶς as subject for the first infinitive, but omitted it for the second one, whereas MT represents exactly the opposite. Hex has accordingly omitted ὑμᾶς from the first clause, but added it after διασκεδάσαι.

26:16 The apodosis begins with the divine statement "and I will do thus to you." The adverb οὕτως represents זאת of MT, which an anonymous marginal s reading has translated by ταυτα. The statement simply introduces the threats which follow in the next clauses.

The second clause has God state "and I will bring together upon you ἀπορίαν," literally a "difficulty, something that admits of no solution," In MT the corresponding word is בהלה "terror." This is then followed in MT by four such matters which terrorize, none of which is fully certain as to its meaning.[15] ἀπορίαν is a less specific term than בהלה, and is a general term which can include a variety of evils. In other words, the translator took the first word as the genus and the remainder as species. The use of τε in LXX probably is intended to differentiate between ἀπορίαν and the nominals which follow, thus "even ...."

The first of these is את השחפת. The word occurs only here and at Dt 28:27. In both cases it is rendered by τὴν (τε) ψώραν "itch, mange." Hex has placed this

---

14. See Ulrich 62.
15. Theod renders the clause up to this point by καὶ ἐπισκέψομαι ἐφ᾽ ὑμᾶς σπουδῇ.

one under the obelus as having no counterpart in MT, and then adding σπουδη before τὴν ἀπορίαν (as a doublet reading) under the asterisk. Origen here followed the lead of Theod, but also retained τὴν ἀπορίαν. The root בהל does mean "hasten, hurry," often in dismay or terror.

The next item is ואת הקדחת which also occurs only here and at Dt 28:22. It probably means a "burning fever," from the root קדח "to light a fire, kindle." LXX has in its slot "καὶ τὸν ἴκτερον "jaundice," obviously not understanding the word. In Dt it is translated by πυρέτῳ "fever," This is followed by מכלות עינים "destroying eyes" (possibly then "creating blindness"). LXX understood this as a separate affliction καὶ σφακελίζοντας τοὺς ὀφθαλμοὺς ὑμῶν "and making your eyes to fester," though hex corrects by omitting the καί. The participle actually means "making gangrenous." In the tradition, a popular M V reading has a singular participle, but the more difficult plural is original; the plural simulates the plural מכלות of MT. In MT the participle modifies the two nouns השחפת and הקדחת, but in LXX the nouns are masculine; the translator simply was inattentive, and the popular M V variant is an attempt to "correct" the Greek. Hex has placed ὑμῶν under the obelus, since MT reads עינים, i.e. without a suffix.[16] The last affliction is ומדיבת נפש "and causing life to wither away," rendered by καὶ τὴν ψυχὴν ὑμῶν ἐκτήκουσαν "and making your life melt away." The ὑμῶν has no counterpart in MT, and hex has placed it under the obelus.

The remainder of the verse is quite straightforward. It reads: "and you shall sow your seed in vain, and your enemies shall eat (it)." MT has אכלהו, with the suffix referring to זרע, and hex has added αυτα (referring to σπέρματα) to represent it.

26:17 To "set my face against you" means to be adamently opposed to. This then means that God will see to it that πεσεῖσθε ἐναντίον τῶν ἐχθρῶν ὑμῶν. The verb in MT is the Ni נגפתם "be smitten,"[17] and LXX's translation is a free interpretation, but does get the general sense of the Hebrew.

In the third clause MT states "that those who hate you רדו בכם," i.e. "shall rule over you." LXX has διώξονται ὑμᾶς "shall pursue you," presumably read-

---

16. Theod has for this list τὴν ἀνεμοφθορίαν καὶ τὸν συμφρυγμὸν συντελοῦνται ὀφθαλμούς.
17. Sym translates the clause somewhat more accurately by προσκόψετε πρὸ τῶν ἐχθρῶν ὑμῶν.

ing רדפו under the influence of the final clause "and there is no one רדף you;" either verb makes sense, and which is original is not completely certain, though רדפו is almost certainly secondary in view of רדף of the final clause.[18]

The verse ends with a genitive absolute conditioning φεύξεσθε. οὐθενὸς διώκοντας ὑμᾶς is concessive,[19] i.e. "you will flee, although there is none pursuing you." In MT this is a coordinate nominal clause: ואין רדף אתכם.

26:18 The threats come in stages. The next stage is introduced by (καὶ ἐὰν) ἕως τούτου μὴ ὑπακούσητέ μου "and if up to this juncture you have not obeyed me." The τούτου is plural in MT: אלה, referring to the various stages of discipline outlined in vv.16—17. The singular adequately renders the intent of the Hebrew.

The punishment will then increase. The use of προσθήσω plus an infinitive represents a literal rendering of a Hebrew idiom meaning "to repeat, or continue" an action. Here the complementary infinitive παιδεῦσαι is unmarked. The unmarked infinitive occurs 45 times in Lev (of which 36 occur with complete support in the tradition). On the other hand, 10 cases of the marked infinitive occur, but only three with full support for the article. Here the B Byz+ text does add τοῦ before παιδεῦσαι, but it is unlikely to be original. The articulation of infinitives tends to mark later Greek,[20] and the unmarked infinitive is to be preferred here as well.[21] I would translate the clause: "I will discipline you seven times more because of your sins."

The infinitive is modified by the adverb ἑπτάκις "seven times." This represents שבע of MT correctly, but the tradition found it difficult not to concretize it, either by the popular addition of πληγαις before it, or reading πληγαις επτα with the V b z+ text, or by πληγας επτα of the Byz text. These are all influenced by an awareness of πληγὰς ἑπτά of v.21; the more difficult text of Lev is certainly original. The prepositional phrase, ἐπί plus the dative, is causal; thus "because of your sins."

26:19 The first clause states "I will break up τὴν ὕβριν τῆς ὑπερηφανίας ὑμῶν." MT has את גאון עזכם "the arrogance of your strength." What is meant is Israel's

---

18. According to Hesychius Sym read *in servitutem redigent vos*, and Theod had *erudiunt a vos*. Sym must have read רדו, but Theod's reading is puzzling.
19. See SS 177.
20. See Mayser II 1.323.
21. See THGL 82.

arrogant reliance on its own strength. In LXX it is ὑπερηφανίας which means "arrogance," whereas ὕβριν lies in the same semantic field, and the structure might be translated by "the insolence of your arrogance," in other words "your excessive arrogance." Oddly, the translator did not use some such word as ἰσχύς or some form of κράτος; the translator certainly knew what עז meant, but he thought of "the arrogance of strength" in the sense of "strong, powerful arrogance," which he realized by a superlative ὕβριν τῆς ὑπερηφανίας. The rendering is unique, imaginative, and not at all inaccurate.

The second clause in MT reads "And I will make your skies like iron, and your land like copper." The point made by the figure is that the skies will produce no moisture, and the land no produce. LXX renders the verb נתתי by θήσω,[22] but then continues with τὸν οὐρανὸν ὑμῖν σιδηροῦν καὶ τὴν γῆν ὑμῶν ὡσεὶ χαλκῆν. The second simile is literally rendered, but instead of את שמיכם כברזל LXX renders ברזל by an adjective, disregards the preposition, and translates the suffix by a dative of advantage. What LXX says is "I will set for you an iron sky." Hex could hardly overlook this, and so added ὡς before οὐρανοῦν under the asterisk, and a few witnesses also changed the adjective to σιδηρον ad sensum.

26:20 MT begins with ותם, with כחכם "your strength" as its subject, and modified by לריק, thus "your strength will be expended in vain." The translator rendered this freely; instead of תם he simply used ἔσται, resulting in "and your strength will be in vain," or possibly "will become vain." In other words, he understood the verb תמם as "be finished, come to an end," and so "be finished εἰς κενόν" being tautological, a simple ἔσται εἰς κενόν was sufficient.

V.b puts this into concrete terms: "And your land will not produce its seed, and the tree of your field will not produce fruit." The Hebrew has את יבולה "its produce" as modifier of the first verb תתן, and one might have expected γένημα, but LXX chose σπόρον, which is not incorrect, but it only occurs here in OT for יבול. It does fit well contextually. MT has for the subject of the last clause עץ הארץ, which LXX translates as "τὸ ξύλον τοῦ ἀγροῦ ὑμῶν. One might have expected the translator to understand עץ as a collective, but he chose the singular as reflecting a singular noun in Hebrew. In this clause the translator also chose an unusual rendering for הארץ, viz. τοῦ ἀγροῦ, which is practically a calque for

---

22. Sym has ἑτοιμάσω (retroverted from Syh).

השדה; in fact, it occurs only once elsewhere for הארץ in OT at Job 5:25. But this is peculiarly apt in this context. MT had no equivalent for ὑμῶν, and hex in consequence placed the pronoun under the obelus.

26:21 A further stage: καὶ ἐὰν μετὰ ταῦτα πορεύησθε πλάγιοι καὶ μὴ βούλησθε ὑπακούειν μου "And if afterwards you should walk contrariwise, and not want to obey me." MT has the first clause somewhat differently: ואם תלכו עמי קרי. The noun קרי is derived from קרה "to meet, encounter," and so a meeting but in a hostile sense, thus "if you continue in hostile fashion with me." The adjective πλάγιοι means "obliquely, sideways,"[23] and so metaphorically "crooked, treacherous,"[24] which constitutes LXX's attempt at rendering קרי. μετὰ ταῦτα is either an odd misunderstanding of עמי or simply a contextual gloss. Origen apparently took it in the former sense, i.e. for עמי, and transposed the phrase after πορεύησθε, i.e. to equal the order of תלכו עמי. This again illustrates how mechanically he worked in the hex. The *b z+* text represents a clearer comprehension of עמי by its gloss πρός με after the verb, a plus which must ultimately be based on MT.

The apodosis begins in MT with ויספתי, rendered in LXX by προσθήσω. The Byz text has woodenly introduced καὶ to equal the Hebrew, but it reads better without it. The verb is to be understood literally, "I will add." Furthermore, the Hebrew prepositional phrase עליכם is idiomatically rendered by ὑμῖν, so "I will add to you seven plagues according to your sins."

26:22 MT says "I will send (והשלחתי) against you את חית השדה," i.e. "the beasts of the field." LXX renders the phrase expansively by τὰ θηρία τὰ ἄγρια τῆς γῆς "the wild beasts of the land." שדה is only seldom translated by γῆ (8/9 times) though see 27:21. In fact, its most common translation is ἀγρός (210 times),[25] but the translator uses two words, ἄγρια and γῆς, either of which could represent שדה. Hex solved it by omitting τὰ ἄγρια, but it is by no means clear that Origen was right; see comment on ἀγρός at v.20. It seems to me that the translator purposely used the fuller structure in view of the context. The next three clauses all contain third singular verbs for which τὰ θηρία τὰ ἄγρια is the

---

23. Sym has ἐναντίοι.
24. According to LS sub πλάγιος II.
25. According to the count in Dos Santos.

subject. It is the "wild beasts of the land" who "will devour you and destroy your cattle and decimate you," and "wild beasts" is a most appropriate term, e.g. over against τὰ κτήνη ὑμῶν. Note the Classical use of singular verbs with neuter plural subjects.

In the tradition, a popular B text has ποιησω instead of ποιήσει. This would make God the subject of the third clause. In other words, the wild beasts devour you and destroy your cattle, but God himself will make you ὀλιγοστούς. It is of course wrong, though it does make sense in view of the opening clause: ἀποστελῶ.

The last clause shows the result of this activity of the wild beasts: "and your ways (or roads) shall become desolated." This also reflects the cut of the Masoretes, who divided the verse at this point, leaving only ונשמו דרככם as v.b.

26:23 The protasis for the next stage. MT begins with a negative condition "and if by these you should not be disciplined towards me," and follows with "ἀλλά you should conduct yourselves in a hostile fashion towards me." The translator first rendered באלה by ἐπὶ τούτοις, which he placed between καί and ἐάν. Hex reordered this by transposing ἐάν after καί. He also disregarded לי, thus reading "and because of these should you not be disciplined." Then the positively constructed contrast reads "but you should conduct yourselves (πορεύεσθε) towards me contrariwise." The verb is a present subjunctive, since "going, acting, conducting yourselves" is a process. This contrasts with the aorist of v.a. For πορεύησθε ... πλάγιοι and its Hebrew counterpart see comment at v.21. It should be noted that עמי "with me" becomes πρός με "towards me," which is a reasonable understanding in this context.

26:24 LXX twice uses κἀγώ, once to render אף אני, and once for גם אני. These two are the only cases of crasis in the entire book.[26] In both cases they are used to direct special attention to the first person subject, exactly like their Hebrew counterparts. The verb πορεύσομαι is used in the same sense as in v.23: "I will conduct myself." In this verse and in v.28 בקרי "with hostility" occurs as descriptive of God. To contrast this with קרי describing the human attitude towards God, the translator uses πλαγίῳ as an adjectival modifier of θυμῷ, For LXX God

---

26. See THGL 100.

is not to be described as πλάγιος; such contrariness must be rooted in divine anger, hence "in angry reaction," or "in adverse anger." The use of θυμῷ πλαγίῳ is a leveling with v.28, which see. Hex was bothered by θυμῷ πλαγίῳ and changed this to πλαγιως, omitting θυμῷ entirely as having no counterpart in MT. This change, however, obviates the distinction which the translator apparently intended.

That God will act in angry hostility towards the recalcitrant people is clear from the next clause: "and I will smite you, even I, seven times because of your sins." The preposition ἀντί "over against, because of" renders על correctly. This contrasts with v.21 where the preposition ב is used rather than על, and is accordingly rendered by κατά, but comp v.18 where על is used, and rendered by ἐπί plus a dative noun. The translator is not consistent in his renderings.

26:25 The first clause reads "and I will bring on you a sword wrecking the vengeance of the covenant." The term δίκην διαθήκης refers to the vengeance demanded by the covenant. God's covenant ensures the blessings of the covenant for obedient children, but curses, i.e. "vengeance," for the disobedient. The genitive is in other words a subjective one; the covenant exacts vengeance. The construction ἐκδικοῦσαν δίκην represents a cognate structure נקמת נקם in Hebrew. I would translate "wrecking or exacting vengeance." The C text has παταξω instead of ἐπάξω, which is probably a careless error palaeographically stimulated.

This in turn means that "you will flee into your cities." καταφεύξεσθε uniquely renders נאספתם "you will gather yourselves." The translator avoids a passive state on the part of the disobedient Israelites; this does not constitute something which is imposed on the people; they themselves try to escape the divine judgment by fleeing to the apparent safety of the city walls.

But there is no escape. "I will send θάνατον to you." MT has שלחתי דבר בתוככם. The verb ἐξαποστελῶ is clearly original, though επαποστελω is read by b n+, and αποστελω, by C' x+ ἐξαποστέλλω occurs seven times for the Pi שלח in Lev, αποστέλλω obtains only once (16:10), and επαποστέλλω never occurs. In fact, the last one occurs only once in the Pentateuch for the Pi (Dt 28:48), and once for the Hi (Exod 8:21). The word θάνατον is always used in OT to translate דבר "pest." It is a true calque, and must be understood in the sense of דבר. It had already been used three times in Exod (5:3 9:3,15), and recurs once each in Num and Dt. Presumably, the intent of the Exod translator was to indicate the deadly character of the pest. In MT the prepositional phrase is בתוככם, but LXX has εἰς ὑμᾶς. The preposition is correctly used in modification of ἐξαποστελῶ as a verb of movement.

The final clause reads "and you will be delivered εἰς χεῖρας ἐχθρῶν"; the Hebrew has ביד אויב "into the power of an enemy." LXX uses the plural, which makes excellent sense in view of the plural verb. The use of εἰς χεῖρας vs εἰς χεῖρα is arbitrary; both, however, mean "into the hand(s) of," i.e. into the power of. In the tradition, most witnesses add υμων after ἐχθρῶν; this has no basis in Hebrew, and is simply an ad sensum gloss.

26:26 MT's "when I break for you the staff of bread" means "when I cut off your bread supply." The Greek has expressed this differently. The first person subject is not recognized, but ὑμᾶς is the subject of the infinitive θλῖψαι. The verb θλίβω is usually transitive, but it can have a stative meaning "be constricted, hemmed in," so here ἐν τῷ θλῖψαι σιτοδείᾳ ἄρτων "when you are constricted by want of bread." The term σιτοδεία is a hapax legomenon in OT, but its intent is clear; it means a need for food, and so famine. Here it is best rendered by "want of (bread)." The translator has neutralized the action by not making God the actor creating the famine. But this is hardly an intentional avoidance of divine activity, since throughout this section it is God who is the actor.

In such a time of scarcity "καί ten women will bake your bread in one oven and will give back your bread by weight." The καί is added in imitation of the Hebrew. What is meant by this statement is that grain will be so scarce that ten women will pool their grain in a single oven, because even the grain for ten families can easily be baked in a single oven. When the baking is finished, one gets bread doled out by weight; comp Ezek 4:10 for a measured daily portion: ἐν σταθμῷ εἴκοσι σίκλους τὴν ἡμέραν. But this will not suffice to still your hunger: καὶ φάγεσθε καὶ οὐ μὴ ἐμπληθῆτε.

26:27 The phrase ἐπὶ τούτοις is probably influenced by v.23, for which see comment ad loc. That this is due to the Greek of v.23 is clear from MT; at v.23 באלה occurred, but here it is the singular בזאת. μὴ ὑπακούσητέ μου is contrasted with πορεύσησθε πρός με πλάγιοι. The latter is a copy of v.23b; cf comments ad loc. The adversative ἀλλά is also taken from v.23, but it is a peculiarly fitting rendering for the coordinate conjunction in MT. An A B V *O x+* text has "corrected" this to καί, which may well be a recensional correction.[27]

26:28 This verse begins the apodosis for v.27. It starts typically with a conjunction והלכתי "And I will go"; LXX not only imitates the Hebrew by its initial καί, but also adds a reflexive αὐτός, thus "I myself will go," thereby once again placing the stress on the divine origin of the punishment; it is God himself who will go. This addition gives better balance to v.b where ἐγώ also occurs to give added emphasis to the divine subject, but here with a Hebrew parent text: אף אני. For ἐν θυμῷ πλαγίῳ see the discussion at v.24. In v.28, however, the ἐν θυμῷ has a parent text in בחמת, and is undoubtedly the source for the θυμῷ πλαγίῳ of v.24.

V.b has a close parallel in v.24b, but differs in three respects. The most important is the change of verb from πατάξω/הכיתי to παιδεύσω/יסרתי. This is a case of divine chastisement rather than of smiting. παιδεύω has an element of correction in it, though basically it remains punishment, as the elaborations in the verses that follow show. Instead of κἀγώ our verse has ἐγώ, and instead of ἀντί it has κατά. The translator hardly intended any semantic difference in the use of the different prepositions; rather it illustrates his love of variation. For details of interpretation see comments at v.24.

In the tradition, ἐγώ has been amplified to και εγω by hex, so as to represent MT's אף אני. The Byz variant καγω is probably borrowed from v.24.

26:29 The word σάρξ is singular in Lev, except where the context is plural as in this verse; the plural occurs elsewhere only at 21:5 (with αὐτῶν), and at 25:49 (οἰκείων τῶν σαρκῶν αὐτοῦ). The hunger will be so severe that parents will eat the flesh of their children.

26:30 The first clause in MT reads והשמדתי את במתיכם "and I shall exterminate your high places." LXX renders the verb by ἐρημώσω "make desolate," which is unique in OT. I suspect that the translator misread the word as והשמותי from the root שמם, which is commonly rendered by ἐρημόω or ἐξερημόω. Also unusual, but not unique, is the rendering for the noun: τὰς στήλας "pillars," for which see comment at v.1. στήλη also occurs for במת three times in Num (21:28 22:41

---

27. See THGL 131.

33:52).²⁸ The word במת occurs only here in Lev, and aside from the three cases in Num, obtains in the Pentateuch only in Dt 32:13 33:29. It then becomes common in the later literature, and is there most often rendered by ὑψηλός. It may be noted that the first four times that the word occurs in the Pentateuch it was interpreted by στήλη. The word also gave trouble to the Dt translator. At 32:13 it was rendered by τὴν ἰσχύν (τῆς γῆς), a probable reference to the land's fertility; see Note at Dt 32:13. At Dt 33:29 במותימו is translated by ἐπὶ τὸν τράχηλον αὐτῶν, for which see Note ad loc. This means that the Pentateuch translators never rendered the word correctly, though the notion of a place connected with idolatrous worship does occur. Was the notion of "high places" as place fo idolatrous worship unknown to the Alexandrian trnaslators?

The second clause also created a problem. MT's text reads והכרתי את חמניכם. Precisely what a חמן was is uncertain; traditionally it was thought to be a sun-pillar, but more recently, to be an incense altar. What is clear is that it was associated with illicit cult.²⁹ To the Greek translator they were idols, i.e. τὰ ξύλινα χειροποίητα "wooden hand-crafted objects"; cf comment at v.1.

The next clause is also somewhat problematic. In MT it reads "I will place your corpses on פגרי גלוליכם." The word גלולי occurs only here and at Dt 29:16(17) in the Pentateuch, and in both cases is rendered by εἴδωλα. The term is a pejorative one, a pun on גללים "dung-pellets," thus "dung-idols." But odd is the collocation "corpses of your idols." It is, of course, engendered by פגריכם. So "I will put your carcasses on the carcasses of your idols." Reference to the lifeless carcasses of idols is highly ironic. LXX rationalized this by translating פגרי by τὰ κῶλα, so "I will place your limbs on the limbs of your idols," which is less bizarre than the Hebrew. κῶλον thereafter became the most frequently used translation for פגר.

For the final clause see comment at v.15, and comp v.11. The Attic future προσοχθιεῖ is original, while the O C⁾ s z text reads the Hellenistic προσοχθισει.

26:31 The verb θήσω is used with a double accusative, thus "I will set your cities as deserts," i.e. I will translate your cities into deserts. For the second clause some uncertainty centers about מקדשיכם. Sam and many Hebrew mss, as well as

---

28. See Dorival 69—70.
29. Tar are no help at all. Tar⁰ has חניסנסיכון; Tar⁾ makes it מנחשיכון, and Tarᴺ, טעוותכון. All are agreed on their illicit nature, but on nothing else.

Pesh, witness to a singular noun. This would make the reference to a single sanctuary. The singular may well be an attempt at correcting the text. After all, the tradition of a central sanctuary at Jerusalem was well-known. But both MT and LXX read the plural, i.e. "your sanctuaries." Israel did have various holy places, and the plural is to be preferred.

The third clause in MT states: "and I will not smell בריח ניחחכם. The nominal ריח ניחוח occurs frequently in Lev, and is normally rendered by ὀσμὴ εὐωδίας, for which see Notes at Gen 8:21 and Exod 29:18. In fact, out of 45 occasions of ניחח 44 are translated by εὐωδίας. Here, however, what God refuses to smell is τῆς ὀσμῆς τῶν θυσιῶν ὑμῶν "the odor of your sacrifices." The rendering is unique in OT, and must have been an intentional change. Elsewhere the nominal is always in a positive context; e.g. a κάρπωμα might be offered for a sweet-smelling savour to the Lord. The term normally describes a sacrifice of some kind as being, or intended for, an ὀσμὴ εὐωδίας. But here the context is uniquely negative. God will not signal acceptance; in fact, he will not smell the "smell of your sacrifices." Here it shows God as rejecting Israel's sacrifices.

26:32 The ἐγώ is not necessary to the sense, and the Byz text actually omits it, but it is based on MT, where אני serves to call special attention to God as the actor. One might render: "it is I who will desolate your land." MT lacks "your," and hex has placed ὑμῶν under the obelus to indicate that lack. The translator simply levelled with the context of v.31: "your cities ... your sanctuaries ... your sacrifices."

MT uses the same root in both clauses, i.e. שמם, but in the Hi in the first clause "to desolate, lay waste," and in the Qal for the second "be appalled, horror stricken." The translator perforce used different lexemes. As in v.31 he used ἐξερημώσω for השמתי, and for שממו he has θαυμάσονται "be appalled, stupified." The verb is modified by ἐπ' αὐτῇ for עליה. The use of ἐπί with the dative shows cause or occasion.[30] The O text changed the dative to an accusative, but the dative is original. The subject of the verb is "your enemies who are inhabiting it," with αὐτῇ here also referring to "your land." Since God will "lay waste your land," and "your enemies are inhabiting it," an exilic condition for Israel is suggested.

---

30. See LS sub ἐπί B.III.1.

26:33 God will scatter Israel among the nations; comp Dt 4:27 28:64. MT has אתכם אזרה, and hex has transposed διασπερῶ ὑμᾶς to equal the word order of MT.

The second clause in MT reads והריקתי אחריכם חרב "and I will unsheathe a sword after you." The picture of the Lord actually himself taking the sword out of the scabbard in pursuit of the Israelites was overly graphic for the translator, who rendered by καὶ ἐξαναλώσει ὑμᾶς ἐπιπορευομένη ἡ μάχαιρα "and the sword shall suddenly (i.e. coming by surprise) destroy you."[31] The translator removed the figure of God as an active warrior cutting down Israel to a personified sword moving swiftly to annihilate the people.[32] Origen apparently took ἐπιπορευομένη to occupy the אחרי slot, and so transposed ὑμᾶς ἐπιπορευομένη to equal the word order of MT.

In MT "your land shall be שממה, and your cities shall be חרבה," but the translator made no distinction between the two words using ἔρημος/-μοι. I would render "your land shall be a desert, and your cities shall be deserts."

26:34 The verb εὐδοκήσει "shall be pleased with, enjoy" exactly renders the Hebrew תרצה. The point being made is that with the people dispersed or destroyed the land can enjoy the Sabbath years due the land; for the year of the jubilee see chapter 25 passim. Enjoying the Sabbath years means that no one will be left to seed the land, so that the land will lie fallow "all the days of its desolate state." MT has no equivalent for "its," which was added ad sensum.

That desolate state is explicated by καὶ ὑμεῖς ἔσεσθε ἐν τῇ γῇ τῶν ἐχθρῶν ὑμῶν. MT has no verb here, but the copula is necessary in Greek.[33] Hex has placed ἔσεσθε under the obelus, since MT simply reads אתם. In MT the clause is a nominal one, and LXX's addition of the future verb changes the sense. In the Hebrew it simply states a condition which explains the days of its desolation"; I would render the clause in MT as "while you are in the land of your enemies." Oddly enough, the A B n+ text has a καί before "all the days." This can only be a copyist error in origin, since it does not make much sense.[34]

---

31. See Lee 89.
32. Lee 89 maintains that the translators did not recognize ריק in the sense of "draw (a sword)," and attempted to render its other sense "empty out," but I am doubtful about the translation overlooking this well-known meaning of הריק.
33. See SS 80.
34. See THGL 102–103.

The adverb τότε occurs twice, introducing both v.a and b; this exactly equals the אז of MT, indicating precisely "at that time," i.e. when the land is uninhabited.

V.b simply restates the content of v.a: "then the land shall rest (i.e. engage in Sabbath rest) and enjoy its Sabbath years."

26:35 For πάσας τὰς ἡμέρας τῆς ἐρημώσεως αὐτῆς see v.34, where the structure is exactly the same as here, in both MT and LXX. The subject of σαββατιεῖ as well as of ἐσαββάτισεν is "the land." The opening temporal construction modifies σαββατιεῖ, i.e. "it (the land) shall not rest all the days of its desolation."

The relative clause is introduced by ἅ, which refers to τὰ σάββατα of v.34, thus "the (sabbaths) which it did not rest." This is further explicated by "in your sabbaths when you were occupying it." The implied charge is that Israel had not celebrated the jubilee years when it dwelt in the land. Note the proper use of the imperfect κατῳκεῖτε, i.e. "when you were inhabiting it."

In the tradition, the Byz text shows a different syntactic pattern. By adding καί before σαββατιεῖ the temporal structure preceding it no longer modifies the verb, but is taken with v.34 in modification of εὐδοκήσετε 2°.

26:36 In MT a pendant construction is introduced by a conjunction, והנשארים בכם, and as for those who are left among you." This is followed by והבאתי, i.e. "As for those left ..., and I will bring ...." LXX incorporates the pendant into the clause by a dative participle modified by ἐξ ὑμῶν "and to those who are left from you (I will bring)." This simplified, but correctly interpreted, the unusual Hebrew construction. What God will bring into their hearts is δειλίαν "timidity, faintheartedness," which correctly renders the hapax legomenon מרך, a noun derived from רכך. Incidentally, the B x+ text shows how a palaeographically stimulated variant can create a meaningless text. It reads δουλειαν for δειλίαν, but "slavery, servitude" makes little sense here.

What sending fright into their hearts means psychologically is clear from the next two clauses, which I would translate "When the sound of a leaf being borne (φερομένου for נדף "driven") chases them, they shall flee as those fleeing from battle." The least little sound will cause the exiles to panic. The ὡς structure simplifies the parent text which reads מנסת חרב. What MT says is "(they shall flee) the flight of a sword." LXX's rendering is free, but interprets correctly what is intended by the Hebrew.

In fact, "and they shall fall, although no one is pursuing." The genitive absolute is here used concessively.[35] The form οὐθενός with *theta* rather than with *delta* is the preferred form in the papyri of the last three centuries BCE,[36] whereas in later Greek the old Attic ουδενος became popular. In fact, in Modern Greek οὐθείς has completely disappeared.[37] The F M majority text also reads ουδενος, but the oldest uncials, A B G, read the *theta* form.

26:37 The opening clause in MT reads וכשלו איש באחיו כמפני חרב "and they shall stumble, a man over his fellow, as though from the sword," i.e. "even though none is pursuing." The translator apparently found the idea of stumbling in the context of battle odd, and changed the verb to ὑπερόψεται "overlook," thus disregard.[38] The verb occurs later in the verse at vv.40,43,44 as well, but with different equivalents in the parent text; see also 20:4. LXX also renders איש by ὁ ἀδελφός, thus "and brother shall disregard brother as in warfare." What the Greek says is that such panic shall be engendered that normal regard of brother for brother will be suspended. Actually the Greek makes the figure of a man stumbling over his brother in hasty flight due to fright somewhat more abstract, a free paraphrase of what MT says. In the tradition, the majority F M text has added αυτου after τὸν ἀδελφόν. This equals אחיו, and is probably recensional (possibly hex) in origin.[39] The clause ends in MT with ורדף אין. This resembles the concluding ואין רדף of v.36, and is also rendered by a genitive absolute concessively intended,[40] though the participle is rendered differently by κατατρέχοντος, i.e. "though no one is running (him) down," i.e. chasing, pursuing. The change in lexeme is simply for variety's sake.

The last clause puts it negatively. "There shall be for you no תקומה before your enemies." LXX renders this idiomatically by "you shall not be able to withstand (ἀντιστῆναι) your enemies," which is clearly what MT intended.

---

35. See SS 177.
36. See Mayser I.I.148—149.
37. See Bl-Debr 33.
38. I find the rendering of Harlé-Pralon "dédaignera" peculiar. The disregard of ὑπερόψεται need hardly be "scornful, disdainful."
39. See SS 97.
40. See SS 179.

26:38 The Greek translates MT literally: "and you will perish among the nations, and the land of your enemies will devour you." The b text mistakenly changed ἡ γῆ to πληγη, but this is an error due to careless reading. Enemies conceivably might be considered a plague, but that would hardly devour; it would kill. The notion of devouring is figurative, and not to be understood literally as in the case of Korah and his associates in Num 16:31—33.

36:39 LXX has a shorter text than MT. V.a reads in MT "And those who are left among you ימקו in their iniquities in the land of איביכם." Sam, as well as many Hebrew mss, read איביהם; this was also read by LXX, which text may be translated "And those who are left from you (ἀφ' ὑμῶν) shall be destroyed (καταφθαρήσονται) on account of their sins (διὰ τὰς ἁμαρτίας αὐτῶν) in the land of their enemies."[41] The use of ἀφ' ὑμῶν for בכם is idiomatic after καταλειφθέντες, and has been "corrected" in Theod to read ἐν ὑμῖν. The translator chose to render ימקו freely by καταφθαρήσονται. The verb מקק in the Ni means "to fester, rot," but when applied to people, "to pine or waste away." The verb occurs twice, and is translated by The Three consistently by τακήσονται. LXX also used τακήσονται in v.b. The verb τήκω means "to melt away," hence "be dissolved." In v.a the translator used a more general notion "be destroyed."

V.b in MT reads ואף בעונת אבתם אתם ימקו "and even on account of the iniquities of their fathers with them they shall pine away."[42] LXX has only τακήσονται, having overlooked from איביהם to אתם, because of homoioteleuton. LXX thus reads the ἐν structure of v.a with τακήσονται, i.e. "in the land of their enemies they shall waste away." Hex has added και εν ταις αμαρτιαις πατερων αυτων μετ αυτων in the proper place after ἐχθρῶν αὐτῶν. The hex addition became popular, but in the majority F M text was copied in the wrong place afer ἁμαρτίας αὐτῶν. Though theoretically the shorter text of Lev could have been

---

41. Aq translates v.a by καὶ περιλειπόμενοι ἐν ὑμῖν τακήσονται ἐν ἀνομίᾳ αὐτῶν ἐν γαίαις ἐχθρῶν ὑμῶν; Theod has καὶ οἱ καταλειφθέντες ἐν ὑμῖν τακήσονται διὰ τὰς ἁμαρτίας αὐτῶν ἐν ταῖς γαῖς τῶν ἐχθρῶν αὐτῶν, whereas Sym reads οἱ δὲ περιλειφθέντες ὑμῶν τακήσονται διὰ τὰς ἁμαρτίας ὑμῶν ἐν ταῖς γαίαις τῶν ἐχθρῶν αὐτῶν. It should be noted that only Aq follows MT in reading "of your enemies."
42. Aq translates καίπερ ἐν ἀνομίαις πατέρων αὐτῶν αὐτοὶ τακήσονται; Theod has καὶ ἐν ταῖς ἁμαρτίαις πατέρων αὐτῶν μετ' αὐτῶν τακήσονται, and Sym renders καὶ διὰ τὰς ἁμαρτίας πατέρων αὐτῶν σὺν ταῖς ἑαυτῶν τακήσονται. Note how אתם is rendered differently by each of The Three.

created by parablepsis from one αὐτῶν to another, the shorter text alone can explain the somewhat complicated text history of the passage. The reading of Lev is supported inter alia by both A and B.

26:40 With v.40 begins a message of hope, vv.40 and 41 constituting the condition for the new hope given as a divine promise in vv.42—45.

V.40 begins with "and they shall confess their sins and the sins of their fathers," probably better "and when they shall confess...." What these sins consisted of is detailed in two ὅτι clauses. The first one reads ὅτι παρέβησαν καὶ ὑπερεῖδόν με "that they transgressed and disregarded me." For ὑπερεῖδον see comment at v.37. This is an attempt at rendering MT's במעלם אשר מעלו בי "in their acting treacherously (by) which they acted treacherously against me." The translator made two clauses, first rendering the bound infinitive plus pronominal suffix by παρέβησαν, which is an adequate equivalent, though syntactically a different structure. The rendering of the relative clause is oddly done. In trying to make a distinction between the infinitival structure and the relative clause, he may have read מעלו as עלמו, since at 20:4 יעלימו was translated by ὑπερίδωσιν; see comment ad loc.

The second ὅτι clause reads καὶ ὅτι ἐπορεύθησαν ἐναντίον μου πλάγιοι "and that they walked contrariwise before me." MT has a relative clause: ואף אשר הלכו עמי בקרי. For a closely similar structure see comment at v.21. In contrast to v.21, however, עמי is rendered by ἐναντίον μου. For the variation in the rendering of עמי see comment at v.24. The term קרי occurs only in this chapter (see also vv.21,23,24,27,28,41), and is always rendered by some form of πλάγιος.

26:41 For "and as for me I conducted myself with them in angry reaction," see the comments at v.24. The change of ἐπορεύθην to πορευσομαι in F z+ is not to be taken as recensional (cf אלך), but rather as influenced by v.24. Since MT's בקרי is rendered by ἐν θυμῷ πλαγίῳ, hex has placed θυμῷ under the asterisk, but see comment at v.24.

The next clause has καὶ ἀπολῶ for והבאתי. This need not mean that the translator read והאבדתי as BHS suggests. Rather the translator avoided the repetition of an exile already well-stated, e.g. in v.33. The change to the future makes a literal rendering of הבאתי senseless; after all, they are already in the land of their enemies. Modern translators have tended to mistranslate והבאתי by making it a past tense, thereby voiding the problem, but this is not what MT says. The future verb ἀπολῶ is clearly not prospective, but is to be taken as deliberative, i.e. "and I would be destroying them in the land of their enemies."[43] God is preparing to wreak further destruction on the exiled Israel.

In view of such action the following τότε clauses become meaningful. The first reads: "Then their uncircumcised heart shall be turned about," which interprets MT's או אז יכנע לבבם הערל. The או has rightly been disregarded as a corrupt dittograph of אז; What is of import is the rendering of יכנע "be humbled" by ἐντραπήσεται. The humbling of their uncircumcized heart means genuine repentance, a turning about. The figure of circumcision of the heart is well-known from prophetic literature, but see also Note at Dt 10:16.

The second coordinate τότε clause reads εὐδοκήσουσιν τὰς ἁμαρτίας αὐτῶν. εὐδοκέω is the most common rendering for the Hebrew רצה (21 times).[44] It can hardly mean "enjoy" as at v.34, and is to be understood as metonymic for the causative notion: "to make acceptable, making satisfaction for."[45] I would translate the clause by "then they shall render satisfaction for their sins."[46]

26:42 Once the two τότε conditions take effect, God will remember the patriarchal covenants. MT has an unusual text in that it reads בריתי יצחק, בריתי יעקב and בריתי אברהם.[47] What MT says is "I will remember my covenant Jacob, (or better my Jacob covenant), and my Isaac covenant and my Abraham covenant I will remember." This is admittedly an odd construction. I would understand these resp as meaning "my covenant with Jacob, ... with Isaak, and ... with Abraam," on the understanding that these covenants are obviously with "me." LXX simplifies by omitting in each case the suffix, i.e. "the covenant of Yakob ... the covenant of Isaak ... the covenant of Abraam." Hex has added μου after all three

---

43. See Porter 424—425.
44. According to Dos Santos.
45. Sym has understood ירצו in that way by his ἱλάσονται.
46. Schl sub εὐδοκέω discusses this clause as follows: *h.e. poenas, quas pro peccatis patientur, placide et humiliter quasi poenitentes acceptabunt. Posset etiam per antiphrasin et ironice accipi, q.d. tunc displicebunt illis peccata eorum, s. ea exosa habebunt et abominabuntur.*
47. GK 128d suggests that the suffix might be a case of dittography, but this is hardly convincing. If the suffixal form had occurred only once, either with יעקב or with יצחק, this might suffice, but it occur three times, and the third time with אברהם.

cases of διαθήκης, so as to represent MT more exactly. What is unclear in the Greek is where to divide the clauses. I have divided after Ἰακώβ simply because the Masoretes did so, but one could also divide after Isaak.

26:43 The opening clause states that "the land shall be forsaken מהם," which is rendered by ἐγκαταλειφθήσεται ἡ γῆ ὑπ' αὐτῶν. A popular F M V text has απ instead of ὑπ', which may well be recensional, but this is by no means certain, since in cursive script the two vowels are readily confused in these contexts. In any event, they did leave the land, and the personal agent interpretation is sensible. MT has the subject before the verb, and the hex transposition of ἡ γῆ before the verb became popular; in fact even cod B supports it, though it is certainly secondary.[48]

This is followed by a τότε clause. The translator added τότε to make clear that the action of the clause follows temporally on the abandonment predicted in the first clause. The τότε clause uses προσδέξεται to translate תרץ. This would then mean that "the land will accept its sabbaths when it is rendered desolate on their account." The verb προσδέχομαι means to accept readily or favorably, hence it is an adequate rendering for תרץ. MT reads בהשמה מהם "while it was deserted without them." מהם occurred in the first clause as well (see above), but here it modifies השמה,[49] and means "without them." The translator understood the מן differently, however, as his δι' αὐτούς shows.

The next clause uses αὐτοί to place stress on the change in subject of προσδέξονται in imitation of MT's הם. The verb again represents the verb ירצו, and is best rendered "(and it is they who) must accept (i.e. accept responsibility for) their lawless acts." The verb is again the same, but with ἀνομίας/עון as modifier has a somewhat different nuance, hence the notion "accept responsibility for."

The reason for this acceptance of responsibility is given in an ἀνθ' ὧν structure, which correctly interprets the unusual יען ביען of MT.[50] It is because "my judgments ὑπερεῖδον." For the verb in the sense of "neglect" see comment at v.37. Furthermore, "they treated my statutes with contempt τῇ ψυχῇ αὐτῶν." MT says "my statutes געלה נפשם," i.e. the subject is נפשם. I would render the Greek

---

48. See THGL 103—104.
49. See GK 67y.
50. For which see GK 158b.

by "they treated my statutes with contempt in their person," i.e. they personally treated .... In the tradition, the x+ text changed the structure to read προσωχθισεν η ψυχη αυτων, which equals MT exactly. The x text is not usually recensional in character, and the equation may be accidental.

26:44 The verse begins in MT with וְאַף גַּם זֹאת, which probably means "and even also this," i.e. nonetheless or nevertheless. MT then continues with a בהיותם structure "when they were." The translator simplified this by καὶ οὐδ' ὣς ὄντων αὐτῶν "nor while they were," using οὐδ' to anticipate the negative with the verb, οὐχ ὑπερεῖδον. The use of a genitive absolute construction is, however, related to the main structure by means of pronouns, αὐτούς and αὐτοῖς. I would translate LXX as "Nor while they were in the land of their enemies, did I neglect them nor treat them with contempt." For ὑπερεῖδον see comment at v.37.

The ὥστε plus infinitive clause represents לכלתם, i.e. a marked infinitive. ὥστε ἐξαναλῶσαι interprets the Hebrew correctly "so as to destroy completely." This is followed in unusual fashion by an articulated infinitive,[51] τοῦ διασκεδάσαι. The first infinitive is unarticulated, and I suspect the differentiation to be intentional on the part of the translator. In Lev infinitives are seldom articulated, but here it is for a purpose; for the use of marked infinitives in Lev see comment at v.18. It points out what the first one involves; it involves God's shattering "my covenant τὴν πρὸς αὐτούς." In MT this covenant is אתם "with them," but to the translator the divine covenant is unidirectional; it is God's covenant towards them; it is instigated by God. The Lord and Israel are not equal partners; the source is God, and the recipients are Israel.

What v.44 has said is that the Lord has not neglected the people even in their exilic surroundings; he has not in any real sense abandoned them for a very good reason: ὅτι ἐγώ εἰμι κύριος ὁ θεὸς αὐτῶν.[52] A popular F text has εγω γαρ instead of ὅτι ἐγώ; this is merely a stylistic variant. ὅτι and γάρ can be used interchangeably, and both occur frequently in Lev (ὅτι 44 times, and γάρ 34). Since MT has no equivalent for εἰμι hex has omitted it. What the ὅτι clause insists on is that because God is the Lord their God he cannot abandon his people.

---

51. See THGL 82.
52. The Others read ὅτι ἐγὼ κύριος ὁ θεὸς αὐτῶν; after all, the Hebrew lacks the verb.

26:45 MT has God say: I will remember להם ברית ראשנים, i.e. "for their sake the covenant of ancestors." For ראשנים see Note at Dt 19:14. The translator has reinterpreted this. For להם he has αὐτῶν, which modifies "covenant," and has taken ראשנים as a singular adjective, i.e. τῆς διαθήκης τῆς προτέρας "the former covenant"; possibly the translator misread ראשנים as ראשון "former." A majority text has omitted both articles, which omission may be recensional (though not hex), since this coincides with MT; the omission may be Byz in origin. The relative clause which follows in MT then refers to the ראשנים, thus "whom I brought out." LXX has made of the relative pronoun a temporal notion: ὅτε, "when I brought them out." This then defines the time of "the former covenant," made possible by reading ראשנים as τῆς προτέρας. A popular stylistic change transposes αὐτῶν after διαθήκης, which is contrary to MT, and only made possible by the failure to render the preposition in מהם.

LXX has added after "land of Egypt" the well-known phrase ἐξ οἴκοι δουλείας. This is an ex par expansion, and was correctly placed under the obelus by hex. The phrase "before the nations" represents the open display of the redemptive act of the exodus. A popular gloss has added παντων, i.e. "all the nations." It is obviously secondary.

The purpose of the exodus is given by the articulated infinitival structure "to be their God"; in other words, the purpose of the redemptive act of the exodus from Egypt is to inaugurate the covenant from God's side; it was done in order for him to be their God. The short self-identification formula ἐγώ εἰμι κύριος concludes and authenticates the divine instructions of ch.26.

26:46 The subscription. The structure is nominal, with ταῦτα as subject, and "the judgments and the statutes and the law" as predicate. The Hebrew has the first two nouns reordered, i.e. "the statutes and the judgments." The A B x+ text has added μου after both κρίματα and προστάγματα, thus making God the speaker. That these are mistaken is clear, since the relative clause which follows is in third person, ὃν ἔδωκεν κύριος. The translator has changed התורת to the singular ὁ νόμος. νόμος in the singular more naturally applies to "Law" in general or to the Pentateuch, as in "the Law and the Prophets" or "the law of Moses."[53] One suspects that to the Alexandrian translator the torah meant the law in the sense of

---

53. According to Hesychius The Others used the plural *leges*, i.e. νόμοι.

the aggregate of all divine instruction, which he found more meaningful than "instructions, teachings." That this is correct is clear from the relative clause; see below. ἔδωκεν is used as rendering for נתן, and occurs 1491 times in OT, followed in frequency by τίθημι (139 times), and παραδίδωμι (132); then follow ἐπιτίθημι (68) and ἀποδίδωμι (23); the remainder is insignificant.[54] δίδωμι is here used Hebraically in the sense of "place, put," which is legitimate for נתן rather than for δίδωμι. The relative clause, however, modifies only νόμος, thereby clarifying what the translator meant; it is "the law which the Lord had placed between him and (between) the Israelites at Mount Sina by the hand of Moses." What the translator intended was to identify the instructions which are here subscribed as the Law given by the Lord at Mount Sina.

---

54. The count is that of Dos Santos.

Chapter 27

27:2 In MT איש is followed by כי יפלא נדר "should he make a special vow," which LXX renders by ὃς ἂν εὔχηται εὐχήν, "who might vow a vow." The notion of יפלא נדר means "to discharge a vow," though the verb does carry with it the notion of something extraordinary. LXX has disregarded the special nature of יפלא; see also 22:21.[1]

The content of the vow is expressed in MT by בערכך נפשת "according to the evaluation of human beings," i.e. the vow is the equivalent value of a human being. For בערכך see comment at 5:15. The translator was equally elliptical with his ὥστε τιμὴν τῆς ψυχῆς αὐτοῦ. In fact, a number of witnesses inserted δουναι after the conjunction.[2] The infinitive was added to relieve the elliptical ὥστε τιμήν, but the more difficult reading of Lev is original. What LXX probably means is "who might vow a vow so as to yield an equivalent value of his person (to the Lord)." LXX has changed נפשת "people" to τῆς ψυχῆς αὐτοῦ, and hex has omitted αὐτοῦ as having no correspondent in MT. What is meant is: should someone pledge a vow to give to the Lord the equivalent value of his own person. Vv.3—8 then give the various equivalency values.

In the tradition, the initial ἄνθρωπος is omitted by the A B x+ text, but whenever איש כי introduces a casuistic law in Lev the איש is always rendered either by ἄνθρωπος, ἀνήρ or an indefinite pronoun, and the omission is secondary.[3] Also to be noted is the fact that (ἐρεῖς) πρὸς αὐτούς becomes αυτοις in the A B O+ text. But only seldom does the dative occur after a verb of saying or speaking to render the preposition אל. In fact, only four cases obtain in the book, whereas a πρός phrase occurs 61 times. Only when the pattern "speak to ... and you shall say πρός ..." occurs, does the dative occur regularly to modify the imperative.[4]

---

1. Theod and Aq have ἐὰν θαυμαστήσῃ; according to Hesychius Sym had interpreted this as *si superaverit*.
2. Harlé-Pralon rendered this freely by "de manière que se soit la valeur de sa propre vie."
3. See THGL 116.
4. See THGL 79—80.

27:3 The first in the scale is the value of the male between the ages of twenty and sixty. This is expressed by an ἀπό ... ἕως pattern. The ἕως translates ועד, but Lev throughout disregards the *waw*. MT also begins the verse with a conjunction, but the translator fortunately also disregarded that as well. It should be noted that ערכך has become a set form to indicate "rate, price, value, assessment;" In fact, in v.b the word is rendered by αὐτοῦ ἡ τιμή "his price"; this is set at fifty didrachms of silver. The didrachm is used by Lev to render שקל "shekel." The standard for the didrachm is τῷ σταθμῷ τῷ ἁγίῳ. At Exod 30:13 this is given as κατὰ τὸ δίδραχμον τὸ ἅγιον. One might well have expected a similar rendering here, since MT has בשקל הקדש, but once again Lev's love for variation comes into play, and שקל is rendered by σταθμῷ "measure, weight, standard." For the value of the didrachm as well as for the variant spellings of the word itself see Note at Exod 30:13. The preposition is not rendered, nor is it necessary in Greek, the dative by itself being sufficient.[5] In the tradition, hex (i.e. ms 426) has added υιον before ἑξακονταετοῦς to represent MT's בן ששים. It should also be noted that for vv.4—8 the O text throughout has added αυτου after ἡ τιμή, even though MT reads ערכך. If this is hex, it must mean that Origen understood ערכך as "its rate, price." In any event, an αυτου does not fit at all in the context. I suspect that the consecution αὐτοῦ ἡ τιμή in v.3 promoted the hex "correction" to η τιμη αυτου, and this in turn stimulated the additions of αυτου in the following verses.

27:4 MT presents a conditional statement concerning women parallel to v.3, which LXX shortens to a simple statement;[6] i.e. instead of "and if it is a woman, then the price ...," LXX has changed the "and" sensibly to a contrastive δέ, and created a single clause by changing והיא היא to a single word ἔσται, and by making "the woman" genitive: "but the price of a female is thirty didrachms." The term for "price" here is συντίμησις, which contrasts with τιμή used in vv.3,5—8. It also occurs in v.18 in contrast to vv.16—17,19. The Hebrew term throughout is ערכך,[7] but the translator introduces a new and relatively rare term, συντίμησις, which is reserved in Lev to indicate "price, rate, value," in contrast to the usual, i.e. it shows a parallel rate, a contrastive price.

---

5. See SS 129.
6. For the construction see SS 80.
7. For the use of ערכך see SS 97.

27:5 The rate for younger people, i.e. those from five to twenty years of age. For ערכך see comment at v.3. The price for the male youngster is two-fifths of that of the mature male, i.e. twenty didrachms, and for the female, one-third that of the mature female, i.e. ten didrachms. For didrachms see comment at v.3. As in v.3, which see, hex has added υιος before εἴκοσι to represent the Hebrew idiom "son of (twenty years)" to signify age.

27:6 The rate for children. The age for children is given as "from a month to five years." Again LXX shortens by omitting the conditional particle ἐάν. Hex again introduces υιου before πενταετούς to represent the Hebrew text literally. The rate given also differs for the sexes; for the male child the price is five silver didrachms, but for the female, only three didrachms. MT repeats כסף "silver" for the three didrachms as well,[8] as well as ערכך before "three didrachms." The majority of witnesses follows hex in adding αργυριου to equal MT, and hex has added η τιμη before τρία, again to represent the second ערכך.

27:7 The rate for senior citizens, i.e. from sixty years old and upward. Odd is the use of ἑξηκονταετῶν, but only O changes to εξηκονταετους as at v.3; in fact, the -ετους inflection is used throguhout this section. The change is of course similar; the singular adjective would hardly be correct when it refers to "sixty year olds and upward"; the plural is intentional, and correctly used. The sexes are differentiated by a μέν ... δέ construction, i.e. "if it be a male ..., but if female," rendering MT's ול ... אם. The rate for the male "shall be fifteen silver didrachms," but if female, "ten didrachms." MT has no equivalent for "silver," and hex has placed ἀργυρίου under the obelus to indicate that fact. On the other hand, the Byz text has added αργυριον at the end of the phrase to balance the "silver didrachms" designated for the male, as in v.6.

In the tradition, ἐὰν δὲ θήλεια was changed to της δε θηλειας in the F M majority text, but this is due to the influence of v.6, and not original text.

27:8 For the meaning of ταπεινὸς ᾖ see the discussion on ταπεινωθῇ at 25:39— 40. The case being discussed is that of someone who is too poor to pay the τιμὴν

---

8. Pesh's Ambrosian Codex 7a1 attests to the second כסף as well, but most mss omit it with Lev.

τῆς ψυχῆς αὐτοῦ to the Lord (v.2).[9] What the protasis means is "but if he should be in such straightened circumstances that he cannot afford the price."[10]

The apodosis begins with στήσεται "he shall present himself." The middle voice is used to translate העמידו "one shall make him stand." Since the subject is indefinite, either a passive or a middle would be adequate as a rendering. Hex has wrongly added an αυτον to indicate the suffix of the Hebrew. The priest must then evaluate him, i.e. adjust the rate. The verb τιμήσεται is neatly used to determine the τιμή for him.

V.b. then instructs the priest as to the standard he is to employ for this evaluation; he is to do this καθάπερ ἰσχύσει ἡ χεὶρ τοῦ εὐξαμένου. MT has the verb השיג with יד as subject. This is an idiom meaning "one can afford," literally "the hand can attain, reach." This idiom also occurs at 5:11, where it is rendered by εὑρίσκῃ (αὐτοῦ) ἡ χείρ, similarly at 14:21 as ἡ χεὶρ (αὐτοῦ μη) εὑρίσκῃ; at 25:26 it becomes εὐπορηθῇ τῇ χειρί, and at v.49 as εὐπορηθεὶς ταῖς χερσίν, and in each case it refers to an individual not being able to afford something. Only here is the verb translated by ἰσχύσει, i.e. "as the ability of the one making a vow can attain." Since τιμήσεται αὐτὸν ὁ ἱερεύς which concludes the verse is an exact repetition of the end of v.a, a majority F M text has introduced it by ουτως; this certainly improves the text rhetorically, but it has no basis in the parent text, and constitutes an ad sensum gloss.

27:9 Vv.9—13 describe the regulations concerning an animal which has been presented to the Lord as a δῶρον. MT presents the protasis in v.9 rather strangely as a subject without a predicate, and one must for good sense supply a linking verb, thus "if (there should be) cattle from which a sacrifice (קרבן) is to be offered (יקריבו) to the Lord." The translator has added a preposition before "cattle," i.e. a partitive ἀπό,[11] and made δῶρον the subject, and the ἀπό structure the predicate, all of which is sensible. V.a may then be translated "but if a sacrifice (δῶρον) to the Lord be of cattle from those which may be offered."

This is then followed by ὃς ἂν δῷ ἀπὸ τούτων τῷ κυρίῳ ἔσται ἅγιον. Only the last two words can constitute the apodosis for v.a, i.e. "it shall be holy." The relative clause can best be understood as the subject of v.10; its equivalent in MT

---

9. According to Hesychius Aq read *si excessit*; cf f.n. at 25:35.
10. For the comparative מן see SS 149.
11. See SS 165.

is quite different; it has כל אשר יתן ממנו ליהוה as the subject of יהיה קדש, i.e. "everything which he shall give from it (i.e. from the sacrifice) shall be holy." What makes this difficult is ממנו, which can not refer to בהמה which is feminine, but must refer to קרבן. The translator obviously was puzzled by this, and by using the plural, ἀπὸ τούτων,[12] could make it refer to "cattle." But why he should have translated כל אשר by ὃς ἄν is baffling; this simply does not fit the context. Or did he mean to say "(regardless of) who might give some of these to the Lord?" This is a possible understanding of the clause, but it remains the subject of v.10. I would render v.b as "whoever might give any of these to the Lord, it shall be holy." Then follows the predicate of the whoever clause: "may not substitute ...)."[13]

27:10 MT forbids two actions: לא יחליפנו ולא ימיר אתו, which LXX combines into one: οὐκ ἀλλάξει αὐτό. It is quite uncertain which of the two verbs the translator read. In Gen the verb ἀλλάσσω translates some form of חלף four times, but in Lev המיר is rendered five (or six) times by ἀλλάσσω, and once it barely renders פדה (v.27). Note also that v.b begins with (ἐὰν δὲ) ἀλλάσσων ἀλλάξῃ, which already translates המר ימיר as well. In fact, it never translates the verb חלף, so I would suggest that it is ולא יחליפנו which has been omitted, probably an error due to homoioteleuton. Origen, however, understood it differently, and hex has added και ουκ αντερει αυτω under the asterisk after ἀλλάξει αὐτό. It might be noted that the hex gloss is transposed (including the asterisk) after πονηρῷ by n, but this is hardly sensible. Since the two verbs are synonyms, it is also possible that the translator compressed the two into a single verbal form. What might not be substituted is καλὸν πονηρῷ οὐδὲ πονηρὸν καλῷ. The dative expresses means, as does ב in MT, i.e. "good by bad nor bad by good."[14]

---

12. Also a partitive ἀπό; see SS 167.
13. I must protest against R.Sollamo's characterization of this as "a good example of the kind of mess a translator may produce. He begins freely, but then ended in total failure"; see Greenspoon—Munnich 50, and see especially her summarizing characterization of the translator on p.53. Admittedly, at times his work is hard to understand, and the odd relative clause here is such a case. But one owes it to the translator to try to understand what he intended to say to the reader. One might prefer a more rigid adherence to accepted grammatical rules of concord and anaphora, but it remains his work, not ours, and it means that the modern reader must grapple with what the translator tried to say.
14. According to Hesychius Sym read *deterius* for πονηρόν.

The Hebrew cognate free infinitive המר is rendered by a present participle in LXX, ἀλλάσσων (ἀλλάξῃ). This is part of the protasis: "but should he actually substitute αὐτὸ κτῆνος κτήνει," i.e. an animal for an animal. MT has no equivalent for αὐτό, and hex has also omitted it; it is indeed otiose. The word κτῆνος is usually collective, signifying domestic animals, but here it refers to a single such animal. In such an exchange "it shall be along with the exchange holy." MT repeats "shall be" for both "it" and "its exchange," but LXX has only one ἔσται. MT reads תמורתו and LXX also omits "its," but hex makes up for this by adding αυτου after ἄλλαγμα, though the possessive is unnecessary in Greek composition.[15] MT has קדש, whereas LXX has the plural ἅγια; this was intentional on the part of the translator, since both "it" and "the substitute" are considered holy. A popular A F V variant text does read the singular, but this is not necessarily recensional; it is likely singular by attraction to the nearer element of a compound subject. But note also v.33.[16]

27:11a But suppose such an animal would be ritually unclean, what then? Such an animal is characterized as ἀφ' ὧν οὐ προσφέρεται ἀπ' αὐτῶν δῶρον τῷ κυρίῳ. The passive present tense verb is a good interpretation of the active indefinite plural יקריבו. I would translate this as "from which a sacrifice may not be offered to the Lord."

27:11b—12 Such an unclean animal "one must set before the priest." Then τιμήσεται αὐτὸ ὁ ἱερεύς.[17] The evaluation shall be made ἀνὰ μέσον καλοῦ καὶ ἀνὰ μέσον πονηροῦ. An evaluation between good and bad probably means that he must rate it as to how good or bad it is.

The conclusion reads "and as the priest might evaluate it, so shall it be established." In the "as" clause the subjunctive τιμήσηται is used, though its counterpart in MT is the noun ערכך; i.e. MT says: "according to the evaluation of the priest so shall it be (יהיה)." In v.12 τιμήσεται renders the cognate Hi verb העריך. A popular A F M V text has changed the subjunctive τιμήσηται to the future indicative. In later Greek the distinction did blur, but after the particle ἄν LXX uses the subjunctive, not the future. Here the use of the future in v.a proba-

---
15. See SS 98.
16. See THGL 119.
17. According to Hesychius Sym read *statuit pretium sacerdos*.

bly contributed to the confusion, but the future is clearly secondary.[18] One might note that $C^{'}$ $s+$ have changed the future in v.a to the aorist subjunctive, which could not possibly be taken seriously as a real variant reading. That the translator does pay attention to the context, and does not translate words in isolate fashion is clear from his use of στήσεται to render יהיה; the standard has been applied, and the evaluation is set, established.

27:13 Possibly the owner of the κτῆνος, once having presented it as a δῶρον, would prefer actually to redeem it. This is fully possible, but he must add τὸ ἐπίπεμπτον πρὸς τὴν τιμὴν αὐτοῦ. MT introduces the apodosis with a waw, but LXX uses normal Greek, i.e. has no apodotic καί.

In the tradition, B* and 59 read αυτον instead of αὐτό, but this is a copyist error; the antecedent must be κτῆνος, which is neuter. The Byz text has changed πρός to επι. This is, however, secondary, possibly influenced by ἐπίπεμπτον, though more likely taken over from one of The Three, since MT has על. The verb modified is προσθήσεται, and the cognate πρός is expected.

27:14 Vv.14—15 deal with a dedicated house. איש כי is rendered by καὶ ἄνθρωπος plus ὅς, in which a relative pronoun is used to render כי. This is not uncommon, occurring nine times in Lev.[19] The protasis presupposes "a man who would dedicate his house as holy to the Lord." Actually both MT and LXX have cognate expressions here; MT's יקדש plus קדש becomes ἁγιάσῃ ... ἅγιαν in LXX, but this is difficult to reproduce in English, possibly "sanctify ... as sacred" might reproduce what was intended. The apodosis repeats v.12a with grammatically necessary adjustments, i.e. αὐτό becomes αὐτήν, and the adjectives are also feminine, καλῆς and πονηρᾶς; for the meaning of ἀνὰ μέσον καλῆς καὶ ἀνὰ μέσον πονηρᾶς also see comment at v.12a.

Similarly, the parallel to v.14b is found in v.12b, though MT is quite different. Instead of the prepositional phrase כערכך הכהן, "the evaluation of the priest," v.14 uses a verbal structure כאשר יעריך אתו הכהן, which LXX translates correctly by ὡς ἂν τιμήσηται αὐτὴν ὁ ἱερεύς. As in v.12 a popular variant, including A B V as support, read τιμησεται, i.e. the future indicative, but see comment at v.12; only the subjunctive can be original. The remainder reads

---
18. See THGL 128.
19. See THGL 74.

οὕτως στηθήσεται. In the tradition, b n+ read στησεται with v.12, but the passive makes the distinction between יהיה of v.12 and יקום at v.14. The distinction was clearly intended.

27:15 LXX has as protasis ἐὰν δὲ ὁ ἁγιάσας αὐτὴν λυτρῶσαι τὴν οἰκίαν αὐτοῦ. This is what MT says, though it has no counterpart to αὐτήν, and hex has placed it under the obelus.[20]

LXX does not introduce the apodosis with an apodotic καί in spite of MT's ויסף. The verb προσθήσει is modified by ἐπ' αὐτό representing עליו. Unfortunately, αὐτό has no grammatical antecedent, and it is again a case of Lev using a neuter pronoun ad sensum.[21] In the Hebrew the suffix of עליו refers on the analogy of v.13 to ערכך. MT does not have עליו immediately after the verb, but rather at the end of the clause (i.e. after ערכך). Hex has "fixed up" the text by omitting ἐπ' αὐτό and then adding the phrase επ αυτην after τιμῆς; this equals MT exactly, with the αυτην referring to τιμῆς.

27:16 Vv.16—21 deal with regulations concerning the dedication of land which is part of one's patrimony. The protasis speaks of a man who "would dedicate ἀπό the field of his possession to the Lord." This makes clear that what is being dedicated is part of his patrimony, since the ἀπό is clearly partitive; comp 25:24.[22]

The apodosis is introduced by καί in imitation of the Hebrew. MT states that the price shall be לפי זרעו, which is in turn followed by זרע. The translator disregarded the זר, and simply has κατὰ τὸν σπόρον αὐτοῦ. Origen was obviously puzzled by this odd text, and tried to "correct" it by changing αὐτοῦ to του σπορου, though just what "the seed of the seed" was supposed to convey is unclear. It should be added that the Masoretes tried to make sense of this by placing זרעו under the *ethnach*, i.e. they made זרע the onset of v.b. Modern translators understand זרע חמר שערים as meaning "a homer of barley seed." The word seed is actually otiose, but represents the זרע of MT. I would understand the prepositional phrase to mean "according to the seed required for it"; in other words, the αὐτοῦ is to be understood as an objective genitive.

---

20. According to Hesychius Aq translated אם המקדיש יגאל by *si sanctificans adfinem fecerit*. I am not clear what Greek verb is intended by the Latin.
21. See Huber 33—36 for examples of incongruence in gender; he does not cite this one, however.
22. See SS 161.

V.b then sets the price of such seed; it is "a cor of barley for fifty silver drachmas."[23] A cor is a dry measure which equals slightly more than five bushels.[24] The term κόρος also occurs for חמר at Num 11:32, and usually as כור in Tar.[25]

27:17 LXX follows the ואם of Qumran texts[26] and Sam rather than the אם of MT by its ἐὰν δέ. This dedication might be ἀπὸ τοῦ ἐνιαυτοῦ τῆς ἀφέσεως; this contrasts with the next verse, and must mean "as of the year of release." In other words, the dedication has taken place during the year of release. For the regulations concerning the year of release see ch.25. The regulation under this condition is simply: "it shall remain according to its price." LXX has ערכך and the αὐτοῦ of LXX is epexegetical. What is meant by στήσεται is that there will be no deviation from the rate that was set; it will hold itself steady.

27:18 A problem arises with the value rating if the dedication of land takes place between the years of release. MT says "and if after the jubilee he should dedicate his field." LXX, so as to make doubly clear that this condition contrasts with that of v.17, adds ἔσχατον before "after the release." It is used here adverbially in the sense of "later on, subsequently." It has no equivalent in MT, but is added to make sure that the dedication occurs "later on after the release." In such a case "the priest shall make a reckoning for him of the money (i.e. the silver) according to the years that are left up to the (next) year of release." This accords with the rules given at 25:14—16. This will then ἀνθυφαιρεθήσεται from its συντιμήσεως. For συντιμήσεως see comment at v.4. The verb is well-attested in the third century BCE in the sense of "deduct, abstract." What is meant is that the assessment of value will be proportionate to the number of years remaining until the next year of release.

---

23. The genitive is a genitive of price; see SS 128.
24. According to Eupolemus 33.1 ὁ κόρος ἐστὶν ἀρταβῶν ἕξ, i.e. approximately 60 gallons, cited from C.R.Holladay, Fragments from Hellenistic Jewish Authors. Volume I: Historians, p.122. But this is a liquid measure. As a dry measure it is approximately 5.2 bushels.
25. For a discussion of the term see Lee 116—117.
26. Both 4QLev—Num[a] and 11QpaleoLev[a] read ואם; see DJD XII 162.

27:19 This verse is a parallel to v.15. In both cases "the one dedicating" seeks to redeem what he has dedicated; in this case it is the field. The two differ in MT in that here it is not simply יגאל, but גאל יגאל. LXX, however, disregarded the free infinitive, and simply has λυτρῶται as in v.15.[27] At v.15 the subject was ὁ ἁγιάσας αὐτόν, but MT had only המקדיש. Here, however, MT does have אתו after the participle; the translator had simply levelled the text of v.15 to agree with v.19. In the tradition, hex has added λυτρούμενος before the verb to represent the free infinitive of MT.

The apodoses of the two verses are identical in MT, except for the concluding clause; v.19 reads וקם לו, whereas v.15 has והיה לו. In LXX both read καὶ ἔσται αὐτῷ. For the rest v.19 lacks the problematic ἐπ' αὐτό of v.15, and instead of τὴν τιμῆς reads πρὸς τὴν τιμὴν αὐτοῦ. This has ערכך עליו as counterpart in MT, and is a free rendering of the Hebrew. The Greek is more idiomatic here in that a πρός phrase rather than a simple genitive modifies προσθήσει.

27:20 Conversely, "should he not redeem the field, and should sell the field to another person, he can no longer redeem it." The verbs λυτρῶται and ἀποδῶται are both governed by the ἐάν particle, i.e. the verbs are both in the subjunctive. In MT the second clause reads ואם מכר, i.e. "and if he has sold." LXX does not repeat ἐάν but simply joins the two verbs by καί.

It is uncertain whether the subject of ἀποδῶται is the same as that of λυτρῶται. The land had been dedicated to the Lord, but the owner had not redeemed it. The land was in a sense indentured, and it has been suggested that the owner could not sell it, but only a sanctuary official could sell it.[28] But this seems to me to void a plain reading of the text. Once the owner sells the property, he loses the right of redemption.

Furthermore, the apodosis in MT reads לא יגאל עוד with the verb vocalized in the Ni, thus "it is no longer redeemable." In the tradition, the V 426 b n+ text omits the αὐτόν, which omission may well be recensional, possibly hex, since it equals MT.

---

27. For a possible shorter parent text see THGL 111.
28. See especially Harlé-Pralon who translate "et qu'on vend le champ à un autre homme." In fact, they make the comment: "Il faut supposer que le vendeur du champ est quelqu'un parmi les membres du personnel du sanctuaire."

27:21 בצאתו ביבל "when it goes out at the jubilee" is rendered by a genitive absolute, ἐξεληλυθυίας τῆς ἀφέσεως "when the release has gone out," i.e. as soon as the release has come to an end. In MT the suffix of בצאתו refers to השדה; it is the field that "goes out" in the jubilee year.

In any event, at that time "the field shall be holy to the Lord." The translator has understood this as contrasting with v.20, since he begins with the adversative ἀλλ'. In other words, it is no longer redeemable; it is beyond redemption. In the tradition, a popular F M text has glossed ἅγιος with αινετος, but this is a direct import from 19:24, which see. This is barely sensible here, and should not be taken seriously.

This is holy ὥσπερ ἡ γῆ ἡ ἀφωρισμένη "as the land which has been set aside." This is, however, not what MT says, which has כשדה החרם "as the field of the ban," i.e. a field which has been placed under the ban. For the חרם/ἀνάθεμα see discussion at v.28. First of all, the rendering of שדה by γῆ is highly unusual. It only occurs eight times in all of OT, whereas ἀγρός renders it 210 times.[29] It is unique in Lev, whereas ἀγρός occurs 16 times. Furthermore, the participle does not render חרם, but is probably based on 25:34 οἱ ἀγροὶ οἱ ἀφωρισμένοι which may not be sold. This may well reflect an avoidance on the part of the translator of the field's being placed under the ban, particularly in view of a) that it is holy to the Lord, and b) what this involves as shown in v.b.

That the promised field is holy to the Lord means τῷ ἱερεῖ ἔσται κατάσχεσις. What is meant by τῷ ἱερεῖ is not certain; is it the priest who has been evaluating the land (v.18), or does it refer to the priestly class in general? The text does not specify, though probably the latter was intended. In MT the counterpart to κατάσχεσις is אחזתו. The translator did not render the suffix, since it is otiose in Greek;[30] hex has, however, added αυτου to represent it.

27:22 Vv.22—25 deal with land purchased, i.e. a field which is not part of his patrimony. V.22 contains only the protasis, for which vv.23—24 are the apodosis. In contrast to vv.16—21 the dedicated field is את שדה מקנתו which is not part of the field of his possession, i.e. of his patrimony. LXX changes the structure by means of a partitive ἀπό phrase plus a relative clause, ἀπὸ τοῦ ἀγροῦ οὗ

---

29. According to Dos Santos.
30. See SS 98.

κέκηται. By using a relative clause the translator has rendered מקנתו, with the verbal inflection taking care of the pronominal suffix.³¹

The Hebrew relative clause is rendered by a second relative clause, which also contains a partitive ἀπό.³² It translates the Hebrew correctly by ὃς οὐκ ἔστιν ἀπὸ τοῦ ἀγροῦ τῆς κατασχέσεως αὐτοῦ.

27:23 MT introduces the apodosis with a conjunction, but LXX does not in conformity with good Greek style. Here the Greek uses the simplex λογιεῖται to render חשב, rather than προσλογιεῖται as at v.18; there it was modified by αὐτῷ, but here by πρὸς αὐτόν; the intent is, however, exactly the same. What reckoning the priest shall make for him is τὸ τέλος τῆς τιμῆς ἐκ τοῦ ἐνιαυτοῦ τῆς ἀφέσεως, i.e. "the full amount of the assessment (reckoned) from the year of release." MT has מכסת הערכך "the proportion of the assessment," which is determined עד שנת היבל "up to the year of the jubilee." MT assesses the price based on the remaining years up to the jubilee year. The Greek puts it the other way around, the price being determined ἐκ the year of release. What is meant is a full assessment from which is removed the elapsed time from the year of release. The two versions agree on the outcome of the computation. In the tradition, the Byz text has changed the ἐκ to εως, thereby equalling MT exactly; the revision is probably based on one of The Three.

Furthermore, the assessment is to be paid immediately: "he must pay τὴν τιμήν in that day ἅγιον to the Lord." Understandably, a popular M variant text has changed ἅγιον to αγιαν, i.e. "the price in that day as holy to the Lord." But the translator used the neuter, since he intended rightly to make the adjective refer to τὸ τέλος (τῆς τιμῆς); it is the full amount of the assessment that constitutes a sacred gift to the Lord.

27:24 In accordance with the regulations concerning the Sabbatical year of ch.25, land reverted to the original owner in the year of release; cf 25:13 and passim. In contrast to MT, LXX, supported by Pesh, begins the verse with καί. "And in the year of release the field must be returned to the man from whom he had bought it." MT expresses this by אשר קנהו מאתו. This is followed by οὗ ἦν ἡ κατάσχεσις τῆς γῆς "whose had been the possession of the land." In the tradi-

---

31. See SS 58.
32. See SS 158—159.

tion, hex unnecessarily added παρ αυτου, which, however, had been adequately and correctly rendered by the genitive relative pronoun οὗ.[33] The equivalence here as in the Exod passage probably describes an ideal sacred didrachm. For variant spellings of δίδραχμον see Note at Exod 30:13 as well.

27:25 According to MT: every price shall be בשקל הקדש, "according to the shekel of the sanctuary." LXX has rendered this by a dative,[34] i.e. by a plural adjectival phrase σταθμίοις ἁγίοις "in accordance with holy balances, scales." For σταθμίοις see comment at 19:35. "Holy balances" meant standard scales; these were used to guard against falsified weights and measures; see 19:35—36.

The section ends with a learned note, also found at Exod 30:13, though without ἔσται. The Greek obol was, however, only one-sixth of a drachm; see Note at Exod 30:13.

27:26 No first-born among the cattle could be dedicated to the Lord, since all first-born already belonged to the Lord. Lev begins with καὶ πᾶν πρωτότοκον, which follows Sam, MT lacking כל. MT uses a cognate verb יבכר vocalized as Pu. LXX did not reproduce the cognate, but simple used γένηται, which is fully adequate. After all, a first-born is automatically born "first." The Greek begins with καί, whereas MT begins with אך. The first clause reads: "And every first-born which might be born among the cattle shall be to the Lord."[35]

This then means that "no one may dedicate it, whether young bull or sheep; the Lord's it is." This time LXX renders יקדיש by the compound καθαγιάσει rather than the simplex. The two are similar in meaning, and can hardly be distinguished in English.

איש is correctly rendered by οὐθείς, since איש here means "someone, τις."[36]

---

33. See SS 58.
34. See SS 129.
35. Theod and Sym have πλὴν πρωτότοκον ὃ ἂν (or ἐὰν) πρωτότοκον γένηται τῷ κυρίῳ ἐν τοῖς κτήνεσιν, whereas Aq translates πλὴν πρωτότοκον <ὃ> πρωτοτοκευθήσεται τῷ κυρίῳ ἐν κτήνει.
36. Theod translates by οὐχ ἁγιάσει ὁ ἀνὴρ αὐτὸ ἐὰν μόσχος ἐὰν ἐκ ποιμνίου τῷ κυρίῳ ἐστιν; Aq differs slightly with his οὐχ ἁγιάσει ἀνὴρ αὐτὸ ἐὰν βοῦς ἐὰν βόσκημα τῷ κυρίῳ ἐστιν. Sym has a shorter version: οὐχ ἁγιάσει οὐδεὶς ἐάν τε βοῦς ἐάν τε βόσκημα τῷ κυρίῳ ἐστιν.

27:27 τῶν τετραπόδων covers more than בהמה; the translator probably wanted a more inclusive term than κτήνων here in view of v.26 where both μόσχον and πρόβατον are mentioned. The variant *b* text reads κτηνων which is obviously recensional. As in Exod 13:13 LXX uses "exchange" rather than "redeem," though elsewhere throughout the chapter ἀλλάσσω occurs only for המיר. It should be noted that the Byz text changes ἀλλάξῃ to the more literal λυτρωσεται. The exchange could be made in accordance with its price, plus one-fifth, i.e. "he must add the fifth πρὸς αὐτό." MT has חמשתו, and hex has added αυτου after ἐπίπεμπτον to represent it.[37] The reverse is the case with τιμὴν αὐτοῦ, where MT has no equivalent for the pronoun. The neuter pronoun has ἐπίπεμπτον as its antecedent, whereas in MT עליו refers to ערכך. The Byz text has changed the phrase to επ αυτην (i.e. referring to τιμήν), obviously through mediate Hebrew influence, since MT has עליו. The following clause, καὶ ἔσται αὐτῷ, has no counterpart in MT, but is ex par; cf vv.15,19,31.

Since unclean animals could hardly be dedicated to the Lord for sacrifice, the alternative to their redemption is πραθήσεται κατὰ τὸ τίμημα αὐτοῦ. Why the translator should change from τὴν τιμήν to the hapax legomenon τὸ τίμημα is not known; probably he wanted to avoid using the same phrase twice in the same verse. The word is synonymous with τιμή.

27:28 Vv.28—29 deal with that which is ἀνάθεμα. This is the first occurrence of the word in the Pentateuch. In Greek the term was not initially pejorative, but referred to anything dedicated, but in LXX the term is a calque for חרם, since it is only used to translate √חרם, and so only the meaning of חרם is relevant. A חרם is something which has been placed under the extermination ban. The root meaning is that of extreme devotion to deity; it is very holy, hence separate, exclusive, and as such taboo. So something designated as חרם has been devoted to destruction, and can refer not only to property, but also to people and even to cities. Such objects are usually associated with God's enemies, particularly with idolators or objects associated in some way with them. Anything placed under the חרם had to be completely destroyed; cf Lexx sub חרם. See also Note at Dt 7:26. This use of ἀνάθεμα became prevalent in later Christian literature where it is

---

37. See SS 97.

used to indicate the object of a curse, thus something accursed.[38] To retain the sense of the Greek word it may best be rendered by "something devoted."

The reference in πᾶν ἀνάθεμα which a person might devote to the Lord is all-inclusive; it can be ἀπὸ πάντων ὅσα αὐτῷ ἐστιν, and can range from ἀνθρώπου ἕως κτήνους, as well as from ἀγροῦ κατασχέσεως αὐτοῦ. MT does not use the idiom "from ... up to" here, but simply lists "from men and cattle and from the field ...," whereas LXX uses the more common ἀπό ... ἕως ... ἀπό.

The rule concerning anything devoted to the Lord is that it may be neither sold nor ransomed; the devotion is absolute. In fact, it is most holy, ἅγιον ἁγίων; "it shall belong to the Lord." The translator has rendered the nominal הוא ליהוה "it is the Lord's" by the future ἔσται; this future is not to be taken as the prospective, but as an omnitemporal truth; that which is most holy shall always belong to the Lord.[39] The Byz text has changed the ἔσται to εστιν, obviously a variant reading inspired by the Hebrew. In the tradition, αναθημα, the old Classical spelling, is a popular variant, but the Hellenistic ἀνάθεμα is to be preferred,[40] for which see Note at Dt 7:26.

27:29 MT begins with כל חרם; LXX prefixes the conjunction καί, but renders only the כל as πᾶν, and hex has added αναθεμα to represent חרם. In any event, the πᾶν is intended as an abbreviation for παν αναθεμα, as the neuter form shows. The specific חרם which v.29 details is that which involves people, i.e. "anything which might be devoted ἀπὸ τῶν ἀνθρώπων. People who are devoted to the Lord may not be ransomed, but must actually be put to death. MT has no counterpart to the adversative conjunction, but simply orders מות יומת. The free infinitive is translated by the dative noun θανάτῳ, i.e. "with death he must be put to death." It represents the translator's way of rendering the free infinitive, i.e. placing strong stress on the verbal idea, and the structure θανάτῳ θανατωθήσεται must be understooood as a stereotype for the Hebrew.

27:30 Since a new notion is introduced, LXX does not begin with a conjunction as MT does. Vv.30—33 deal with the tithe. For the tithe of the land see Gen 28:22, and comp 14:20. What is meant by τῆς γῆς in the initial structure πᾶσα

---

38. See Bauer sub voce.
39. See Porter 423—424.
40. See THL 135.

δεκάτη τῆς γῆς is clarified by "from the seed of the land and the fruit of trees." The term ξυλίνου is an adjectival nominal used in a collective sense as is the Hebrew העץ. MT repeats the preposition before פרי, i.e. as מפרי; it also lacks a conjunction, though many mss as well as Sam read ומפרי, as did LXX.

The predicate is τῷ κυρίῳ ἐστιν, i.e. every tithe belongs to the Lord; in fact, it is ἅγιον τῷ κυρίῳ. The neuter adjective is here nominalized as is קדש in the Hebrew.

27:31 Here the cognate participle λυτρούμενος is used to render the free infinitive גאל. It also serves in the Hebrew fashion to put stress on the verbal idea, thus: "(should a man) actually redeem (his tithe)." An A B x+ text has substituted the noun λυτρω and transposed it after the verb, but the participle is to be preferred; note too that the word order is erratic in the variant text as well.

The general rule of adding a fifth to the price (see vv.13,15,19,27 and comp 5:16 22:14) is to apply. As at v.27 hex has added αυτου after ἐπίπεμπτον to represent the suffix of חמשתו.[41] MT also reads ממעשרו, i.e. with a partitive מן, thus "some of his tithe." The preposition is, however, almost certainly the result of dittography. The neuter αὐτό must refer to ἐπίπεμπτον in contrast to MT's עליו in which the suffix refers to מעשר. The majority M text has changed πρὸς (αὐτό) to επ, which must also ultimately be based on the Hebrew. The final clause, καὶ ἔσται αὐτῷ, has no basis in MT; for its source see comment at v.27. Its omission by a popular M text could well be recensional, possibly, though probably not, hex.

27:32 MT defines "every tithe of cattle and sheep as כל אשר יעבר תחת השבט "everyone that crosses over under the rod," whereas LXX has a καί introducing it. This is hardly sensible in a conjunctive sense, and should probably be translated by "even." LXX translates the structure by καὶ πᾶν ὃ ἂν ἔλθῃ ἐν τῷ ἀριθμῷ ὑπὸ τὴν ῥάβδον. A majority F M text has "corrected" ἔλθῃ to διελθῃ; this is clearly a recensional attempt to reproduce יעבר. The translator has interpreted יעבר by ἔλθῃ ἐν τῷ ἀριθμῷ; what is intended by the expansion is that passing through (a narrow gate) enabled one to count off every tenth animal; this was done "under the rod," i.e. the rod would mark the tenth animal in some way;

---

41. See SS 97.

comp Jer 33:13 Ezek 20:37. Every tenth animal (τὸ δέκατον) would be ἅγιον to the Lord, i.e. would constitute the Lord's portion.[42]

27:33 MT states: "Not may one make a distinction between good and bad (i.e. between good and bad animals) nor may he exchange it." The translator has harmonized this with v.10 so as to clarify what is meant. V.10 had prohibited exchanging καλὸν πονηρῷ or πονηρὸν καλῷ. Only the first of these alternatives is applicable, and so he interprets: "not may you exchange καλὸν πονηρῷ," i.e. a good one with a bad one. In other words one may not fob off a bad one on to the Lord. This free interpretation does do justice to what MT intended. The Byz text added ουκ επισκεψεται ανα μεσον και πονηρου και at the beginning; this represents an attempt to render MT's לא יבקר בין טוב לרע; others have added πονηρον καλω after καλὸν πονηρῷ, which is a gloss taken from v.10. Only the text of Lev can be original.

But suppose "you should actually exchange it," what then? This will be no advantage to the owner, since "also its exchange shall be holy." MT is somewhat clearer with its והיה הוא ותמורתו יהיה קדש "and it shall be and its exchange shall be holy." In LXX the "and it shall be" is omitted. Hex has added και εσται αυτο before καί,[43] thereby reaching the same end. In any event, "it may not be ransomed."[44]

27:34 The subscription to the book. The regulations of the book are identified as "the commandments which the Lord commanded τῷ Μωυσῇ πρὸς τοὺς υἱοὺς Ἰσραήλ in Mount Sina." The verb ἐνετείλατο is modified by both a dative showing indirect object, and a πρός phrase designating those for whom the commandments were intended. MT uses את for the first one, and אל for the second.

In the tradition, a popular A B F V text adds εισιν after αὗται. In spite of its impressive support, it is secondary, as the usage in Lev makes clear. Nominal clauses with demonstrative pronouns of nearer definition as subject are translated without a linking verb (except for 8:5) throughout Lev; in fact, the pattern occurs 24 times without the verb "to be."[45]

---

42. Harlé-Pralon render this clause idiomatically and accurately by "et tout dixième animal qui vient en compte sous la houlette."
43. But see THGL 119.
44. According to Hesychius Aq read *affinis non efficietur*.
45. See THGL 108.

APPENDIX A

Proposed changes in the critical text of Lev

2:4 For κλιβάνῳ ἐκ σεμιδάλεως, read κλιβάνῳ, ἐκ σεμιδάλεως
4:10 For σωτηρίου, read σωτηρίου·
4:21,24 For ἁμαρτία read ἁμαρτίας
5:6 For προβάτων, ἀμνάδα read προβάτων ἀμνάδα,
5:7 For ἰσχύσῃ read ἰσχύῃ
5:10,12 For ἁμαρτία read ἁμαρτίας
5:12 For τῶν read ἐπὶ τῶν
10:4 For Προσέλθατε read Προσέλθετε
10:9 For ὑμῶν· read ὑμῶν
10:12 Omit πρὸς 2°
13:19 For τηλαυγὴς read τηλαυγής,
13:56 Tr, ἢ ἀπὸ τοῦ δέρματος post κρόκης
15:23 For κάθηται read καθῆται
16:6,11 For αὐτοῦ 1° read αὑτοῦ
16:17 For αὐτοῦ 2° read αὑτοῦ
16:24 For αὐτοῦ 4° read αὑτοῦ
16:27 For αἷμα read αἷμα αὐτῶν
18:7 Omit καὶ 2°
21:1 Omit λέγων
22:18,22 For θεῷ read κυρίῳ
23:3 For ποιήσεις· read ποιήσετε·
23:21 For ἡμέραν κλητήν· read ἡμέραν· κλητὴ
24:9 For ἁγίων read ἁγίων, and for κυρίῳ, read κυρίῳ
25:22 For παλαιά· read παλαιὰ and for ἐνάτου, read ἐνάτου·
25:44 For σοι read σοι,
26:5 For ἀλόητος read ἄμητος
26:12 For μου λαός. read μοι ἔθνος.

APPENDIX B

Terms for Sacrifices

It is well-known that the Hebrew word חטאת can mean not only "sin" or the "guilt" associated with sin, but is also used to designate the sacrifice demanded for it.[1] The usual Greek rendering, ἁμαρτία, (243 out of 275 occurences) only meant "failure," and then in a religious context, "sin" or "guilt,"[2] but had no notion of "sacrifice" before the time of the LXX, which introduced it.

Accordingly, the translator was faced with the problem of terminology; he wanted to make crystal clear the distinction between חטאת as "sin, guilt" and חטאת as a sacrifice dealing with the pheomenon of חטאת. The earlier translators, Gen and Exod, had not solved the problem, but Lev did. The חטאת sacrifice was always to be rendered by the genitive.

The term ἁμαρτία occurs 98 times in Lev. Of these 34 do not refer to the sacrifice; of these 12 are cases of the accusative singular used in the sense of "guilt", whereas all cases in which the plural is used refer to "sin." Nine cases modify the verb (ἐξ)ιλάσκομαι, seven in a περί phrase and twice with ἀπό.

The remaining 68 cases refer to the sacrifice for sin; in every case only the genitive occurs. Of these the fullest (and clearest) rendering of the חטאת sacrifice is the articulated περὶ τῆς (omitted in two cases) ἁμαρτίας which occurs 26 times.

In 25 cases an unarticulated περί phrase either with or without an article modifying ἁμαρτίας is used to designate the sin offering. And at 6:25 an articulated ἁμαρτίας modifies ὁ νόμος in the collocation "the rule of the sin offering."

---

1. Milgrom 253—254 rightly objects to the common rendering of חטאת by "sin offering," preferring the translation "purification offering." Since LXX uses the term ἁμαρτίας which does not mean "purification," I shall for the sake of clarity use the term "sin offering" for both the Hebrew and Greek sacrifice, in the full awareness that the Hebrew term has a somewhat different connotation.
2. See LS s.v.

There are eight cases in which the nominal τῆς ἁμαρτίας is articulated, seven of which modify a preceding noun. Thus at 4:8 8:14 τοῦ μόσχου is modified by τοῦ τῆς ἁμαρτίας, i.e. "the bullock which is that of the sin offering"; this then serves to specify the sacrificial animal intended for the sin offering; see also 4:20 τὴν μόσχον τὸν τῆς ἁμαρτίας. This is similar to 4:29 τὴν χίμαιραν τὴν τῆς ἁμαρτίας. At vv.25,34 the antecedent for the article is τοῦ αἵματος, i.e. "of the blood which is of the sin offering." At v.33 the relevant passage reads τὴν κεφαλὴν τοῦ τῆς ἁμαρτίας, in which the τοῦ refers to τὸ πρόβατον or τὸ δῶρον of v.32, thus "the head of that which is of the sin offering." Only one case obtains in which the article has no referent, but simply serves to nominalize the notion of the sin offering; at 6:17 the passage reads ὥσπερ τὸ τῆς ἁμαρτίας καὶ ὥσπερ τὸ τῆς πλημμελείας, which means that the same applies both to the sin offering and to the trespass offering.

This leaves four cases in which the unarticulated genitive noun modifies ἐστιν. In Lev these were all wrongly inflected in the nominative, and all of them should be changed to the genitive; see Appendix A. In Lev these read as follows: (I give only the Greek ms evidence).

- 4:21 ἁμαρτία A B 58-82-381′ 46c-52′-551 537 53′-129 54 85c 318 55 319 426] περι αμαρτιας Fb 19′; της αμαρτιας 72; αμαρτιας rell
- 4:24 ἁμαρτία (ἐστίν) A B F 15-64*-72-708 56′-129 509-619 318 126-628 59 426] υπερ αματιας 527 319; αμαρτ 71; + γαρ 53′ 55; αμαρτιας Fb rell
- 5:9 ἁμαρτία (γάρ ἐστιν) F 551 129-246 426] περι αμαρτιας 319; αμαρτιας Fb 802 rell
- 5:12 ἁμαρτία (ἐστίν) A B* F M 72 129 619 121* 18 59] περι γαρ αμαρτιας 319; αμαρτ 71; αμαρτιας γαρ Fb 19′ 53′-246 527 126; + γαρ 318; αμαρτιας rell

In all four cases the majority reading is the genitive. At 4:21 the next word begins with a *sigma*, and haplography/dittography could be an influencing factor, but this can hardly be argued in the other three cases. It would be much easier to explain the nominative as an early copyist correction; after all, an εστιν would normally govern a predicative nominative rather than a genitive. In all cases the genitive must have been original in accordance with the distinction made by the translator; in each case it is not "sin," but "sin offering" that is intended. What such statements mean is "it is of a sin offering"; i.e. it concerns, deals with a sin offering.

A parallel case obtains with אשם. Again the noun can refer either to some offence or guilt as well as to the sacrifice for such an offence. In Lev, wherever the sacrifice is intended, the word is rendered either by the genitive πλημμελείας or a relative clause with the cognate verb (5:6,15 14:21). It is never rendered by the nominative, only by the genitive, except for 5:18 εἰς πλημμέλειαν, even in modification of verbs, viz of φέρω (5:15) or of προσάγω (14:12 19:21), where one would normally expect an accusative. As in the case of ἁμαρτίας it may be governed by περί, or the articulated nominal may in turn be articulated. Except for the case of 6:17 discussed under τὸ τῆς ἁμαρτίας above, the articulated nominal τῆς πλημμελείας occurs only in ch.14. At v.13 it is nominalized as at 6:17 in the clause ἔστιν γὰρ τὸ περὶ ἁμαρτίας ὥσπερ τὸ τῆς πλημμελείας. In three cases, vv.14,17,25, τοῦ τῆς πλημμελείας modifies τοῦ αἵματος, and twice, vv.24,25, τὸν τῆς πλημμελείας refers to τὸν ἀμνόν. Clearly here too the genitive nominal is used in analogy to ἁμαρτίας to designate the sacrifice intended for the אשם.

Other sacrificial designations are not problematic. The שלמים sacrifice is always (except at 7:18[8] where it is omitted) and only translated by the singular (τοῦ) σωτηρίου. The general term for sacrifice זבח is usually translated by θυσία, i.e. 32 out of 35 occurrences, and מנחה also becomes θυσία 34 out of 36 times. The Alexandrian considered both to be general terms for sacrifice, but they are distinctive in their contexts. The מנחה was a θυσία in its own right, whereas זבח usually occurs as a θυσία governing τοῦ σωτηρίου or τῆς αἰνέσεως (but see 22:29).

The term אשה is rendered only by κάρπωμα in Num, but Lev is quite inconsistent. Over half of the instances (19 out of 35) are also rendered by κάρπωμα, but θυσία is used nine times, and even ὁλοκαύτωμα obtains seven times. One case is clearly a textual one, 24:7, where instead of אשה LXX has προκείμενα; obviously this can not be taken as based on the MT reading. As far as the Alexandrian was concerned, an אשה was some kind of sacrifice not clearly defined.

The word עלה "burnt offering" is usually translated by either ὁλοκαύτωμα (40 times) or by its cognate ὁλοκαύτωσις (seven times). The remaining 16 occurrences of עלה are all rendered by nouns derived from the root καρπο-: κάρπωμα (11 cases), κάρπωσις and ὁλοκάρπωμα (two each), and one case of ὁλοκάρπωσις.³ Just how the Alexandrian distinguished between אשה and עלה is not clear, since for both, κάρπωμα and ὁλοκαύτωμα are used, though admittedly in reverse popularity. The general term θυσία is never used for עלה, however, although a quarter of the instances of אשה were rendered by θυσία.

The general term קרבן occurs 40 times in the book, and is always (except for 1:2 where δωρεῖται is used) translated by δῶρον, which is obviously a calque for the Hebrew word. The מנחה "grain sacrifice" occurs 36 times in the book. Once, at 9:40 σεμίδαλιν occurs in its slot, for which see comment ad loc. Once, at 2:13 it was rendered by θυσιασμάτων for the sake of variety, and in all other cases it is translated by θυσία. Other types of sacrifices such as the אזכרה or the תודה sacrifices are seldom mentioned, and neither occasions any surprise. The former occurs only six times and becomes μνημόσυνον five times, and ἀνάμνησις once. The term תודה occurs only five times, four times becoming αἴνεσις and once as (εὐχὴ) χαρμοσύνης (for which see comment at 22:29).

---

3. This is based on my own examination of MT and the Greek. This contrasts with the count and analysis based on HR, which is inaccurate.

Index of Greek Words and Phrases

A

ἄβατος, 253
ἀγγεῖον, 157, 221
ἅγια, 16, 77
ἁγιάζω, 103, 162, 251, 364
ἁγιασμός, 175
ἁγιαστήριον, 175
ἅγιος, 43, 162, 175, 290, 318
ἅγιος τῶν ἁγίων, 16
ἀγνοέω, 41
ἄγνος, 384
αγρός, 200
ἀδικέω, 65, 297
ἀδίκημα, 249
ἀδικία, 285
ἄδικος, 296, 298
ἀετός, 147
ἄζυμος, 368
ἄθυτος, 293
αἷμα, 38, 262, 299
αἱμορροέω, 239
αἰνετός, 305
αἴξ, 29, 260
αἵρεσις, 355
αἴρω, 229
ἀκαθαρσία, 90
ἀκάθαρτος, 144, 152
ἀκουσίως, 34, 46
ἀκρίς, 150
ἄκρος, 109
ἄλας, 22

ἀλήθεια, 102
ἁλιάετος, 148
ἀλλογενής, 350, 360
ἀλλότριος, 129
ἅλς, 22
ἁμαρτάνω, 34
ἁμαρτάνω ἀπό, 34
ἁμάρτημα, 49
ἁμαρτία, 41, 48, 89, 293, 300
ἁμαρτίας, 45
ἀμνός, 201, 209, 373
ἄμωμος, 24, 356
ἀνάγω, 145
ἀνακαλέω, 1
ἀνάμνησις, 15, 391
ἀνάπαυσις, 257, 366, 377
ἀναπληρόω, 176
ἀναποιέω, 84, 371
ἀναφέρω, 23, 78, 207, 370
ἄνθρωπος, 226, 320, 342, 351
ἄνθρωπος ἄνθρωπος, 260
ἀνόμημα, 271, 321
ἀνομία, 321
ἀνταποδίδωμι, 285
ἀντί, 269
ἅπαν, 77
ἀπαρχή, 21, 352, 369
ἅπας, 111
ἀπέναντι, 264
ἀπερικάθαρτος, 305
ἀπό, 155, 210
ἀποκάθημαι, 239, 323
ἀποκαλύπτω, 275, 323
ἀποκιδαρόω, 132

ἀποκτείνω, 316
ἀπολλύω, 267, 379
ἀπολλύω ἐκ, 90
ἀποξύω, 217
ἀποπίπτω, 295
ἀποπομπαῖος, 244
ἀποπομπή, 245
ἀποσπάω, 359
ἀποτίθημι, 394
ἀποτίνω, 397
ἀποφέρω, 95, 324
ἅπτομαι, 228, 348
ἅπτομαι ἀπό, 54
ἀρέσκω, 142
ἄρην, 27
ἀρνός, 8
ἁρπαγή, 65
ἀρσενικός, 74
ἄρσην, 79, 356
ἄρτοι, 351, 390
ἄρτος, 17, 85
ἀρχιερεύς, 35
ἄρχων, 45, 282, 314
ἀσεβέω, 321
ἀσέβημα, 280
ἀσπάλαξ, 154
ἀσχημοσύνη, 275
ἄτεκνος, 324
ἀτμίς, 246
ἀττακής, 150
αὐλή, 24, 73, 113
αὐτά, 81, 208, 255, 264, 375
αὐτό, 12, 63
αὐτοῦ, 210
αὐτόχθων, 257, 286, 316, 386

ἀφαγνίζω, 220
ἀφαίρεμα, 86, 95, 126, 137, 352
ἀφαιρέω, 19, 39, 95, 112, 370
ἄφεδρος, 173, 233
ἀφίημι, 45, 245
ἀφορίζω, 95, 215, 327, 329, 370
ἀφόρισμα, 95, 137
ἀφόρισμα ἀφορίζω, 138

B

βάπτω, 43, 156
βάπτω ἀπό, 204
βάσις, 80
βδέλυγμα, 146, 283, 321
βδελύσσω, 147, 161, 288, 328
βεβηλόω, 294, 339
βεβήλωσις, 334
βιβάζω, 283, 322
βιβρώσκω, 73, 77, 147, 292
βοῦς, 7
βραχίων, 95, 126
βροῦχος, 150
βρῶσις, 92, 293
βύρσα, 106
βωμός, 5

Γ

γαλῆ, 154
γάρ, 96, 139, 276, 335
γενεά, 323
γεννάω, 276
γένος, 323, 340

γερουσία, 117
γῆ, 270
γλαύξ, 148
γλωσσότμητος, 357
γονορρυής, 226
γόνος, 225
γράμμα, 307
γρύψ, 148
γυνή, 280
γυνὴ ἥτις, 173

Δ

δάκτυλος, 37, 105
δασύπους, 144
δασύς, 384
δέ, 217
δεκτός, 3, 261, 292
δέρμα, 106
δέχομαι, 293, 360
δέω, 35
δήλωσις, 102
διαθήκη, 392
διαθρύπτω, 17
διαιρέω, 9
διακρίνω, 394
διάνοια, 300
διὰ παντός, 75
διαπαύω, 21
διαποστέλλω, 54
διαστέλλω, 255, 357
διατρίβω, 201
διαφυλάσσω, 302
διαχέω, 216
διάχυσις, 220

δίδωμι, 398
δίκαιος, 311
δικαιοσύνη, 299
δικαίωσις, 399
δὶς, 175
διχηλέω, 143
διχοτόμημα, 6
δόλος, 299
δόμα, 383
δόξα, 119, 127
δράγμα, 369, 372
δύω, 349
δῶρα, 334
δῶρον, 1, 24, 75, 120, 262

Ε

ἐὰν μέν, 23, 35
ἑβδομάς, 372
ἐγγαστρίμυθος, 308
ἐγγίζω, 332
ἐγκάθημαι, 285
ἔγκητος, 212
ἐγχώριος, 286
ἐγώ, 273, 318
ἐγώ εἰμι, 295
ἐγὼ κύριος, 364
ἔθνος, 299
εἴδωλον, 291
εἶπεν, 272
εἶπον, 135
εἰς ἄφεσιν, 255
εἰς τὸν αἰῶνα, 32
εἰσφέρω, 248
ἐκβάλλω, 339

ἐκβεβλόω, 335
ἐκδέρω, 5
ἐκδίδωμι, 332
ἐκεῖ, 325
ἐκεῖνος, 92
ἐκζητέω, 139
ἐκθερίζω, 294
ἐκθλίβω, 359
ἐκκλησιάζω, 99
ἑκούσιος, 87, 355, 383
ἐκπορνεύω, 316
ἐκτομίας, 359
ἐκτρίβω, 79
ἐκφέρω, 40, 219
ἐκχέω, 40, 262
ἔκχυσις, 40
ἔλαιον, 19, 205
ἐλασσονέω, 322
ἐλεγχμός, 300
ἐλέγχω, 68, 300
ἐλεκτός, 76
ἐμπίπτω, 156
ἐμπυρισμός, 133
ἔναντι κυρίου, 30, 36, 68, 98, 110, 130, 207
ἐνδελεχῶς, 389
ἐνδογενής, 276
ἔνδον, 156
ἐνδύω, 337
ἐνιαύσιος, 370
ἔνοχος, 319
ἐντέλλομαι, 260
ἔν τι, 35
ἐντομίς, 307
ἐξαγορεύω, 55

ἐξάγω, 364
ἐξαιρέω, 216
ἐξαλείφω, 217
ἐξάπινα, 333
ἐξαποστέλλω, 284
ἐξεκκλησιάζω, 99
ἐξέρχομαι, 215
ἐξηγέομαι, 223
ἐξιλάσκομαι, 4, 105, 177, 245
ἐξιλασμός, 378
ἐξίστημι, 128
ἐξόδιος, 381
ἐξολεθρεύω, 262
ἑορτάζω, 384
ἑορτή, 357, 365, 368
ἑορτὴ σκηνῶν, 380
ἐπακολουθέω, 291
ἐπανατρυγάω, 295
ἐπανήκω, 215
ἐπαοιδός, 308
ἐπαύριον, 370, 372
ἐπέρχομαι, 218, 244
ἐπί, 26, 61, 85, 332
ἐπιβαίνω, 228
ἐπιβάλλω, 129
ἐπίθεμα, 95, 112, 209, 372
ἐπίκλητος, 376
ἐπίπεμπτος, 63
ἐπίσαγμα, 228
ἐπισκοπή, 303
ἐπιστοιβάζω, 5
ἐπισυνίστημι, 299
ἐπιτελέω, 76
ἐπιτήδευμα, 273
ἐπιτίθημι, 5, 7, 23, 24, 47, 95, 105, 252, 370

ἐπιτίθημι δόμα, 95
ἐπιτίθημι ἐπί, 102
ἐπιχέω, 22, 158
ἐπονομάζω, 393
ἔποψ, 149
ἐπωμίς, 101
ἔργον, 257
ἐρεικτός, 22
ἐρεύγομαι, 146
ἔριφος, 8
ἕρπετον, 149, 154, 348
ἕρπω, 154, 160
ἐρῳδιός, 149
ἐσθίω, 73, 159, 269, 368
ἑσπέρα, 153
ἑσπερινός, 367
ἔσται, 226
ἐστιν, 277
ἐσχάρα, 18
εὐλαβής, 238
εὐλογέω, 127
εὑρίσκω, 59, 207
εὐφραίνω, 128, 385
εὐχή, 87, 355, 383
ἔφειλος, 342
ἐφίστημι, 267
ἔχω, 150, 344
ἕως, 371
ἕως ἄν, 175

Z

ζάω, 221, 245, 275
ζητέω, 139
ζυγόν, 311

ζύμη, 20
ζυμίτης, 86
ζυμωτός, 20
ζώνη, 100
ζωνύω, 104

H

ἤ, 319, 352
ἡμέρα, 114
ἧπαρ, 25

Θ

θανατόω, 320
θέμα, 390
θερίζω, 369
θερισμός, 295, 376
θῆλυς, 49
θήρευμα, 269
θηρεύω, 269
θηριάλωτος, 52
θλαδίας, 359
θνησιμαῖος, 52
θυγάτηρ, 352
θυμίαμα, 38
θυμόω, 139
θύρα, 5, 24
θυσία, 7, 14, 72
θυσιάζω, 392
θυσιαστήριον, 5, 44
θυσία σωτηρίου, 23
θύω, 263, 292

I

ἰάομαι, 220
ἶβις, 148
ἱερεύς, 331
ἱκανός, 177
ἱλαστήριον, 241, 247
ἱμάτιον, 152, 338
ἵν, 371
ἵνα, 140
ἵστημι, 243, 283
ἰσχύω, 57
ἰτέα, 384

K

καθά, 97
καθαιρέω, 157, 218
καθάπερ, 115, 259
καθαρίζω, 105, 123, 177, 208, 237, 251
καθαρισμός, 230
καθαρός, 158, 230
καθέζομαι, 174
κάθημαι, 234
καθίζω, 227
καθότι, 211
καιρός, 366
καίω, 71, 388
κακοποιέω, 54
κακῶς εἶπον, 298
καλαβώτης, 154
κάλλυνθρον, 384

κάμηλος, 144
κανοῦν, 110
καρπόω, 4
κάρπωμα, 92, 358
κάρπωσις, 39, 358
κατά, 247
κατακαίω, 40, 79, 321
κατακάρπωσις, 70
καταλείπω, 20, 88, 205
καταμανθάνω, 214
κατὰ μέλη, 122
καταπέτασμα, 37
καταράκτης, 148
καταράομαι, 393
καταράσσω, 298
καταστραγγίζω, 58
κατατέμνω, 334
κατ' αὐτῆς, 55
καταφυτεύω, 304
κατενώπιον, 43
κατεσθίω, 130
κατοικέω, 273
κατοικία, 32, 366, 373
κατοικίζω ἐν, 386
κατοχεύω, 301
καῦσις, 69
κέδρινος, 199
κέρας, 47
κεφάλαιον, 67
κιβδηλός, 302
κιβωτός, 241
κίδαρις, 104
κινέω, 163
κλάδος, 384
κλάσμα, 76

493

κλέπτω, 296
κλῆρος, 244
κλητός, 365, 375
κλίβανος, 16, 83, 157
κλώθω, 199
κλωστός, 200
κοιλάς, 214
κοιλία, 108
κοιμάω, 232
κοιτασία, 322
κοίτη, 232, 281
κόκκινος, 199
κολοβόκερκος, 358
κολοβόριν, 341
κομίζω, 323
κόραξ, 148
κοτύλη, 202, 209
κρεανομέω, 108
κρέας, 87, 145
κριός, 80, 107
κριὸς τελειώσεως, 108
κρίσις, 311
κροκόδιλος χερσαῖος, 154
κτῆνος, 143
κτῆσις, 212
κτίζω, 249
κυθρόπους, 157
κύκλῳ, 105
κυκνός, 149
κύριος, 298
κυρίου, 248
κυρτός, 342
κωφός, 298

Λ

λάγανον, 110
λαλέω, 314
λαμβάνω, 52, 96, 111
λανθάνω, 55, 61
λάρος, 148
λατρευτός, 368
λατρεύω, 282
λέγων, 1
λειχή, 343, 358
λεπίς, 145
λέπρα, 212
λεπράω, 347
λεπρός, 198, 347
λεπτός, 246
λίβανος, 72
λινοῦς, 69
λοβός, 25, 109
λόγιον, 101
λόγοι, 116
λοιπόν, 376
λοιπός, 20
λούω, 159, 201, 229
λύτρον, 302
λύχνος, 388

Μ

μαι, 278
μαρτύρια, 247
μαρτύριον, 99
μαρυκάομαι, 152
μάταιος, 265

μέλι, 20
μέλος, 5
μέν, 85
μερίς, 74
μετὰ ταῦτα, 214
μετὰ τοῦτο, 207, 214
μέτρον, 311
μηνίω, 300
μηρίον, 25, 81
μηρυκισμός, 145, 152
μιαίνω, 54, 284, 315
μίασμα, 89
μισθός, 297
μισθωτός, 297, 350
μίτρα, 102
μνημόσυνον, 15, 19, 377
μοσχάριον, 117
μόσχος, 38, 260
μυγαλῆ, 154
μυρηκιάω, 357
μῦς, 154
μυσερός, 284
μῶμος, 341, 360, 398

N

νέος, 22, 373
νεοσσὸς περιστερῶν, 59
νεφέλη, 246
νεφρός, 25
νίζω, 229
νόμιμα, 135
νόμιμος, 32, 96, 286
νόμος, 69, 163, 223, 274, 301, 312
νόμος αἰώνιος, 76

νυκτερίς, 149

Ξ

ξύλον, 71, 199
ξυράω, 200, 201

Ο

ὅδε, 139
οἶδα, 386
οἰκεία, 278
οἰκεῖα σαρκός, 275
οἰκεῖος, 275, 280, 331
οἰκέτις, 302
οἰκογενής, 351
οἰφί, 60
οἰωνίζομαι, 306
ὁλοκάρπωμα, 253
ὁλοκάρπωσις, 118
ὁλόκαυτος, 77
ὁλοκαύτωμα, 3, 203, 374
ὅλος, 45
ὁ μέγας, 337
ὄμνυμι, 296
ὅμοιος, 148
ὁμολογία, 355
ὁμοπάτριος, 277
ὄνειδος, 322
ὄνομα, 296, 315, 337, 397
ὄνος, 228
ὃν τρόπον, 113
ὀνυχίζω, 143
ὀνυχιστήρ, 143

ὁπλή, 143
ὅπως ἄν, 263
ὁράω, 127, 213, 386
ὁρκισμός, 52
ὅρκος, 54
ὀρνίθιον, 199
ὀρνιθοσκοπέω, 306
ὀσμὴ εὐωδίας, 7, 29
ὅστις, 348
ὀσφύς, 28, 81
ὅτι, 287, 289, 335, 343
ὅτι γάρ, 139
οὗτος, 163
οὗτος ὁ νόμος, 69
οὕτως, 241
ὀφιομάχης, 151
ὀφρύς, 201
ὄψις, 307

Π

πάλιν, 217
"πᾶν, 231
παρά, 36, 243
παραθήκη, 65
παρατάσσω, 6
παρθένος, 339
πάροικος, 350
παροράω, 65
πᾶς, 233
πᾶς ὅς, 288
πάσχα, 367
πατρικός, 352
πεδίον, 200
πελικάν, 149

πέμπτος, 67
πένομαι, 207
περὶ αἰνέσεως, 85
περιαιρέω, 25
περὶ ἁμαρτίας, 50, 244
περικαθαρίζω, 305
περισκελής, 242
περιστερά, 10
περὶ τῆς ἁμαρτίας, 42
περιτίθημι, 104
πετεινόν, 12, 149
πηγή, 158, 323
πίμπλημι, 124
πλάγιος, 8
πλημμέλεια, 202
πλημμελέω, 41, 68
πλήν, 158
πλήρης, 246
πλήρης τὴν δράκα, 15
πληρόω, 114
πλησίον, 65, 297, 310, 320, 398
πλύνω, 152, 231
ποιέω, 237, 248
ποίησις, 101
πόρνη, 339
πορφυρίων, 149
πούς, 108
πρεσβύτερος, 42
πρόβατον, 7, 201
πρός, 44, 224
προσάγω, 2, 31, 100, 104, 243, 356
προσγίγνομαι, 286, 314
προσέρχομαι, 275, 309
προσέχω, 346

προσήλυτος, 257, 286, 295, 310
πρόσθεμα, 305
προσκεῖμαι, 266
προσκολλάω, 309
προσοχθίζω, 285, 287
προσπορεύομαι, 310
προσραίνω, 37
προσσιελίζω, 228
πρόσταγμα, 32, 274, 288
προστάσσω, 199
πρὸς τῇ, 44
πρὸς τήν, 44
προσφέρω, 2, 9, 31, 100
προσχέω, 5, 24, 80, 107
πρότερον, 58
προτίθημι, 298, 391
πρωτογένημα, 373
πτερόν, 11
πτερύγιον, 145
πτίλος, 342
πτωχός, 295
πῦρ, 128, 129
πῦρ ἀλλότριον, 240
πυρεῖον, 246
πώγων, 307

Ρ

ῥαντίζω, 78
ῥέω, 225, 235
ῥύσις, 224, 323
ῥῶς, 295

C

σάββατα, 291
σάββατα σαββάτων, 257, 380
σαββατίζω, 380
σάββατον, 291
σάλπιγξ, 377
σάρξ, 174
σαύρα, 154
σβέννυμι, 69, 128
σεμίδαλις, 14, 86, 118, 202
σίκερα, 134
σίκλος, 62
σισόη, 306
σκάνδαλον, 298
σκέλος, 150
σκεῦος, 103, 155, 221
σκηνή, 238, 262, 380
σπέρμα, 158, 281
σπέρμα σπόριμον, 158
σπερματίζω, 173
σπερματισμός, 283
σποδιά, 40
στάθμιον, 311
στέαρ, 28, 96, 110
στέατα, 125
στηθύνιον, 126
στικτός, 307
στολή, 70, 253
στραγγίζω, 10, 58
στρουθός, 148
συγγένεια, 316, 324
συγγενής, 279
συγγενής, ἡ, 324
συκοφαντέω, 296

συλλέγω, 295
συμβιβάζω, 135
συναγωγή, 40, 100, 119, 130, 242, 396
σύνθεσις, 38
συνίστημι, 225
συντάσσω, 400
συντελέω, 251, 294, 383
σύντριμμα, 398
σφάγιον, 359
σφάζω, 30, 263
σφόνδυλος, 58
σωτηρίου, 138, 374

T

τὰ ἅγια, 131
τὰ ἐνδόσθια, 39
ταπεινόω, 256
τελειόω, 258, 337
τελείωσις, 98, 110
τελευτάω, 331, 338
τετελειωμένος τὰς χεῖρας, 36
τετράπους, 283
τήγανον, 17, 83
τῆς ἁμαρτίας, 74
τίκτω, 173
τιμή, 62
τὸ ἅγιον, 240
τὸ ἅγιον τοῦ ἁγίου, 259
τὸ δειλινόν, 75
τόπος, 205
τόπος ἅγιος, 139
τὸ πρωί, 75
τὸ πρωὶ πρωί, 71

τὸ πρῶτον, 124
τοῦ, 39
τρυγών, 10
τυφλός, 341
των, 366

Υ

ὕδατα, 145
ὕδωρ, 159, 221
ὑποδύτης, 100
ὑπολείπω, 377
ὕσσωπος, 199
ὑφαίνω, 302
ὑψόω, 322

Φ

φαλάκρωμα, 333
φέρω, 56, 370
φθάρμα, 360
φθείρω, 307
φοβέω, 290
φοῖνιξ, 384
φρύγω, 22
φύλαγμα, 116, 350
φυράω, 75, 202
φωνή, 52
φῶς, 388

X

χαμαιλέων, 154

χαραδριός, 149
χαρμοσύνη, 362
χείρ, 111
χήρα, 339
χίμαιρα, 48
χίμαρος, 46, 242, 260
χιτών, 70, 100, 242
χοιρογρύλλιος, 144
χοῦς, 217, 270, 312
χρῖσις, 97
χριστός, 36, 339
χρίω, 75
χρώς, 227
χωλός, 341
χῶμα, 270
χωρίς, 124
χωρισμός, 281
χωρισμὸς τῆς ἀφέδρου, 173

ὥσπερ ἀφή, 213
ὥστε, 245
ὠτότμητος, 341

Ψ

ψεύδω, 66, 296
ψόα, 28
ψυχή, 34, 163, 267, 307, 331, 348, 378
ψυχὴ ἐάν, 34
ψυχὴ ἦ ἄν, 63
ψώρα ἀγρία, 342
ψωραγριάω, 358

Ω

ὡραῖος, 384
ὡς ἄν, 212

Index of Hebrew Words and Phrases

א

אב	337
אבנט	100
אבת	308
אדמדם	188
או	46
אוב	329
אזוב	199
אזכרה	14
אזרח	286, 270
אחזה	212
אחר	207
אחרי כן	214
איל	107
איש	226
איש איש	260, 224
אך	158
אכל	293, 73
אכלה	159
אליה	81, 28
אלילים	291
אל מחוץ	222
אם ואב	332, 290
אני	326
אני יהוה	298
אסף	383
אפד	101
אפה	83, 60
אצבע	105
ארבה	150

אשה	254, 173, 82, 7
אשך	343
אשם	202, 54
אשמת העם	35
את	6

ב

בגד	192
בגדים	99, 70
בדד	190
בהן	109
בהק	187
בהרת	187, 170
בוא	278
בזאת	241
בטא	54
בכורים	374
בלול	371, 84
בלע	333
בני	117
בן נכר	360
בנפש	269
בעד	120
בעל	333
בער	71
בערכך	62
בקר	7
בקרת	303
בקש	308
בשבעה	55

בשגגה 34	**ה**
בשר 70, 174, 224, 227, 242	
בתולים 339	האביד 379
	הבדיל 327
ג	הביא 17, 248
	הגיש 18
גבח 188	הדר 384
גבן 342	ההן 371
גור 309, 266, 257	הוא 234
גורל 243	הונה 310
גזל 65	הוסיף 305
גזר 253	הזיר 238
גלח 184	הזנות 308
גפן 302	הזריע 173
גר 286, 270, 257	החיה 143
גרב 343	החתים 225
גרה 145	היה 328
גרר 145	הכהן הגדול 337
	הלולים 305
ד	המזבחה 29, 82
	המכסה 125
דבק 309	המציא 122
דבר 130, 117	הן 140
דברים 116	הניף 95, 370
דד 324	הסגיר 172, 219
דדה 279, 324	הסיר 26
דוה 239, 173	העביר 282
די שה 57	העלה 207
דל 207	העמיד 243
דם 93	הפשיט 5
דמיו בו 319	הקדש 63, 353
דמם 130	הקהיל 99
דרש 139	
דרת 34	

הקטיר............... 30, 22, 7		חזה 94	
הקטר 76		חטא 220, 123, 105, 34	
הקצה 218, 217		חטאת 252, 206, 77, 38	
הקציע 218, 216		חלב 110, 92, 28	
הקרב 278		חלה 390, 16	
הקריב 243, 100, 30, 9		חלות 390	
הראה 192		חלל 294	
הרביע 301		חלץ 216	
הרים 18		חלק 74	
השבית 20		חלת לחם 110	
השחית 307		חמץ 86, 19	
השיג 211, 59		חק 97	
		חקה 301, 286, 32	
ו		חקות 135	
		חרוץ. 357	
והנה 218		חרם 342	
ז		**ט**	
זב 239		טבל 43	
זבח 292, 265, 88, 23		טהור 137	
זבח השלמים 39		טהר 237, 177	
זוב 224		טוח 217	
זכר 356		טמא 190	
זמה 321, 308, 280		טמאת 249	
זנה 340		טרפה 91	
זקן 307, 183, 42			
זרע 341, 158		**י**	
זרק 5			
		יבלת. 357	
ח		יד. 36	
		ידבר 272	
חבש 104			
חדש 373			
חול 135			

כפרים	378	ידנעי	329
כפרת	241	ידע	386
כפת	384	ידענים	308
כרות	359	יותרת	81
כרם	302	ילפת	343
כרעים	150, 40	ימים	146
כשב	7	ירא	298, 290
כתבת קעקע	307	ירך	8
כתות	359	ישב	201
		יתר	205

ל

לבב	300	כ	
לבן	188	כאשר	99
לבנה	72	כבה	69
לבש	100	כבוד	120
להורת	223, 135	כבס	194, 78
להניף תנופה	94	כבש	373, 201
לחם	353, 334, 29, 16	כהה	173
לחם אלהים	344	כהן	209
ליהוה	90	כהש	296
למלך	282	כי	379, 341, 287, 173, 139
לפני יהוה	80	כי אם	332
לקח	335, 47	כירים	157
לקט	295	כל	231
לראות	214	כלאים	301
לרבעה	322	כלה	251
לריח	111	כלי	155
לריח ניחח	261	כליל	77
לרצון	292, 3	כמשפט	59
		כנען	212
		כסלים	81
		כסף	351
		כף	124
		כפר	251, 177, 4

מ

מאור 388
מגבעות 104
מדברה 245
מדה 311
מול 304, 174
מולדת אב 277
מועד 99
מוציא 364
מוקש 298
מושב 191
מושבת 373
מות יומת 318
מזבח 5
מזבח העלה 39, 25
מחיה 181, 177
מחלל 337
מחתה 246
מטהר 202
מים 146
מים חיים 230
מין 148
מכוה 181
מכשל 298
מלא את יד 337, 258, 36
מלא קמץ 14
מלואים 98
מלח 20
מלך 314
ממארת 193
מנחה 118, 72, 13
מסכה 292
מספחת 173
מעוך 359

מעיל 100
מעין 158
מעל 61
מעשה 273
מפריס 144
מצה 58
מצוה 34
מצות 110
מצנפת 102
מצרע 198
מקדש 340, 315, 175
מקדש הקדש 259
מקור 323
מקרא 375, 365
מראה 184, 179
מרבכת 75
מרוח 343
מרח 343
מרכב 228
משורה 311
משח 75
משחת 360, 97
משכב 226
משכבי אשה 283
משכן יהוה 262
משמרת 350, 288, 116
משפחה 316
משפט 399, 286
משקל 311

נ

נבלה 91, 53

נשיא	45	נגע	170, 54
נתוק	359	נדבה	355
נתח	8	נדה	233, 173
נתן	267, 252, 129, 5	נדר	355
נתק	184	נדת טמאה	281
		נושן	175
		נותר	205
ס		נותרת	19
		נזר	346, 339, 102
סכות	380	נחלה	213
סל	110	נחלים	146
סלת	13	נחרף	302
סמך	394, 252, 105, 24	נחש	306
ספחת	170	נטר	300
		נכרת	90
ע		נמצה	10
		נמרט	188
עבת	384	נסלח	44
עגל	117	נסלח מן	304
עד־	160	נעלם	54
עדה	396, 99, 41	נעשה	83
עדת	388, 242	נפל	156
עול	299	נפש	307, 267, 34, 13
עולל	295	נפש החיה	163
עון	293, 285, 252	נפשת	338
עונן	306	נצתה	11
עור	192, 106	נקב	393
עז	260, 29, 7	נקבה	49
עזאזל	244	נקם	300
עין	195	נקף	306
עלה	253, 244, 118, 7, 4	נראה	213, 118
עלם	62	נשא	132
		נשא עון	271, 52
		נשבע	66
		נשחת	77

עם	323	פרע	132
עמיו	331	פרש	394, 40
עמית	398, 65	פשה	193, 173
עמר	369	פשע	252, 249
ענה	256	פשתים	191
ענן	246	פת	76, 16
ענף	384	פתח	264, 113, 24, 5
עפר	269	פתת	16
עצה	28		
עצים	6	**צ**	
עצרת	381		
ערבים	384, 367	צאן	7
ערוה	279	צדק	311
ערך	391, 5	צהב	185
ערלים	305	צוה	400, 97
ערף	58	צמר	191
עשה	244	צפור	199
עשק	297, 65	צרבת	180
		צרוע	189
פ		צרע	348
		צרעת	170
פאת	307, 294	צרר	280
פאת פנים	188		
פגול	293, 89	**ק**	
פחתת	195		
פנה	291	קבב	393
פסח	367	קדש	336, 103
פעלה	297	קהל	250, 242, 41
פקד	285	קיא	285
פקדון	65	קלה	21
פר	260, 38	קלוט	358
פרוע	190	קלל	393, 298
פרח	197, 175	קמץ	72
פרכת	388		
פרס	144		

שבתון	257	קנין	351
שבתות	372	קצר	294
שבת שבתון	257	קרא	190
שדה	263, 200	קרב	131, 40, 25
שוב	177	קרב לפני	240
שופר	377	קרבן	335, 262, 120, 20, 1
שוק	95	קרח	188
שור	260	קרחה	333
שחט	203		
שטף	229	**ר**	
שים	101		
שכבה	322, 281	ראה	215, 172
שכבת זרע	231	ראש	333, 183, 40
שכיר	297	ראש השנה	377
שכן	249	ראשית	369
שכרא	134	רבעה	284
שלח	284	רגם	330
שלם	397	רום	18
שלמים	138, 85	רחץ	6
שמה	325	רכיל	299
שמח	385	רנן	128
שם לאלהים	283	רע	297, 65
שמן	210, 103	רצון	261
שם קדשים	315	רק	228
שעטנז	302	רקיק	110
שעיר	265, 260, 242	רקק	228
שפך	216	רר	225
שפך הדשן	40		
שפם	190	**ש**	
שקץ	146		
שקר	296, 66	שאר	275, 19
שרוע	342	שארה	280
שרט	334, 307	שאת	189, 170
		שבעתים	175
		שבתא	291

שרף 114
שרץ 53, 146, 160, 348

ת

תבואה 305
תבל 284, 321
תבלל 342
תודה 55, 85, 362
תועבה 283
תורה 80
תורת הבהמה 163
תושב 350
תחת 180
תמיד 389
תמים 356
תמר 384
תנוך 109
תנופה 95, 137
תנור 157
תפיני 75
תרומה 86, 95, 137, 352
תרועה 377
תשוסת יד 65

Index of Grammatical and Textual Items

A

absolute use of ἐντέλλομαι: 120
absolute use of λαμβάνω: 116
absolute use of ἄγω: 176
accusative of extent of time: 121, 175, 199, 236, 239
accusative of time: 241
accusative, use of: 122
accusative with ἐπί: 33
active infinitive with δεῖ: 35
active verb for Ho: 201
active verbs: 85
adverbial accusative: 92
adverbial ἐνώπιον: 193
adverbial ἔξω: 223
adverbial ὅλον: 49
adverbials: 32, 127, 167
agentive use of ἐκ: 93
ambiguity removed: 102
analogy: 58
aorist as default tense: 101
aorist passive participle, use of: 209
apposite phrases: 3
apodotic καί: 14, 36, 69, 179, 184
apposition: 58, 132
appositive construction: 72, 76
Aramaic conditional particle: 227
articulated infinitive: 109

articulated infinitives with μετά: 226
articulation of proper nouns: 132
asseverative γάρ: 144
asyndetic clauses: 236
attributive participle: 56
awkward Hebraism: 24

C

calque: 6, 10, 14, 34, 161, 174, 171, 189
carelessness of LXX: 54
cases with ἐπί: 9, 74
cases with πρός: 48
causal כי: 95
change in number: 6, 49, 85, 88, 114, 137, 199
change in referent: 9
change in syntactic cut: 91
change in tense: 205
change in voice: 123
change of tense: 195
change of voice: 140
clarifying gloss: 55, 56, 60, 91, 88, 144, 178
clarifying paraphrase: 193
clause without predicate: 78
cognate accusative: 70, 240
cognate dative noun: 229

cognate free infinitive: 197, 228, 239
cognate noun: 106
cognate structure, rendering of: 175
collective: 41, 52, 116, 164
collectives: 53, 94
comitative expression: 56
comparative degree: 50, 189
comparative degree plus genitive: 221
comparison: 41
complementary infinitive: 220
compounds in Hellenistic Greek: 61
conditional εἰ particle: 146
conflation: 44
congruence: 77
congruence ad sensum: 78
contextual free infinitive: 75
contextual guess: 80
contextualization: 32
contextual rendering: 165
contrastive δέ: 61, 76, 164, 208, 225
contrast marker: 9
coordinate structures: 66
coordination: 52, 55

D

dative of advantage: 199
declarative future: 172
default aorist: 237
default aorist subjunctives: 59

default neuter pronoun: 16, 32, 68, 139
deliberate future: 205
different parent text: 35
different vocalization: 90
difficult syntax: 71
direct speech marker: 1
distributive: 74
dittograph: 216
dittography: 73, 196, 226
double accusative: 13, 36, 62, 66, 101, 106, 138, 221
double entendre: 50
double reading: 182
doublet: 51, 88, 174, 213, 226, 234
doublet gloss: 200

E

editorial change: 16, 137
envelope statement: 202
ex par gloss: 230
expiation: 36
explicative καί: 88, 233
explicative structure: 245

F

faulty punctuation: 58
final *nu* in cursive script: 89
free infinitives: 95
future indicative, use of: 67
future passive, use of: 198

future, use of: 173

homophones: 94

G

gender of ὕσσωπος: 200
genitive absolute: 238
genitive construction, use of: 217
genitive/dative: 92
genitive, intent of: 69
genitive of source: 185
genitive, use of: 93
genitive with ἐπί: 109
grammatical concord disregarded: 52
grammatical interruption: 245
grammatical patterns: 67

H

hapax legomenon: 15, 163, 229
haplography: 181
haplography/dittography: 232
Hebraic ἀπό: 215
Hebraic syntagms: 86, 246
Hebraisms: 16, 224, 227, 229
Hebrew nominal clause: 23, 30
Hellenistic euphemism: 174
Hellenistic inflections: 133
Hellenistic spelling: 163
holiness demanded: 171
homoiarchon: 145
homography: 102
homoioteleuton: 57, 70, 88, 119, 197

I

idiosyncratic grouping of mss: 67
imperative, use of: 118
incongruity of number: 155
indefinite active plural: 82
indefinite plurals: 42, 52, 85, 146
indefinite plural verb: 223
indefinite relative pronoun: 235
indefinite singular: 204
independent γάρ clause: 145
instrumental dative: 108, 228
instrumental ἐν: 68, 170, 231
interruptive structure: 79
intransitive verb: 181
introductory particles: 3

L

lapsus oculi: 198, 221
leveling: 3, 71, 76, 87, 134, 197, 201
Leviticus Syh: 111
locatives: 29, 89

M

marked infinitive: 102
masculine pronoun, odd use of: 75
masculine pronoun for ψυχή: 66
metonymy: 190, 198

N

neologism: 85
neuter noun as adverb: 61
neuter plural, congruence of: 198
neuter plurals as collectives: 147
neuter plural subject: 202
neuter pronoun as compromise: 213
neuter pronoun, odd use of: 18
neuter pronoun, use of: 72, 88, 167, 207
neuter singular as collective: 205
nominal clause: 198
nominalization: 90
nominative pendant: 234, 235
nominative prepositional phrase: 164
number leveling: 129

O

objective genitive: 64
objective modifier with infinitive: 212
oxymoron: 201, 208

P

palaeographic confusion: 68
palaeographic error: 19
paraphrastic construction: 243
paraphrastic rendering: 67
paratactic rendering: 118
participial structure: 58, 206
partitive ἀπό: 14, 38, 47, 56, 118, 166, 214
partitive genitive: 57, 145
partitive genitive as subject: 164
partitive preposition: 2, 47
participle of attendant circumstance: 7, 21
passive: 83
passive deponent: 201
passive future, use of: 235
passive structure: 120
passive transforms: 24, 89
passive, use of: 120, 173
pattern: 102
pendant accusative: 110, 124, 128, 200
pendant nominative: 84, 90, 95, 101, 166, 208
pendant subject: 92
perfect passive participle: 199
perfect passive, use of: 206
perfect tense, use of: 192
permissive future: 143
positive adjective plus ἀπό: 172
positive degree with ἀπό: 190
postcedent referent: 100
post-hexaplaric corrections: 111
predicate nominative: 181
prehex readings: 33
preposition ב, meaning of: 89
present middle participle, use of: 209

present participle, use of: 204, 206
present subjunctive: 192
present subjunctive, meaning of: 63, 136
present subjunctive, use of: 188, 237, 238, 239
present tense, use of: 41, 57, 83, 152, 198, 202, 211
priestly judgment: 183
proleptic pronouns: 155
punctuation: 227
purposive futures: 168
purposive infinitive: 86, 142, 172

Q

quantification by hex: 53
questionable text: 12

R

rationalization: 81
rationalization of change of text: 119
rationalization of text: 58
rationalization of word order: 201
recapitulative article: 206
recapitulative phrase: 237
regulatory future: 149
relative clause: 217

S

set patterns: 31
simplex/compound: 8, 68, 143
stylistic change: 53, 228
stylistic improvement: 87
subject change, reason for: 34
subjective genitive: 218
subject of coordinate verbs: 108
subject of infinitive: 79
subordinating participle: 117, 130, 129, 222
superlative: 16
Syh: 227, 242
synecdoche: 102, 116
synonymous parallelism: 131
synonyms: 68, 112, 197, 219
syntactic levels: 216

T

temporal clause: 177
textual change: 50, 59, 62, 65, 133, 138, 207, 238
timer: 89, 198, 210, 228, 226
timer plus ἐγενήθη: 117
transitive καίω: 73

U

uncertain modifications: 227
uncertain reference: 36
uncertain text: 114
unclear reference: 133
unusual aorist, use of: 212

V

variation, love of: 31, 40, 56, 175
variation, purpose of: 8
vocalization: 84
voice distinction: 204

W

word order: 104

General Index

A

Aaronids as asssistants: 123
Aaronids, duties of: 25
ablutions ordered: 201
abnormal discharge: 242
abominations: 54, 155
adjuration: 52
affliction: 171
altar: 6
altar access limited: 34
altar area: 37
altar base: 15, 87
altar of sacrifice: 42
animal sacrifice: 23
anointed priest: 37
anointing of altar: 105
anointing of tent: 105
appointed allotment: 103
aquatic animals, rules for: 146
assembly: 100
atonement: 5, 62, 70, 109
atonement for a house: 231
atonement, meaning of: 209
atonement, means of: 49
atonement, need for: 243

B

baked sacrifices: 17
basis for abstinence: 136
basis for avoiding defilement: 170
"before the Lord": 37, 130
blessing of the people: 131
blood forbidden as food: 96
blood, rules concerning: 40
booty: 66
burnt offering: 3, 29, 60, 82, 121, 177, 243

C

cedar wood: 199
censer: 129
chronic case: 177
chronic mildew: 202, 227
clarification of ambiguity: 19
clarification of text: 11
clean animals defined: 143
clean insects, characteristics of: 153
cleansing of altar: 39
cleansing ritual: 198, 202, 233
communicable defilement: 156
community of Israel: 43
condition of poverty: 59
confession, nature of: 57
consecration of Aaron: 106
constricted discharge: 226
consummation sacrifice: 112
contagion: 79, 83, 175
contagion by contact: 237
contagious impurity: 160, 228

contagious infection: 228
contamination by contact: 231
contamination of corpses: 165
contextual translation: 15
copulation: 235
courtyard area: 4
cultic impurity: 156

D

daily holocausts: 29
daubing of extremities: 215
declaration: 57
declaration of cure: 179
declarative judgment: 202
decontamination: 230
dedicatory gift: 87
defilement: 53
demand for holiness: 169
desecration by impurity: 244
diagnosis: 174, 181, 183, 196, 222, 229
disposal of waste: 43
divine revelation: 131
divine summons: 1
domesticated animals: 156
door vs doors: 25
double standard: 176

E

elders: 45
elevation offering: 98
entrusted deposit: 65
ephah: 63
ephod: 101
exegetical interpretation: 66, 130

F

fat and blood: 38, 94
fat for sacrifice: 27
feeling of guilt: 51
fine flour: 14
fire: 130
first fruits: 26
flying insects: 152
formulae: 217, 232, 225, 244
formulaic penalty: 96
frankincense: 14
fried sacrifices: 17

G

gifts: 1
gifts to the Lord: 100
girdle: 101
grain offering: 13
greater exactness: 65
guilt sacrifice: 58
guilt transfer: 5

H

harmonization: 11
high priest: 36
high priestly duties: 121
high priest's vestments: 99
holy place: 77, 141
horns of the altar: 39
hyssop: 200

I

impurity by touch: 94
inadvertent action: 44
inadvertent sin: 34
inauguration of public cult: 117

incense: 129
incense altar: 39
inflammation: 170
instructions to new priests: 119
instructions to worshipers: 97
instruments of purification: 231
intentional abbreviation: 91

J
joint-ownership: 66

L
laws of purity, basis for: 169
laying on of hands: 4
leaven: 77
leavened loaves: 86
leaven forbidden, reason for: 23
leprosy as mold: 218
leprosy, meaning of: 171
linen garments: 73
liquid measure: 203
loins: 32
Lord's portion: 98

M
mark: 170
meal offering: 75
memorial sacrifice: 15, 127
mildew: 200
mildew not contagious: 220
Moses as mediator: 1
mourning rites: 134
mystery religions: 38

O
offering of fat: 87
olive oil: 14

open sore: 182
oracle pouch: 102
ordination ceremony: 99, 107
ordination sacrifice: 103
ownership: 69

P
pagan practices: 33
people of the land: 54
perpetual offering: 80
place of assembly: 100
pollution: 53
praise offering: 85
praise sacrifice, nature of: 86
presentation of offering: 9
priestly action: 173
priestly allotments: 140
priestly clothing: 71
priestly declaration: 182
priestly dues: 79
priestly examination: 171, 177, 194, 196, 205, 222
priestly judgment: 187
priestly portions: 100
priestly prerogatives: 206
priestly role in cult: 7
priestly share of sacrifice: 97
priestly succession: 81
prohibition: 38
propitiation as prerequisite: 122
purification of offering: 126
purification rite: 126
purification ritual: 108

Q
quadruped: 212

quarantine: 174, 177, 187, 190, 204, 228
quarantine of menstruant: 236

R

redemptive motif: 171
regulations: 70
regulations for sin offering: 82
reinfection of house: 225
removal of ashes: 72
removal of guilt: 49
repayment: 69
restitution: 68
reuse of scraped stones: 224
rite of purification: 229
rites of purification: 232
ritual declaration: 229
ritually clean: 193
ritual of tresspass offering: 86
robe: 101

S

sacredness of cult: 131
sacrifice for deliverance: 23
sacrifice for deliverance ritual: 85
sacrifice of birds: 13
sacrifice of sheep: 29
sacrifices of the poor: 211
sacrificial female animal: 55
saddle: 230
salt: 25
salt of the covenant: 24
scaly infection: 190
scar: 170
semen discharge: 224
sin by inadvertence: 57

sin, nature of: 34
sin offering: 35, 52, 60, 90, 107, 121, 177, 209, 243
sin offering, purpose of: 209
spermatorrheic: 227
sprinkling of blood: 61
sprinkling ritual: 207, 214
strange fire: 130
strong drink prohibited: 135
subject change, reason for: 27
subscription: 37, 103, 171, 179, 208, 216, 232, 233, 244
substitute sacrifice: 60
summary: 172
swearing of an oath: 66
symbolic transfer: 4

T

tautology: 54
the divine glory: 132
theophanic fire: 132
theophany: 121
transfer of guilt: 46
trespass offering: 68, 65, 90, 204
tunic: 101
turban: 103
types of cloth: 200

U

uncertain reference: 27
unclean animals: 146
unclean aquatic creatures: 147
unclean creepers: 158
unclean fowl: 149
unclean state of worshiper: 92
undergarment: 101

V

validity of regulation: 37
very holy: 85
voluntary offering: 89
votive offering: 89

W

wave offering: 99
white rash: 194
wild animals: 157

www.ingramcontent.com/pod-product-compliance
Lightning Source LLC
Chambersburg PA
CBHW021112300426
44113CB00006B/122